DELL CROSSWORD
DICTIONARY

By **KATHLEEN RAFFERTY**

Published by
Dell Publishing Co., Inc.
1 Dag Hammarskjold Plaza
New York, New York 10017

ISBN: 0-440-16314-5

Printed in the United States of America

Four previous editions
New reissued edition
First printing—February 1983
Third printing—March 1983

ABOUT THIS BOOK . . .

Looking for an "Assam silkworm"? Can't find a "Brazilian coin"? Don't know a "candlenut tree"? You will—with the aid of this book.

The purpose of this dictionary is to give puzzlers the pleasure of COMPLETING, down to the last three letter word, every crossword that they begin. It is meant to eliminate the frustration of filling in "all but a few" of those final puzzle squares. Here, in handy, workmanlike form, is a complete 384-page reference book that can be used by puzzle solvers to find all of those little-known, but much-used, crossword words.

This DELL CROSSWORD DICTIONARY contains the exclusive new cross referenced Word-Finder. We believe this book is the most useful book ever published exclusively for crossword solvers.

It is the outgrowth of many years of exhaustive research and was prepared by the editor of the three famous DELL CROSSWORD magazines, OFFICIAL CROSSWORD PUZZLES, DELL CROSSWORD PUZZLES and POCKET CROSSWORD PUZZLES—all leaders in the puzzle world.

KATHLEEN RAFFERTY
Compiler and Editor

ABBREVIATIONS USED IN THIS BOOK

abbr. .... abbreviation
Abyssin. .... Abyssinia(n)
Afgh. .... Afghanistan
Afr. .... Africa(n)
Am. .... American
Arab. .... Arabia(n)
Arch. .... Architecture
A.-S. .... Anglo-Saxon
Austr. .... Austria(n)
Austral. .... Australia(n)
Babyl. .... Babylonian
Bibl. .... Biblical
biol. .... biology
bot. .... botany; botanical
Braz. .... Brazil(ian)
Cent. Am. .. Central America(n)
Chin. .... Chinese
comb. form .... combining form
Dan. .... Danish
Du. .... Dutch
Du. E. Ind. ... Dutch East Indies
E. .... East
Egyp. .... Egypt(ian)
E. Ind. .... East Indies
Eng. .... England; English
Eur., Europ. .... Europe(an)
fort. .... fortification
Fr. .... France; French
geol. .... geology; geological
geom. .... geometry
Ger. .... German(y)
Goth. .... Gothic
govt. .... government
Gr. .... Greek
Hebr. .... Hebrew
Her. .... heraldry
Himal. .... Himalayan
Holl. .... Holland
Ind. .... India(n)
Indo-Chin. ...... Indo-Chinese
Ir. .... Ireland; Irish
Is. .... Island

Ital. .... Italian; Italy
Jap. .... Japan(ese)
Lat. .... Latin
math. .... mathematics
med. .... medical
Medit. .... Mediterranean
Mex. ...... Mexican; Mexico
milit. .... military
Min. .... Minor
mus. .... music; musical
myth. .. mythological; mythology
N., No. .... North
naut. .... nautical
N. Hebr. .... New Hebrides
N. T. .... New Testament
N. Z. .... New Zealand
Nor. .... Norway; Norwegian
O. Eng. .... Old English
P. I. .... Philippine Islands
P. R. .... Puerto Rico
Pacif. .... Pacific
Pers. .... Persian
pert. .... pertaining
pharm. .... pharmacy
philos. .... philosophical
poet. .... poetry
Polyn. .... Polynesia(n)
Port. ..... Portugal; Portuguese
Pruss. .... Prussian
R. C. .... Roman Catholic
Rom. .... Roman
Russ. .... Russian
S. .... South
S. Afr. .... South Africa(n)
Scot. .... Scottish
Sp. .... Spanish
Teut. .... Teutonic
Turk. .... Turkey; Turkish
W. .... West
W. Ind. .... West Indian
WW .... World War
zool. .... zoology

TABLE OF CONTENTS

Every essential two-, three- and four-
letter word in the English language.
Cross-referenced to Definitions section for utmost aid to solving. You
can complete unfinished puzzle words
with this section.

DEFINITIONS SECTION

CROSSWORD DEFINITIONS AND ANSWERS

HOW TO USE THIS SECTION:

Here are crossword DEFINITIONS, arranged alphabetically.

Look up the DEFINITION of a crossword word, and you will find, in bold-face type, the word you want.

There are two kinds of crossword definitions. One is the almost unvarying definition: "Bitter vetch" or "Vetch" is used to define ERS. If you look in this dictionary under "B" for "bitter vetch" or under "V" for "vetch" you will find it there.

The other kind of definition, far more common, is the more varied definition where the puzzle-maker can choose from among many descriptive words when he defines a puzzle word: "India nurse," "Oriental nurse," "Oriental maid," "Oriental nursemaid" are all used in crossword puzzles as definitions for AMAH. For efficiency's sake, crossword words with varying definitions are listed here under the ESSENTIAL definition word. In the case of AMAH, the listing is under "nurse," "maid," and "nursemaid."

So, if you don't find your wanted word under the first word of the definition given, look for it under the other words of the definition.

The length of a word is important to crossword solvers, and so, when a definition fits two or more words the words are arranged according to length. For example: adage . . . . SAW, MAXIM, PROVERB.

Remember to use also the efficiently arranged reference word lists in the SPECIAL SECTION, beginning on page 187.

5

A

Aaron's brother ...... MOSES
Aaron's sister .... MIRIAM
Aaron's miracle worker .. ROD
Aaron's son, oldest .... NADAB
abaca .... LINAGA
abaca, top-quality ..... LUPIS
Abadan's land .... IRAN
abalone shell money
ULLO, UHLLO
abandon . MAROON, DISCARD
abandoned .... DERELICT
abate .... EBB, LESSEN
abatement .... LETUP
abbess .... AMMA
abbey: Sp. .... ABADIA
abbot: Lat. .... ABBAS
abbreviations
PTA, SRO, NATO (1949
pact)
abdominal .... VENTRAL
Abel's brother .... CAIN
abhor HATE, DETEST, LOATHE
Abie's girl .... ROSE
Abijah's son .... ASA
ability ...... POWER, TALENT
abject .... BASE
abode, blissful .... EDEN
abode of dead HADES, SHEOL
abode of dead: Egypt.
AALU, AARU
abound .... TEEM
abounding .... RIFE
about .. OF, RE, ANENT, CIRCA
about: Lat. .... CIRCITER
above ..... O'ER, OVER, UPON
abrade .... RUB, CHAFE
Abraham's birthplace ..... UR
Abraham's brother
HARAN, NAHOR
Abraham's father ..... TERAH
Abraham's nephew ...... LOT
Abraham's son
ISAAC, ISHMAEL
Abraham's wife SARAH, SARAI
abrasive .... EMERY
abrogate .... ANNUL
abrupt flexure .... GENU
Absalom's cousin ..... AMASA
Absalom's sister ..... TAMAR
abscond .. ELOPE, LEVANT
absence, license for ... EXEAT
absent ..... OFF, OUT, AWAY,
GONE
absolute .... UTTER, PLENARY
absolve sins .... SHRIVE

absorbed .... RAPT
abstruse .... ESOTERIC
abundance, in ...... GALORE
abundant ...... RIFE, AMPLE
abuse: India ... GALI, GALEE
abuse ... VIOLATE, MISTREAT
abusive, be .... REVILE
abusive charges .... MUD
abut ...... ADJOIN, BORDER
abyss ... GULF, HOLE, CHASM
Abyssinian .... KAFA, KAFFA
Abyssin. fly .... ZIMB
Abyssin. grain .... TEFF
Abyssin. Hamite AFAR, AGAO,
BEJA, AFARA
Abyssin. language ...... SAHO
Abyssin. mountain wolf
KABERU
Abyssin. ruler's title .. NEGUS
Abyssin. ox .. GALLA, SANGA,
SANGU
Abyssin. Semitic dialect
GEEZ, GHESE
Abyssin. tree .... KOSO
Abyssin. tribesman ..... SHOA
Abyssin. vizier .... RAS
accent .... TONE
accent, Irish .. BLAS, BROGUE
access .... ENTREE
accommodate .... LEND
"—accompli" .... FAIT
according to . ALA, AUX, ALLA
accost ...... HAIL, GREET
account entry .. ITEM, DEBIT,
CREDIT
accumulate .... AMASS,
HOARD, ACCRUE
accumulation .... FUND
accustomed .... USED, WONT,
ENURED
acetic acid ester ... ACETATE
acetone derivative .. ACETOL
acetylene ..... ETHIN, ETHINE
Achilles' adviser .... NESTOR
Achilles' father ..... PELEUS
Achilles' mother ..... THETIS
Achilles' slayer ...... PARIS
acid, kind of .. AMINO, BORIC
acid radical ... ACYL, ACETYL
acidity .... ACOR
acknowledge .... OWN
acknowledge frankly .. AVOW
acorns, dried ...... CAMATA
acoustics apparatus .. SIRENE
acquainted .... VERSANT
acquiesce .... ASSENT

6

a acquiesce, fully ..... ACCEDE
acquire .... WIN, GAIN, REAP
acrobat of India .... NAT
Acropolis of Thebes . CADMEA
across: comb. form
.... TRAN, TRANS
acrostic, Hebrew .... AGLA
act ...... DEED, FEAT, EMOTE
act: Lat. ..... ACTU, ACTUS
action, put into .... ACTUATE
action word .... VERB
active .. SPRY, AGILE, BRISK,
.... LIVELY, NIMBLE
actor .... HISTRIO, HISTRION
actor's group .... TROUPE
actor's hint .... CUE
actor's valet .... DRESSER
actual .... REAL, TRUE
actual being .... ESSE
actuality .... FACT
adage .... SAW, MAXIM,
.... PROVERB
Adam's ale .... WATER
Adam's 1st mate: legend
.... LILITH
Adam's grandson ...... ENOS
Adam's son ABEL, CAIN, SETH
adapt .... FIT
adept .... ACE
add on AFFIX, ANNEX, ATTACH
adder, common .... ASP
additions .... ADDENDA
addition, bill's .... RIDER
adequate .... DUE, FULL,
.... AMPLE, EQUAL
adhere .... CLING, STICK,
.... CLEAVE
adherent .... IST
adhesive .. GUM, GLUE, PASTE
ADJECTIVE ENDING, see SUF-
FIX, ADJECTIVE
adjust ..... FIX, SET, ADAPT,
.... ATTUNE, ORIENT
adjutant .... AIDE
adjutant bird .... ARGALA,
.... HURGILA, MARABOU
admonish ... WARN, EXHORT,
.... REPROVE
admonisher .... MONITOR
adolescence .... TEENS,
.... YOUTH, NONAGE
adopted son of Mohammed ALI
Adriana's servant ...... LUCE
adroit ...... READY, HABILE,
.... SKILLFUL
adulterate .. DEBASE, DEFILE,
.... DENATURE
advance guard .... VAN
advantage .... USE, GAIN,
.... PROFIT, BENEFIT

c adventitious lung sound . RALE
adventure ..... GEST, GESTE
adviser, woman ...... EGERIA
Aeetes' daughter .... MEDEA
Aegir's wife .... RAN
Aeneas' wife .... CREUSA
Aeneid author VERGIL, VIRGIL
Aesir .. TIU, TYR, ULL, FREY,
.... LOKE, LOKI, ODIN, THOR,
.... VALE, VALI, DONAR,
.... FREYA, BRAGI, WODEN,
.... BALDER
affectionate ... FOND, WARM,
.... LOVING, TENDER
affirm .. AVER, POSIT, ASSERT
affirmative .... AY, AYE,
.... YEA, YES
affirmative vote .... AY, AYE,
.... YEA, YES
afflict ...... TRY, VEX, PAIN,
.... DISTRESS
affluence ..... EASE, RICHES,
.... WEALTH
affray .... BRAWL, FIGHT,
.... MELEE
Afghan prince .. AMIR, AMEER
Afghan title .... KHAN
afresh .... ANEW
d afraid: obsolete ...... REDDE
AFRICAN .... see also SOUTH
AFRICAN and AFRICAN in
SPECIAL SECTION
AFRICAN ANTELOPE
.... see ANTELOPE
Afr. bass .... IYO
Afr. bustard .... KORI
Afr. cotton garment .... TOBE
Afr. disease .... NENTA
Afr. worm .... LOA
Afr. grass, millet-like ... FUNDI
Afr. hornbill .... TOCK
Afr. plant .... ALOE
Afr. scrub .... BITO
Afr. soldier .... ASKARI
Afr. squirrel .... XERUS
Afr. stockade .... BOMA
Afr. tableland ...... KAROO
Afrikaans ..... TAAL, BOERS
aft .... ABAFT, ASTERN
after awhile .... ANON
aftermath .... ROWEN
afterpart of ship's keel
.... SKAG, SKEG
afterpiece, comic .... EXODE
aftersong .... EPODE
again .... ENCORE
against .... CON, ANTI,
.... CONTRA, VERSUS
agalloch wood .. AGAR, ALOE,
.... GAROO
Agamemnon's son .. ORESTES

7

agate stone .... ACHATE
age .... EON, ERA, AERA,
RIPEN, PERIOD
aged .... OLD, ANILE, SENILE
agave fiber .... ISTLE
agency, depression-era .. N R A
agency, govt. ... E C A, F H A
agency, wage, price .... E S A
agency, ration-book ...... O P A
agency, World-War II .. O P A
agent .... DOER, FACTOR,
FACIENT
agents acted through .. MEDIA
aggregate . SUM, MASS, TOTAL
agitate .... STIR
agitation ...... STIR, DITHER,
TUMULT
agitation, be in state of
SEETHE
agnomen .... NAME
agree ..... GIBE, JIBE, TALLY,
ASSENT, CONCUR
agreeable: old Eng. ... AMENE
agreeableness of letters
EUTONY
agreement ...... MISE, PACT,
CONCORD, ENTENTE
agriculture goddess . CERES,
VACUNA, DEMETER
Agrippina's son ...... NERO
Ahasuerus' minister .. HAMAN
ahead ON, BEFORE, FORWARD
Ahiam's father ...... SACAR
aid .. ABET, ASSIST, SUCCOR,
FURTHER
aim ..... END, GOAL, ASPIRE
aims, with the same .... AKIN
air.. AER, ARIA, MIEN, TUNE
air apparatus ...... AERATOR
air current, ascending
THERMAL
air, fill with .... AERATE
air, fresh .... OZONE
air passage ..... FLUE, VENT
air spirit .... SYLPH
air, upper .... ETHER, AETHER
aircraft, motorless ... GLIDER
airplane ...... JET, AERO
airplane: Fr. .... AVION
airport marker ...... PYLON
airport, Paris .... ORLY
airship . AERO, BLIMP, PLANE
airy ...... LIGHT, ETHEREAL
ait .... ISLE
Ajax, tale about .... MYTH
Ajax's father ..... TELAMON
akin .... SIB
alang grass .... LALANG
alarm SCARE, SIREN, AROUSE
alas! .. ACH, HEU, OCH, OIME
alas: Irish .. OHONE, OCHONE
alas: poetic .... AY
Alaska glacier .... MUIR

ALBANIAN see COINS, TRIBES,
GAZETTEER in SPECIAL
SECTION
Albanian dialect .. GEG, CHAM,
GHEG, TOSK
albatross, sooty ...... NELLY
alchitran .... TAR, PITCH
alcohol radical .... AL
alcohol, solid STERIN, STEROL
alcoholic drink ... GIN, RUM,
RHUM
Alcott heroine ...... JO, AMY,
MEG, BETH
alcove ...... BOWER, RECESS
alder tree: Scot. .... ARN
ale mug .... TOBY
ale, sour .... ALEGAR
alewife fish ...... POMPANO
ALEUTIAN see TRIBES, GAZET-
TEER in SPECIAL SECTION
Alexandrian theologian ARIUS
Alexander victory
ISSUS, ARBELA
alfalfa ... LUCERN, LUCERNE
Alfonso's queen .... ENA
alga .... NORI
alga, one-cell ...... DIATOM
algae genus, fan-shaped
PADINA
algarroba tree ...... CALDEN
ALGERIA—see SPECIAL SEC-
TION
Algerian governor .... DEY
ALGONQUIN .... see Page 192
Ali Baba's word ...... SESAME
Ali, caliph descendants ALIDS
Alien in Hebrew territory .. GER
alienate ... WEAN, ESTRANGE
align ... TRUE, ALINE, RANGE
alkali ..... LYE, REH, USAR
alkaline solution .... LYE
alkaloid ... CAFFEIN, CAFFEINE
alkaloid, calabar bean
ESERINE
all: Lat. .... TOTO
all religions, believer in
OMNIST
all right ...... OKAY, OKEH
allanite .... CERINE
allay ...... CALM, ASSUAGE,
RELIEVE
alleged force .... OD
allegory, religious .. PARABLE
Allepo native .... SYRIAN
aleviate ...... EASE, ALLAY,
LESSEN
alley .... MIB, MIG
alliance .... UNION, LEAGUE
alliance, Western ...... NATO
alligator .... LAGARTO

alligator pear ...... AVOCADO
alligator, S.A. ...... CAIMAN, CAYMAN
allot .... METE, GRANT ASSIGN, PORTION
allotment ... QUOTA, RATION
allow .... LET
allowance TARE, TRET, RATION
alloy .... MOKUM, OROIDE
alloy, aluminum ...... DURAL
alloy, copper .... BRASS
alloy, copper-tin ..... BRONZE
alloy, gold-silver: Egyp. ASEM
alloy, lead-tin . CALIN, TERNE
alloy, non-ferrous ..... TULA
alloy, yellow .... AICH
allspice .... PIMENTO
allure .... TICE, TOLE, TEMPT, ENTICE
allusion .... HINT
almond emulsion .... ORGEAT
almost .... ANEAR
alms box or chest ..... ARCA
aloe .... AGAVE
aloe derivative ...... ALOIN
aloes product .... ALOIN
alone, on stage .. SOLA, SOLUS
along .... ON, BESIDE
alp .... PEAK
alpaca .... PACO
alphabet letter, old .... RUNE
Alps, Austro-It. TIROL, TYROL, TIROLO
Alps, one of .... BLANC
Alps pass .... CENIS
Alps, river rising in .. RHONE
Altar constellation ..... ARA
altar end of church .... APSE
altar screen .... REREDOS
altar shelf . GRADIN, RETABLE
altar side curtain ..... RIDDEL
altar top .... MENSA
alternate .... ROTATE
alternative ...... OR, EITHER
alumni .... GRADS
always .. AY, AYE, EER, EVER
amadou .... PUNK
amass .... HOARD, GATHER
amateur TIRO, TYRO, NOVICE
Amazon cetacean ..... INIA
Amazon tributary .. APA, ICA
ambary .... DA
ambary hemp ...... NALITA
ambassador .. ENVOY, LEGATE
amber fish RUNNER, MEDREGAL
Amen-Ra's wife .... MUT
amend ALTER, EMEND, REVISE
amendment, document . RIDER
amends, make .... ATONE
ament .... CHAT

Am. artist ..... WEST, HICKS, HOMER, MARIN, PEALE, BENTON, COPLEY, INNESS, CORBINO, ALBRIGHT
AMERICAN INDIAN ...... see INDIANS, Page 192
Am. aloe fiber .... PITA, PITO
Am. author ADE, POE, AMES, BAUM, HARTE, WYLIE, YERBY, CORWIN, FERBER, HERSEY, KANTOR, MORLEY
Am. author, illustrator .. PYLE
Am. capitalist .... ASTOR
Am. caricaturist .. REA, NAST
Am. dramatist AKINS, BARRY, ODETS, CROUSE
Am. editor .... BOK
Am. educator .... MANN
Am. explorer BYRD, FREMONT
Am. general LEE, OTIS, GREENE
Am. humorist .. ADE, NYE, COBB, NASH, ROGERS
Am. jurist .... TANEY
Am. inventor . IVES, MORSE, TESLA, EDISON
American: Mex. ..... GRINGO
Am. nature writer BEEBE, SETON
Am. nighthawk .... PISK
AM. PAINTER see AM. ARTIST
Am. patriot ..... HALE, OTIS, ALLEN, REVERE
Am. philanthropist ..... RIIS
Am. philosopher ..... EDMAN
Am. pianist ARRAU, DUCHIN, LEVANT
Am. poet POE, AUDEN, BENET, FROST, GUEST, RILEY, STEIN, MILLAY
Am. poetess .. STEIN, LOWELL
Am. sculptor .... CALDER
AM. SINGER ... see SOPRANO
Am. statesman CLAY, BARUCH, DULLES
Am. suffragist .... CATT
Am. surgeon .... PARRAN
AM. WRITER see AM. AUTHOR
AMERIND (means any American Indian) See pages 192, 193
amide, pert. to .... AMIC
a mine: Corn. .... BAL
ammonia compound .. AMIN, AMIDE, AMINE
ammoniac plant ...... OSHAC
ammunition SHOT, SHRAPNEL
ammunition, short for: AMMO, AMMU
ammunition wagon .. CAISSON
among ...... IN, MID, AMID
amorously, stare . LEER, OGLE
amount assessed ..... RATAL

a amount staked in gambling .... MISE
amuse .... DIVERT
ampere .... WEBER
amphibian
FROG, TOAD, ANURAN
amphibian, order HYLA, ANURA
amphitheater .... ARENA
amphitheater, natural CIRQUE
amplification factor ... MU
amulet .... CHARM, PERIAPT
analyze .... ASSAY, DISSECT
analyze grammatically PARSE
ancestor of Irish .. IR, ITH,
MIL, MILED
ancestor of man, Hindu MANU
ancestral .... AVITAL
ancestral spirit, P. I. ANITO
ancestral spirits LARES, MANES
anchor ..... FIX, TIE, MOOR,
KEDGE
anchor part .... FLUKE
anchor, small, light ... KEDGE
anchor tackle .... CAT
anchovy sauce .... ALEC
ancient Asiatic .... MEDE
ancient Briton .... CELT
ancient Chinese ...... SERES
ancient city, Asia Minor MYRA,
NICAEA
ancient country ...... GAUL
Ancient Egyp. kingdom SENNAR
ancient flute .... TIBIA
ancient Greece division
AETOLIA
ancient invader, India
SAKA, SACAE
b ancient people of Gaul REMI
ancient Persian .... MEDE
ancient Persian money . DARIC
ancient philosophy ... YOGA
ancient race .... MEDES
ancient Slav
VEND, WEND, VENED
ancient times ... ELD, YORE
ancient tribe of Britons ICENI
ancient weight .... MINA
and .. TOO, ALSO, PLUS, WITH
and: Lat. .... ET
and not .... NOR
and so on: abbr. ...... ETC.
Andes cold higher region PUNA
Andes grass .... ICHU
Andes mountain .... SORATA
andiron .... DOG
"Andronicus,—" ...... TITUS
anecdotage or anecdotes
ANA, TALES
anent .... RE, ABOUT, BESIDE
anent, close — .... TO
anesthetic ...... GAS, ETHER
Angel of Death ...... AZRAEL
angel, Pers. .... MAH

c anger .... IRE, RAGE
RILE, CHOLER
anger, fit of .. PIQUE, TEMPER
angle, 57 degrees .... RADIAN
angle of leaf and axis ... AXIL
angle of leafstalk ...... AXIL
angle of stem, pert. to . AXILE
Anglo-Saxon "G" . YOK, YOGH
A.-S. god of peace ..... ING
A.-S. lord's man THANE, THEGN
A.-S. king .... INE
A.-S. money (coin) ...... ORA
A.-S. slave .... ESNE
A.-S. warrior .. THANE, THEGN
Angora goat .... CHAMAL
angry .... HOT, MAD,
SORE, IRATE
animal, Afr. .... CIVET, GENET,
POTTO, ZEBRA, GENETTE
animal, ant-eating ... ECHIDNA
animal, aquatic .. SEAL, OTTER,
WHALE, DUGONG,
WALRUS, MANATEE
animal, arboreal .... TARSIER
animal, Austral. .... ECHIDNA
animal, badgerlike, Java
TELEDU
animal body .... SOMA
animal, draft ...... OX, OXEN
d animal, fabulous ... DRAGON
animal, giraffelike ... OKAPI
animal, India .... DHOLE
animal, Madagascar
FOSSA, FOUSSA
animals of area ..... FAUNA
animal-plant life ...... BIOTA
animal, Peru .... ALPACA
animal, sea .... SEAL, CORAL,
WHALE, WALRUS,
DUGONG, MANATEE
animal, S. Afr. .... ZORIL
animal, S. Am. .. APARA, COATI
animal trail ...... RUN, SLOT,
SPUR, SPOOR
animating principle .... SOUL
ankle TALUS, TARSI, TARSUS
ankle, pert. to ..... TARSAL
Annamese measure ..... TAO
ANNAMESE see also ANNAM
in SPECIAL SECTION
Annapolis student PLEB, PLEBE
annatto seeds. Sp. ACHIOTE
anneal .. TEMPER, TOUGHEN
annex .... ADD, ELL,
WING, ATTACH
annihilate .... DESTROY, DIS-
CREATE
ANNIVERSARY . see WEDDING
announce .... HERALD
annoy ... IRK, TRY, VEX, RILE,
PEEVE, TEASE, BOTHER,
MOLEST, PESTER, DISTURB

a annual, as winds .... ETESIAN
annuity, form of .... TONTINE
annul .... UNDO, VOID,
  CANCEL, REVOKE
annular die .... DOD
annulet; Her. .... VIRE
anoint ... OIL, ANELE, ENELE
another ... NEW, ADDITIONAL
ant ...... EMMET, PISMIRE
antarctic bird ...... PENGUIN
antarctic icebreaker ..... ATKA
antecedent . PRIOR, ANCESTOR
antelope, Afr. ..... GNU, KOB,
 BISA, GUIB, KOBA, KUDU,
 ORYX, POKU, PUKU, TORA,
 ADDAX, ELAND, ORIBI,
 RHEBOK
antelope, Afr., large .. IMPALA
antelope, Afr., small .. DUIKER
antelope, Ind.
 SASIN, NILGAI, NILGAU
antelope, Siberian ...... SAIGA
antelope, tawny .... ORIBI
antenna HORN, PALP, AERIAL
  FEELER
antenna, with nodose
  NODICORN
anthracite, inferior .... CULM
anti-aircraft shells .... FLAK
anti-tank gun .... PIAT
b antic ... DIDO, CAPER, PRANK
antique red color . CHAUDRON
antiseptic ..... EUPAD, EUSOL,
 IODIN, SALOL, CRESOL,
 IODINE
antiseptic, mercury
 EGOL, METAPHEN
antitoxin ...... SERA, SERUM
antler point .... SNAG, TINE,
  PRONG
antler, unbranched ...... DAG
antlers, stag's ...... ATTIRE
"Anthony and Cleopatra" character .... IRAS
anvil ...... INCUS, TEEST
anxiety .... CARE
any: dialect .... ONI
any one .... AN
aoudad .... ARUI
apathy .. ENNUI, DOLDRUMS
ape .... ORANG
ape, long-tailed, India ... KRA
appelation ...... NAME, TITLE
APERTURE . see also OPENING
aperture .... GAP, HOLE,
 SLOT, VENT, ORIFICE
apex, at the .... APICAL
aphasia, motor ...... ALALIA
aphorism . SAW, RULE, SUTRA
Aphrodite .... VENUS

c Aphrodite, got apple from
  PARIS
Aphrodite, love of .. ADONIS
Aphrodite's mother ... DIONE
Aphrodite's son .... EROS
apocopate .... ELIDE
Apocrypha, book from ESDRAS
Apollo's instrument ..... BOW,
  LUTE, LYRE
Apollo's mother LETO, LATONA
Apollo's sister
  DIANA, ARTEMIS
Apollo's son .... ION
Apollo's twin ...... ARTEMIS
Apollo's vale, sacred . TEMPE
apoplexy, plant .... ESCA
Apostle (12) ..... JOHN, JUDE
 (THADDEUS), JAMES, JUDAS,
 PETER (SIMON PETER), SI-
 MON, ANDREW, PHILIP,
 THOMAS (DIDYMUS), MAT-
 THEW (LEVI), MATTHIAS,
 BARTHOLOMEW
Apostle, Capernaum MATTHEW
Apostles, teaching of DIDACHE
apparent ..... OVERT, PLAIN,
  EVIDENT
apparition . SPECTER, SPECTRE
appear .. LOOK, LOOM, SEEM
appearance . AIR, MIEN, GUISE
d appease ...... CALM, ALLAY
  PLACATE
appellation ..... NAME, TITLE
append .... ADD, AFFIX,
  ATTACH
appendage, caudal ..... TAIL
appetizer . CANAPE, APERITIF
apple .. POME, TREE, FRUIT,
  PIPPIN
apple acid .... MALIC
apple seed .... PIP
apple tree .... SORB
apple tree genus .... MALUS
apple, winter ...... ESOPUS
apples, crushed ... POMACE
apple-like fruit ...... POME
appoint . SET, NAME, CHOOSE
apportion DEAL, METE, ALLOT
appraise RATE, VALUE, ASSESS
apprise ..... ADVISE, NOTIFY
approach ..... NEAR, ANEAR,
  ACCESS
appropriate, .. APT, FIT, MEET
appropriate, not INAPT, UNFIT
apricot, Jap. .... UME
apricot, Korean . ANSU, ANZU
apricots .... MEBOS
apropos ...... PAT, FITTING
apteryx .... KIWI
aptitude ..... FLAIR, ABILITY

11

a aptitude, natural .... FLAIR, TALENT
aquamarine .... BERYL
AQUATIC . see SEA or MARINE
Arab .... GAMIN, SEMITE
Arab cloak, sleeveless .. ABA
Arab drink ...... BOSA, BOZA, BOZAH
Arab name .... ALI
Arab's state of bliss .... KEF
Arabia, people of .... OMANI
ARABIAN . see ARAB, ARABIA, SPECIAL SECTION
Arabian chief . SAYID, SAYYID
Arabian chieftain AMIR, EMIR, AMEER, EMEER
Arabian chieftian's domain EMIRATE
Arabian cloth .... ABA
Arabian district .... TEMA
Arabian garment .... ABA
Arabian jasmine .... BELA
Arabian judge .... CADI
"Arabian Nights" dervish AGIB
Arabian noble .. AMIR, EMIR, AMEER, EMEER
Arabian nomadic tribesman SLEB
Arabian sailboat . see VESSEL, ARAB
Arabian sleeveless garment ABA
b Arabian tambourine TAAR, DAIRA, DAIRE
Arabic jinni, evil AFRIT, AFREET, AFRITE
Arabic letter . GAF, KAF, MIM, WAW, ALIF, DAHL
Arabic script .... NESKI
Arabic surname .... SAAD
arachnid . MITE, TICK, SPIDER
Arawakan language ... TAINO
arbitrator . UMPIRE, REFEREE
arboreal .... DENDRAL
arc .... LINE, CURVE
arch of heaven .... COPE
arch, pointed .... OGIVE
archaeology, mound .... TERP
archangel .... URIEL
archbishop .... PRIMATE
archbishop, Canterbury BECKET
archer in Eng. ballad CLIM, CLYM
archetype .. MODEL, PATTERN
archfiend .... SATAN
architect's drawing . EPURE
architecture, school of BAUHAUS
architecture, type DORIC, IONIC
ARCTIC ...... see GAZETTEER
Arctic NORTH, POLAR, FRIGID

c arctic air force base ... THULE
arctic dog .... SAMOYED
arctic gull genus ..... XEMA
arctic plain .... TUNDRA
Arden .... FOREST
ardor .. ELAN, ZEAL, FERVOR
area measure . RADII, RADIUS
area, small .... AREOLA
areca .... BETEL
arena .... FIELD
Ares' mother .... ENYO
Ares' sister .... ERIS
ares, 10 .... DECARE
Argonaut .. JASON, ACASTUS
Argonauts' leader .... JASON
Argonauts' ship .... ARGO
argument .... AGON, DEBATE, HASSLE
arhat .... LOHAN
aria ...... AIR, SOLO, SONG, TUNE, MELODY
arias .... SOLI
aridity, having ..... XERIC
arikara .... REE
arise .... REBEL, ACCRUE, APPEAR
arista .... AWN
Arizona aborigine ..... HOPI
d ARIZONA ... see also SPECIAL SECTION
ARIZONA INDIAN see page 192
Ark, porter of: Bible .... BEN
Ark's landing place . ARARAT
arm .... LIMB, TENTACLE
arm, movable with verniers ALIDADE
arm of sea . BAY, FIRTH, FRITH
armadillo .... APAR, APARA
armadillo, Braz. . TATU, TATOU
armadillo, giant . TATU, TATOU
armadillo, large 12-banded TATOUAY
armadillo, 6-banded . PELUDO
armadillo, small .. PEBA, PEVA
armadillo, 3-banded .. APAR, APARA, MATACO, MATICO
armed band .... POSSE
armed galley of old Northmen AESC
ARMOR .... see also SPECIAL SECTION, page 194
armor bearer ...... ARMIGER
armor, body .... CUIRASS
armor, chain .... MAIL
armor, horse .. BARD, BARDE
armor, leg .... JAMB, JAMBE
armor, leg below knee GREAVE
armor, lower body .... CULET

12

a armor part .... LORICA
armor part, throat .. GORGET
armor, skirt .... TACE, TASSE,
TASSET
armor, thigh .. CUISH, TUILE,
CUISSE, TUILLE
armpit .... ALA
army .... HOST, TROOPS
army group .... CADRE
army provisioner ...... SUTLER
aroid, an ...... ARAD, ARUM
aromatic herb
DILL, MINT, SAGE
aromatic herb, carrot genus
CARUM
aromatic herb-plant ... NARD
aromatic seed
CUMIN, CUMMIN
aromatic seed, plant .. ANISE
aromatic substance . BALSAM
aromatic weed .... TANSY
around .... CIRCA
arouse .... FIRE, STIR, PIQUE
arpeggio .... ROULADE
arquebus support ...... CROC
arraign .... ACCUSE, INDICT
arrange ...... FIX, SET, FILE,
DISPOSE
arangement: comb. form . TAX,
TAXI, TAXO, TAXEO, TAXIS
b arrangement, pert. to .. TACTIC
array .. DECK, ORDER, ATTIRE
arrest .... NAB, HALT
arrest writ .... CAPIAS
arris .... PIEN
arrow .... BOLT, DART
arrow, body of .... STELE
arrow, fit string to ..... NOCK
arrow, spinning .... VIRE
arrow wood .... WAHOO
arrowroot ...... PIA, ARARU
arroyo .... HONDO
art: Lat. .... ARS
art style ...... DADA, GENRE
Artemis . UPIS, DELIA, PHOEBE
Artemis' twin .... APOLLO
Artemis' victim ...... ORION
artery, largest ...... AORTA
artery of neck ...... CAROTID
artful .... SLY, WILY
arthritis aid ACTH, CORTISONE
Arthur's foster brother .. KAY
Arthurian lady
ENID, ELAIN, ELAINE
article ...... AN, THE, ITEM
article, Fr. ...... LA, LE, DES,
LES, UNE
article, Ger. ...... DAS, DER
article, Sp. .. EL, LA, LAS, LOS
articulated joint ...... HINGE
artifice .. RUSE, WILE, TRICK

c artificial language ... RO, IDO
ARTIST .... see also PAINTER
and under Country
of each artist
artist, primitive ...... MOSES
artless .... NAÏVE
arum family plant TARO, CALLA
arum plant .... ARAD, AROID
Aryan .... MEDE, SLAV
as . QUA, LIKE, SINCE, WHILE
as far as .... TO
as it stands: mus. ...... STA
as written: mus. .... STA
asafetida .... HING
asbestos .... ABISTON
ascent .... UPGO, CLIMB
ascetic, ancient ...... ESSENE
asceticism, Hindu ..... YOGA
ash, fruit, seed ...... SAMARA
ash key .... SAMARA
ashy pale .... LIVID
ASIA .. see also SPECIAL SEC-
TION
Asia Minor district, old IONIA
Asia Minor region, pert. to
EOLIC, AEOLIC
Asia native, S.E. ...... SHAN
Asiatic ancient people . SERES
d Asiatic country .. see page 210
Asiatic cow .... ZO, ZOH
Asiatic evergreen ...... BAGO
Asiatic fowl .... SAT
Asiatic gangster ..... DACOIT
Asiatic sardine ...... LOUR
Asiatic shrub .... TEA, TCHE
Asiatic tree .... ACLE,
ASAK, ASOK, ASOKA
"— asinorum" .... PONS
askew .... WRY, AGEE,
ALOP, AWRY
aspect .. SIDE, FACET, PHASE
asperse .... SLANDER
aspire .... HOPE
ass, wild
KULAN, ONAGER, QUAGGA
assail ...... BESET, ATTACK
ASSAM .... see also SPECIAL
SECTION, Page 191
Assam hill tribe .... AKA
Assam mongol .... NAGA
Assam silkworm .. ERI, ERIA
Assam tribe, Naga Hills
AO, NAGA
assault ...... ONSET, STORM
assault, prolonged .... SIEGE
assayer .... TESTER
assaying cup .... CUPEL
assemble .... MEET, MUSTER,
COLLECT

a assembly ...... DIET, SYNOD
SESSION, GATHERING
assembly, A.-S. ...... GEMOT,
GEMOTE
assembly, China, Hawaii . HUI
assembly, Dutch ...... RAAD
assent, solemn ...... AMEN
assert ... AVER, POSIT, STATE
assert formally ... ALLEGATE
assess ... TAX, LEVY, VALUE
assessment RATE, SCOT RATAL
asseverate .... AVER
assignor of property . CEDENT
assimilate . ABSORB, DIGEST
assistance AID, HELP, SUPPORT
assistant .... AIDE
associate . ALLY, COLLEAGUE
association, trade GILD, GUILD
assuage .... MITIGATE
ASSYRIAN .. see also SPECIAL
SECTION, Page 198
Assyrian king .... PUL
Assyrian queen, myth
SEMIRAMIS
asterisk .... STAR
astern .... AFT, BAFT, ABAFT
astringent ... ALUM, STYPTIC
astringent, black ...... KATH
astringent fruit ...... SLOE
astrologer of India ... JOSHI
b astronomical ...... URANIC
astron. luminous "cloud"
NEBULA
Aswan, ancient ..... SYENE
asylum ..... HAVEN, REFUGE
at all .... ANY
at any time .... EVER
at odds .... OUT
at the home of: Fr. .... CHEZ
Atahualpa, king .... INCA
atap palm .... NIPA
atelier .... STUDIO
Athamas' wife .... INO
Athena ... PALLAS, MINERVA
Athena, appellation, title ALEA
Athena, possession of
EGIS
Athenian .... ATTIC
Athenian bronze coin CHALCUS
Athenian demagogue .. CLEON
Athens, last king of . CODRUS
athlete, famous ..... THORPE
a-tiptoe .... ATIP
atmospheric pressure, of BARIC
at no time: poet. ..... NEER
atoll's pool .... LAGOON
atom part .... PROTON
atomic machine
BETATRON, RHEOTRON
atomic physicist BOHR, RABI,
UREY, FERMI, PAULI, COMP-
TON, MEITNER, MILLIKAN

c atomic submarine .... SKATE,
SARGO, TRITON, NAUTILUS
atone for .... REDEEM
attach .... ADD, FIX, TIE,
APPEND
attack .... BESET, ONSET
attack, mock .... FEINT
attar .... OTTO
attempt ... TRY, STAB, ESSAY
attendant, hunter's
GILLY, GILLIE
attention .. EAR, CARE, HEED
attest ...... VOUCH, CERTIFY
attic ...... LOFT, GARRET
Attica resident ...... METIC
Attila .... ATLI, ETZEL
attitudinize .... POSE
attribute .. IMPUTE, ASCRIBE
attune .... KEY, ACCORD
auction .... SALE
audience ..... EAR, HEARING
auditory ...... OTIC, AURAL
auger .... BORE, BORER
augment .... EKE
augur .... BODE, PORTEND
augury ..... OMEN, PORTENT
auk genus . ALCA, ALLE, URIA
auk, little ... ROTCH, RÖTCHE
aura, pert. to .... AURIC
d aureola .... HALO
auric acid salt ...... AURATE
auricle .... EAR
auricular ...... OTIC, EARED
aurochs .. TUR, URUS, AURUS
aurora .... EOS, DAWN
auspices .... EGIS, AEGIS
Australasian harrier-hawk
KAHU
Australasian shrub genus
HOYA
AUSTRALIA . see also SPECIAL
SECTION
Australian boomerang . KILEY
Austral. food .... KAI
Austral. gum tree
KARI, TUART
Austral. hut ..... MIAM, MIMI
Austral. marsupial
TAIT, KOALA
Austral. scaly-finned fish
MADO
Austral. tree, timber .. PENDA
Austrian folk dance .. DREHER
Austr. violinist ...... MORINI
author .... PARENT
author, boys' . ALGER, HENTY
author, nature stories . SETON
authoritative .... MAGISTRAL
author unknown: abbr. . ANON

a authority, name as CITE, QUOTE
auto, old .. JALOPY, JALOPPY
automaton .... ROBOT
automaton: Jew. legend GOLEM
automobile "shoe" TIRE, TYRE
ave .... HAIL
avena .... OAT
avenger: Hebr. .... GOEL
average ...... PAR, MEAN,
NORM, USUAL, MEDIAL
averse ...... LOTH, LOATH
Avesta division
YASNA, GATHAS, YASHTS
avid .... KEEN, EAGER
avifauna .... ORNIS
avocado, Mex. .... COYO
avoid ...... SHUN, ESCHEW

c avouch .... AVER, ASSERT
away ... OFF, GONE, ABSENT
aweather, opposed to .. ALEE
aweto .... WERI
awkward .... INEPT
awkward fellow .... LOUT
awn .... ARISTA
awned .... ARISTATE
awry .... AGEE, AJEE, AGLEY
axilla .... ALA
axilla, pert. to .... ALAR
axillary .... ALAR
axis deer .... CHITAL
Aztec god, sowing .... XIPE
Aztec "Noah" (hero) ... NATA
Aztec "Noah's" wife ... NANA
Aztec spear .... ATLATL

B

babbler: Scot. ..... HAVEREL
Babism, founder .... BAB
babul tree pods ...... GARAD
baby animal: Fr. ...... TOTO
baby carriage .... PRAM
b BABYLONIAN GODS, DEITY,
see also GODS and also SPE-
CIAL SECTION on page 198
Babylonian abode of dead
ARALU
Babylonian chief gods ... EA,
ANU, BEL, HEA, ENKI
Babylonian chief goddess
ISTAR, ISHTAR
Babylonian chief priest of
shrine .... EN
Babylonian city .... IS
Babylonian division ... SUMER
Babylonian hero ...... ETANA
Babylonian lunar cycle
SAROS
Babylonian neighbor
ELAMITE
Babylonian numeral ... SAROS
Babylonian priestess . ENTUM
Babylonian purgatory . ARALU
Bacchanals' cry ...... EVOE
bacchante .... MAENAD
Bacchus' follower ..... SATYR
Bacchus' son .... COMUS
back ... AID, AFT, FRO, ABET,
HIND, REAR, SPONSOR
back, call .... REVOKE
back door .... POSTERN
back, flow .... EBB, RECEDE
back, lying on ...... SUPINE
back of neck .... NAPE
back, pert. to ...... DORSAL

back, take .... RETRACT
back, thrust .... REPEL
back, toward ...... RETRAL
back: Zool. ..... NOTA, NOTUM
d backbone ...... CHINE, SPINE
bacteria-free .... ASEPTIC
bacteriologist's wire ... OESE
bacteriostatic subst. . CITRININ
badge, Jap. .... MON
badger .... DAS, BAIT
badgerlike animal
PAHMI, RATEL
badgers, Old World .... MELES
baffle .... FOIL, POSE, ELUDE
bag .... SAC
bag net .... FYKE
bagatelle .... TRIFLE
bagpipe, hole in LILL
bagpipe sound .... SKIRL
bailiff, old Eng. ...... REEVE
baize fabric .... DOMETT
baker bird .... HORNERO
baking chamber ... OST, KILN,
OAST, OVEN
baking pit .... IMU
balance .. REST, POISE, SCALE
balance, sentence ... PARISON
Balance, The .... LIBRA
balancing weight .... BALLAST
Balder's killer LOK, LOKE, LOKI
Balder's wife .... NANNA
baldness .... ACOMIA
Balkan .... SERB
ball, low .... LINER
ball, to hit
LOB, BUNT, SWAT

a

ball, yarn thread ...... CLEW
ballad .... LAY, DERRY
ballet jump .... JETE
ballet skirt .... TUTU
ballet turn .... FOUETTE
balloon basket CAR, NACELLE
ball-rope missile
                    BOLA, BOLAS
balm of Gilead ...... BALSAM
balsalike wood ...... BONGO
balsam ... FIR, TOLU, RESIN
Balt .... ESTH
BALTIC ... see also SPECIAL
     SECTION
Baltic Finn .... VOD
Baltimore stove .... LATROBE
Balto-Slav .... LETT
Baluchistan tribe ...... REKI
Baluchistan tribesman . MARI
"Bambi" author ...... SALTEN
bamboo .... REED
bamboo shoots, pickled ACHAR
Bana's daughter: Hindu USHA
banal .... STALE, TRITE
banana genus .... MUSA
banana, kind of ... PLANTAIN
banana, Polyn. .... FEI
band .... BELT, TAPE,
               STRIP, FILLET
band: Arch. .. FACIA, FASCIA
band, muscle, nerve . TAENIA
band, narrow .. STRIA, STRIAE
bandage ..... STUPE, TAENIA
bandicoot .... RAT

b

bandmaster, Am. ..... SOUSA
banish ...... EXILE, RELEGATE
bank .... RELY, DEPEND
bank, of a river .. RIPARIAN
bank, river .... RIPA
banker, India . SARAF, SHROFF
banner .... FLAG,
     ENSIGN, BANDEROLE
banter ... CHAFF, PERSIFLAGE
BANTU   see also TRIBES in
     SPECIAL SECTION, Page 191
Bantu ...... KAFIR, KAFFIR
Bantu, Congo ... RUA, WARUA
Bantu language .... ILA
Bantu nation .... GOGO
Bantu-speaking tribe
          RAVI, RORI, PONDO
Bantu, tribesman ..... DUALA
baobab, dried .... LALO
baobab leaves, powdered LALO
baptism font .... LAVER
baptismal basin .... FONT
bar .... RAIL, INGOT,
         HINDER, STRIPE
bar legally .... ESTOP
bar, supporting .... FID
barb, feather .... HARL, HERL

c

Barbados native .... BIM
barbarian .... HUN, GOTH
Barbary ape .... MAGOT
barber .... SHAVER, TONSOR
bard, Goth. .... RUNER
bare ...... BALD, MERE, NUDE
bargain .... DEAL, PALTER
bargain: Dutch ...... KOOP
barge .... HOY
bark .... BAY, YAP, YIP
bark, bitter .. NIEPA, NIOTA
bark, inner .... CORTEX
bark, lime tree .. BAST, BASTE
bark, medicinal .... COTO
bark, paper mulberry .. TAPA
bark, pert. to .... CORTICAL
bark remover ...... ROSSER
bark, rough exterior ... ROSS
barking .... LATRANT
barn owl genus ...... TYTO
barometric line ..... ISOBAR
barony, Jap. .... HAN
barracuda, small SPET, SENNET
barrelmaker .... COOPER
barrel slat .... STAVE
barren land .... USAR
Barrie character ...... ALICE
barrow, Russ. ...... KURGAN
base .... LOW, VILE
base, architectural
          SOCLE, PLINTH

d

base, attached by .... SESSILE
baseball position: abbr. ... LF,
               RF, SS
Bashan, king of .... OG
bashful ..... COY, SHY, TIMID
basilica, Rome ..... LATERAN
basin: Geol. .... TALA
basis of argument ... PREMISE
basket .... KISH, CABAS,
          PANIER, PANNIER
basket, coarse .... SKEP
basket, Eng. .... PED, CAUL
basket, fish .. WEEL, CRAIL,
          CREEL, WICKER
basket grass, Mex. .... OTATE
basket, large ...... HAMPER
basket, strip .... RAND
basketball player .... CAGER
basketry rod .... OSIER
Basra native .... IRAQI
bass, Europ. .... BRASSE
basswood .... LINDEN
bast fiber .... RAMIE
bat .... RACKET
batfish .... DIABLO
bathe .... LAVE
bathing-suit .... MAILLOT
baths, Roman ..... THERMAE
Bathsheba's husband
          URIA, URIAH

16

a baton .... ROD
batrachian ...... FROG, TOAD
batter .... RAM
battering machine ...... RAM
battery plate .... GRID
battle, Am. Rev. ... CONCORD
battle area .... SECTOR
battle, Arthur's last .. CAMLAN
battle ax ...... TWIBIL, TWIBILL
battle, Civil War, Tenn. SHILOH
battle cry, Irish ... ABU, ABOO
battle, Eng.-Fr. CRECY, CRESSY
battle formation ...... HERSE
battlel, Franco-Pruss. .. SEDAN
battle, 100 Years War
          CRECY, CRESSY
"Battle Hymn of Republic"
  author .... HOWE
battle, WWI .. MARNE, SOMME,
          YPRES, VERDUN
battlefield .... ARENA
bauble .... BEAD
bay ..... COVE, BIGHT, INLET
bay, Orkney, Shetland ... VOE
bay tree .... LAUREL
bay window .... ORIEL
bazaar .... FAIR
be foolishly overfond ... DOAT,
          DOTE
b be silent: music ...... TACET
be still .... SH, HUSH, QUIET
beach .... SHORE, STRAND
beach cabin .... CABANA
beads, prayer ...... ROSARY
beak .... NEB, NIB, BILL
beam, supporting
     TEMPLET, TEMPLATE
bean .... SOY, URD, LIMA
bean, E. Ind. .... URD
bean, field .... PINTO
bean, green .... HARICOT
bean, poisonous ... CALABAR
bean, S. Am. .... TONKA
bean tree .... CAROB
bear STAND, YIELD, ENDURE
Bear constellation ...... URSA
bear, nymph changed to
          CALLISTO
bear, Austral. .... KOALA
bear witness . VOUCH, ATTEST
beard of grain .. AWN, ARISTA
bearded seal .... MAKLUK
bearer, Ind. .... SINDAR
bearing .... MIEN, ORLE
bearing plate .... GIB
bear's-ear .... ARICULA
beast of burden ...... ASS,
          BURRO, LLAMA
beat ..... WIN, CANE, DRUB,
     FLAP, POMMEL, PULSE
beat about: naut. ...... BUSK

c beater, mortar .... RAB
beauty, goddess of: Hindu
     SRI, SHRI, SHREE, LAKSHMI
beauty, Greek .... LAIS
beaver .... CASTOR
beaver skin .... PLEW
beche-de-mer ...... TREPANG
beckon .... NOD
bed .... KIP, PALLET
bed of dry stream ..... DONGA
bed of press, handle . ROUNCE
bed: slang .... DOSS
Bedouin headband cord . AGAL
bee, honey, genus ..... APIS
bee house ...... APIARY, HIVE
bee, male .... DRONE
bee tree .... LINDEN
bees, pert. to .... APIAN
bee's pollen brush .... SCOPA
beech tree genus ..... FAGUS
beechnuts .... MAST
beefwood: Polyn. ...... TOA,
          TOOA, BELAH
beehive, straw .... SKEP
Beehive State .. see page 209
beer ..... ALE, BOCK, LAGER
beer, Afr. millet ..... POMBE
beer ingredient .. HOPS, MALT
beer mug .... STEIN
beer, P. I. rice ...... PANGASI
d beet variety .... CHARD
Beethoven's birthplace . BONN
beetle .... DOR, ELATER
beetle, burrowing ..... BORER
beetle, click .... ELATER
beetle, fruit-loving .... BORER
beetle genus, ground .. AMARA
beetle, ground ...... CARAB
beetle, sacred Egypt. . SCARAB
beetle, wood .... SAWYER
befall .... HAP
before .... ERE, PRE,
          ANTERIOR
before: obs. .... ERER
before: naut. .... AFORE
beget .... EAN, SIRE
"Beggar's Opera" dramatist
          GAY
beginner .... TIRO, TYRO,
     NOVICE, NEOPHYTE
beginning .... GERM, ONSET,
     ORIGIN, INITIAL
beginning .... NASCENCY
behave toward .... TREAT
behind .... AFT, AREAR,
          ASTERN
behold .... LO, ECCE, VOILA
behoove .... DOW
beige .... ECRU
being .... ENS, ENTITY

a being, abstract ... ENS, ESSE, ENTIA
being, essential .... ENS
Bela, son of .... IRI
beleaguerment .... SIEGE
Belem .... PARA
belief .... CREED, FAITH, TENET
believe .... TROW, CREDO, CREDIT
believer in god of reason DEIST
bell, alarm .... TOCSIN
bell, sacring .... SQUILLA
bell tower .... BELFRY, CAMPANILE
bell's tongue ...... CLAPPER
bellbird, N.Z. .... MAKO
bellowing .... AROAR
below: nautical .... ALOW
belt .... CEST, SASH
belt, sword ...... BALDRIC, BAWDRIC, BALDRICK
ben .... BENE
bench ...... EXEDRA, SETTLE
bench, judge's .. see JUDGE'S BENCH
bench in a galley ..... BANK
bend ...... SNY, FLEX, GENU, STOOP, FLEXURE
benediction .... BENISON
benefactor .... PATRON
beneficiary: Law .... USES
b benefit .... BOON, AVAIL
Bengal native .... KOL
Bengal singer .... BAUL
Benjamin's first born ... BELA
bent .... PRONATE
bequeath .... WILL
bequest .... DOWER
Berber .... RIFF
Bermuda arrowroot ARARU, ARARAO
Bermuda grass . DOOB, DOUB
berserk ...... AMOK, AMUCK
beseech .... PRAY, OBTEST, ENTREAT
beside .... BY
besides TOO, YET, ALSO, ELSE
bestow .... AWARD, CONFER, IMPART
bets, fail to pay WELCH, WELSH
betel leaf ...... BUYO, PAUN
betel nut .... SERI, SIRI, BONGA, SIRIH
betel palm .. ARECA, PINANG
betel pepper .... IKMA, ITMO
Bethuel's son .... LABAN
betoken .... DENOTE
betroth .... AFFY
between: prefix .... INTER
Bevan's nickname ...... NYE

c bevel .... BEZEL, SLANT
bevel out .... REAM
bevel ship timber ..... SNAPE
bevel to join ... MITER, MITRE
BEVERAGE ... see also DRINK
beverage .... ADE, ALE, TEA, BEER
beverage, curdled .... POSSET
beverage, hot wine ... NEGUS
beverage, Polyn.
KAVA, KAWA
beverage, S. Am. ...... MATE
bewitch .... HEX, SPELL
beyond: comb. form .. ULTRA
Bhutan pine .... KAIL
biased person .... BIGOT
BIBLICAL .. see also SPECIAL SECTION
Biblical city .... DAN, BABEL, EKRON
Biblical character .. ARA, IRA, ERI, ARAN, ATER, ONAN
Biblical country EDOM, ENON, SEBA, SHEBA
Biblical driver .... JEHU
Biblical judge .... ELI, ELON, GIDEON, SAMSON
Biblical king . OG, ASA, AGAG, AHAB, ELAH, OMRI, SAUL, HEROD, NADAB
d Biblical kingdom .... ELAM, MOAB, SAMARIA
Biblical land .... NOD
Biblical lion .... ARI
BIBLICAL MEASURE .... see HEBREW MEASURE
BIBLICAL MOUNT see Page 197
Biblical name ... ED, ER, IRI, ONO, REI, TOI, ABIA, ADER, ANER, ANIM, ASOM, DARA, ENOS, IRAD, IVAH, REBA, ABIAM, AHIRA, AMASA, ASEAS
Biblical name for part of Arabia SHEBA
Biblical ornaments ..... URIM
Biblical priest, high ..... ELI, AARON, ANNAS
Biblical region .. ARAM, EDAR
Biblical ruler .... IRA
Biblical sacred objects .. URIM
Biblical serpent . NEHUSHTAN
Biblical son .... HAM
Biblical spy .... CALEB
Biblical tower .... EDAR
Biblical town in Samaria ENON
BIBLICAL TRIBE .... see Page 197
Biblical weed .... TARE
Biblical well; spring AIN, ESEK
Biblical wild ox .... REEM

18

a Biblical witch's home .. ENDOR
Biblical woman RAHAB, LEAH
Biblical word .. SELAH, MENE
Biblical word of reproach RACA
bicarbonate .... SODA
bice blue .... AZURITE
bicker .... CAVIL
bicycle for two ..... TANDEM
biddy .... HEN
"— bien" .... TRES
big casino .... TEN
bile .... GALL
bill .... DUN, NEB, BEAK
bill of fare .. MENU, CARTE
bill, part of .... CERE
billiard shot .. CAROM, MASSE
billow .... SEA, WAVE
bind ...... TAPE, SWATH
biography ..... LIFE, MEMOIR
biological .. BIOTIC, BIOTICAL
biological reproductive body
                    GAMETE
biotic community .... BIOME
bird ..... CLEE, COCK, CROW,
DOVE, FINK, GLED HUIA,
IIWI, JACU, KALA KIWI,
KOEL, KORA, KUKU KYAH,
LARK, LOON, LORO LORY,
LOUN, LOWA, LULU, LUPE,
MAKO, MAMO, MIRO,
MOHO, MORO, MYNA,
b NENE, PAPE, PEHO, PISK,
RAIL, RAYA, ROOK RUFF,
RURU, RYPE SKUA SMEE,
SMEW, SORA STIB SWAN,
TEAL, TERN, TOCK TOCO,
TODY, UTUM, WAEG,
WREN, YENI, YUTU,
DRAKE, ROBIN, SERIN, EL-
ANET, SHRIKE, SISKIN,
bird, Am. .... TOWHEE
bird, Arctic .. BRANT, FULMAR
bird, Austral. .... EMU KOEL,
              COOEE. COOEY
bird, black ANI, ROOK, RAVEN
bird, blue .... JAY
bird, C. & S. Am. ..... COIN,
          CONDOR, CONDORES
bird cry .... CAW, COO
bird, diving ..... AUK, LOON,
              LOUN, SMEW
bird, ducklike .... COOT
bird, extinct .... MOA,
              DODO, MAMO
bird, Europ. ... GLEDE, TEREK
bird genus .... CRAX, RHEA
bird, gull-like .... TERN
BIRD, HAWAIIAN .... see
          HAWAIIAN BIRD
bird house .... COTE
bird, hunting .... FALCON

c bird, India .... SARUS
          SHAMA, ARGALA
bird, laughing .... LOON
bird life .... ORNIS
bird, long-legged
          AGAMI, STILT
bird, marsh .... RAIL,
          SORA, BITTERN
bird, mythical .... ROC
bird, national .... EAGLE
bird nest collector OOLOGIST
bird of prey ..... ERN, ERNE,
          HAWK, KITE, EAGLE,
          CORMORANT
bird, orange .... ORIOLE
bird order ... PICI, RASORES
bird, oscine .. CHAT, ORIOLE
BIRD, OSTRICHLIKE ..... see
          OSTRICHLIKE BIRD
bird, Persian .... BULBUL
BIRD, SEA .... see SEA BIRD
bird, shore RAIL, SORA, SNIPE,
          WADER, AVOCET, PLOVER
bird, small .... TIT, PIPIT
bird, small brown ...... WREN
BIRD, S. AM. .... see
          S. AMER. BIRD
bird, swimming LOON, GREBE
bird, talking . MYNA, MYNAH
d bird, tropical ... ANI, ANO,
          TROGON, JACAMAR
bird, U. S.
          COLIN, VEERY, TANAGER
BIRD, WADING .... see
          WADING BIRD
bird, wading, Afr.
          UMBER, UMBRETTE
bird, water see WADING BIRD
BIRD, WEB-FOOTED ..... see
          WEB-FOOTED BIRD
bird, W. Ind. .... TODY
bird, white-plumed .. EGRET
bird, white-tailed .. ERN, ERNE
birds .... AVES
bird's beak ...... NEB, NIB
bird's cry ..... CAW, WEET
birds of region ...... ORNIS
birds' route .... FLYWAY
biretta .... CAP
birth, by .... NEE
birth, of one's .... NATAL
birthmark
          MOLE, NEVUS, NAEVUS
birthplace, Apollo, Diana DELOS
birthplace, Constantine's
          NIS, NISH
birthplace, Mohammed's
          MECCA
birthplace, Muses, Orpheus
          PIERIA

19

a birthstone .... Jan., **GARNET;**
Feb., **AMETHYST;** March,
**JASPER, AQUAMARINE,
BLOODSTONE;** April, **DIA-
MOND;** May, **AGATE, EM-
ERALD;** June, **PEARL,
MOONSTONE;** July, **ONYX,
RUBY;** Aug., **CARNELIAN,
SARDONYX, PERIDOT;**
Sept., **SAPPHIRE;** Oct.,
OPAL; Nov., **TOPAZ;** Dec.,
TURQUOISE, ZIRCON
birthwort, Europ. . **CLEMATITE**
bishop .... **PRELATE**
bishop of Rome .... **POPE**
bishopric .... **SEE**
bishop's attendant ... **VERGER**
bishop's hat
HURA, MITER, MITRE
bishop's office .... **LAWN**
bishop's seat ..... **SEE, APSE**
bishop's title, East ... **ABBA**
bite .... **CHAM, MORSEL**
bite upon .... **GNAW**
biting .... **ACERB, ACRID**
bitter .... **ACERB, ACRID**
bitter almonds compound
AMARINE
bitter drug .... **ALOE**
bitter vetch .... **ERS**
b bittern .... **HERON**
bivalve ...... **CLAM, MUSSEL**
bivalve genus .... **PINNA**
bizarre .... **OUTRE**
black ...... **JET, EBON, INKY
RAVEN, SABLE, TARRY,
NIGRINE**
black and blue .... **LIVID**
black buck .... **SASIN**
black gum tree genus **NYSSA**
black haw .... **SLOE**
black kelpie .... **BARB**
black nightshade .... **DUSCLE**
Black Sea arm .. **AZOF, AZOV**
blackbird
ANI, MERL, MERLE, RAVEN
blackbird, Europ.
OSSEL, OUSEL, OUZEL
blackbird: variant ...... **ANO**
blacken .... **INK, SOOT**
black-fin snapper ..... **SESI**
blackfish .... **TAUTOG**
Blackmore heroine ... **LORNA**
blacksnake .... **RACER**
blacksmith's block ... **ANVIL**
blackthorn fruit .... **SLOE**
blackwood, India .... **BITI**
blade .... **OAR**
Blake's symbolic figure .. **ZOA**
Blake's symbolic figures **ZOAS**
blanch .... **ETIOLATE**

c blanket, cloak-like .. **PONCHO**
blanket, coarse wool .. **COTTA**
blanket, horse .... **MANTA**
blanket, Sp.-Am. ..... **SERAPE**
blast furnace, stone in .. **TYMP**
blaubok, S. Afr. ...... **ETAAC**
blaze star .... **NOVA**
bleach .... **CHLORE**
bleaching vat .... **KEIR, KIER**
bleak .... **RAW**
blesbok .... **NUNNI**
bless .... **SAIN**
bless: Yiddish .... **BENSH**
blessing
BOON, GRACE, BENEFICE
blight .... **NIP**
blight of drought, India **SOKA**
blind, as hawks .... **SEEL**
blind dolphin .... **SUSU**
blind god, Teut. **HOTH, HODER**
blind, impulse to ruin ... **ATE**
blindness .... **CECITY**
blister . **BLEB, BULLA, BULLAE**
block, small arch
DENTEL, DENTIL
block, wood .... **NOG**
blockhead .... **ASS, DOLT**
blood factor .... **RH**
blood, lack of red
ANEMIA, ANAEMIA
d blood of gods .... **ICHOR**
blood, part of .... **SERUM**
blood, pert. to ...... **HEMAL,
HEMIC, HAEMAL, HAEMIC**
blood vessel .... **VEIN**
blood vessel, main .... **AORTA**
blood, watery part of
SERA, SERUM
blood sucker .... **LEECH**
blood-sucking parasite .. **TICK**
blouse, long .... **TUNIC**
blow ..... **COUP, CRIG, ONER,
SWAT, WAFT**
blubber, piece of ..... **LIPPER**
blubber, to strip ..... **FLENSE**
blue ..... **CADET, PERSE,
SMALT, COBALT**
blue-dye yielding herb **WOAD**
blue dyestuff .... **WOAD**
"Blue Eagle" .... **NRA**
blue-footed petrel ...... **TITI**
blue grass (genus) .... **POA**
blue grape anthocyanin
ENIN, OENIN
blue gray
CHING, MERLE, SLATE
blue, greenish .... **BICE,
SAXE, TEAL, EMAIL**
blue mineral .... **IOLITE**
blue-pencil .... **EDIT**
blue pointer shark ..... **MAKO**

20

a blue pine .... LIM
Bluebeard's wife .... FATIMA
bluebonnet .... LUPINE
bluff .... CRUSTY
bluish-white metal ..... ZINC
blunder .... ERR
blunt .... DULL
blushing .... ROSY
boa, ringed .... ABOMA
boast ...... BRAG, VAUNT
boastful air .... PARADO
BOAT . see also SHIP, CANOE,
GALLEY, VESSEL
boat .... ARK, TUB, PUNT
boat, assault .... LST
boat, Ceylon, India
DONI, DHONI
boat, collapsible
FALTBOAT, FOLDBOAT
boat, dispatch .... AVISO
boat, E. Ind. ... DONI, DHONI
boat, Egypt .... BARIS
boat, Eskimo . BIDAR, CAYAK,
KAYAK, UMIAK, OOMIAC,
OOMIAK, UMIACK
boat, fishing
TROW, DOGGER, CORACLE
boat, fishing, North Sea COBLE
boat, flat-bottomed
SCOW, BARGE
b boat, freight .... LIGHTER
boat front ...... BOW, PROW
boat, Ind. landing . MASOOLA
boat, landing ... LCI, LST
boat, Levantine .... BUM
boat, light .... WHERRY
boat, mail .... PACKET
boat, Malay ..... PAHI, PRAH,
PRAO, PRAU, PROA,
PRAHU, PRAHO
boat, Manila Harbor . BILALO
boat, military .... PONTOON
boat, Nile 2-masted . SANDAL
boat, P. I. .. BANCA, BANKA
boat, racing .. SCULL, SHELL
boat, river
BARGE, FERRY, PACKET
boat, river, Chin. ... SAMPAN
boat, small .... DORY
boat, 3-oar ...... RANDAN
boat, used on Tigris
GUFA, KUFA
boat, with decks cut
RASEE, RAZEE
bob bait for fish .... DIB
bobbin .. PIRN, REEL, SPOOL
bobbins, frame for .... CREEL
bobwhite .... COLIN
Boche .... HUN
bodice, India .... CHOLI
bodily motion, pert. to GESTIC

c body .... SOMA, LICHAM
body, heavenly . STAR, COMET
body of laws .... CODE
body of men .... FORCE
body of persons ... CORPS
body of retainers ... RETINUE
body of writing .... TEXT
body, part of
THORAX, THORACES
body, pert. to SOMAL, SOMATIC
body, trunk of . TORSE, TORSO
body; zool. .... SOMA
Boer general .... BOTHA
bog FEN, MIRE, QUAG, MARSH
boggy .... FENNY
boil .... STEW, SEETHE
boil down .... DECOCT
boiled rice without salt: P. I.
CANIN
boiler, disk for hole in .. SPUT
"Bolero" composer ..... RAVEL
boll weevil .... PICUDO
Bolshevik leader ..... LENIN
bolt .... SCREEN
bomb, defective ...... DUD
bombardment, short, intense
RAFALE
bombast .... ELA
bombastic TURGID, OROTUND
Bombyx .... ERI
d bond .... NEXUS
bond-stone .... PERPEND
bondman ..... SERF, VASSAL
bonds, chem. with 2 double
DIENE
bone .... OS
bone, ankle TALUS, ASTRAGAL
bone, arm .... ULNA
bone, arm, pert. to .. ULNAR
bone, breast
STERNA, STERNAL, STERNUM
bone, ear ..... ANVIL, INCUS
bone: Greek .... OSTE
bone, leg .... FEMUR,
TIBIA, FIBULA, TIBIAE
bone, pelvic, hip ...... ILIUM
bone, pert. to ...... OSTEAL
bone scraper .... XYSTER
bone, skull .... VOMER
bones .... OSSA
bones, dorsal .... ILIA
bones, end of spine .. SACRA
bones, hip .... ILIA
bonnet monkey ZATI, MUNGA
bonnyclabber .... SKYR
bony .... OSTEAL
book .... MO, TOME, PRIMER
book, case for FOREL, FORREL
book, largest .... FOLIO
book, manuscript
CODEX, CODICES

21

a book, map .... **ATLAS**
book, Bible . see SPECIAL SEC-
TION, Page 196
books of devotions ... **MISSAL**
book of feasts, Catholic **ORDO**
book of hours . **HORA, HORAE**
book palm, tree .... **TARA**
book, The .... **BIBLE**
books, Bible .... **GOSPEL**
bookbinding style ...... **YAPP**
bookkeeping entry
DEBIT, CREDIT
booklet .... **BROCHURE**
boor **OAF, CLOD, LOUT, CHURL**
boat, Eskimo .... **KAMIK**
booth .... **STALL**
booth, Oriental market
SUQ, SOOK, SOUK
bootlace .... **LACET**
booty ..... **LOOT, PELF, SWAG**
booty, take .... **REAVE**
borax, crude .... **TINCAL**
border ..... **HEM, RIM, EDGE,**
RAND, SIDE, MARGE
border on .... **ABUT**
bore .... **TIRE, EAGRE,**
WEARY, CALIBER
borecole .... **KAIL, KALE**
boredom .... **ENNUI**
boric acid salts ...... **BORATE**

b born .... **NEE**
born, being ...... **NASCENT**
born: old Eng. .... **NATE**
Bornean squirrel shrew
PENTAIL
Borneo native . **DYAK, DAYAK**
boron, pert. to .... **BORIC**
borough .... **BURG**
borrowed stock: Irish law **DAER**
bosh .... **ROT, POOH**
boss .... **STUD**
boss on shield .... **UMBO**
Bostonian .... **HUBBITE**
botanical suffix ..... **ACEAE**
botanist .... **MENDEL**
botch .... **FLUB, MESS**
both ears, involving use of
BINAURAL
bother ... **ADO, FUSS, TODO,**
TEASE, MOLEST, PESTER
bo-tree .... **PIPAL**
bottle, glass water .. **CARAFE**
bottle, oil, vinegar
CRUET, FLASK
bottomless pit ... **ABADDON**
boundary ...... **LINE, MERE,**
METE, LIMIT
boundaries, mark off
DEMARCATE
bounder .... **CAD**
bounding line .... **SIDE**

c bounds .... **AMBIT**
bouquet .... **AROMA**
bovine .... **OX, COW**
bovine, male .... **STEER**
bow of ship .... **PROW**
bow, low Oriental
SALAM, SALAAM
bow-shaped .... **ARCATE**
bower .... **ARBOR**
bowfin .... **AMIA**
bowl: cricket .... **YARK**
bowling term .... **SPARE**
bowstring hemp **IFE, PANGANE**
box ..... **BIN, BINN, CASE,**
CIST, SPAR, CHEST
box canyon: Sp. ..... **CAJON**
box, ecclesiastic ...... **ARCA**
box, metal .... **CANISTER**
box opener .... **PANDORA**
box, papyrus rolls, Rom.
CAPSA
box, sacred, ancient Rom. **CIST**
box sleigh .... **PUNG**
boxing glove, Rom. ... **CESTUS**
boxing term .... **KO, TKO**
BOY'S NAME ..... see MAN'S
NAME
boy ... **BUB, BUD, LAD, TAD**
boys in blue .... **ELI'S**
B.P.O.E. member .... **ELK**

d brace .... **PAIR, TRUSS**
braced aback: nautical **ABOX**
bracing .... **TONIC**
brag .... **BOAST, VAUNT**
Brahman rule . **SUTRA, SUTTA**
Brahmany bull .... **ZEBU**
braid ... **PLAT, PLAIT, QUEUE**
braid, kind of .... **LACET**
brain canal-passage .... **ITER**
brain, layer in .... **OBEX**
brain opening ... **LURA, PYLA**
brain, part .... **PIA**
brain: P. I. .... **UTAC**
brain ridges .... **GYRI**
brain tissue .... **TELA**
brain ventricle opening **PYLA**
branch ... **ARM, LIMB, RAMI,**
RAME, RAMUS, SPRIG
branch-like **RAMOSE, RAMOUS**
branchia .... **GILL**
branch of learning ..... **ART**
brass, man of . **TALOS, TALUS**
brassart .... **BRACER**
"Brave Bulls" author .... **LEA**
brawl .... **MELEE, FRACAS**
BRAZIL .... see also SPECIAL
SECTION
Brazil capital .... **RIO**
Brazil dance .... **SAMBA**
Brazil drink .... **ASSAI**
Brazil heron .... **SOCO**

a Brazil Negro .... MINA
Brazil plant .... YAGE, YAJE
Brazil red .... ROSET
Brazil rubber tree ULE, HULE
Brazil tree .... APA, ANDA
breach .... GAP
bread, hard-baked ..... RUSK
bread crumbs, dish with
                      PANADA
breadfruit: P. I. ...... RIMA
breadfruit: P. R. .. CASTANA
bread-tree seeds ...... DIKA
break .... SNAP
break in .... STAVE
breakers .... SURF
breakwater .... MOLE, PIER
breastbone, of .... STERNAL
breastplate .... URIM
breastwork .... PARAPET
breastplate, Gr.
             THORAX, THORACES
breath of life .... PRANA
breathed .... SPIRATE
breathing, harsh
             RALE, STRIDOR
breech-cloth, Polyn. .... MALO
breeches: Scot. ...... TREWS
breed .... REAR, RAISE
Bremen's river ...... WESER
breviary .. PORTAS, PORTASS
b brewer's ferment .. LOB, LOBB
brewer's vat .... TUN
brewing .... MALTING
brewing, one
             GAAL, GAIL, GYLE
bribe .... SOP
brick carrier .... HOD
brick, sun-dried ..... ADOBE
bricklayer .... MASON
bricklayer's helper ...... CAD
bridal wreath .... SPIREA
bridge .... SPAN
bridge, floating ... PONTOON
bridge, maneuver .. FINESSE
bridge, Mississippi ... EADS
bridge part TRESSEL, TRESTLE
brief .... SHORT, TERSE
brigand .... LATRON
Brigham Young U. site PROVO
bright .... APT, NITID
bright colored fish
             BOCE, OPAH, WRASSE
bright: music .... ANIME
brilliance .. ECLAT, ORIENCY
brilliant group ...... PLEIAD
bring forth .... EAN
bring on oneself ...... INCUR
bring together ..... COMPILE
bring up ...... REAR, RAISE
brisk: music ...... ALLEGRO
bristle .... SETA

c bristles .... SETAE
bristle, pert. to .... SETAL
bristly .... SETOSE
Britain's ancient inhabitant
                      PICT
BRITISH   also see ENGLISH
British conservative .... TORY
British king, legendary LUD,
      BELI, BRAN, BRUT, LUDD,
      NUDD
Britisher, early .... PICT
Brittany; city, ancient .... IS
broach .... RIMER
broad band: Her. ..... FESS
broadbill, E. Ind. ...... RAYA
broadbill duck ...... SCAUP
broken glass to remelt .. CALX
broken seed coats ..... BRAN
broken spike of grain .. CHOB
broken stone, etc. ... RUBBLE
Bronte heroine .... EYRE
bronze, Rom. money .... AES
brood .... SET, NIDE, COVEY
brook, small ..... RUN, RILL
broom of twigs ...... BESOM
broom-corn millet
             HIRSE KADIKANE
brother .. FRA, FRIAR, FRATER
brought up .... BRED
brow of hill; Scot. ..... SNAB
d brown .... TAN, SEAR, SEPIA,
      UMBER, BISTER, RUSSET,
      SIENNA, SORREL
brown kiwi .... ROA
brown, pale .... ECRU
brown, red-yellow .... PABLO
brown-skinned race .. MALAY
brown sugar ...... PANELA
brown, yellowish dull .. DRAB
browned .... RISSOLE
brownie .... NIS, NIX, NISSE
Browning poem, girl in PIPPA
browse .... GRAZE
Brunnehilde's mother ... ERDA
brushwood .. TINET, TINNET
brusque ...... BLUNT, TERSE
Brythonic .... CORNISH
Brythonic sea god ...... LER
bubble .... BLEB
buck, 4th year .... SORE
Buddha .... FO
Buddha, Jap. AMIDA, AMITA
Buddha's foe .... MARA
Buddha's mother ..... MAYA
Buddha's tree .... PIPAL
Buddhist angel ...... DEVA
Buddhist church in Jap. . TERA
Buddhist language .... PALI
Buddhist monastery, Jap. TERA
Buddhist Mongol .... ELEUT
Buddhist monk ... BO, LAMA

23

Buddhist

a Buddhist monument .. **STUPA**
Buddhist novice ...... **GOYIN**
Buddhist pillar .... **LAT**
Buddhist priest .... **LAMA**
Buddhist relic .... **STUPA**
Buddhist sacred city .... **LASSA**
Buddhist sacred dialect **PALI**
Buddhist sacred mountain **OMEI**
Buddhist saint **LOHAN, ARHAT**
Buddhist scripture .... **SUTRA,
SUTTA**
Buddhist sect, Jap. .... **ZEN**
Buddhist shrine **TOPE, STUPA,
DAGABA, DAGOBA, DAG-
HOBA, DHAGOBA**
Buddhist spirit of evil . **MARA**
buds, pickled .... **CAPERS**
buffalo, India
ARNA, ARNI, ARNEE
buffalo pea .... **VETCH**
buffalo, water, P. I. .. **CARABAO**
buffet .... **SLAP, SMITE, TOSS**
buffoon .. **FOOL, MIME, ZANY,
CLOWN, MUMMER, JESTER**
bug .... **BEETLE**
bugaboo: S. Afr. **GOGA, GOGO**
bugle call
TATOO, TATTOO, TANTARA
bugle note .... **TIRALEE**
build .... **REAR, ERECT**
builder .... **ERECTOR**
b builder, jetty-dam ...... **EADS**
building site .... **LOT**
building wing ... **ELL, ANNEX**
bulb, edible .... **SEGO**
bulb, Indian food
CAMAS, CAMASS, CAMMAS
bulb-like stem .... **CORM**
BULGARIAN ... see also SPE-
CIAL SECTION
Bulgarian czar .... **BORIS**
bulge, as eyes .... **BUG**
bulk .... **MASS**
bull, girl carried off on **EUROPA**
bull, sacred Egyp. ...... **APIS**
bullet, size of
CALIBER, CALIBRE
bullet sound .... **ZIP, PHIT,
PHUT, PIFF**
bullfight .... **CORRIDA**
bullfight cry .... **OLE**
bullfighter on foot ... **TORERO**
bullfighter's queue .... **COLETA**
bullfinch, Eng. .... **ALP**
bully .... **HECTOR**
bulrush .... **TULE**
Bulwer-Lytton heroine .. **IONE**
bumblebee .... **DOR**
bumpkin .... **LOUT**
bunch .... **TUFT, WISP**
bunch grass .... **STIPA**
bundle .... **BALE, PACK**

c bundle, small .... **PACKET**
bundle, twig, stick .... **FAGOT**
bundling machine .... **BALER**
bungle .... **BOTCH**
bunting .. **ESTAMIN, ETAMINE,
ORTOLAN, ESTAMENE**
bunting bird .... **CIRL**
buoy, Eng. .... **DAN**
buoy, kind of **CAN, NUN, NUT,
BELL, SPAR, WHISTLING**
buoyancy .... **FLOTAGE**
burbot .... **LING**
burbot genus .... **LOTA, LOTE**
Burchell's zebra ...... **DAUW**
burden ... **LADE, LOAD, ONUS**
burden bearer .... **ATLAS**
burglar .... **YEGG**
burial place, Polyn. .... **AHU**
BURMA ... see also SPECIAL
SECTION
Burma Buddhist (native) **MON**
Burma chief .... **BO, BOH**
Burmese capital, ancient **AVA**
Burmese demon (devil) .. **NAT**
Burmese gibbon .... **LAR**
Burmese governor **WUN, WOON**
Burmese hill-dweller ..... **LAI**
Burmese hills .... **NAGA**
Burmese knife .. **DAH, DHAO**
Burmese language . **WA, PEGU**
Burmese mongoloid ..... **LAI**
d Burmese native (s) **WA,LAI,WAS**
Burmese premier .... **UNU**
Burmese 3-string viol ... **TURR**
Burmese wood sprite ... **NAT**
burn incense .... **CENSE**
burn .... **ASH, CHAR, SERE**
Burnett, Frances, heroine **SARA**
burning bush .... **WAHOO**
burning, malicious .... **ARSON**
burnish .... **RUB**
burrowing animal **MOLE, RATEL**
burst asunder .... **SPLIT**
burst forth .... **ERUPT**
bury ...... **INTER, INHUME**
bush or bushy clump .... **TOD**
bushel, fourth of ..... **PECK**
Bushmen .... **SAN, SAAN**
bushy .... **DUMOSE**
business .... **TRADE**
business cartel .... **TRUST**
"Bus Stop" author ..... **INGE**
bustard genus .... **OTIS**
bustle .... **ADO, TODO**
bustle about .... **FISK**
busy, to be .... **HUM**
but ...... **YET, ONLY, STILL**
butcher's hook .... **GAMBREL**
butter, illipe .... **MAHUA**
butter, India .....**GHI, GHEE**
butter, liquid ..... **GHI, GHEE**

24

a butter tree .... SHEA
butter tub .... FIRKIN
butterbur .... OXWORT
butterfly, ... IO, SATYR
butterfly, large .... IDALIA
butterfly-lily .... SEGO
button .... STUD
button, part of ...... SHANK
buyer .... VENDEE
buyer: Law .... EMPTOR

c buzzard .... BUTEO
buzzing sound .. WHIR, WHIZ
by .... AT, PER, PAST,
ALONG, BESIDE
by birth .... NEE
by hand, bred .... CADE
by means of .... PER
bygone .... AGO
Byron poem .... LARA
Byzantine capital .... NICAEA

C

C, mark under ..... CEDILLA
caama .... ASSE
cab, Near East .... ARABA
cabal .... PLOT
cabbage .... COLE, KAIL,
KALE, KEAL
cabbage type .... SAVOY
cabin, main .... SALOON
cabinet, open, bric-a-brac
ETAGERE
cactus fruit, edible .. COCHAL
cactus, genus .... CEREUS
cactus-like .... CACTOID
caddis fly worm .... CADEW
Caddoan Indian .... REE
b cadet .... LAD
Cadmus' daughter ...... INO
Caen's river .... ORNE
Caesar's conspirator-slayer
CASCA, BRUTUS, CASSIUS
cafe .... CABARET
caffein in tea
THEIN, THEINA, THEINE
caffein-rich nut .. COLA, KOLA
cage .... MEW
Cain's brother .... ABEL
Cain's land .... NOD
Cain's son .... ENOCH
Cain's wife, Byron poem
ADAH
cake, rich ... TORTE, TORTEN
cake, small .... BUN, BUNN
calabar bean alkaloid
ESERIN, ESERINE
calamity .... WOE, DISASTER
calcium oxide .... LIME
calf of leg, pert. to ... SURAL
calf's cry .... BLAT
caliber .... BORE, DIAMETER
calico colors, mix ...... TEER
calico horse . PINTO, PIEBALD
calico-printing method . LAPIS
California army base ... ORD
Calif. fish .... RENA, REINA
Calif. fort .... ORD

Calif. herb .... AMOLE
Calif. motto .... EUREKA
Calif. shrub, berry .... SALAL
Calif. wine valley ...... NAPA
Caliph .... ALI, IMAM
call .. CRY, DUB, DIAL, NAME,
ROUSE, WAKEN, MUSTER
call for hogs .... SOOK
call forth .. EVOKE, SUMMON,
ELICIT, EVOCATE
call, to attract attention
HEY, PST, HIST, PIST
calling .. METIER, VOCATION
Calliope's sister ...... ERATO
calm ..... LAY, COOL, LULL,
d QUIET, STILL, PLACID, SE-
RENE, SMOOTH, SOOTHE
calorie ..... THERM, THERME
calumniate .... MALIGN
calumny .... SLANDER
Calvinists, Scotch .. BEREANS
calyx leaf .... SEPAL
cam .... TAPPET
cambric .... PERCALE
cambric grass .... RAMIE
CAME .... see COME
camel: Anglo-Ind. ..... OONT
camel hair cloth .... ABA
camel hair robe .... ABA
camel-like animal .... LLAMA
Camelot lady .... ENID
cameo stone .... ONYX
camera platform ..... DOLLY
Cameroons tribe .... ABO
"Camille" author .... DUMAS
camlet .... PONCHO
camp, fortified ...... TABOR
camp, pert. to ...... CASTRAL
camphor, kind of ..... ALANT
campus, restrict. to Eng. GATED
Canaanite month .... BUL
Canada goose ..... OUTARDE
canal bank .... BERM, BERME
canal betw. N. and Balt. Seas
KIEL

25

a canary yellow ...... MELINE
canasta play .... MELD
cancel . DELE, ANNUL, ERASE
candid .... OPEN, FRANK
candidates list . LEET, SLATE
candle .... DIP, TEST, TAPER
candle holder
            SCONCE, GIRANDOLE
candle wick . SNAST, SNASTE
candlenut tree .... AMA
candlenut tree fiber ..... AEA
cane .... RATTAN, MALACCA
Canio's wife "I pagliacci"
                          NEDDA
canister, tea, alloy for . CALIN
canna plant .... ACHIRA
cannabis .... HEMP
cannon .... MORTAR
cannon, old
        MOYENNE, ROBINET
CANOE .. see also BOAT
canoe, Afr. .. BONGO, BUNGO
canoe, Hawaii ...... WAAPA
canoe, Malabar ...... TONEE
canoe, Malay (South Seas) out-
    rigger ... PAHI, PRAH,
    PRAO, PRAU. PROA,
    PRAHO, PRAHU
canoe, Maori .... WAKA
b canoe, P. I. .. BANCA, BANKA
canon .... LAW, RULE
canonical hour .. SEXT (noon),
    LAUDS, NONES, PRIME,
    MATINS, TIERCE
canopy COPE, SHADE, TESTER
cant TIP, TILT, SLANG, CAREEN
cant-hook .... PEAVY, PEEVY,
        PEAVEY, PEEVEY
cantankerous command SCAT
cantata, pastoral .. SERENATA
canticle, Scripture ...... ODE
"Cantique de Noel" composer
                          ADAM
CANTON .. see the country in
    SPECIAL SECTION
canvas .. DUCK, TUKE, SAILS
canvas, piece of ...... TARP
canvas shelter .... TENT
canyon mouth .... ABRA
canyon, small ...... CANADA
CAP .... see HEADGEAR
capable .... ABLE
Cape .... NES, RAS,
        NASE, NAZE, NESS
cape, early .... COPE
cape, fur .... PALATINE
Cape Horn native ...... ONA
cape, Pope's .. FANON, ORALE
Cape Verde native .... SERER
Capek creature ...... ROBOT

c caper .... DIDO, LEAP, ANTIC
CAPITAL .. see SPECIAL SEC-
                          TION
caprice WHIM, FANCY, VAGARY
captain, fiction .... AHAB
captain, Nile ...... RAIS, REIS
capture BAG, NAB, NET, SEIZE
car .... SEDAN
car, last CABOOSE, CAMBOOSE
car, old make .... REO
caracal .... LYNX
Caradoc .... BALA
caravan .... CAFILA
caravansary
        CHAN, KAHN, SERAI
caravel, Columbus NINA, PINTA
carbolic acid ...... PHENOL
carbon, powdery ...... SOOT
CARD .. see also GAME, CARD
card ... ACE, PAM, SIX, TEN,
    TWO, FOUR, JACK, KING,
    NINE, TREY, KNAVE,
    POSTAL
card game like bridge .. VINT
card game, 3-handed ... SKAT
card game, old ...... TAROT
card game, Sp. ...... OMBER,
                          OMBRE
card holding .... TENACE
card in euchre ...... BOWER
card, playing
        TAROC, TAROT, TAROCCO
d card wool ...... TUM, TEASE
cards, highest ...... HONORS
care for .... RECK, TEND
care, heavy .... CARK
careen ...... TIP, LIST, TILT
caress .... PET
cargo ...... LOAD, PORTAGE
cargo, put on ... LADE, LOAD
"Carmen" composer .. BIZET
carnation .... PINK
carnelian .... SARD
carnivore, Afr. .... RATEL
carol .... NOEL, SING
carol singer .... WAIT
carom .... RICOCHET
carousal ORGY, BINGE, SPREE
carouse .... REVEL
carp .... ID, CAVIL
carp, Jap. .... KOI
carp, red-eyed .... RUD, RUDD
carpet, Afgh. .. HERAT, HERATI
carpet, Caucasian BAKU, KUBA
carpet, India .... AGRA
carpet, Pers. .. KALI, SENNA
carriage .. GIG, MIEN, POISE,
    CALASH, LANDAU, CARIOLE
carriage: Fr. ...... FIACRE
carriage, India ...... EKKA
carriage, Java, Oriental SADO

26

a carried away .... RAPT
carrier, of Orient .... HAMAL
Carroll heroine .... ALICE
carrot-family plant .. ANISE
carrot-like herb genus . MEUM
carrot ridges .... JUGA
carry ...... LUG, BEAR, TOTE
carry across water .... FERRY
carry on (a war) ...... WAGE
cart, heavy .... DRAY
carte .... MENU
Carthage, of .... PUNIC
Carthage queen .... DIDO
cartograph .... MAP
cartoonist
  ARNO, CAPP, NAST, KIRBY
carve in itaglio ...... INCISE
case, grammatical ... DATIVE
case of explosives ... PETARD
case, toilet, small
             ETUI, ETWEE
casing, bore-hole ...... LINER
cask .. KEG, TUB, TUN, BUTT,
  CADE, TIERCE, PUNCHEON
cassava .. AIPI, JUCA, YUCA
cassia leaves .... SENNA
cast, founded .. FUSIL, FUSILE
cast metal mass . PIG, INGOT
cast off . MOLT, SHED, MOULT
b caste AHIR, BICE, GOLA, JATI
caste, agricultural .... MEO
caste, gardener ...... MALI
caste, low KOLI, KULI, PARIAH
caste, Tamil merchant
             CHETTY
caster ...... CRUET, ROLLER
casting mold .... DIE
castor-oil bean poison .. RICIN
castor-oil plant .... KIKI
Castor's killer .... IDAS
Castor's mother ...... LEDA
cat .... ANGORA
cat, Afr.
  CIVET, GENET, GENETTE
cat, Am.
  PUMA, COUGAR, OCELET
cat cry .. MEW, MIAU, MIAW,
  MIAOU, MIAOW, MIAUL
cat genus .... FELIS
cat-headed goddess, Egypt BAST
cat, spotted
  PARD, MARGAY, OCELET
cat, tailless .... MANX
catalogue .... LIST, RECORD
catamaran ...... BOAT, RAFT
catapult .... ONAGER
cataract .... FALLS
catch .... NAB, HAUL, HOOK,
  SNAG, TRAP, DETENT
catchword .... CUE, SLOGAN

c catechu-like resin ...... KINO
category ... GENRE, SPECIES
cater ...... PANDER, PURVEY
caterpillar .... LARVA
caterpillar hair .... SETA
caterpillar, N. Z. ...... WERI
catfish, Egypt ...... DOCMAC
catfish, S. Am. ...... DORAD
cathedral .... MINISTER
cathedral city, Eng. .... ELY
cathedral, famous . CHARTRES
cathedral passage ..... SLYPE
cathedral, Russian .. SOBOR
Catholic, Greek UNIAT, UNIATA
Catholic tribunal ...... ROTA
catkin .... AMENT, AMENTA
catnip .... NEP
catspaw DUPE, TOOL, STOOGE
cattail ...... TULE, MATREED
cattail India, narrow .. REREE
cattail, N. Z. ...... RAUPO
cattle, breed of ...... DEVON
cattle dealer .... DROVER
cattle genus .... BOS
cattle stealing, crime of
          ABIGEAT
CAUCASIAN .... see
      CAUCASUS NATIVE
Caucasian bharal .... TUR
Caucasian goat .. TUR, TEHR
Caucasian ibex .... ZAC
d Caucasian language
         ANDI, AVAR
Caucasian Moslem
        LAZ, LAZZI
Caucasian race in China
       LOLO, NOSU
Caucasus native
  SVAN, SVANE, OSSET
caucho tree .... ULE
caudal appendage ...... TAIL
caulk lightly .... CHINSE
cause ...... CAUSA, REASON
caustic ... LYE, LIME, ACRID,
  ERODENT, MORDANT
caustic poison ...... PHENOL
cauterize .... SEAR
cautery plant .... MOXA
cautious WARE, WARY, CHARY
"Cavalleria Rusticana"
  heroine .... LOLA
cavalryman .. ULAN, UHLAN
cavalryman, Turk., Alg.
      SPAHI, SPAHEE
cave: archaic .... ANTRE
cave explorer ... SPELUNKER
cave: poet .... GROT
cavern . CAVE, GROT, GROTTO
caviar .... ROE, IKRA
caviar fish .. SHAD, STERLET
cavil .... CARP, OBJECT

27

a cavity ...... ATRIA, ANTRA, SINUS, ANTRUM
cavity, ear, nose .... ANTRUM
cavity, in a rock . VUG, VOOG, VUGG, VUGH, GEODE
cavy .... APEREA
ceasel ...... HALT, AVAST
Cecrops' daughter .... HERSE
cedar, E. Ind. ...... DEODAR
Celebes ox .... ANOA
celebrated .... EMINENT
celery-like plant .... UDO
cella .... NAOS
cellulose acetate ... ACETOSE
cellulose: comb. form . CELLO
Celt .... ERSE, GAEL
Celt, legendary IR, ITH, MILED
Celtic .... ERSE, MANX, WELSH
Celtic church early center IONA
Celtic dart .... COLP
Celtic god .... TARANIS
Celtic goddess
ANA, ANU, DANA, DANU
Celtic mother of gods
ANA, ANU, DANA, DANU
Celtic name meaning black
DHU
Celtic Neptune .... LER
b Celtic paradise ..... AVALON
Celtic sea god .... LER
Celtic sun god ... LUG, LUGH
cement LUTE, PUTTY, SOLDER
cement well lining ... STEEN
cenobite .... MONK
censure . BLAME, CHIDE, SLATE
center .... HUB, CORE, FOCI, FOCUS, HEART
center away from .... DISTAL
center, toward ...... ENTAD
centerpiece .... EPERGNE
centesimal unit GRAD, GRADE
centesiml, 100 .... LIRA
centipede: Tahiti ..... VERI
central .... MID, FOCAL
Cent. Am. gum tree
TUNO, TUNU
Cent. Am. tree .... EBO, EBOE
central line .... AXIS
central points .... FOCI
century plant .... AGAVE
century plant fiber . PITA, PITO
cere .... WAX
cereal .... FARINA
cereal grain ...... OAT, RYE
cereal grass ..... OAT, RYE, WHEAT, MILLET
cereal grass, E. Ind. ... MAND, RAGI, RAGGI, RAGGEE

c cereal grass egnus ... SECALE
cereal plant: obs .... RIE
cereal spike ...... COB, EAR
ceremonial chamber ... KIVA
Ceres' mother .... OPS
certificate, money ..... SCRIP
cerulean blue COELIN, COELINE
cervine animal .... DEER
cesspool .... SUMP
cetacean . ORC, WHALE, NARWAL, NARWHAL, PORPOISE
cetacean, dolphinlike, genus
INIA
Ceylon ape .... MAHA
Ceylon foot soldier .... PEON
Ceylon governor ... DISAWA
Ceylon moss .... AGAR
Ceylon native
VEDDA, VEDDAH, WEDDAH
Ceylon standstone ..... PAAR
Ceylon trading vessel .. DONI
chafe RUB, FRET, FROT, GALL
chaff .... BANTER
chaffinch ..... CHINK, SPINK
chain .... CATENA
chain, nautical .... TYE
chainlike .... CATENATE
chair .... SEDAN
chair part ..... RUNG, SPLAT
d chaise .... GIG
chalcedony .... ONYX, AGATE
chalcedony, red ...... SARD
Chaldean astron. cycle .. SAROS
Chaldean city .... UR
chalice
AMA, AMULA, CALIX, GRAIL
chalice veil .... AER
chalky silicate .... TALC
challenge DARE, DEFY, GAGE
chamber .... ROOM, CAMERA
chamber, pert. to .. CAMERAL
champagne, Marne ...... AY
chance .... HAP, LOT, LUCK
chances, excess of ..... ODDS
chanced upon .... MET
chancel port .... BEMA
chancel screen .... JUBE
chancel seat .. SEDILE, SEDILIA
change .... FLUX, VARY, ALTER, AMEND
change appearance .. OBVERT
change direction CANT, KANT, TACK, TURN, VEER
change: music .... MUTA
channel .... GAT, MEDIA, STRIA, MEDIUM, STRIAL
Channel Island .... SARK
channel marker .... BUOY
channels .... MEDIA

28

chant .... INTONE
chanticleer .... COCK
chantry .... CHAPEL
chaos .... NU, NUN
chaos, Babyl. .... APSU
chaos, Egypt ...... NU, NUN
chaos, Maori myth .... KORE
Chaos' son .... EREBUS
chap: S. Afr. .... KEREL
chapel, private .... ORATORY
chapel, sailor's ...... BETHEL
chaperon: Sp. DUENA, DUENNA
chaplain .... PADRE
chaplet .. ANADEM, WREATH
chapped .... KIBY
character .... NATURE
characteristic .... TRAIT
charcoal: Pharm. .. CARBO
charge .... FEE, COST,
        DEBIT, INDICT
charge solemnly .... ADJURE
charged particle .... ION
charger .... STEED
chariot, ancient Briton
    ESSED, ESSEDA, ESSEDE
chariot race site .... CIRCUS
chariot, religious RATH, RATHA
charity .... ALMS
Charlemagne, race sub-
    dued by .... AVARS
Charlemagne's father .. PEPIN
Charlotte —, dessert .. RUSSE
charm .... JUJU,
    SPELL, AMULET, GRIGRI
Charon, payment for .. OBOL
Charon, river of .... STYX
chart .... MAP
Charybdis, rock opp. .. SCYLLA
chasm GAP, ABYSS, CANYON
chaste .... PURE, VESTAL
chat, friendly ... COSE, COZE
Chateaubriand heroine,
    novel .... ATALA
chatelaine bag .... ETUI
chatter GAB, GAS, YAP, PRATE
chatterbox .... PIET
cheat ...... RENIG, RENEGE
cheat .... BAM,
    CON, FOB, FUB, GIP, GYP,
    BILK, MUMP, COZEN, SHARP
cheaters: slang .... GLASSES
check .... NIP, TAB, REIN,
    STEM, BRAKE, STUNT
checking block .... SPRAG
cheek ... GENA, JOLE, JOWL
"cheek" GALL, BRASS, NERVE
cheek, pert. to .... MALAR
cheek-bone .... MALAR
cheer .... OLE, RAH,
    BRAVO, ELATE, ENCORE
cheer pine .... CHIR

cheer up .... LIVEN
cheerless .... SAD, DRAB
cheese ...... EDAM, STILTON
cheese, Dutch .... EDAM
cheese, hard brown . MYSOST
cheese, soft .... BRIE
cheesy .... CASEOUS
cheetah, Ind. . YOUSE, YOUZE
chela .... CLAW
Chemical compound .... IMID,
    AMIDE, AMINE, IMIDE,
    IMINE, ESTER
CHEMICAL ELEMENT .... see
        SPECIAL SECTION
chemical ending OL, INE, ENOL
chemical prefix ... ACI, OXA,
        AMIDO, AMINO
chemical salt .... SAL, ESTER,
        NITRE, BORATE
CHEMICAL SUFFIX .. see SUF-
        FIX, CHEMICAL
chemical unit .... TITER
chemist's pot ...... ALUDEL
cherish .. FOSTER, TREASURE
cherry .... GEAN
cherry red .... CERISE
chess piece .... MAN
chess term,—passant .... EN
chessman .... KING, PAWN,
    ROOK, QUEEN, BISHOP,
    CASTLE, KNIGHT
chest, acacia wood ..... ARK
chest, antique .... CIST, KIST
chest, sacred ARK, ARCA, CIST
chest sound .... RALE
chestnut, Eur. ...... MARRON
chestnut, Polyn. ...... RATA
chevrotain . NAPU, MEMINNA
chew .... BITE, CHAM, GNAW
chew, leaf to .... COCA
chewink .... TOWHEE
Chibcha chief's title .... ZIPA
chick-pea .... GRAM
chicken snake .... BOBA
chide ...... SCOLD, BERATE,
        REPROVE
chief .... ARCH, HEAD, MAIN
chief, Afr. tribe ...... KAID
chief, Am. Ind. ...... SACHEM
chief: Chinook ...... TYEE
chief deity, Panopolis .... MIN
chief in Italy .... DUCE
chief, India ...... SIRDAR
Chief Justice 1921-30 .. TAFT
Chief Justice 1941-46 . STONE
chief, Moslem .... RAIS, REIS
chief Norse god ...... ODIN,
    WODAN, WODEN, WOTAN
chief officer, India .. DEWAN,
        DIWAN
chief, Pres. .... MIR

29

a
child . . . . TIKE, TYKE
child of streets . ARAB, GAMIN
"Child of the Sun" . . . . INCA
child, pert. to . . . . FILIAL
child: Scot. . . . . BAIRN
child: Tagalog, P. I. . . . . BATA
Chilean proletariat . . . . ROTO
Chilean timber tree . . . . PELU
Chilean volcano . . . . ANTUCO
chill . . . . ICE, AGUE
chills and fever
. . . . AGUE, MALARIA
chimney: dialect . . . . . . LUM
chimney pipe . . . . FLUE
chin . . . . MENTA, MENTUM
China . . . . CATHAY
China blue . . . . NIKKO
China grass . . . . BON
Chinese . . SERES, SERIC, SINIC
Chinese aborigine YAO, MANS
Chin. aboriginal population
division . . . . MIAO
Chin. are . . . . MU
Chin. boat . . . . JUNK
Chin. brick bed . . . . . K'ANG
Chin. Causasian tribesman LOLO
Chin. characters in Jap. MANA
Chin. club . . . . TONG
CHIN. COIN . . see also COINS
Page 190
Chin., coin, bronze LI
b
Chin., coin, early . . . . . . PU
Chin. Communist . MAO, CHOU
Chin. cult . . . . JOSS
Chin. department . . . . . . FU
Chin. dialect . . . . WU
Chin. division . . . . MIAO
Chin. dynasty HAN, KIN, SUI,
WEI, YIN, CH'IN, CHOU,
HSIA, T'ANG, MING, SUNG,
TS'IN, YUAN
Chin. factory . . . . HONG
Chin. feudal state . . . . . WEI
Chin. flute . . . . TCHE
Chin. god . . . . . GHOS, JOSS
Chin. govt. section HIEN, HSIEN
Chin. guild . . . . HUI
Chin. idol . . . . . . GHOS, JOSS
Chin. instrument, stringed KIN
Chin. kingdom, old
WU, SHU, WEI
CHIN. MEASURE . . . . see also
pages 188, 189
Chin. measure of length TSUN
Chin. mile LI
Chin. monetary unit . . . . YUAN
CHIN. MONEY see also page 190
Chin. negative principle . . YIN
Chin. noodles . . . . MEIN
Chin. official . . KUAN, KWAN
Chin. philos. principle LI, YANG

c
Chin. plant . . . . UDO
Chin. pottery . . . . CHUN,
KUAN, MING, TING
Chin. ruler . . YAO, YAU, YAOU
Chin. secret society . . . . TONG
Chin. shop: Du. E. Ind. . TOKO
Chin. silk . . . . PONGEE
Chin. wax, wax insect . . PELA
Chin. wormwood . . . . MOXA
Chin. yellow . . . . SIL
chinin . . . . COYO
chink . . . . . . RIFT, RIMA, RIME
chink-like . . . RIMAL, RIMATE
chinky . . . . . . RIMAL, RIMOSE,
RIMOUS
chip . . . . NICK
chip of stone . SPALL, GALLET
chipmunk . . . . HACKEE
chirp CHEEP, TWEET, TWITTER
chisel, primitive . . . . . . CELT
chisel, very broad . . . . TOOLER
chocolate powder . . . . PINOLE
chocolate source . . . . CACAO
choice . . . . . . CREAM, ELITE,
PRIME. SELECT
choke up . . . . . . DAM, CLOG
choler . . . . . . IRE, BILE, RAGE
choose . . . . OPT. ELECT
chop . . . AXE, CUT, HEW. LOP
chop fine . . . . MINCE
d
chopped . . . . HEWN
choral music
MOTET, CANTATA
chord, 3 tones . . . . TRINE
chore . . . . JOB, CHARE
Chosen . . . . COREA, KOREA
Christ's thorn . . NABK. NUBK
Christmas . . . . . NOEL, YULE
Christmas crib . . . . . CRECHE
chromosome . . . . . . IDANT
chronicle . . ANNAL, ANNALS
chrysalis . . . . PUPA
chrysanthemum . . MUM. KIKU
chub. Europ. . . . . . . CHEVIN
chunk . . . . GOBBET
church . . . . FANE
church bench . . . . PEW
church, body of . . . . . NAVE
church calendar . . . . . ORDO
church contribution . . . TITHE
church council . . . . . SYNOD
church court . . . . ROTA
church dignitary POPE, BISHOP,
PRELATE, CARDINAL
church dish . . . . PATEN
church, India . . . . . SAMAJ
church living . . . . . BENEFICE
church maintenance, canon's
PREBEND
church officer . . . . . . ELDER

church official ..... SEXTON, VERGER
church part .... APSE, BEMA, NAVE, ALTAR
church, Pope's .... LATERAN
church porch ...... PARVIS
church property ...... GLEBE
church reader ...... LECTOR
church recess ...... APSE
church, Scot. .... KIRK, KURK
church vessel . AMA, PIX, PYX
churchman ...... PRELATE
churl CEORL, VILLAIN, VILLEIN
churl: var. .... CARLE
churn plunger ...... DASHER
cibol .... ONION
cicatrix .... SCAR
cigar ...... CLARO, SMOKE, CORONA, CHEROOT
cigar, cheap .. STOGY, STOGIE
cigarette, medicinal .. CUBEB
cigarfish .... SCAD
cincture .... BELT
cinnamon, kind of ... CASSIA
cion .... GRAFT
cipher .... ZERO, OUGHT
cipher system .... CODE
Circe's home .... AEAEA
circle .... CIRC, CIRQUE, RONDURE
circle of light .. HALO, NIMB
circle, part of .... ARC
circle segment ...... SECTOR
circuit .... LAP, TOUR, AMBIT, ORBIT
circuit judge, court .... EYRE
circular motion ...... GYRE
circular plate .. DISC, DISK
circular turn .... LOOP
circular saw ...... EDGER
cirque, geol. .... CWM
cistern .... BAC, VAT
citation .... CITAL
cite .... QUOTE, ADDUCE
citron .... ETROG, CEDRAT, ETHROG
citrus fruit .... LIME, LEMON, ORANGE, SHADOCK, SHADDOCK
CITY .. see also TOWN and GAZETTEER
city, ancient, Asia Min. . MYRA, TYRE, SARDES, SARDIS
city, ancient Thessalian LARISSA
city: Gr. .... POLIS
City of a Hundred Towers PAVIA
City of Bridges ...... BRUGES
City of God .... HEAVEN
City of Kings .... LIMA
City of Lights .... PARIS

City of luxury ...... SYBARIS
City of Masts ...... LONDON
City of Rams ...... CANTON
City of Refuge ...... MEDINA
City of Saints ...... MONTREAL
City of the Prophet ... MEDINA
City of the Seven Hills . . ROME
City of the Violet Crown ATHENS
City of Victory ...... CAIRO
city, pert. to .. CIVIC, URBAN
city, Philistines' ..... EKRON
city political division .. WARD
civet, Chinese .... RASSE
civet, Indian .... ZIBET
civet, Java .... DEDES
civet, Madagascar .... FOSSA, FOUSSA
civetlike cat GENET, GENETTE
civic goddess, Gr. ..... ALEA
Civil War commander ... LEE, POPE, GRANT, EWELL, MEADE, SCOTT, SYKES, HOOKER, CUSTER, FORREST, JACKSON
civil wrong or injury .... TORT
claim ...... ASSERT, DEMAND
clam genus .... MYA
clam, giant .... CHAMA
clam, razor .... SOLEN
clamor .... DIN, NOISE
clamp .... VICE, VISE
clan ...... GEN, SEPT, TRIBE
clan chieftain successor TANIST
clan, division: Gr. ...... OBE
clan, Gr. .... GENOS
clan, head of .... ALDER
clarinet socket .... BIRN
clash ...... JAR, COLLIDE
clasp . HASP, ENFOLD, INFOLD
clasp for a cape ...... MORSE
class .... ILK, CASTE, GENUS, GENERA, SPECIES
class leader, Eng. ..... DUX
class, lowest Jap. ..... HEIMIN
class, scientific GENUS, GENERA
classic tongue .... LATIN
classification .... RATING
classification method . . SYSTEM
classify .. RANK, RATE, SORT, TYPE, GRADE
claw .... NAIL, TALON, UNGUIS, UNGUES
claw, crustacean's CHELA, CHELAE
claw ornament .... GRIFF
claw: zool. ... UNCI, UNCUS
clay .... BOLE, ARGIL, LOESS
clay, baked .... TILE

31

clay bed .... GAULT
clay, building: Sp.
.... ADOBE, TAPIA
clay-covered .... LUTOSE
clay, friable .... BOLE
clay layer .... SLOAM, SLOOM
clay, melting pot ...... TASCO
clay mineral .... NACRITE
clay molding plate ...... DOD
clay pigeon shooting .. SKEET
clay pipe .... TD
clay plug .... BOTT
clay, porcelain ...... KAOLIN
clay, potter's .... ARGIL
clayey .... BOLAR
clayey soil BOLE, MALM, MARL
cleansing agent .... BORAX
clear NET, RID, LUCID, LIMPID,
AUDIBLE, TRANSPARENT
clear, as anchor ..... AWEIGH
clear of charges .... ACQUIT
clearing of land, Eng. .. SART
cleave REND, RIVE, CLING
cleaving tool .... FROE
cleft .... REFT, RIFT, RIMA
Clemenceau's nickname TIGRE
clement .... MILD
Cleopatra's attendant ... IRAS
Cleopatra's handmaid .... IRAS
Cleopatra's needle .. OBELISK
Cleopatra's serpent ..... ASP
clergyman ABBE, CANON,
VICAR, CURATE, PRIEST,
RECTOR
cleric, Fr. .... ABBE
clerical cap .... BIRETTA
clerical, not .... LAIC, LAICAL
clever .... APT, HABILE
click beetle ..... DOR, DORR,
ELATER
climb ..... GRIMP, SCALE
climbing plant ... IVY, VINE,
LIANA, LIANE
cling ...... STICK, ADHERE
clingfish .... TESTAR
clinging, for .... TENENT
Clio, sister of .... ERATO
clip .. CUT, MOW, SNIP, SHEAR
clique .... SET
CLOAK ... see also GARMENT
cloak .... ABA, WRAP, CAPOT,
CAPOTE, MANTLE
cloak, Ind. .... CHOGA
cloak, Rom. . SAGUM, ABOLLA,
ABOLLAE
cloak, woman's ..... DOLMAN
clock, ship-form .... NEF
clog-like shoe .... PATTEN
cloister .... MONASTERY
"Cloister-Hearth" author READE

close eyes of .... SEEL
close, keep .... HUG
close: musical .... CODA
close to AT, BY, NEAR, ANEAR
close, to fit .... FAY, FADGE
closed, as wings .... PLIE
closing measure, music . CODA
CLOTH ...... see also SILK,
COTTON, FABRIC
cloth, bark .... TAPA
cloth, figured old ..... TAPET
cloth measure .... ELL
cloth, old wool ..... CHEYNEY
cloth, stout .... BRIN
cloth strip, India ...... PATA
cloth used in mourning CRAPE
cloth, wrapping ...... TILLOT
clothe . GIRD, VEST, ENDUE
clothes moth .... TINEA
clothespress, old Dutch . KAS
clothing . DUDS, GARB, GEAR,
TOGS, RAIMENT
cloud .... SMUR, CIRRI,
NUBIA, CIRRUS
cloud dragon, Vedic ...... AHI
cloud, luminous ..... NIMBUS
clouds, broken .... RACK
clouds, wind-driven RACK, SCUD
cloudberry .... MOLKA
cloudy .... DULL, LOWERY
clout .... HIT, SWAT
cloven-footed ...... FISSIPED
clover .... HUBAM,
ALSIKE, MELILOT
clown .... APER, GOFF, ZANY
clown, Shakesperean LAVACHE
cloy .... PALL, SATE, ACCLOY
club member, Gr. .... ERANIST
club, women's .... ZONTA
clubfoot TALIPED, TALIPES
clumsily, handle PAW, BOTCH
clumsy ...... INEPT, OAFISH
cluster .... NEP, TUFT
cluster, grape ...... RACEME
cluster pine ...... PINASTER
coach dog ...... DALMATIAN
coach, Eastern .... ARABA
coagulate .... GEL, CLOT
coal dust ...... COOM, SMUT
coal, heat-treated .... COKE
coal, live .... EMBER
coal refuse .... CULM
coal scuttle .... HOD
coal, size of .. EGG, NUT, PEA
coalfish .... CUDDY
coalition .... UNION, MERGER
coarse .... GROSS
coarse sugar, E. Ind. .. RAAB
coast bird ...... GULL, TERN
coast dweller ...... ORARIAN
coastal range, India .... GHAT

COAT .... see also GARMENT
coat .... LAYER
coat, animal .... PELAGE
coat, Arab .... ABA
coat, soldier's .... TUNIC
coat with alloy ...... TERNE
cob .... SWAN
cobbler .... SUTOR
cobra . HAJE, NAGA, MAMBA
cobra genus .... NAIA, NAJA
cocaine source . COCA, CUCA
cockatoo, Austral. ... GALAH
cockatoo, palm . ARA, ARARA
cockboat .... COG
cockpit .... ARENA
coconut, dried ...... COPRA
coconut fiber ... COIR, KOIR,
                 KYAR, COIRE
coconut, Ind. ..... NARGIL
coconut palm, P. I. .... NIOG
cocoon insect .... PUPA
cocoon, silkworm ..... CLEW
cod genus .... GADUS
cod, pert. to .... GADOID
cod, young .... SCROD
code ...... LAW, CIPHER
codfish, Eur. .... POOR
coffee ... RIO, JAVA, MOCHA
coffee-chocolate flavor MOCHA
coffer-dam, Egypt .... SADD
coffin stand .... BIER
cognizant .... AWARE
cognomen .. NAME, EPITHET
cohere .... BIND
coil .... WIND, TWINE,
             TWIST, WREATHE
COIN ..... see also SPECIAL
             SECTION, Page 190
coin ...... RIN, YEN, SPECIE
coin, cut edges of ...... NIG
coin, edging .... REEDING
coin, gold .... LEV
coin, mill .... NURL
coin money .... MINT
coin, pewter .... TRA
coin, reverse side ..... VERSO
coin, silver .... SCEAT
coin tester, Orient
             SARAF, SHROFF
coin, tin .... TRA
coincide .... JIBE, AGREE
colander .... SIEVE
cold .... ALGID, GELID
cold, producing ..... ALGIFIC
cold tableland, Andes. .. PUNA
collar ETON, FICHU, GORGET
collar, clerical ...... RABAT,
             RABATO, REBATO
collar, deep ...... BERTHA
collar, wheel-shaped ... RUFF
collect ...... AMASS, GARNER

collection .... ANA, SET
collection .... SORTITE
collection, motley ...... RAFT
collection of facts ...... ANA
collection of sayings .... ANA
COLLEGE DEGREE . see DEGREE
college, Iowa .... COE
college, N.J., East Orange
                    UPSALA
college official .... DEAN
college quadrangle .... QUAD
colloquialism .... IDIOM
colonists greeting to Ind. NETOP
colonize .... SETTLE
colonizer .... OECIST
colonnade .... STOA
colony, Eng. ...... CAROLINA
colony, Fr. .... ALGERIA
color .... DYE, HUE, TINT
color ... ASH, BAY, RED, TAN,
        BLUE, FAON, FAWN, GRAY,
        GREY, HOPI, JADE, LIME,
        NAVY, NILE, PINK, PUCE,
        ROSE, SAXE, AMBER, BEIGE,
        CORAL, CREAM, EBONY,
        HENNA, IVORY, MAUVE,
        MOCHA, SEPIA, UMBER,
        CERISE, CITRON, COBALT,
        MAROON, RESEDA, SEVPES,
        SIENNA, SORREL, CAR-
        MINE, CELESTE, CITRINE,
        MAGENTA
color brown sugar .. CARAIBE
color, changer, photo .. TONER
color, neutral GREGE, GREIGE
color, purplish-brown .. PUCE
color, slightly .... TINT, TINGE
color, stripe of ...... PLAGA
color, terrapin ...... FEUILLE
Colorado park .... ESTES
coloring agent ...... RUDDLE
coloring matter in fustic MORIN
colorless .... DRAB
colorless alkaloid .... ESERIN
colorless oil .... CETANE
columbite, variety of DIANITE
Columbus' birthplace GENOA
Columbus' city sailed from
                    PALOS
Columbus' ship . NINA, PINTA
column, Buddhist-Hindu, build
        ing .... LAT
column, Gr. .... DORIC, IONIC
column, memorial ...... LAT
column, twisted TORSE, TORSO
columns, arranged in TABULAR
coma .... TRANCE
comb horse .... CURRY
comb wool ..... CARD, TEASE
combat, field, place of . ARENA
combat, knight's ...... JOUST

33

Combat

a

combat, scene of ..... ARENA
combination .. UNION, CARTEL
combination, card .... TENACE
COMBINING FORMS:
above .... SUR
air ...... AER, AERI, AERO
all .... PAN, OMNI
ass .... ONO
bad .... MAL
bee .... API
beyond .... SUR
black .... MELA
blood .... HEMO
body ...... SOMA, SOMATO
bone .... OSTEO
both .... AMBI
boundary .... ORI
bread .... ARTO
bristle .... SETI
cetacean .... CETO
Chinese .... SINO
communications ...... TEL
contemporary .... NEO
daybreak .... EO
dry .... XER
ear .... OTO, AURI
earth .... GEO
egg .... OO, OVI
eight .... OCT, OCTO
equal .... ISO, PARI

b

eye .... OCULO
far .... TEL, TELE
fat .. SEBI, STEAT, STEATO
fearful .... DINO
feast day .... MAS
female .... GYNE
firm .... STEREO
five .... PENTA
fellower .... IST
food .... SITO
foot ..... PED, PEDI, PEDO
four-parted .... TETRA
fruit .... CARPO
gas .... AER, AERO
gate .... PYLE
glade .... NEMO
gland .... ADEN
gray .... POLIO
great .... MEGA
gums .... ULO
hair .... PIL, PILI
half .... DEMI, SEMI
heat ..... THERM, THERMO
hundred .... CENTI, HECTO
idea .... IDEO
ill .... MAL
individual .... IDIO
inner .... ENTO
in zoology .... EAE
late, latest .... NEO
line .... STICH

c

many .... POLY
medicine .... IATRO
middle .... MEDI
milk .... LACT, LACTO
monster .... TERAT
mountain .... ORO
mouth ...... STOM, STOMO
moving .... KINO
narrow .... STENO
neck types .... DERA
needle .... ACU
nerve .... NEURO
new .... NEO
nine .... ENNE, ENNEA
nose .... NASI
not .... UN, NON
numerical .... UNI
numerous .... MULTI
oil .... OLEO
one .... UNI, MONO
on this side .... CIS
other .... HETER
outside .... ECTO
peculiar .... IDIO
power .... DYNA
powerful .... MEGA
quality .... ACY
recent ...... NEO, CENE
reversal .... ALLO

d

ribbon .... TENE
round .... GYRO
sad .... TRAGI
seeds .... CARPO
seizure of illness ... AGRA
self .... AUT, AUTO
shoulder .... OMO
small .... STENO
solid .... STEREO
speak .... LALO
star .... ASTRO
stone .... LITH
strange .... XENO
sun .... HELIO
ten .... DECA
thin .... SERO
third .... TRIT
thread .... NEMA
threefold, thrice ..... TER
tooth .... ODONT
touch .... TAC
thought .... IDEO
thousand .... MILLE
up .... ANO
vapor .... ATMO
various ...... VARI, VARIO
watery .... SERO
white .... ALBO
whole .... TOTO
wind .... ANEMO
within .... ENT, ESO,
        ENDO, ENSO, ENTO

a
without .... ECT
wood .... XYLO
worker .... ERGATE
come . ENSUE, ACCRUE, ARRIVE
come back .... RECUR
come forth .... ISSUE,
    EMERGE, EMERSE
come forth from .. JET, GUSH,
    SPEW, EMANATE
comedian's foil ...... STOOGE
comedy .... FARCE
"Comedy of Errors" servant
    LUCE
comfort ...... EASE, SOLACE
comfortable .... COSH, SNUG
comforter .... SCARF
command ...... BID, FIAT,
    ORDER, DICTATE
command: archaic ..... HEST
command to horse
    GEE, HAW, HUP
commander, Egypt ... SIRDAR
commander, Moslem
    AGA, AGHA
commander, fortress
    CAID, QAID
commentary: Hebrew .. BIUR
commission, milit. .. BREVET
commodity .... WARE, STAPLE
common ... VULGAR, GENERAL
common brant ...... QUINK

b
common: Hawaiian ...... NOA
common man .... PLEB
commonplace .. BANAL, TRITE
commotion .. ADO, STIR, TO-DO
commune, Dutch, Holland EDE
COMMUNE see its country in
    GAZETTEER
communion cup .... AMA
communion dish ...... PATEN
communion service .... MASS
communion table ..... ALTAR
compact ...... DENSE, SOLID
companion .... PAL, MATE
comparative conjunction THAN
comparative suffix ending . ER
compass point ... NE, SE, SW,
    ENE, ESE, NNE, NNW, SSE,
    SSW, WNW, WSW
compass point, mariner's
    RHUMB
compassion ...... PITY, RUTH
compel ...... MAKE, FORCE,
    COERCE
compendium .... SYLLABUS
compensate .... PAY
compensation, N. Z. .... UTU
competent .... ABLE
complain ...... FRET, FUSS,
    GRIPE, REPINE
complainant ...... RELATOR
complete ...... TOTAL, UTTER,
    ENTIRE, PLENARY

c
completely ...... ALL, QUITE
completely occupy . ENGROSS
complication .... NODE, NODI
comply ...... OBEY, YIELD
composer, Am. . NEVIN, SOUSA,
    FOSTER, COPLAND
composer, Eng. ...... ARNE,
    ELGAR, COATES
composer, Fr. .. LALO, AUBER,
    BIZET, IBERT, RAVEL
composer, Ger. .... ABT, BACH,
    WEBER
composer, Roum. ..... ENESCO
COMPOSITION see also MUSIC
composition . ESSAY, THEME
composition, mus. ...... OPUS,
    ETUDE, MOTET, RONDO,
    SUITE, SONATA, CON-
    CERTO, FANTASIA
composition of selections
    CENTO
composition, operatic . SCENA
composition, sacred .. MOTET
compositor .... TYPO
compound, organic ... AMIDE
compound with oxygen . OXIDE
comrade-in-arms ...... ALLY
concave .... DISHED
conceal: law .... ELOIN
concealed .... INNER, PERDU
concealed obstacle .... SNAG
concede .... ADMIT,

d
    GRANT, YIELD
conceive .... IDEATE
concern .... CARE
concerning ...... RE, INRE,
    ABOUT, ANENT
conch .... SHELL
conciliate .... ATONE
conciliatory gift .... SOP
concise BRIEF, SHORT, TERSE
concluding passage music
    CODA
concoct .... BREW
concrete mixer ...... PAVER
concur . JIBE, AGREE, ASSENT
condescend ... DEIGN, STOOP
condiment .... SALT,
    CURRY, SPICE
condition .. IF, STATE, STATUS
condition in agreement
    PROVISO
conduct .... LEAD, GUIDE
conductor .... MAESTRO
conductor's stick ...... BATON
conduit . MAIN, DRAIN, SEWER
cone .... STROBIL, STROBILE
cone of silver .... PINA
confection .... COMFIT
confection, nut ..... PRALINE
confederate .... ALLY
Confederate soldier ...... REB
confederation .... LEAGUE
conference .... PALAVER

35

Confess

a
- confess .... **AVOW, ADMIT**
- confession of faith ... **CREDO**
- confidence .... **FAITH, TRUST**
- confidences .... **SECRETS**
- confident .... **RELIANT**
- confidential ...... **ESOTERIC**
- confine ..... **BOX, HEM, PEN, CAGE, CRAMP**
- confined .... **PENT**
- confront .... **MEET**
- confused, make ...... **ADDLE**
- confusion .... **BABEL**
- congealed dew .... **RIME**
- conger .... **EEL**
- congregate ... **MEET, GATHER**
- conical mass of thread .. **COP**
- coniferous tree .... **FIR, YEW, PINE, CEDAR, SPRUCE**
- conjunction .... **OR, AND, BUT, NOR**
- connect ... **JOIN, LINK, UNITE**
- connecting strip of land **ISTHMUS**
- connection **NEXUS, CORRELATION**
- connective .... **AND, NOR**
- connective tissue .... **FASCIA**
- connubial .... **MARITAL**
- conquer .... **MASTER**
- conqueror, Mex. **CORTES, CORTEZ**

b
- Conrad's "Victory" heroine **LENA**
- conscript .... **DRAFT**
- consecrate .... **BLESS**
- consecrated .... **OBLATE**
- consequence ...... **OUTCOME**
- conservative .... **TORY**
- consider .... **DEEM, RATE, TREAT, REGARD**
- consonant, hard ..... **FORTIS**
- consonant, unaspirated . **LENE**
- conspire .... **PLOT**
- Constantine VIII's daughter **ZOE**
- constellation ...... **ARA, LEO, APUS, ARGO, LYNX, LYRA, PAVO, URSA, VELA, ARIES, CANIS, CETUS, DRACO, LIBRA, MENSA, ORION, VIRGO, AQUILA, GEMINI, PISCES, TAURUS**
- constellation, Altar ...... **ARA**
- constellation, Aquila .. **EAGLE**
- constellation, Ara .... **ALTAR**
- constellation, Aries . **RAM**
- constellation, Balance . **LIBRA**
- constellation, Bear.... **URSA**
- constellation, Bull ..**TAURUS**
- constellation, Crab .. **CANCER**
- constellation, Crane ... **GRUS**
- constellation, Crow .. **CORVUS**

c
- constellation, Dog ..... **CANIS**
- constellation, Dragon . **DRACO**
- constellation, Hunter .. **ORION**
- constellation, Lion ...... **LEO**
- constellation near South Pole **APUS**
- constellation, northern .. **LEO**
- constellation, Peacock .. **PAVO**
- constellation, Ram .... **ARIES**
- constellation, Southern .. **ARA, APUS, ARGO, GRUS, PAVO, VELA, INDUS**
- constellation's main star . **COR**
- constitution supporter **CARTIST**
- constrictor ... **BOA, ABOMA**
- constructor .... **ERECTOR**
- consume: obs. .... **ETE**
- container .... **BOX, CAN, TIN, TUB, VAT, URN, CASE**
- containing ore .... **ORY**
- contempt, exclamation of **PISH**
- contempt, look of .... **SNEER**
- contend .... **VIE, COPE, DEAL, COMPETE**
- contest ...... **AGON, BOUT**
- continent: abbr. ...... **NA, SA, AFR, EUR**
- continue .... **LAST, ENDURE, RESUME**
- contort . **WARP, GNARL, TWIST**

d
- contradict ..... **DENY, REBUT, NEGATE**
- contrition .... **REMORSE**
- contrive ...... **MAKE, DEVISE**
- control .... **STEER**
- controversial .... **ERISTIC**
- controversy .... **DEBATE**
- conundrum . **ENIGMA, RIDDLE**
- convert to Judaism ...... **GER**
- conveyance of estate . **DEMISE**
- convoy .... **ESCORT**
- cony ... **DAS, DAMAN, GANAM**
- cook in cream ... **SHIR, SHIRR**
- cooking odor .... **NIDOR**
- cooking pot .... **OLLA**
- cooky .... **SNAP**
- cool .... **ICE**
- coolie woman ..... **CHANGAR**
- Cooper novel .... **PILOT**
- copal .... **ANIME**
- copper .... **CENT**
- Copperfield, Mrs. ..... **DORA**
- copse ...... **HOLT, COPPICE**
- Coptic bishop .... **ANBA**
- copy ... **APE, MODEL, ECTYPE**
- copy, court record .. **ESTREAT**
- coral .... **POLYP**
- cord .... **LINE, RAIP, ROPE, WELT**
- cord, hat or Bedouin .... **AGAL**
- cord, Hawaii .... **AEA**

cordage fiber DA, COIR, ERUC, FERU, HEMP, IMBE, JUTE, RHEA, ABACA, SISAL
cordage tree .... SIDA
Cordelia's father ..... LEAR
"Cordiale,—" ...... ENTENTE
core ..... AME, PITH, HEART
core, casting mold ... NOWEL
core material of earth .. NIFE
core to fashion metal ... AME
core, wooden .... AME
cork .... SPILE
Cork Country port ..... COBH
cork, extract of .... CERIN
cork, flat .... SHIVE
cork helmet .... TOPI, TOPEE
corkwood .... BALSA
corm .... BULB
corn crake bird .... RAIL
corn crake genus ...... CREX
corn, hulled .... HOMINY
corn, India .. RAGEE, RAGGEE
corn lily .... IXIA
corn meal .... MASA
cornbread .... PONE
corner NOOK, TREE, ANGLE
cornerstone .... COIN, COYN, COIGN, QUOIN, COIGNE
cornice support ...... ANCON
Cornish prefix: town .... TRE
Cornish prefix in names . LAN, ROS
cornu .... HORN
Cornwall mine .... BAL
corolla part .... PETAL
corona AUREOLA, AUREOLE
coronach, Scot. .... DIRGE
coronation stone ..... SCONE
corpulent .... OBESE
corral: Sp. .... ATAJO
correct . OKEH, TRUE, AMEND, EMEND, REVISE
correct behaviour, Chin. .. LI
correlative ...... OR, NOR
correspond JIBE, AGREE, TALLY
corridor .... HALL
corrie .... CWM
corrode ... EAT, RUST, ERODE
corrupt .... TAINT, VENAL, VITIATE
corrupt with money ... BRIBE
corsair .... PIRATE
corset bone .... BUSK
cortege .... RETINUE
corundum .... EMERY
cos lettuce .... ROMAINE
Cos, pert. to .... COAN
cosmic cycle .... EON
cosmic order: Vedic .... RITA
Cossack .... TATAR
Cossack chief ...... ATAMAN

Cossack headman .. HETMAN
Cossack regiment .POLK, PULK
cosset .... PET
costa .... RIB
coterie .... SET
cottage, Ind. .... BARI
cotton batting .... BATT
cotton, Bengal .... ADATI
cotton, Egypt .... SAK, PIMA, SAKEL
cotton fabric .. JEAN, LAWN, LENO, DENIM, SURAT, MADRAS
cotton fabric, corded CANTOON
cotton machine .... GIN
cotton, matted .... BATT
cotton tree .... SIMAL
cottonwood, Texas ... ALAMO
couch .... LAIR
cougar ..... PUMA, PANTHER
council .... SOVIET
council, ecclesiastical . SYNOD
council, king's .... WITAN
"Council of—" .... TRENT
counsel .... REDE
counselor .... MENTOR
count .... ENUMERATE
count, Ger. .... GRAF
counter .... BAR
counter, in cards ..... MILLE
countercurrent .... EDDY
countermand .... REVOKE
counterpart .... LIKE
countersink .... REAM
counting frame ..... ABACUS
COUNTRY see also GAZETTEER, beginning on Page 210
country, ancient ...... ELAM
country, ancient, Asia Min., Gr. EOLIS, AEOLIA, AEOLIS
country, ancient, Bib. . SHEBA
country, ancient Greek .. ELIS
country bumpkin RUBE, YOKEL, RUSTIC
country: law .... PAIS
COUNTY. see also GAZETTEER, beginning on Page 210
county: Dan. .... AMT
county: Eng. .... SHIRE
county: Nor. .... AMT, FYLKE
county: Swed. .... LAN
couple .... TWO, PAIR
courage .... METTLE
courier ..ESTAFET, ESTAFETTE
course .... WAY, ROAD, TACK, ROUTE
course, complete ..... CYCLE
course, meal . SALAD, ENTREE
course, part of ..... LAP, LEG
court .... AREA

court action .... **SUIT**
court, A.-S. ..**GEMOT, GEMOTE**
court, church .... **ROTA**
court cry .... **OYES, OYEZ**
court hearing .... **OYER**
court, inner .... **PATIO**
court, Jap. ..... **DARI, DAIRO**
court, old English ...... **LEET**
court order .... **ARRET**
court panel .... **JURY**
court, pert. to church . **ROTAL**
court proceeding ...... **TRIAL**
courtly .... **AULIC**
courtway .... **AREA**
courtyard .... **PATIO**
Covenant, — of the ....**ARK**
cover inner surface ..... **LINE**
covering — **TEGMEN, TEGUMEN**
covey .... **BEVY, BROOD**
cow .... **BOSSY, BOVINE**
cow house .... **BYRE**
cows .... **KINE, BOSSIES**
coward .... **CRAVEN**
cowboy garment ..... **CHAPS**
cowboy, S. Am. ..... **GAUCHO**
cowfish .... **RAY, TORO**
cowl .... **HOOD**
cowlike .... **COUS**
coxcomb .... **FOP**
coy .... **ARCH**
coyotillo .... **MARGARITA**
coypu .... **NUTRIA**
cozy .... **HOMY, SNUG**
cozy place .... **DEN, NEST**
crab-eating mongoose ... **URVA**
crab, front of .... **METOPE**
crack . **SNAP, CHINK, CREVICE**
crackling .... **CREPITANT**
crackpot .... **NUT**
craft .... **ART, TRADE**
craftsman .... **ARTISAN**
crafty .... **SLY, FOXY, WILY**
craggy hill .... **TOR**
cramp .... **KINK**
crane arm .... **GIB, JIB**
crane genus .... **GRUS**
crane, India .... **SARUS**
crane, pert. to .... **GRUINE**
crane, ship's .... **DAVIT**
cranelike bird ...... **CHUNGA**
cranelike bird, S. Amer.
.... **SERIEMA**
cranial nerve ... **VAGI, VAGUS**
cravat .... **TIE**
crave.**ASK, BEG, LONG, DESIRE**
craw.**MAW, CROP**
crayon ...... **CHALK, PASTEL**
craze .... **FAD, MANIA**
crazy .... **LOCO, LUNY, WILD**

cream .... **ELITE**
credit transfer system .. **GIRO**
creed .... **CREDO, NICENE**
creek .... **RIA, KILL**
creek: N.Y. .... **VLEI**
creeper .... **IVY**
creeping .. **REPENT, REPTANT**
Cremona .... **AMATI**
crescent moon's point .. **CUSP**
crescent-shaped ...... **LUNATE**
crescent-shaped figure .. **LUNE**
crescent-shaped mark . **LUNULA**
crest .**TOP, COMB, PEAK, TUFT**
crest, sharp rugged mountain
.... **ARETE**
crested as birds .... **PILEATE**
Cretan princess .... **ARIADNE**
Cretan spikenard ...... **PHU**
CRETE . see SPECIAL SECTION
crevice .. **CREVAS, CREVASSE**
crew .... **MEN, GANG,**
TEAM, EIGHT
cribbage pin or score ....**PEG**
cribbage term ...... **NOB, NOBS**
cricket .... **GRIG**
cricket, ball in ...... **EDGER**
cricket, field parts .**ONS, OFFS**
cricket, run in .... **BYE**
cricket term **OVER, TICE, YORK**
crime, Eccl. .... **SIMONY**
Crimean river .... **ALMA**
criminal .... **FELON**
crimp .... **CURL, GOFFER**
crimson ..... **RED, CARMINE**
crippled .... **HALT, LAME**
criticize .... **SLATE**
criticize in a small way
.... **CARP, CAVIL**
crocodile, India ..... **GAVIAL**
crocodile-head god, Egyp.
.... **SOBK, SEBEK**
crocus .... **IRID**
crocus bulb .... **CORM**
Croesus' land .... **LYDIA**
crony ... **PAL, CHUM, BUDDY**
crony: old Eng. .... **EME**
crooked ...... **AGEE, AWRY**
crooner, early ...... **VALLEE**
crop .... **MAW, CRAW**
crop, spring, India .... **RABI**
cross ..... **IRATE, TRAVERSE**
cross church .... **ROOD**
cross-examine .... **GRILL**
cross of life, Egypt .... **ANKH**
cross oneself .... **SAIN**
cross out .... **DELETE**
cross-stroke .... **SERIF**
cross timber, ship .... **SPALE**
crossbeam .... **TRAVE, TREVE**
crossbill genus .... **LOXIA**
crossbow .... **RODD**

a crossing, fence .... STILE
crosspiece .BAR, RUNG, CLEAT
crosspiece, vehicle .. EVENER
crossthreads ... WEFT, WOOF
crosswise .... THWART
crossword champion, former
.... COOPER
crow . ROOK, CRAKE, CORVUS
crow: Eng. .... BRAN
crow, Guam .... AGA
crow, kind of .... DAW
crowd, common .. MOB, RUCK
crowd together . HERD, SERRY
crowded .... SERRIED
crown .... CAP, PATE,
.... TIARA, DIADEM
crown colony, Brit.
.... ADEN, BAHAMAS
crown of Osiris or Egypt .ATEF
crown: poetic .... TIAR
crown, Pope's triple
.... TIAR, TIARA
crucial point ... CRUX, PIVOT
crucible .... CRUSET
crucifix .... ROOD
crude RAW, ROUGH, COARSE
crude metal .... ORE
crude sugar-molasses MELADA
cruel person .... SADIST
cruet ...... AMA, CASTER
b cruising .... ASEA
crumbled easily ..... FRIABLE
Crusader's foe .... SARACEN
Crusader's headquarters ACRE
crush ...... MASH, SUBDUE
crustacean .. CRAB, ISOPOD,
.... SHRIMP, LOBSTER
crustacean order, one of
.... DECAPOD
cry ... HO, HOA, SOB, HOWL,
.... WAIL, WEEP, LAMENT
cry, Austral. .. COOEE, COOEY
cry for silence, court
.... OYES, OYEZ
crystal-clear ...... PELLUCID
ctenophores, no tentacle NUDA
Cuban dance .... CONGA
Cuban rodent .... PILORI
Cuban secret police .. PORRA
Cuban timber tree .... CUYA
cubic decimeter ...... LITER
cubic measure . CORD, STERE
cubic meter .... STERE
cubicle .... CELL
cubitus .... ULNA
Cuchulain's wife EMER, EIMER
cuckoo, black, keel-billed ANI
cuckoo, Oriental . COEL, KOEL
cuckoopint .... ARUM
cucumber ...... CUKE, PEPO
cud .... QUID, RUMEN

c cudgel .... BAT, CLUB, DRUB,
.... BASTE, STAVE, STICK
cue .... HINT
cue, music .... PRESA
cuff fastener .... TAB
cuirass .... LORICA
cull .... SORT
culmination ... ACME, APEX
cultivate land ... HOE, PLOW,
.... TILL, HARROW
cultivation method, Bengal
.... JUM, JOOM
cultivation, soil .... TILTH
culture medium ...... AGAR
cunning ... ART, CUTE, FOXY,
.... WILY, DEDAL, CALLID,
.... DAEDAL
cup .... CRUSE
cup, assaying .... CUPEL
cup, ceremonial .... AMA
cup, gem cutting ...... DOP
cup stand of metal .... ZARF
cup to hold gem ...... DOP
cupbearer .... SAKI
cupbearer of gods .... HEBE
cupboard ...AMBRY, CLOSET
Cupid .... AMOR, EROS
Cupid's title .... DAN
cupola .... DOME
cur .... MUT, MUTT
d curare ...... URALI, OORALI
curassow .... MITU
curassow genus ...... CRAX
curdling powder .... RENNET
cure-all .. ELIXIR, PANACEA
cure by salting ...... CORN
cure with salt grass .... DUN
curfew .... BELL
curios .... VIRTU
curl COIL, FRIZ, WIND, FRIZZ
curl of hair .... FEAK, TRESS,
.... RINGLET
curling, mark aimed at .. TEE
currant genus .... RIBES
current ...... AC, DC, EDDY,
.... RIFE, TIDE, STREAM
curt ...... BRUSK, BRUSQUE
curve .... ARC, BOW, ESS,
.... ARCH, BEND, SINUS
curve in a stream HOEK, HOOK
curve, plane ...... ELLIPSE,
.... PARABOLA
curve, sigmoid or double .ESS
curved handle .... BOOL
curved in . ADUNC, CONCAVE
curved out .... CONVEX
curved plank, vessel's .. SNY
Cush, son of .... SEBA
cushion ..... PAD, HASSOCK
custard .... FLAN
custard apple ...... ANNONA

a
custard cake .... ECLAIR
custard dish .... FLAN
custody .... CHARGE
custom .... LAW, WONT,
     HABIT, USAGE
custom, India ...... DASTUR
custom: Lat. .... RITUS
custom: obs. .... URE
customer .... PATRON
customs .... MORES
cut . HEW, LOP, MOW, DOCK,
  GASH, HACK, KERF, REAP,
  SLIT, SNEE, SNIP, TRIM,
  SEVER, SHEAR, SLIVE,
  CLEAVE, TREPAN
cut down .... FELL
cut edges of coins ...... NIG
cut of meat .... LOIN
cut off ... DOCK, SNIP, ELIDE
cut off, as mane ..... ROACH
cut out .... EXCISE
cut: Shakespeare ..... SLISH
cut vertically
  SCARP, ESCARP, ESCARPE
cutter .... SLED
cutting .... SECANT, INCISAL

c
cutting tool ... AX, ADZ, AXE,
  HOB, SAW, SAX, SYE, ADZE
cuttlefish ..... SEPIA, SQUID
cuttlefish fluid .... INK
Cyclades, one of, see GAZET-
  TEER
cycle, astronomical ... SAROS
cyclorama .... CYKE
cylinder, moving .... PISTON
cylindrical .... TERETE
cyma .... GOLA
cyma recta or reversa .. OGEE
cymbal, Orient .... ZEL
cymbals, India .... TAL
Cymbeline's daughter IMOGEN
Cymric deity
    GWYN, LLEU, LLEW
Cymry .... WELSH
cypher system .... CODE
cyprinoid fish .... ID, IDE,
    CARP, CHUB
Cyrus' daughter .... ATOSSA
cyst .... WEN
Czar .... IVAN, FEDOR
Czech .... SLAV
Czech, Eastern .... ZIPS

D

b
Dadaist .... ERNST
dado, pedestal ..... SOLIDUM
Daedalus' son ...... ICARUS
dagger . DIRK, SNEE, BODKIN
dagger, ancient SKEAN, SKENE
dagger, Ir. DHU, SKENE, SKEAN
dagger, Malay ... CRIS, KRIS,
  CREES, KREES, CREESE,
    KREESE
dagger: obs. .... SNEE
dagger, thin ..... STILETTO
Dahomey Negro . FON, FONG
daily .... DIURNAL
dais .... ESTRADE
daisy .MOON, OXEYE, SHASTA
Dallas school .... SMU
dam .... WAER, WEIR
dam, Egypt ..... SADD, SUDD
dam site .... ASWAN
damage . MAR, HARM, IMPAIR
Damascus river ...... ABANA
damp .... DANK
damselfish .... PINTANO
dance ...... HOP, JIG, REEL,
  GALOP, GAVOT, POLKA,
  TANGO, RUMBA, REDOWA,
  RHUMBA, GAVOTTA, GA-
  VOTTE
dance, country . REEL, ALTHEA
dance, Gr. ...... HORMOS
dance, Israeli .... HORA

d
dance, lively ......JIG, REEL,
  GALOP, POLKA, BOLERO
dance, old Eng. ...... MORRIS
dance, Sp. .. TANGO, BOLERO
dance, stately, old
  PAVAN, MINUET, PAVANE
dance step .... PAS, CHASSE,
    GLISSADE
dancer ...... KELLY, SHAWN,
  BOLGER, ZORINA, ASTAIRE
dancing girl, Egypt ... ALMA,
    ALME, ALMEH
dancing girl, Jap. ..... GEISHA
dandy FOP, DUDE, JAKE, TOFF
DANISH .. see also DENMARK
  in SPECIAL SECTION
Danish astronomer .. BRAHE
Dan. borough (in Eng.) . BORG
Dan. chieftain .... JARL, YARL
Dan. division, territorial . AMT
Dan. fjord .... ISE
Dan. king ..... CNUT, KNUT,
    CANUTE
Dan. measure .... ALEN
Dan. money ..... ORA, ORAS
Dan. physicist .... BOHR
Dan. speech sound .... STOD
dank .... WET
Dante's patron .... SCALA
Danube city ...... ULM, LINZ
Danube, old name of .. ISTER

a Danube tributary
    INN, OLT, ISAR, PRUT
daring .... BOLD, NERVE
dark ...... MIRKY, MURKY
dark horse .... ZAIN
dark rock .... CHERT
dark wood ..... TEAK, EBONY
darkness ...... MIRK, MURK
darling: Ir. . ROON, ACUSHLA,
    ASTHORE
darnel .... TARE
dart along .... FLIT
"Das Rheingold" role .. ERDA
dash .... ELAN
date, pert. to .... DATAL
date plum .... SAPOTE
date, Roman ... IDES, NONES
"David Copperfield" character
    DORA, HEEP, DARTLE
David's captain .... JOAB
David's commander .. AMASA
David's daughter ..... TAMAR
David's father .... JESSE
David's nephew ...... AMASA
David's ruler, one of ..... IRA
David's son ...... SOLOMON
David's wife ...... MICHAL
dawn ..... DEW, EOS, AURORA
dawn, pert. to .... EOAN
day, Hebr. .... YOM
b day, Rom. ......IDES, NONES
day-breeze, It. .... ORA
days: Lat. .... DIES
day's march .... ETAPE
daybreak .... DAWN
dazing larks, device for DARE
deacon's stole .... ORARION
dead ... FLAT, AMORT, INERT
dead, abode of HADES, SHEOL
dead, region of: Egypt AMENTI
dead trees .... DRIKI
deadly ...... FATAL, LETHAL
deadly carrot .... DRIAS
deadly sins, 7 ENVY, LUST, AN-
    GER, PRIDE, SLOTH, GLUT-
    TONY, COVETOUSNESS
dealer .... MONGER
dealer, cloth DRAPER, MERCER
dean ...... DOYEN, DOYENNE
dearth .... WANT
death ...... MORT, DEMISE
death deity: Rom. ..... MORS
death note on hunter's horn
    MORT
death notice .... OBIT
death rattle .... RALE
debate—debatable
    AGON, MOOT
debauchee ...... RAKE, ROUE
debris, rocky .... SCREE

c decade .... TEN
decamp ..... ELOPE, LEVANT
decay, dental .... CARIES
decay tree ...... CONK, KONK
deceit .... SHAM, WILE,
    FRAUD, GUILE
deceive .. BILK, DUPE, FOOL,
    GULL, TRICK, ILLUDE
decelerate .... RETARD
deception . HOAX, STRATAGEM
decide: Rom. law ...... CERN
decimal unit .... TEN
deck, ship's .... POOP
decks, cut away RASEE, RAZEE
declaim ...... RANT, RAVE,
    ORATE, RECITE
declaration in whist . MISERE
declare .... AVER, AVOW,
    STATE, AVOUCH
declare, in cards ...... MELD
decline .... EBB, SINK,
    WANE, REFUSE
declivity ..... SCARP, SLOPE
declivity in menage . CALADE
decorate ..... DECK, ADORN
decorated letter .... FAC
decorated wall part .... DADO
decorous .... STAID, DEMURE
decoy .... LURE, PLANT
decrease ...... EBB, WANE,
    LESSEN, RECEDE
d decree .... ACT, FIAT,
    CANON, EDICT, ORDAIN
decree, Fr. law ...... ARRET
decree, Moslem ...... IRADE
decree, Rom. law .. DECRETE
decree, Russian ..... UKASE
deduce .... INFER
deed .... GEST, GESTE
deeds .... ACTA
deer, Asia ...... AHU, KAKAR,
    SAMBAR, SAMBUR,
    SAMBHAR, SAMBHUR
deer, barking .... KAKAR
deer, Chile, Andes .... PUDU
deer, female . DOE, ROE, HIND
deer, genus, E. Ind. .... RUSA
deer, India .... AXIS
deer, Jap. .... SIKA
deer, Kashmir ...... HANGUL
deer, red .... ROE, HART
deer, S. Am. ...... GEMUL,
    GUEMAL, GUEMUL
deer, spotted .... CHITAL
deer, Tibet .... SHOU
deer track .... SLOT
deerlet .... NAPUS
deerlike .... CERVINE
defamation .... LIBEL
defeat, chess .... MATE
defeat utterly ... BEST, ROUT

41

a defect, weaving .... SCOB
defendant's plea ...... NOLO
deference .... RESPECT
defraud .... GYP, BILK,
GULL, CHEAT
defy .... DARE
degrade ..... ABASE, LOWER,
DEBASE
degrading .... MENIAL
degree .... GRADE, STAGE
degree .. (dental) DDS, DDSC;
(engineer) CE, EE; (divin-
ify) DD; (science) BSC;
(arts) BA, MA, MFA; (law)
LLB, LLD
degree, extreme .... NTH
degree taken, Cambridge
INCEPTOR
degrees, angle of 57.30
RADIAN
deified sky, Rom. .... CAELUS
DEITY . see also GOD, GOD-
DESS and SPECIAL SECTION
deity .... GOD
deity, Buddhist ... DEV, DEVA
deity, Hindu ..... DEV, DEVA
deity, Jap. ... AMIDA, AMITA
deity, primeval .... TITAN
deity, Sumerian .... ABU
b deity, Syrian .... EL
delay WAIT, DETAIN, LINGER
delay, law .... MORA, MORAE
delicacy .... FINESSE
delight .... REVEL
delusion: Buddhism ... MOHA
demand NEED, CLAIM, INSIST
demeanor .... AIR
Demeter's daughter
CORA, KORE
demigod .... HERO
demolish ..... RASE, RAZE
demon ... IMP, DEVIL, FIEND
demon, Arab, Moslem, Oriental
JIN, JINN GENIE,
GENII, JINNI, JINNEE
demon, Hindu ASURA, DAITYA
demon, sun-swallowing, Hindu
myth .... RAHU
demon, Zoroastrian
DEV, DIV, DEVA
demonstrative pronoun
THAT, THIS, WHOM
den ...... DIVE, LAIR, HAUNT
denary .... TEN
denial .... NO, NAY
DENMARK . see also DANISH
and SPECIAL SECTION
denomination .... SECT
denote .... MEAN, SHOW,
INDICATE
denoting unfit ships in Lloyd's
registry .... AE

c dense .CRASS, THICK, STUPID
density .... DORD
dental tool .... SCALER
deny .... NEGATE
depart .... BEGONE, DECAMP
depart fast VAMOSE, VAMOOSE
depart: Lat. .... VADE
departed .. GONE, LEFT, WENT
department, Chin. .. FU, FOO
departure .... EXODUS
dependent .... MINION
depict .... DRAW, PAINT,
DESCRIBE
deplore .... LAMENT
deposit, alluvial DELTA, GEEST
deposit, clayey .... MARL
deposit, geyser ...... SINTER
deposit, mineral ...... LODE
deposit, river
ALLUVIA, ALLUVIUM
deposit, wine cask .. TARTAR
depressed .... SAD
depression .... DENT, FOVEA
deprivation .... LOSS
deprived .... REFT
depute .... SEND
deputy .... AGENT, VICAR
derby .... BOWLER
deride .... GIBE, JIBE
derrick ..... CRANE, STEEVE
d dervish, "Arab. Nights" .. AGIB
dervish, Moslem ...... SADITE
descendant ...... SON, CION
descendant, Fatima's
SAID, SEID, SAYID
descendants, male line . GENS
descent, deep .... SCARP
descriptive term .... EPITHET
desert dweller ..... EREMITE
desert, Mongolia ...... GOBI
desert plant .... AGAVE
deserter .... RAT
deserve .... EARN, MERIT
design .... AIM
desire .... YEN, URGE,
WANT, WISH
desire eagerly .... ASPIRE
desirous .... FAIN
desolate ...... LORN, BLEAK
despoil .... RUIN
despot ... CZAR, TSAR, TZAR,
TYRANT, DICTATOR
dessert ... ICE, PIE, MOUSSE,
TRIFLE
destiny . DOOM, FATE, KARMA
destroy .... RASE, RAZE,
DECIMATE
destruction .... RUIN
detach .... WEAN
detachable button .... STUD
detail .... ITEM

detain **CHECK, DELAY, ARREST**
detecting device ..... **SONAR**
detective .... **TEC, DICK**
detent .... **PAWL**
determination .... **WILL**
determine ...... **FIX, DECIDE, RESOLVE**
detest .... **HATE, LOATHE**
dethrone .... **DEPOSE**
detonator .... **CAP**
"— deum" .... **TE**
devaluate .... **DEBASE**
developed compound animal **ZOON**
Devi .... **UMA**
deviate .. **ERR, LAW, DIVERGE**
deviation .... **LAPSE**
deviation from course ... **YAW**
devil . **DEMON, DEUCE, SATAN**
devil: Gypsy .... **BENG**
devil, Moslem **SHAITAN, SHEITAN**
devil, Russian folklore . **CHORT**
devil worship ..... **SATANISM**
devilfish .... **MANTA**
Devon river .... **EXE**
devotee .... **FAN, IST**
devotion, nine-day .. **NOVENA**
devoutness .... **PIETY**
dewberry .... **MAYES**
dewy .... **RORAL, RORIC**
dexterity .... **ART**
dexterous .... **CLEVER**
diadem .... **TIARA**
diagonal .... **BIAS**
DIALECT .. see also LANGUAGE
dialect .**IDIOM, LINGO, PATOIS**
dialect, Chin. ...... **CANTON**
dialect, Ethiopic ..... **TIGRE**
dialect, Gr. ... **DORIC, IONIC**
diamond corner .... **BASE**
diamond fragments .... **BORT**
diamond holder .... **DOP**
diamond, impure industrial **BORT**
diamond, perfect .. **PARAGON**
diamonds, low quality .. **BORT**
Diana .... **ARTEMIS**
Diana's grove ...... **NEMUS**
Diana's mother .... **LATONA**
diaphanous ..... **THIN, SHEER**
diaphragm, pert. to . **PHRENIC**
diatonic note .... **MI**
diatribe . **SCREED, HARANGUE**
dibble .... **DAP, DIB**
Dickens character .. **PIP, TIM, DORA, GAMP, HEEP, FAGIN, DORRIT**
Dickens' pseudonym .... **BOZ**
"Die Fledermaus" girl . **ADELE**
die for making drain pipe **DOD**
die, gambling . **TAT, TESSERA**

"Dies—," "Day of Wrath" **IRAE**
diet .... **BANT, FARE**
differ ...... **VARY, DISAGREE**
difference between solar and
lunar year .... **EPACT**
different .... **OTHER, DIVERS**
difficulty ...... **RUB, KNOT**
dig ..... **GRUB, PION, DELVE**
digest .... **PANDECT**
digit, foot .... **TOE**
digraph **AE, EA, OA, OE, SH, TH**
dike .... **LEVEE**
dilation .... **ECTASIA**
dilatory ...... **SLOW, TARDY, REMISS**
dilemma .... **FIX**
dill herb .... **ANET**
dilute .... **THIN, WATER**
dim, become .**BLEAR, DARKLE**
diminish .. **EBB, BATE, SINK, WANE, ABATE, TAPER**
diminish front: military . **PLOY**
dingle .... **DALE, DELL, GLEN**
dining room, ancient .. **OECUS**
diocese center .... **SEE**
Dioscuri .... **ANAX**
dip .... **DAP, DIB, DOPP, DUNK, LADE**
dip out .... **BAIL**
diplomacy .... **TACT**
diplomat ... **ENVOY, CONSUL, ATTACHE**
diphthong .... **AE, IA, OA, UO**
Dipper constellation ... **URSA**
direct .... **AIM, LEAD**
direct attention ...... **REFER**
direct steering of boat . **CONN**
dirge .... **LINOS, LINUS**
dirigible .... **BLIMP**
dirk .... **SNY, SNEE**
dirty lock .... **FRIB**
disable .... **LAME, MAIM**
disagreeable .... **ILL**
disappear gradually **EVANESCE**
disavow ..... **DENY, RECANT**
disbeliever .... **ATHEIST**
disburse .... **SPEND, EXPEND**
discard **DROP, SCRAP, REJECT**
discernment .... **TACT**
discharge .... **EMIT, FIRE, SACK, SHOOT**
discharged .... **SHOT**
disciple .... **APOSTLE**
disciple: India ...... **CHELA**
disciplinarian .... **MARTINET**
disclaim .... **DENY**
disclose ...... **BARE, REVEAL**
discolored ..... **DOTY, LIVID**
disconcert ..... **FAZE, ABASH**
discourse . **HOMILY, DESCANT**
discourse, art of .. **RHETORIC**

discover . SEE, SPY, ESPY, FIND
discriminate . . . . SECERN
discuss . . . . . . TREAT, DEBATE
discussion group . . . . . . FORUM
disease . . MAL, POX, HIVES
disease, Afr. . . . . NENTA
disease cause . . . . VIRUS
disease, diver's . . . . BENDS
disease, fowl . . . . PIP, ROUP,
　　　　　　　　　　　PEROSIS
disease, fungus . . . . . . ERGOT
disease, grape-vine
　　　　　　　ESCA, ERINOSE
disease, plant . . SMUT, SCALD
disease, skin . . . . ECZEMA
disease spreader
　　　　　　VECTOR, CARRIER
disease, tropical . . . . . SPRUE
disembark . . . . LAND
disembodied spirit: Chin.
　　　　　　　　　KUEI, KWEI
disencumber . . . . RID
disengage . . . . FREE
disfigure . . . . . . MAR, DEFACE
disgrace . . . . SCANDAL
disguise . . . . MASK
disgust, word of . . . . AW
DISH . . . . . . also see VESSEL
dish . . . . PLATE
dish, Hawaiian . . . . POI
dish, highly seasoned
　　　　　　　　　OLIO, OLLA
dish, hominy . . . . POSOLE
dish, Hungarian . . . . . GOULASH
dish, It. . . . . RAVIOLI
dish, main . . . . ENTREE
dish, meat . . STEW, RAGOUT
dish, Mex. . . TAMAL, TAMALE,
　　　　　　　　　　　　TAMALI
dish, stemmed . . . . . COMPOTE
dishearten . . . DAUNT, DETER
dishonor . . SHAME, VIOLATE
dishonorable . . . . BASE
disinclined . . . . AVERSE
disinfectant CRESOL, PHENOL,
　　　　　　CRESSOL, CRESSYL
disk, ice hockey . . . . . PUCK
disk, like a . DISCAL, DISCOID
disk, metal . . . . PATEN
dislocate . . . . LUXATE
dismal . . . . DREAR
dismantle . . . . STRIP
dismay . . APPAL, DAUNT
dismiss . . . . DEMIT, FIRE
dismounted . . . . ALIT
disorder . . . . . . MESS, DERAY,
　　　　　　　　　　　CLUTTER
disorderly flight . . . . . . ROUT
disparaging . . . . SNIDE
disparaging remark . . . . SLUR
dispatch . . . . . . SEND, HASTE

dispatch boat . . . . AVISO
dispelled . . . . GONE
display . . . AIR, SHEW, SHOW,
　　　　　　　　ARRAY, EVINCE
display proudly
　　　　　　VAUNT, OSTENT
displease . . . . VEX, MIFF,
　　　　　　　　ANGER, ANNOY
disposed . . . . PRONE
disposition . . MOOD, TEMPER
dispossess . . . . . . OUST, EVICT
disprove . . . . REFUTE
disputable . . . . MOOT
dissertation . . THESES, THESIS
dissolute person . RAKE, ROUE
dissonant . . . . ATONAL
distance, at-from a OFF, AFAR
distant . . FAR, YON, REMOTE
distilling vessel . . MATRASS
distinctive air . . AURA, MIEN,
　　　　　　　　　　　CACHET
distracted . . . . DISTRAIT
distraint: old Eng. law . . NAAM
distribute . DEAL, DOLE, METE
DISTRICT . . . see also REGION
district . . . . AREA, ZONE
district, old Eng. court
　　　　　　　　　SOC, SOKE
disturb . . . . . . ROIL, MOLEST
disturbance . . . . ROW, RIOT
ditch . . . . FOSS, RINE,
　　　　　　　FOSSE, TRENCH
ditch, castle . . . . MOAT
ditch, fort . . . . RELAIS
ditch millet . . . . HUREEK
ditto . . . . SAME
divan . . . . SOFA
dive . . . . . . DEN, HEADER
dive bomber . . . . STUKA
diverge . . . . DEVIATE
divers . . . . SEVERAL
divest . . . . . . STRIP, DEPRIVE
divide . . . . PART, SHARE
divide for study . . . DISSECT
divided . . . . REFT, SPLIT
divider . . . . MERIST
dividing wall, membrane, parti-
　　tion . . . . SEPTA, SEPTUM
divination by lots: Lat.
　　　　　　　SORS, SORTES
"Divine Comedy" author
　　　　　　　　　　　DANTE
divine favor . . . . GRACE
divine law: Rom. . . . . . . FAS
divine revelation TORA, TORAH
divine utterance . . . ORACLE
divinity . . . . DEITY
divorce bill, Jewish law
　　　　　　　　GET, GETT
divorce, Moslem . . . . . TALAK
"— dixit" . . . . IPSE
dizziness, pert. to . . . . DINIC

44

a docile .... TAME
dockyard barge ...... LUMP
doctor ... INTERN, INTERNE
Dr. Brown's dog hero ... RAB
Dr. Jekyll's other self .. HYDE
doctrinaire .... ISMY
doctrine . ISM, DOGMA, TENET
documents, box for . HANAPER
dodder .... AMIL
dodo genus .... DIDUS
doe .... HIND
doe, young .... TAG, TEG
dog ...... CANIS, CANINE
dog ... POM, CHOW, PEKE,
    BASSET, POODLE, SPANIEL
dog, chops of .... FLEWS
dog-faced ape .... AANI
dog-fisher .... OTTER
DOG, GUN see DOG, HUNTING
dog, Hungarian PULI, KUVASZ
dog, hunting (bird) . ALAN,
    ALAND, ALANT, BASSET,
    BEAGLE, SETTER, COURS-
    ER, HARRIER, POINTER
dog, John Brown's ...... RAB
dog, large .... ALAN
dog, "Odyssey" ...... ARGOS
dog salmon .... KETA
dog, small-toy .... POM, PUG,
                        PEKE
b dog snapper, fish ...... JOCU
dog, Sputnik's .... LAIKA
dog star .... SEPT, SOPT,
                SEPTI, SIRIUS
dog, tropical .... ALCO
dog, Welsh .... CORGI
dog, wild, Austral. .... DINGO
dog, wild, India ..... DHOLE
doge, office of .... DOGATE
dogfish .... SHARK
dogma .... TENET
dogwood .... OSIER, CORNEL
dole .... METE
dolphin fish .... DORADO
dolphin genus .... INIA
dolphin-like cetacean ... INIA
dolt .... ASS, OAF, CLOD,
                LOUT, DUNCE
domain .... BOURN, REALM,
    BOURNE, DEMENE, ESTATE,
    DEMESNE
dome .... CUPOLA
dome-shaped .... DOMOID
Domesday Book money .. ORA
domestic .... MAID, LOCAL
domestic animal .... ASS, CAT,
    COW, DOG, HOG, PIG,
    RAM, SOW, MULE
domestic slave .... ESNE
domesticated .... TAME
dominion ... REALM, EMPERY

c domino .... MASK
Don Juan's mother .... INEZ
donkey .... ASS, MOKE,
                BURRO, NEDDY
doom ... CONDEMN, DESTINE
doom palm, Afr. .... DUM
door .... PORTAL
door: Lat. .... JANUA
door part .... JAMB, SASH,
                SILL, LINTEL
door section .... PANEL
doorkeeper, Masonic ... TILER
dorado, color .... CUIR
Doric frieze slab .... METOPE
dormant ... ASLEEP, LATENT
dormouse .... LOIR
dormouse, garden .... LEROT
dormouse genus ...... GLIS
dorsal .... NOTAL
dote .... DRIVEL
dots, paint with ..... STIPPLE
dotted with figures ... SEME
double . DUAL, TWIN, BINATE
double cocoon ...... DUPION
double dagger .... DIESIS
double, Egypt .... KA
double salt .... ALUM
double tooth .... MOLAR
doubletree .... EVENER
d dovkie ..... ROTCH, ROTGE,
                ROTCHE
Dovyalis .... ABERIA
dowel ..... PIN, COAG, COAK
dower, pert. to .... DOTAL
dower property .... DOS
down ...... FUZZ, PILE, EIDER
down, facing. PRONE, PRONATE
down quilt .... DUVET
"downunder" native clan .. ATI
downward, curve .... DEFLEX
dowry .... DOS, DOT
drag .. LUG, TUG, HAUL, SNIG
dragnet .... TRAWL
dragon, like a .. DRACONTINE
dragon of darkness, Bibl.
                        RAHAB
drain . SAP, DEPLETE, VITIATE
drain .... SUMP, SEWER
dram, small .... NIP
DRAMA ..... see also PLAY
Dravidian KOTA, MALE, NAIR,
    TODA, TULU, TAMIL
draw ...... TIE, TOW, LIMN,
                PULL, DEPICT
draw forth .... EDUCE
draw from .... DERIVE
draw out . EDUCE, ATTENUATE
draw tight: naut. ...... FRAP
drawing curve ...... SPLINE
drawing room .... SALON
dreadful .... DIRE
dream, day .... REVERIE

45

Dream

a
"Dream Girl" playwright . RICE
dregs .... FAEX, LEES,
.... DROSS, SEDIMENT
drench ...... SOUSE, TOUSE
drenched ...... WET, DEWED
DRESS ... see also GARMENT
dress .... GARB, CLOTHE,
.... ACCOUTER
dress, as stone .... DAB, NIG
dress feathers .... PREEN
dress leather ..... DUB, TAN
dress up ...... TOG, PREEN
dressed .... CLAD
dressing wounds, material for
.... LINT, LINTS
dried berry: Sp. .... PASA
dried up .... SERE
drift .... TREND
drill .... BORE, TRAIN
drilling rod ...... BAR, BIT
DRINK ... see also BEVERAGE
drink .... GULP, SWIG,
.... QUAFF, IMBIBE
drink, Christmas
.... NOG, WASSAIL
drink, fermented ..... MEAD
drink, honey .... MEAD
drink, hot .... TODDY
drink, hot milk ...... POSSET
drink of gods ...... NECTAR
drink of liquor .. NIP, BRACER

b
drink, old honey ..... MORAT
drink, palm .... NIPA
drink, rum-gin ..... BUMBO
drink slowly ...... SIP, SUP
drink, small ...... NIP, PEG,
.... DRAM, SLUG
drink to excess . TOPE, BOUSE
drink, whiskey ...... STINGER
drinking bowl .... MAZER
drinking cup, Gr. ... HOLMOS
drinking vessel ... CUP, MUG,
.... TIG, TYG, JORUM,
.... STEIN, TANKARD
drive .... RIDE, URGE, IMPEL
drive away .... SHOO, DISPEL
drive back
.... ROUT, REPEL, REPULSE
drive in .... TAMP
drivel .... DROOL, SLAVER
driver, fast reckless ... JEHU
drizzle . MIST, SMUR, SMURR
droll .... ODD
dromedary, female ... DELUL
dromedary, swift ... MEHARI
drone ...... BEE, DOR, HUM
droop ...... LOP, SAG, WILT
drooping .... ALOP
drop ..... DRIB, FALL, SINK,
.... GUTTA, GLOBULE
drop a fish line or bait .. DAP
drop, one .... MINIM

c
drop: Prov. Eng. ..... SIE, SYE
dropsy .... EDEMA
dross . SLAG, SPRUE, SCORIA
drought-tolerant plant .. GUAR
drove .... HERD, RODE
drove of horses ...... ATAJO
drowse .... NOD
drudge .... MOIL, TOIL, LABOR
drug .... DOPE, SINA, ALOES,
.... OPIATE, DILANTIN
drug, Hippocrates' ... MECON
drugged bliss .... KEF
drum-call to arms ... RAPPEL
drum roll, reveille ..... DIAN
drum, small . TABOR, TABOUR,
.... TABRET
drum, W. Ind. .... GUMBY
drumbeat ...... DUB, TATTOO,
.... TATTOO
drunkard .... SOT, SOAK,
.... SOUSE, TOPER
dry .... SEC, ARID, SERE
dry, as wine .... SEC
dry bed of river ..... WADI
dry goods dealer .... DRAPER
dub .... NAME, KNIGHT
duck .... ANAS, SMEE,
.... TEAL, PEKIN
duck, Arctic .... EIDER

d
duck, breed of .... ROUEN
duck, diving .... SMEW
duck eggs, Chin. ..... PIDAN
duck, fresh water ..... TEAL
duck genus .. AEX, AIX, ANAS
duck, like a .... ANATINE
duck lure .... DECOY
duck, male .... DRAKE
duck, Muscovy .... PATO
duck, pintail .... SMEE
duck, ring-necked ..... DOGY
duck, river .... TEAL, EIDER,
.... SHOVELER
duck, sea ..... COOT, SCAUP
duck, sea, northern .. SCOTER
duck-shooting boat ... SKAG
duck to cook: Fr. ..CANETON
duct: anat. ..... VAS, VASA
dude .... FOP, DANDY
due, India ...... HAK, HAKH
duet .... DUI, DUO
dugout canoe
.... BANCA, PIROGUE
dugout, India .DONGA, DUNGA
duke's dominion ..... DUCHY
dulcimer .... CITOLE
dulcimer, Oriental ... SANTIR
dull . DRY, DUN, DRAB, LOGY,
.... BLUNT, PROSY, BORING
dull color .. DUN, MAT, DRAB,
.... MATTE, TERNE
dull in finish ... MAT, MATTE

a dull silk fabric .... GROS
dullard .... BOOR
Dumas hero
  ATHOS, ARAMIS, PORTHOS
dummy whist .... MORT
dung beetle .... DOR
dunlin bird .... STIB
dupe .... USE, FOOL
duration measure ...... TIME
dusk .... EVE
dusky ... DIM, DARK, SWART
dusty: Scot. .... MOTTY
DUTCH .... see also NETHER-
  LANDS, SPECIAL SECTION
Dutch: bit .... DOIT
  cupboard .... KAS
  donkey .... EZEL
  "mister" .... HEER
  out .... UIT
  woman .... FROW
Dutch cheese .... EDAM
Dutch commune .... EDE
Dutch early geographer .. AA
Dutch fishing boat .. DOGGER
Dutch measure, old .. AAM
Dutch meter .... EL
Dutch minor coin ...... DOIT
Dutch news agency, old ANETA
Dutch painter
  LIS, HALS, LELY, STEEN
Dutch two-masted vessel KOFF
duty .... CHORE, TARIFF
dwarf .. RUNT, STUNT, TROLL

c dwarf cattle, S. Am.
  NATA, NIATA
dwell ...... BIDE, LIVE, ABIDE
dwelling .... ABODE
dwindle .... PETER
Dyak knife .... PARANG
Dyak, sea .... IBAN
dye base .... ANILINE
dye, blue .... WOAD
dye, blue-red ...... ORSELLE
dye gum .... KINO
dye, indigo .... ANIL
dye, lichen
  ARCHIL, ORCHAL, ORCHIL
dye plant .... ANIL
dye, red AAL, ANATO, AURIN,
  EOSIN, ANATTA, ANATTO,
  AURINE, EOSINE, ANNAT-
  TA, ANNATTO, ANNOTTO,
  ARNATTO
dye, red, poisonous
  AURIN, AURINE
dye stuff .. EOSINE, MADDER
dye, yellow .... WELD,
  WOLD, WOALD
dyeing apparatus ..... AGER
dyeing reagent .... ALTERANT
dyestuff from lichens . LITMUS
dyewood tree .... TUI
dynamite inventor .... NOBEL
DYNASTY see CHIN. DYNASTY
dynasty, first Chin. ..... HSIA
dynasty, It. .... SAVOY

E

b eager .. AGOG, AVID, ARDENT
eagle ....ERN, ERNE
eagle, Bible .... GIER
eagle, tried to mount to heaven
  on .... ETANA
eagle, sea .... ERN, ERNE
eagle's nest
  AERY, EYRY, AERIE, EYRIE
eaglestone ... ETITE, AETITES
ear .... LUG, HANDLE
ear canal .... SCALA
ear cavity .... UTRICLE
ear doctor .... AURIST
ear inflamation .... OTITIS
ear of wheat: archeol.
  SPICA, SPICAE
ear, pert. to .... OTIC, AURAL
ear, prominence
  TRAGI, TRAGUS
ear shell .. ORMER, ABALONE
ear stone .. OTOLITE, OTOLITH
earache .. OTALGY, OTALGIA
eared seal .... OTARY

d early Britisher .... PICT
early Christian priest .. ARIUS
earnest
  ARDENT, INTENT, SINCERE
earnest money: law .... ARRA,
  ARLES, ARRHA
earth .... GEO
earth deposit in rocks .. GUHR
earth: dial. .... ERD
earth god, Egypt.
  GEB, KEB, SEB
earth goddess ..... GE, ERDA,
  GAEA, GAIA
earth goddess, Khonds' .. TARI
earth goddess, Rom.
  CERES, TERRA
earth, kind of .... LOAM
earth, pert. to .... GEAL
earth's surface, made on
  EPIGENE
earthenware maker .. POTTER
earthly .... TERRENE
earthquake . SEISM, TEMBLOR

47

earthquake, pert. to . SEISMIC
earthquake, shock of . TREMOR
earthwork, Rom. . . . . . . AGGER
East . . ASIA, LEVANT, ORIENT
E. African native . . . . SOMALI
E. Afr. spiritual power . . NGAI
E. Indian animal . . . . TARSIER
E. Ind. dye tree . . . . . DHAK
E. Ind. fruit DURIAN, DURION
E. Ind. grass . . . . KASA
E. Ind. herb . . PIA, SESAME
E. Ind. herb root CHAY, CHOY
E. Ind. palm . . . . NIPA
E. Ind. plant . . JUTE, SESAME
E. Ind. shrubby herb . . . SOLA
E. Ind. tanning tree . . AMLA,
AMLI
E. Ind. term of address SAHIB
E. Ind. timber tree . . ACH, SAJ,
SAL, SAIN, SAUL, TEAK
E. Ind. tree, large . . . . SIRIS
E. Ind. vine . . . AMIL, GILO,
ODAL, ODEL, SOMA
E. Ind. vine, milky . . . SOMA
E. Ind. weight . . . . . . TOLA
E. Ind. wood, strong, heavy
ENG
E. Ind. woody vine ODAL, GILO
East Indies . . . . . . INDONESIA
east wind . . . . EURUS
east wind's opposite . . . AFER
Easter . . . . . PASCH, PASCHA
Eastern . . . . ORTIVE
Eastern Catholic . . . . . UNIAT
Eastern Church doxology DOXA
Eastern European . . . . . SLAV
Eastern garment . . . . . . SARI
Eastern name . . ALI, ABOU
Eastern title . . . . . . AGA, RAS
Eastern Turkey tribesman
KURD
easy . . . . SOFT
easy gait . . . . LOPE
easy job
SNAP, CINCH, SINECURE
eat away . . . . ERODE
eat voraciously
RAVEN, RAVIN, RAVINE
eaten away . . . . EROSE
eating away
CAUSTIC, ERODENT
eccentric person . . . . . GINK
eccentric piece, rotating CAM
ecclesiastic . . . . PRELATE
ECCLESIASTICAL see CHURCH
eclipse . . . . DIM
eclipse demon, Hindu
KETU, RAHU
ecru . . . . BEIGE
Ecuadorian extinct Indians
CARA
edentate genus . . . . . MANIS
edge . . . . HEM, LIP, RIM,
ARRIS, BRINK, MARGE
edged unevenly . . . . . . EROSE
edging . . . . PICOT

edging, make . . . . TAT
edible fungus . . . . CEPE
edible root . . . . . . OCA, YAM,
TARO, CASAVA, CASSAVA
edible shoot, Jap. . . . . . . UDO
edict . . . LAW, FIAT, DECREE
Edinburgh: poet . . . . . EDINA
edit . . . . . . REVISE, REDACT
editorial "I" . . . . WE
Edom district . . . . TEMAN
Edomite . . . . OMAR
Edomite city . . . . PAU
Edomite duke UZ, ARAN, IRAM
Edomite king, ruler . . . BELA
educated . . . BRED, LETTERED
educator, Am. . . . . MANN
educe . . . . . . EVOKE, ELICIT
Edward Bradley's pseudo. BEDE
eel, marine . . . . CONGER
eel: old Eng. . . . . ELL
eel-shaped amphibian . . . OLM
eel, S. Am. . . . . CARAPO
eel, young . . . . ELVER
eelworm . . . . NEMA
Eghbal's land . . . . IRAN
effervescent, to make AERATE
effigy . . . . IDOL
effluvium . . MIASM, MIASMA
effort . . . . DINT, ASSAY,
NISUS, TRIAL
effusive . . . . GUSHING
eft . . . . EVET, NEWT
egg . . . . OVUM
egg dish . OMELET, OMELETTE
egg drink . . . . . . NOG, NOGG
egg, insect . . . . NIT
egg-shaped
OOID, OVAL, OVATE, OVOID
egg-shaped ornaments . . OVA
egg white, raw . . . . . . GLAIR
eggs . . . . OVA, ROE
ego . . . . SELF
Egypt, pert. to . . . . . . COPTIC
Egyptian bird . . . . IBIS
Egyp. Christian . . . . . . COPT
Egyp. city, ancient
SAIS, THEBES
Egyp. cobra . . . . HAJE
Egyp. crown . . . . ATEF
Egyp. dog-headed ape, deity
AANI
Egyp. gateway . . . . . . PYLON
Egyp. god of creation . . PTAH
EGYPTIAN GODS—GODDESSES
—DEITY see also GODS and
SPECIAL SECTION
Egyp. guard . . . . GHAFIR
Egyp. heaven
AALU, AARU, IALU, YARU
Egyp. immortal heart
AB, HATI
Egyp. king . MENES, RAMESES
Egyp. lute . . . . NABLA

a

Egyp. nationalist party . WAFD
Egyp. precious alloy ... ASEM
Egyp. primeval chaos .... NU
Egyp. queen of gods .... SATI
Egyp. sacred bird . BENU, IBIS
Egyp. sacred bull ...... APIS
Egyp. season .... AHET
Egyp. tambourine ..... RIKK
Egyp. thorn .... KIKAR
Egyp. writing surfaces PAPYRI
eh?: obs. .... ANAN
eight days after feast . UTAS
eight, group of
OCTAD, OCTET, OCTAVE
eight, set of .... OGDOAD
eighth day of feast .... UTAS
eighth day, on ..... OCTAN
eighth note .... UNCA
Eire legislature .... DAIL
ejaculation, mystic ..... OM
eject ..... EMIT, OUST, SPEW
elaborate .... ORNATE
Elam, capital of ...... SUSA
eland .... IMPOFO
elanet .... KITE
elasmobranch fish RAY, SHARK
Elbe, river to .... EGER, ISER
Elbe tributary .... EGER, ISER
elbow .... ANCON
elder .... SENIOR

b

elder son of Zeus ...... ARES
elder statesmen, Jap. .. GENRO
eldest: law ... AINÉ, EIGNE
electric catfish .... RAAD
electric force .... ELOD
electric force unit ..... VOLT
electric reluctance unit .. REL
electric unit ES, AMP, MHO,
OHM, REL, PERM, FARAD,
HENRY, AMPERE
electrified particle ..... ION
electrode ANODE, CATHODE
electromagnet .... RELAY
electron tube
TRIODE, KLYSTRON
elegance .... GRACE
elegant .... FINE, POSH
elegist .... POET
elegy .... NENIA
ELEMENT, non-metallic and metallic, gaseous on page 195
elemi .... ANIME
element, radioactive of URANIC
elephant goad ...... ANKUS
elephant: India .... HATHI
elephant's cry ...... BARR
elephant's ear ...... TARO
elevated ground MESA, RIDEAU
elevation of mind . ANAGOGE
elevator: Brit. .... LIFT

c

elf .... SPRITE
elf. Egypt. .... OUPHE
elfin .... FEY
Elia .... LAMB
elicit .... EDUCE
elide .... DELE, OMIT
Elija .... ELIAS
eliminate .. DELETE, REMOVE
Elizabeth I, name for ORIANA
elk, Am. .... WAPITI
elk, Europ. .... MOOSE
elk, Europ. genus .... ALCES
elliptical ..... OVAL, OVOID
elm .... ULM, ULME
elm fruit seed ...... SAMARA
elongated .... PROLATE
else .... OTHER
elude .... DODGE, EVADE
elver .... EEL
emaciation .. TABES, MACIES
emanation .... AURA
emanation, star ...... BLAS
embankment ... DAM, BUND,
DIKE, DYKE, DIGUE, LEVEE
embellish
GILD, ADORN, DECORATE
embellished .... ORNATE
ember .... ASH, COAL
emblem . INSIGNE, INSIGNIA

d

emblem of authority ... MACE
emblem of U.S. ...... EAGLE
embrace
HUG, CLASP, ENARM, INARM
embrocation ..... LINIMENT
embroidery frame
TABORET, TABOURET
emend .... EDIT
emerald ... BERYL, SMARAGD
emerge RISE, ISSUE, EMANATE
emetic .... IPECAC
eminent .... NOTED
emit .... REEK, EXUDE
emmer .... SPELT
emmet .... ANT
Emperor of Russia
CZAR, TSAR, TZAR
emphasis .. ACCENT, STRESS
empire .... REALM
employ ... USE, HIRE, PLACE
employed for wine, meas AAM
employees ...... PERSONNEL
employer ...... BOSS, USER
employment .... PLACE
emporium ..... MART, STORE
Empress, Byzant .... IRENE
Empress, Russian . CZARINA,
TSARINA, TZARINA
empty .... VOID, INANE,
DEPLETE
emulate .... RIVAL
enamel ware ...... LIMOGES

49

a enchantress .. CIRCE, MEDEA
encircle ... ORB, GIRD, GIRT, RING, EMBAY
encircled GIRT, RINGED, SURROUNDED
encircling band ...... ZONE
enclose .... MEW
enclosure ... MEW, PEN, REE, STY, CORRAL
enclosure, cattle ...... ATAJO
enclosure: Sp. Am. .. CANCHA
encomium .... ELOGE
encompass . GIRD, GIRT, RING
encompassed by ...... AMID
encore .... BIS
encounter .... MEET
encourage .... ABET
end TIP, FINIS, LIMIT, OMEGA
end: music .... FINE
end result .... PRODUCT
end, tending to an .... TELIC
endeavor . TRY, ESSAY, NISUS
ENDING .. see also SUFFIX or type of ending
ending, comparative . IER, IOR
ENDING, NOUN see SUFFIX, NOUN ENDING
ending, plural ...... EN, ES
ending, superlative ..... EST
endow ...... DOWER, INVEST
b endue .... ENDOW
endure .. BEAR, LAST, WEAR
endure: dial. .... BIDE
energy ..... PEP, VIM, ZIP, POWER, VIGOR, VIGOUR
energy, potential .... ERGAL
energy unit ERG, RAD, ERGON
enfeeble WEAKEN, DEBILITATE
engage HIRE, ENTER, CHARTER
engender .... BEGET, BREED, PROMOTE, GENERATE
engine, donkey ..... YARDER
engine of war .... RAM
engine part .... STATOR
engine, rotary ..... TURBINE
engineer, Am. .... EADS
engineer, military ... SAPPER
English actor .... EVANS
Eng. actress .... (Nell) GWYN, TERRY, NEAGLE
Eng. architect .... WREN
Eng. author .... MORE, WEST, ARLEN, BACON, CAINE, DE-FOE, DORAN, ELIOT, HARDY, READE, SHUTE, WAUGH, WELLS, AMBLER, AUSTEN, BARRIE, BELLOC, BRONTE, ORWELL, STERNE
Eng. car .... ROVER
Eng. cathedral city ELY, YORK
Eng. city, historic COVENTRY

c Eng. college .. ETON, BALIOL
ENG. COMPOSER see COMPOSER, ENG.
Eng. country festival ... ALE
Eng. dramatist SHAW, PEELE, DRYDEN
Eng. emblem .... ROSE
Eng. essayist .. SALA, STEELE
Eng. explorer .. ROSS, CABOT
Eng. historian .... BEDE
Eng. king BRAN, CNUT, KNUT, CANUTE
Eng. monk .... BEDE, BAEDA
Eng. murderer .... ARAM
Eng. musician .... ARNE
ENG. NOVELIST ... see ENG. AUTHOR
Eng. painter ... OPIE, ORPEN
Eng. philosopher .... HUME, JOAD, BACON, SPENCER
Eng. playwright ..... SHAW
Eng. poet .... GRAY, AUDEN, BLAKE, BYRON, CAREW, DONNE, ELIOT
Eng. queen .... ANNE, MARY
Eng. rebel leader, 1450 . CADE
Eng. royal house YORK, TUDOR
Eng. scholar, schoolmaster ARAM
Eng. school, boys' ..... ETON
Eng. sculptor .... EPSTEIN
d Eng. spa ... BATH, MARGATE
Eng. spy .... ANDRE
Eng. statesman .. EDEN, PITT
Eng. theologian ... ALCUIN
Eng. woman politician ASTOR
ENG. WRITER ..... see ENG. AUTHOR and ENG. ESSAYIST
engraver .. CHASER, ETCHER, GRAVER
engraver, famous . PYE, DORE
engraver's tool ...... BURIN
engrossed .... RAPT
enigma .... RIDDLE
enlarge DILATE, EXPAND, INCREASE
enlarge a hole .... REAM
enlarging, as chimneys EVASE
enmity .... ANIMUS
Enoch's father .... CAIN
enough .... ENOW
enrol .... ENTER, ENLIST
ensign .... FLAG
ensnare .... NET, WEB
entangle .... MAT, MESH
enter .... ENROL
entertain AMUSE, DIVERT, REGALE
enthusiasm ELAN, ARDOR, VERVE, SPIRIT
enthusiastic .... RABID

50

entice............ BAIT, LURE,
    TOLE, TEMPT, ALLURE
enticement .... TICE
entire man .... EGO
entity .... ENS, ENTIA
entomb .... INURN
entrance
    ADIT, DOOR, GATE, PORTAL
entrance halls .... ATRIA
entreat ...... PRAY, PLEAD
entreaty .... PLEA
entry, separate .... ITEM
entwine
    WEAVE, ENLACE, WREATHE
enumerate .... COUNT
envelop
    WRAP, ENFOLD, INFOLD
environment .... MILIEU
envoy .... LEGATE
envy .... COVET
enzyme ...... ASE, LOTASE,
    RENNIN, MALTASE
eon .... OLAM
ephah, 1/10 .... OMER
epic poetry ... EPOS, EPOPEE
epoch .... ERA
epochal .... ERAL
epode .... POEM
eponymous ancestor ... EBER
equal IS, ARE, TIE, EVEN, PEER
equality .... PAR, PARITY
equally .... AS
equilibrium .... POISE
equine .... HORSE
equip .... FIT, RIG
equitable .. JUST, IMPARTIAL
equivalence .... PAR
equivocate .... EVADE
era .... EPOCH
eradicate ... ERASE, UPROOT
eral .... EPOCHAL
erase ...... DELE, DELETE
erect .... REAR, RAISE
ergo .... HENCE
Eris' brother .... ARES
ermine, summer .... STOAT
Eros .... CUPID
errand boy .... PAGE
error, publication ... TYPO,
    ERRATA, ERRATE, ERRATUM
Esau's .... EDOM
Esau's brother ..... JACOB
Esau's father-in-law ... ELON
Esau's grandson ... OMAR
Esau's home .... SEIR
Esau's wife .... ADAH
escape LAM, ELUDE, EVADE
eschew .... SHUN
escutcheon band ...... FESS
Esdra's angel .... URIEL
eskers .... OSAR
Eskimo .... ITA

Eskimo boat
    KIAK, KYAK, KAYAK
Eskimo boot ...... MUKLUK
Eskimo coat
    PARKA, NETCHA, TEMIAK
Eskimo curlew .... FUTE
Eskimo house
    IGLU, IGLOE, IGLOO, IGLOU
Eskimo settlement .... ETAH
Eskimo summer hut ... TOPEK
Eskimos of Asia YUIT, INNUIT
esoteric .... INNER
espy .... SEE, SPY
esquire .... ARMIGER
essay .. TRY, TEST, ATTEMPT
essay, scholarly
    THESIS, TREATISE
essence: Hindu religion . RASA
essence, rose .... ATTAR
essential oils fluid ... NEROL
essential part .... CORE, PITH
"— est" (that is) .... ID
establish ..... BASE, FOUND
established value ...... PAR
estate, landed, large ... MANOR
estate manager ... STEWARD
estate, not held by feudal ten
    ure ALOD, ALLOD, ALODIUM
esteem .... HONOR,
    PRIZE, ADMIRE, HONOUR
ester, hydriodic acid .. IODIDE
ester, liquid .... ACETIN
ester, oleic acid .... OLEATE
estimate .... RATE, APPRAISE
Estonian .... ESTH
estuary .... RIA
estuary, Brazil .... PARA
estuary, S. Am. ..... PLATA
Eternal City .... ROME
eternity .. AGE, EON, OLAM
ether compound ..... ESTER
etheral ..... AERY, AERIAL
ETHIOPIA see also ABYSSINIA
Ethiopia .... CUSH
Ethiopian title .... RAS
Ethiopic .... GEEZ
ethos, opposed to ... PATHOS
Etruscan god .... LAR
Etruscan Juno .... UNI
Etruscan Minerva ... MENFRA
Etruscan title, peer LAR, LARS
eucalyptus secretion
    LAAP, LARP, LERP
eucalyptus tree .... YATE
Eucharist case ..... PIX, PYX
Eucharist cloth
    FANO, FANON, FANUM
Eucharist spoon ...... LABIS
Eucharist wafer .... HOST
eulogy .... ELOGE
euphorbia .... SPURGE

51

Eurasian

a
Eurasian dock plant . **PARELLE**
eureka red . . . . **PUCE**
Euripides heroine . . . . **MEDEA**
EUROPEAN see also specific
   word, as FISH, ANIMAL,
   etc.
European . . . . . . **POLE, SLAV**
Eur. colorful fish . . . . . **BOCE**
EUROP. FISH . see FISH, EUR.
European, in Moslem East
                FRANGI
Europ. iris . . . . **ORRIS**
Europ. kite . . . . **GLED, GLEDE**
Europ. porgy . . . . **PARGO**
Eurytus' daughter . . . . . **IOLE**
evade . . . . **SHUN,**
    DODGE, ELUDE, SHIRK
evaluate . . . . . . **RATE, ASSESS**
Evangelist . . . . **LUKE, MARK**
Evans, Mary Ann . . . . . . **ELIOT**
Eve's grandson . . . . **ENOS**
even . . . . **EEN, LEVEL, PLANE**
even if . . . . **THO**
evening party . . . . . . **SOIREE**
evening prayer . . . . . . **VESPER**
eventual lot . . . . **FATE**
ever . . . . **EER**
evergreen . . **FIR, YEW, PINE,**
   CAROB, CEDAR, OLIVE,
   SAVIN, LAUREL, SABINE,
b
   SAVINE, SPRUCE
evergreen, bean . . . . . **CAROB**
evergreen genus
   OLAX, ABIES, CATHA
evergreen, red-berry
           YEW, WHORT
evergreen, tropical . . **CALABA**
everlasting . . **ETERN, ETERNE**
evict . . . . **OUST**
evident **CLEAR, PLAIN, PATENT**
evil . . . . **MAL**
evil god, Egypt. . . **SET, SETH**
evil intent: law . . . . . **DOLUS**
evil spirit, Haiti . **BAKA, BOKO**
evil spirit, Hindu . . . . **ASURA**
evolve . . . . **EDUCE**
ewe, old . . . . **CRONE**
exact **BLEED, DEMAND, EXTORT**
exacerbate . . . . **IRE**
exact point . . . . **TEE**
examine . . . **PRY, SPY, SCAN**
excavate . **DIG, PION, DREDGE**
excavation for extracting ore
               STOPE
excavation, mine . **PIT, STOPE**
exceed . . . . **TOP**
exceedingly: music . . . . **TRES**
excellence . . . . **VIRTU**
excellent . . . . **AONE**
except . . . . **BUT, SAVE**
excess . . . . **LUXUS, NIMIETY**

c
excess, fill to . . . **GLUT, SATE**
excess of solar year . . **EPACT**
exchange medium, Chin. **SYCEE**
exchange premium, discount
                AGIO
exchequer . . . . . . **FISC, FISK**
excite . . . . **ELATE, ROUSE**
excited . . . . **AGOG, MANIC**
excitement, public
       FUROR, FURORE
exclamation . . **AH, EH, HA, HI,**
   MY, OH, OW, UM, ACH,
   AHA, AUH, BAH, BAW, FIE,
   FOH, GRR, HAH, HAW,
   HAY, HEM, HEP, HEU, HEY,
   HIC, HIP, HOI, HOY, HUH,
   OHO, OUF, PAH, PEW, POH,
   PUE, SOH, TCH, TCK, TUT,
   UGH, WEE, WHY, WOW,
   YAH, YOI, YOW, ALAS,
   PHEW, ALACK
exclamation, Fr. . . . . **HEIN**
exclamation, Ger. . . . . **HOCH**
exclamation Ir. . . . . **ADAD,**
   AHEY, ARAH, ARRA, ARRO,
   BOOH, EHEU, OCHONE
exclude . . **BAR, OMIT, DEBAR**
exclusive . . . . **SOLE**
exclusive set . . **ELECT, ELITE**
exclusively . . . . **ONLY**
d
excoriate . . . . **ABRADE**
excrete from skin . . . . **EGEST**
excuse . . **PLEA, ALIBI, REMIT**
excuse, court **ESSOIN, ESSOINE**
execrated . . . . **CURST, SWORE**
exemplar . . **MODEL, PATTERN**
exhaust
   SAP, TIRE, SPEND, DEPLETE
exhausted . . . . **EFFETE**
exhibits leaping . . . . **SALTATE**
exigency . . . . **NEED**
exist . . . . **LIVE**
exist . . all forms of verb "BE"
exist, beginning to . **NASCENT**
existence . . . . . . **ENS, ESSE**
existentialist leader . . **SARTRE**
existing **ALIVE, BEING, EXTANT**
exit . **LEAVE, DEPART, EGRESS**
expand . . . . **DILATE, DISTEND**
expanse . . . . **SEA**
expatriate . . . . **EXILE**
expectation . . . . **HOPE**
expedite . . **HURRY, HASTEN**
expedition . . **SAFARI, SUFFARI**
expert . . **ACE, ONER, ADEPT**
expiate . . . . **ATONE**
explain . . . . **DEFINE**
explode . . . . **POP,**
   DETONATE, FULMINATE
exploit
   DEED, FEAT, GEST, GESTE

a
explosive .... CAP, TNT, GAINE, TONITE
explosive sound .. POP, CHUG
expose .... AIR, DISPLAY
expression, elegant . ATTICISM
expression, local ..... IDIOM
expressionless .... WOODEN
expunge DELE, ERASE, DELETE
extend .... JUT, LIE, REACH, BEETLE
extend the front .... DEPLOY
extensive .... AMPLE
extent .... AREA
external .... EXOTERIC
external covering HIDE, HUSK, PEEL, PELT, RIND, SKIN
extinct wild ox .... URUS
extirpate .. ROOT, ERADICATE
extort ...... BLEED, EXACT
extra ...... ODD, SPARE
extra leaf .... INSERT
extra, theatrical ..... SUPE
extract DRAW, ELICIT, EVULSE
extraneous .... EXOTIC
extraordinary person, thing ONER

c
extravagance .... ELA
extreme .... ULTRA
extreme unction, give ANELE, ENELE
exudate, plant GUM, LAC, RESIN
exude .... EMIT, OOZE, REEK
exult .... ELATE
eye ...... ORB, SEE, OGLE
eye cosmetic ... KOHL, KUHL
eye inflammation . STY, IRITIS
eye, inner coat ..... RETINA
eye, layer .... UVEA
eye of bean .... HILA, HILUM
eye of insect ..... STEMMA
eye, part of the .... IRIS, UVEA, CORNEA, RETINA
eye, pert. to .... OPTIC
eye socket .... ORBIT
eye, symbolic .... UTA
eye-worm, Afr. .... LOA
eyelash ...... CILIA, CILIUM
eyes: old Eng. .... NIE
eyestalk .... STIPE
eyewink ..... LOOK, GLANCE
eyot .... ISLE, ISLET

F

b
Fabian .... SHAW
fable ... APOLOG, APOLOGUE
fable writer ... ESOP, AESOP
fabled bird .... ROC, RUKH
"Fables in Slang" author ADE
fabric .... REP, ACCA BAFT, DRAB, DUCK, IKAT, LAWN, LENO, MOFF, REPP, SILK, SUSI, TAPA, TUKE, CRAPE, CREPE, MOIRE, NINON, ORLON, RAYON, CANVAS, COVERT, MANTUA, MOHAIR
fabric, Angora ...... CAMLET, MOHAIR
fabric, coarse cotton . SURAT
fabric, coarse wool TAMIN, TAMINE
fabric, corded .... REP, REPP, PIQUE
fabric, cotton LENO, MULL, DENIM, MANTA, SCRIM, CALICO, CRETON, NANKIN, PENANG, NANKEEN, CRETONNE
fabric, curtain .. NET, SCRIM
fabric, felt-like ...... BAIZE
fabric, fig'd DAMASK, PAISLEY
fabric from remnants MUNGO
fabric, Ind. .. SHELA, SHELAH

d
fabric, knitted ...... TRICOT
fabric, light wool .. ALPACA
fabric,lustrous POPLIN,SATEEN
fabric, mourning ALMA, CRAPE
fabric, net .. TULLE, MALINE
fabric, plaid .. MAUD, TARTAN
fabric, printed BATIK, BATTIK
FABRIC, RIBBED see RIBBED FABRIC
fabric, satin .. PEKIN, ETOILE
fabric, satiny SATINET, SATINETTE
fabric, sheer ...... GAUZE, BEMBERG, ORGANZA
fabric, short nap ...... RAS
fabric, silk .... SURAH, PONGEE, SAMITE, TOBINE
fabric, silk,gold,medieval ACCA
fabric, silk, thick ..... GROS
fabric, stiff .... WIGAN
fabric stretcher TENTER, STENTER
fabric, striped .. SUSI, DOREA, DORIA, DOOREA, MADRAS
fabric, thick .... DRAB
fabric, twilled .... REP
fabric, upholstery BROCATEL, BROCATALL, BROCATELL, BROCATELLE

53

Fabric

a fabric, velvet-like ..... PANNE
fabric, voile-like .... ETAMINE
fabric, wool .. SERGE, TAMIN, TAMIS, MERINO, TAMINE, TAMINY, TAMISE, TAMMIN, ESTAMIN, ETAMINE, STAMMEL, ESTAMINE
fabric, worsted .... ETAMINE
fabricate .... MAKE
fabulist ..... ESOP, AESOP
fabulous bird .. ROC, RUKH
face MAP, MUG, PHIZ, FACADE
face with stone ...... REVET
facet of gem . BEZEL, BEZIL, CULET, COLLET
facile .... EASY
facing glacier .... STOSS
fact .... DATUM
fact, by the law ...... FACTO
faction .. SECT, SIDE, CABAL
factor .... GENE
factory .... PLANT
facts .... DATA
faculty .... SENSE
fade ..... DIE, DIM, WITHER
"Faerie Queene" iron man TALUS
"Faerie Queene" lady .. UNA
failure .... DUD, FLOP
fainting: med. .... SYNCOPE
b fair . BAZAR, FERIA, BAZAAR, KERMIS, KIRMES
fair . JUST, CLEAR, IMPARTIAL
fair-haired .. BLOND, BLONDE
fair-lead, naut. .... WAPP
fairy . ELF, FAY, PERI, SPRITE
fairy fort .... LIS, LISS
fairy king .... OBERON
fairy queen .. MAB, TITANIA
fairy, Serbo-Croat . VILA, VILY
fairylike creature ...... PERI
faith, article of ...... TENET
faith, pert. to .... PISTIC
faithful .... LEAL, TRUE, STANCH, STAUNCH
falcon ..... SACER, SAKER, LANNER, MERLIN, SAKERET
falcon, Asia LAGGAR, LUGGAR
falcon genus .... FALCO
falcon-headed god MENT, MENTU
falcon, Ind. SHAHIN, SHAHEEN
falcon of sea .... ERN, ERNE
falconer's bait .... LURE
fall DROP, PLAP, PLOP, SPILL
fall back .... RETREAT
fallacy ...... IDOLA, IDOLUM
fallow-deer, female .... TEG
false excuse ... SUBTERFUGE
false friend . IAGO, TRAITOR
false fruit of rose ...... HIP

c false god .... IDOL
Falstaff's follower ..... NYM
fame .... ECLAT, KUDOS, RENOWN, REPUTE
famed .... NOTED
familiar .... VERSANT
familiar saying .... SAW, TAG
family, Florentine .... MEDICI
family, Genoese ...... DORIA
family: Scot. .... ILK
famous .... NOTED
fan .... ROOTER
fan palm genus .... INODES
fan's stick .... BRIN
fanatical .... RABID
fancy .. IDEA, WHIM, IDEATE
fanfare .... TANTARA, TANTARO, TANTARARA
fanning device PUNKA, PUNKAH
fare .... DIET
farewell .. AVE, VALE, ADIEU
farinaceous .... MEALY
farinaceous food SAGO, SALEP
farm group .... GRANGE
farm, small, Sp. Am. CHACRA
farm, Sw. small leased . TORP
farm: Swedish ...... TORP
farm, tenant .... CROFT
farmer .... KULAK, GRANGER
d farmyard, S. Afr. ...... WERF
Faroe Is. wind .... OE
Faroe judge .... FOUD
Farouk's father ...... FUAD
fashion ...... FORM, MODE, MOLD, MODEL, STYLE
fasten ... BOLT, LOCK, NAIL, SEAL, SNIB, TACK, RIVET
fasten: naut. BELAY, BATTEN
fastener ... NUT, PIN, BRAD, CLIP, HASP, NAIL, SNAP, STUD, CLASP, RIVET, CLEVIS, COTTER
fastener, wire ...... STAPLE
fastener, naut. .... BITT
fastener, wood FID, NOG, PEG, PIN
fastening .... LATCH
fastidious .... NICE
fasting month .... RAMADAN
fasting period .... LENT
fat . LARD, LIPA, SUET, OBESE
fat, animal . ADEPS, TALLOW
fat: comb. form STEAT, STEATO
fat, liquid part ...... ELAIN, OLEIN, ELAINE, OLEINE
fat, natural .... ESTER
fat, of .... SEBAIC
fat, solid part STEARIN, STEARINE
fatal ...... FUNEST, LETHAL

54

a fate .... LOT, DOOM, KISMET
fateful .... DIRE
Fates, Gr. & Rom. .... MOIRA,
     MORTA, PARCA, CLOTHO,
     DECUMA, MOIRAI, PAR-
     CAE, ATROPOS, LACHESIS
father .... SIRE, BEGET
father: Arab. .... ABU, ABOU
father: Hebr. .... ABBA
father of modern engraving PYE
father's side, kinship on
     AGNAT, AGNATE
fathom .... PROBE, SOUND
fatigue ... FAG, TIRE, WEARY
Fatima's husband .... ALI
fatty .... ADIPOSE
fatty gland secretion ... SEBUM
fatuous .... INANE
faucet .. TAP, COCK, SPIGOT
fault find .... CARP, CAVIL
faultfinder . MOMUS, CAVILER
faulty .... BAD
faux pas .... ERROR, GAFFE
favor .... BOON
favorable vote .. AY, AYE, YES
favorite .... PET, IDOL
fawn color .... FAON
fawning favorite .... MINION
fear .... PHOBIA
fearful .... TREPID
b feast .... REGALE
feast day: comb. form .. MAS
feather PENNA, PINNA, PLUME
feather grass .... STIPA
feather palms .... EJOO, IROK
feather: zool. .... PLUMA
feathers, cast .... MEW
feathers of o-o .... HULU
feathered scarf .... BOA
feeble . PUNY, WEAK, DEBILE
feel .... SENSE
feel one's way ...... GROPE
feeler PALP, PALPI, ANTENNA
feet, having .... PEDATE
feet, pert. to PEDAL, PEDARY
feign .... ACT, SHAM
feline .... CAT, PUMA
felis leo .... LION
fellow .... GUY, LAD, BOZO,
     CHAP, DICK, CHAPPY,
     CHAPPIE
felt ...... GROPED, SENSATE
female animal, parent
     DAM, DOE
female camel .... NAGA
female disciple at Joppa
     DORCAS
female insect .... GYNE
fence of shrubs ...... HEDGE
fence of stakes ... PALISADE
fence step .... STILE

e fence, sunken, hidden
     AHA, HAHA
fence to restrain cattle .. OXER
fencer's cry .. HAI, HAY, SASA
fencing dummy .... PEL
fencing position CARTE, SIXTE,
     QUARTE, QUINTE, TIERCE,
     SECONDE, SEPTIME
fencing sword ... EPEE, FOIL
fencing term .... TOUCHE
fencing thrust ...... LUNGE,
     PUNTO, REMISE, RIPOST,
     RIPOSTE, REPRISE
fend .... WARD
fennel: P. I. .... ANIS
"Ferdinand the Bull" author
     LEAF
feria, pert. to .... FERIAL
ferment .... YEAST
ferment: med. .... ZYME
fermented milk dessert LACTO
fern, climbing, P. I. .... NITO
fern, Polyn., edible .... TARA
fern root, N. Z. .... ROI
fern "seed" .... SPORE
fern species .... WEKI
fern spore ..... SORI, SORUS
Ferrara ducal family ... ESTE
ferrum .... IRON
ferryboat .... BAC
d ferryboat, Afr. .... PONT
fertilizer ... MARL, GUANO
fervent .... ARDENT
fervor .. ZEAL, ZEST, ARDOR
fester .... RANKLE
festival .... ALE, FAIR, FETE,
     GALA, FERIA, FIESTA, KER-
     MIS, KIRMES
festival, Creek Indian .. BUSK
festival, Gr.
     AGON, DELIA, HALOA
fetid .... OLID, RANK
fetish .... OBI, JUJU, OBIA,
     ZEME, ZEMI, CHARM,
     OBEAH, GRIGRI
fetish, P. I. .... ANITO
fetter .... GYVE, IRON
feud, opposed to .. ALOD, AL-
     LOD, ALODIUM, ALLODIUM
feudal benefice .... FEU
feudal estate FEOD, FEUD, FIEF
feudal land .... BENEFICE
feudal service, form of AVERA
feudal tax .... TAILAGE,
     TALLAGE, TAILLAGE
feudal tenant .... VASSAL
fever, intermittent
     AGUE, TERTIAN
feverish .... FEBRILE
fez .... TARBUSH,
     TARBOOSH, TARBOUCHE

a fiber .... JUTE, PITA, RAFFIA, STAPLE, THREAD
fiber, bark ... TAPA, OLONA, TERAP
fiber, coarse .... ADAD
fiber, cordage .... DA, COIR, FERU, HEMP, IMBE, JUTE, RHEA, ABACA, SISAL
fiber from palm .... ERUC
fiber, hat or basket .. DATIL
fiber knot .... NEP
fiber plant ISTLE, IXTLE, IXLE, RAMIE
fiber plant, Brazil .... CAROA
fiber plant, E. Ind. SANA, SUNN
fiber, textile .... SABA
fiber, tropical IXLE, ISTLE, IXTLE
fiber woody .... BAST, BASTE
fictional submarine character NEMO
fiddle, medieval .... GIGA
fiddler crab genus .... UCA
field LEA, ACRE, WONG, CROFT
field deity ...... PAN, FAUN
field, enclosed: law .... AGER
field, stubble .... ROWEN
fifth segment crustacean CARPOS

b fig marigold, Afr. ..... SAMH
figs, Smyrna .. ELEME, ELEMI
fight .... CLEM, FRAY, MELEE, AFFRAY
figurative use of word . TROPE
figure .... SOLID
figure, equal angles ISAGON, ISOGON
figure, 4-sided .... TETRAGON
figure, geom. .... SECTOR
figure of speech TROPE, SIMILE, METAPHOR
figure, oval .... ELLIPSE
figure, 10-sided ... DECAGON
figwort .... MULLEIN
Fiji chestnut .... RATA
Fiji tree .... BURI
filament ...... FIBER, HAIR
filament, flax .. HARL, HARLE
filament, plant ELATER, THREAD
filch .... STEAL
file .... ROW
file, coarse .... RASP
file, three-square single-cut CARLET
filled to capacity SATED, REPLETE
fillet, architectural ORLE, ORLO
fillet, narrow heraldic ORLE, ORLO, LISTEL
fillet, shaft's .... ORLE, ORLO

c fillip .... SNAP
film, old green ...... PATINA
filthy .... VILE
filthy lucre .... PELF
finale: music .... CODA
finally: Fr. .... ENFIN
finback whale .... GRASO
finch . MORO, LINNET, SISKIN
finch, Europ. TARIN, TERIN, SERIN
finch, S. Afr. .... FINK
find fault .... CARP, CAVIL
fine, as a line ...... LEGER
fine, punish by .... AMERCE
fine, record of ..... ESTREAT
finesse ...... ART, SKILL
Fingal's kingdom .... MORVEN
finger .... DIGIT
finger, cymbals ... CASTANETS
finger, 5th . PINKIE, MINIMUS
finger inflammation ... FELON
finger nail half-moon LUNULA, LUNULE
fingerless glove .... MIT, MITT
fingerprint pattern .. WHORL
finial ornament, slender EPI
finisher .... EDGER, ENDER
finishing tool ..... REAMER
FINLAND, FINNISH see also SPECIAL SECTION

d Finland .... SUOMI
Finn in Ingria .... VOT, VOTE
Finns .... SUOMI
Finnish god .... JUMALA
Finnish poetry ...... RUNES
Finnish steam bath . SAUNA
fire basket .... CRESSET
fire bullet .... TRACER
fire god .... VULCAN
fire god, Hindu . AGNI, AKAL, CIVA, DEVA, KAMA, SIVA
fire in heart: Buddhism RAGA
fire opal: Fr. ...... GIRASOL
fire, sacrificial, Hindu . AGNI
fire worshipper PARSI, PARSEE
firearm GUN, RIFLE, MAUSER, PISTOL, CARBINE, REVOLVER
firecracker .... PETARD
fired clay .... TILE
firedog .... ANDIRON
fireplace GRATE, INGLE, HEARTH
fireplace side shelf .... HOB
firewood bundle BARIN, FAGOT
firewood, Tex. .... LENA
firework .... GERB
firm FAST, STANCH, STAUNCH
firm: Hawaii .... HUI
firmament .... SKY
firn .... NEVE
firs, true .... ABIES

a first PRIME, INITIAL, ORIGINAL
first American-born white
child .... DARE
first appearance ..... DEBUT
first born: law .... EIGNE
first fruits of a benefice
ANNATES
first miracle site ...... CANA
first mortal, Hindu ..... YAMA
first part in duet ..... PRIMO
first principles .... ABCS
first-rate .... ACE
firth: Scot. .... KYLE
fish .. ANGLE, TRAWL, TROLL
fish .... ID, EEL, IDE, CARP,
DACE, HAKE, HIKU, JOCU,
LIJA, LING, MADO, MASU,
OPAH, ORFE, PEGA, PETO,
PIKE, POGY, ROUD, RUDD,
SCAD, SCUP, SESI, SHAD,
SIER, SKIL, SOLE, SPET,
TOPE, TUNA, ULUA, PAR-
GO, POWAN, POWEN,
ROACH, SKATE, CONGER,
MULLET, SABALO, TOM-
COD
fish, ancient .. ELOPS, ELLOPS
fish, Atlant. TAUTOG, ESCOLAR
fish, boneless .... FILET, FILLET
fish, bony ... CARP, TELEOST
fish, butterfly .... PARU
b fish by trolling .... DRAIL
fish, Calif. surf .... SPRAT
fish, carplike
RUD, DACE, ROUD, RUDD
fish cleaner .... SCALER
fish, climbing .... ANABAS
fish, cod-like ... CUSK, HAKE,
LING
fish, colorful
BOCE, OPAH, WRASSE
fish, Congo .... LULU
fish, Cuban .... DIABLO
fish, cyprinoid
ID, IDE, ORF, ORFE
fish, edible .... SPRAT
fish eggs .... ROE
fish, Egypt. .... SAIDE
fish, elongated EEL, GAR, PIKE
fish, Europ. .. ID, BOCE, DACE,
BREAM, SPRAT, UMBER,
BARBEL, BRASSE, PLAICE,
SENNET, WRASSE
fish, flat .... DAB, RAY, SOLE,
BRILL, FLUKE, FLOUNDER
fish, Florida .... TARPON
fish, food . SOD, CERO, HAAK,
HAIK, HAKE, LING, SHAD,
TUNA, TUNNY, SARDINE
fish, food: Ind. .... HILSA
fish, fresh water
IDE, BASS, DACE, ESOX
fish from boat .... TROLL

c fish, game .... BASS,
MARLIN, TARPON, TARPUN
fish, gobeylike .. DRAGONET
fish, Gr. Lakes . CISCO, PERCH
fish, Hawaiian .... AKU
fish, herringlike ...... SHAD
fish, hook for GIG, GAFF, DRAIL
fish, lancet .... SERRA
fish line ..... SNELL, TRAWL
fish line cork .... BOB
fish, linglike .... COD
fish, long-nosed .... GAR
fish, mackerellike
CERO, TUNNY, TINKER
fish, many .... SHOAL
fish, marine BONITO, TARPON
fish measure .... MEASE
fish, Medit. .... NONNAT
fish, nest-building .... ACARA
fish net
SEINE, TRAWL, SPILLER
fish, N. Z. .... IHI
fish, No. Pacif. .... INCONNU
fish, parasitic ...... REMORA
fish, perch-like ...... DARTER
fish, Pers. myth .... MAH
fish pickle .... ALEC
fish, piece of ... FILET, FILLET
fish, pikelike .... GAR
d fish-pitching prong PEW, GAFF
fish-poison tree .... BITO
fish, predatory .... GAR
fish, river .... BLAY
fish, Russian .... STERLET
fish sauce .... ALEC, GARUM
fish sign .... PISCES
fish, silvery .... MULLET
fish, small . ID, IDE, DARTER
fish, snouted .... SAURY
fish, S. Am. ... ARAPAIMA
fish, sparoid .... SAR, SARGO
fish, spiny .... GOBY, PERCH
fish, sucking ...... REMORA
fish, trap ..... WEEL, WEIR
fish, tropical
SARGO, ROBALO, SALEMA
fish, warm sea
GUASA, GROUPER
fish, W. Ind.
BOGA, CERO, TESTAR
fish whisker .... BARBEL
fish with moving line .. TROLL
fish with net ... SEINE, TRAWL
fish, young .... FRY
fisherman's hut, Orkney
SKEO, SKIO
fishhook line-leader ... SNELL
fishhook part .... BARB
fishing expedition: Scot. DRAVE
fishing grounds, Shetlands
HAAF

57

fissure .... RENT, RIFT, RIMA, RIME, CLEFT
fissures, full of RIMOSE, RIMOUS
fist .... NEAF
fit .. APT, RIPE, SUIT, ADAPT
fit for cultivation ... ARABLE
fit for human consumption POTABLE
fit of sulks .... HUFF
five-dollar bill .... VEE
five-franc piece .... ECU
five, group of .... PENTAD
five in cards .... PEDRO
fix or fixed .... SET
fixed charge .... FEE
fixed income person . RENTIER
fixed payment .... KIST
flaccid .... LIMP
flag .... JACK, ENSIGN, BANDEROLE
flag, flower, blue .... IRIS
flag, military .... GUIDON
flag, pirate .... ROGER
flag, small BANNERET, BANNERETTE
flagellants .... ALBI
flag's corner .... CANTON
flank .... SIDE
flank: dialect .... LEER
flannel .... LANA
flap .... TAB, LOMA
flap, as sails .... SLAT
flare .... FUSEE, FUZEE
flaring edge .... LIP, FLANGE
flashed lightning ... LEVINED
flask, drinking ... CANTEEN
flat ... EVEN, LEVEL, PLANE
flat-bottomed boat ARK, DORY, PUNT, SCOW
flat, music .... MOL, MOLLE,
flatfish .... DAB, RAY, SOLE, BRILL, FLUKE, FLOUNDER
flatten out .... CLAP
flattened . OBLATE, PLANATE
flatter .... PALP
flattery .... PALAVER
flavor .... LACE, TANG, AROMA, SAPOR, SEASON
flavoring plant .. HERB, LEEK, MINT, ANISE, BASIL
flavoring root ..... LICORICE
flax fiber .... TOW
flax, like .... TOWY
flax, prepare .... RET
flee .... LAM, BOLT
fleece .... FELL, WOOL
fleece, poorest .... ABB
fleet .... NAVY
fleet, esp. Span. ARMADA, ARMADO, ARMATA
fleet, merchant ..... ARGOSY
fleur-de-lis .... LIS, LYS, LISS

fleur-de-lis, obs. ...... LUCE
flexible .... LITHE
flexible wood: dial. ... EDDER
flight ...... HEGIRA, HEJIRA
flight of ducks .... SKEIN
flight organ .... WING
flight, pert. to .... AERO
flightless bird EMU, KIWI, WEKA, PENGUIN
flip .... SNAP
flit .... FLY, GAD
float BUOY, RAFT, SWIM, WAFT
floating .... NATANT
floating vegetation on Nile SADD, SUDD
floating wreckage .. FLOTSAM
flock of quail .... BEVY
flock of swans .... BANK
flock, pert. to ...... GREGAL
flock, small .... COVEY
flog BEAT, LASH, WHIP, SWINGE
flood .... SEA, EAGRE, SPATE, FRESHET, TORRENT
floodgate ..... CLOW, SLUICE
flora and fauna ...... BIOTA
floral leaf .... BRACT, SEPAL
Florentine family .... MEDICI
Florida tree .... MABI
flounder DAB, SOLE, FLUKE, PLAICE
flour sieve .... BOLTER
flour, unsorted Ind. ATA, ATTA
flourish, music .... ROULADE
flourishing: dialect .... FRIM
flow .... RUN, FLUX
flow out .... EMIT, SPILL
flow, to stop STANCH, STAUNCH
flower cluster CYME, ANADEM, RACEME
flower extract ATAR, OTTO, ATTAR, OTTAR
flower, fall ASTER, COSMOS, SALVIA
flower, field .... GOWAN
flower, genus of .... ROSA
flower-goddess, Norse . NANNA
flower-goddess, Rom. . FLORA
flower leaf ... BRACT, SEPAL
flower, Oriental ...... LOTUS
flower part .... PETAL, SEPAL, CARPEL, SPADIX
flower, showy .... CALLA
flower spike .... AMENT
flowering plant .... ARUM
fluctuate .... WAVER
fluent .... GLIB
fluff, yarn .... LINT

a fluid, aeriform .... GAS
fluid, medical .. SERA, SERUM
fluid, serous ... SERA, SERUM
fluidity unit .... RHE
flume .... SHUTE, SLUICE
flushed .... RED
flute, ancient Gr. .. HEMIOPE
flute, India ... BIN, MATALAN
flute, small .... FIFE
flutter .. FLAP, WAVE, HOVER
fly GNAT, SOAR, WING, AVIATE
fly agaric .... AMANITA
fly aloft .... SOAR
fly, artificial .... HARL,
    HERL, CAHILL, CLARET
fly, kind of .... BOT
fly, small ..... GNAT, MIDGE
fly, S. Afr. .... TSETSE
flycatcher .... TODY, ALDER,
    PEWEE, PHOEBE
flying .... VOLANT, VOLITANT
"Flying Dutchman" saver
    SENTA
flying fox .... KALONG
flying lemur .... COLUGO
flying, of .... AERO
flying saucer .... UFO
foam .... SUD, SUDS
focus .... CONCENTRATE
fodder pit .... SILO
fodder storage place .... SILO
b fodder, to store .... ENSILE,
    ENSILO, ENSILAGE, ENSILATE
fog .... MIST
fog horn .... SIRENE
fog: old Eng. .... RAG
foist .... FOB, PALM
fold .... LAP, PLY, PLIE,
    RUGA, PLEAT, CREASE
fold of skin .... PLICA
folded .... PLICATE
folds, arrange in ..... DRAPE
folio .... PAGE
folk dance, Slavic ...... KOLO
folklore being ...... TROLL
folkway .... MOS
folkways .... MORES
follow .... DOG, TAIL,
    ENSUE, TRACE, SHADOW
follow suit, not RENIG, RENEGE
follower .. IST, ITE, ADHERENT
foment .... ABET
fondle .... PET, CARESS
fondness: Ir. .... GRA
font .... LAVER, STOUP
food .... FARE, MEAT,
    MANNA, ALIMENT, PABULUM
food bit .... ORT
food, farinaceous .... SAGO
food for animals .... FORAGE
food forbidden Israelites
    TEREFA

c food, Hawaii .... POI
food: Maori, N. Z. .... KAI
food of gods .... AMRITA,
    AMREETA, AMBROSIA
food: Polyn. .... KAI
food, provide .... CATER
food, soft invalid's ..... PAP
foods, choice .... CATES
fool ASS, DOLT, GABY, RACA,
    SIMP, IDIOT, NINNY
fool's bauble ...... MAROTTE
fool's gold .... PYRITE
foolish .. DAFT, ZANY, INANE,
    SILLY, HARISH, ASININE
foot, animal's ..... PAD, PAW
foot, Chin. .... CHEK
foot, Gr. poet. ...... IONIC
foot, having .... PEDATE
foot part, horse's .... PASTERN
foot, poet. ...... IAMB, IAMBIC,
IAMBUS, ANAPEST, ANAPAEST
foot soldier .... PEON
foot soldier, Ir. . KERN, KERNE
foot, two-syllable
    SPONDEE, TROCHEE
foot, verse ... IAMB, DACTYL,
    ANAPEST, ANAPAEST
football position: abbr. ... FB,
    HB, LE, LT, QB, RE, RT
d footless ...... APOD, APODAL
footless animal APOD, APODE
footless animal genus . APODA
footlike .... PEDATE
footlike part .... PES
footpad .... WHYO
footstalk, leaf .... STRIG
footstool HASSOCK, OTTOMAN
for .... PRO
for example .... EG
for fear that .... LEST
for shame .... FIE
forage plant .. GUAR, ALSIKE,
    LUCERN, ALFALFA, LUCERNE
foramen .... PORE
foray .... RAID
forbidden
    TABU, TABOO, BANNED
Forbidden City .... LASSA
forbidding .... STERN
force ..... VIS, DINT, DRIVE,
    IMPEL, POWER, ENERGY,
    VIOLENCE
force, alleged
    OD, BIOD, ELOD, ODYL
force, hypothetical ...... OD
force, unit of .... DYNE
force, with .... AMAIN
foreboding .... OMEN
forefather .... SIRE
forefoot .... PUD
forefront .... VAN

forehead, of the ... **METOPIC**
forehead strap .... **TUMP**
foreign in origin ..... **EXOTIC**
foreign trade discount . **AGIO**
foreigner: Hawaii .. **HAOLE**
foreigners' quarter, Constantinople .... **PERA**
foremost part
      BOW, VAN, FRONT
foremost segment, insect's
              ACRON
foreordain .... **DESTINE**
foreshadow .... **BODE**
forest: Brazil .... **MATTA**
forest clearing .... **GLADE**
forest: obsolete .... **WOLD**
forest ox .... **ANOA**
forest partly inundated . **GAPO**
forest, pert. to
  SILVAN, SYLVAN, NEMORAL
forest, P. I. .... **GUBAT**
forest warden .... **RANGER**
forestall ... **AVERT, PREVENT**
foretell .... **AUGUR, INSEE**
foreteller .... **SEER**
foretoken .... **OMEN**
forever .... **AY, AYE**
forever: Maori .... **AKE**
forever: poet. **ETERN, ETERNE**
forfeit .... **LOSE, LAPSE**
forfeits, Jap. .... **KEN**
forgetfulness fruit .... **LOTUS**
forgetfulness water .... **LETHE**
forgive .... **REMIT**
forgiving .... **CLEMENT**
forgo .... **WAIVE**
form a network .... **PLEX**
form: Buddhism .... **RUPA**
form into line . **ALIGN, ALINE**
form, pert. to .... **MODAL**
form, philos. .... **EIDOS**
formal choice .... **VOTE**
formation, military . **ECHELON**
former .... **ERST**
former ruler **CZAR, TSAR, TZAR**
formerly .... **NEE, ERST, ONCE**
formerly: pref. .... **EX**
formic acid source ..... **ANT**
formicid .... **ANT**
formula .... **LAW**
forsaken .... **LORN**
fort ...... **DIX, ORD, REDAN,
CITADEL, REDOUBT, RAVELIN**
fort, N. Z. .... **PA, PAH**
forth .... **OUT**
forth, issuing ..... **EMANANT**
forthwith .... **NOW**
fortification
  REDAN, RAVELIN, REDOUBT

fortification, ditchside
  SCARP, ESCARP, ESCARPE
fortification, felled trees
              ABATIS
fortification, slope .... **TALUS**
fortified place ...... **LIS, LISS**
fortify .... **ARM, MAN**
fortunate (India) .... **SRI**
fortune: Gypsy .... **BAHI**
forty days fast ..... **CARENE**
forty: Gr. .... **MU**
forward .... **ON, AHEAD**
fossil, mollusk ...... **DOLITE**
fossil resin .... **RETINITE**
fossil worm track .. **NEREITE**
foul smelling
  OLID, FETID, REEKY
found .... **BASE**
found, thing .... **TROVE**
foundation . **BED, BASE, BASIS**
fountain .... **FONS**
four, group of .... **TETRAD**
four-inch measure .... **HAND**
fourth calif (caliph) .... **ALI**
fourth estate .... **PRESS**
fowl ... **HEN, CAPON, POULT**
fowl's gizzard, etc. .. **GIBLET**
fox .... **TOD**
fox, Afr. .... **FENNEC**
fox hunter's coat ..... **PINK**
fox, S. Afr. .... **ASSE, CAAMA**
"Fra Diavolo" composer **AUBER**
fraction ... **PART, DECIMAL**
fragment, pottery
  SHARD, SHERD, SHEARD
fragments .... **ANA, ORTS**
fragrant .... **OLENT**
frame, supporting
  TRESSEL, TRESTLE
framework .... **TRUSS**
France .... **GAUL**
franchise .... **CHARTER**
Franciscan .... **MINORITE**
frank ...... **OPEN, HONEST**
Franks, pert. to ...... **SALIC**
frankincense ..... **OLIBANUM**
Frankish law .... **SALIC**
Frankish peasant . **LITI, LITUS**
fraud .... **SHAM**
fraught .... **LADEN**
fray .... **MELEE**
free .... **RID, GRATIS**
free-for-all .... **FRAY, MELEE**
free from discount .... **NET**
free from knots: obs. .. **ENODE**
freebooter .... **PIRATE**
freedman, Kentish law . **LAET**
freehold land, Turkey.. **MULK**
freeman ..... **CEORL, THANE**
freight-boat .... **ARK**

a freight car ...... GONDOLA
FRENCH WORDS: (accent
marks omitted throughout)
according to .... ALA, AUX
after .... APRES
again .... ENCORE
airplane .... AVION
alas .... HELAS
all .... TOUT
among .... ENTRE
and .... ET
angel .... ANGE
annuity .... RENTE
arm .... BRAS
article .... LA, LE, DE,
(plural) DES, LAS, LES, UNE
at the home of .... CHEZ
aunt .... TANTE
baby .... BEBE
bacon .... LARD
back .... DOS
ball .... BAL
bang! .... PAN
bath .... BAIN
beach .... PLAGE
beast .... BETE
before .... AVANT
begin .... ETRE
bench .... BANC
b between .... ENTRE
beware .... GARE
bitter .... AMER
black .... NOIR, NOIRE
blue .... BLEU
bread crumbs .... PANURE
bridge .... PONT
business house ...... CIE
but .... MAIS
cabbage .... CHOU
cake .... GATEAU
carefully groomed . SOIGNE
carriage .... FIACRE
charmed .... RAVI
chicken .... POULE
child .... ENFANT
clear .... NET
climax, theatre ...... CLOY
cloth .... DRAP
cloud .... NUAGE
coarse cloth ...... BURE
connective .... ET
cowardly .... LACHE
cup .... TASSE
dance, formal ...... BAL
dare .... OSER
daughter .... FILLE
deal .... DONNE
dear .... CHER, CHERI
deed .... FAIT
defy .... DEFI

c department ... see SPECIAL
SECTION, GAZETTEER
depot .... GARE
detective force ... SURETE
devil .... DIABLE
dirty .... SALE
donkey .... ANE
down with .... ABAS
dream .... REVE
duck to cook ... CANETON
dugout .... ABRI
duke .... DUC
dungeon .... CACHOT
ear of grain .... EPI
east .... EST
egg .... OEUF
elegance .... LUXE
enamel .... EMAIL
equal .... PAREIL
evening .... SOIR
exaggerated .... OUTRE
exclamation .... HEIN
exist .... ETRE
fabric .... RAS, DRAP
father .... PERE
fear .... PEUR
finally .... ENFIN
fingering .... DOIGTE
fire .... FEU
d five .... CINQ
for .... CAR
friend ...... AMI, AMIE
froth .... BAVE
full .... PLEIN
game .... JEU, JEUX
gift .... CADEAU
god .... DIEU
golden .... DORE
good .... BON
good-bye ADIEU, AU REVOIR
grain ear .... EPI
gray .... GRIS
gravy .... JUS
grimace .... MOUE
ground .... TERRE
half-mask .... LOUP
hall .... SALLE
handle .... ANSE
head .... TETE
health .... SANTE
here ICI
hill .... PUY
his .... SES
house .... MAISON
hunting match ...... TIR
husband .... MARI
idea .... IDEE
(French words continued on
pages 62 and 63)

French

a **FRENCH:**

impetuosity	**ELAN**
in	**DANS**
income, annual	**RENTE**
is	**EST**
island	**ILE**
kind	**SORTE**
king	**ROI**
lamb	**AGNEAU**
land	**TERRE**
laugh	**RIRE**
laughter	**RISEE**
law	**LOI, DROIT**
leather	**CUIR**
lift	**LEVE**
lily	**LIS**
little	**PEU**
lively	**VIF**
lodging place	**GITE**
low	**BAS**
maid	**BONNE**
mail	**POSTE**
mask, half	**LOUP**
material	**DRAP**
May	**MAI**
meat dish	**SALMI**
milk	**LAIT**
mine	**AMOI**
mother	**MERE**
mountain	**MONT**
museum	**MUSEE**
nail	**CLOU**
name	**NOM**
near	**PRES**
network	**RESEAU**
night	**NUIT**
no	**NON**
nose	**NEZ**
nothing	**RIEN**
number, one	**UNE**
nursemaid	**BONNE**
of	**DE**
one	**UNE**
our	**NOS, NOUS**
out	**HORS**
outbreak	**EMEUTE**
over	**SUR**
oyster farm	**PARC**
petticoat	**JUPE, COTTE**
picnic spot	**BOIS**
pinion	**AILE**
poem	**DIT**
pork	**SALE**
pout	**MOUE**
preposition	**DES**
pretty	**JOLI, JOLIE**
pronoun	**CES, ILS, MES, TOI, UNE, ELLE**
queen	**REINE**
quickly	**VITE**

rabbit	**LAPIN**
railway station	**GARE**
read	**LIRE**
rear	**ARRIERE**
reception	**ACCUEIL**
rent	**LOUER**
river	**RIVIERE**
roast	**ROTI**
royal edict	**ARRET**
saint: abbr.	**STE**
salt	**SEL**
salted	**SALE**
school	**ECOLE, LYCEE**
scow	**ACON**
sea	**MER**
security	**RENTE**
senior	**AINE**
servant	**BONNE**
she	**ELLE**
sheath	**ETUI**
sheep	**MOUTON**
shelter	**ABRI**
shine	**LUSTRE**
shooting match	**TIR**
sickness	**MAL**
silk	**SOIE**
situated	**SISE**
small	**PETIT**
smitten	**EPRISE**
soldier	**POILU**
some	**DES**
son	**FILS**
soul	**AME**
spirit	**AME**
star	**ETOILE**
state	**ETAT**
stocking	**BAS**
storm	**ORAGE**
summer	**ETE**
superior quality	**LUXE**
superfluous	**DETROP**
surnamed	**DIT**
sweetmeat	**DRAGEE**
that	**CE, CET, QUE, QUI, CELA**
thee	**TE**
there!	**VOILA**
they	**ILS**
thirty	**TRENTE**
this	**CE**
thou	**TOI**
to be	**ETRE**
to go	**ALLER**
to love	**AIMER**
too much	**TROP**
under	**SOUS**
upon	**SUR**
us	**NOUS**
verb	**ETRE**
verse	**RONDEL**

FRENCH:

very	TRES
vineyard	CRU
wall	MUR
water	EAU
wave	ONDE
weapon	ARME
well	BIEN
wine	VIN
wine, delicacy of	SEVE
wine-plant	CEP
wing	AILE
with	AVEC
with the	AU
without	SANS
wood	BOIS
yesterday	HIER
you	TOI
your	VOTRE
Fr., annuity	RENTE
Fr. art group	FAUVES
Fr. artist	DORE, DUFY, GROS, COROT, DEGAS, MANET, MONET, BRAQUE, DERAIN, RENOIR, CHAGALL, CHIRICO, MATISSE, UTRILLO
Fr. artist cult	DADA
Fr. author	SUE, GIDE, HUGO, LOTI, ZOLA, CAMUS, DUMAS, RENAN, STAEL, VERNE, RACINE, SARTRE, COCTEAU
Fr. Calvinist	CALAS
Fr. chalk	TALC
Fr. coin, old	SOU
Fr. commercial company	CIE
FR. COMPOSER see COMPOSER, FR.	
Fr. dramatist	RACINE
Fr. ecclesiastic city	SENS
Fr. explorer	CARTIER
Fr. fort, battle of Verdun	VAUX
Fr. general	FOCH, HOCHE GAMELIN
Fr.-Ger. river basin	SAAR
Fr. guerillas	MAQUIS
Fr. Guiana tribesman	BONI
Fr. historical area	ANJOU
Fr. honeysuckle	SULLA
Fr. illustrator	DORE
Fr. island	ILE
Fr. lace-making town	CLUNY
Fr. marshal	NEY, MURAT
FR. NOVELIST see FR. AUTHOR	
FR. PAINTER see FR. ARTIST	
Fr. philosopher	COMTE
Fr. premier, former	LAVAL
Fr. priest	ABBE, PERE
Fr. protectorate	TUNIS
Fr. psychologist	BINET

Fr. Revolution month	NIVOSE, FLOREAL, PRAIRAL, VENTOSE, BRUMAIRE, FERVIDOR, FRIMAIRE, MESSIDOR, PLUVIOSE, THERMIDOR
Fr. revolutionist	MARAT
Fr. sculptor	RODIN
Fr. security	RENTE
Fr. singer	PIAF, SABLON
Fr. soprano	PONS, CALVE
Fr. statesman	COTY
FR. WRITER . see FR. AUTHOR	
Frenchman	GAUL
frenzied	AMOK
frequently	OFT
fresh	NEW, SPICK
fresh supply	RELAY
freshet	FLOOD, SPATE
freshwater worm	NAID, NAIS
fretted	EROSE
Frey's wife	GERD
friar	FRA, MONK
friar, mendicant	SERVITE
friend: law	AMY
Friendly Islands	TONGA
friends	KITH
friendship	AMITY
frigate bird, Hawaiian	IWA
Frigg's brother-in-law	VE
Frigg's husband	ODIN
fright	FUNK, PANIC
frighten	FLEY, ALARM, SCARE
frill, neck	RUFF, JABOT
fringe of curls	FRISETTE
fringe: zool.	LOMA
frisk	PLAY, ROMP
frisky	PEART
FROCK see GARMENT	
frog	TOAD
frog genus	RANA
frogs, order of	ANURA
frogs, pert. to	RANINE
frolic	LARK, PLAY, ROMP, CAPER, SPORT, SPREE
from head to foot	CAP-A-PIE
from: Lat.	DE
from: prefix	AB
front	VAN, FORE, FACADE
front page weather box	EAR
front, to extend	DEPLOY
frontier post	FORT
frontiersman	BOONE, CARSON
frost	ICE, HOAR, RIME
frosty	RIMY
froth	FOAM, SPUME
frothlike	SPUMY, YEASTY
frown	LOUR, GLOOM, LOWER, SCOWL, GLOWER
frugal	CHARY
fruit	BERRY, OLIVE
fruit, Afr.	PECEGO

Fruit

a
fruit, aggregate .... ETAERIO
fruit decay .... BLET
fruit dish
    COMPOTE, COMPOTIER
fruit, dry .... ACHENE
fruit, fleshy ...... PEAR, PEPO
fruit, hard-shelled NUT, GOURD
fruit, India .... BEL
fruit-jelly .... RHOB
fruit, lemonlike .... CITRON
fruit of maple ...... SAMARA
fruit pigeon, Polyn. ..... LUPE
fruit, plumlike .... SLOE
fruit, pulpy .... UVA, DRUPE
fruit shrub, E. Ind. ... CUBEB
fruit, small, 1-seeded
  AKENE, ACHENE, ACHENIUM
fruit, southern .... PAPAW
fruit squeezer .... REAMER
fruit, tropical . DATE, MANGO
fruit, vine .... MELON
fruit, yellow tropical
  PAPAW, PAPAYA, PAWPAW
fruitdots, fern . SORI, SORUS
fruiting spike .... EAR
frustrate .. SCOTCH, THWART
fry lightly .... SAUTE
Fuegon Indian .... ONA
fuel . LOG, COAL, COKE, PEAT
fuel ship ...... OILER, TANKER
fuel, turf .... PEAT, PEET
fugue theme .... DUX
fulcrum, oar .... THOLE
full .... PLENARY
full and clear ..... OROTUND
fullness .... PLENUM
fulmar ... NELLY, MALDUCK
fume .... REEK, SMOKE

c
fun .... SPORT
function .... GO, USE, WORK
function, trig. .. SINE, COSINE
fundamental
    BASIC, ELEMENTAL
funeral bell KNELL, MORTBELL
funeral music .... DIRGE
funeral notice .... OBIT
funeral oration .... ELOGE
funeral pile .... PYRE
funeral song .... NENIA
fungi, tissue in ..... TRAMA
fungus .... AGARIC
fungus, edible
  MOREL, MORIL, TRUFFLE
fungus, white-spored AMANITA
fur ...... SEAL, VAIR, GENET
  MARTEN, NUTRIA, MINIVER
fur cape .... PELERINE
fur: Her. . PEAN, VAIR, VAIRE
furbelow ...... FRILL, RUFFLE
Furies, Gr. .... ERINYS
ERINNYS, ERINYES, ERINNYES
Furies, one of
  ALECTO, MEGAERA, TISI-
             PHONE
Furies, Ram. .... DIRAE
furlongs, eight .... MILE
furnish crew .... MAN
furnish with .... ENDOW
furnishings, mode of . DECOR
furrows, with RIVOSE, RUTTED
further .... AID, YET
furtive .... SLY, SNEAKY
fury .... IRE
furze .... WHIN, WHUN,
  GORSE, GORST, GORSTE
fuse partly .... FRIT
fuss .... ADO, TO-DO

b
gabl .... TARO
Gad, son of .... ARELI
gadget .... GISMO
Gael .... SCOT
Gaelic . ERSE, CELTIC, KELTIC
Gaelic poem .... DUAN
Gaelic sea god .... LER
gaff .... SPAR
gain ..... GET, WIN, EARN
gait . LOPE, CANTER, GALLOP
gait, horse's .. PACE, RACK
Galahad's mother .... ELAINE
Galatea's beloved ..... ACIS
Galilee town .... CANA
galla ox ..... SANGA, SANGU
gallery, art .... SALON
gallery: hist. .... ALURE

d
gallery, open .... LOGGIA
gallery protecting troops
      ECOUTE
galley, armed, old Northmen's
    AESC
galley, fast
    DROMON, DROMOND
galley, 1 oar bank UNIREME
galley, 2 oar banks BIREME
galley, 3 oar banks TRIREME
gallop, rapid .... TANTIVY
gallop slowly .... LOPE
Galsworthy heroine .... IRENE
Galway Bay, Isles in ... ARAN
gamble .... GAME
gambling place ..... CASINO

a gambol .... DIDO, CAPER
   game .. LOTO, BINGO, LOTTO
   game, Basque .... PELOTA
   game, board .. CHESS, HALMA
   game, card ..... LU, LOO, NAP,
     PAM, PUT, FARO, CINCH,
     MACAO, MONTE, OMBER,
     OMBRE, STUSS, TAROT,
     WHIST, BASSET, CASINO,
     ECARTE, ROUNCE, CA-
     NASTA
   game, child's .... TAG
   game, dice .... LUDO
   game, follow .... STALK
   game, gambling
     FARO, PICO, STUSS
   game, Hawaii .... HEI
   game, Ind. guessing . CANUTE
   game, It. guessing ...... MORA
   game of skill ... POOL, CHESS
   game piece .. MAN, DOMINO
   gamecock .... STAG
   gamekeeper .... RANGER
   gaming cube ...... DIE, DICE
   Ganges boat .... PUTELI
   gangplank .... RAMP
   gangster MUG, THUG, WHYO
   gannet, common ...... SOLAN
   gannet genus .... SULA
   gap ...... HIATUS, LACUNA
   gap in hedge
b   MUSE, MEUSE, MUSET
   gar fish .... SNOOK
   garland ...... LEI, ANADEM
   GARMENT . see COAT, BLOUSE
   garment .... ROBE
   garment, Arab .... ABA
   garment, bishop's
     CHIMAR, CHIMER, CHIMERE
   garment, church ...... COTTA
   GARMENT, CLERICAL OR EC-
     CLESIASTIC, see GAR-
     MENT PRIESTLY
   garment, fitted ...... REEFER
   garment, India, Hindu .. SARI,
     SAREF BANIAN, BANYAN
   GARMENT, LITURGICAL
     see GARMENT PRIESTLY
   garment, loose CAMIS, CAMUS,
     CYMAR, SIMAR, CAMISE
   garment, Malay .... SARONG
   garment, Moslem ...... IZAR
   garment, N Afr. .... HAIK
   garment, Old Ir. ...... INAR
   garment, outer
     CAPOTE, PALETOT
   garment, Polyn. ...... PAREU
   garment, priestly ALB. COPE,
     AMICE, EPHOD, STOLE
   garment, rain ..... PONCHO
   garment, scarflike .... TIPPET

c garment, Turk. .... DOLMAN
   garment, woman's
     BODICE, MANTUA
   garnishment .... LIEN
   garret .... ATTIC
   garter snake genus .... ELAPS
   gas .... FUEL, NEON
   gas apparatus ...... AERATOR
   gas, charge with .... AERATE
   gas, colorless .... OXAN
   gas, inert .... ARGON, XENON
   gas, radioactive
     RADON, NITON
   GASEOUS ELEMENT
     see ELEMENTS, SPECIAL
     SECTION, Page 195
   gaseous sky "cloud" NEBULA
   GASTROPOD see also MOL-
     LUSK
   gastropod .... WELK, WILK,
     WHELK, LIMPET
   gastropod, Haliotis . ABALONE
   gate .... PORTAL
   gate, water .... SLUICE
   gateway .... PYLON
   gateway, Buddhist temple
     TORAN, TORANA
   gateway, Pers. .... DAR
   gateway, Shinto temple TORII
   gather ..... AMASS, GLEAN,
     GARNER, MUSTER
   gather, as grouse ...... LEK
d gather in bundles ... SHEAVE
   gathers, put in
     SHER, SHIR, SHIRR
   gaunt .... SPARE
   Gawain's father .... LOT
   gazelle .... ARIEL
   gazelle, Afr. .... ADMI, DAMA,
     MOHR, KORIN, MHORR
   gazelle Asia .... AHU
   gazelle black-tailed .... GOA
   gazelle Pers. .... CORA
   gazelle, Sudan .... DAMA
   gazelle, Tibetan .... GOA
   gear .... CAM
   gear tooth .... COG
   gear wheel, smallest . PINION
   Geb's consort .... NUT
   Gelderland city .... EDE
   gelid .... ICY, COLD
   GEM .... see also STONE
   gem ...... JADE, ONYX, OPAL,
     RUBY, SARD, AGATE, PEARL,
     STONE, GARNET, SPINEL,
     EMERALD, PERIDOT
   gem-bearing earth, Burma
     BYON
   gem, carved .... CAMEO
   gem facet .... BEZEL, BEZIL,
     CULET, COLLET
   gem weight .... CARAT
   Gemini's mortal half . CASTOR

Gender

a   gender, a .... NEUTER
genealogy .... TREE
GENERAL, CIVIL WAR
   see CIVIL WAR COMMANDER
general, Morocco ..... KAID
general Sitting Bull defeated
                CUSTER
generation .... AGE
Genesis matriarch ..... SARAI
genie, Egypt. .... HAPI
genip tree .... LANA
genipap wood .... LANA
gentle . MILD, TAME, TENDER
gentle breeze .... AURA
gentle heat .... TEPOR
genuflect . see ...... KNEEL
GENUS . see PLANT or
        ANIMAL named
genus of plants .... ARUM
geode .... VUG, VOOG, VUGG,
               VUGH
geological division LIAS, LYAS
geol. epoch BALA, ECCA, LIAS,
      MUAV, ERIAN, UINTA,
      PLIOCENE
geol. formation .... TERRAIN,
     TERRANE, TERRENE
geol. period .... DYAS,
     EOCENE, MIOCENE
geol. stage .... RISS, ACHEN
geol. vein angle ...... HADE

b   geometric ratio ...... SINE
geometric solid
    CONE, CUBE, PRISM
geometrical lines ..... LOCI,
     LOCUS, SECANT
geometry rule .... THEOREM
geometry term ...... VERSOR
geophagy .... PICA
George Sand novel .... LELIA
Geraint's wife .... ENID
geranium lake color NACARAT
germ . BUG, VIRUS, MICROBE
germ-free
   ASEPTIC, ANTISEPTIC
germs, produced by .. SEPTIC
GERMAN . see also TEUTONIC
GERMAN WORDS: (umlauts
omitted throughout)
 "A" .... EIN
above .... UBER
again .... UBER
alas .... ACH
article ..... DAS, DER, EIN
ass .... ESEL
beer .... BIER
blood .... BLUT
conjunction .... UND
count .... GRAF
donkey .... ESEL
dumpling .... KNODEL
eat .... ESSEN

c   eight .... ACHT
evening .... ABEND
everything .... ALLES
exclamation .... HOCH
four .... VIER
gentleman . HERR, HERREN
hall .... AULA, SAAL
heaven .... HIMMEL
hunter .... JAGER
"I" .... ICH
ice .... EIS
iron .... EISEN
is .... IST
it .... ES
league (s) .. BUND, BUNDE
love .... LIEBE
mister .... HERR
nation .... VOLK
never .... NIE
new .... NEUE
no .... NEIN
noble .... EDEL
old .... ALT
one .... EIN, EINE
out of .... AUS
pronoun .... ICH
people .... VOLK
school hall .... AULA
softly .... LEISE

d   song .... LIED
spirit .... GEIST
state .... STAAT
steel .... STAHL
temperament ..... GEMUT
than .... ALS
the .... DAS, DER
three .... DREI
thunder .... DONNER
title .... VON, PRINZ
town .... STADT
us .... UNS
very .... SEHR
with .... MIT
without .... OHNE
yes .... JA
you .... SIE
your ..... IHR, DEIN, EUER

German .... BOCHE
Ger. admiral .... SPEE
Ger. bacteriologist ..... KOCH
Ger. camp, war ..... STALAG
GER. COMPOSER
   see COMPOSER, GER.
Ger.-Czech region .. SUDETEN
Ger. district, old ...... GAU
Ger. dive bomber .... STUKA
Ger. emperor .... OTTO
Ger. highway .... AUTOBAHN
Ger. John .... HANS

66

a

Ger. king .... OTTO
Ger. landscape painter . ROOS
Ger. name prefix .... VON
Ger. philosopher KANT, HEGEL
Ger. physicist . OHM, ERMAN
Ger. president .... EBERT
Ger. princely family .... WELF
Ger. theologian .... ARND
Ger. title .. VON, GRAF, PRINZ
Ger. tribal region
.... GAU, GAUE, GAUS
Germanic deity ...... DONAR
Germanic letter .... RUNE
gesture dance, Samoa; Fiji SIVA
get out! . SCAT, SHOO, SCRAM
ghastly .... LURID
ghost .... HANT, SPOOK,
.... SPECTER, SPECTRE
ghost, India .... BHUT
ghost-town state: abbrev.: . UT
giant .... TITAN
giant, frightful .... OGRE
giant, Hindu myth ..... BANA
giant, killed by Apollo .. OTUS
giant, Norse, Scand. myth
..... YMER, YMIR, JOTUM, MIMIR
giant Rom. .... CACA
giant, 1000-armed, Hindu BANA
giants. Bibl. .... ANAK, EMIM
gibbon, Malay .... LAR
gift, receiver of ..... DONEE

b

gig .... NAPPER
gigantic person .... TITAN
"Gil —" LeSage novel . BLAS
Gilead's descendant ... ULAM
Gilgit language, Kashmir SHINA
gills, four .... PINT
gilt .... DORE
gin .... TRAP
gingerbread tree ...... DUM
ginkgo tree .... ICHO
GIPSY .... see GYPSY
giraffe-like animal .... OKAPI
girasol .... OPAL
girder .... TRUSS
girdle ...... OBI, CEST SASH
girl .... SIS. CHIT,
.... DAME, SKIRT
GIRL'S NAME
.... see WOMAN'S NAME
girth, saddle .... CINCH
gist .... NUB, PITH
give: law .... REMISE
give reluctantly .... GRUDGE
give up . CEDE, WAIVE, YIELD
give up wholly ..... DEVOTE
give way .... YIELD
glacial hill .... PAHA
glacial ice block, pinnacle
.... SERAC
glacial ridge .. AS, OS, ASAR,
.... KAME, OSAR, ESCAR,
.... ESKAR, ESKER

c

glacial snow field FIRN, NEVE
glacial stage .... WURM
glacier chasm
.... CREVAS, CREVASSE
glacier, facing a ...... STOSS
gladiolus .... IRID
gladly .... FAIN
gland .... PINEAL, THYROID
gland, edible .... NOIX
glass .... LENS
glass, blue .... SMALT
glass bubble .... BLEB
glass defect .... TEAR
glass, flatten ...... PLATTEN
glass furnace mouth . BOCCA
glass ingredient .... SILICON
glass-like material .... PLASS
glass maker .... GLAZIER
glass, molten ...... PARISON
glass, partly fused FRIT, FRITT
glass, transparent .. UVIOL
glass vial . AMPULE, AMPOULE
glassmaker's oven LEER, LEHR
glasswort .... KALI
glassy .... HYALINE
glazier's tack .... BRAD
gleam .... GLINT
glide .... SKIM, SLIP
.... SKATE. SLIDE

d

glittering piece ..... SPANGLE
global .... ROUND, SPHERAL
globe .... ORB. SPHERE
gloom .... MIRK MURK
gloomy .... DARK, DOUR
.... DREAR, DREAPY
"Gloomy Dean" .... INGE
glossy-surfaced ..... GLACE
glottal stop: Dan. ..... STOD
glove leather .... KID, NAPA
.... MOCHA, SUEDE
glove shape, unstitched TRANK
glowing .... CANDENT
glucoside, root .... GEIN
glut SATE, GORGE, SATIATE
gnarl .... NUR, KNUR, NURR
gnat, small .... MIDGE
gnome .... NIS, GREMLIN
go .... WEND
go astray .... ABERRATE
go astray slightly ..... ERR
go back .... REVERT
go forth .... FARE
go hence: Lat. .... VADE
go on! .... GARN, SCAT
go shufflingly . MOSY, MOSEY
goad ... PROD, SPUR, INCITE
goal .... AIM, END
goat, Alpine mountain . IBEX
goat antelope .... GORAL
goat, Asian .... JAGLA

a goat, genus .... **CAPRIA**
goat god .... **PAN**
goat, wild . **TUR, IBEX, TAHR, TAIR, TEHR, THAR**
goatsucker .... **POTOO**
gob .... **TAR**
Gobi Desert .... **SHAMO**
goblet .... **HANAP**
goblin, Egypt .... **OUPHE**
goblin ... **POOK, PUCA, PUCK**
goblin, Norse .... **NIS, NISSE, KOBOLD**
goby, small .... **MAPO**
GOD . see also DEITY, and see also SPECIAL SECTION
god, Babyl. **EA, ABU, ANU, BEL**
GOD, CHIEF see CHIEF NORSE GOD, also BABYLONIAN CHIEF GOD
god: Chin. .... **SHEN**
god: Hebrew .... **EL**
god: Jap. .... **KAMI**
god: Lat. .... **DEUS**
god of alcoholic drinks, **SIRIS**
god of Arcadia .... **PAN**
GOD OF CHAOS .. see CHAOS
god of darkness—evil, Egyp. **SET, SETH**
god of dead, Hindu ... **YAMA**
god of dead, Rom. .... **ORCUS**
b god of discord, Norse **LOK, LOKE, LOKI**
god of earth, Babyl. .. **DAGAN**
GOD OF EARTH, Egyptian see EARTH GOD
god of evil: Egyp. .. **SET, SETH**
god of evil, to ward off **BES, BESA**
god of fertility, Norse .. **FREY**
god of fields, flocks, forest **PAN, FAUN**
god of fire ... **AGNI, VULCAN**
god of Hades ... **DIS, PLUTO**
god of harvests ..... **CRONUS**
god of light, Norse **BALDR, BALDER, BALDUR**
god of love, Gr. ..... **EROS**
god of love, Rom. **AMOR, CUPID**
god of love, Vedic ... **BHAGA**
god of mirth . **COMUS, KOMOS**
god (goddess) of mischief **ATE**
god of michief, Norse **LOK, LOKE, LOKI**
GOD OF MOON see MOON GOD
god of music .... **APOLLO**
god of north wind .. **BOREAS**
god of pleasure ... **BES, BESA**
god of procreation, Egyp. **MIN**
god of prosperity, Teutonic **FREY**
god of revelry, Gr. .. **COMUS, KOMOS**
god of ridicule ..... **MOMUS**
GOD OF SEA ... see SEA GOD
GOD OF SKY ... see SKY GOD

c God of Southeast Wind: Gr. **EURUS**
GOD OF STORMS see STORM GOD
GOD OF SUN ... see SUN GOD
god of thunder **THOR, DONAR**
god of Tuesday **TIU, TIW, TYR**
GOD OF UNDERWORLD see UNDERWORLD GOD
god of war, Assyrian **ASUR, ASSUR**
god of war, Babyl. . **IRA, IRRA**
god of war, Gr. .... **ARES**
god of war, Norse **TY, TYR, TYRR**
god of war, Rom. ...... **MARS**
god of war, Teut. .... **ER**
god of wind, Norse .... **VAYU**
god of wind, storm, Babylonian **ZU, ADAD, ADDA, ADDU**
god of winds, Gr. .... **AEOLUS**
god of wisdom, Babyl. **NABU, NEBO**
god of wisdom, Norse .. **ODIN**
god of youth .... **APOLLO**
god skilled with bow, Norse **ULL**
god, Sumerian .... **ABU**
god, unknown, Hindu .... **KA**
gods, Chief Teut., Norse **AESIR**
gods: Lat. .... **DI**
d gods, mother of .... **RHEA**
gods, mother of: Ir. **ANA, ANU**
GODS, QUEEN OF see QUEEN OF GODS
gods, the .... **DEI, DII**
GODDESS see also SPECIAL SECT.
GODDESS, CHIEF see BABYLONIAN CHIEF GODDESS
goddess, cow-headed .... **ISIS**
goddess: Latin .... **DEA**
GODDESS, MOTHER see MOTHER GODDESS
goddess of agriculture **CERES, DEMETER**
goddess of art or science **MUSE**
goddess of astronomy **URANIA**
goddess of beauty: Norse **FREYA**
goddess of betrothal, Norse **VOR**
goddess of chase **DIAN, DIANA**
goddess of crops, Rom. **ANNONA**
goddess of dawn, Gr. .... **EOS**
goddess of dawn, Rom. **AURORA**
goddess of dawn, Vedic **USAS**
goddess of dead .. **HEL, HELA**
goddess of deep, Babyl. **NINA**
goddess of destiny, Norse **URD, URTH**
goddess of destruction .. **ARA**
goddess of discord . **ATE, ERIS**
goddess of earth, Teut. **ERDA**

goddess of earth .. GE, ERDA, GAEA, GAIA, TARI
goddess of earth: Rom. CERES, TERRA
goddess of faith, Rom. . FIDES
goddess of fate, Rom. NONA, PARCA
goddess of fate, Teutonic NORN
goddess of fertility ASTARTE
goddess of fertility, Anatolian MA
goddess of field, Rom. FAUNA
goddess of flowers, Gr. CHLORIS
goddess of flowers, Norse NANNA
goddess of flowers, Rom. FLORA
goddess of grain CERES, DEMETER
goddess of harvest ... OPS
goddess of harvest, Attica CARPO
goddess of healing ..... EIR
goddess of hearth .... VESTA
goddess of heavens, Egyp. NUT
goddess of hope ...... SPES
goddess of hunt DIAN, DIANA
goddess of infatuation ATE
goddess of justice MA, MAAT
goddess of love ...... VENUS, ASTARTE, APHRODITE
goddess of love, Babylonian ISTAR, ISHTAR
goddess of love, Norse FREYA, FREYJA
goddess of magic HECATE
GODDESS OF MATERNITY see MATERNITY GODDESS
goddess of mischief .... ATE
GODDESS OF MOON see MOON GODDESS
goddess of nature CYBELE, ARTEMIS
GODDESS OF NIGHT, NORSE see NIGHT, NORSE
goddess of night: Rom. NOX, NYX
goddess of peace IRENE, EIRENE
goddess of plenty .... OPS
goddess of prosperity: Rom. SALUS
goddess of retribution .. ATE
goddess of retribution, Gr. ARA
goddess of revenge . NEMESIS
GODDESS OF SEA see SEA GODDESS
goddess of seasons ... HORAE
goddess of splendor, Hindu UMA
goddess of truth, Egypt. MA, MAAT
GODDESS OF UNDERWORLD see UNDERWORLD GODDESS

goddess of vegetation . CORA, KORE, CERES
goddess of vengeance ... ARA
goddess of victory ..... NIKE
goddess of volcanoes, Hawaii PELE
goddess of war, Gr. ... ENYO
goddess of wisdom ATHENA, PALLAS
goddess of woods ..... DIAN, DIANA, ARTEMIS
goddess of youth ...... HEBE
goddess, queen . HERA, JUNO
goddesses of destiny .. FATES
goddesses of fate, Gr. MOERAE
goddesses of fate, Norse NORNS
Goethe drama ...... FAUST
Goethe heroine ..... MIGNON
golconda .... MINE
gold ...... AU, CYME, GILT
gold alloy, ancient .... ASEM
Gold Coast Negro .... GA
Gold Coast tong. CHI, TWI, TSHI
gold-colored metal . ORMOLU
gold, cover with .... GILD
gold deposit .... PLACER
gold district-field, Afr. .. RAND
gold: Her. .... OR
gold mosaic .... ORMOLU
gold, pert. to .... AURIC
golden .... AUREATE
Golden Fleece keeper AEETES
Golden Fleece seeker JASON
golden in color DORE, DURRY
golden oriole .... PIROL
golden, oriole, Eur. .. LORIOT
golden-touch king ... MIDAS
golf attendant ..CADY, CADDY
golf club ..... IRON, CLEEK, MASHIE, PUTTER
golf club, part .... TOE
golf club socket ..... HOSEL
golf hole .... CUP
golf pro .... SNEAD
golf score .... PAR
golf stroke-shot .. PUT, BAFF, CHIP, LOFT, PUTT, DRIVE, SCLAFF
golf term ..... LIE, PAR, TEE
golfer .... TEER
gomuti .... ARENGA
gondolier's song BARCAROLE, BARCAROLLE
gone .... OUT, AWAY
gone by .... AGO, PAST, YORE
gonfalon .... BANNER
good-bye: Fr. ADIEU, AU REVOIR
good digestion .... EUPEPSIA
good health, in ...... PEART
"Good King" .... HAL
good news EVANGEL, EVANGILE

a "Good Queen Bess," name for ORIANA
good: Tagalog ...... MABUTI
goods .... WARES
goods in sea .... JETSAM
goods sunk at sea LAGAN, LIGAN
goose barnacle genus . LEPAS
goose cry ..... HONK, YANG
goose genus .... ANSER
goose, male .... GANDER
goose, sea .... SOLAN
goose, wild .... BRANT
gooseberry .... FABES
gopher tortoise .. MUNGOFA
gorge .... GLUT, CHASM, FLUME, RAVINE
Gorgons, one of .... MEDUSA
gorse .. WHIN, WHUN, FURZE
goshawk genus ASTUR, BUTEO
gospel . EVANGEL, EVANGILE
gossamer .... WEB
gossip .... EME
gossip: India .... GUP
Gottfried's sister ...... ELSA
gourd fruit .... PEPO
gourd rattle .... MARACA
gourmet .... EPICURE
gout of knee ..... GONAGRA
government .... STATE

b government control ... REGIE STATISM
governor .... REGENT
governor, Mecca SHERIF, SHEREEF
governor, Persia .... SATRAP
governor, Turkish ...... BEY
GOWN .... see GARMENT
grace .... ADORN
Graces' mother ..... AEGLE
Graces, The ..AGLAIA, THALIA
graceful .... GAINLY
grackle .... DAW, MINA, MYNA, MYNAH
grade .... RANK, RATE, SORT, STEP
gradient .... SLOPE
Graf —, ship .... SPEE
graft .... CION, SCION
grafted: Her. .... ENTE
Grail, Holy, finder of .. BORS
grain ..... OAT, RYE, SEED, WALE, SPELT, MILLET
grain beetle ...... CADELLE
grain, chaff of .... BRAN
grain, coarse .... SAMP
grain given Romans . ANNONA
grain sorghum, Ind... DARI, DORA, DURR, MILO, CHENA, DARRA, DARSO, DURRA, DHURRA, DOURAH, HEGARI

c grain, sorghum, U. S. FETERITA
grain, stalks of ..... HAULM
grain to grind .... GRIST
gram molecule .... MOL
grammatically, describe PARSE
grampus .... ORC
granary, India GOLA, GUNJ, GUNGE
grandparental .... AVAL
grandson, Adam's, Eve's ENOS
grant ... CEDE, MISE, REMISE
grant, India, Hindu ... ENAM
grant of rights PATENT, CHARTER
granular snow ... FIRN, NEVE
grape .... UVA, MUSCAT, CATAWBA, CONCORD
grape conserve ...... UVATE
grape disease .... ESCA
grape genus .... VITIS
grape jelly .... SAPA
grape juice DIBS, MUST, STUM
grape juice sirup ..... SAPA
grape-like .. UVA, UVAL, UVIC
grape-like fruit .... UVA
grape refuse .... MARC
grape, white .... MALAGA
grapefruit . POMELO, PUMELO
graphite .... KISH
grasp .... SEIZE

d grass ... POA, REED, DARNEL
grass, Andes .... ICHU
grass, blue .... POA
grass, coarse .. REED, SEDGE
grass genus ...... AIRA, COIX, AVENA, STIPA
grass, kind of .... RIE
grass, marsh .... REED SEDGE, FESCUE
grass, N. Afr. .... ALFA
grass, pasture ...... GRAMA
grass rope: Sp. .... SOGA
grass, rope-making MUNG, MUNJ
grass, sour .... SORREL
grass stem .... CULM
grass tuft .... HASSOCK
grass, yard, wire ...... POA
grasshopper .... GRIG
grassland SAVANNA, SAVANNAH
grassland, S. Afr. ..... VELDT
grasslands, Western .. RANGE
grate ..... JAR, RASP, GRIDE
gratify SATE, ARRIDE, PLEASE
grating .. GRID, GRILL, GRILLE
gratuitous .... FREE
gratuity .... FEE, TIP
gratuity, customer .... PILON
grave .... SOBER

gravestone, Gr. & Rom. STELA, STELE, STELAE, STELAI
graving tool .... STYLET
Gray, botanist .... ASA
gray .... OLD, HOAR, ASHEN, SLATE
gray kingbird .... PIPIRI
gray, mole .... TAUPE
gray parrot .... JAKO
gray plaid, gray shawl MAUD
grayish-brown .. DUN, TAUPE
graze ...... AGIST, BROWSE
grease .. OIL, LARD, AXUNGE
great barracuda .... PICUDA
Great Barrier Island, N. Z. OTEA
"Great Emancipator" ... ABE
great: Gypsy .... BARO
greater ...... MORE, MAJOR
Greece, ancient name HELLAS
Greece, modern ...... ELLAS
greedy .... AVID

Greek Letters, Numbers:
Greek A, One .... ALPHA
Greek B, Two .... BETA
Greek D, Four ...... DELTA
Greek E, Eight .... ETA
Greek I, Ten .... IOTA
Greek M, Forty .... MU
Greek N, Fifty .... NU
Greek O, 800 ...... OMEGA
Greek P, Eighty .... PI
Greek R, 100 .... RHO
Greek T, 300 .... TAU
Greek Z, Seven ...... ZETA
Greek 90 .... KOPPA
Greek 900 .... SAMPI
Gr. ancient .... ATTIC
Gr. assembly .... AGORA
Gr. athletic contest .. AGON
Gr. authors .. ZENO, AESOP, HOMER, PLATO, TIMON, HESIOD, PINDAR, SAPPHO, STRABO, THALES, PLUTARCH
Gr. city, ancient ELIS, SPARTA
Gr. city, word for ... POLIS
Gr. colony, ancient ... IONIA
Gr. column .... DORIC, IONIC
Gr. commonalty .... DEMOS
Gr. community ...... DEME
Gr. dialect .... EOLIC, AEOLIC
Gr. district, ancient ATTICA
Gr. drama .... MIME
Gr. festival city ..... NEMEA
Gr. galley TRIREME, UNIREME
Gr. garment .... CHITON
Gr. ghost .... KER
GREEK GODS, GODDESSES see SPECIAL SECTION and see GODS, GODDESSES
Gr. hero ...... AJAX, JASON

Gr. historian .... CTESIAS
Gr. January ...... GAMELION
Gr. legendary hero ..... IDAS
Gr. marketplace ..... AGORA
Gr. meeting place of voters PNYX
Gr. musical term MESE, NETE
Gr. myth. flier ..... ICARUS
Gr. native .... CRETAN
Gr. patriarch .... ARIUS
Gr. philosopher PLATO, THALES
Gr. poet ... ARION, HOMER, PINDAR
Gr. poetess . SAPHO, SAPPHO
Gr. poetry, simple ... DORIC
Gr. priest .... MYST
Gr. princess .... IRENE
Gr. province .... NOME
Gr. resistance group .. EDES
Gr. rose .... CAMPION
Gr. sculptor .... PHIDIAS
Gr. shield .... PELTA
Gr. slave .... PENEST
Gr. statesman ... ARISTIDES
Gr. temple .... NAOS
Gr. theologian ...... ARIUS
Gr. township-commune . DEME
Gr. underground ...... ELAS
Gr. vase .... PELIKE
Gr. weight, old .. MNA, MINA
green .... NILE, VERD, VERT, OLIVE, RESEDA
green chalcedony .... JASPER
green cheese ...... SAPSAGO
green chrysolite .... PERIDOT
green copper arsenate ERINITE
green fly .... APHID
green: Her. .... VERT
Green Mountain hero .. ALLEN
green parrot: P. I. ... CAGIT
green stone JADE, PERIDOT
greenish yellow OLIVE, RESEDA
Greenland Eskimo ...... ITA
Greenland geol. div. ... KOME
Greenland settlement, town, base .... ETAH
Greenland's colonizer .. ERIC
greeting . AVE, HAIL, SALUTE
gridiron .... GRILL
grief ...... DOLOR, DOLOUR
griffon genus .... GYPS
grimalkin .... CAT
grinding .... MOLAR
grindstone, Indian ... MANO
grit .... SAND
grivet .... WAAG
grivet monkey .... TOTA
grommet, naut. ..... BECKET
groom, India SAIS, SICE, SYCE
groove .... RUT, SCARF

71

a
groove, pilaster STRIA, STRIAE
grooved .... LIRATE, STRIATE
grope .... FEEL
gross .... CRASS
ground grain .... MEAL
ground wheat-husk .... BRAN
groundhog .... MARMOT
group .... BAND, BODY, CREW, TEAM
group, animal ..... NID, NYE, HERD, NIDE, COVEY, DROVE, CLUTCH
grouper .... MERO
grouse .... PTARMIGAN
grouse, red: Scot. MUIRFOWL
grove, small-tree .... COPSE
grow .... WAX, RAISE
grow together ..... ACCRETE
growing out .... ENATE
growl ...... YAR, GNAR, YARR, SNARL
growth, skin .... WEN
grub .... LARVA
grudge .... SPITE
gruel, maize .... ATOLE
gruesome . GRISLY, MACABRE
guarantees ...... SURETIES
b guard .... SENTRY
guard, as door .... TILE
guardhouse .... BRIG
guardian, alert ARGUS, CERBERUS
Guatemala fruit ...... ANAY
guava .... ARACA
Gudrun's husband ATLI, SIGURD
Guenon monkey ..... MONA
guest house .... INN
Guiana tree .... MORA
guide ... LEAD, PILOT, STEER
guiding .... POLAR
guiding rule .... MOTTO
Guido's note ..... UT, ELA
guild, merchants' .... HANSE
guillemot ..... COOT, MURR, MURRE
guilty .... NOCENT
guinea fowl's young .... KEET
guinea pig .... CAVY
gulch: Sp. .... ARROYO
GULF, .. also see GAZETTEER
gulf, Ionia sea .... ARTA
gulf, Medit. .... TUNIS

c
gull ...... MEW, SKUA, TERN, WAEG, XEMA
gull, fork-tailed ...... XEMA
gull genus ... LARI, XEMA
gulls, of, like .... LARINE
gullet ...... MAW, CRAW
gullible person . DUPE, GULL
"Gulliver's Travels," men YAHOOS
gully: Afr. .... DONGA
gulp .... SWIG
gum .... RESIN, BALATA
gum arabic ACACIA, ACACIN, ACACINE
gum, astringent ...... KINO
gum resin ... ELEMI, LOBAN, MYRRH
gum resin, aromatic .. MYRRH
gum, Somaliland ..... MATTI
gumbo .. OCRA, OKRA, OKRO
gumbo limbo tree .. GOMART
gums .... ULA
gun .... GAT
gun, British .... STEN
gun, fire, burst of .... SALVO
gun, Ger. .... BERTHA
d gun, kind of .... BREN
gun lock catch .... SEAR
gun, P. I. .... BARIL
gun, slang .... ROD, HEATER ROSCOE
gun: S. Afr. .... ROER, ROHR
gunny cloth .... TAT
gusto .... ZEST
gutta mixture .... SOH
gutta, Sumatra ...... SIAK
guy-rope . STAT, STAY, VANG
gym feat .... KIP
gymnast .... TURNER
gypsum, kind of YESO, GESSO, YESSO, SELENITE
gypsy ... ROM, CALE, CALO, ROAMER, ROMANY
gypsy boy .... ROM
gypsy gentleman ...... RYE
gypsy girl .... CHAI
gypsy husband .... ROM
gypsy lady .... RANI
gypsy married woman . ROMI
gypsy: Sp. .... GITANO
gypsy tent, camp ..... TAN
gypsy village .... GAV
gypsy word .... LAV
gypsy word for paper, book LIL

H

H .... AITCH
habit ... RUT, WONT, USAGE
habitat plant form ..... ECAD
habitation .... ABODE
habituate ... ENURE, INURE
habituated .... USED
hackney coach, Fr. . FIACRE
hackneyed ... STALE, TRITE
Hades .. DIS, ORCUS, PLUTO,
SHEOL, TARTARUS
Hades: Old Eng. .... ADES
Hades, place before . EREBUS
Hades river
STYX, LETHE, ACHERON
hag .... CRONE
haggard .... DRAWN
Haggard, H. Rider, novel SHE
hail .... AVE, GREET
hail: naut. .... AVAST
hair, arrange .... COIF
hair, caterpillar ...... SETA
hair coat .... MELOTE
hair-do, old .... TETE
hair dressing ...... POMADE
hair, false RAT, WIG, TOUPEE
hair, head of .... CRINE
hair, knot of . BUN, CHIGNON
hair, lock of ... CURL, TRESS
hair net .... SNOOD
hair, remove .... EPILATE
hair, rigid .... SETA
hair, rough, matted ... SHAG
hair shirt .... CILICE
hair, standing ...... ROACH
hair unguent ...... POMADE
hairless: Sp. Am. ..... PELON
hairlike process
CILIA, CILIUM
hairy PILAR, COMOSE, PILOSE
Haiti bandit .... CACO
Halcyone's husband ... CEYX
half .... MOIETY
half-boot .... PAC
half-breed . MESTEE, MUSTEE
half-caste .... METIS
half-moon figure ..... LUNE
halfpenny: Brit. ...... MAG
half-way .... MID
halfway house .... INN
hall: Ger. ...... AULA, SAAL
hallow .... BLESS
halo .... NIMB, CORONA,
NIMBUS, AUREOLA, AUREOLE
halt .... LAME, STOP
halting place, troops' . ETAPE
Hamilton's party ... FEDERAL

Hamite .... SOMAL, BERBER,
SOMALI
Hamitic language AGAO, AGAU
hamlet .. BURG, DORP, TOWN
Hamlet's castle ... ELSINORE
hammer .... KEVEL
hammer head part ..... PEEN
hammer, heavy ...... MAUL
hammer, large ..... SLEDGE
hammer, lead ...... MADGE
hammer, tilt .... OLIVER
hamper ... CRAMP, FETTER,
TRAMMEL
Ham's son .... CUSH
hand ... PUD, NEAF, MANUS
hand, pert. to ...... CHIRAL
hand, whist .... TENACE
handbill .... LEAF
handcuff .... MANACLE
handle ...... EAR, LUG, PAW,
ANSA, HILT, KNOB,
HELVE, TREAT
handle, bench plane ... TOTE
handle, having ..... ANSATE
handle roughly .. PAW, MAUL
handle, scythe ...... SNATH,
SNEAD, SNEED, SNATHE
handstone for grinding . MANO
handwriting .... SCRIPT
handwriting on the wall MENE,
TEKEL, UPHARSIN
hang ...... DRAPE, DROOP,
HOVER, IMPEND
hank of twine .... RAN
Hannibal's defeat ..... ZAMA
Hannibal's victory ... CANNAE
happen ..... OCCUR, BEFALL,
BETIDE, CHANCE
happening .... EVENT
happiness god, Jap.
EBISU, HOTEI
harangue .... ORATE,
TIRADE, DIATRIBE
Haran's son .... LOT
harass .... NAG, BESET
harbinger .... HERALD
harbor .... BAY, COVE,
PORT, HAVEN
hard cash .... SPECIE
harden .... GEL, SET,
ENURE, INURE, INDURATE
hardship .... TRIAL
hardtack .... PANTILE
hardwood ...... ASH, OAK
Hardy novel heroine .... TESS
hare: dialect .... WAT

73

a

hare, genus	LEPUS
hare, young, 1 year	LEVERET
harem	ZENANA, SERAGLIO
harem room	ODA
harlot of Jericho, Bibl.	RAHAB
harm	BANE, DAMAGE, INJURE
harm: old Eng.	DERE
harm: poetic	BALE
harmful	NOCENT
harmonize	ATTUNE
harmony . UNISON, CONCORD
harp, ancient	TRIGON
Harp constellation	LYRA
harp guitar key	DITAL
harp, kind of	EOLIC
harp, Nubian	NANGA
harpy, Gr. myth	AELLO
harquebus projection	CROC
harrow	DRAG
harsh to taste	ACERB
hartebeeste	ASSE, TORA, CAAMA, KAAMA
harvest	REAP
harvest festival, Rom.	OPALIA
harvest goddess	OPS
harvest, India . RABI, RABBI
has not: Old Eng.	NAS
hashish	BHANG
hasty pudding	SEPON
HAT	see HEADGEAR

b

hat: Anglo-Ir.	CAUBEEN
hat plant	SOLA
hat, straw . MILAN, PANAMA
hatchet, archeol.	HACHE
hatchet, stone	MOGO
hatred	ODIUM, AVERSION
hatred: Buddhism	DOSA
hatter's mallet	BEATER
haul tight, naut. BOUSE, TRICE
haunt, low . DEN, DIVE, NEST
hautboy	OBOE
haven	LEE
having buttery account: Oxford	BATTEL
having holes, as cheese	EYEY
having true luster when uncut	NAIF
hawl: P.I.	MANO
haw, as cattle	HOI
Hawaiian bird . IO, O-O, IIWI
Hawaiian bird, extinct	MAMO
Hawaiian bird, red-tailed	KOAE
Hawaiian blueberry .	OHELO
Hawaiian chant	MELE
Hawaiian cloth . TAPA, KAPA
Hawaiian cudweed . . ENAENA
Hawaiian dance	HULA
Hawaiian farewell, greeting	ALOHA
Hawaiian feather cloak	MAMO
Hawaiian fern	HEII

c

Hawaiian floral emblem	LEHUA
Hawaiian food	POI
Hawaiian food-game fish	ULUA
Hawaiian garland	LEI
Hawaiian god	KANE
Hawaiian goddess, fire .	PELE
Hawaiian goose	NENE
Hawaiian gooseberry . .	POHA
Hawaiian governor, 1st .	DOLE
Hawaiian grass	HILO
Hawaiian hawk	IO
Hawaiian herb	HOLA
Hawaiian loincloth	MALO
Hawaiian musical instrument	PUA
Hawaiian porch	LANAI
Hawaiian president, 1st	DOLE
Hawaiian royal chief . . .	ALII
Hawaiian shrub	AKIA
Hawaiian staple	POI
Hawaiian starch	APII
Hawaiian timber tree .	OHIA
Hawaiian tree	KOA, AULU, ALANI, ILIAHI
Hawaiian tree, dark . . .	AALII
Hawaiian tree fern	PULU
Hawaiian vine	IE
Hawaiian volcano goddess	PELE
Hawaiian windstorm . . .	KONA

d

hawk	KITE
hawk, falconry	BATER
hawk, fish	OSPREY
hawk genus	BUTEO
hawk-head god, Egypt.	HORUS
hawk, India	SHIKRA
hawk-like bird	KITE
hawk, Scot.	ALLAN
hawk, young	BRANCHER
hawks	IOS
hawk's cage	MEW
hawk's leash	LUNE
hawthorn	MAY
hawthorn berry	HAW
hay, spread to dry	TED
haystack	RICK
hazard . . . DARE, RISK, PERIL
hazardous	CHANCY
haze: Old Eng.	HASE
hazelnut	FILBERT
hazy, make . . . . DIM, BEDIM
"he remains": Lat.	MANET
head	NOB, LEAD, PATE, POLL, TETE, CAPUT, CHIEF, CAPITA, LEADER, NODDLE, NOODLE
head covering . . . CAP, HAT, TAM, HOOD, VEIL, BERET
head covering, fleecy . NUBIA
head, crown of	PATE
head, having round . . RETUSE
head, membrane covering	CAUL

a head, Moslem .... RAIS, REIS
head of Benjamin's clan .. IRI
head, shaved ...... TONSURE
head: slang .... NOGGIN
head wrap ... NUBIA, SHAWL
headband, Gr. ...... TAENIA
HEADDRESS
        see also HEADGEAR
headdress, bishop's
            MITER, MITRE
headgear, brimless ... TOQUE
headgear, clerical
        BERETTA, BIRETTA
headgear, dervish ...... TAJ
headgear, kind of .. PANAMA
headgear, military ..... SHAKO
headgear, Moslem . TARBUSH,
    TARBOOCH, TARBOOSH,
            TARBOUCHE
headgear, poetic .... TIAR
headgear, priest's
        BERETTA, BIRETTA
headgear, tropics
    TOPI, TERAI, TOPEE
headgear, Turk. .... FEZ
headland . RAS, CAPE, NASE,
            NESS, NOZE
headless: Her. .... ETETE
headstrong .... RASH
healing goddess .... EIR
health, in good .... FIT
b health-drinking word
            SALUD, PROSIT
health resort .... SPA
heap .... PILE, RAFF, RAFT
hear ye! .... OYES, OYEZ
hearing: law .... OYER
hearken .. HEAR, HEED, LIST,
            ATTEND, LISTEN
heart .... COR, CORE
heart auricle . ATRIA, ATRIUM
heart contraction ... SYSTOLE
heart, immortal, Egyp. ... AB
heart trouble ...... ANGINA
heartleaf .... MEDIC
heartless .. CRUEL, SARDONIC
heat .... WARM, CALOR
heated to whiteness CANDENT
heath .... MOOR
heath genus .... ERICA
heathen .... PAGAN
heathen god .... IDOL
heather ...... LING, ERICA
heating apparatus, vessel ETNA
heave upward .... SCEND
heaven . SION, ZION, URANO
heaven, eagle-borne flier to
            ETANA
heaven personified: Babyl.
            ANU
heavens, pert. to ... URANIC
heavenly .... EDENIC

c heavenly being ...... ANGEL
            SERAPH, SERAPHIM
heavenly Jerusalem SION, ZION
heavy blow .... ONER
HEBREW see also JEWISH
            and BIBLICAL
Hebr. Bible books ... NEBIIM
Hebr. Bible pronounciation aid
        GRI KRI, KERE, KERI,
        QERE QERI, QUERI
Hebr. drum .... TOPH
Hebr. dry measure . CAB, KAB
Hebr. lyre .... ASOR
Hebr. measure .. KOR, EPHA,
            OMER, EPHAH
Hebr. precept .... TORA
HEBREW PROPHETS . see
    SPECIAL SECTION, Page 196
Hebr. proselyte .... GER
Hebr. reclaimer ...... GOEL
Hebr. teacher ..... RAB, REB
Hebr. universe ...... OLAM
Hebrews' ancestor, legend
            EBER
Hector's mother .... HECUBA
hedge plant .... PRIVET
hedgerow; Eng. .... REW
heed .... HEAR, MIND,
            OBEY, RECK
heel .... CAD, CALX
d height .... STATURE
heir .... SON, SCION,
        HERITOR, LEGATEE
held, able to be .... TENABLE
Helen: Ital. .... ELENA
Helen of Troy's mother . LEDA
Helen's lover .... PARIS
helical .... SPIRAL
Helios .... SUN
hell .... HADES, SHEOL
Hellespont swimmer LEANDER
helm position .... ALEE
helmet, light ...... SALLET
helmet, medieval
            ARMET, HEAUME
helmet, Rom. .... GALEA
helmet-shaped ... GALEATE
helmet-shaped part ... GALEA
helmsman .... PILOT
Heloise's husband ... ABELARD
help . AID, ABET, BACK, TIDE,
    ASSIST, SUCCOR, SUCCOUR
helper .... AIDE
Helvetic .... SWISS
hem in .... BESET
hemp .. TOW, RINE, RAMIE
hemp, Afr. .... IFE
hemp, India ... KEF, BANG,
    KEEF, KEIF, KIEF, BHANG,
    DAGGA, RAMIE
hemp, Manila .... ABACA

75

Hemp

a
hemp narcotic ..... **CHARAS**
hemp shrub, India
.... **PUA, POOA, POOAH**
hen .... **LAYER**
hen harrier, Europ. .. **FALLER**
hence ...... **SO, OFF, AWAY**
Hengist's brother .... **HORSA**
Henry IV birthplace .... **PAU**
"Henry IV" character .. **PETO**
"Henry V" knave ...... **NYM**
"Henry VI" character .. **IDEN**
hep .... **ONTO**
her: obs. .... **HIR**
Hera's son .... **ARES**
herald .... **USHER**
HERALDIC TERMS see also
SPECIAL SECTION, Page 194
heraldic bearing **ORLE, FILLET**
heraldic cross .... **PATEE**
heraldic wreath .... **ORLE**
herald's coat .... **TABARD**
herb ... **RUE, LEEK, MINT,
MOLY, WORT, ANISE, TANSY,
YARROW, OREGANO**
herb, aromatic **BASIL, DITTANY**
herb, bitter ..... **RUE, ALOE**
herb, carrot family ... **ANISE**
herb eve .... **IVA**
herb, fabulous **MOLY, PANACE**
herb, forage .... **SULLA**

b
herb genus .... **ABFA
GEUM, RUTA, ALETRIS**
herb, medicinal . **ALOE, SENNA**
herb of grace .... **RUE**
herb, smoke-charm .. **MUNGO**
herb with aromatic root **NONDO**
herb, wooly .... **POLY**
Hercules' captive ..... **IOLE**
Hercules, monster slain by
.... **HYDRA**
Hercules' mother .. **ALCMENE**
herd .... **DROVE**
herd of horses ...... **CAVIYA**
herd of whales .. **GAM, POD**
herdsman, Swiss ..... **SENN**
hereditary right ...... **UDAL**
hereditary factor . **GEN, GENE**
heretic, 4th cent.
.... **ARIAN, ARIUS**
heretofore .... **ERENOW**
Hermes' mother ..... **MAIA**
Hermes' son .... **PAN**
hermit . **EREMITE, ANCHORITE**
hero, legendary .... **PALADIN**
Hero's love .... **LEANDER**
heroic ...... **EPIC, EPICAL**
heroic poem **EPIC, EPOS, WORK**
heroic song .... **EDDA**
heron .... **EGRET**
heron brood, flock .... **SEDGE**
heron, kind of .... **BITTERN**

c
herring ... **ALEC, BRIT, SILL**
herring, grayback .... **CISCO**
herring keg .... **CADE**
herring small Eur. .... **SPRAT**
hesitate
..... **DEMUR, FALTER, TEETER**
hesitation syllable .. **ER, UM**
Hesperides, one of .. **AEGLE**
Heyward, Du Bose, heroine
.... **BESS**
Hezekiah's mother ..... **ABI**
hiatus .... **GAP, LACUNA**
hickory tree .... **SHELLBARK**
hidden .... **INNER, ARCANE,
COVERT, LATENT**
hide .... **VEIL, CACHE**
hide of beast .... **FELL, SKIN**
hide, thongs of ...... **RIEM**
hide, undressed .... **KIP**
hides, Russian leather . **JUFTI**
hiding in .... **PERDU**
high in pitch: mus. ..... **ALT**
high on scale .... **ELA**
high priest **ELI, AARON, ANNAS**
highest note .... **ELA**
highest point . **APEX, ZENITH**
highway .... **ITER, PIKE**
highway, Alaska-Canada **ALCAN**
highwayman .. **PAD, LADRONE**
hike .... **TRAMP**

d
hill .... **TOR**
hill, broad ... **LOMA, LOMITA**
hill dweller, Ceylon ... **TODA**
hill dweller, India .... **DOGRA**
hill, flat-topped ...... **MESA**
hill fort: Ir. .... **RATH**
hill, isolated .... **BUTTE**
hill, pointed .... **TOR**
hill, Rome
.... **CAELIAN, PALATINE**
hill, S. Afr. .... **KOP, BULT**
hill: Turk. .... **DAGH**
hillock .... **TUMP**
hillside: Scot. .... **BRAE**
hilltop .... **KNAP**
hit, sword .... **HAFT, HANDLE**
Himalayan animal ... **PANDA**
Himal. broadmouth .... **RAYA**
Himal. ibex .... **KYL**
Himal. monkshood .... **ATIS**
Himal. mountain ...... **API**
Himal. wild goat **KRAS, TAHR,
TAIR, THAR**
hind .... **ROE, BACK, REAR**
hinder by fear ...... **DETER**
hindrance ...... **BAR, LET**
Hindu age, cycle ..... **YUGA**
Hindu ancestor ...... **MANU**
Hindu ascetic .... **JOGI,
YATI, YOGI, FAKIR,
SADHU, FAKEER**

a Hindu bible .... **VEDA**
Hindu charitable gift .. **ENAM**
Hindu cymbal .... **TAL**
Hindu deity ... **DEVA, RAMA, SIVA, SHIVA**
HINDU DEITY . see also **GOD** and see SPECIAL SECTION
Hindu divorce law .... **TALAK**
Hindu female slave .... **DASI**
Hindu festival .... **HOLI**
Hindu festival, religious **PUJA**
Hindu gentlemen **BABU, BABOO**
HINDU GODS .. see SPECIAL SECTION, Page 200, and also GOD
Hindu guitar .... **BINA, VINA, SITAR**
Hindu holy man ...... **SADH**
Hindu laws, giver of .. **MANU**
Hindu legendary hero .. **NALA**
Hindu life energy ...... **JIVA**
Hindu, low caste ...... **KORI**
Hindu magic .... **MAYA**
Hindu mantra .... **OM**
Hindu mendicant ...... **NAGA**
Hindu monastery ...... **MATH**
Hindu "Olympus" ..... **MERU**
Hindu philosophy ...... **YOGA**
Hindu poet ...... **TAGORE**
Hindu prince **RAJA, RANA, RAJAH**
b Hindu progenitor, myth **MANU**
Hindu queen .. **RANI, RANEE**
Hindu religious adherent **JAIN, JAINA**
Hindu rites .... **ACHARA**
Hindu sacred literature . **VEDA**
Hindu sacred word ...... **OM**
Hindu scripture ..... **AGAMA**
Hindu scriptures, pert. to **VEDIC**
Hindu sect, one of **SEIK, SIKH**
Hindu teacher .... **GURU**
Hindu temple .... **DEUL**
Hindu term of respect . **SAHIB**
Hindu title .... **AYA, SRI**
Hindu trader **BANIAN, BANYAN**
Hindu unknown god ...... **KA**
Hindu, unorthodox .. **JAINA**
Hindu widow, suicide . **SUTTEE**
Hindu woman's garment **SARI, SAREE**
Hindu word .... **OM**
Hindu writings .... **VEDA**
Hinduism, elixir **AMRITA, AMREETA**
Hindustani .... **URDU**
hinge, kind of .... **BUTT**
hint ... **TIP, CLEW, POINTER**
hip ...... **COXA, ILIA, ILIAC**
hipbone, of the .... **ILIAC**

c Hippocrates' birthplace .. **KOS**
Hippodrome .... **ARENA**
hire .... **LET, RENT, ENGAGE, CHARTER**
hired carriage .... **HACK**
hired labor: S. Afr. .... **TOGT**
history .... **LORE**
hitherto .... **YET**
Hittites ancestor .... **HETH**
hive for bees .... **SKEP**
hives .... **UREDO**
hoard ...... **AMASS, STORE**
hoarder .... **MISER**
hoarfrost .... **RIME**
hoarfrost: Eng. .... **RAG**
hoary .... **OLD, GRAY**
hoax .... **RUSE, CANARD**
hobgoblin .... **PUCK, SPRITE**
hock, horse's .... **GAMBREL**
hockey ball .... **ORR**
hodgepodge .... **MESS, OLIO**
hog cholera ...... **ROUGET**
hog deer .... **AXIS**
hog, female .... **GILT**
hog plum, W. Ind. **AMRA, JOBO**
hog, wild .. **BOAR, PECCARY**
hog's heart, liver, etc. **HASLET**
Hogan, golfer .... **BEN**
hoist .... **HEAVE**
hold, as in war ...... **INTERN**
d hold back .... **DETER**
hold fast: naut. ...... **BELAY**
holding device . **VISE, TONGS**
hole for molten metal .. **SPRUE**
hole in embankment ... **GIME**
hole in mold .... **GEAT**
hole-in-one .... **ACE**
holidays, Roman ...... **FERIA**
HOLLAND see NETHERLANDS SPECIAL SECTION
hollow .... **DENT, HOWE**
holly .... **HOLM, ILEX**
holly, U. S. .... **ASSI, YAPON, YUPON, YAUPON**
holm oak .... **ILEX**
"Holy Hill," Gr. ...... **ATHOS**
Holy Land city .... **DAN**
holy orders, give .... **ORDAIN**
holy water font ...... **STOUP**
homage .... **HONOR**
home .... **ABODE**
home of gods, Norse.. **ASGARD**
"Home Sweet Home" author **PAYNE**
homeopath school-founder **HERING**
Homer's epic ...... **ODYSSEY**
hominy, Indian coarse . **SAMP**
honey .... **MEL**
honey-badger .... **RATEL**

a honey buzzard .... PERN
honey drink .. MEAD, MORAT
honey eater bird
    IAO, MOHO, MANUAO
honeybee .... DESERET
honeycomb, like a .... FAVOSE
honor .... EXALT, REVERE
honorarium .... TIP
honorary commission BREVET
Honshu bay .... ISE
Honshu port .... KOBE
hooded garment ...... PARKA
hoodoo ...... JINX, JYNX
hoof .... UNGUES, UNGUIS
hook, bent into .... HAMATE
hook, double curve ..... ESS
hook, engine .... GAB
hook for pot .... CLEEK
hook money ... LARI, LARIN
hooks .... HAMI
hookah .... NARGILE
hooked .... HAMUS,
    HAMATE, HAMOSE, FALCATE
Hoover Dam lake .... MEAD
hope goddess, Rom. ... SPES
hop-picker's basket .... BIN
hop plant .... LUPULUS
hopscotch stone .... PEEVER
Horae, one of ...... DIKE,
    EIRENE, EUNOMIA
Horeb .... SINAI
b horizontal stripe ...... BAR
horizontal timber .... LINTEL
horn .... CORNU
horn, crescent-moon .. CUSP
horn, Hebr SHOFAR, SHOPHAR
horn quicksilver .... CALOMEL
horn-shaped structure CORNU
horn sounded for kill .. MORT
horn tissue, bit of .... SCUR
horneblende .... EDENITE
hornless, Eng dial. .... NOT
hornless stag ..... POLLARD
hors d'oeuvre ...... CANAPE
horse .... BAY, COB, NAG, ARAB,
    MARE, MERE, ROAN,
    MOUNT, STEED, EQUINE,
    JENNET
horse, Austral. ...... WALER
horse, Barbary native .. BARB
horse blanket ...... MANTA
horse breed ...... MORGAN
horse, brown
    BAY, ROAN, SORREL
horse color BAY, ROAN, SORREL
horse dealer, Eng. .... COPER
horse disease of ... SPAVIN
horse, draft .... SHIRE
horse genus .... EQUUS
horse; gypsy . GRI, GRY, GRAS
horse-mackerel ...... SCAD

c horse-man, myth ... CENTAUR
horse, piebald .... PINTO
horse, race .... PACER
horse-radish, fruit of .... BEN
horse, saddle ...... MOUNT
horse, small .... GENET,
    GENNET, JENNET, GENETTE
horse, Sp. Am. ..... CABALLO
horse, swift ARAB, COURSER
horse, talking, Gr. ... ARION
horse, war .... CHARGER
horse, white-flecked . ROAN
horse, wild Asiatic . TARPAN
horse, young .. COLT, FOAL
horsehair .... SETON
horsemanship, art of MANEGE
horses, goddess of .. EPONA
horse's sideways tread . VOLT
horseshoe gripper ..... CALK
horseshoeing stall
    TRAVE, TREVE
Horus' mother .... ISIS
Hosea's wife .... GOMER
host ...... ARMY, HORDE
hostelry .... INN
hot air chamber ..... OVEN
hot iron to sear .... CAUTER
hot spring, eruptive .. GEYSER
Hottentot .... NAMA
hourly .... HORAL
d house ROOF, VILLA, COTTAGE
house, like a ...... DOMAL
house, mud, Afr. .... TEMBE
house urn: Rom. .. CAPANNA
housefly genus ...... MUSCA
housefly genus, lesser FANNIA
household MENAGE, MAINPOST
household god .. LAR, LARES
howl .... ULULATE
howling monkey MONO, ARABA
hub .. NAVE, BOSTON CENTER
hubbub . ADO, STIR, TUMULT
hue .... COLOR TINGE
huge .... VAST, ENORM
Huguenot leader .... ADRETS
hull .... POD, HUSK
humble .... ABASE
hummingbird
    AVA, TOPAZ, COLIBRI
humorist .... WIT
humpback salmon
    HADDO, HOLIA
Humphreys, Mrs. (pseudo.)
    RITA
hundred .... CENTUM
hundredweight ...... CENTAL
Hungarian dog .... PULI
Hungarian hero ...... NAGY
Hungarian king ...... BELA
Hungarian people .. MAGYAR
Hungarian pianist .. SANDOR

a

Hungarian playwright MOLNAR
Hungarian violinist ... AUER
Huns, king of
ATLI, ETZEL, ATTILA
hunt, Ind. .... SHIKAR
hunter .... ORION, NIMROD
hunter, India ...... SHIKARI
hunting cry . HO, YOI, TOHO,
HALLOO, YOICKS, TALLY-
HO
hunting hat .... TERAI
hunting hound .... ALAN
huntress .... ATALANTA
huntsman .... JAGER
HUNTSMAN'S CRY see HUNT-
ING CRY
hup: army .... ONE
hurdy-gurdy .... LIRA, ROTA
hurry .... HIE, HASTEN
hurt .... MAR, ACHE, LESION

c

hurt: old Eng. .... DERE
hurtful .... MALEFIC
husband's brother .... LEVIR
hush .... SH, HSH
husk, cereal .... BRAN
hut, India .... BARI
hut, Mex. .... JACAL
hydrate, as lime ...... SLAKE
hydraulic pump .... RAM
hydrocarbon TOLAN, ETHANE,
OCTANE, RETENE, TERPENE
hydrogen compound .. IMINE
hydrogen isotope .. PROTIUM
hymn .... ODE
hymn of praise ..... ANTHEM
hypnotic state ..... TRANCE
hypothetical force
OD, BIOD, ELOD, ODYL
hypothetical force of .. ODIC
hyson .... TEA

I

I .... EGO
"I have found it" ... EUREKA
"I love": Lat. .... AMO
Iago's wife .... EMILIA
Iberians ...... IBERI, IBERES

b

Ibex .... KYL, TUR, KAIL
Ibsen character .. ASE, NORA
ice block, glacial ..... SERAC
ice mass ...... BERG, FLOE
ice, slushy ..... SISH, LOLLY
Iced .... GLACE
Iceland epic, literature, tales
EDDA
Icelandic narrative .... SAGA
Icy .... GELID
"id —" (that is) .... EST
Idea, Plato .... EIDOS
Ideal .... UTOPIAN
ideal republic, imaginary
OCEANA
Ideal state .... UTOPIA
identical .... ONE, SAME
ideology .... ISM
idiocy .... ANOESIA
idiot ...... AMENT, CRETIN
idle .... OTIANT, OTIOSE
idle, to be .... LAZE, LOAF
idol: archaic .... PAGOD
idol: philos. .... EIDOLON
idolatrous .... PAGAN
ids, pert. to .... IDIC
Idumaea .... EDOM
if ever .... ONCE
if not .... ELSE
ignoble .... BASE

d

ignominy .... SHAME
ignorance, Hindu philos. TAMAS
ignorant . STUPID, UNAWARE
ignore .... ELIDE
Igorot's neighbor tribesman ATA
ill .... EVIL
ill-will ...... SPITE, RANCOR
illumination unit ...... LUX
illusion .... CHIMERA
illusory riches .... MINE
Image .... IDOL,
IDOLON, IDOLUM, EIDOLON
Image, pert. to ...... ICONIC
image, religious . ICON, IKON
imagine: arch. .... WIS
imbecile .... AMENT,
ANILE, CRETIN
imbibe .... SIP, GULP, DRINK
imitate .. APE, MIME, MIMIC
imitation .... MIMESIS
imitation gems ...... PASTE
immature seed .... OVULE
immature: zool. ..... NEANIC
immeasurable .. BOUNDLESS
immediately .... NOW, ANON
immense .... VAST
immerse . DIP, DUNK, DOUSE
immigrant, Greek .... METIC
immunizing substance
SERUM, HAPTEN, HAPTENE
Imou pine .... RIMU
Impair . MAR, DAMAGE, SPOIL
impart .... GIVE, LEND
impartial .... EVEN
impede .... ESTOP, HAMPER
impel .... URGE

a impertinent ... **PERT, SAUCY**
IMPLEMENT .. see also **TOOL**
implement, pounding . **PESTLE**
implement to skid logs **TODE**
implied .... **TACIT**
import .... **SENSE**
important, critically ... **VITAL**
importune .... **URGE**
impose .... **LAY**
impost .... **TAX**
imposture .... **SHAM**
impoverish .... **IMPOOR**
impressionist painter **DEGAS,**
MANET, MONET, RENOIR
imprison .... **IMMURE**
improve .... **AMEND**
improvise music ...... **VAMP**
impudence .... **LIP,**
BRASS, CHEEK, NERVE
impure metal product **MATTE**
in addition .. **TOO, ALSO, YET**
in agreement .... **UNITED**
in disagreement .... **OUT**
In half, in — .... **TWO**
"in medias —" .... **RES**
In name only ...... **NOMINAL**
in same place .... **IBID**
in so far as .... **QUA**
in the know .... **AWARE**
In the matter of ...... **INRE**
in the past .... **OVER**
b in the very near future.. **ANON**
in unison .... **ONE**
in very truth .... **AMEN**
inability to hear .... **ASONIA**
inactive .... **INERT**
inadequate .... **SCANT**
inborn .... **NATIVE**
incarnation, Hindu .... **RAMA,**
AVATAR
incense ingredient
GUM, SPICE, STACTE
Incense receptacle, Rom
ACERRA
Incense, Somali ...... **MATTI**
Incentive .... **GOAD, MOTIVE**
incessantly .... **EVER**
inch, .001 of .... **MIL**
incidentally .... **OBITER**
incinerate .... **CREMATE**
incite .... **EGG, PROD, URGE,**
IMPEL, SET ON, SUBORN
inciter .... **EGGER**
inclination .... **BENT**
incline **TEND, SLOPE, TREND**
inclined .... **APT, PRONE**
inclined way .... **RAMP**
income, annual, Fr. ... **RENTE**
incompletely .... **SEMI**
inconsiderable .... **NOMINAL**
increase .... **WAX, RISE**
incrustation .... **SCAB**

c Incursion, predatory ... **RAID**
indeed: Ir. ...... **ARU, AROO**
indentation
CRENA, CRENAE, CRENELET
index mark .... **FIST**
INDIA, INDIAN ...... see also
SPECIAL SECTION and see
also **HINDU**
India farmer .... **MEO**
India minstrel .... **BHAT**
India native chief ... **SIRDAR**
India native servant .. **MATY**
India: poet. .... **IND**
India, swamp belt of .. **TERAI**
INDIAN .. see also page 192
Indian .... **SAC**
INDIAN, ALGONQUIN .... see
page 192
Indian, Arawak ...... **ARAUA**
Indian, Arikara .... **REE**
Indian, Athapasca ..... **TAKU**
Indian buzzard .... **TESA**
Indian corn .... **MAIZE**
Indian corn: N. Z. ... **KANGA**
Indian elk .... **SAMBAR**
Indian farmer, Fla. .. **CALUSA**
Indian in Chaco ...... **TOBA**
Indian mahogany tree . **TOON**
Indian mulberry **AL, AAL, ACH**
Indian of Jalisco ..... **CORA**
Indian of Keresan ..... **SIA**
Indian of Mex., scattered **CORA**
d Indian ox .... **ZEBU**
Indian, Panamint ..... **KOSO**
INDIAN, PLAINS see page 193
Indian race .... **JAT**
Indian shell currency
ULO, UHLLO
INDIAN, SIOUAN see page 193
Indian, S. Peru ..... **CHANCA**
INDIAN TREE see **TREE**. INDIA
Indian warlike ...... **APACHE**
Indian weight ... **SER, TOLA**
Indian, whaler .... **HOH**
Indian yellow .... **PURI,**
PIURI, PURREE
indicating succession **ORDINAL**
indict .... **ARRAIGN**
indifferent to pain
STOIC, STOICAL
indigo plant .... **ANIL**
indistinct, make ..... **BEDIM**
indite .... **PEN, WRITE**
individual ...... **ONE, SELF**
Indo-Chin. native **LAO,MRU,TAI**
Indo-Chin. tribe **TAI,LAOS,SHAN**
Indo-Chin. tribes ..... **MOI**
Indo-European **ARYA, ARYAN**
Indo-Malayan animal .. **NAPU**
Indolent .... **OTIOSE, SUPINE**
Indonesian .... **ATA, NESIOT**

induce .... LEAD
Indus tribesman .... GOR
ineffectual .... VAIN
inelastic .... LIMP
inert .... SUPINE
infatuation .... ATE
infertile moor .... LANDE
infinity .... OLAM
infirm ...... ANILE, SENILE
inflamed, be .... RANKLE
inflammable liquid . ACETONE
inflammation: med. . ANGINA
inflexible ...... IRON, RIGID
inflict ...... DEAL, IMPOSE
inflorescence RACEME, SPADIX
inflorescence, racemose AMENT
influence .... AFFECT
informer. slang .... NARK
infusion .... TEA
ingenuous .... NAIVE
inhabitant .... ITE
inhabitant of a town ... CIT
inheritance .... ENTAIL
inheritor .... LEGATEE
initiate. OPEN, BEGIN, START
initiate, Gr. ... EPOPT, EPOPTA
injure ... MAR, HARM, MAIM
injury ..... LESION, TRAUMA
inlaid .... MOSAIC
inlaid decoration ...... BUHL
inlet ARM, BAY, RIA, FIORD
inlet: Dutch .... ZEE
inlet, Orkneys .... VOE
inn .... KHAN,
  HOSTEL, POSADA, HOSPICE
Inn, "Canterbury Tales" TABARD
inn, Oriental .... SERAI
Inn, Turkish .... IMARET
inner .... ENTAL
inner meaning . CORE, HEART
inner parlor: Scot. ...... BEN
Innkeeper
  PADRONE, BONIFACE
Insect ANT, BEE, BUG, DOR,
  FLY, FLEA GNAT, MITE,
  APHID, CADEW, EMESA,
  BEETLE CADDIS, CICADA,
  CICALA, MANTIS
Insect, adult .... IMAGO
Insect body
  THORAX, THORACES
insect, immature ...... PUPA,
  LARVA, INSTAR
insect mature .... IMAGO
Insect order .... DIPTERA
Insect, plant sucking ... APHID
insect, ruinous APHID, BORER
insertion mark ...... CARET
inset .... PANEL
insidious .... SLY
insincere talk .... CANT
insipid, become .... PALL

Insist .... URGE, PRESS
Inspire .... IMBUE
install .... INSTATE
instance .... CASE
Instant .... MO, TRICE
Instar PUPA, IMAGO, LARVA
instigate EGG, ABET, INCITE
instruct .... BRIEF, EDUCATE
INSTRUMENT see also MU-
  SICAL INSTRUMENT
Instrument, Afr. reed
  GORA, GORAH, GOURA
instrument, Chin. ancient KIN
instrument Hebr. .. TIMBREL
instrument, India .... RUANA
instrument Jap. .... SAMISEN
instrument lutelike BANDORE
instrument, lyrelike ... KISSAR
instrument, math. .... SECTOR
instrument, medieval . ROCTA
instrument, naut.
  PELORUS, SEXTANT
Instrument, Sp. .... CASTANET
instrument, stringed ... LYRE
  NABLA, REBAB REBEC
  SAROD, SITAR, VIOLA
  CITHER, CITHARA, CITH
  ERN, CITTERN, GITTERN
Instrument, surveying TRANSIT
instrumentally MEDIA, MEDIUM
insulate .... ISLE
insult .... CAG
insurgent .... REBEL
intact .... WHOLE
intellect .... MIND
  NOUS, MAHAT, REASON
Inter ...... BURY, INHUME
intercharged ..... PERMUTED
interdict .... BAN
interferometer ..... ETALON
interior, ancient temple CELLA
interjection for silence .. TST
interlace .... WEAVE
interlock .... LINK
international language RO, IDO
inter. money unit ... BANCOR
international pact .. ENTENTE
Interpret .... REDE
intersect .... MEET
interstice, small
  AREOLA, AREOLE
Interstices, with .. AREOLAR
intervening law ..... MESNE
interweave TWINE, RADDLE
intimidate AWE, COW, DAUNT
Intone .... CHANT
Intoxicant: India ...... SOMA
intoxicated .... SOSH
intricate ... DEDAL, DAEDAL,
  GORDIAN

81

a intrigue .... CABAL
introduce
  BROACH, INSERT, PRESENT
introducer of jetties for deep-
  ening .... EADS
inundation .... SPATE
inveigle ...... LURE, ENTICE
inventor, claim of rights PATENT
inventor, elevator ...... OTIS
inventor, sewing machine HOWE
inventor, steam engine .. WATT
invest .... ENDOW, ENDUE,
  INDUE, CLOTHE, ORDAIN
invested .... CLAD
investigate .... PROBE
investigator .... TRACER
invite .... ASK, BID
involve . ENTAIL, ENTRAMMEL
Io butterfly .... KIHO
iodine source .... KELP
ion, negative .... ANION
ion, positive .... CATION
Ionian city .... TEOS
iota .... JOT, MITE
Iowa college town .... AMES
ipecac source .... EVEA
IRAN ..... see also PERSIAN
Iran, former part of .. ELAM
Iranian .... TAT, KURD
b Iranian Turk .... SART
irascible .... TESTY
irate .... MAD
Ireland ...... EIRE, ERIN
Ireland, old name ... IERNE
Ireland personified ... IRENA
iridescent gem .... OPAL
iris .... FLAG
Iris, Florentine, European ORRIS
iris, layer of .... UVEA
iris, of a layer .... UVEAL
iris root .... ORRIS
IRISH ..... see also IRELAND
Irish .... ERSE
Ir. alphabet, early
  OGAM, OGUM
Ir. ancestor IR, MIL, ITH MILED
Ir. assembly .... DAIL
Ir. church .... KIL
Ir. city, ancient ...... TARA
Ir. clan, ancient ...... SEPT
Ir. competitive meet ... FEIS
Ir. crowning stone, — Fail LIA
Ir. dramatist .... SYNGE
Ir. exclamation .. ARU, AROO,
  ARRA, WHIST, WURRA
Ir. fairies .... SHEE
Ir. family .... CINEL
Ir. Free State .... EIRE
Irish-Gaelic .... ERSE
Ir. goddess, battle BADB, BODB

c IR. GODS' MOTHER see page 200
Ir. kings' home .... TARA
Ir. law, tribe .... CINEL
Ir. lower house parliament DAIL
Ir. nobleman .... AIRE
Ir. poet
  AE, COLUM, MOORE, YEATS
Ir. rebel group .... IRA
Ir. tribe .... SIOL
Ir. writing .. OGAM, OGHAM
Irishman .. AIRE, CELT, MICK
iron disulfide .... PYRITE
iron, pert. to .... FERRIC
ironwood ..... ACLE, COLIMA
irony .... SATIRE
Iroquoian .... ERIE
Iroquois demon ...... OTKON
irrational number ..... SURD
irregularity .... JOG
irrigation ditch FLUME, SLUICE
irritate .... VEX, GALL, RILE,
  NETTLE, RANKLE
Isaac's son
  EDOM, ESAU, JACOB
Ishmael .... PARIAH
Ishmael, son of ..... DUMAH
Ishmael's mother .... HAGAR
isinglass .... MICA
Isis, husband of ...... OSIRIS
ISLAM ...... see MOSLEM
d island ... OE, AIT, CAY, KAY,
  KEY, EYOT, HOLM, ILOT,
  ISLE, ATOLL, ISLET, ISLOT
ISLAND AEGEAN .... see
  GAZETTEER
Island, Argyll .... IONA
island, coral .... ATOLL
island, Dodecanese .... COO,
  KOS, CASO, LERO, SIMI
Island, Great Barrier .. OTEA
island, Gr. (fine marble) PAROS
Island, Gr., pert. to .. CRETAN
island, inhabiting an NESIOTE
ISLAND, INNER HEBRIDES
  see HEBRIDES GAZETTEER
Island, Ionian .... ZANTE
Island, Micronesia .. PONAPE
island, near Ireland .... ARAN
island, near Italy ..... CAPRI
island, off Scotland ... IONA,
  ARRAN
Island, Riga Gulf ..... OESEL
island, river AIT, EYOT, HOLM
island, South Seas .... ARU,
  TAITI, TAHITI, OTAHEITE
Island, west of Sumatra . NIAS
Islands, Gulf of Bothnia ALAND
Islands, Irish .... ARAN
Islands, off Timor ..... LETI
Isle of Man, pert. to .. MANX
islet .... AIT, CAY, HOLM
isolate .... ENISLE

82

Israel .... JACOB
ISRAEL, KING OF .. see KING
                    OF ISRAEL
ISRAELITE . see also HEBREW
            and BIBLICAL
ISRAELITE JUDGE .. see
            BIBLICAL JUDGE
ISRAELITE KING .. see KING
                    OF ISRAEL
Israelite tribe .... DAN
Israelites ...... SION, ZION
issue EMIT, EMERGE, EMANATE
isthmus .... NECK
istle fiber ...... PITA, PITO
it proceeds: music ...... VA
ITALIAN WORDS: (accent marks
omitted throughout)
  arts .... ARTES
  article .... LA
  canal (s) CANALE, CANALI
  chest .... CASSO
  custom house .... DOGANA
  day-breeze .... ORA
  dear .... CARA, CARO
  dough .... PASTA
  drink .... BEVERE
  enough .... BASTA
  evening .... SERA
  enthusiasm .... ESTRO
  feast .... FESTINO
  field .... CAMPO
  food .... PASTO
  from beginning ... DACAPO
  gentleman .... SER
  goodby .... ADDIO
  gondola cabin ..... FELZE
  hamlet ... CASAL, CASALE
  hair .... PELO
  hand .... MANO
  harbor .... PORTO
  harp .... ARPA
  hatred .... ODIO
  Helen .... ELENA
  holiday .. FESTA, FESTE
  host .... OSTE
  Italy .... ITALIA
  judge .... PODESTA
  lady .... DONNA, SIGNORA
  lake .... LAGO
  little .... POCO
  love .... AMORE
  lover .... AMOROSO
  mother .... MADRE
  mountain peak .... CIMA
  nine .... NOVE
  ninth .... NONO

  one .... UNO
  paste .... PASTA
  peak .... CIMA
  pronoun .... MIA
  right .... DESTRO
  Rome .... ROMA
  sign .... SEGNO
  somebody .... UNO
  street .... CALLE
  three .... TRE
  time .... TEMPO
  tour .... GIRO
  town .... CASAL, CASALE
  you .... TU
  voice .... VOCE
  well .... BENE
  with .... CON

Italian actress .... DUSE
It., ancient
        ITALI, OSCAN, SABINE
It. astronomer .... GALILEO
It. author .... SILONE
It. car .... FIAT
It. cathedral city ..... MILAN
It. commune .... ESTE
It. composer .... BOITO,
        GUIDO, VERDI, ROSSINI
It. day breeze .... ORA
It. family .... ESTE,
        CENCI, DORIA, MEDICI
It. family royal name .. ESTE
It. gambling game .... MORA
It. gentleman .... SER
It. guessing game .... MORA
It. lady .... DONA, SIGNORA
It. millet ...... BUDA, MOHA
It. painter .... RENI,
        LIPPI, VINCI, ANDREA,
        CRESPI, GIOTTO
It. poet
        DANTE, TASSO, ARIOSTO
It. resort .... LIDO
It. rice dish ...... RISOTTO
It.: Rome .... ROMA
It. sculptor .... LEONI
It. singer .... AMATO
It. title, early .... SER
It. university city BARI, PADUA
It. violin maker ...... AMATI
It. wine .... ASTI
Italy .... ITALIA
Itch .... PSORA
itemize .... LIST
ivory nut .... ANTA, TAGUA
ivy crowned .... HEDERATED
ivy thicket .... TOD

83

J

Jack in cribbage .... NOB
Jack-in-the-pulpit ARAD, AROID
Jack tree .... JACA
Jackal, Afr. .... THOS
Jackal, India .... KOLA
Jackal, N. Afr. .... DIEB
Jackdaw .... DAW
Jackdaw: Scot. .... KAE
JACKET .. see also GARMENT
Jacket . ETON, JUPE, BOLERO
Jacket, armor .... ACTON
Jacket, Malay .... BAJU
Jackson heroine .... RAMONA
Jacob's brother .. EDOM, ESAU
Jacob's son . DAN, GAD, ASER,
              LEVI, ASHER
Jacob's twin brother ... ESAU
Jacob's wife .. LEAH, RACHEL
Jaeger gull .... SKUA, ALLAN
Jagged line .... ZAG, ZIG
Jai alai .... PELOTA
Jamashid .... YIMA
James II daughter ..... ANNE
Janizaries, Chief of .... DEY
JAPANESE: see also SPECIAL
         SECTION
Jap. aborigine ... AINO, AINU
Jap. admiral .... ITO
Jap.-Am. .... ISSEI,
         KIBEI, NISEI, SANSEI
Jap. army reserve ...... HOJU
Jap. army second line .. KOBI
Jap. art of self-defense . JUDO
Jap. badge, family ..... MON
Jap. badge, imperial . KIRIMON
Jap. beer, rice ... SAKE, SAKI
Jap. beverage .... SAKE
Jap. box, girdle .... INRO
Jap. bush clover ...... HAGI
Jap. cedar .... SUGI
Jap. celery-like vegetable UDO
Jap. cherry .... FUJI
Jap. clogs .... GETA
Jap. deer .... SIKA
Jap. drama ..... NO, KABUKI
Jap. emperor's title .. TENNO
Jap. festival .... BON
Jap. fish .... TAI, FUGU
Jap. food, seaweed
              KOBU, KOMBU
Jap. gods .... KAMI
Jap. happiness god
              EBISU, HOTEI
Jap. harp .... KOTO
Jap. herb, stout .... UDO

Jap. Immigrant .... ISSEI
Jap. mile measure .... RI
Jap. monastery .... TERA
Jap. national park ..... ASO
Jap. naval station .... KURE
Jap. news agency ... DOMEI
Jap. nobleman .... KUGE
Jap. outcast
         ETA, YETA, RONIN
Jap. outer garment
       MINO, HAORI, KIMONO
Jap. parliament .... DIET
Jap. perfecture .... FU
Jap. persimmon .... KAKI
Jap. plane .... ZERO
Jap. plant .... UDO
Jap. primitive ... AINO, AINU
Jap. province, old .. ISE, KAI
Jap. receptacle .... INRO
Jap. salad plant .... UDO
Jap. salmon .... MASU
Jap. sash, kimono ...... OBI
Jap. school of painting KANO
Jap. ship name .... MARU
Jap. sock .... TABI
Jap. statesman .... ITO
Jap. straw cape ...... MINO
Jap. sword ... CATAN, CATTAN
Jap. vegetable .. UDO, GOBO
Jap. verse .... UTA
Jap. village .... MURA
Jap. volcano .... FUJI
Jap. writing .... KANA
Japheth, son of ..... GOMER
Jar ... EWER, OLLA, CRUSE
Jar ring .... LUTE
Jar, wide-mouthed ..... OLLA
Jargon . CANT, ARGOT, PATOIS
Jason's father ...... AESON
Jason's 2d wife .... CREUSA
Jason's ship .... ARGO
Jason's wife .... MEDEA
Jaunty .... PERK
Java plum: P. I. .... DUHAT
Javanese carriage .... SADO
Javanese language KAVI, KAWI
Javanese poison tree ... UPAS
Javelin, Afr. ASSAGAI, ASSEGAI
Javelin game .. JERID, JEREED
Javelin, Rom. .... PILUM
Jeer .... GIBE, SCOFF
Jeer at ..... TAUNT, DERIDE
Jehoshaphat, father of .. ASA
Jehovah .... GOD
Jehovah: Hebr. .... JAH,
       JAVE, JAVEH, YAHWEH

84

e jejune .. DRY, ARID, BARREN
jelly base .... PECTIN
jelly fruit .... GUAVA
jelly, meat .... ASPIC
jeopardize .... ENDANGER
Jericho, land opposite . MOAB
jersey, woolen ...... SINGLET
Jerusalem, ancient name
                 SALEM
Jerusalem: poet ...... ARIEL
jest .... JAPE
jester ...... MIME, BUFFOON
jet, U.S. .. SABRE, SCORPION
Jether, son of .... ARA
jetty .... MOLE
Jew .... SEMITE
JEWEL ... see GEM, STONE
jewelry setting .... PAVE
jewels, adorn with ... BEGEM
JEWISH ... see also HEBREW
Jewish ascetic ...... ESSENE
Jewish benediction .. SHEMA
Jewish bride .... KALLAH
Jewish ceremony ... SEDAR,
                 SEDER
Jewish feast of tabernacles
               SUCCOTH
Jewish festival . PURIM, SEDER
Jewish law, body of TALMUD
Jewish marriage contract
               KETUBA
b Jewish offering ... CORBAN
Jewish prayer book . MAHZOR
Jewish scholar .... RAB
Jewish sect, ancient ESSENES
Jewish teacher .. REB, RABBI
Jewish title of honor
          RAB, GAON
Jezebel's husband ..... AHAB
Joan of Arc's victory ORLEANS
Job's-tears .... COIX
jog .... TROT, NUDGE
John: Gaelic, Scot. IAN, EOAN
John: Ir. .... EOIN, SEAN
John: Russ. .... IVAN
johnny-cake .... PONE
Johnson, Dr., hero . RASSELAS
join ...... LINK, PAIR, SEAM,
      WELD, YOKE, MERGE,
       UNITE, ATTACH
join corners ... MITER, MITRE
join wood .... RABBET
joining bar .... YOKE
joint HIP, KNEE, NODE, HINGE
joint part ... TENON, MORTISE
joke with KID, RIB, JAPE, JOSH
joker .... WAG, WIT
Jordan city, ancient region
              PETRA
Joseph's father ...... JACOB
Joseph's nephew ...... TOLA

c Joshua tree .... YUCCA
Joshua's father .... NUN
jostle .... JOG, ELBOW
jot .... IOTA, TITTLE
journey ... ITER, RIDE, TOUR,
      TREK, TRIP, TRAVEL
journey in circuit ...... EYRE
joy ..... DELIGHT, RAPTURE
joyous .... GLAD
Judah, city in .. ADAR, ENAM
Judah's son .... ER, ONAN
Judaism scriptures
          TORA, TORAH
Judge DEEM, RATE, ARBITER
JUDGE, BIB. ... see BIBLICAL
              JUDGE
Judge in Hades ...... MINOS
judge of dead, Egypt. ..OSIRIS
judge's bench .... BANC
judge's chamber ... CAMERA
judges' rule, Israel KRITARCHY
judgment, Fr. law ..... ARRET
JUDICIAL see also LEGAL, LAW
judicial assembly ..... COURT
jug, large beer ...... RANTER
jug shaped like man ... TOBY
jug, wide-mouthed ..... EWER
juice .... SAP
juice, thickened ...... RHOB
jujitsu .... JUDO
jujube .... BER, ELB
Jules Verne character .. NEMO
d Juliet's betrothed .. PARIS
Juliet's father, family CAPULET
jumble ...... PI, PIE, MESS
jump: music .... SALTO
jumping disease, Malay LATA
jumping rodent ... JERBOA
juncture, line of ...... SEAM
June bug .... DOR
Jungfrau's site .... ALPS
jungle clearing ...... MILPA
juniper .... GORSE,
     SAVIN, SABINE, SAVINE
juniper, Europ. .... CADE
juniper tree, Bibl. EZEL, RETEM
Jupiter .... JOVE
Jupiter's moon, inner ... IO
Jupiter's wife ... HERA, JUNO
jurisdiction .... VENUE
jurisdiction, old Eng. SOC, SOKE
jurisprudence .... LAW
jury list .... PANEL
jury, writ summoning . VENIRE
just .... MORAL
justice, goddess of . MA, MATT
jute .... DESI
Jutlander .... DANE
jutting rock .... TOR
juxtaposition, place in APPOSE
jynx .... SPELL

85

K

Kaffir language .... XOSA
Kaffir tribe .... ZULU
Kaffir war club .... KIRI
Kaffir warrior .... IMPI
Kalmuck .... ELEUT, ELEUTH
Kandh language .... KUI
kangaroo, male ..... BOOMER
kangaroo, young .... JOEY
Katmandu's country .. NEPAL
kava .... AVA
kava bowl .... TANOA
Kaw .... AKHA
Keats poem-1820 .... LAMIA
keel .... CAREEN
keel, at right angle to ABEAM
keel block wedge .. TEMPLET
keel, having no ...... RATITE
keel, kind of .... FIN
keel, part of .... SKEG
keel-shaped part
          CARINA, CARINAE
keen . ACUTE, SHARP, ASTUTE
keep account of .... TAB
keepsake .... TOKEN
keeve .... KIVER

b Kentucky coffee tree . CHICOT
Kentucky college ..... BEREA
kerchief .... MADRAS
kernel .... NUT
ketch, Levant .... SAIC
ketone, liquid .... ACETONE
ketone, oily ...... CARONE
kettledrum NAKER, ATABAL,
     ATTABAL, TIMPANI, TIM-
     PANO, TYMPANO
key .... ISLE
key fruit .... SAMARA
key notch .... WARD
key part .... BIT
key-shaped ..... URDE, URDY
keyed up .... AGOG
Khedive's estate ...... DAIRA
kid, undressed ...... SUEDE
kidney .... NEER
kidney bean .... BON
kidneys, pert. to ..... RENAL
killer whale .... ORCA
kiln ...... OST, OAST, OVEN
kiloliter .... STERE
kind
   ILK, SORT, GENRE, SPECIES
kind: Gr. .... GENOS
kindle: dialect .... TIND
kindly .... BENIGN
kindness .... LENITY
kindred .... SIB

king ..... REX, REY, REGES
king —, cartoon character
                      AROO
King Alfred's city: abbr. . LON
king, Amalekite ...... AGAG
King Arthur's abode . AVALON,
          AVALLON, CAMELOT
King Arthur's burial place
          AVALON, AVALLON
King Arthur's court CAMELOT
King Arthur's father . UTHER
King Arthur's fool . DAGONET
King Arthur's lance ... RON
King Arthur's mother IGERNA,
     IGERNE, YGERNE, IGRAINE
King Arthur's queen
     GUINEVER, GUINEVERE
KING, BIBLICAL ...... see
                BIBLICAL KING
King Ethelred "The —"
                   UNREADY
king, Gr. .... MINOS
King Gradlon's capital .... IS
king, Hebrew .... HEROD
king, Midianite .... REBA
king, mythical .... MIDAS
king of beasts .... LION

d King of Colchis' daughter
                     MEDEA
king of Crete .... MINOS
king of elves ...... ERLKING
king of gods, Egypt.
     AMEN, AMON, AMUN
king of Greece, ancient MINOS
king of Israel .. AHAB, ELAH,
     OMRI, SAUL, NADAB
king of Jews .... HEROD
king of Judah ... ASA, AHAZ,
     AMON, UZZIAH
king of Judea .... HEROD
king of Naples ...... MURAT
king of Persia ...... CYRUS
king of Sodom .... BERA
king, pert. to ..... REGNAL
king, Phrygian ...... MIDAS
king, rich ...... CROESUS
king, Spartan AGIS, LEONIDAS
king, Teut. Visigoth . ALARIC
king's bodyguard .... THANE
king's yellow .... ORPIMENT
KINGDOM . see also COUNTRY
kingdom, ancient ..... MOAB
KINGDOM, BIB. . see page 197
kingfish .... HAKU, OPAH
kinkajou .... POTTO
kinship, Moslem law .. NASAB
Kipling hero .... KIM

a

kismet	FATE
kiss	BUSS, SMACK
kitchen, ship's	GALLEY
kitchen tool	CORER, RICER, GRATER
kite, bird	GLED, GLEDE, ELANET
kittiwake gull, Shetlands	WAEG
kitty, feed the	ANTE
kiwi	ROA
knave	ROGUE
knave, in cribbage	NOBS
knave of clubs	PAM
knead	ELT
knead, in massage	PETRIE
knee: Lat.	GENU
kneecap	ROTULA, PATELLA
KNIFE	see also DAGGER
knife	CHIV, STAB, MACHETE, MACHETTE
knife, Burmese	DAH, DOW
knife dealer	CUTLER
knife, Eskimo	ULU
knife, large	SNY, SNEE
knife, loop-cutting	TREVAT, TRIVAT, TRIVET
knife, P. I.	BOLO
knife, single-edge	BOWIE
knife, surgical	SCALPEL
knight	SIR, RITTER, TEMPLAR
knight, heroic	PALADIN
knight, make	DUB
knight, medieval	BEVIS
knight's mantel	TABARD

c

knight's wife	DAME
knitting stitch	PURL
knob: anat.	CAPUT
knobbed	TOROSE
knobkerrie	KIRI
knoblike	NODAL
knockout	KO, KAYO
knot	MILE, NODE, NODI, SNAG, GNARL, KNURL, NODUS
knot, fiber	NOIL, NOYL
knot in wood	BURL, KNAR, KNOR, KNUR, NURL
knot, insecure	GRANNY
knot lace	TAT, TATT
knot, like a	NODAL
knot of thread	BURL
knots, fiber	NEP
knots, having	NODED
know	KEN, WIST
knowledge	KEN, LORE
knowledge, pert. to	GNOSTIC
knowledge, pure	NOESIS
known as milo maize, grain	MILO
knucklebones, sheep	DOLOS
kobold	NIS, NISSE
Kol dialect	HO
kopecks, 100	RUBLE
Koran chapter	SURA
Koran interpreters	ULEMA
Korea	CHOSEN
Korean president	RHEE
Korean soldier	ROK
Kronos' wife	RHEA
kurrajong tree	CALOOL

L

b

"La Boheme" heroine	MIMI
Laban, daughter of	LEAH
label	TAG, PASTER
LABOR GROUP	see UNION
laborer, China	COOLY, COOLIE
laborer, India	TOTY
Labrador tea	LEDUM
labyrinth	MAZE
lac	RESIN
lace	BEAT, LASH
lace, barred	GRILLE, GRILLEE
lace, Fr.	CLUNY, ALENCON
lace, gold, silver	ORRIS
lace, metal tip of	AGLET, AIGLET
lace, square hole	FILET
lacerate	RIP, TEAR
laceration	RIP, TEAR
lack	NEED, WANT
lack of power	ATONY

d

Laconian clan group	OBE
Laconian subdivision	OBE
ladder, scale fort wall with	SCALADE, SCALADO, ES-CALADE, ESCALADO
ladderlike	SCALAR
lady, India	BIBI
"Lady of the Lake" outlaw	DHU
ladylove, in poetry	DELIA
lagoon	LIMAN
lake	MERE
lake, Afr. salt	SHAT, SHOTT
lake, Blue Nile source	TANA
Lake Erie battle officer	PERRY
Lake, Great (5)	ERIE, HURON, ONTARIO, MICHIGAN, SU-PERIOR
lake, mountain	TARN
lake near Galilee sea	MEROM
lake, resort	TAHOE

lake: Scot. .... LOCH
Lake Tahoe trout ...... POGY
lake whitefish ...... POLLAN
lama, head .... DALAI
lamb ...... EAN, EWE, YEAN
lamb, holy .... AGNUS
lamb: Lat. .... AGNI, AGNUS
lamb, young .... COSSET
Lamb's pen name ...... ELIA
Lamech, ancestor of ... CAIN
Lamech's son
        NOAH, JABAL, JUBAL
lament .... KEEN, WAIL,
        WEEP, GRIEVE, PLAINT
lamentation .... LINOS
lamp black .... SOOT
lamprey .... EEL
lance head .... MORNE
lance, mythical .... RON
lance rest, breastplate FAUCRE
lance, short .... DART
Lancelot's beloved ... ELAINE
lancer, Ger. .... ULAN, UHLAN
lancewood .... CIGUA
land, absolute property ALOD,
    ALLOD, ALODIUM, ALLODIUM
land amid water . ISLE, ISLET
land breeze .... TERRAL
land, church's ...... GLEBE
land held in fee simple
                ODAL, UDAL
land: law .... SOLUM
LAND MEASURE .... see also
    AREA in SPECIAL SECTION
land measure
    AR, ARE, ROD, ACRE, ROOD
land ownership, pert. to ODAL
land snail genus .... CERION
land spring .... LAVANT
land, tilled, plowed: Sp.
            ARADA, ARADO
land under tenure: Scot. .. FEU
landing place .... KEY, PIER,
        QUAI, QUAY, LEVEE
landing place, India
                GAUT, GHAT
landing ship .... LST
landmark .... COPA
landmark: Sp. ...... SENAL
lands .... ACRES
language, Aramaic ... SYRIAC
language, Assam .... AO, AKA
language, dead ...... LATIN
language, early It. .... OSCAN
language, Egypt. ..... COPTIC
language, Finnish ... UGRIC
language form, peculiarity
                    IDIOM
language, Gilgit .... SHINA
language, Hittite .... PALA
language, Indic .... HINDI

language, Indo-Chin. ..... AO,
    WA, AKA, ANU, LAI, LAO,
    MRO, MRU, PWO, SAK,
    AHOM, AKHA, AMOY,
    BODO, GARO, KAMI, NAGA,
    RONG, SGAU, SHAN
language, Ir. . CELTIC, KELTIC
language, Kandh .... KUI
language, Kashmir ... SHINA
language, Mossi ... MO, MOLE
language, N. Afr. ... BERBER
language of Bible days
                    ARAMAIC
language, P. I.
        TAGAL, TAGALOG
language, Scot. CELTIC, KELTIC
language, Semitic ... ARABIC
language, Siberian
        ENISEI, YENISEI
language, S. Afr. ...... TAAL
language, Sudanic . MO, MOLE
language, synthetic .. RO, IDO
language, Welsh
            CELTIC, KELTIC
languages, E. Europ. ... UGRIC
languish ...... FLAG, PINE
languor, drug-induced
            KEF, KAIF, KIFF
langur .... MAHA
lantern feast .... BON
Laomedon's father .... ILUS
Laomedon's son
            PRIAM, TITHONUS
Laos aborigine ... KHA, YUN
lapel .... REVER
lapidate .... STONE
Lapp's sledge .. PULK, PULKA
larboard .... APORT
larch . TAMARAC, TAMARACK
large amount .... SCAD
lariat .... LAZO, ROPE,
        LASSO, REATA, RIATA
lariat, metal eye of
    HONDA, HONDO, HONDOO
larva .... GRUB
larva of fly ...... BOT, BOTT
lash .... TIE, WHIP
lasso
    ROPE, REATA, RIATA, LARIAT
last .... FINAL, OMEGA
last but one .... PENULT
"Last Days of Pompeii" char-
    acter .... IONE
last Imam .... MAHDI
last section .... FINALE
Last Supper picture ... CENA
Last Supper room . CENACLE
latching: naut. ...... LASKET
late ... NEW, TARDY, RECENT
late, one at school .... SERO
lateen-rigged boat ..... DOW,
        DHOW, SETEE, MISTIC

latent .... DORMANT
lateral .... SIDE
lath .... SLAT
LATIN ...... see also ROMAN
LATIN:
  abbot .... ABBAS
  above ..... SUPER, SUPRA
  about .... CIRCITER
  across .... TRANS
  act .... ACTU, ACTUS
  after .... POST
  aged .... AET (abbr.)
  all .... TOTO
  alone ..... SOLO, SOLUS
  and .... ET
  and others ... ETAL (abbr.)
  around .... CIRCUM
  art .... ARS
  backward .... RETRO
  before .... ANTE
  behold .... ECCE
  being .... ESSE
  believe, I .... CREDO
  beneath .... INERA
  bird .... AVIS
  book .... LIBER
  blessed .... BEATA
  bronze .... AES
  but .... SED
  cattle .... PECORA
  country ...... RUS, RURIS
  cup .... CALIX
  custom .... RITUS
  day .... DIEM
  days .... DIES
  depart! .... VADE
  divination by lots ... SORS,
                 SORTES
  door .... JANUA
  earth .... TERRA
  egg .... OVUM
  eight .... OCTO
  error .... LAPSUS
  event .... REI
  evil ...... MALA, MALUM
  fate .... NONA
  field .... AGER
  fields .... AGRI
  fire .... IGNIS
  first .... PRIMUS
  fish .... PISCES
  force .... VIS
  from .... DE
  go! .... VADE
  god .... DEUS
  goddess .... DEA
  gods .... DI
  gold .... AURUM
  good ..... BONUM, BONUS
  grandfather .... AVUS
  he .... ILLE

  he remains .... MANET
  he was .... ERAT
  head .... CAPUT
  high .... ALTA
  himself .... IPSE
  I love .... AMO
  in so far as ...... QUA
  is .... EST
  itself .... IPSO
  ivory .... EBUR
  journey .... ITER
  knee .... GENU
  lamb .... AGNI, AGNUS
  land .... AGER
  learned .... DOCTUS
  life .... VITA, ANIMA
  lo .... ECCE
  man .... VIR
  mass .... MISSA
  mine .... MEUM
  more than .... SUPER
  mountain .... MONS
  name .... NOMEN
  nose, of the ...... NAS
  not .... NON
  observe .... NOTA
  offense ..... MALA, MALUM
  once .... SEMEL
  or .... AUT
  other .... ALIA
  over .... SUPER
  pardon .... VENIA
  palm .... VOLA
  part .... PARS
  partly .... PARTIM
  peace .... PAX
  pin .... ACUS
  pledge .... VAS
  possessive .... SUA
  power .... VIS
  pronoun .... SUA
  property .... BONA
  quickly .... CITO
  rate .... RATA
  religious law ...... FAS
  right .... DEXTER
  same .... IDEM
  scarcely VIX
  see .... VIDE
  side .... LATUS
  table .... MENSA
  tail .... CAUDA
  that is .... "ID EST"
  that one .... ILLE
  the same .... IDEM
  thing .... RES

Latin

(continued from page 89)

this one .... HIC, HAEC
thus .... SIC
throat .... GULA
to be .... ESSE
to use .... UTOR
tooth .... DENS
toward .... AD
twice .... BIS
under .... SUB
unless .... NISI
vein .... VENA
voice .... VOX
water .... AQUA
we .... NOS
well .... BENE
where .... UBI
within .... INTRA
without .... SINE
wool .... LANA
wrong ..... MALA, MALUM

Latvia, native of ...... LETT
laugh .... FLEER
laugh, able to ...... RISIBLE
laughing .... RIANT
laughing, pert. to ... GELASTIC
laurel .... BAY, DAPHNE
laurel bark, medicinal ... COTO
lava .... AA, LATITE, SCORIA
lava, rough .... AA
lavender, Eur. .... ASPIC
lavish affection ...... DOTE
law
    JURE, RULE, CANON, EDICT
law, abstract .... JUS
law, D. E. Ind. .... ADAT
law excluding women from
    reign .... SALIC
law of Moses .. TORA, TORAH
law, Rom. .... JUS, LEX
lawful ...... LEGAL, LICIT
lawgiver, Gr.
    DRACO, MINOS, SOLON
lawgiver, Hebr. ...... MOSES
lawmaker .... SOLON
lawyer .... LEGIST
lawyers' patron saint ... IVES
lay .... PUT, DITTY
layer .... PLY, LAMINA,
    STRATA, STRATUM
layer of a plant .... PROVINE
layer, wood .... VENEER
layman .... LAIC
lazar .... LEPER
lazy .... OTIOSE
lead-colored .... LIVID
lead: music . PRESA, PRECENT
lead, ore .... GALENA

lead, pellets of .... SHOT
lead, pencil ..... GRAPHITE
lead sulphide, native GALENA
lead telluride ...... ALTAITE
lead, white .... CERUSE
leaden color, having ... LIVID
leader, fishing ...... SNELL
leader of movement .... VAN
leader, Rom. .... DUX
leaf appendage ..... STIPEL
leaf-cutting ant ...... ATTA
leaf division .... LOBE
leaf, fern .... FROND
leaf, flower .... BRACT, SEPAL
leaf-miner beetle ..... HISPA
leaf of book .... FOLIO
leaf vein .... RIB
league, Ger. .... BUND
league, trading ..... HANSE
Leah's father .... LABAN
Leah's son .... LEVI
lean ... CANT, GAUNT, SPARE
lean-to .... SHED
Leander's love ...... HERO
"Leaning Tower" city .. PISA
leap: LUNGE, VAULT, CURVET
leap: music .... SALTO
leap: Scot. .... LOUP, LOWP,
    STEND
leaping .... SALTANT
learned . ERUDITE, LETTERED
learning .... LORE
learning, man of
    SAGE, PEDANT, SAVANT
Lear's daughter ..... REGAN
Lear's faithful follower KENT
least bit .... RAP
leather bottle ...... MATARA
leather flask, Gr. ...... OLPE
leather, glove
    KID, NAPA, MOCHA, SUEDE
leather, kind of ... ELK, BOCK
leather, prepare—make into
    TAN, TAW
leather, soft
    NAPA, ALUTA, SUEDE
leather thong, hawk's . BRAIL
leatherfish .... LIJA
"leatherneck" ...... MARINE
leave
    GO, QUIT, EXEAT, DEPART
leave destitute ..... STRAND
leave of absence, school EXEAT
leaven .... YEAST
leave-taking .... CONGE
leaves, having: Her. . POINTE
leaving .... ORT
leavings ... DREGS, RESIDUE
Lebanese port, old .... TYRE
ledge, fort .... BERM, BERME
ledger entry
    ITEM, DEBIT, CREDIT

lee, opposed to ...... STOSS
leeangle .. LEAWILL, LEEWILL
leer .... OGLE
Leeward Island .... NEVIS
left: comb. form ...... LEVO
left-hand .... LEVO
left-hand page .. VO, VERSO
left, to turn .... HAW
leftover .... ORT
leg, covering, ancient PEDULE
leg, front of .... SHIN
leg joint, animal ...... HOCK
leg-like part .... CRUS
leg of mutton, lamb . GIGOT
leg, part of ... SHIN, SHANK
leg, pert. to calf of .. SURAL
legal action suit .. RES, CASE
legal claim .... LIEN
legal delays .... MORAE
legal injury .... TORT
legal job .... CASE
legal matter .... RES
legal offense .. DELIT, DELICT
legal order .... WRIT
legal paper .... DEED
legal profession ... BAR, LAW
legal prosecution ...... SUIT
legend ... MYTH, SAGA, TALE
legion division, Rom. COHORT
legislate .... ENACT
legislative assembly, Afr. RAAS
legislator .. SOLON, SENATOR
legislature ... DIET, SENATE
legislature: Sp. ..... CORTES
legume ... PEA, POD, BEAN
leisure .... REST, OTIUM
lemur .... MAKI, INDRI,
    LORIS, AYE-AYE, SEMIAPE
lemur, Afr. .... GALAGO
lemur, Asia, Ceylon LORI, LORIS
lemur, Ceylonese ...... LORI
lemur, flying ..... COLUGO
lemur, ruffed .... VARI
lemuroid .... POTTO
lengthily, address . PERORATE
Leningrad's river ...... NEVA
lens, hand .... READER
lentil .... ERVUM
leopard .... PARD
Leporidae, one of the .. HARE
leprosy .... LEPRA
Lepus genus, one of ... HARE
lerp .... LAAP
Lesbos, poet of ...... ARION
"Les Etats —" .... UNIS
less .... MINUS
lessen BATE, ABATE, MITIGATE
let HIRE, RENT, LEASE, PERMIT
let bait drop .... DAP
let it stand! ...... STA, STET

let up .... ABATE
lethal .... FATAL
lethargy
    COMA, STUPOR, TORPOR
letter .. AR (18), EF (6), EM
    (13), EN (14), EX (24),
    WY (25), BEE (2), CEE (3),
    DEE (4), ESS (19), GEE (7),
    JAY (10), PEE (16), TEE
    (20), VEE (22), WYE (25),
    ZED (26), ZEE (26), AITCH
    (8)
letter, according to . LITERAL
letter, Ang.-Sax. .. EDH, ETH
letter, early Gr. .... SAN
LETTER, GR. and NUMBER see
    also GREEK LETTER
letter, Gr. .. MU, NU, PI, XI,
    CHI, ETA, PHI, PSI, RHO,
    TAU, BETA, IOTA, ZETA,
    ALPHA, DELTA, GAMMA,
    KAPPA, OMEGA, SIGMA,
    THETA, LAMBDA, EPSI-
    LON, OMICRON, UPSILON
letter, Hebr. .. HE (5), PE (17),
    AIN (16), MEM (13),
    NUN (14), SIN (21), TAV
    (22), TAW (22), VAU
    (16), WAW (16), ALEF
    (11), AYIN (16), BETH
    (2), CAPH (11), ELEF (1),
    KAPH (11), KOPH (19),
    QOPH (19), RESH (20),
    SADE (18), SHIN (21),
    TETH (9), YODH, (10),
    ALEPH (13), GIMEL (3),
    LAMED (12), DALETH (4),
    LAMEDH (12)
letter of resignation .. DEMIT
letters, sloping ...... ITALICS
lettuce, kind of COS, ROMAINE
Levantine ketch ...... SAIC
levee .... DIKE, DYKE
level EVEN, RASE, RAZE, PLANE
leveling slip .... SHIM
lever ..... PRY, PEVY, PEAVY,
    PEEVY, PEAVEY, PEEVEY,
    TAPPET
levy ... TAX, CESS, IMPOST
Lew Wallace hero ...... HUR
Lhase holy man ...... LAMA
Lhasa's country ...... TIBET
liability .... DEBT
liana .... CIPO
liang .... TAEL
liar .... ANANIAS
Liberian native .... VAI, VEI
Liberian tribes . GI, KRA, KRU
license: slang ...... READER
lichen .... MOSS
lichen genus USNEA, EVERNIA

91

a lichen, kind **PARELLA, PARELLE**
lie in wait .... **LURK**
Liege, town near ...... **ANS**
liegeman .... **VASSAL**
lieu .... **STEAD**
life .... **BIOS, BIOTA**
life: Lat. .... **VITA, ANIMA**
life, of .... **VITAL**
life principle .... **PRANA**
life principle, Hindu . **ATMAN**
life prolonger ...... **ELIXIR**
life, relating to
   BIOTIC, BIOTICAL
life tenant .... **LIVIER**
lifeless **AMORT, AZOIC, INERT**
lifetime .... **AGE**
lifted with effort ...... **HOVE**
ligament .... **BOND**
light ...... **LAMP, KLEIG,
   KLIEG, TAPER, ILLUME**
light and fine, as lines **LEGER**
light as a line .... **LEGER**
light bulb filler ..... **ARGON**
light, circle of
   HALO, NIMB, NIMBUS
light intensity unit ..... **PYR**
light, kind of .... **ARC**
light ring .... **CORONA**
light, science of .... **OPTICS**
light, sun's ...... **AUREOLA,
   AUREOLE**
b light unit **PYR, LUMEN, HEFNER**
lighter, lamp .... **SPILL**
lighter, make ...... **LEAVEN**
lighthouse .... **PHAROS**
lightning: poet. ...... **LEVIN**
ligulate .... **LORATE**
like .... **AS, AKIN**
likely .... **APT**
likeness ...... **ICON, IMAGE**
likewise not .... **NOR**
lily .... **LIS, LYS, ALOE,
   ARUM, SEGO, CALLA**
lily family plant ...... **CAMAS,
   CAMASS, CAMMAS**
lily genus .... **ALOE**
lily genus, plantain ... **HOSTA**
Lily Maid of Astolat
   ELAIN, ELAINE
lily, palm .... **TI**
limb .... **ARM, LEG, MANUS**
limber .... **LITHE**
lime, to hydrate ..... **SLAKE**
lime tree ...... **TEIL, TEYL**
limestone, grainy .... **OOLITE**
limestone, Irish ...... **CALP**
limestone, soft **MALM, CHALK**
limicoline bird **SNIPE, PLOVER**
limit .... **TERM, BOURN,
   STENT, STINT, BOURNE**
limn .... **DRAW, PAINT**
Lindbergh's book .... **WE**

c linden ...... **LIN, TEIL, TEYL**
line .... **ROW, RANK**
line, cutting ...... **SECANT**
line, fine, on type letter **CERIF,
   SERIF, CERIPH**
line, fishing .... **SNELL**
line, in a .... **AROW**
line, intersecting .... **SECANT**
line inside of .... **CEIL**
line, math .... **VECTOR**
line, naut. . **EARING, MARLINE**
line not forming angle **AGONE**
line on a letter ...... **SERIF**
line, pert. to ...... **LINEAR**
line, thin ..... **STRIA, STRIAE**
line, waiting .... **CUE, QUEUE**
line with stone **STEAN, STEENE**
lines, marked with
   RULED, STRIATE, STRIATED
lines, telescope-lens ..**RETICLE**
linen .... **CREA**
linen, fine ..... **LAWN, TOILE**
linen, household, table **NAPERY**
linen, one caring for royal
   NAPERER
linen tape, braid ...... **INKLE**
linger .... **WAIT, TARRY**
lingo .... **ARGOT**
lingua .... **GLOSSA**
liniment .... **ARNICA**
d link .... **YOKE, CATENATE**
links connected ... **CATENAE**
linnet .... **TWITE, LENARD**
lion .... **LEO, SIMBA**
lion group .... **PRIDE**
lion killed by Hercules **NEMEAN**
lion of God .... **ALI**
lionet .... **CUB**
lips, pert. to .... **LABIAL**
liqueur ..... **CREME, NOYAU**
liqueur, sweet .... **GENEPI**
liquid element
   BROMIN, BROMINE
liquid, made **FUSIL, FUSILE**
liquid, without ... **ANEROID**
liquor **GIN, RUM, RYE, GROG**
liquor, malt .... **ALE, PORTER**
liquor, oriental ..... **ARRACK**
liquor, P. I. .... **VINO**
liquor, Russian **VODKA, VODKI**
liquor, sugar-cane
   TAFIA, TAFFIA
Lisbon's river .... **TAGUS**
lissome .... **SVELTE**
list .... **ROTA, SLATE,
   ROSTER, CATALOG, CATA-
   LOGUE**
list of persons
   ROTA, PANEL, ROSTER
list, one of a .... **ITEM**
listen .... **HARK, HEAR**
listless, be .... **MOPE**

listlessness .. ENNUI, APATHY
liter, Dutch .... AAM, KAN
literary collection .... ANA
literary extracts
     ANALECTA, ANALECTS
literary master ...... STYLIST
literary scraps, bits
     ANA, NOTES
literate . LEARNED, LETTERED
lithograph .... CHROMO
Lithuanian ..... BALT, LETT
litter, E. Ind. . DOOLI, DOOLY,
    DOOLEE, DOOLEY, DOOLIE
"Little Boy Blue" poet .. FIELD
little casino .... TWO
little chief hare .... PIKA
little: music .... POCO
liturgy .... RITE
live ... all forms of verb "BE"
live oak, Calif. ...... ENCINA
lively ... PERT, BRISK, PEART
lively, make .... PERK
lively: music
    VIVO, DESTO, ANIMATO
lively person .... GRIG
lively song .... LILT
liver .... HEPAR
liver, pert. to ...... HEPATIC
liverwort genus ...... RICCIA
livid .... BLAE
living in currents .... LOTIC
Livonian LIV
lixivium .... LYE, LEACH
lizard . GILA, GECKO, GUANA,
    SKINK, VARAN, IGUANA
lizard, Am. ... ANOLE, ANOLI
lizard, beaded .... GILA
lizard, changeable CHAMELEON
lizard genus .. UTA, AGAMA
lizard, large . GILA, MONITOR
lizard, old world .... SEPS
lizard, small ... EFT, GECKO
lizard, starred ...... AGAMA
lizard, tropical ...... AGAMA
lizardlike .... SAURIAN
llamalike animal .... ALPACA
load .... LADE, ONUS
loadstone .... MAGNET
loaf, small: dial. ...... BAP
loam .... LOESS
loam, India .... REGUR
loath .... AVERSE
loathe .... ABHOR
lobster box .... CAR
local .... TOPICAL
locale .... SITE
locality .... AREA,
    LOCUS, VENEW, VENUE
location .. SITE, SPOT, PLACE
lock .... CURL, TRESS

locks, Panama Canal . GATUN
lockjaw .. TETANUS, TRISMUS
locust .... ACACIA,
    CICADA, CICALA
locust, N. Z. .... WETA
lodge, soldier's ...... BILLET
lofty dwelling .... AERIE
log birling contest .... ROLEO
log drive, escape work on SNIB
log, spin floating ...... BIRL
log splitter .... WEDGE
logarithm unit .... BEL
loge .... STALL
logger's implement .. PEAVY,
    PEAVEY
logic, omission of step in
    proof .... SALTUS
logician .... DIALECTOR
Lohengrin's wife ...... ELSA
Loire, city on .... BLOIS
loiter .... LAG
Loki's daughter ... HEL, HELA
Loki's son .... NARE
Loki's wife .... SIGYN
London district ...... SOHO
long .... YEN, PINE,
    CRAVE, YEARN, ASPIRE
long ago .... ELD, YORE
long journey . TREK, ODYSSEY
long line (fishing) with hooks
    TROT
long live! .... VIVA, VIVE
long-suffering .... MEEK
look .... LO, SEE
look after ..... MIND, TEND
look askance .... LEER
look at ... EYE, SCAN, VIEW
look here! .... HIST
look narrowly ... PEEK, PEEP,
    PEER
look slyly ..... LEER, OGLE
loom, heddles of ...... CAAM
loom, lever in .... LAM
loon genus .... GAVIA
loon, kind of .... DIVER
loop, edging .... PICOT
loophole .... MUSE, MEUSE
looplike structure, anat. ANSA
loose .... LAX
loose coat PALETOT, MANTEVIL
loose robe .... SIMAR
loosen ...... UNDO, UNTIE
lop .. SNED, PRUNE, SNATHE
lopsided ...... ALOP, ALIST
loquat tree .... BIWA
Lord High Executioner in
    "Mikado" .... KOKO
Lord: Jacobite Church ... MAR
lord, Oriental .... KHAN
lord, Pers. .... KAAN,
    KAUN, KAWN, KHAN
lord, privileged ... PALATINE

93

lord, Scot. .... LAIRD
lore, Norse .... RUNE
lorica .... CUIRASS
"Lorna Doone" character RIDD
lose .... AMIT
"Lost Chord" finale ... AMEN
lot .... FATE
Lotan's father .... SEIR
Lot's birthplace .... UR
Lot's father .... HARAN
Lot's son .... MOAB
lottery prize .... TERN
lotus enzyme ...... LOTASE
Lotus poet .... LOTE
lotus tree .... SADR
loud: music .... FORTE
loud-voiced one ... STENTOR
loudness, measurement unit
PHON
loudspeaker for high sound
TWEETER
loudspeaker for low sound
WOOFER
Louis XVI's nickname .. VETO
Louisiana county .... PARISH
Louisiana native .... CREOLE
lounge ...... LOAF, LOLL
love JO, GRA, ADORE, AMOUR
love: Anglo-Irish ...... GRA
love apple .... TOMATO
love feast .... AGAPE
LOVE GOD see GOD OF LOVE
LOVE GODDESS see GOD-
DESS OF LOVE
love, inflame with
ENAMOR, ENAMOUR
love knot .... AMORET
love to excess .. DOAT, DOTE
lover .... ROMEO
"Love's Labour's Lost" con-
stable .... DULL
loving
FOND, AMATIVE, AMATORY
low ...... MOO, BASE
low caste Hindu .. PASI, TELI
low caste Indian .... DOM,
MAL, GADDI
Lowell, poetess .... AMY
lower ABASE, DEBASE, NETHER
lower: arch. .... VAIL
lower jaw, bird's .... MALA
lower world gods, Rom. MANES
lowest deck .... ORLOP
lowest part of base .. PLINTH

lowest point .... NADIR
loyal .... LEAL,
TRUE, STANCH, STAUNCH
loyalist .... TORY
lozenge .... PASTIL, ROTULA
TROCHE, PASTILE, PASTILLE
loyalty fulfilling religious
obligations: Rom. .PIETAS
Lubeck, pert. to ...... LUBS
lucerne .... MEDIC, ALFALFA
luck: Ir. .... CESS
luck, pert. to .... ALEATORY
lucky stroke .... FLUKE
lugubrious .... SAD
lukewarm .... TEPID
lumber along .... LOB, LOBB
Lumber State ... see page 208
lumberman .... SAWYER
lumberman's boot ...... PAC
lumberman's boots
PACS, OVERS
lumberman's hook ..... PEVY
PEAVY, PEEVY, PEAVEY,
PEEVEY
luminaire .... LAMP
luminary .... STAR
lump .... NUB, WAD,
CLOT, NODE, SWAD
lunar crater .... LINNE
lunar god, Phrygian ... MEN
luncheon .... TIFFIN
lurch .... CAREEN
lure ...... BAIT, DECOY
luster ...... GLOSS, SHEEN
lusterless . DIM, MAT, MATTE
lustrous .... NITID
lute, Oriental .... TAR
luxuriant ..... LUSH, RANK
luxuriate .... BASK
Luzon native .... ATA, ITA
AETA, ATTA, TAGAL,
TAGALA
Luzon negrito .... ATA,
AETA, ITA, ATTA
Luzon pagan .... ITALON
Lynette's knight .... GARETH
lynx, Afr. .... SYAGUSH
lynx, Pers. .... CARACAL
lyrebird genus .... MENURA
lyric .... ODE, MELIC
lyric Muse .... ERATO
Lytton heroine .... IONE

M

macaque Indian ...... BRUH, RHESUS
macaw .... ARA, ARARA
macaw, Braz.
    ARA, ARARA, MARACAN
mace-bearer .... BEADLE
macerate .... RET, STEEP
machine, finishing ... EDGER
machine, grain cleaner AWNER
machine gun ... BREN, STEN
machine, hummeling . AWNER
machine, ore-dressing VANNER
machine part
    CAM, PAWL, TAPPET
machine, rubber .. EXTRUDER
mackerel net .... SPILLER
mackerel, young ...... SPIKE
Madagascar mammal . LEMUR
Madagascar native .... HOVA
madam .... MUM, MAAM
madder .... RUBIA, MUNJEET
madder, common Eu. GARANCE
madder shrub genus .. EVEA
madness .... MANIA
mafura tree .... ROKA
maggot .... LARVA
Magi, one of .... GASPAR
magic .... RUNE
magic: Hindustan JADU, JADOO
magic, pert. to ..... GOETIC
magic stone .... AGATE
magic: W. Ind. .... OBEAH
magician .... MAGE,
    MAGI, MAGUS, MERLIN
magistrate, Athens . ARCHON
magistrate, It. ...... DOGE
magistrate, Rom. .... EDILE,
   AEDILE, CONSUL, PRETOR
magnate ... MOGUL, TYCOON
magnifying glass ...... LENS
Magog, ruler of ...... GOG
magpie ... MAG, PIE, MAGG,
   PIET, PIOT, PYAT, PYET,
   NINUT, PIANET
magpie genus .... PICA
mah-jongg piece ...... TILE
mahatma
   ARAHT, ARHAT, ARAHAT
mahogany pine ..... TOTARA
mahogany, Sp. ...... CAOBA
mahogany streak ...... ROE
mahogany tree, Ind. ... TOON
MAHOMET . see MOHAMMED
MAHOMETAN .. see MOSLEM
maid .... LASS, BONNE
maid, lady's .... ABIGAIL
maid-of-all-work ..... SLAVEY
maid, Oriental
   AMA, IYA, AMAH, EYAH
maiden .... DAMSEL

maiden name, signifying . NEE
maiden of myth .... IO
mail .... POST, SEND
mail, coat of BRINIE, BYRNIE
mail, India DAK, DAUK, DAWK
main point .. NUB, GIST, PITH
maintain AVER, HOLD, ASSERT
maize .... CORN
maize bread .... PIKI
maize genus .... ZEA
major: music .... DUR
major third: Gr. mus. . DITONE
make .... RENDER
make as one: obs. ..... UNE
make evident .... EVINCE
make fast: naut. ..... BELAY
make good by action REDEEM
make happy .... ELATE
make public: Old Eng. DELATE
Makua .... KUA
malarial fever .... AGUE
malarial poison
    MIASM, MIASMA
Malay apple .... KAWIKA
Malay conce
  PRAH, PRAO, PRAU, PROA
Malay chief or headman DATO,
    DATU, DATTO
Malay dagger ... CRIS, KRIS,
  CREES, KREES, CREESE,
    KREESE
Malay lanseh tree .... DUKU
Malay law .... ADAT
Malay lugger .... TOUP
Malay negrito ..... ATA, ITA
Malay nerve ailment .. LATA
MALAY OUTRIGGER see
    MALAY CANOE
Malay title of respect . TUAN
Malay ungulate ...... TAPIR
Malay verse form ... PANTUN
Malay vessel
  PRAH, PRAO, PRAU, PROA
Malay, word meaning dark
    AETA
Malayan ape .... LAR
male cat .... GIB, TOM
male figure, used as support
    ATLAS, TELAMON
male swan .... COB
malefic .... EVIL
malic acid, fruit with
   ATTA, APPLE, GRAPE
malign .... REVILE
malignant .... EVIL
malignant spirit .. KER, KERES
malleable ... SOFT, DUCTILE
mallet .... MALL, GAVEL
malt drink, pert. to ..... ALY
malt infusion .... WORT
maltreat .... ABUSE

MAMMAL .. see also ANIMAL
mammal, sea aquatic .. SEAL OTTER, WHALE, DUGONG, MANATEE
mammoth .... GIANT
man-eating monster ... LAMIA
man, handsome ..... ADONIS
man, rich .... CROESUS
man's name   ELI, GUY, IAN, IRA, JOB, LEE, RAY, REX, ADAM, ALAN, AMOS, BRAM, CARL, DANA DION, EBEN, EMIL, ENOS, ERIC, EVAN, EZRA, HANS, HUGH, HUGO, IVAN, JOEL, JOHN, JOSE, JUAN, JUDE, KARL, KNUT, LEON, LUKE, MARC, MARK, NEIL, NOEL, OTTO, OWEN, PAUL, SEAN, SETH, TEIG, BASIL, CALEB, CLARE, ENOCH, HIRAM, HOMER, SERGE, STEVE, TERRY, DEXTER, GASPAR, GEORGE, OLIVER, SAMSON, STEVEN, WARREN
man's nickname AL, ABE, ALF, BEN, BOB, DON, GUS, JIM, JOE, KIT, LEW, LON, LOU, MAC, MAT, MAX, MOE, NED, PAT, ROB, SAM, SID, SIM, TED, TOM, ABIE, ALGY, ANDY, BART, BERT, BILL, BONY, DAVE, DAVY, DICK, DODE, FRED, GENE, JACK, JAKE, JOCK, JOEY, MART, MIKE, MOSE, NOLL, PETE, PHIL, RUBE, TOBY, TONY, WALT, ZACH, ZEKE
manageable .... YARE
manager .... GERENT
Manasseh, city of ..... ANER
Manasseh's son of ... AMON
mandarin's home   YAMEN, YAMUN
manducate .... EAT
maned .... JUBATE
manger ...... CRIB, CRECHE
mangle .... MAUL
mango, P. I. ...... CARABAO
mania .... CRAZE
manifest .... SHOW, OVERT, ATTEST, EVINCE
manifestation .... AURA
manifestation of god of lower world .... SERAPIS
maniple FANO, FANON, FANUM
manner   AIR, WAY, MIEN, MODE
manner of walking ... GAIT
manners .... MORES
manor .. DEMENE, DEMESNE

mantis crab .... SQUILLA
mantle .... CAPE
manual training, Swed. SLOID, SLOYD
manuao .... IAO
Manxman .... GAEL
many .... MAINT
many-colored   PIED, PINTO, MOTLEY
many-colored stone ... AGATE
Maori tattooing ...... MOKO
Maori village .. KAIK, KAIKA
Maori wages .... UTU
Maori war club .... MERE, MARREE
Maori war-club wood .. RATA
map .... PLAT
map in a map ...... INSET
maple fruit, seed .. SAMARA
maple genus .... ACER
maple tree top .... SPILE
mar .... DEFACE
marabou .... ARGALA
marble MIB, MIG, TAW, MIGG, AGATE, AGGIE, MARMOR, MEALIE, SHOOTER
marble, Belgian RANCE, RANSE
marble, choice .. ALAY, ALLEY
Marble, It. .... CARRARA
marble, Rom. ...... CIPOLIN
marble, white .... DOLOMITE
marbles, game at ..... TAW
March King .... SOUSA
more: Gypsy .... GRASNI
margin . RIM, EDGE, MARGE
marginal reading, Hebrew Bible .... KRI
margosa tree .... NIM, NEEM
Marie Wilson, character played by .... IRMA
MARINE .. see also SEA
marine annelid .... LURG
marine fish, E. Ind. .. DORAB
marine measure, Jap. .... RI
marine snail   WELK, WILK, WHELK
marine snail genus .. NERITA
marine turtle genus .. CARETTA
marine worm ...... SYLLID
marionette maker ... SARG
mark   STIGMA, STIGMATA
mark, diacritic TILDE, MACRON
mark of omission ..... CARET
mark, reference   OBELI, OBELUS, OBELISK
mark, short vowel ... BREVE
marked with spots: bot. NOTATE
marker, Gr. & Rom. .... STELA, STELE, STELAE, STELAI

market .... **MART, SELL,
VEND, RIALTO**
market: India .... **PASAR**
market, Oriental
SUQ, SOOK, SOUK
market place **BAZAR, BAZAAR**
market place, Gr. ... **AGORA**
marksman .... **AIMER**
marmalade tree
MAMEY, SAPOTE
marmoset .... **MICO**
marmoset, S. Am. .. **TAMARIN**
"Marner, —" Eliot novel **SILAS**
marriage, absence of **AGAMY**
marriage notice **BAN, BANNS**
marriage portion, pert. to
DOTAL
marriage portion: Scot.
DOS, DOTE
marriage settlement .. **DOS,
DOT, DOWRY, DOWERY**
marriage vows .... **TROTH**
marriageabe .... **NUBILE**
marrow .... **PITH**
marry .... **WED, WIVE**
Mars .... **ARES**
Mars' outer satellite . **DEIMOS**
Mars, pert. to .... **AREAN**
"Marseillaise" author . **LISLE**
marsh .... **BOG, FEN,
SLUE, LIMAN, SWALE**
marsh elder .... **IVA**
marsh fever .... **HELODES**
marsh gas .... **METHANE**
marsh hen .... **RAIL**
marsh mallow ...... **ALTEA**
marsh marigold ...... **CAPER**
marsh plant
REED, SEDGE, FESCUE
marshal, Waterloo .... **NEY**
marshy **PALUDAL, PALUDINE**
marsupial, arboreal
COALA, KOALA, POSSUM
marten .... **SOBOL**
martyr, 1st Christian **STEPHEN**
marvel .... **MIRACLE**
Mascagni heroine .... **LOLA**
MASCULINE
see also **MALE, MAN'S**
mashy .... **IRON**
masjid .... **MOSK, MOSQUE**
mask, half .... **DOMINO**
mask topknot, Gr. .... **ONKOS**
masons' pickax ..... **GURLET**
masquerade cloak .. **DOMINO**
mass ...... **GOB, WAD, BULK**
mass book .... **MISSAL**
mass meeting .... **RALLY**
mass, pert. to .. **MISSATICAL**
mass, rounded .... **BOLUS**
mast .... **SPAR**

mast: obs. .... **SPIR**
mast, support .... **BIBB**
mast, wood for ...... **POON**
master' archaic .... **DAN**
master, India
MIAN, SAHEB, SAHIB
master, pert. to ...... **HERILE**
master, S. Afr. ...... **BAAS**
master-stroke .... **COUP**
mastic tree .... **ACOMA**
masticate ..... **CHAW, CHEW**
mat, ornamental ..... **DOILY**
match, friction ..**FUSEE, FUZEE**
match, wax .... **VESTA**
matchmaker .... **EROS**
MATERIAL ... see also **FABRIC**
maternity goddess, Egypt. **APET**
matgrass .... **NARD**
math quantity **SINE, OPERAND**
math ratio quantity **PI, SINE**
math term hyperbolic function
COSH, SECH, SINH, TANH
matter: law .... **RES**
matter-of-fact ..... **LITERAL**
matter: philos. .... **HYLE**
mattress case .... **TICK**
mature .... **AGE, RIPE, RIPEN**
mature reproductive cell
GAMETE
maul .... **MALLET**
Mau Mau territory .. **KENYA**
Mauna — .... **LOA**
mausoleum, at Agra ... **TAJ**
maw: dialect .... **MAA**
maxilla ...... **JAW, MALA**
maxim .. **SAW, ADAGE AXIOM**
GNOME, MOTTO SAYING
maxwell per ampere turn **PERM**
May 1, Celtic ...... **BELTANE**
May fly .... **DUN**
MAYAN ..see **MAYAN INDIAN**
page 192
Mayan year .... **HAAB**
Mayan year-end days .. **UAYEB**
mayor, Sp. **ALCADE, ALCALDE**
meadow .... **LEA MEAD**
meadow barley .... **RIE**
meadow grass genus .... **POA**
meadow mouse ..... **VOLE**
meadow saxifrage .... **SESELI**
meadowsweet **SPIREA, SPIRAEA**
meager .... **SCANT**
LENTEN, SCANTY
meal .... **REPAST**
meal, boiled .... **MUSH**
meal, fine .... **FARINA**
meal, grain **PINOLA, PINOLE**
meal, Indian, Hindu **ATA, ATTA**
meal, light .... **BEVER**

Meaning

a
meaning ... **SENSE, PURPORT**
meantime .... **INTERIM**
MEASURE .. Area, Liquid, Dry
    Length, Distance
       see SPECIAL SECTION
measure .... **EM, EN, GAGE,
      METE, PACE, GAUGE**
MEASURE, BIB. . see HEBREW
               MEASURE
measure, Chin. length .... **LI**
"Measure for Measure"
    character ...... **ANGELO**
MEASURE, DRY, BIB. .... see
    HEBREW DRY MEASURE
measure, Jap. distance .. **RI**
measure of distance, Ang.-Ind.
               COSS
measure of spirits ...... **PEG**
measure, old Arab ...... **SAA**
measure, old length .... **ELL**
measure, poetry ...... **SCAN**
measure, square .... **AR, ARE**
meat, cut of ...... **HAM, RIB,
     CHOP, LOIN, FILET,
     STEAK, FILLET**
meat on skewer .... **CABOB,
      KABOB, KEBAB**
meat roll, fried .... **RISSOLE**
Mecca pilgrim garb .. **IHRAM**
Mecca shrine ...... **CAABA,
     KAABA, KAABEH**

b
Mecca, trip to .... **HADJ**
mechanical man ..... **ROBOT**
mechanical part ...... **CAM**
mechanics, branch of **STATICS**
mechanics of motion
           DYNAMICS
meddle ...... **PRY, TAMPER**
Medea's father ...... **AEETES**
median line of valve .. **RAPHE**
medical .... **IATRIC**
medical fluid .... **SERUM**
medicinal capsule ... **CACHET**
medicinal fruit shrub .. **ALEM**
medicinal gum ...... **KINO**
medicinal herb ...... **ALOE,
    IPECAC, BONESET**
medicinal plant ...... **ALOE**
medicinal plant, leaves **SENNA**
medicinal tablet .... **TROCHE**
medicine man ...... **SHAMAN**
medicine man, S. Am.
         PEAI, PIAY
medieval lyric .... **ALBA**
medieval society . **GILD, GUILD**
medieval tale, poem . **LAI, LAY**
Medina Arab .... **AUS**
MEDITERRANEAN .. see also
        GAZETTEER
Mediterranean, East of **LEVANT**
Medit. grass .... **DISS**

c
Medit. herb genus ..... **AMMI**
Medit. island: It .... **RODI**
Medit. resort .... **NICE**
medlar .... **MESPIL**
medley .... **OLIO**
Medusa's slayer .... **PERSEUS**
meet .... **SIT**
meeting .... **TRYST, SESSION**
meeting, political ... **CAUCUS**
megapode .... **MALEO**
melancholy **SAD, BLUE, DREAR**
melancholy: poet. ..... **DOLOR**
mellow .... **AGE, RIPE**
melodic .... **ARIOSE**
melodious .... **ARIOSO**
melody ...... **AIR, ARIA,
    TUNE, MELOS**
melon ...... **PEPO, CASABA**
melt together .... **FUSE, FUZE**
melted .... **MOLTEN**
membership .... **SEAT**
membrane ...... **WEB, TELA,
    VELA, VELUM**
memento .... **RELIC**
memorabilia .... **ANA**
memorandum ... **CHIT, NOTE**
memorial post, Indian **TOTEM**
memory, pert. to
   MNESIC, MNEMONIC

d
Memphis chief god .... **PTAH**
Memphis street, famous **BEALE**
men .... **SONS**
mendacious person .... **LIAR**
mender, chief ...... **TINKER**
mendicant, Mos.
    FAKIR, FAKEER
Menelaus' wife ...... **HELEN**
menhaden fish ...... **POGY**
menhaden, young .. **SARDINE**
Mennonite .... **AMISH**
Menotti heroine ..... **AMELIA**
men's party .... **STAG**
mental .... **PHRENIC**
mental deficiency ... **AMENTIA**
mental deficient **IDIOT, MORON**
mention .... **CITE**
Mercator ...... **MAP, CHART**
mercenary . **VENAL, HIRELING**
merchandise .... **WARES**
merchant .... **TRADER**
merchant: India ...... **SETH**
"Merchant of Venice" heiress
          PORTIA
merchant ship ...... **ARGOSY**
merchant vessel, Gr. **HOLCAD**
Mercury, Gr. ...... **HERMES**
Mercury's wand .. **CADUCEUS**
mercy, show .... **SPARE**
mere .... **SIMPLE**
merely .... **ONLY**

a merganser duck SMEW, GAR-BILL
merge .... MELD
merit .... EARN
merriment .... GLEE
merry-go-round .. CAROUSAL, CAROUSEL, CARROUSAL
"Merry Widow" composer LEHAR
"Merry Wives" character PISTOL
mesh .... NET, WEB
Mesopotamia .... IRAK, IRAQ
Mesopotamian boat GUFA, KUFA
Mesopotamian city ... URFA
mesquite bean flour .. PINOLE
mess, to make a .... BOTCH
mestizo .... METIS
metal .... TIN, MONEL
metal alloy .... BRASS, MONEL, BRONZE
metal, bar of .... INGOT
metal bar on house door RISP
metal casting .. PIG, INGOT
metal, coat with PLATE, TERNE
metal-decorating art . NIELLO
metal disk .... MEDAL
metal dross .... SLAG
metal filings .... LEMEL
metal fissure .... LODE
b metal leaf .... FOIL
metal mixture ...... ALLOY
metal refuse .... SCORIA
metal spacer: print. .... SLUG
metal suit .... MAIL
metal sulfide, impure . MATTE
metal white .... TIN
metallic rock .... ORE
metalwart, lacquered ... TOLE
metalwork, god of .. VULCAN
metarabic acid .... CERASIN
meteor .... LEONID
meteor, exploding BOLIS, BOLIDE
meter, Dutch .... EL
meter, one-millionth . MICRON
meters, 100 sq. ... AR, ARE
metheglin .... MEAD
method .... PLAN, ORDER
Methuselah's grandson . . NOAH
methyl-phenol CRESOL, CRESSOL
metric measure .. AR, ARE, GRAM, KILO, LITER, METER, STERE, DECARE, HECTARE
metric "quart" .... LITER
metrical beat .... ICTUS
metrical unit .... MORA
metropolitan .... URBAN
mew .... GULL
mew, cat's .... MIAU, MIAW, MIAOU, MIAUL

c Mexican dollar .... PESO
Mex. mush .... ATOLE
Mex. painter .... RIVERA
Mex. persimmon ... CHAPOTE
Mex. plant .... JALAP
Mex. president .... ALEMAN, CALLES, MADERO
Mex. resin tree ...... DRAGO
Mex. rodent .... TUCAN
Mex. slave .... PEON
Mex. spiny tree .... RETAMA
Mex. timber tree ... ABETO
Mex. wind instrument CLARIN
mezzanine .... ENTRESOL
miasma .... MALARIA
mica, kind of ..... BIOTITE
mica of muscovite .... TALC
microbe .... GERM
microspores .... POLLEN
middle .... MESAL, MESNE, MEDIAN
middle, in the ..... ATWEEN
middle, toward ...... MESAD
middling .... SOSO
MID-EAST land .... IRAK IRAQ
Midgard Serpent slayer THOR
midge .... GNAT
midship, off .... ABEAM
d "Midsummer Night's Dream" character .. PUCK, SNUG
midwife: India ...... DAHI
mien .... AIR
might .... POWER
mignonette .. GREEN, RESEDA
migrate .... TREK
migratory worker OKIE, ARKIE
Mikado's court . DAIRI, DAIRO
Milanion's wife ... ATALANTA
Milan's "Met" ... LA SCALA
mild .... SHY, MEEK, SOFT, BLAND, GENTLE
mildness .... LENITY
mile: naut. .... KNOT
mile, part of, Burma ... DHA
Miled, son of .. IR, ITH, EBER
milestone .... STELE
milfoil .... YARROW
military award .... DSO
military cap .... KEPI
military command .. AT EASE
military group CADRE, CORPS
military maneuvers . TACTICS
milk, coagulated ..... CURD
milk coagulator ..... RENNIN
milk, curdled ..... CLABBER
milk, part of SERUM, LACTOSE
milk, pert. to .... LACTIC
milk: pharm. .... LAC
milk protein ...... CASEINE

a milk, watery part of ... WHEY
milkfish ...... AWA, SABALO
Milky Way .... GALAXY
mill .... QUERN
MILLET
   see also GRAIN SORGHUM
millet, India JOAR, JUAR, CHENA
millimeter, 100th part MICRON
millstone support ..... RYND
millwheel board .... LADE
millwheel bucket ...... AWE
Milton, masque by .. COMUS
Milton rebel angel .... ARIEL
mime .... APER
mimic ... APE, APER, MIME
mimicking, practice of . APISM
mimosa .... ACACIA
minced oath . GAD, GED, GEE,
   LUD, DRAT, EGAD, HECK,
   OONS, SWOW, MAFEY,
   MACKINS
mind .... CARE, TEND
mind, opposite of: Hindu
   ATTA, ATMAN
mind: philos. .... NOUS
Mindanao native, Indonesian
   ATA, AETA, MORO
mine ceiling .... ASTEL
mine entrance .... ADIT
mine narrow veins .... RESUE
b mine passage .... STULM
mine roof support ..... NOG
mine shaft drain pit ... SUMP
mine step .... LOB
mineral, alkaline .... TRONA
mineral, blue ...... IOLITE
mineral group ..... URANITE
mineral group, pert. to SALIC
mineral, hard
   SPINEL, SPINELLE
mineral, lustrous ...... SPAR
mineral, raw, native ... ORE
mineral salt .... ALUM
mineral, soft .... TALC
mineral spring .... SPA
mineral tar .... BREA
mineral, transparent .. MICA
mineral used gun-powder NITER
Minerva .... ATHENA
minim .... DROP
mining refuse .... ATTLE
mining road .... BORD
mining tool .... GAD, BEELE
minister, Moslem VIZIR, VIZIER
minister (to) .... CATER
mink, Amer. .... VISON
minority, legal ...... NONAGE
Minos' daughter ... ARIADNE
Minotaur's slayer .. THESEUS
minstrel .... RIMER
minstrel, medieval .. GOLIARD
minstrel, Norse SCALD, SKALD

c mint .... COIN
mint, Europ. .. CLARE, CLARY,
   CLARRY, HYSSOP, DITTANY
mint genus .... MENTHA
mint herb .... SAGE
mints, the .... NEPETA
minus .... LESS
minute ... WEE, TINY, SMALL
mira .... STAR
miracle, scene of first . CANA
mirage . ... SERAB
miscellany .... ANA
mischief .... HOB
mischievous spirit ..... PUCK
misconceive .... ERR
Mishnah section ABOT, ABOTH
Mishnah section festivals
   MOED
misinterpret .... ERR
mislay .... LOSE
misplay .... ERROR
misrepresent .... BELIE
Miss Dombey's suitor . TOOTS
missile ...... DART, SNARK
missile, guided ... JUNO, NIKE,
   THOR, ATLAS, TITAN,
   BOMARC, JUPITER, PERSH-
   ING, REGULUS, REDSTONE,
   BOLD ORION, MINUTEMAN
mist ... HAZE, SMUR, MISLE
mist: Eng. .... RAG
d mistake, stupid ...... BONER
mistakes .... ERRATA
mistakes, make ...... ERR
mite .... ACARI, ATOMY,
   ACARID, ACARUS
mite genus . ACARI, ACARUS
mite, tick, order of
   ACARIDA, ACARINA
mitigate EASE, ABATE, ALLAY
mix .... STIR, ADDLE, KNEAD
mixture .... OLIO
mixture, mineral .... MAGMA
Moab city, chief .... UR
Moab king .... MESHA
Moabites, Bibl. ...... EMIM
moat .... FOSS, FOSSE
"Moby Dick" pursuer .. AHAB
moccasin .... PAC
mock .... GIBE, JIBE, FLEER,
   TAUNT, DERIDE
mock blow .... FEINT
mock orange ...... SYRINGA
mockingbird genus .. MIMUS
model, perfect .... PARAGON
moderate .... BATE,
   ABATE, LESSEN
modernist .... NEO
modest ...... SHY, DEMURE
modify .... VARY, ALTER,
   EMEND, TEMPER
Mogul emperor ...... AKBAR

MOHAMMEDAN . see MOSLEM
Mohammedanism ..... ISLAM
Mohammed's adopted son ALI
Mohammed's birthplace MECCA
Mohammed's daughter FATIMA
Mohammed's descendant
SAID, SEID, SAYID
Mohammed's son-in-law .. ALI
Mohammed's supporters
ANSAR
Mohammed's title .... ALI
Mohammed's tomb city
MEDINA
Mohammed's uncle ... ABBAS
Mohammed's wife .... AISHA
Mohawk, city on ...... UTICA
Mohicans, last of the UNCAS
moiety .... HALF
moist ... WET, DAMP DANK,
DEWY, UVID HUMID
moist spot, rock-ledge .. SIPE
moisten .. DAMPEN, IMBRUE
moisture, having medium
MESIC
mojarra fish .... PATAO
molasses . TREACLE, TRIACLE
molasses, rum made from
TAFIA
mold .... MUST
mold, hole in casting GIT, GEAT
molded clay .... PUG
molding . CYMA, GULA, OGEE,
TORUS, REGLET, REEDING
molding, concave
CONGE, SCOTIA
molding, convex
OVOLO, TORUS, ASTRAGAL
molding, curved CYMA, OGEE
molding, edge of . ARIS, ARRIS
molding flat .... FILLET
molding, rounded TORI, TORUS
molding S-shaped ..... OGEE
molding, square ...... LISTEL
moldings, quarter-round OVOLI
moldy .... MUSTY
mole ...... NEVUS, NAEVUS
mole cricket, S. Am. CHANGA
mole genus .... TALPA
molecule part .... ION
molelike mammal .. DESMAN
MOLLUSK
see also GASTROPOD
mollusk .... CLAM, CHITON,
MUSSEL, ABALONE
mollusk, bivalve ..... SCALLOP
mollusk, chamber-shelled
NAUTILUS
mollusk, gastropod
SNAIL, ABALONE
mollusk genus .ARCA, MUREX
OLIVA, ANOMIA
mollusk, largest ..... CHAMA
mollusk's rasp organ .RADULA
molt .... MEW, SHED

molten rock .. LAVA, MAGMA
moment .... MO, JIFF, TRICE
Monaco, pert. to
MONACAN, MONEGASQUE
monad .... ATOM, UNIT
monastery .... MANDRA
monastery church .. MINISTER
MONEY .. see also SPECIAL
SECTION COINS
money ... CASH, CUSH, GELT
money, Amer. Ind. . WAMPUM
money, bronze .... AES
money certificate BOND, SCRIP
money, copper .... AES
money: dialect ...... SPENSE
money early Eng. ...... ORA
money drawer .... TILL
money exchange fee ... AGIO
money, fishhook .LARI, LARIN
money, medieval ...... ORA
money of account ...... ORA
money, piece of ...... COIN
money premium .... AGIO
money, put in ...... INVEST
money reserve .... FUND
money, shell SEWAN, SEAWAN
money, trade unit .. UNITAS
moneylender ...... USURER
moneylender, Ind. .. MAHAJAN
Mongol . HU, ELEUT, TATAR,
ELEUTH, TARTAR
Mongol dynasty .... YUAN
Mongol warrior ...... TATAR
Mongolian tent .... YURT
Mongoloid ... TURK, DURBAN
Mongoloid in Indo-China SHAN
mongrel .... CUR, MUTT
monitor lizard .... URAN
monk . FRA, FRIAR, CENOBITE
monk, Buddhist .... ARAHT,
ARHAT, ARAHAT
monk, Eng. ..... BEDA, BEDE
monk, Gr. Church .. CALOYER
monk, head .... ABBOT
monk settlement SCETE, SKETE
monk's hood .... COWL
monk's title ... FRA, ABBOT
monkey ..... APE, LAR, SAI,
SIME, SIMIAN, MARMOSET
monkey, Afr. .... MONA,
WAAG, GRIVET
monkey, Asia ...... LANGUR
monkey, capuchin ...... SAI
monkey, Chin. .... DOUC
monkey genus ...... CEBUS
monkey, guenon .... NISNAS
monkey, howling ..... ARABA
monkey, P. I. ...... MACHIN
monkey puzzle ...... PINON
monkey, red, Afr. .... PATAS
money, small .... LEMUR

101

a monkey, S. Am. ... SAKI, TITI, ACARI, ARABA, SAJOU, TETEE, PINCHE, SAGUIN, SAMIRI, SAIMIRI, SAPA-JOU
monkey, spider, genus QUATA, ATELES, COAITA
monkshood .... ATIS, ATEES, ACONITE
monolith .... MENHIR
monopoly ... TRUST, CARTEL
monosaccharide .... OSE
Mons, language of .... PEGU
monster . GOUL, GOWL, OGRE
monster, Gr. myth . CHIMERA
monster, half-man-bull MINOTAUR
monster: med. .... TERAS
monster, 100 eyes .... ARGUS
monster slain by Hercules HYDRA
month, Egypt. .... AHET, APAP, TYBI
month, first day, Rom. CALENDS, KALENDS
month, Hindu ... ASIN, JETH, KUAR, MAGH
month, in last ...... ULTIMO
month, Jewish ancient .... AB (11th), BUL (8th), ZIF (8th), ABIB (7th), ADAR (6th), ELUL, (12th), IYAR (8th), NISAN (7th), SEBAT (5th), SIVAN (9th), TEBET (4th), TIZRI (1st), TEBETH (4th), TISHRI (1st)
b month, Moslem ...... RABIA, RAJAB, SAFAR, SHABAN, RAMADAN
month, Nisan .... ABIB
monument, stone LECH, CAIRN, DOLMEN, CROMLECH
moon . LUNA, DIANA, PHOEBE
moon, age at beginning of calendar year .... EPACT
moon angel .... MAH
moon flower .... ACHETE
moon god, Babyl. . SIN, ENZU
moon goddess ..... ASTARTE
moon goddess, Gr. . SELENA, SELENE, ARTEMIS
moon goddess, Rom. . LUNA, DIAN, DIANA
moon nearest earth, point PERIGEE
moon valley .... RILL, RILLE
moor grass .... NARD
moorhen .... GORHEN
Moorish .... MORISCAN
moose genus .... ALCES
mop .... SWAB, SWOB

c Moqui, one of ....HOPI
morals overseer ..... CENSOR
morass ...... QUAG, MARSH
moray .... EEL
Mordecai, enemy of . HAMAN
more .... PLUS
more! .. BIS, PIU, ENCORE
more than enough ..... TOO, EXTRA, EXCESS
More's Island .... UTOPIA
morepork, N. Z. . PEHO, RURU
morindin dye .... AL
moringa seed .... BEN
morning glory ...... IPOMEA
morning music ..... AUBADE
morning: P. I. ...... UMAGA
morning prayer ..... MATINS
morning song .... MATIN
Moro .... SULU, LANAO
Moro chief ..... DATO, DATU, DATTO
Moro mantle .... JABUL
Moroccan Berber ..... RIFF
Moroccan land, public . GISH
Moroccan native .... MOOR
moron ...... AMENT, IDIOT
morose .. BLUE, GLUM, GRUM
morsel .... ORT
d mortar implement ... PESTLE
mortar ingredient ..... LIME
mortar mixer .... RAB
mortar tray .... HOD
mortise insert ...... TENON
Mosaic law ... TORA, TORAH
mosaic piece ..... TESSERA
Moselle, river to ..... SAAR
Moses, law given to here SINA, SINAI
Moses' brother ..... AARON
Moses' death mountain . NEBO
Moses' father-in-law . JETHRO
Moses' spy in Canaan . CALEB
MOSLEM .... see also MECCA
Moslem .... TURK
Moslem ablution before prayer WIDU, WUDU, WUZU
Moslem, Afr. .... MOOR
Moslem beggar FAKIR, FAKEER
Moslem bible .... KORAN
Moslem call to prayer ADAN, AZAN
Moslem chief .... AGA, IMAM, DATTO
Moslem chief gold coin DINAR
Moslem converts ..... ANSAR
Moslem deity . JANN, ALLAH
Moslem demon . JANN, EBLIS
Moslem Easter .... EED
Moslem fast ..... RAMADAN
Moslem festival ..... BAIRAM

a Moslem fiat .... IRADE
Moslem fourth Caliph .... ALI
Moslem grant of property
WAKF, WAQF, WUKF
Moslem guide .... PIR
Moslem holy city .... MECCA
Moslem holy man
IMAM, IMAUM
Moslem, hostile to Crusaders
SARACEN
Moslem in Turkestan .... SALAR
Moslem judge ... CADI, CAZI,
CAZY, KADI, KAZI, KAZY
Moslem leader IMAM, IMAUM
Moslem marriage MOTA, MUTA
Moslem marriage settlement
MAHR
MOSLEM MORO ... see MORO
CHIEF
Moslem mystic .... SUFI
Moslem name .... ALI
Moslem Negroids .... MABA
Moslem noble .... AMIR, EMIR,
AMEER, EMEER
Moslem, N. W. India .... SWAT
Moslem official .... AGA
Moslem, orthodox .... HANIF
Moslem, P.I. .... MORO
Moslem potentate .... AGA
Moslem prayer .... SALAT
Moslem prayer place .... IDGAH
Moslem priest IMAM, IMAUM
b Moslem prince AMIR, EMIR,
AMEER, EMEER
Moslem principle ... IJMA
Moslem pulpit ...... MIMBAR
Moslem reformer ... WAHABI
Moslem religion ...... ISLAM
Moslem religious college
ULEMA
Moslem ruler .... HAKIM
Moslem saber ..... SCIMITAR
Moslem saint .... PIR
Moslem school .... MADRASA
Moslem spirit JINN, JINNI
Moslem spiritual guide PIR
Moslem teacher ALIM, COJA
Moslem temple
MOSK, MOSQUE
Moslem theologians ULEMA
Moslem title AGA, RAIS,
REIS, SEID, SIDI, SYED,
SYUD, CALIF, SAYID,
SEYID, CALIPH
Moslem tunic JAMA, JAMAH
Moslem weight .... ROTL
Moslem woman's dress IZAR
Moslems, Sunnite .... SART
Moslemized Bulgarian POMAK
mosque .... MASJID
mosque, central ...... JAMI
mosque, Jerusalem ... OMAR
mosque student ...... SOFTA

c mosquito, genus, yellow-fever
AEDES
mossbunker fish ...... POGY
moss of Ceylon ...... AGAR
moth .... IO, LUNA,
EGGER, TINEA
moth, clearwing, genus SESIA
moth, clothes .... TINEA
moth, green .... LUNA
mother goddess; Baby. ERUA
mother goddesses, Hindu
MATRIS
mother of Arthur ... IGRAINE
mother of gods .... RHEA
MOTHER OF IRISH GODS .see
page 200
mother-of-pearl ...... NACRE
mother-of-pearl shell. ABALONE
mother turned to stone NIOBE
mother's side, related on
ENATE, ENATIC
mother's side, relation on
ENATE, ENATION
motherless calf DOGY, DOGIE
motion, producing .... MOTILE
motionless .... INERT, STILL
motive ... CAUSE, REASON
motmot, S. AM. ... HOUTOU
motor part .... ROTOR
mottled ...... PIED, PINTO
d mottled as wood ... ROEY
MOULDING . see MOLDING
mound .. TUMP, BARROW
mound, Polyn. .... AHU
Mount of Olives ..... OLIVET
mountain, Alps ...... BLANC
mountain ash SORB, ROWAN
mountain, Asia Minor ... IDA
mountain, Bibl HOR, NEBO,
SEIR, SINA, HOREB,
SINAI, ARARAT
(see others on page 197)
mountain chain ... SIERRA
mountain climbing staff PITON
mountain crest .... ARETE
mountain, Crete .... IDA
mountain, Edom .... HOR
mountain, fabled Hindu MERU
mountain, famous ... IDA
mountain, Gr. .... HELICON
mountain in Thessaly .. OSSA
mountain lion ...... PUMA
mountain mint .... BASIL
mountain, Moab ...... NEBO
mountain pass .... COL
mountain pass, Alps .. CENIS
mountain pass, India
GAUT, GHAT
mountain peak .... ALP
mountain pool .... TARN
mountain recess ...... CWM
mountain ridge .... ARETE

a mountain ridge, Port. . SERRA
mountain, 2nd highest N.A. LOGAN
mountain sickness PUNA, VETA
mountain spinach .... ORACH
mountain spur .... ARETE
mountains, Asia ...... ALTAI
mountains, myth. .. KAF, OAF
mourn .... WEEP, GRIEVE, LAMENT
mournful .... SAD, DIRE
mourning band ...... CRAPE
mouse .... VOLE
mouse, field .... VOLE
mouse genus .... MUS
mousebird .... COLY, SHRIKE
mouth .... OS, ORA
mouth, away from ... ABORAL
mouth open .... AGAPE
mouth, river .... DELTA
mouth, tidal river ..... FRITH
mouth, toward .... ORAD
mouthful .... SIP, SUP
mouthlike orifice ..... STOMA
mouthpiece .... REED, BOCAL
move .... STIR, AFFECT
move a camera .... PAN
move back .... EBB, RECEDE
move to and fro
WAG, FLAP, SWAY

b movement: biol. ...... TAXIS
movement, capable of MOTILE
movement: music ..... MOTO
movement, with: music
CONMOTO
movie: Sp. .... CINE
moving part .... ROTOR
mow, barn's .... LOFT
mow of hay .... GOAF
mowed strip .... SWATH
Mowgli's bear friend . BALU, BALOO
Mozambique native ..... YAO
muck .... MIRE
mud .... MIRE, MURGEON
mud deposit .... SILT
mud, slimy .... OOZE
mud, stick in .... MIRE
mud, viscous .... SLIME
mud, volcano .... SALSE
muddle .... MESS, ADDLE
muddy .... ROIL
muffin .... GEM
mug .... STEIN, NOGGIN
mug, small .... TOBY
mugger .... GOA
mulatto .... METIS
mulberry bark cloth .. TAPA
mulberry genus ..... MORUS
mulberry, India .... AL, AAL
mulct .... FINE, AMERCE
mullet, red .... SUR

c multiform .... DIVERSE
multiplicand: math. FACIEND
multiplier: math. ... FACIENT
multitude ..... HOST, HORDE
mum .... ALE
munch .... CHAMP
mundane .... TERRENE
Munich's river ...... ISAR
municipal officer, Sp. ALCADE, ALCAID, ALCAIDE, ALCAYDE
muntjac deer . KAKAR, RATWA
murder by suffocation . BURKE
murder fine, Scot. ..... CRO
murderer, first .... CAIN
murmuring sound
CURR, PURL, PURR
Musci, plant of ...... MOSS
muscle .... THEW, SINEW
muscle coordination, lack of
ATAXIA
muscle, deep, pert. to
SCALENE
muscle, kind of
ERECTOR, LEVATOR
muscle, like .... MYOID
muscle, round, rolling . TERES
muscle, stretching .. TENSOR
muscles .... BRAWN
muscular action, irregular
ATAXIA

d muscular spasm .... TIC
Muse, chief ...... CALLIOPE
muse in reverie .... REVE
Muse of astronomy .. URANIA
Muse of comedy ..... THALIA
Muse of dancing TERPSICHORE
Muse of history ...... CLIO
Muse of lyric poetry
CLIO, ERATO
Muse of music ..... EUTERPE
Muse of poetry ...... ERATO
Muse of sacred lyric
POLYMNIA
Muse of tragedy MELPOMENE
Muses, 9 .... PIERPIDES
Muses' region .... AONIA
Muses, The .... NINE
musette .... OBOE
museum head ... CURATOR
mush .... ATOLE, SEPON
mushroom ... MOREL, MORIL
mushroom cap ...... PILEUS
music: as written ...... STA
music character .... DOT, CLEF, REST
music drama .... OPERA
music for nine ...... NONET
music for three .... TRIO
music for two .... DUET
music from the sign: abbr. DS

a
music hall .... ODEA, ODEON, ODEUM
music interval .... TRITONE
music: it proceeds .... VA
music lines .... STAFF
music piece
SERENATA, SERENATE
music, sacred
CHORAL, CHORALE
music symbols, old .. NEUME
MUSICAL ... see also MUSIC
musical beat .... TAKT
musical composition, India
RAGA
musical direction . STA, TACET
musical instrument ... ASOR, DRUM, FIFE, GIGA, HARP, HORN, LUTE, LYRE, OBOE, PIPE, REED, TCHE, TUBA, TURR, VINA, VIOL, CELLO, RAPPEL, SPINET, CLAVIER, HELICON, OCARINA
musical sign DOT, CLEF, REST
musical study .... ETUDE
musical work .... OPUS
musician, 11th century GUIDO

c
musket ball, India ...... GOLI
Musketeer .... ATHOS, ARAMIS, PORTHOS
mussel, fresh-water .... UNIO
must .... STUM
mustache monkey ..MOUSTOC
mustard family plant .. CRESS
musteline animal
OTTER, RATEL
mustiness .... FUST
mutilate .... MAIM
muttonbird .... OII
muttonfish .... SAMA
'My Name is —" ..... ARAM
mysteries .... ARCANA
mysterious .... OCCULT
mystery .... RUNE
mystic word, Hindu ..... OM
mystic writing .... RUNE
mythical land ..... LEMURIA
mythical stream ...... STYX
mythical submerged island
ATLANTIS
mythical warrior .... ARES
MYTHOLOGY ... see SPECIAL SECTION, Page 198

N

b
nab .... GRAB, ARREST
Nabal's wife: Bibl. ... ABIGAIL
NaCl .... SALT
nahoor shep .... SNA
nail .... CLAW, TALON, UNGUES, UNGUIS
nail, hooked .... TENTER
nail, mining, surveying . SPAD
nail, thin .... BRAD
nail with aperture ..... SPAD
nails, 100 lbs. .... KEG
namaycush .... TOGUE
NAME ...... see also MAN'S NAME, WOMAN'S NAME
name .. DUB, TERM, CLEPE, NOMEN, TITLE, ENTITLE
name: Dan. .... NAAM
name plate, shop's ... FACIA
named ... Y-CLEPT, Y-CLEPED
namely .... VIZ
Naomi, name claimed by MARA
Naomi's daughter-in-law RUTH
naos .... CELLA
nap, coarse, long ..... SHAG
nap-raising device .. TEASEL, TEASLE, TEAZEL, TEAZLE
nap-raising machine .... GIG
nap, to raise .... TEASE
napoleon, game like ... PAM

d
Napoleon's brother-in-law
MURAT
Napoleon's isle .... ELBA
Napoleon's marshal general
NEY
Napoleonic victory JENA, LODI
Narcissus, nymph who loved
ECHO
narcotic ...... DOPE, DRUG, HEROIN, OPIATE
narcotic, India BANG, BHANG
narcotic plant .... DUTRA
narcotic shrub
KAT, KAAT, KHAT
narcotic shrub, S. Am.
COCA, CUCA
narrate .... TELL
narrow ..... LINEAL, STRAIT
nasal .... RHINAL
Nata's wife: myth. .... NANA
nation: Ger. .... VOLK
nation, pert. to ..... STATAL
NATIVE ...... see TRIBES in SPECIAL SECTION, Page 191
native ..... ITE, RAW, NATAL, ENDEMIC, INDIGENE
natural luster, having .. NAIF
natural talent . DOWER, FLAIR
nature .... OUSIA, ESSENCE
nature goddess ..... CYBELE

105

Nature

a nature principal: Hindu . . GUNA
nature spirit . . . . NAT
nature story writer . . . SETON
nautical . . . . MARINE
nautical cry
    AHOY, OHOY, AVAST
Navaho hut . . . . HOGAN
naval hero . . . . PERRY
navy jail . . . . BRIG
near AT, NIGH, ABOUT, CLOSE
Near East native ARAB, TURK
Near East river valley WADI
near the ear . . . . . . PAROTIC
near to . . . . BY, ON
nearest . . . . NEXT
nearsighted person . . . MYOPE
nearsightedness . . . . MYOPIA
neat . . . . . TIDY, TOSH, TRIG,
    TRIM, SPRUCE
neat cattle . . . . NOWT
neatly . . . . FEATLY
necessitate . . . . ENTAIL
neck, nape of . . . . NUCHA
necklace . . . BEADS, RIVIERE
neckline shape
    VEE, BOAT, CREW
neckpiece . . . . ASCOT, STOLE
neckpiece, feather . . . . . BOA
neckpiece, woman's . . . FICHU
NECKTIE . . . . see TIE
b need . . . . . . WANT, REQUIRE
needle . . . . . . PROD, BODKIN
needle bug . . . . NEPA
needle case . . . . ETUI
needlefish . . . . GAR
needlelike bristle . . . ACICULA
needle-shaped . . . . . ACUATE,
    ACERATE
negative . . . . . . NE, NO, NAY,
    NON, NOT
negative pole . . . . . . CATHODE
neglect . . . . OMIT
neglected school subject:
    abbr. . . . . LAT.
negligent . . . . LAX
negotiate . . . . TREAT
negrito . ATA, ATI, ITA, AETA,
    ATTA
NEGRO . . . see also TRIBES in
    SPECIAL SECTION
Negro dance . . . . JUBA
Negro: India . . . . HUBSHI
NEGRO TRIBE . . see SPECIAL
    SECTION
Nelson's victory site . . . NILE
nematocyst . . . . CNIDA
nemesis . . . . BANE
Nepal Mongoloid . . . . . . RAIS
Nepal native . . . . KHA
Nepal people . . . . RAIS
nephew . . . . NEPOTE

c nephew, Fijian . . . . VASU
Neptune . . . . LER
Neptune's spear . . . TRIDENT
nerve cell . . . . NEURON
nerve-cell process . . . . . AXON
nerve layers, brain . . . . ALVEI
nervous . . . . EDGY
nervous disease . . . . CHOREA
nest . . . . NID, NIDE,
    NIDI, NIDUS
nest, eagle's . . . AERY, AERIE,
    EYRY, EYRIE
nested boxes . . . . INRO
nestling . . . . EYAS
net . . . . CLEAR
net, fishing . . . . SEINE,
    STENT, TRAWL
net of hair-lines . . . . RETICLE
NETHERLANDS
    see SPECIAL SECTION
netlike . . . . RETIARY
nettle family . RAMIE, RAMEE
network . . . . WEB, MESH,
    RETE, RETIA
neuroglia . . . . GLIA
neve . . . . FIRN
— Nevis, Gt. Brit. peak . BEN
new . . . . NOVEL, RECENT
New Caledonia bird . . KAGU
New England state: abbr. . RI
d New Guinea area . . . . PAPUA
New Guinea tribesman KARON
New Guinea victory . . . GONA
New Guinea wild hog . . . BENE
New Jerusalem foundation
    JASPER
new, lover of . . . . NEO
new star . . . . NOVA
new wire . . . . MUST
New York harbor isle . . . ELLIS
New Zealand aborigine . ATI
N.Z. bird . . . . . . HUIA, KAKI,
    PEHO, RURU
N.Z. clan . . . . ATI
N.Z. evergreen . . . . TAWA
N.Z. fruit pigeon . . . . . KUKU
N.Z. laburnum . . . . GOAI
N.Z. mollusk . . . . PIPI
N.Z. native . . . . MAORI
N.Z. native fort . . . . UA, PAH
N.Z. parson bird . . . . . . KOKO
N.Z. plant . . . . KARO
N.Z. rail bird . . . . WEKA
N.Z. scabbard fish . . . . HIKU
N.Z. shrub . . . . KARO
N.Z. shrub, poisonous . . TUTU
N.Z. subtribe . . . . HAPU
N.Z. timber tree . GOAI, HINO,
    MIRO, PELU, RATA, RIMU,
    HINAU, HINOU, KAURI,
    KAURY, TOTARA

106

a N.Z. tree .. AKE, KOPI, NAIO,
PUKA, TORO
N.Z. tree, lightwood .. WHAU
N.Z. tribe .... ATI
N.Z. Wages .... UTU
N.Z. wood hen .... WEKA
news agency, Eng. .. REUTERS
news agency, Europ. .. ANETA
news agency, Jap. .. DOMEI
news agency, Rus. Soviet TASS
news paragraph .... ITEM
newspaper service .. AP, UP,
INS, UPI, REUTERS
newspapers .... PRESS
newt .... EFT, EVET, TRITON
nibble .. GNAW, KNAB, KNAP
niche .... RECESS
Nichols' hero .... ABIE
Nick Charles' dog ..... ASTA
Nick Charles' wife .... NORA
nickel steel alloy ..... INVAR
nicotine acid .... NIACIN
nictitate .... WINK
Niger delta native ..... IJO
NIGERIA
see SPECIAL SECTION
Nigerian Negro .... ARO, IBO
Nigerian tribe .... EDO
NIGERIAN TRIBE OR PEOPLE
see also SPECIAL SECTION,
page 191
b niggard .... MISER
nigh .... NEAR
night, Norse ...... NATT, NOTT
nightingale, Pers. ... BULBUL
nightjar .... POTOO
nightmare demon, Teut. MARA
nightmare, the .... INCUBUS
nightshade, black
MOREL, MORIL
Nile, as god .... HAPI
Nile Island .... RODA
Nile native .... NILOT
Nile sailboat .... CANGIA
Nile valley depression .. KORE
Nile, waste matter on
SADD, SUDD
Nilotic Negro .... JUR, LUO,
LWO, SUK
nimble .... SPRY, AGILE
nimbus .... HALO, NIMB
nimrod .... HUNTER
nine-angled polygon NONAGON
nine, based on ...... NONARY
nine, group of ...... ENNEAD
nine inches .... SPAN
nine, music for ...... NONET
Nineveh's founder .... NINUS
ninth day, every .... NONAN
ninth: mus. .... NONA
niton .... RADON

c nitrogen .... AZO, AZOTE
Noah, pert. to ...... NOETIC
Noah's landing ..... ARARAT
Noah's 1st son ... SEM, SHEM
Noah's 2nd son ...... HAM
Nobel prize, literature '04
MISTRAL
Nobel prize, science ... UREY
noble, nobleman .DUKE, EARL,
LORD, PEER, BARON, COUNT
noble: Ger. .... GRAF, RITTER
NOBLEMAN ..... see NOBLE
nobleman, Jap. .... KAMI
nocturnal mammal
BAT, LEMUR
nod .... BOW, BECK
Nod, west of .... EDEN
nodding .... NUTANT
noddy tern: Hawaii .... NOIO
node ...... KNOB, KNOT,
KNUR, NODUS
"— noire" .... BETE
nomad ...... ARAB, SCENITE
Name in Greece .... ELIS
nomenclature .... NAME
nominal value .... PAR
nominate .... NAME
non-gypsy: Romany .... GAJO
non-Jew .... GOI, GOY
non-Moslem of Turkey or
d Ottoman Empire RAIA, RAYA
non-professional .. LAY, LAIC
non-union worker ..... SCAB
nonchalant .... COOL
none: dialect .... NIN
nonsense PISH, POOH, HOOEY
nonsense creature .... GOOP
noodles: Yiddish
FARFEL, FERFEL
nook, sheltered ...... COVE
noose .... LOOP
Norn, one of URD,URTH,WYRD
Norse "Adam" .... ASKR
Norse bard ... SCALD, SKALD
Norse chieftain .. JARL, YARL
Norse epic .... EDDA
Norse explorer ... ERIC, LEIF
NORSE GOD or GODDESSES
see also GODS and GOD-
DESSES and see also SPE-
CIAL SECTION, Page 200
Norse gods .... VANS,
AESIR, VANIR
Norse letter .... RUNE
Norse myth. hero EGIL, EGILL
Norse myth. king ...... ATLI
Norse myth. "Life" force . LIF
Norse myth. woman ... IDUN
Norse neighbor .... FINN
Norse- poetry .... RUNES
Norse prose .... EDDA
Norse sea goddess ..... RAN
Norseman .... DANE, SWEDE

107

a

North African ...... BERBER
N. Afr. outer garment .. HAIK
North Carolina college ELON
North Carolinian .. TARHEEL
North Caucasian language
    UDI, AVAR, UDIC, UDISH
North, Mrs. of fiction PAMELA
North Sea fishing boat COBLE
North Sea, river into
    ELBE, TEES
North Star .... POLARIS
North Syrian deity .... EL
northern .... BOREAL
northern Scandinavian .. LAPP
northern tribe, China .. HU
northernmost land .... THULE
Northumberland river .. TYNE
Norway coin .... ORE
Norway territorial division AMT
Norwegian author HAMSUN
Norwegian composer GRIEG
Norwegian county AMT, FYLKE
Norwegian saint ..... OLAF
nose ...... CONK, NASI,
    NASUS, SNOOP
nose, having large .. NASUTE
nose, having snub ... SIMOUS
nose openings . NARES, NARIS
nose, snub .... PUG
nostrils ..... NARES, NARIS

b

nostrils, of .... NARIC,
    NARIAL, NARINE
"— Nostrum," Mediterranean
    MARE
not at home .... OUT
not ever: poet. .... NEER
not genuine .... TIN
not in style ..... OUT, PASSE
not long ago .... LATELY
not moving .. INERT, STATIC
not one ...... NARY, NONE
not so great ... LESS, FEWER,
    SMALLER
notch ... KERF, NICK NOCK,
    CRENA, CRENAE
notched . SERRATE, SERRATED
note .... CHIT, MEMO
note, double, whole .. BREVE
note, Guido's .... UT, ELA
note, Guido's low .... GAMUT
note, half .... MINIM
note, high, highest ..... ELA
note, marginal
    POSTIL, APOSTIL
note: music .. DI, DO, FA, FI,
  LA, LE, LI, ME, MI, RA, RE,
  RI, SE, SI, SO, TE, TI, SOL
note, old Gr. musical ... NETE
note, old musical ...... ELA
NOTE, SCALE .... see NOTE:
    MUSIC
notes, furnish with ANNOTATE

c

notes in Guido's scale . ELAMI
nothing . NIL, NIX, NUL, NULL,
    ZERO, NIHIL
notion .... BEE, IDEA
notion, capricious ..... WHIM
notional .... IDEAL
notorious .... ARRANT
Nott's son .... DAG
notwithstanding ...... YET
nought ...... ZERO, NULL
NOUN ENDING
    see SUFFIX, noun
noun form .... CASE
noun suffix of condition . ATE
noun with only 2 cases
    DIPTOTE
nourish ...... FEED, FOSTER
nourishment ...... PABULUM
Nova Scotia .... ACADIA
novel, advocate of.... NEO
novel by A. France .... THAIS
novelty .... FAD
novice .... TIRO, TYRO
now: dial. .... NOO
noxious .... MIASMIC
Nubian .... NUBA
nucha .... NAPE
nuclear element .... PROTON
nudge .... POKE
nuisance .... PEST
nullify .... NEGATE

d

nullify, legally .... VOID
number, describable by SCALAR
number under 10 ..... DIGIT
number, whole ..... INTEGER
numbered Bib. .... MENE
numerous MANY, MULTIPLE
nun, Franciscan ..... CLARE
nun, head .... ABBESS
nun's dress .... HABIT
nunbird .... MONASE
nuque .... NAPE
nurse, Oriental, India AMA,
  IYA, AMAH, AYAH, EYAH
nurse, Slavic .... BABA
nursemaid: Fr. ...... BONNE
nut ..... COLA, KOLA, LICHI,
    ALMOND, CASHEW,
    LICHEE, LITCHI
nut, beverage ... COLA, KOLA
nut, hickory .... PECAN
nut, pert. to .... NUCAL
nut, P. I. .... PILI
nut, pine .... PINON
nut, stimulating ..... BETEL
nut tree, Afr. ... COLA, KOLA
nuts for food .... MAST
nuthatch genus ...... SITTA
nutlike drupe .... TRYMA
nutmeg husk .... MACE
nutria .... COYPU

a nutriment ... FOOD, ALIMENT
nutritive .... ALIBLE
nymph ...... MAIA, LARVA
nymph, fountain ...... EGERIA
nymph, laurel ...... DAPHNE
nymph Moslem ...... HOURI

c nymph, mountain .... OREAD
nymph, ocean ..... OCEANID
nymph, water NAIAD, NEREID
nymph, wood DRYAD, NAPEA,
        NAPAEA, HAMADRYAD
Nyx's daughter .... ERIS

O

O, plural .... OES
oaf .... LOUT
oak, Calif. .... ENCINA
oak, dried fruit of .. CAMATA
oak, evergreen .... HOLM
oak mass .... EVERNIA
oak, Turkey .... CERRIS
oakum, seal with .... CALK
oar ... ROW, BLADE, PROPEL
oar at stern .... SCULL
oasis, N. Afr. .. WADI, WADY
oat genus .... AVENA
oats as rent ...... AVENAGE
oath, knight's .... EGAD
oath, old-fashioned ODS, EGAD
oath, say under .... DEPOSE
obeisance, Oriental
        BOW, SALAAM
b obey .... HEED, MIND
object .. AIM, CAVIL, DEMUR
object of art .... CURIO
objection, petty ...... CAVIL
objective .... AIM, GOAL
obligation .... TIE, DEBT,
        DUTY, ONUS
oblique .... CANT, BEVEL,
        SLANT, SLOPE
obliterate ... ERASE, EFFACE
obliteration ...... RASURE
oblivion .... LETHE, LIMBO
oblivion stream ...... LETHE
obscure .... DIM, FOG, DARK,
        BEDIM, CLOUD
obscure, render .... DARKLE
observe . SEE, NOTE, BEHOLD,
        REMARK, CELEBRATE
obstinate .... SET, HARD
obstruction, petty ..... CAVIL
obtain .... GET
obvious .... OPEN, PATENT
obvious, not SUBTLE, SUBTILE
occasional .... ODD
Occident .... WEST
occipital protuberances .. INIA
occultism .... CABALA
occupant .... TENANT
occupation .... TRADE
occupy .... USE, FILL
occurrence .... EVENT

oceanic .... PELAGIC
oceanic tunicate ...... SALP
ocean's rise, fall ...... TIDE
ocher, black .... WAD, WADD
octave, designating high . ALT
octave of church feast .. UTAS
octopus .... POULPE
octoroon
        METIS, MESTEE, MUSTEE
odd-job man .... JOEY
Odin
        WODAN, WODEN, WOTAN
Odin's brother ...... VE, VILI
Odin's granddaughter . NANNA
Odin's son ... TY, TYR, THOR,
        TYRR, VALE, VALI
Odin's wife .... RIND
odor .... AROMA, SCENT
ODYSSEUS..see also ULYSSES
Odysseus' companion ELPENOR
d Odysseus' friend ... MENTOR
Odyssey beggar .... IRUS
Odyssey singer ...... SIREN
Oedipus' father ...... LAIUS
Oedipus' mother ... JOCASTA
of speed of sound .... SONIC
of the age: abbr. .... AET
off .... AWAY
offend .... CAG
offense .... CRIME
offense: law .. MALA, MALUM
offer .... BID, TENDER
offered up .... OBLATE
offhand .... CASUAL
office, ecclesiastic .. MATINS
office, priest's ...... MATINS
office, R. C. curia
        DATARY, DATARIA
officer, church ...... BEADLE
officer, court: Scot. ... MACER
officer, municipal: Scot. BAILIE
officer, Rom. .... LICTOR
officer, synagogue ... PARNAS
officer, university
        DEAN, BEADLE, BURSAR
official, Moslem ...... HAJIB
official, Rom.
        EDILE, AEDILE, TRIBUNE
official, subordinate .. SATRAP
official, weights ...... SEALER
offspring ...... SONS, HEIRS

109

o ogygian . . . . AGED
Ohio college town . . . . . . ADA
oil . . . . FAT, LARD, LUBE,
ATTAR, OLEUM
oil beetle . . . . MELOE
oil bottle . . . . CRUCE, CRUET,
CRUSE, CRUIZE
oil, cruet . . . . AMPULLA
oil, edible . . . . ACEITE
oil, orange . . . . NEROLI
oil, pert. to . . . . OLEIC
oil, rub with . . . . ANOINT
oil-yielding Chinese tree TUNG
oil-yielding tree . . EBO, EBOE
oilfish . . . . ESCOLAR
oilstone . . . . HONE
oily ketone . . . . IRONE
ointment . . . . . . BALM, NARD,
SALVE, CERATE, POMADE
Ojibway secret order
MEDA, MIDE
O.K. . . . . ROGER
okra . . . . . . GOMBO, GUMBO
old . . . AGED, ANILE, SENILE
"Old Curiosity Shop" girl NELL
old English army . . . . . FYRD
old Eng. gold piece . . . RYAL
old Eng. rune . . WEN, WYN
old Greek coin . . . . . . OBOL
old Irish coin . . . . RAP
old Persian money . . DARIC
old person . . . . DOTARD
old Sp. gold coin . . . . DOBLA
OLD TESTAMENT see BIBLICAL
and SPECIAL SECTION
Old Testament objects URIM
b Old Test. people. . PHUD, PHUT
old times . . . . . . ELD, YORE
old-womanish . . . . . . ANILE
oleaginous . . . . OILY
oleander genus . . . . NERIUM
oleic acid salt . . . . OLEATE
oleoresin . . . . ANIME,
ELEMI, BALSAM
olive fly genus . . . . . DACUS
olive genus . . . . OLEA
olive, inferior . . . . . . MORON
olive, stuffed . . . . . . PIMOLA
Oliver's nickname . . . . . NOLL
Olympian deity-god-goddess
ARES, HERA, APOLLO,
ATHENA, HERMES, AR-
TEMIS, DEMETER
Olympus, mountain near OSSA
Olympus queen . . . . HERA
Olympus, region by . . PIERIA
omen . . . . BODE, PRESAGE
omission, vowel . . . . ELISION
omit . . . . . DELE, PASS, SKIP
omit in pronunciation. . ELIDE

c omitted, having part
ELLIPTIC, ELLIPTICAL
onager . . . . ASS
once: dial. . . . . ANES
one . . . . AIN, UNIT
one-base hit . . . . SINGLE
one behind other . . . TANDEM
one-eighth Troy ounce . . DRAM
one-eyed giant . . . . CYCLOPS
one-horse carriage . . . . SHAY
one hundred sq. meters
AR, ARE
one hundred thousand rupes
LAKH
one, music by . . . . SOLI, SOLO
one-spot . . . . ACE
one thousand . . . . MIL
one-year record . . . . . ANNAL
O'Neill heroine . . . . . . ANNA
onion . . . . CEPA
onion, Welsh . . . . CIBOL
onionlike plant . . CIVE, LEEK,
CHIVE, SHALLOT, ESCHALOT
only . . . . MERE, SAVE, SOLE
onward . . . . . . AHEAD, FORTH
onyx, Mex. . . . . TECALI
oorial . . . . SHA
ooze . . . . LEAK, SEEP, SEIP,
SIPE, SYPE, EXUDE
open . . . . . AJAR, OVERT,
BROACH, PATENT, UNWRAP
d open court . . . . AREA
open plain . . . . VEGA
opening . . . . GAP, HOLE,
RIFT, SLOT, VENT, HIATUS
opening, long . . . RIMA, SLOT
opening, mouthlike
STOMA, STOMATA
opening, slit-like . . . . . RIMA
opening, small . . . . . . PORE
opera . . AIDA, BORIS, ORFEO
opera, Beethoven . . . FIDELIO
opera, Bizet . . . . CARMEN
opera composer, modern
BRITTEN, MENOTTI
opera, Gounod . . . . . . FAUST
opera hat . . . . GIBUS
opera heroine . . AIDA, ELSA,
MIMI, SENTA, ISOLDE
opera house, Milan . . . SCALA
opera, Massenet
MANON, THAIS
opera, Puccini . . . . . . TOSCA
opera scene . . . . SCENA
opera singer . . . . MELBA
opera soprano, star . . . ALDA,
PONS, BORI, RISE,
RAISA, STEBER
opera star . . . . DIVA
opera, Verdi . . . AIDA, ERNANI
opera, Wagner . . . . . RIENZI
operate . . . . . . RUN, MANAGE
operetta composer . . . . FRIML

110

a

opium poppy seed ..... MAW
opossum, S. Am. ..... QUICA
opponent .. FOE, ANTI, RIVAL
opportune .... TIMELY
opportunity .... CHANCE
oppose .... IMPUGN
opposed, one .... ANTI
opposed to solo .... TUTTI
opposite .... REVERSE
opposite extremities ... POLES
Ops' daughter ...... CERES
Ops' husband ..... SATURN
optical glass .... LENS
optical illusion ..... MIRAGE
optical instrument lines
.... RETICLE
optimistic ... ROSY, ROSEATE
oracle, Apollo's ...... DELOS
oracle, Gr. . DELPHI, DELPHOI
oral .... PAROL
orange-red stone ...... SARD
orange tincture, Her. ... TENNE
orangutan, Malay ..... MIAS
orarion .... STOLE
orator ...... OTIS, RHETOR
orb of day .... SUN
orbit point .. APSIS, APOGEE
orchid genus .... DISA
orchid leaves for tea
.... FAAM, FAHAM
orchid tuber .... SALEP

b

ordain .... DECREE
order .... BID, FIAT,
.... ARRAY, EDICT, DECREE
order, one of Catholic MARIST
order, put in ... TIDY, SETTLE
orderliness .... SYSTEM
ordinance .... LAW
ordnance piece ..... MORTAR
ore deposit ... LODE, MINE
ore of iron ... OCHER, OCHRE
ore receptacle ..... MORTAR
organ .... EAR, EYE
organ of algae .... PROCARP
organ part .... STOP
organ pipe .... REED
organ pipe, displayed MONTRE
organ prelude .... VERSET
organ, seed-bearing ... PISTIL
organ stop ..... REED, SEXT,
DOLCAN, CELESTE, MELODIA
organism, 1-cell
.... AMEBA, AMOEBA
organism, simple
.... MONAD, MONAS
organization .... SETUP
orgy .... REVEL
Orient .... EAST
Oriental ...... ASIAN, TATAR
Oriental dwelling .... DAR

c

Oriental lute .... TAR
Oriental nursemaid .... AMA,
...... IYA, AMAH, AYAH, EYAH
Oriental plane tree .. CHINAR
Oriental porgy .... TAI
Oriental potentate ...... AGA
Oriental sailing ship .. DHOW
Oriental servant ...... HAMAL
Oriental ship captain .. RAS
Oriental weight .... ROTL
orifice PORE, STOMA, OSTIOLE
orifices, sponge ..... OSCULA
origin .... SEED
original .... NEW
original sin .... ADAM
originate
.... ARISE, START, CREATE
Orinoco tributary ...... ARO
oriole, golden .... LORIOT
ornament .... FRET
ornament, curly ... SCROLL
ornament in relief .. EMBOSS
ornament, spire .... EPI
ornamental border ... DADO
ornamental grass .. EULALIA
ornamental nailhead ... STUD
Orpheus' destination .. HADES
Orpheus' instrument .. LYRE
orris .... IRIS
orris-root ketone, oil .. IRONE
oscillate .... WAVE
osier .... WITHE

d

Osiris, brother .... SET
Osiris' wife, sister ..... ISIS
ostentation .... POMP
ostracism ... TABU, TABOO
ostrich, Am. .... RHEA
ostrich-like bird
.... EMU, EMEU, RATITE
Otaheite apple .... HEVI
Othello was one ...... MOOR
Othello's lieutenant, foe . IAGO
otherwise .... ELSE
otic .... AURAL
otologist .... AURIST
otter brown, color ... LOUTRE
otter genus .... LUTRA
Ottoman .... TURK
Ottoman court ..... PORTE
Ottoman official ..... PASHA
"Our Mutual Friend," ballad-
seller in .... WEGG
oust .... EJECT, EVICT
out .... AWAY, FORTH
out-and-out ...... ARRANT
out: Dutch .... UIT
out of style .... PASSE
out of the way ...... ASIDE
outbreak, unruly ...... RIOT
outburst, sudden ...... SPATE
outcast
.... LEPER, PARIAH, ISHMAEL

outcome, final ...... UPSHOT
outcry .... CLAMOR
outer .... ECTAL
outer portion of earth .. SIAL
outfit   KIT, RIG, GEAR, SUIT
outfit, queer .... GETUP
outlet .... VENT
outlook .... PERIMETER
outlook .... VISTA
outmoded .... PASSE
OUTRIGGER see MALAY CANOE
outward .... ECTAD
ova ... . EGGS
oval ... ELLIPTIC, ELLIPTICAL
oven .... KILN OAST
oven, annealing .. LEER LEHR
oven, Polyn. native ...... UMU
over ...... ATOP, ABOVE,
    AGAIN, ENDED, ACROSS
overnice .... FINICAL
overnice person .... PRIG
over: poet. .... OER
over there .... YON, YONDER
overact .... EMOTE
overcoat .. ULSTER, PALETOT
overdue payment ... ARREAR
overflow .... DEBORD
overfond, be .... DOAT, DOTE
overjoy .... ELATE
overlay .... CEIL
overripe grain .... BRITE
overseer, ranch: Sp. Am.
                    CAPORAL
overshadow ...... DOMINATE
overshoe
    GOLOE, GALOSH, GALOSHE
overskirt   PANIER, PANNIER
overspreading mass .... PALL

overt .... OPEN, FRANK
overwhelm .... DELUGE
overwhelming amount ... SEA
Ovid's "— Amatoria" ... ARS
ovule .... SEED
ovum .... EGG
owala tree .... BOBO
owl, barn, Samoa .... LULU
owl, eagle . BUBO, KATOGLE
owl, horned .... BUBO
owl, S. Asia .... UTUM
owl's cry .... HOOT
own up to .... AVOW
ownership, of land, old law
                ODAL, UDAL
ox, extinct wild ...... URUS
ox, forest .... ANOA
ox, long-haired ...... YAK
ox of Caesar's time ... URUS
ox, wild .... ANOA
ox, wild: India ...... GAUR
        GOUR, ZEBU, GAYAL
oxalis, S. Amer. .... OCA
oxen .... KINE
oxhide strap .... REIM, RIEM
oxide .... CALX
oxidize .... RUST
oxygen compound OXID, OXIDE
oxygen, form of ...... OZONE
oxygen radical ...... OXYL
oyster bed material
        CULCH, CUTCH, CULTCH
oyster drill .... BORER
oyster farm: Fr. ...... PARC
oyster, young .... SPAT
oysterfish .... TAUTOG
Ozarks, town west of in Okla.
                    ADA
Oz books author ..... BAUM

pace .... RATE, STEP
pachisi, kind of ...... LUDO
pachyderm .... ELEPHANT
Pacific aroid food plant TARO
Pacific Island cloth ... TAPA
Pacific pine .... HALA
Pacific shrub .... SALAL
pacify
    CALM, SOOTHE, PLACATE
pack .... WAD, STOW
pack animal .... ASS,
    BURRO, LLAMA, SUMPTER
pack horse .... SUMPTER
pack down ..... RAM, TAMP
package, India .... ROBBIN
package of spun silk . MOCHE
pad .... TABLET

padded jacket under armor
                    ACTON
padnag ...... TROT, AMBLE
Padua, town near ..... ESTE
pagan god .... IDOL
page, "Love's Labor Lost"
                    MOTH
page number .... FOLIO
pageantry .... POMP
"Pagliacci" character . CANIO
"Pagliacci" heroine . NEDDA
pagoda Chinese .... TA, TAA
pagoda ornament .. EPI, TEE
paid notice .... AD
pail .... SKEEL
pain, dull .... ACHE
pain reliever
        OPIATE, ANODYNE
paint, face ... FARD, ROUGE

a pain-killer alkaloid source **COCA**
painted bunting: Creole . **PAPE**
PAINTER   see also ARTIST
        and country of each artist
painter, modernist
                KLEE, MIRO, ERNST
painting style .... **GENRE**
painting, wall .... **MURAL**
pair .... **DUO, DIAD,**
            DUAD, DYAD MATE
pair of horses .. **SPAN, TEAM**
pairing .... **MATING**
palanquin .... **JAUN**
palanquin bearer .... **HAMAL**
palanquin, Jap. .... **KAGO**
palatable, very .... **SAPID**
pale .... **WAN ASHY,**
            ASHEN PASTY
pale color .... **PASTEL**
pale-colored .... **MEALY**
Palestine in Jewish use **ERETS**
palisade: fort .... **RIMER**
Pallas .... **ATHENA**
pallid .... **WAN PALE**
palm ..... **TI, COCO TALA,**
TALIPAT, TALIPOT, TALI-
PUT
palm, Afr. .... **DUM**
palm, Asia ... **ARENG, BETEL**
palm betel .... **ARECA**
b palm book .... **TARA**
palm Brazil .... **ASSAI**
palm climbing ..... **RATTAN**
palm cockatoo .... **ARARA**
palm, dwarf genus .... **SABAL**
palm fiber **DOH, TAL,** RAFFIA
palm fiber, S. Amer **DATIL**
palm genus .... **ARECA**
palm genus Asia .... **ARENGA**
palm juice, fermented **SURA**
palm leaf
        OLA, OLE, OLAY, OLLA
palm-leaf mat .... **YAPA**
palm lily .... **TI**
palm liquor .. **BENO, BINO**
palm, N. Z. .... **NIKAU**
palm, nipa .... **ATAP ATTAP**
palm off .... **FOB FOIST**
palm, palmyra leaf .... **OLA,**
            OLE, OLLA, OLAY
palm sago, Malay .. **GOMUTI**
palm sap .... **TODDY**
palm starch .... **SAGO**
palm, W. Ind. **GRIGRI, GRUGRU**
palmetto .... **SABAL**
palmyra leaf .... **OLA, OLE,**
            OLAY, OLLA
palmyra palm .... **BRAB**
palp .... **FEELER**
palpitation .... **PALMUS**

c pamper ... **COSHER, COSSET**
pamphlet .... **TRACT**
panacea .... **ELIXIR**
Panama gum tree **COPA, YAYA**
Panama, old name .. **DARIEN**
Panama tree, large **CATIVO**
Panay negrito .... **ATI**
panda .... **WAH, BEAR**
panel .... **PANE**
panel of jurors ..... **VENIRE**
pang .... **THROE**
pangolin .... **MANIS**
panic .... **FEAR, FUNK**
pannier .... **DOSSER**
Panopolis, chief god of . **MIN,**
                KHEM
pant .... **GASP**
pantry ... **AMBRY, LARDER,**
            SPENCE BUTTERY
papal cape .... **FANO FANON,**
FANUM, ORALE, PHANO,
FANNEL
papal church ..... **LATERAN**
papal collar .... **FANO FANON,**
FANUM, ORALE, PHANO,
FANNEL
papal court ...... **SEE CURIA**
papal fanon .... **ORALE**
papal letter ... **BULL, BULLA**
d papal scarf .... **ORALE**
papal veil ..... **FANO FANON,**
FANUM, ORALE, PHANO,
FANNEL
papal vestment .... **FANO,**
FANON FANUM, ORALE,
PHANO FANNEL
paper folded once ..... **FOLIO**
paper imperfect poor
        CASSE CASSIE, RETREE
paper lighting .... **SPILL**
paper measure **REAM, QUIRE**
paper mulberry .... **KOZO**
paper mulberry bark ... **TAPA**
paper size
        DEMY, POTT, OCTAVO
paper, thin crisp .... **PELURE**
par, 2 under .... **EAGLE**
Para, Brazil, capital **BELEM**
parade ..... **MARCH, STPUT**
paradise .... **EDEN**
paradise Buddhist .... **JODO**
paradise like .... **EDENIC**
"Paradise Lost" angel **ARIEL**
paragraph .... **ITEM**
parallelogram .... **RHOMB**
paralysis .... **PARESIS**
parapet, solid portion of
                MERLON
parasite .... **LEECH**

113

a parasite in blood ...... TRYP
parasitic insect MITE, ACARID
parasitic plant MOSS, DODDER
paravane .... OTTER
Parcae .... FATES
Parcae, one of
    NONA, MORTA, DECUMA
parcel of land ... LOT, PLAT
parchment, book
    .....FOREL, FORREL
pardon .... REMIT, CONDONE
pardon, general ... AMNESTY
pare .... PEEL
Paris art exhibit ..... SALON
Paris, first bishop of
    DENIS, DEYS
Paris section .... PASSY
Paris subway .... METRO
Paris thug .... APACHE
Paris' father .... PRIAM
Paris' wife .... OENONE
parish head .... RECTOR
parley .... PALAVER
Parliament report . HANSARD
parol .... ORAL
paroxysm .... FIT, SPASM
parrot
    KEA, LORY, VASA, VAZA
parrot, Brazil .. ARA, ARARA
parrot-fish

b   LORO, LUIA, SCARID
parrot, hawk .... HIA
parrot, monk .... LORO
parrot, N. Z. large KEA, KAKA
parrot, P. I., green ... CAGIT
parrot, sheep-killing .... KEA
parrot's bill, part of ... CERE
parrotlike .... ARINE
parry .... FEND, EVADE
Parsi priest .... MOBED
Parsi scripture ..... AVESTA
parsley camphor ...... APIOL
parsley, plant kin to
    ANISE, CELERY
parson bird
    POE, TUE, TUI, KOKO
parsonage .... MANSE
part .... ROLE, SOME, PIECE,
    BREAK, SEVER, SHARE,
    CLEAVE, ELEMENT
part, Greek play
    EXODE, EXODOS
part of church .... BEMA
    NAVE, AISLE, ALTAR
part of horse's foot . PASTERN
part of speech . NOUN, VERB
parted .... PARTITE
participle ending .... ING
parti-colored ... PIED, PINTO

c parti-colored horse
    ROAN, CALICO
particle ..... ACE, BIT, ION,
    JOT, ATOM, IOTA, DROP,
    MITE, MOTE, GRAIN,
    SHRED, TITTLE
particle, electrically charged
    ION
particle in cosmic rays MESON
particle of chaff ..... PALEA
particle, small
    JOT, ATOM, IOTA, MOTE
particular .... ITEM
Partlet .... HEN, BIDDY
partnership: Hawaii HUI, HOEY
partridge call ... JUCK, JUKE
partridge, sand ..... SEESEE
partridge, snow ...... LERWA
party .... SECT
parvenu .... UPSTART
pasha .... DEY
pass .... HAND, ELAPSE
pass a rope through .. REEVE
pass between peaks .... COL
pass by .... BYGO
pass on .... RELAY
pass over . OMIT, SKIP, ELIDE
pass through .... REEVE
pass through mountains . COL,
    DEFILE
passable .... SOSO

d passage .... GUT, ITER
    CANAL, TRANSIT
passage, bastion ... POSTERN
passage, covered ... ARCADE
passage: hist. .... ALURE
passage: music
    TUTTI, STRETTA
passage out ... EXIT, EGRESS
passageway ADIT, HALL, AISLE
Passover .... PASCH, PASCHA
Passover meal SEDAR, SEDER
passport endorsement
    VISA, VISE
past AGO, GONE, OVER, AGONE
paste .... STRASS
pasteboard .... CARD
pasted-up art work . COLLAGE
pastel .... TINT
pastoral .... IDYLLIC
pastoral place ..... ARCADIA
pastoral poem .. IDYL, IDYLL
pastoral staff . PEDA, PEDUM
pastry
    PIE, FLAN, TART, ECLAIR
pasture .... LEA
pasture: N. Eng. .... ING
pasture, to .... AGIST
pasty .... DOUGHY
pat .... DAB, TAP
pat, very .... APT
Patagonian cavy ..... MARA
patchwork, literary ... CENTO

patella .... ROTULA
paten ...... ARCA, ARCAE
patent from monarch . BERAT
path: Anglo-Ir. ..... CASAUN
path: math. .... LOCUS
path of planet ...... ORBIT
pathos, false ...... BATHOS
patriarch Jacob ..... ISRAEL
patriarch's title .... NASI
patron .... CLIENT
patron saint of France
            DENIS, DENYS
patronage ..... EGIS, AEGIS
pattern .... NORM, TYPE,
    IDEAL, MODEL, PARAGON
pattern, large square DAMIER
Paul, Apostle .... SAUL
— Paulo, Brazil .... SAO
Paul's birthplace .... TARSUS
paulownia tree .... KIRI
pause .... REST
pause: poet, & music
    SELAH, CESURA, CAESURA
paver .... TUP
paver's mallet .... TUP
pavilion .... TENT
paving stone ... FLAG, SETT
paw .... PUD, FOOT
pawl .... DETENT
pawn .... HOCK
Pawnee Indian rite ... HAKO
Pawnee tribes .... CHAUI
pay ... ANTE, WAGE, REMIT
pay dirt .... ORE
pay, fixed .... STIPEND
pay for another ...... TREAT
pay homage: feudal law
            ATTORN
pay one's part .... ANTE
pay out .... SPEND
payable .... DUE
paymaster, India ..... BUXY
payment back ...... REBATE
payment for a bride, S. Afr.
            LOBOLA
payment for death, feudal CRO
payment for homicide . ERIC
payment, press for ... DUN
payment to owner: Fr. law
            CENS
pea .... LEGUME
peace .... PAX
peace god, Anglo-Saxon . ING
peace of mind .... REST
peaceful . IRENE, IRENICAL
peach, clingstone .... PAVY
peacock ...... MAO, PAVO
peacock blue .... PAON
peacock butterfly .... IO
peacock fish ...... WRASSE
peacock genus .... PAVO
peacock: Kipling .... MAO

peak ...... ALP, TOR, ACME,
        APEX, PITON, ZENITH
peak: Scot. .... BEN
peanut .... MANI, GOOBER
pear, autumn .... BOSC
pear cider .... PERRY
pearl blue color ..... METAL
Pearl Buck heroine ... OLAN
pearl, imitation ..... OLIVET
pearl millet ... BAJRA, BAJRI
pearlweeds .... SAGINA
peasant CARL, CEORL, CHURL
peasant, India .... RYOT
peasant, Scot.
        COTTAR, COTTER
peat .... TURF
peat spade .... SLADE
pecan tree .... NOGAL
peccary, collared ... JAVALI
peck ..... DAB, NIP, KNIP
pedal .... TREADLE
peddle .. HAWK, SELL, VEND
peddle: Eng. .... TRANT
pedestal .... GAINE
pedestal part . DADO, PLINTH
peduncle, plant ..... SCAPE
peel BARK, PARE, RIND, SKIN
peep-show .... RAREE
PEER ...... see also NOBLE
peer .... PEEK, PEEP
Peer Gynt's mother ..... ASE
peevish .... PETULANT
peg .... KNAG
peg, golf .... TEE
peg, wooden
    NOG, TRENAIL, TREENAIL
Pegu ironwood .... ACLE
Peleg's son .... REU
pellucid ..... CLEAR, LIMPID
pelma .... SOLE
pelota court ...... FRONTON
pelt ... FELL, SKIN, STONE
pelvic bone, pert. to ... ILIAC
pelvic bones .... ILIA
pen name, Dickens .... BOZ
pen name, G. Russell .... AE
pen name, Lamb ..... ELIA
pen point .... NEB, NIB
pen-text .... RONDE
penman, Yutang .... LIN
penalty .... FINE
pendulum weight ...... BOB
Penelope's father ... ICARIUS
penetrate
    GORE, ENTER, PERMEATE
penitential season .... LENT
penmanship .... HAND
pennies .... PENCE
Pennsylvania sect ... AMISH
Pentateuch ... TORA, TORAH

People

a

PEOPLE .. see also TRIBES in
SPECIAL SECTION
people .... MEN, FOLK,
ONES, RACE, DEMOS
people, ancient Asian .. SERES
people: Ger. .... VOLK
people: Ir. .... DAOINE
people, Nigerian BENI, BENIN
people: Sp. .... GENTE
people, spirit of ..... ETHOS
people, the .... DEMOS
pepper, climbing ..... BETEL
pepper, garden ... PIMIENTO
pepper plant, Borneo ... ARA
pepper shrub
AVA, CAVA, KAVA, KAWA
pepper vine .... BETEL
Pequod's captain ...... AHAB
"per —" ... DIEM, ANNUM
perceive SEE, SENSE, DESCRY
perception EAR, TACT, SENSE
perch .... SIT, ROOST
perch genus .... PERCA
perchlike fish ...... DARTER
percolate OOZE, SEEP, LEACH
peregrine .... ALIEN
perenially shifting sands region
AREG
perfect ...... IDEAL, MODEL
perforate .... BORE, DRILL,
PUNCH, RIDDLE
perform .... RENDER
performer

b

DOER, ACTOR, ARTISTE
perfume
ATAR, OTTO, AROMA, ATTAR
perfume base .... MUSK
perfume with incense . CENSE
perfumed pad ...... SACHET
Pericles' consort .... ASPASIA
periphery .. RIM, PERIMETER
period .... DOT
period, time
AGE, EON, ERA, STAGE
periodic as Med. winds
ETESIAN
permit .. LET, ALLOW, LICENSE
permission .... LEAVE
pernicious, something ... PEST
perplex .... BAFFLE,
CONFUSE, BEWILDER
Persephone .... CORA, KORE
Persephone's husband
HADES, PLUTO
Persia .... IRAN
Persian .... IRANI
Persian coin, ancient . DARIC
Pers. demigod .... YIMA
Pers. elf .... PERI
Pers. enameled tile .... KASI
Pers. fairy .... PERI
Pers. governor, old ... SATRAP
Pers. headdress, ancient TIARA

c

Pers. lord ..... KAAN, KHAN
Pers. mystic .... SUFI
Pers. native .... LUR
Pers. poet .... OMAR
Pers. potentate ...... SHAH
Pers. priestly caste .... MAGI
Pers. province, ancient . ELAM
Pers. race, tribesman
LUR, KURD
Pers. rug . SENNA, HAMADAN
Pers. ruler .... SHAH
Pers. ruler of dead .... YIMA
Pers. sect .... BABI
Pers. sprite .... PERI
PERS. TITLE ...... see TITLE,
PERSIAN
Pers. tribe member .... LUR
Pers. weight .... SER
persimmon, E. Ind. GAB, GAUB
person of mixed blood
METIS, MESTIZO
person, overnice ...... PRIG
personage .... NIBS
personification of folly ... ATE
personification of light: Polyn.
AO
personnel .... STAFF
perspiration . SUDOR, SWEAT
perspire ...... EGEST, SWEAT
pert girl ...... CHIT, MINX
pertaining to the chin MENTAL

d

pertinent .... APT, PAT
perturb .... DERANGE,
DISTURB, AGITATE, TROUBLE
PERU INDIAN .. see page 193
peruse .... CON, READ, SCAN
peruser .... CONNER
Peruvian fertility goddess
MAMA
Peruvian plant .... OCA
pervade .... PERMEATE
pester ...... ANNOY, TEASE
pestle .... PILUM
pestle vessel ...... MORTAR
pet .... CADE
pet lamb ..... CADE, COSSET
"Peter Pan" dog ..... NANA
"Peter Pan" pirate ..... SMEE
petiole .... STIPE
Petrarch's love ...... LAURA
petrol .... GAS
peyote .... MESCAL
phantoms .... EIDOLA
Pharaoh .... RAMESES
Pharaoh after Rameses I .SETI
phase .... FACET, STAGE
pheasant brood
NID, NYE, NIDE
pheasant, Himal. CHIR, CHEER
pheasant, India ...... MONAL
Phidias statue ...... ATHENA
philippic .... TIRADE
PHILIPPINE ISLANDS
see also SPECIAL SECTION

Philippine Islands attendant .... ALILA
P.I. bast fiber ..... CASTULI
P.I. cedar .... CALANTAS
P.I. chief DATO, DATU, DATTO
P.I. DWARF see P. I. NEGRITO
P.I. dyewood tree
.... TUI, IPIL, TUWI
P.I. food .... POI, SABA
P.I. fort .... COTA, KOTA
P.I. grass ...... BOHO, BOJO
P.I. lighter .... CASCO
P.I. lizard .... IBID, IBIT
P.I. Moslem .... MORO
P.I. negrito, native, dwarf
.... ATA, ATI, ITA,
.... AETA, ATTA
P.I. palm wine .. BENO, BINO
P.I. peasant .... TAO
P.I. poisonous tree ... LIGAS
P.I. rice ...... PAGA, MACAN
P.I. sash .... TAPIS
P.I. servant .... ALILA
P.I. shrub, rope NABO, ANABO
P.I. skirt .... SAYA
P.I. tree ..... DAO, IBA, TUA,
.... TUI, BOGO, DITA, IFIL,
.... IPIL, YPIL
P.I. warrior .... MORO
Philistine city .... GATH,
.... GAZA, EKRON
Philistine deity, principal
.... DAGON
philosopher's stone ... ELIXIR
philosophical element ... RECT
philosophical theory MONISM
philosophy, pert. to Gr.
.... ELEATIC
phloem .... BAST
phoebe ...... PEWEE, PEWIT
Phoebus ...... SOL, SUN
Phoenician city .... TYRE
Phoenician goddess . ASTARTE
Phoenician port ...... SIDON
Phoenician princess .. EUROPA
phonetic notation system
.... ROMIC
phonetical sound ... PALATAL
phosphate of lime .. APATITE
photo-developing powder
.... METOL
photography solution ... HYPO
Phrygian god .... ATTIS
Phrygian lunar god .... MEN
physical SOMAL, SOMATIC
physician .. GALEN, MEDIC
physician's group ...... AMA
physician's symbol CADUCEUS
physicist, Am. .... EINSTEIN
physicist, Eng. ...... BOYLE
physicist, Fr. .... CURIE
physicist, Nobel prize-winner
.... 1944 .... RABI
physiological individual . BION

piano, upright ...... CLAVIAL
pick, miner's: Eng.
.... MANDREL, MANDRIL
pick out ...... CULL, GLEAN
picket .... PALE
pickled bamboo shoots ACHAR
pickled meat .... SOUSE
pickling fluid .... BRINE
pickling herb .... DILL
pickpocket .... DIP
"Picnic" author ...... INGE
picture ... DRAW, PORTRAIT
picture border .... MAT
picture, composite . MONTAGE
picturesque .... SCENIC
pie, meat, small ...... PASTY
piebald .... PINTO
piebald pony ... PIED, PINTO
piece of eight ...... REALS
piece out .... EKE
piece, thin .... SLAT
pier .... KEY, DOCK,
.... MOLE, QUAI, QUAY
pier, architectural ..... ANTA
pier support ... PILE, PILING
pierce.. GORE, STAB, SPEAR
pig HOG, SOW, SHOAT, SHOTE
pig, wild .... BOAR
pig, young ...... ELT, GRICE
pigs .... SUS
pigs' feet ...... PETTITOES
pigs, litter of ...... FARROW
pigs, red .... DUROC
pigeon .. NUN, BARB, DOVE,
.... POUTER, ROLLER
pigeon hawk .... MERLIN
pigeon pea DAL, TUR, GANDUL
piglike animal ..... PECCARY
pigment, blue-green .... BICE
pigment, brown ...... SEPIA
pigment, brown, from soot
.... BISTER, BISTRE
pigment, deep blue .. SMALT
pigment, red .... LAKE
pigment test crystalline DOPA
pigment, without .... ALBINO
pigmentation, lack of
.... ACHROMA
pigtail .... CUE, QUEUE
pike, full grown . LUCE, LUCET
pike, walleyed ...... DORE
pilaster .... ANTA
pilchard . FUMADO, SARDINE
pilchard-like fish ...... SPRAT
pile ..... NAP, HEAP, SPILE
pile driver .... OLIVER
pile driver ram .... TUP
pile of hay .... RICK, STACK
pilfer .... STEAL
pilgrim .... PALMER

a
pilgrimage city ...... MECCA
pilgrimage to Mecca ... HADJ
pill, large .... BOLUS
pillage .. LOOT, SACK, STEAL
pillage .... RAPINE
pillar, as of ore ...... JAMB
pillar, Hindu .... LAT
pillar, resembling ... STELAR
pillar, tapering ..... OBELISK
pillow .... BOLSTER
pilot .... GUIDE, STEER
pimento or —spice ...... ALL
pin .... BROOCH
pin, firing .... TIGE
pin, gunwale .... THOLE
pin, machine .... COTTER
pin, metal .... RIVET
pin, pivot .... PINTLE
pin, rifle firing .... TIGE
pin, Roman .... ACUS
pin, small, very LILL
pin, splicing .... FID
pin, wooden ... FID, NOG, PEG,
     COAG, COAK, DOWEL
pin wrench .... SPANNER
pinafore .... TIER
pincer claw .... CHELA
pinch .... NIP
pinched with cold .... URLED
Pindar work .... ODE

b
pine-cone, like a ... PINEAL
pine, Mex. ... OCOTE, PINON
pine, Scot. .... RIGA
pine, textile screw
     ARA, PANDAN
pineapple NANA, PINA, ANANA
pineapple genus ...... PUYA
pinfeather .... PEN
pinion .... WING
pink .... DAMASK
pinnacle .... TOP, APEX
pinnacle, ice .... SERAC
pinniped .... SEAL
pinochle score, term
     DIX, MELD
pint, half .... CUP
pintado fish .... SIER
pintail .... SMEE
pinworm . ASCARID, ASCARIS
pious Biblical Jew ..... TOBIT
pipe, ... TUBE, RISER
pipe, Irish .... DUDEEN
pipe joint, fitting ...... TEE
pipe, pastoral .... REED
pipe, tobacco
     BRIAR, BRIER, DUDEEN
pipe, water HOOKAH, NARGILE
pipe with socket ends
     HUB, HUBB
pipelike .... TUBATE
pique .... PEEVE

c
pirate ..... ROVER, CORSAIR
pirate in War of 1812 LAFITTE
pismire .... ANT, EMMET
pistil part .... CARPEL
pistol .... DAG, DAGG,
     MAUSER, SIDEARM
pistol: slang .... HEATER
pit .... HOLE, ABYSS, STONE
pit for roots, Maori .... RUA
pit: medical .... FOSSA
pit, small .. FOVEA, LACUNA
pitch ..... KEY, TAR, TONE
pitcher .... JUG, EWER
pitcher's false move .... BALK
pith .... NUB, GIST
pith helmet ... TOPI, TOPEE
pithy .... TERSE
pithy plant .... SOLA
pitiful quality ...... PATHOS
pittance .... DOLE
pitted .... FOVEATE
pity .... RUTH
placard .... POSTER
place ...... SET, LIEU, LOCI,
     SPOT, LOCUS, STEAD, LO-
     CALE
place before .... APPOSE
place, camping .... ETAPE
place case is tried .... VENUE
place in office again . RESEAT

d
place, in relation ..... POSIT
place, market ...... FORUM
place of shelter . GITE, HAVEN
placid ...... CALM, SERENE
plagiarize .... STEAL
plague .... PEST, TEASE
plain, arctic ...... TUNDRA
plain, Argentine ..... PAMPA
plan, Asia .... CHOL
plain, Palestine .... ONO
plain, Russia .... STEPPE
plain, S. Am. .... LLANO
plain, treeless .... SAVANNA
plain, treeless Arctic TUNDRA
plain, upland . WOLD, WEALD
Plains Indian ... see page 193
plainly woven .... UNI
plait .... PLY, BRAID
plan .... PLOT, INTEND
plane, Fr. .... SPAD
plane, Ger. .... STUKA
plane, Jap. .... ZERO
plane part .... FLAP,
     NOSE, TAIL, WING
plane, Russ. fighter .... MIG
planets (in order of distance
     from sun) MERCURY (1), VE-
     NUS (2), EARTH (3), MARS
     (4), JUPITER (5), SATURN
     (6), URANUS (7), NEPTUNE
     (8), PLUTO (9)

118

a planets in distance from Earth
(closest first)

1—VENUS		5—SATURN
2—MARS		6—URANUS
3—MERCURY		7—NEPTUNE
4—JUPITER		8—PLUTO

planets in size (largest first)

1—JUPITER		6—VENUS
2—SATURN		7—PLUTO
3—NEPTUNE		8—MARS
4—URANUS		9—MERCURY
5—EARTH		

planetarium .... ORRERY
planetary aspect CUST, TRINE
plank's curve on ship .... SNY
plant .... SOW, SEED
plant, bayonet .... DATIL
plant broom .... SPART
plant, bulb
    CAMAS, CAMASS, CAMMAS
plant cutter bird .... RARA
plant cutting   SLIP, PHYTON
plant disease ... RUST, SMUT
plant joined to another GRAFT
plant life .... FLORA
PLANT LILY ...... see LILY
plant, lily-like
    CAMAS, CAMASS, CAMMAS
plant louse .... APHID
plant, male .... MAS
b plant, medicinal, S. Am.
    ALOE, SENNA, IPECAC
plant modified by environment
    to abnormal development
        ECAD
plant, mustard family
    KALE, CRESS
plant organ .... LEAF
plant pod .... BOLL
plant, poisonous .... LOCO
plant, sea-bottom .. ENALID
plant stem: bot. .... CAULIS
plant stem tissue .... PITH
plant used as soap .. AMOLE
plants of area .... FLORA
plantain lily genus .... HOSTA
plantation, osier ...... HOLT
planter .... SEEDER
plaster .... SMEAR
plaster, artist's painting GESSO
plastic .... LUCITE
plate, battery ...... GRID
plate, Eucharist ...... PATEN
plate, reptile's ...... SCUTE
plate to hurl ...... DISCUS
plateau .... MESA
plateau, Andes ...... PUNA
platform .... DAIS, STAGE
platform, ancient ..... BEMA

c platform, mine shaft
        SOLLAR, SOLLER
platinum, of .... OSMIC
platinum wire loop .... OESE
Plato's "Idea" .. EIDE, EIDOS
play .... DRAMA
play on words .... PUN
play, part of .... ACT, SCENE
play unskillfully ...... STRUM
player .... ACTOR
playing card, old it. .. TAROT
playwright .... INGE
plea, to end: law ... ABATER
plead ...... SUE, ENTREAT
pleading: lay .... OYER
please .... SUIT
pleasing .... NICE
pleasure god, Egypt.
        BES, BESA
pledge .... VOW,
    GAGE, OATH, PAWN,
    TROTH, ENGAGE
pledge, Rom. law ...... VAS
plexus ...... RETE, RETIA
pliable .... WAXY
pliant .... LITHE
plinth ...... ORLO, SOCLE
plot .... LOT,
    PLAT, CABAL, CONSPIRE
plow, cutter COLTER, COULTER
d plow part ... SHETH, SHEATH
plow, sole of .... SHARE
plowed field ... ERD, ARADA
plug .... BUNG,
    CORK, SPILE, STOPPER
plum ...... GAGE, SLOE
plume . EGRET, PREEN AIGRET
plummet .... FATHOM
plump child .... FUB
plunder ... ROB, LOOT, PREY,
    SACK, BOOTY, RAVEN,
    RAVIN, REAVE, PILFER,
    RAPINE, RAVAGE, RAVINE
plunder ruthlessly .. MARAUD
plunge ...... DIVE, DOUSE
plural ending ...... EN, ES
plus .... AND
Pluto ... DIS, HADES, ORCUS
Pluto's mother-in-law DEMETER
pneumonia, kind of ... LOBAR
Po tributary .... ADDA
pochard .... SMEE
pocket billiards ...... POOL
pocket gopher, Mex. ... TUZA
pod, cotton .... BOLL
pods for tanning ...... PIPI
Poe poem .... RAVEN
poem ... ODE, ELEGY, EPODE
poem division, or part CANTO
poem, 8 line .... TRIOLET

119

a
poem, long heroic **EPIC, EPOS**
poem, love ...... **SONNET**
poem, lyric ..... **ODE, EPODE**
poem, mournful ...... **ELEGY**
poem, of a .... **ODIC**
poem, old Fr. .... **DIT**
poem, sacred .... **PSALM**
poet .... **BARD, ODIST**
poet, A.-S. .... **SCOP**
poet, Bengal .... **TAGORE**
poet, blind, epic .... **HOMER**
poet, lyric .... **ODIST**
poet, Norse .. **SCALD, SKALD**
poet, poor .... **RIMER**
poetry .... **EPOS, POESY**
poetry, early .... **RUNE**
poetry, Finnish ...... **RUNES**
poetry, mournful, pert. to
ELEGIAC
poetry, Norse god of
BRAGE, BRAGI
poi, source of .... **TARO**
point **END, TIP, BARB, PUNTO**
point in moon's orbit nearest
earth .... **PERIGEE**
point of curve .... **NODE**
point of land .... **SPIT**
point of moon .... **CUSP**
point of view .... **ANGLE**

b
point on mariner's compass
RUMB
point on tooth's crown . **CUSP**
point, tennis or golf ... **ACE**
point won .... **GOAL**
pointed .... **SHARP, ACUATE**
pointed arch .... **OGEE**
pointed end .... **CUSP**
pointed missile **DART, SPEAR**
pointed remark .... **BARB**
pointed staff .... **PIKE**
pointer .... **WAND**
pointless .... **INANE**
poison ...... **BANE, TAINT**
poison, arrow .... **INEE, UPAS,
URALI, URARE, URARI,
CURARE, CURARI**
poison, hemlock .... **CONINE**
poison, India **BISH, BISK, BIKH**
poisonous protein
RICIN, RICINE
poisonous weed .... **LOCO**
poke .... **JAB, PROD, NUDGE**
poker stake ..... **POT, ANTE**
pokeweed .... **POCAN, SCOKE**
Polar explorer .... **BYRD**
pole .... **MAST**
pole, Gaelic games
CABER, CABIR
Pole .... **SLAV**
pole, naut. .... **MAST, SPRIT**
pole to handle fish .... **PEW**
pole to pole, from
AXAL, AXIAL

c
polecat, Cape **ZORIL, ZORILLA**
police line .... **CORDON**
policeman ..... **COP, PEELER**
policeman, state ... **TROOPER**
policeman, S. Afr. .... **ZARP**
polish .... **RUB, WAX,
SHINE, LEVIGATE**
POLISH .. see also **POLAND
SPECIAL SECTION**
Polish assembly . **SEIM, SEJM**
Polish cake .... **BABA**
Polish general . **BOR, ANDERS**
Polish title of address
PAN, PANI
polished ..... **SHINY, SLEEK,
URBANE, ELEGANT**
polisher .... **EMERY**
polishing material
RABAT, ROUGE
polite .... **CIVIL**
political booty .... **GRAFT**
pollack fish .... **SEY**
pollen brush . **SCOPA, SCOPAE**
Pollux or Castor ...... **ANAX**
Pollux' mother .... **LEDA**
Pollux' twin .... **CASTOR**
polo stick .... **MALLET**
Polynesian .... **MAORI**
Polyn. "Adam" .... **TIKI**
Polyn. chestnut ...... **RATA**

d
Polyn. cloth .... **TAPA**
Polyn. dance .... **SIVA**
Polyn. deity, demon
AKUA, ATUA
Polyn. drink .... **AVA**
Polyn. for nature's power
MANA
Polyn. god .... **ATEO**
Polyn. god of forest ... **TANE**
Polyn. herb .... **PIA**
Polyn. hero .... **MAUI**
Polyn. island group .. **SAMOA**
Polyn. languages
MAORI, MAHORI
Polyn. lily .... **TI**
Polyn. stone heap ...... **AHU**
pome .... **APPLE**
"Pomp and Circumstance"
Composer .... **ELGAR**
pompous .... **TURGID**
pond . **MERE, POOL, LOCHAN**
ponder ...... **MUSE, PORE**
pontiff .... **POPE**
pony .... **CAVY**
pony, student's .... **CRIB**
pool .... **MERE, TARN,
LAGOON, PUDDLE**
pool: Scot. ...... **DIB, CARR,
LINN, LLYN**
poon tree
DILO, DOMBA, KEENA
poor .... **NEEDY**
poor joe .... **HERON**

a poor player .... DUB	*c* portent .... OMEN, SIGN
poorly ILL	porter, Orient
POPE ...... see also PAPAL	HAMAL, HAMMAL
Pope .. JOHN, PIUS, ADRIAN	Portia's waiting woman
Pope, English .... ADRIAN	NERISSA
Pope John XXIII first name	portico .... STOA
ANGELO	portion
Pope John XXIII last name	PART, SOME, SEGMENT
RONCALLI	portion out
Pope Pius XI .... RATTI	DOLE, METE, ALLOT
Pope Pius XII ...... PACELLI	portray .... DRAW,
POPE'S CAPE, COLLAR ... see	LIMN, DEPICT, DELINEATE
PAPAL CAPE, COLLAR	Portuguese coin .... REI
Pope's triple crown TIAR, TIARA	Port. colony, India ...... GOA
poplar ...... ALAMO, ASPEN	Port. folk tune .... FADO
poplar, white . ABELE, ASPEN	Port. lady .... DONA
poppy red .... GRANATE	Port. man .... DOM
poppy seed .... MAW	Port. navigator .... GAMA
populace, the .... DEMOS	Port. title .... DOM, DONNA
popular girl .... BELLE	pose .... SIT
porcelain	Poseidon .... NEPTUNE
CHINA, SEVRES, LIMOGES	Poseidon's son ...... TRITON
porcelain, ancient ..... MURRA	posited .... SET
porcelain, Chin. ...... JU, KO	position ..... SITUS, STATUS
porcelain, Eng. .... SPODE	position without work
porch ...... ANTA, STOOP,	SINECURE
VERANDA, VERANDAH	positive .... THETIC
porch, Gr. .... STOA	positive pole, terminal ANODE
porch, Hawaiian ..... LANAI	possession, landed ... ESTATE
b porch swing .... GLIDER	possum .... COON
porcupine anteater . ECHIDNA	possum, comic-strip ... POGO
porcupine, Canada ... URSON	post .... MAIL, SEND
pore ...... PORUS, STOMA,	post-hole digger (slick) . LOY
OSTIOLE, STOMATA	*d* postpone .... DEFER
porgy .... SCUP	postulate .... POSIT
porgy, Europ. .... PARGO	posture .... STANCE
porgy genus .... PAGRUS	pot .... OLLA
porgy, Jap. (Oriental) .... TAI	pot, chem. .... ALUDEL
porkfish .... SISI	pot, earthen .... CRUSE
porous rock .... TUFA, TUFF	pot herb .... WORT
porpoise .... DOLPHIN	pot, India LOTA, LOTO, LOTAH
porridge .... POB, BROSE	pot liquor .... BREWIS
porridge, corn meal .... SAMP	pot metal .... POTIN
porride: Sp. Am. ...... ATOLE	potassium .... KALITE
Porsena of Clusium .... LARS	potassium chloride . MURIATE
PORT see also SPECIAL SEC-	potassium nitrate
TION—GAZETTEER	NITER, GROUGH
port .... HAVEN	potation, small ...... DRAM
port, banana, Hondurus . TELA	potato .... SPUD
port, Black Sea ...... ODESSA	potato, sweet . YAM, BATATA
Port Moresby land .. PAPUA	pother .... ADO
port of Rome .... OSTIA	potpourri .... OLIO
port opp. Gibraltar ... CEUTA	potter's blade ...... PALLET
port, South Seas ...... APIA	pottery fragment ... SHARD
port, Suez .... SAID	pottery, pert. to ... CERAMIC
port wine city ...... OPORTO	pouch .... SAC
portable chair ...... SEDAN	pouch-shaped ...... SACCATE
portal .... DOOR, GATE	poultry ...... HENS, BIRDS
portend	poultry disease ... PIP, ROUP
BODE, AUGUR, PRESAGE	pounce .... SWOOP
	pound .... TUND
	pound down ..... RAM, TAMP
	pour .... RAIN, TEEM
	pour off gently ..... DECANT

pour out .... LIBATE
poverty ...... NEED, WANT
powder, astringent ... BORAL
powder, mineral ingredient
.... TALC
powder of aloes ...... PICRA
powdered pumice ...... TALC
power DINT, MANA, FORCE
practical joke .... HOAX
practice .... HABIT
practice exercise, musical
.... ETUDE
praise LAUD, EXTOL, EXTOLL
prance .... CAPER
prank .... DIDO, CAPER
prate .... GAB, YAP
prate: India .... BUKH, BUKK
pray: Yiddish ..... DAVEN
prayer AVE, BEAD, BENE, PLEA,
...... CREDO, MATIN, ORISON
prayer form .... LITANY
prayer, 9-day ..... NOVENA
prayer-rug, Hindu .... ASANA
prayer stick, Am. Ind.
...... BAHO, PAHO, PAJO
prayers, deacon's
...... ECTENE, EKTENE
prayerbook
...... ORDO, PORTAS, PORTASS
praying figure .... ORANT
preacher, Gospel ... EVANGEL

b precepts .... DICTA
precipice, Hawaii ..... PALI
precipitous .... STEEP
preclude ..... AVERT, DEBAR
preconceive .... IDEATE
predicament .... SCRAPE
predicate
...... BASE, FOUND, AFFIRM
predict .... AUGUR,
...... FORECAST, FORETELL
predisposed .... PRONE
preen ...... PLUME, PRINK
preface .... PROEM
prefecture, Jap. ...... KEN
PREFIX:
  about .... PERI
  above .... HYPER
  across ..... DIA, TRANS
  again .... RE
  against .... ANTI
  ahead .... PRE
  an .... AE
  apart .... DIS
  away ..... DE, DI, APO
  back .... ANA
  backward .... RETRO
  bad .... MAL
  badly .... MIS
  beauty .... CALLI
  before .... OB, PRE, ANTE
  blood ...... HAEM, HEMO

c   both .... AMBI
  CHEMICALS .. see page 29
  common .... PRE
  distant .... TEL, TELE
  double .... DI
  down .... DE, CATA
  eight .. OCT, OCTA, OCTO
  equal .... ISO
  far .... TEL, TELE
  faulty .... MIS
  fire .... PYR
  former, formerly ...... EX
  four .... TETRA
  from .... EC
  half .... DEMI, HEMI, SEMI
  ill .... MIS
  mountain .... ORO
  negative ...... IR, NON
  new .... NEO
  not .. IL, IM, IR, UN, NON
  not fully .... SEMI
  numerical .... UNI
  of atmospheric pressure
  .... BARO
  of the stars ...... ASTRO
  on this side .... CIS
  one .... UNI
  out of .... EC, EX

d   outer .... ECT, EXO, ECTO
  outer skin .... EPI
  outside ..... ECT, EXO
  over .... EPI, SUPER,
  .... SUPRA, SUPERB
  partly .... SEMI
  people .... DEMO
  pray .... ORA
  recent .... NEO
  same ... ISO, EQUI, HOMO
  separation .... DIS
  single .... MONO
  ten .... DEC, DECA
  thousand .... KILO
  three .... TER, TRI
  threefold .... TRI
  thrice ...... TER, TRIS
  through ...... DIA, PER
  to .... AP
  together .... COM
  town .... TRE
  turning .... ROTO
  twice .... BI
  two .... DI, DUA
  twofold .... DI
  under .... SUB
  upon .... EPI
  upward .... ANA, ANO
  with .... SYN
  within .... ENDO
  wrong .... MIS

prehistoric implement .. CELT
prehistoric mound ..... TERP
prejudice .... BIAS
prelate, high ...... PRIMATE
prelude .... PROEM
premium, exchange .... AGIO
prepare ...... FIT, GIRD,
    MAKE, ADAPT, EQUIP
prepare for publication . EDIT
prepared opium
    CHANDU, CHANDOO
preposition ..... AT, IN, ON,
    UP, INTO
presage
   OMEN, HERALD, PORTEND
prescribed .... THETIC
prescribed quantity ... DOSE
present . GIFT, GIVE, DONATE
present, be .... ATTEND
present in brief .... SUM
presently ANON, ENOW, SOON
preserve . CAN, JAM, KEEP,
   SAVE, PROTECT, MAINTAIN
preserve in brine CORN, SALT
Presidential nickname .. ABE,
    CAL, IKE, TEDDY
press together .... SERRY
pressure .... DURESS
pressure unit . BARAD, BARIE
pretend . FAKE, SHAM, FEIGN
pretense .... SHAM
pretensions .... AIRS
pretentious .... SIDY
prevail .... WIN
prevail on .... INDUCE
prevalent .... RIFE
prevent .. DETER, PRECLUDE
prevent by law .... ESTOP
prey .... RAVIN
prey upon
   RAVEN, RAVIN, RAVINE
Priam's son
  PARIS, HECTOR, HEKTOR
price .... RATE
price of transportation . FARE
prickle .... SETA
prickles .... SETAE
prickly pear
   TUNA, NOPAL, CACTUS
prickly plant . BRIAR, BRIER,
    .... NETTLE
prickly seed coat . BUR, BURR
pride .... PLUME
PRIEST . see also CLERGYMAN
priest
   FRA, ABBE, CURE, PADRE
priest, Celtic .... DRUID
priest, Gr. .... MYST

PRIEST, HIGH,
       see HIGH PRIEST
priest in "Iliad" .. CALCHAS
priest, Mongol ..... SHAMAN
priest, Moro . SARIP, PANDITA
priestess, Gr. .... AUGE
priestess, Rom. ...... VESTAL
priesthood, Rom. ...... SALII
priestly caste .. MAGI, MAGUS
prima donna .... DIVA
PRIMA DONNA ...... see also
     OPERA SOPRANO
prime minister: Brit. .. EDEN,
     PEEL
primeval .... OLD,
   EARLY, PRIMAL, PRISTINE
prince, Abyssin. .... RAS
prince, Arabian . EMIR, SAYID,
   SAYYID, SHERIF, SHEREEF
prince, India
    RAJA, RANA, RAJAH
prince of Argos ...... DANAE
Prince of Darkness .. SATAN
prince, Oriental ...... KHAN
prince, Persian . AMIR, AMEER
prince, petty .... SATRAP
prince, Slavic .... KNEZ
Prince Val's father .. AGUAR
princeling .... SATRAP
princely .... ROYAL
princess, Gr. myth ..... IOLE
princess, India . RANI, RANEE
principal .... TOP, ARCH
    MAIN, CHIEF
principal commodity .. STAPLE
principle, accepted
   AXIOM, PRANA, TENET
print .... STAMP
print measure ...... EM, EN
printer, 1st colonial .... DAYE
printer's direction ..... STET
printer's mark .... DELE
printer's mistake
    TYPO, ERRATUM
printer's mistakes ... ERRATA
printing plate ...... STEREO
printing roller ...... PLATEN
prison JUG, GAOL, JAIL, QUOD
prison sentence .... RAP
prison spy .... MOUTON
privation .... LOSS
privilege, commercial . OCTROI
prize .... PRY, AWARD
pro .... FOR
"— pro nobis" .... ORA
probe, medical ...... STYLET
problem .... POSER
proboscis .... SNOUT
proboscis monkey ..... KAHA
proceed ... WEND, ADVANCE
proceedings .... ACTA

123

a procession .... TRAIN, PARADE, MOTORCADE
proclaim .... CRY, VOICE, HERALD, DECLARE
prod .... URGE
produce ..... BEGET, YIELD CREATE, INWORK, GENERATE
produce as an effect BEGET
produced, quantity . . YIELD
producing cold ..... ALGIFIC
production, artistic .. FACTURE
profane .... VIOLATE
profane, Hawaiian ...... NOA
profession ART, CAREER, METIER
professional, not LAIC, LAICAL
profit .. GAIN, VAIL, AVAIL
profit, to yield .... NET
profits, taker of: law. PERNOR
profitable ...... FAT, USEFUL
profound .... DEEP
"— profoundis" .... DE
progenitor .... SIRE, PARENT
progeny .... ISSUE
prohibit .... BAN, BAR, VETO, DEBAR, ESTOP
prohibition BAN, VETO, EMBARGO
Prohibition, against ...... WET
project ... JUT, IDEA, PLAN
b projectile .... MISSILE
projecting edge RIM, FLANGE
projecting piece ARM, RIM, TENON, FLANGE
projecting rim .... FLANGE
projecting tooth ...... SNAG
projection EAR, BARB, PRONG
projection, fireplace HOB, HOBB
projection, jagged SNAG, TOOTH
projection, studlike .. KNOP
promenade .... MALL
promise .... WORD
promise to pay ... IOU, NOTE
"Promised Land" fountain AIN
promontory .... CAPE, NASE, NAZE, NESS
promontory, Orkneys .. NOUP
promontory, rocky ...... TOR
promote .... FOSTER
prompt .... CUE, YARE
prone .... APT, FLAT
prong .... TINE, TOOTH
pronghorn .... CABREE, CABRET, CABRIE, CABRIT
pronoun .. IT, ME, US, WE, YE, HER, HIM, ONE, SHE, THAT, THIS, THEE, THEM, THEY, THOU, THESE, THOSE

c pronoun, possessive MY, HER, HIS, ITS, OUR, HERS, MINE, OURS, YOUR
pronounce indistinctly . SLUR
pronounce strongly ... STRESS
pronouncement DICTA, DICTUM
proof, corrected ..... REVISE
proof, printer's ...... GALLEY
proofreader's mark DELE, STET, CARET
prop .... HOLD, STAY, BRACE, BOLSTER, SUSTAIN
propeller .... OAR
proper .... DUE, FIT
properly .... FEATLY
property, hold on ..... LIEN
property, India .... DHAN
property, item of ASSET, CHATTEL
property, landed ...... ESTATE
property owned absolutely ALOD, ALLOD, ALODIUM, ALLODIUM
property, receiver of . ALIENEE
prophesy .... FORETELL
prophet ...... SEER, AUGUR, PREDICTOR, FORETELLER
PROPHETS, BIBLICAL .... see SPECIAL SECTION
prophets .... VATES
d prophetic .. VATIC, VATICAL
proportion .... RATIO
proportionally assess PRORATE
proposition THESES, THESIS, PREMISE
proposition, logic .... LEMMA
proposition: math. . THEOREM
prosecutor .... SUER
prosecutor: abbr. .... DA
proselyte to Judaism .... GER
"— prosequi," ...... NOLLE
Proserpina ..... CORA, KORE
prospect .... VISTA
prosperity .... WEAL
prosperity god, Teut. ... FREY
Prospero's servant .... ARIEL
prostrate ... PRONE, REPENT
protagonist .... HERO
protected .... HOUSED
protection ..... EGIS, AEGIS
protection right, Old Eng. MUND
protective building .. REDAN
protective influence EGIS, AEGIS
Protestant denomination: abbr. ME, PE, BAP, PRESB
prototype .... IDEAL
protozoan order ..... LOBOSA
protuberance JAG, NUB, HUMP, KNOB, KNOT, NODE, WART, KNURL, TORUS

124

a protuberant .... TOROSE
prove: law .... DERAIGN
proverb ..... SAW, ADAGE,
    AXIOM, MAXIM, SAYING
provide ..... ENDOW, ENDUE
provided .... IF
provided that .... SO
province, Rom. ...... DACIA
provisional clause .. PROVISO
proviso .... CLAUSE
provoke .... IRE, RILE,
    ANGER, ANNOY
prow .... BOW, STEM
prune: prov. Eng. .... SNED
pruning knife .... DHAW
Prussian spa, town .... EMS
pry .... NOSE, LEVER, SNOOP
Psalm, 51st ...... MISERERE
Psalmist .... DAVID
Psalms, selection of . HALLEL
Psalms, word in ...... SELAH
pseudonym .... NOM, ALIAS
pseudonym of Louise De La
    Ramee .... QUIDA
psyche .... SOUL
psychiatrist
    JUNG, ADLER, FREUD
Ptah, embodiment of .. APIS
ptarmigan .... RYPE

b pteropod genus ..... CLIONE
pua hemp .... POOA
public ...... OPEN, OVERT
public: Chin. .... KUNG
public esteem ..... REPUTE
public, make .. AIR, DELATE
public vehicle .. BUS, TAXI
publication, style of . FORMAT
publish ..... ISSUE, PRINT
publish illegally ..... PIRATE
Puccini heroine ...... MIMI
puck, hockey ...... RUBBER
pudding ... DUFF, SAGO
pueblo dweller .... HOPI
Pueblo Indian .. HOPI, ZUNI,
    KERES, MOQUI, TANOA
Pueblo sacred chamber . KIVA
Pueblo, Tanoan .... HANO
Puerto Rican plant .... APIO
puff up .... ELATE
puffbird, Brazil ... DREAMER
puffbird genus ..... MONASA
puffer fish .... TAMBOR
Pulitzer poet .... FROST
pull . TOW, TUG, DRAG, HALE
pull with nautical tackle BOUSE
pulley .... SHEAVE
pulp, fruit .... POMACE
pulpit .... AMBO, BEMA
pulpy mass left in cider
    POMACE
pulverize .... MICRONIZE

c pump handle .... SWIPE
pumpkin .... PEPO
punch .... JAB
"Punch and Judy" dog . TOBY
punch, engraver's .. MATTOIR
punctuation mark DASH,COLON
pungent . TEZ, SPICY, TANGY
punish by fine ...... AMERCE
punishment .... FERULE
punishment, of ...... PENAL
punitive .... PENAL
Punjab native .... JAT
punk .... AMADOU
pupa .... INSTAR
pupil of eye .... GLENE
puppet .... DOLL
puppet, famous .. JUDY, PUNCH
puppeteer, famous ... SARG
pure sirup .... CLAIRCE
pure thought .... NOESIS
purification, ancient Roman
    LUSTRUM
purloin .... STEAL
purple
    MAUVE, MODENA, TYRIAN
purple dye source ... MUREX
purple medic ...... LUCERN,
    ALFALFA, LUCERNE
purple ragwort ...... JACOBY
purple seaweed . SION, LAVER

d purport, general ..... TENOR
purpose .... AIM, END,
    GOAL, SAKE, INTENT
purposive .... TELIC
purse net .... SEINE
pursy .... STOUT
push up .... BOOST
put aside .... DAFF
put away .... STORE
put back .... REPLACE
put forth .... EXERT
put in bank .... DEPOSIT
put off .... DEFER
put out .... OUST, EJECT
put up .... ANTE
puzzle .... POSER,
    REBUS, BAFFLE, ACROSTIC
puzzles .... CRUCES
Pygmalian's statue . GALATEA
pygmy .... ATOMY
pygmy people, Congo
    AKKA, ACHUAS
pygmy people, Equatorial Africa
    BATWA, ABONGO, OBONGO
Pylos, kin of .... NESTOR
Pyramus, lover of .. FIREBUG
Pythias' friend ...... DAMON
python .... BOA

125

Q

a
qua .... AS
"— qua non" .... SINE
quack IMPOSTOR, CHARLATAN
quack medicine .. NOSTRUM
quadrant .... ARC
quadrate .... SQUARE
"quae —" which see .. VIDE
quaff .... DRINK
quail .... COLIN, COWER
quake .... SHAKE,
    SHIVER, TREMOR, TREMBLE
Quaker .... FRIEND
Quaker Poet ...... WHITTIER
quaking .... TREPID
qualified .... FIT, ABLE
qualify ...... FIT, ADAPT,
    EQUIP, PREPARE
quality ... CALIBER, CALIBRE
quantity, indeterminate SOME
quantity: math
    SCALER, VECTOR

b
quarrel ...... ROW, FEUD,
    SPAT, TIFF
quarter of a year: Scot. RAITH
quartz .... JASPER
quartz, green ...... PRASE
quartz, translucent ... PRASE
quash law .... CASSARE
quaternion .... TETRAD
quay .... LEVEE
Quebec, district, town . LEVIS
Quebec's patron saint . ANNE
Queen .... CLEO
queen: Moslem .... BEGUM,
    BEEGUM
queen of gods, Egypt. ... SATI
queen of gods, Rom. . HERA,
    JUNO
Queen of Italy ...... ELENA
Queen of Ithaca . PENELOPE
Queen of Roumania .. MARIE
Queen of Scots ...... MARY
Queen of Spain, last .... ENA
Queen, "Romeo and Juliet"
    MAB

c
queenly .... REGAL, REGINAL
Queensland hemp plant . SIDA
Queensland tribe .... GOA
quell .... CALM, CRUSH
quench .... SLAKE
quench steel .... AUSTEMPER
quern .... MILL
query .... ASK
queue .... LINE
question ...... ASK, GRILL
question, hard ...... POSER
quetzal .... TROGON
quibble ...... CAVIL, EVADE
quick .... FAST, AGILE,
    ALIVE, RAPID
quick, music ...... TOSTO
quicken .. HASTEN, ENLIVEN
quickly ...... CITO, APACE,
    PRESTO, PRONTO
quickly, move
    SCAT, SCUD, SKITE
quicksilver ...... HEAUTARIT
quid .... CUD

d
"quid—quo," equivalent PRO
quiescent..LATENT, DORMANT
quiet .... CALM, LULL,
    STILL, SMOOTH
quiet! ...... SH, PST, TST
quilkin .... FROG, TOAD
quill .... PEN, SPINE
quill feathers ...... REMEX,
    REMIGES
quill for winding silk .... COP
quilt .... EIDER, COVER
quince, Bengal .. BEL, BEHL
quinine .... KINA
quintessence ... PITH, ELIXIR
quirt, cowboy's ...... ROMAL
quit .... CEASE, LEAVE
quite .... ALL
quivering .. ASPEN, TREMOR
"quad — demonstrandum"
    ERAT
"Quo Vadis" tyrant character
    NERO
quoits, mark of .... MOT
quote .... CITE

126

R

Ra, consort of .... **MUT**
Ra, son of .... **SU, SHU**
rabbi, law-teaching .. **AMORA**
rabbit cage .... **HUTCH**
rabbit, Europ. . **CONY, CONEY**
rabbit, female .... **DOE**
rabbit fur .... **LAPIN**
rabbit home .... **WARREN**
rabbit, small swamp . **TAPETI**
rabbit, So. Am. ..... **TAPETI**
rabble .... **MOB**
rabies .... **LYSSA**
raccoon-like mammal .. **COATI**
RACE .. see also TRIBES in
        SPECIAL SECTION
race, boat .... **REGATTA**
race, kind of .... **RELAY**
race, short .... **SPRINT**
race-track .... **OVAL**
race-track circuit ..... **LAP**
race-track tipster ..... **TOUT**
races, pert. to ...... **ETHNIC**
Rachel's father ..... **LABAN**
racing boat .... **GIG**
racket, game .... **PELOTA**
radar screen .... **SCOPE**
radiate .... **EMANATE**
radical .... **RED**
radicle .... **STEMLET**
radio advertiser ... **SPONSOR**
radio bulletin ... **NEWSCAST**
radio-guided bomb .... **AZON**
radio wave .... **MICROWAVE**
radio wire .... **LITZ**
radio-TV awards .... **EMMIES**
radioactive counter .. **GEIGER**
radioactive element .. **NITON**
radioactive ray .... **GAMMA**
radium discoverer .... **CURIE**
radium emanation .... **NITON**
radius, pert. to ..... **RADIAL**
radon .... **NITON**
raft, kind of ... **CATAMARAN**
raft, Maori .... **MOKI**
rag doll .... **MOPPET**
rage .... **RAMP, RANT,
            RESE, STORM**
ragged person: Sp. ... **ROTO**
raging monster, Bibl. . **RAHAB**
ragout, game ..... **SALMI**
ragweed genus .... **IVA**
raid .... **FORAY, INROAD**
raid, soldier's .. **COMMANDO**
rail at .... **REVILE**
raid bird **SORA, WEKA, CRAKE**
railing .... **PARAPET**

railroad bridge .... **TRESSEL,
            TRESTLE**
railroad light .... **FLARE**
railroad signal
    TRIMMER, SEMAPHORE
railroad tie .... **SLEEPER**
railroad timber ...... **TIE**
railway station: Fr. .... **GARE**
rain after sunset .... **SEREIN**
rain, fine .... **MISLE**
rain forest .... **SELVA**
rain gauge .... **UDOMETER**
rain serpent, Hindu ... **NAGA**
rain spout: Scot. ..... **RONE**
rain tree .... **SAMAN**
rainbow .... **ARC, IRIS**
rainbow goddess ...... **IRIS**
rainbow, pert. to .... **IRIDAL**
raincoat .... **PONCHO**
rainy .... **WET**
raise **REAR, BREED, ELEVATE**
raised .... **BRED**
raisin: Sp. .... **PASA**
raising device .... **JACK**
Rajah's lady .. **RANI, RANEE**
rake ...... **ROUE, LOTHARIO**
rake with gunfire .. **ENFILADE**
ram **TUP, BUTT, TAMP, ARIES**
ram, male .... **TUP**
ram-headed god, Egypt.
    AMEN, AMON, AMUN
Ramachandra, wife of .. **SITA**
ramble .... **GAD, ROVE**
Ramee, de la, penname **OUIDA**
rammed earth building material
                PISE
rampart .... **AGGER, VALLUM**
range .... **AREA, GAMUT,
            SCOPE, SIERRA**
Rangoon's state .... **PEGU**
rank ... **ROW, RATE, DEGREE**
ranks, press in ...... **SERRY**
rankle .... **FESTER**
ransom .... **REDEEM**
rapeseed .... **COLSA, COLZA**
rapid, more: music . **STRETTA,
    STRETTE, STRETTI, STRETTO**
rapids, river .... **SOO**
rapidly .... **APACE**
rapier .... **BILBO**
rare earth element .. **ERBIUM**
rascal .... **IMP, ROGUE**
rase .... **INCISE**
rasorial .... **GNAWING**
rasp .... **FILE, GRATE**

127

a
raspberry, variety . BLACKCAP
rasse .... CIVET
rat .... DESERTER
rat, Ceylon, India BANDICOOT
rat hare .... PIKA
rate .... ESTIMATE
rate, relative .... AT
ratify .... SEAL
ratio .... RATE
RATIO: MATH see MATH, RATIO
rational .... SANE
rational integer ...... NORM
rational principle ..... LOGOS
rationalize .... THOB
ratite bird ...... CASSOWARY
ratton .... CANE
rattlesnake
　　RATTLER, CROTALUS
rave .... RANT
"Raven" author ...... POE
"Raven" character .. LENORE
ravine
　GAP, DALE, VALE, GORGE
ravine, Afr. ... WADI, WADY
ravine, Arabia . WADI, WADY
rawboned .... LEAN
rawboned animal .... SCRAG
ray fish .... SKATE
rays, like .... RADIAL
rayon .. ACETATE, CELANESE

b
raze .... DEVASTATE
razor-billed auk
　　ALCA, MURR, MURRE
reach across ...... SPAN
react .... RESPOND
read, inability to .... ALEXIA
read metrically ...... SCAN
read publically ..... PRELECT
reader, first ...... PRIMER
reading desk .... AMBO
reading substituted: Bibl.
　　KERE, KERI
ready: dialect ...... YARE
ready-made tie .... TECK
real being, pert. to .. ONTAL
real thing ...... MCCOY
reality .... FACT
realm .... DOMAIN
reamer .... BROACH
rear ERECT, RAISE, ARRIERE
rear, to the
　　AFT, ABAFT, ASTERN
rearhorse .... MANTIS
rearing of horse .... PESADE
reason .... NOUS
reason, deprive of .. DEMENT
reasoning .... LOGIC
reasoning, deductive APRIORI
reata .... LAZO,
　　ROPE, LASSO, LARIAT

c
rebec of India ...... SAROD
Rebecca's hairy son ... ESAU
rebound . CAROM, RICOCHET
rebuff .... SLAP, SNUB
rebuke
　　CHIDE, SCOLD, REPROVE
recalcitrant ...... RENITENT
recant .... RETRACT
recede .... EBB
recent
　NEO, NEW, LATE, NEOTERIC
receptacle .... BIN, BOX,
　　TRAY, VESSEL
reception, a.m. ...... LEVEE
reception Fr. ...... ACCUEIL
reception, India ...... DURBAR
recess .... APSE, ALCOVE
recess, wall .... NICHE
recipient .... DONEE
recite metrically ...... SCAN
reckon ...... ARET, COUNT
reckoning .... TALLY
reclaim .... REDEEM
recline .... LOLL
recluse ASCETIC, EREMITE
　　ANCHORET, ANCHORITE
recoil ...... SHY, RESILE
recommit ...... REMAND
recompense PAY, FEES, MEED
reconnaissance RECCO, RECON
reconnoiter ...... SCOUT
reconstruct ...... REMODEL
record TAB, NOTE, ENROL
　　ENTER, ENTRY, REGISTER
record of investigation REPORT
record ship's .... LOG
record, year's ...... ANNAL
records .... ANNALS
recorded proceedings .. ACTA
recording device ..... TAPE
records one who ..... NOTER
recourse, have ...... REFER
recover strength ..... RALLY
recovery, legal ...... TROVER
recruit .... BOOT
rectifier, current .... DIODE
rectify . AMEND, EMEND
recurring pattern ..... CYCLE
red .... CARMINE
　　MAGENTA, NACARAT
red, Brazil .... ROSET
red cedar ..... SAVIN, SAVINE
red circle: Her. .... GUZE
red currant ...... RISSEL
red deer .... ELAPHINE
red dye root .. CHAY, CHOY
red garden flower .... CANNA
red: Her. .... GULES
red horse ...... BAY, ROAN
red ocher ...... KEEL, KIEL,
　　TIVER, RADDLE, RUDDLE

a reliquary ...... APSE, ARCA, ARCAE, CHEST
relish .... GUSTO
reluctant .... LOATH, AVERSE
rely .... TRUST
remain .... BIDE, STAY
remainder .... REST
remaining .... OVER
remark, witty ... MOT, SALLY
remiss .... LAX
remit .... SEND
remnant ...... END, SHRED
remora fish PEGA, LOOTSMAN
remove . DELE, DOFF, DELETE
remove interior ...... GUT
remove: law .... ELOIN, ELOIGN, ELOIGNE
remunerate .... PAY
rend ...... RIP, TEAR, WREST
render fat .... TRY
rendezvous .... TRYST
renegade .... APOSTATE
renounce ...... ABNEGATE
renovated hat ... MOLOKER
renown ...... FAME, NOTE, EMINENCE, PRESTIGE
rent ...... LET, HIRE, TEAR, TORN, LEASE
rent, old Eng. law .... TAC
renter .... LESSEE
b repair ...... DARN, MEND
repartee ... RIPOST, RIPOSTE
repast .... MEAL
repay .... REQUITE
repay in kind .. RETALIATE
repeat ...... ECHO, ITERATE
repeat: music .... BIS
repeat performance . ENCORE
repeat sign: music .. SEGNO
repeat tiresomely .. DIN, DING
repeated phrase .... REPRISE
repeatedly hit ...... POMMEL
repetition .... ROTE
replete .... FULL
report, small .... POP
repose .... EASE, REST
representation ...... AGENT
reproach .... BLAME, TAUNT
reproach, old term ...... RACA
reproductive body .. GAMETE
reproductive cell .... SPORE
reptile, pert. to .... SAURIAN
repulse .... REPEL
reputation ... NAME, REPUTE
repute .... CHARACTER
request .... PLEA
rescind .... REPEAL
resentment .... IRE
reserve supply .... STORE

c residence .... HOME, ABODE
residence, ecclesiastical MANSE
resident of .... ITE
resign .... QUIT, DEMIT
resin .... GUM, LAC, ANIME, COPAL, ELEMI, JALAP, MYRRH, BALSAM, MASTIC
resin, fossil. AMBER, GLESSITE
resin, fragrant .... ELEMI
resist .... OPPOSE
resist authority ...... REBEL
resisting pressure . RENITENT
resistor, current .. RHEOSTAT
resort .... SPA
resort, Fr. .... PAU, NICE, CANNES
resources .... FUND, MEANS, ASSETS
respect .... ESTEEM
respond .... REACT
rest ...... SIT, EASE, REPOSE
rest, lay at .... REPOSE
restaurant, small .... BISTRO
resthouse ...... CHAN, KHAN
resting .... ABED
restive .... BALKY
restore .... RENEW
d restrain . CURB, REIN, DETER, STINT, TETHER
restrict .... LIMIT
retaliate .... REPAY
retain .... HOLD, KEEP
retaliation .... TALION
retinue ...... SUITE, TRAIN
retort, quick RIPOST, RIPOSTE
retract .... RECANT
retreat .... RECEDE
retreat, cosy DEN, NEST, NOOK
retribution .... NEMESIS
retribution, get ...... VENGE
retrograde .... RECEDE
return .... RECUR, RESTORE
return a profit .... PAY
return blow .... TIT
return on investment .. YIELD
returning .... REDIENT
reunion, hold a ..... REUNE
reveille, call to .... DIAN
revelry, cry of .... EVOE
revelry, drunken ..... ORGY
revenue, church: Scot. ANNAT
reverberate .... ECHO
reverberating .... REBOANT
revere .... HONOR, HONOUR
reverence .... AWE
reversed in order . CONVERSE
reversion to type ... ATAVISM

a revert to state (land) .... ESCHEAT
revise .... EDIT, AMEND
revive wine .... STUM
revoke legacy, grant ADEEM
Revolution hero . HALE, ALLEN
revolutions per minute REVS
revolve SPIN, TURN, ROTATE
revolve logging .... BIRL
revolver GAT, GUN, ROD, COLT
reward .... MEED
rhebok .... PEELE
Rhine city .... MAINZ
Rhine tributary .... AAR
rhinoceros beetle ..... UANG
rhinoceros, black
BORELE, NASICORN
rhinoceros: obs.
ABADA, ABATH
Rhone tributary ..... SAONE
rhythm .... TIME, METER,
METRE, CADENCE
rhythmical accent ...... BEAT
rhythmical swing .... LILT
rib .... COSTA
rib, pert. to .... COSTAL
rib, woman from .... EVE
ribs, with .... COSTATE
ribbed fabric ... REP, CORD,
REPP, PIQUE

b ribbon, badge ...... CORDON
ribbon: comb. form .. TENE
ribbonfish .... GUAPENA
rice .... PADI, PADDY
rice dish ..... PILAU, PILAW
rice field, Java .... PADI
rice grass, P.I. .... BARIT
rice in husk .... PALAY
rice paste, Jap. .... AME
rice polishings .... DARAC
rich man .... MIDAS,
NABOB, NAWAB
rich silk cloth .... CAFFA
riches .... PELF
rid .... FREE
riddle .... ENIGMA
ridge .... ARETE,
SPINE, MOUNTAIN
ridge, camp's .... RIDEAU
ridge, glacial, sandy .... OS,
OSAR, ESKER, OESAR
ridge on cloth .... WALE
ridge on skin .... WELT
ridge, stony .... RAND
ridges, rounded .... GYRI
ridged area, Balkan .... BILO
ridicule .... GUY, MOCK,
RAZZ, DERIDE
ridicule personified, Gr.
MOMUS

c riding academy .... MANEGE
ridging dress .... HABIT
rifle .... KRAG, MINIE
GARAND, CARBINE
rifle ball .... MINIE
rifleman, Ger. .... JAGER
right conduct, Buddhist .. TAO
right conduct: Taoism .... TE
right hand music .... DM
right-hand page . RO, RECTO
right: law .... DROIT
right, pert. to ...... DEXTER
right to speak .... SAY
right, turn .... GEE
rights, of ..... JURAL, UDAL
Rigoletto's daughter .. GILDA
rigorous ..... HARSH, STERN,
STRICT, SEVERE, AUSTERE
rim ..... LIP, EDGE, FLANGE
rim of wheel FELLY, FELLOE
"Rime cold giant" YMER, YMIR
ring .... PEAL, TOLL, KNELL
ring, boxing .... ARENA
ring for reins TERRET, TERRIT
ring, gun carriage .... LUNET
ring, harness pad
TERRET, TERRIT
ring, lamp condensing .. CRIC
ring, little .... ANNULET
ring, naut. ...... GROMMET

d ring of light ..... HALO, NIMB.
NIMBUS, AUREOLA,
AUREOLE
"Ring of the Nibelung" goddess
ERDA
"Ring of the Nibelung" smith
MIME
ring out .... PEAL
ring, part of .... CHATON
ring, rubber jar .... LUTE
ring, seal .... SIGNET
ring-shaped ..... CIRCINATE
ring-shaped piece ... QUOIT
ring, stone of .... CHATON
ringlet .... CURL, TRESS
ringworm .... TINEA, TETTER
ripening agent .... AGER
ripple ...... LAP, RIFF, WAVE
rise above .... TOWER
rise aloft .... TOWER
rise: old Eng. .... RIS
risible .... GELASTIC
rites, religious .... SACRA
ritual .... RITE
RIVER . see also GAZETTEER in
SPECIAL SECTION
river .... RIO
river, Balmoral Castle's .. DEE
river bank .... RIPA
river bank, growing by
RIPARIAN

a river-bank stair, Ind.
                    GAUT, GHAT
   river bed, dry, Afr.
                    WADI, WADY
   river between Europe and Asia
                    KARA
   river, Bremen's ...... **WESER**
   river Caesar crossed
                    RUBICON
   river, Dutch Meuse .... **MAAS**
   river in Baltic .... **ODER**
   river in Essex .... **CAM**
   river in Orleans ...... **LOIRE**
   river in Petrograd .... **NEVA**
   river into Moselle ..... **SAAR**
   river into Rhone ..... **SAONE**
   river islet .... **AIT**
   river, "Kubla Khan" ... **ALPH**
   river, Munich's .... **ISAR**
   river mouth .... **LADE, DELTA**
   river nymph .... **NAIS**
   river to the Humber
                    OUSE, TRENT
   River of Woe ..... **ACHERON**
   river, Southwest ...... **PECOS**
   river: Sp. .... **RIO**
   river: Tagalog .... **ILOG**
   river to Medit. .... **ERBO**
   river valley .... **STRATH**
   rivulet .... **RILL**
   road .... **VIA, PATH,**
                    ITER, AGGER
b road: Roman .... **ITER**
   road: Gypsy .... **DRUN**
   roadhouse .... **INN**
   roam .... **GAD, ROVE**
   roast .... **CALCINE**
   roasted meat strip ... **CABOB**
   roasting rod .... **SPIT**
   rob .... **REAVE, DESPOIL**
   Rob Roy .... **CANOE**
   robber .... **THIEF**
   ROBE .... see also **GARMENT**
   robe .... **MANTLE**
   robe to ankles .... **TALAR**
   "Roberta" composer ... **KERN**
   robot drama .... **RUR**
   rock aggregate .... **AUGE**
   rock, basic igneous .... **SIMA**
   rock cavity .... **VOOG, VUGG,**
                    VUGH, GEODE
   rock, dangerous .... **SCYLLA**
   rock, dark .... **BASALT**
   rock, fine grained .... **TRAP**
   rock, flintlike ...... **CHERT**
   rock, granitoid **DUNITE, GNEISS**
   rock, hard .... **WHIN**
   rock, jutting .... **TOR**
   rock, laminated ... **SHALE,**
                    SLATE, GNEISS
   rock, melted .... **LAVA**
   rock, mica-bearing .. **DOMITE**

c rock, projecting .. **TOR, CRAG**
   rock, rugged .... **CRAG**
   rock snake .... **PYTHON**
   rock whiting genus .... **ODAX**
   rock-wren .... **TURCO**
   ROCKET . see under **MISSILE,**
                    GUIDED
   rocket's goal .... **MOON**
   rockfish ... **RASHER, TAMBOR**
   rockfish, Calif. . **RENA, REINA**
   rockweed .... **FUCI, FUCUS**
   Rocky Mt. peak ...... **ESTES**
   Rocky Mt. range
                    TETON, UINTA
   rocky peak, eminence,
       pinnacle .... **TOR**
   rod ... **POLE, WAND, BATON,**
                    PERCH, STAFF
   rod, barbecue .... **SPIT**
   rod, basketry .... **OSIER**
   rod, billiard .... **CUE**
   rod, chastening ..... **FERULE**
   rodent .... **RAT, HARE**
   rodent genus .... **MUS**
   rodent, rabbit-like ..... **PIKA**
   rodent, S. Am. . **CAVY, DEGU,**
                    PACA, COYPU, AGOUTI
   rodent, W. Ind. ...... **HUTIA**
   Rhoderick Dhu .... **SCOT**
   rogue .... **PICARO**
   roguish .... **SLY, ARCH**
d roister .... **REVEL**
   Roland's destroyer ...... **GAN,**
                    GANO, GANELON
   roll and heave .... **TOSS**
   roll of bread: dialect. ... **BAP**
   roll of cloth .... **BOLT**
   roll of paper .... **SCROLL**
   roll up .... **FURL**
   romaine .... **COS**
   ROMAN GODS
            see **SPECIAL SECTION**
   Rom. assembly .... **COMITIA**
   Rom. authors ... **CATO, LIVY,**
                    OVID, LUCAN, NEPOS,
                    PLINY, CICERO, HOR-
                    ACE, SENECA, SILIUS,
                    VERGIL, SALLUST
   Rom. barracks
                    CANADA, CANNABA
   Rom. box .... **CAPSA**
   Rom. boxing glove .. **CESTUS**
   Rom. bronze .... **AES**
   Rom. brooch .... **FIBULA**
   Rom. building .... **INSULA**
   Rom. cap .... **PILEUS**
   Rom. cavalry body
                    TURM, TURMA
   Rom. circus post ...... **META**
   Rom. clan .... **GENS, GENTES**
   Rom. cloak .. **TOGA, ABOLLA**

a Rom. coin, ancient ...... **SEMIS, DINDER**
Rom. coins .... **AS, AES, ASSES, SOLIDUS**
Rom. Curia court .... **ROTA**
Rom. date ...... **IDES, NONES**
Rom. dictator .... **SULLA**
Rom. dish .... **LANX**
Rom. emperor .... **NERO, OTHO, TITUS**
Rom. farce .... **EXODE**
Rom. galley **TRIREME, UNIREME**
Rom. gaming cube .... **TALUS**
Rom. garment . **TOGA, STOLA, TUNIC, PLANETA**
Rom. goal post in racing **META**
Rom. highway ..... **VIA, ITER**
Rom. historian .. **LIVY, NEPOS**
Rom. judge ... **EDILE, AEDILE**
Rom. law control ... **MANUS**
Rom. legendary king .... **NUMA**
Rom. liquid measure .... **URNA**
Rom. list ..... **ALBE, ALBUM**
Rom. magistrate or official
EDILE, AEDILE, ARCHON, CONSUL, PRETOR, TRIBUNE
Rom. market .. **FORA, FORUM**
b Rom. meal .... **CENA**
Rom. money, copper .... **AES**
Rom. numerals **1-I, 5-V, 10-X, 50-L, 100-C, 500-D, 1000-M**
ROMAN OFFICIAL
see **ROMAN MAGISTRATE**
Rom. patriot .... **CATO**
Rom. philosopher **CATO, SENECA**
Rom. platter .... **LANX**
Rom. pledge .... **VAS**
Rom. poet ... **OVID, LUCAN, HORACE, VERGIL, VIRGIL**
Rom. pound .... **AS**
Rom. province .... **DACIA**
Rom. public games ..... **LUDI**
Rom. public lands ..... **AGER**
Rom. religious festivals **VOTA**
Rom. road .... **VIA, ITER**
Rom. robe .... **TOGA**
Rom. room, principal **ATRIA, ATRIUM**
Rom. scroll .... **STEMMA**
Rom. statesman .... **CATO**
Rom. sword .... **FALX**
Rom. vessel .... **PATERA**
Rom. war garb .... **SAGUM**
Rom. weight .... **AS**

e Rom. well-curb ...... **PUTEAL**
Rom. writer .... **MACER**
romance, tale of **GEST, GESTE**
ROMANIA .... see **RUMANIA**
Rome, a founder of .. **REMUS**
Rome's cathedral church **LATERAN**
Rome's conqueror .... **ALARIC**
Rome's river .... **TIBER**
Romulus' twin .... **REMUS**
rood .... **CROSS**
roof .... **MANSARD**
roof edge .... **EAVE**
roof of mouth ...... **PALATE**
roof of mouth, pert. to **PALATAL**
roof orament .... **EPI**
roof, rounded **DOME, CUPOLA**
roof, rounded like a .. **DOMAL**
roof, truncated .... **HIP**
roofing piece ...... **RAG, TILE**
roofing slate .... **TILE**
roofing timber ...... **PURLIN**
rook's cry .... **CAWK**
room, Eng. college supply **BUTTERY**
room, snug .... **DEN**
room, rooms ... **SPACE, SUITE**
room, architecture .... **OECUS**
room for household goods, linen, etc. .. **EWRY, EWERY**

d room, main, Rom.
ATRIA, ATRIUM
room, mineshaft . **PLAT, PLATT**
room, Rom. .... **ALA**
roomy .... **WIDE**
roost .... **PERCH**
rooster .... **COCK**
root .... **RADIX, RADICES**
root, drug-yielding .... **JALAP**
root, edible .... **OCA, TARO, CASSAVA**
root, tree used for sewing **WATAP**
root, word .... **ETYM**
rootlet ... **RADICEL, RADICLE**
rootstock, edible ...... **TARO**
rootstock, fern (Maori) .. **ROI**
rootstock, fragrant .... **ORRIS**
rope .... **JEFF, LAZO, LASSO, LONGE, REATA, RIATA, LARIAT, MARLINE**
rope, cringle **LEEFANG, LEEFANGE**
rope fiber .. **DA, COIR, FERU, HEMP, IMBE, JUTE, RHEA, ABACA, SISAL**
rope for animals .... **TETHER**
rope guide: naut. ...... **WAPP**
rope loop .... **BIGHT**

133

a rope, naut. .... **FOZ, TYE, STAY,
VANG, HAWSER, RATLIN,
LANIARD, LANYARD, RAT-
LINE, SNOTTER**
rope to tie boat .... **PAINTER**
rope, weave .... **REEVE**
rope, yardarm .... **SNOTTER**
ropes, unite .... **SPLICE**
rosary bead .... **AVE**
rose: Byron .... **GUL**
rose fruit .... **HIP**
rose genus ... **ROSA, ACAENA**
rose-like plant .... **AVENS**
rose of Sharon
        ALTHEA, ALTHAEA
rose oil derivative .... **ATAR,
OTTO, ATTAR, OTTAR**
rose ornament .... **ROSETTE**
rose, Pers. .... **GUL**
rosewood .... **MOLOMPI**
rosolic acid .. **AURIN, AURINE**
rostellum .... **ROSTEL**
roster .... **LIST, ROTA**
rotate .... **ROLL, GYRATE**
rotating muscle ...... **EVERTOR**
rotating part ... **CAM, ROTOR**
rotation producer ... **TORQUE**
rotten .... **PUTRID**
rouge ..... **RADDLE, RUDDLE**
b rough .... **RUDE, UNEVEN**
rough, as country ..... **HILLY**
rough copy .... **DRAFT**
rough in voice .... **GRUFF**
rough rock .... **KNAR**
roughness, sea ...... **LIPPER**
roulette bet ..... **BAS, NOIR,
MILIEU**
round, a ..... **ROTA, ROTULA**
round hand .... **RONDE**
round room .... **ROTUNDA**
Round Table Knight .... **KAY,
BORS, BORT, BALAN,
BALIN, BOHORT, GAR-
ETH, GAWAIN, GALA-
HAD, PELLEAS**
round-up .... **RODEO**
rounded projection ..... **LOBE**
rounder .... **RAKE, ROUE**
roundworm .... **NEMA,
ASCARID, ASCARIS**
rouse . **WAKE, AWAKE, WAKEN**
Rousseau novel, hero .. **EMILE**
route .... **WAY, PATH**
route, plane's fixed .... **LANE**
routine, fixed .... **ROTE**
row .... **LINE, SPAT, TIER**
rowan tree ..... **ASH, SORB**
rowdy: slang .... **B'HOY**
rower .... **OAR**
rower's bench .... **ZYGA,
ZYGON, THWART**

c royal authority .... **SCEPTRE**
royal court, relating to . **AULIC**
royal edict: Fr. .... **ARRET**
royal family, Fr. .... **VALOIS**
royal rights, having **PALATINE**
royal rod . **SCEPTER, SCEPTRE**
royal treasury .... **FISC, FISK**
royalty, Hawaii .... **ALII**
rub harshly .... **GRATE**
rub off .... **ABRADE**
rub out .... **ERASE**
rub roughly .... **SCRAPE**
rub to polish .. **BUFF, SHINE**
rub to soreness ..... **CHAFE**
rubber .... **PARA,
LATEX, CAUCHO, ELASTIC**
rubber, black ...... **EBONITE**
rubber source .... **KOKSAGYZ**
rubber, S. Am. .. **PARA, CEARA**
rubber tree .... **ULE, HULE,
SERINGA**
rubber, wild .... **CEARA**
rubbery substance
        GUTTA, NOREPOL
rubbish .... **ROT, JUNK,
CULCH, RUBBLE**
rubble masonry .... **MOELLON**
rubella .... **MEASLES**
ruby .... **RED**
ruby red quartz .... **RUBASSE**
ruby spinel .. **BALAS, BALASS**
rudder bushing ...... **PINTLE**
rudder fish .... **CHOPA**
ruddle .... **KEEL, KIEL**
rudiment .... **GERM**
rudiments .... **ABC**
rue .... **REGRET**
rue herb genus ...... **RUTA**
ruff, female .... **REE, REEVE**
ruffed lemur .... **VARI**
ruffer .... **NAPPER**
ruffle .... **CRIMP**
ruffle, neck .. **JABOT, RUCHE**
RUG .... see also **CARPET**
rug, long narrow
        KANARA, RUNNER
ruin .... **DOOM**
rule .... **LAW, DOMINEER**
"Rule Britannia" composer
        ARNE
rules, dueling .... **DUELLO**
ruler .... **REGENT**
ruler, Afghanistan .... **EMIR,
AMEER, CALIF, EMEER
CALIPH, SULTAN**
ruler, Arabian . **EMIR, AMEER,
CALIF, EMEER, CALIPH,
SULTAN**
RULER, BIBLICAL .... see
        SPECIAL SECTION

a RULER IN EAST
          see RULER, ARABIAN
ruler, India .... NAWAB
ruler, Morocco
          SHERIF, SHEREEF
ruler, Moslem . EMIR, AMEER,
      CALIF, EMEER, CALIPH,
      SULTÁN
ruler of gods .... ZEUS
ruler, Oriental .... CALIF
ruler, Tunis .... DEY
RUMANIA
      see also SPECIAL SECTION
Rumanian composer . ENESCO
Rumanian folk song . DOINA
Rumanian king's title . DOMN
rumen .... CUD
ruminant ...... DEER, GOAT,
  CAMEL, LLAMA, ANTELOPE
ruminant genus .... CAPRA
ruminant, horned DEER, GOAT
ruminate .... MULL, PONDER
Rumor personified ... FAMA
rumor, to .... BRUIT,
          NORATE, REPORT
b rumple .... MUSS
run at top speed .... SPRINT
run before wind ...... SCUD
run of the mill .... PAR
run out .... PETER
runner .... SCARF,
          STOLO, STOLON
runner, distance ..... MILER
runner, plant STOLO, STOLON
rupees, 100,000 ...... LAC
rural .... RUSTIC, PASTORAL
rural deity .... PAN, FAUNUS
rural poem .... GEORGIC
rush ...... HASTE, SPEED
rush, marsh .... SPART
Russell's viper
          DABOIA, DABOYA
RUSSIA .... see also SOVIET
          and SPECIAL SECTION
Russia, most northern town
                    KOLA
Russian ... RED, RUSS, SLAV,
          KULAK, TATAR
Russ. basso. .... KIPNIS
Russ. author .... BUNIN

c Russ. beer KVAS, QUAS, KVASS
Russ. community ...... MIR
Russ. convention ..... RADA
Russ. cooperative society
                    ARTEL
Russ. council .... DUMA
Russ. dress ...... SARAFAN
Russ. edict .. UKASE, DECREE
Russ. emperor .... CZAR,
          TSAR, TZAR
Russ. fiddle .... GUDOK
Russ. folk dance ...... KOLO
Russ. girl's name ..... OLGA
Russ. hemp .... RINE
Russ. labor union ..... ARTEL
Russ. lagoon .... LIMAN
Russ. Lapland capital .. KOLA
Russ. leather .... YUFT
Russ. liquid measure . STOF,
          STOFF, STOOF
Russ. log hut .... ISBA
Russ. marsh .... LIMAN
Russ. mile .... VERST
Russ. mountain range
          ALAI, URAL
d Russian mts., pert. to ALTAIC
Russ. name, given AKIM, IGOR
Russ. news agency .... TASS
Russ. official .... BERIYA
Russ. opera .... BORIS
Russ. peninsula ...... KOLA
Russ. sea, inland .... ARAL,
          AZOF, AZOV
Russ. secret police
          NKVD, OGPU
Russ. tavern .... CABACK
Russ. tax, old .... OBROK
Rus. tea urn ...... SAMOVAR
Russ. trade guild ..... ARTEL
Russ. vehicle .. ARBA, ARABA
Russ. village .... MIR
Russ. whip .... PLET
Russ. writer .. GORKI, GORKY
Russ. "yes" .... DA
rust .... EAT, ERODE
Rustam's father .... ZAL
rustic ... BOOR, RUBE, CARL,
      CARLE, YOKEL, BUCOLIC,
      PEASANT
Ruth's husband .... BOAZ
Ruth's son .... OBED
rye, disease of ...... ERGOT

S

sable ...... **SOBOL, MARTEN**
sac .... **BURSA**
saccharine source ...... **TAR**
sack fiber .... **JUTE**
sack, to .... **LOOT**
saclike cavity .... **BURSA**
sacred asp, symbol .. **URAEUS**
sacred bull, Egypt. **APIS, HAPI**
sacred chalice .... **GRAIL**
sacred city, India .. **BENARES**
sacred enclosure, Gr. . **SEKOS**
sacred fig .... **PIPAL**
sacred Hindu word ...... **OM**
sacred image ... **ICON, IKON**
sacred lily .... **LOTUS**
sacred object: Oceania . **ZOGO**
sacred picture ... **ICON, IKON**
sacred place .... **SHRINE**
sacred place, Gr.
.... **ABATON, HIERON**
sacred tree, Hindu . **BO, PIPAL**
sacrifice, place of .... **ALTAR**
sacrificial drink, Zoroaster's
.... **SOMA**
sacrificial offerings ... **HIERA**
sad: comb. form ..... **TRAGI**
sad cry .... **ALAS, ALACK**
sad: music .... **MESTO**
saddle horses, fresh . **REMUDA**
saddle knob .... **POMMEL**
saddle, rear of ...... **CANTLE**
safe .... **SECURE**
safe place ..... **PORT, HAVEN**
safe: thief's slang ..... **PETE**
safety lamp .... **DAVY**
safflower .... **KUSUM**
saga .... **EDDA**
sage .... **WISE**
sagacious .... **WISE,
.... ASTUTE, SAPIENT**
sage genus .... **SALVIA**
sail fastener .... **CLEW**
sail-line .... **EARING**
sail nearer wind .... **LUFF**
sail, square .... **LUG**
sail, square, edge of .. **LEECH**
sail, triangular .... **JIB**
sail yard: Scot. .... **RAE**
sail's corner .... **CLEW**
"Sails" of constellation Argo
.... **VELA**
sailboat ...... **YAWL, KETCH**
sailing race .... **REGATTA**
SAILING VESSEL ...... see
.... **VESSEL, SAILING**
sailmaker's awl .... **STABBER**

sailor .... **GOB, TAR, SALT,
.... SEADOG**
sailor, India .... **LASCAR**
St. Anthony's cross .... **TAU**
saint, British .... **ALBAN**
saint, Buddhist
.... **ARAHT, ARHAT, ARAHAT**
St. Catherine's home .. **SIENA**
saint, female: abbr. ...... **STE**
saint, 14th century .... **ROCH**
St. Francis' birthplace . **ASSISI**
St. John's-bread ..... **CAROB**
"St. Louis Blues" composer
.... **HANDY**
saint, Moslem .... **PIR**
St. Paul, deserter from **DEMAS**
St. Vitus dance ..... **CHOREA**
sainte: abbr. .... **STE**
saint's relic box ..... **CHASSE**
salad green .... **UDO, CRESS,
.... KERSE, CRESSE, ENDIVE**
salamander .. **EFT, EVET, NEWT**
salient angle .... **CANT**
Salientia, the .... **ANURA**
sally .... **START, SORTIE**
"Sally in Our Alley" composer
.... **CAREY**
salmon, female .... **HEN**
salmon, male .... **COCK**
salmon net .... **MAUD**
salmon, silver .... **COHO**
salmon, third year ..... **MORT**
salmon, 2 yr. . **SMOLT, SPROD**
salmon, young . **PARR, GRILSE**
salt ..... **SAL, HALITE, SALINE**
salt factory .... **SALTERN**
salt lake, Turkestan ... **SHOR**
salt of tartaric acid . **TARTAR**
salt pond or spring .. **SALINA**
salt, resembling ...... **HALOID**
salt, rock .... **HALITE**
salt, solution . **BRINE, SALINE**
salt tax .... **GABELLE**
salt tree, Tamarisk .... **ATLE**
salted .... **ALAT**
saltpeter ...... **NITER, NITRE**
saltwort .... **KALI**
saltworks .... **SALINA**
salty water .... **BRINE**
salutation .... **AVE**
salutation: Ir. ...... **ACHARA**
Salvation Army leader . **BOOTH**
salver .... **TRAY**
salvia .... **CHIA**
Sambal language ...... **TINO**
sambar deer ... **MAHA, RUSA**
same .... **ILK, DITTO**

136

a	same place: abbr. ...... IBID	*c*	satelllite .... MOON, PLANET
	samlet .... PARR		satellite ... LUNIK, SPUTNIK,
	Samoan maiden ...... TAUPO		PIONEER, EXPLORER,
	Samoan mollusk ...... ASI		VANGUARD, ATLAS-
	Samoan political council FONO		SCORE, DISCOVERER
	Samuel, king killed by . . AGAG		satellite, navigation . TRANSIT
	Samuel, teacher of ...... ELI		satellite, television .... TIROS
	Samuel's son .... ABIA		satellite's path ...... ORBIT
	samurai, straying .... RONIN		satiate ... CLOY, GLUT, SATE
	sanction ...... AMEN, FIAT		satirical .... DRY
	sanctuary ..... BEMA, FANE,		satisfaction Maori ..... UTU
	NAOS, CELLA		satisfy .. SATE, SUIT, PLEASE
	sand .... GRIT		saturate SOAK, IMBUE, STEEP
	sand bar ...... REEF, SHOAL		Saturn, satellite of .... DIONE
	sand expanses ...... AREG		Saturn's rings projection ANSA
	sand hill ..... DENE, DUNE		Saturn's wife .... OPS
	sand island .... BAR		Saturnalia .... ORGY
	sand, sea bottom ...... PAAR		satyr .... FAUN
	sand snake genus ..... ERYX		sauce .... GRAVY
	sandal, Egypt. ...... TATBEB		sauce, Chinese, Oriental . SOY
	sandal, Mex.		sauce, fish .... ALEC
	HUARACHE, HUARACHO		sauce, peppery ..... TABASCO
	sandalwood tree ..... MAIRE		sauce, tomato ..... CATSUP,
	sandarac powder ... POUNCE		CATCHUP, KETCHUP
	sandarac tree .... ARAR		saucy .... PERT
	sandbox tree genus ... HURA		Saul's army leader ... ABNER
	sandpiper .. REE, RUFF, STIB,		Saul's chief herdsman . DOEG
	REEVE, STINT		Saul's father .... KISH
	sandpiper, Europ. ...... TEREK		Saul's grandfather NER, ABIEL
	sandpiper, red .... KNOT		Saul's successor ..... DAVID
	sandpiper, small ..... KNOT,		Saul's uncle .... NER
	PUME, STINT		Sault Ste. Marie .... SOO
	sandstone .... GRIT		saurel fish .... SCAD
b	sandstorm .... HABOOB	*d*	sausage, spiced ... SALAME,
	sandwich .... HERO		SALAMI
	Sandwich Island discoverer		savage .... FERAL
	COOK		Savage Island language .NIUE
	sandy .... ARENOSE		save .... HOARD, STINT,
	Sankhya philos. term .. GUNA		REDEEM, CONSERVE
	Sanskrit dialect .... PALI		saviour .... REDEEMER
	Sanskrit precept		savory .... SAPID, TASTY
	SUTRA, SUTTA		saw .... ADAGE, AXIOM,
	Sanskrit school .... TOL		MAXIM, SAYING
	Sao —, Brazil .... PAULO		saw-leaved centaury
	Sao Salvador .... BAHIA		BEHN, BEHEN
	sap spout .... SPILE		saw, notched like .. SERRATE
	sapodilla .. SAPOTA, SAPOTE		saw notching .... REDAN
	sapota tree .... ACANA		saw, surgical
	Saracen .... MOOR, MOSLEM		TREPAN, TREPHINE
	Sarah's slave .... HAGAR		sawbill duck .... SMEW
	sarcasm .... IRONY		sawlike organ, or part . SERRA
	Sardina gold coin .... CARLINE		sawlike parts SERRAS, SERRAE
	sargeant fish .... SNOOK		sawtooth ridge ...... SIERRA
	Sargon's capital ...... ACCAD		saxhorn .... TUBA
	Sarmatia cave-dwellers TAURI		Saxon god .... ER, EAR
	sartor .... TAILOR		Saxon king ..... INE, ALFRED
	sash, C. Amer. .... TOBE		Saxony natives ...... SORBS
	sash, Jap. kimono ...... OBI		say .... UTTER
	sassafras tree .... AGUE		say again .... ITERATE
	Satan .... DEVIL		saying .. MOT, SAW, ADAGE,
	Satan: Arab. .... EBLIS		AXIOM, MAXIM
			sayings .... LOGIA

a
scabbard fish .... HIKU
scabbard, put into .. SHEATHE
scaffolding .... STAGING
scale .... GAMUT
scale, syllable of .. DO, FA, LA,
　　　　　MI, RE, SO, TI, SOL
scale under blossom
　　　　　　PALEA, PALET
scales, having large SCUTATE
scallop ..... CRENA, CRENAE
scallops, cut in small .. PINK
scalloped .... CRENATE
scalp disease .... FAVI, FAVUS
scamp .... ROGUE, RASCAL
SCANDINAVIAN
　　　　　　see also NORSE
SCANDINAVIAN .... see also
　　SWEDEN, NORWAY, in
　　　　SPECIAL SECTION
Scandinavian .. DANE, SWEDE
Scand., ancient ...... NORSE
Scand. countryman ... GEAT
Scand. explorer .... ERIC
Scand. fertility god ... NJORD
Scand. legend .... SAGA
Scand. measure .... ALEN
Scand. nation ...... GEATAS
Scandinavians in Russia
　　　　　　　ROS, RUS

b
scanty .... SPARSE
scar, resembling a ... ULOID
scarce .... RARE
scarcely: Lat. VIX
scare away .... SHOO
scarf .... BOA, TIE,
　　　　　　ASCOT, ORALE
scarf, long .... STOLE
scarf, Sp. Am. ...... TAPALO
scarlet flower ...... SALVIA
Scarlett O'Hara's home TARA
scatter .. SOW, TED, STREW
scatter: dial. .... SCOAD
scatter on .... LITTER
scattered: Her. ...... SEME
scenario .... SCRIPT
scene ...... VIEW, TABLEAU
scene of action
　　　　　　ARENA, SPHERE
scenic view .... SCAPE
scent .... ODOR, AROMA
scented .... OLENT
schedule .... LIST
scheme .... PLAN, PLOT
schism .... RENT
scholar .... PEDANT
scholars, Moslem .... ULEMA
scholarship .... BURSE
school, boy's .... PREP
school, Fr. .... ECOLE, LYCEE
school grounds ..... CAMPUS

c
SCHOONER .. see also BOAT,
　　　　　　SHIP, VESSEL
schooner, 3-masted .... TERN
sciences .... ARTS
scientific farmer AGRONOMIST
scientific study: abbr. .. ANAT.
scientist, Am. UREY, HOOTON,
　　　PARRAN, COMPTON,
　　　WAKSMAN, MILLIKAN
scientist, Austr. .... MEITNER
scientist, Czech .... CORI
scientist, Dan. .... BOHR
scientist, Eng. ... HOGBEN,
　　　FLEMING, HALDANE
scientist, Ger. .BAADE, HABER
scientist, Ital. .... FERMI
scissors .... SHEARS
scoff ..... GIBE, JEER, JIBE,
　　　　　　RAIL, SNEER
scold ..... JAW, NAG, RATE
scold: dialect .... FRAB
scone: Scot. .... FARL, FARLE
scoop .... DIP
scoot: Scot. .... SKYT, SKITE
scope.. AREA, AMBIT, RANGE
scorch .... CHAR, SEAR,
　　　　　　SERE, SINGE
score .... TALLY
scoria ...... SLAG, DROSS
scorpion fish .... LAPON
Scotch cake .... SCONE
scoter .... COOT
Scotland .... SCOTIA
Scott character ...... ELLEN
Scott heroine .... ELLEN
Scott, poem by ... MARMION
SCOTTISH ...... see Pages
　　　of SCOTTISH WORDS
Scot. alderman .... BAILIE
Scot. author .... BARRIE
Scot. chemist ... URE, DEWAR
Scot. chief landholder
　　　　　　THANE, THEGN
Scot. cultural congress .. MOD
Scot. explorer .... RAE
Scot. highlander ...... GAEL
Scot. king .... BRUCE
Scot. lord .... THANE, THEGN
Scot. pillory .... JOUG
Scot. playwright ..... BARRIE
Scot. poet .... BURNS
Scot. pottage .... BROSE
Scot. proprietor ...... LAIRD
Scot. scholar .... NICOLL
Scot. singer .... LAUDER
SCOTTISH WORDS:
accept .... TAE
advise .... REDE
afraid .... RAD, RADE
age .... EILD

138

a

against	GIN
alder tree	ARN, ELLER
on	AE
animal, lean	RIBE
any	ONY
article	TA
ashes	ASE
ask	AX
at all	AVA
away	AWA
awry	AJEE
babbler	HAVEREL
ball	BA
bank	BRAE
barter	TROKE
beg	SORN
bind	OOP
biscuit	BAKE
blockhead	CUIF, NOWT
bloodhound	LYAM
bone	BANE
bound	STEND
breeches	TREWS
broth	BREE, BROO
brow of hill	SNAB
built	BAG
burden	BIRN
bushel	FOU

b

calves	CAUR, CAURE
came	CAM
catch	KEP
chalk	CAUK
check	WERE
chest	KIST
child	BAIRN
church	KIRK, KURK
comb	KAME
contend	KEMP
court, bring to	SIST
cut	KNAP, SNEG
dairymaid	DEY
damage	TEEN
damaged	LESED
dare	DAUR
devil	DEIL
did not know	KENNA
die	DEE
dig	HOWK
dining room	SPENCE
do	DAE, DIV
do not know	KENNA
dread	DREE
drip	SIE, SYE
dusty	MOTTY
earth	EARD
elder	ELLER
else	ENSE
empty	TOOM
endeavor	ETTLE
endure	DREE

c

extra	ORRA
eye	EE
eyes	EEN, EES
family	ILK
fidget	FIKE
firth	KYLE
fishing expedition	DRAVE
fit of sulks	GEE
flax refuse	PAB, POB
fog	DAG, HAR, HAAR
foretell	SPAE
give	GIE
glimpse	STIME
grandchild	OY, OYE
grant as property	DISPONE
great-grandchild	IEROE
grief	TEEN
have	HAE
hawk	ALLAN
heavy	THARF
hill	BEN, DOD, BRAE, DODD
hillside	BRAE
howl	YOWT
hurt	LESED
injure	TEEN
injured	LESED
intent	ETTLE
keg	KNAG

d

kinsman	SIB
kiss	PREE
knead	ELT
knock	KNOIT
lake	LOCH
leap	LOUP, LOWP, STEND
learning	LEAR
list of candidates	LEET
loaf	SORN
lop	SNATHE
lout	CUIF
love	LOE
loyal	LEAL
marriage portion	DOTE
millrace	LADE
mire	GLAUR
mist	URE
mountain	BEN
mouth, river	BEAL
mouth	BEAL
mud	GLAIR
must	MAUN
name	IAN
near, nearest	NAR
no	NAE
none	NANE
not matched	ORRA
now	NOO
nowhere	NAEGATE
oak	AIK

(Scottish words continued 140)

a

oatmeal dish ...... BROSE
odd .... ORRA
old age .... EILD
once .... ANES
one .... AIN, ANE, YIN
otherwise .... ELS
out .... OOT
own ...... AIN, ANE, AWN
pantry .... SPENCE
parlor .... BEN
payment .... MENSE
paw ground .... PAUT
peat cutter .... PINER
pig .... GRICE
pike .... GED, GEDD
pillory .... TRONE
pipe .... CUTTY
pluck wool .... ROO
pool ...... DIB, CARR,
              LINN, LLYN
present .... GIE
pretty .... GEY
prop .... RANCE
propriety .... MENSE
prune .... SNED
puddle .... DUB
pull .... PU
quagmire .... HAG
quarter of a year .. RAITH
relieve .... LISS

b

revenue, church .... ANNAT
ridge of a hill ...... SHIN
river .... DOON
rowboat .... COBLE
sailyard .... RAE
same .... ILK
scone .... FARL, FARLE
scoot .... SKYT, SKITE
scratch .... RIT
seep .... SIPE
seize .... VANG
self .... SEL
serve .... KAE
sever blow .... DEVEL
sheepfold .... REE
sheepstick .... KED
sheep walk .... SLAIT
shelter ..... BIELD, SHEAL
sift .... SIE
since .... SIN, SYNE
slope .... BRAE
slouch .... LOUCH
sly .... SLEE
small .... SMA
snow .... SNA
so .... SAE
son of .... MAC
song .... STROUD
sore .... SAIR
sorrow .... TEEN
sow .... SOO

e

steward .... MORMAOR
stipend .... ANNAT
stone STANE, STEAN, STEEN
stretch .... STENT
stupid one .... CUIF
suffer .... DREE
summit ...... DOD, DODD
sweetheart .... JO
than .... NA
to .... TAE
toe .... TAE
tone .... TEAN
trench .... GAW
truant, play ...... TRONE
try .... ETTLE
tune .... PORT
turnip .... NEEP
uncanny .... UNCO
uncle .... EME
urge .... ERT
very .... VERA
vex .... FASH
village .... REW
void, to render .... CASS
waterfall .. LIN, LYN, LINN
wealthy .... BIEN
weep .... ORP
week .... OUK
well .... AWEEL

d

weighing machine .. TRON,
                    TRONE
wet .... WAT
whirlpool ..... WEEL, WIEL
whiskey drink ..... ATHOL,
                    ATHOLE
widow's third ..... TERCE
workhouse .... AVER
year, ¼ of .... RAITH
yell .... GOWL
scoundrel ... ROGUE, VARLET
scout unit DEN, PACK, TROOP
scow ...... BARGE, LIGHTER
scow: Fr. .... ACON
scrap, table .... ORT
scraps of literature ..... ANA
scrape .. RAKE, RASP, GRAZE
scrape bottom ..... DREDGE
scratch ...... MAR, RAKE
scrawny animal ..... SCRAG
screamer bird ...... CHAJA
screed .... TIRADE
screen ...... SIFT, SHADE
screen, altar ..... REREDOS
screen, wind .... PARAVENT
script, modern Syriac .. SERTA
script, upright....... RONDE
scripture, early ..... ITALA
scripture passage ...... TEXT
scriptures, occult interpretation
                    CABALA
scrutinize .... EYE, SCAN

140

a
scuffle .... MELEE
sculptor of "Thinker" . RODIN
scum, metal .... DROSS
scup ...... BREAM, PORGY
scuppernong .... MUSCADINE
scuttle .... HOD
scuttle, coal .... HOD
scythe .... SY, SYE
scythe handle SNATH, SNEAD,
                SNEED, SNATHE
sea anemone POLYP, OPELET
sea bird .. ERN, ERNE, GULL,
    SKUA, SCAUP, TERN, FUL-
    MAR, GANNET, PETREL,
    SCOTER
sea bird, north ...... PUFFIN
sea cow . DUGONG, MANATEE
sea cucumber ..... TREPANG
sea demon, Teut. ...... WATE
sea duck .... COOT, ELDER,
            SCAUP, SCOTER
sea eagle ...... ERN, ERNE
sea-ear .... ABALONE
sea: Fr. .... MER
sea girdles .... CUVY
sea god .... LER, TRITON,
                    NEPTUNE
sea god, Gr. NEREUS, TRITON,
                    POSEIDON
sea god, Rom. ...... NEPTUNE
sea god, Teut. .. HLER, AEGIR

b
sea goddess, Norse ..... RAN
sea green .... CELADON
sea gull, Eur. .... MEW
sea, kept bow on ATRY, ATRIE
sea lettuce .... ALGA, LAVER
sea lettuce genus ULVA, ULUA
sea marker .... DAN
sea pheasant .... SMEE
sea robber .... PIRATE
sea mile, Austral. .... NAUT
sea nymph .... NEREID
sea shell .... TRITON
    (see also SHELL)
sea skeleton .... CORAL
sea slug genus .DOTO, ELYSIA
sea snail WELK, WILK, WHELK
sea snake, Asia ...... KERRIL
sea soldier .... MARINE
sea worm SAO, LURG, NEREIS
seal .... SIGIL
seal, eared .... OTARY
seal, fur .... URSAL
seal, letter .... CACHET
seal, official .... SIGNET
seal, papal .... BULLA
seal, young .... PUP
seals, group of .... POD
seamark .... BEACON
seamen: Brit. ...... RATINGS
seamlike ridge .... RAPHE

c
seams of boat, fill ..... CALK
SEAPORT .... see PORT
search .... GROPE
search for ...... HUNT, SEEK
search for food ..... FORAGE
season .... AGE, FALL, SALT,
                TIDE, SPRING
season, church LENT, ADVENT
season, Fr. .... ETE
seasons, goddesses of . HORAE
seasonal phenomenon . EPACT
seasoning ...... SAGE, SALT
seasoning herb .... SAGE,
                BASIL, THYME
seat, chancel .... SEDILE
seat, long ..... PEW, SETTEE
seat of oracle of Zeus DODONA
seat, Rom. .... SELLA
seaweed .. ORE, AGAR, ALGA,
        KELP, ALGAE, LAVER,
        VAREC
seaweed ashes .... KELP
seaweed, brown ...... KELP
seaweed, edible ...... AGAR
seaweed, edible Hawaiian LIMU
seaweed, purple .... LAVER
seaweed, purple, Jap. .. NORI
seaweed, red .... DULSE
Seb, consort of .... NUT

d
secluded .... REMOTE
second ABET, TRICE, MOMENT
second brightest star ... BETA
second-growth crop .. ROWEN
Second Punic War's end,
    site of .... ZAMA
secondary ...... BYE, LESS
second team .... SCRUB
secret ..... RUNE, ARCANE,
        COVERT, MYSTERY,
        ESOTERIC
secret agent .... SKY
secret society, Afr. EGBO, PORO
secret society in Sierra Leone
                        PORO
secrets .... ARCANA
secrets, one learning . EPOPT
secretion, sweet
            LAAP, LERP, LAARP
sect .... CULT
sect, Nepal . ACHAR, ACHARA
section of journey ...... LEG
secular .. LAY, LAIC, LAICAL
secure .. FIX, GET, PIN, FAST,
        NAIL, SAFE, FASTEN
secure firmly MOOR, ANCHOR
secure with rope ..... BELAY
security .... BOND
Sec'y of State, 1933-44 . HULL
sedate .... STAID
sedative .... NEMBUTAL

141

a
sediment .... LEES, SILT, DREGS, SILTAGE
see .... ESPY, LOOK
see: Lat. .... VIDE
seed ...... PIP, PIT, GRAIN, SPORE, PYRENE
seed coat or covering .. ARIL, HULL, HUSK, TESTA, TEGMEN, TESTAE, TEGUMEN, TEGIMINA
seed, edible .... PEA, BEAN, LENTIL, PINOLE
seed, edible, Asia .... SESAME
seed, immature ..... OVULE
seed, lens-shaped .... LENTIL
seed, nutlike ...... PINON
seed, opium poppy .... MAW
seed plant ...... ENDOGEN
seeds, remove .... GIN
sedless plant .... FERN
seek to attain ...... ASPIRE
seem .... LOOK
seesaw .... TEETER
segment last ...... TELSON
segment of body .... SOMITE
segment of circle .... ARC
segment, pert. to .... TORIC
seine .... NET
seize .. NAB, GRAB, GRASP, USURP, ARREST, COLLAR

b
seize: archaic .... REAVE
selections, literary ANA, ANALECTA
self .... EGO
self-assurance ..... APLOMB
self-defense, art of .... JUDO
self-denying ...... ASCETIC
self-education doctrine BIOSOPHY
self-locking nut .... PALNUT
self-reproach ..... REMORSE
sell .... VEND
seller .... COSTER, VENDER, VENDOR
semblance .... GUISE
semester .... TERM
semi-precious stone ONYX, SARD
semicircular room .... APSE
semidiameter ..... RADIUS
semidiameters ..... RADII
Seminole chief .... OSCEOLA
Semitic deity .... BAAL
sen, tenth of .... RIN
senate house ...... CURIA
senate houses ..... CURIAE
Senator, former .... BORAH
send back .. REMIT, REMAND
send money .... REMIT

c
send out ...... EMIT, ISSUE
sending forth ..... EMISSIVE
Senegambia gazelle .. KORIN
senility .... DOTAGE
senior .... ELDER
senior: Fr. .... AINE
senna, source of .... CASSIA
sennet .... SPET
sense .... FEEL
senseless .... INANE
sensitive .... SORE
sentence, analyze .... PARSE
sentenc part ...... CLAUSE
"Sentimental Journey" author STERNE
sentinel, mounted .. VEDETTE
separate SIFT, APART, SECERN
separated .... APART
separation .... SCHISM
sequence, 3-card .... TIERCE
sequester .... ISOLATE
Sequoia national park MUIR
seraglio .... HAREM, SERAI
serene .... SERENO
serf .... ESNE
serf, Rom. .... COLONA
serf, Spartant, ancient HELOT
sergeant fish ...... COBIA
series .... SET, GAMUT
series, in a ..... SERIATIM

d
series of tones ..... SCALE
serious .... GRAVE, EARNEST
sermon .... HOMILY
serow .... JAGLA
SERPENT .. see also SNAKE
serpent, Egypt. myth APEPI
serpent goddess, Egypt. .BUTO
serpent Gr. .... SEPS
serpent, large .BOA, PYTHON
serpent monster ... ELLOPS
serpent myth. .... BASILISK
serpent worship .... OPHISM
serpentine .... OPHITE
servant .... BOY, MAN, MAID, MENIAL
servant, India ..... HAMAL, FERASH, HAMMAL
servant, man's ...... VALET
servant, P. I. .... BATA
servants, for ...... MENIAL
serve soup .... LADLE
server .... TRAY
service, religious .... MASS
service tree .... SORB
servile .... MENIAL
serving boy .... PAGE
sesame ...... TIL, TEEL
sesame oil .... BENI, BENNE
sesame sed ...... GINGILI
session, hold ..... SIT, MEET

142

a

set aside .... DEFER
set in type .... PRINT
set limits to .... STINT
set price .... RATE
set system .... ROTE
set thickly .... STUD
setback .... REVERSE
Seth's brother .... CAIN
Seth's mother .... EVE
Seth's son .... ENOS
setting ...... SCENE, MILIEU
setting sun, Egyp. god of TEM,
          TUM, ATMU, ATUM
settled .... ALIT
settler .... BOOMER
seven .... SEPT
Seven Dwarfs .. DOC, DOPEY,
  HAPPY, GRUMPY, SLEEPY,
  SNEEZY, BASHFUL
seven, group of ... HEPTAD,
  PLEIAD, SEPTET, SEPTETTE
"Seventh Heaven" heroine
                       DIANE
seventh order, of .... SEPTIC
seventh, pert. to ... SEPTAN
sever ...... CUT, LOP, REND
severe .... STERN
severely criticize ...... PAN,
          SLATE, ROAST

b

sew hawk's eyelids ... SEEL
"Seward's —," Alaska . FOLLY
sexes, common to both
                     EPICENE
shabby .... WORN
shabby woman .... DOWD
shackle .... BOND, GYVE,
          IRON, FETTER
shad .... ALLIS, ALOSA,
          ALOSE, ALLICE
shaddock . POMELO, PUMELO
shade .... HUE, SCREEN
shade of difference . NUANCE
shade of meaning .. NUANCE
shaded walk .... MALL
shadow .... TAIL
shadow, eclipse ..... UMBRA
shaft ...... POLE, SPINDLE
shaft column, feather . SCAPE
shaft horse .... THILLER
shaft of column ...... FUST
shaft, wooden .... ARROW
shafter .... HORSE
shake .... JAR, JOLT, NIDGE
Shakespeare's elf ..... PUCK
Shakespeare's theatre . GLOBE
Shakespare's wife ... ANNE
Shakesperian clown . BOTTOM
Shakesperian forest . ARDEN
Shakesperian king ..... LEAR

c

Shakesperian shrew ... KATE
Shakesperian villain ... IAGO
shallow receptacle ..... TRAY
sham .... FAKE
Shamash, wife of ... AI, AYA
"Shane," star of ..... LADD
Shang dynasty .... YIN
shank .... CRUS, SHIN
shanks .... CRURA
shanty .... HUT
shape .... FORM, MOLD
shaped like a club . CLAVATE
shaped like a needle
          ACUATE, ACERATE
shaping tool .. LATHE, SWAGE
share ...... LOT, RATION
share .... PARTAKE
shark .... TOPE
shark, Eur. smalll ...... TOPE
shark, long-nosed ..... MAKO
shark, nurse .... GATA
shark parasite fish .. REMORA
sharp .... ACERB,
          ACUTE, ACUATE
sharp .... CHEAT
sharp ridge .... ARETE
sharpen . EDGE, HONE, WHET
sharpshooter . JAGER, SNIPER
shavetail: abbr. .... LT
shawl ...... MAUD, PAISLEY

d

shea tree .... KARITE
sheaf of grain: Her. ... GERB
shear .... CLIP
sheath, petiole ...... OCREA
Sheba: Lat. .... SABA
shed, as feathers
          MOLT, MOULT
shed for sheep .... COTE
sheen .... GLOSS
sheep ... EWE, RAM, MERINO
sheep, Afr. domestic ... ZENU
sheep, Afr. wild
          ARUI, UDAD, AOUDAD
sheep, Asia wild ... ARGALI
sheep, Asia, wild, mountain
  SHA, SNA, RASSE, URIAL,
  BHARAL, NAHOOR, OORIAL
sheep cry .... BAA, MAA
sheep diesase . COE, GID, ROT
sheep dog .... COLLIE
sheep, Eng. black-faced LONK
sheep, femal .... EWE
sheep genus .... OVIS
sheep in 2nd year
          TEG, TEGG, BIDENT
sheep, India, wild . SHA, SNA,
  URIAL, NAHOOR, OORIAL
sheep, large-horned
          AOUDAD, ARGALI
sheep, Leicester .... DISHLEY
sheep, male .... RAM, TUP

Sheep

a
sheep, N. Afr. wild
    ARUI, UDAD, AOUDAD
sheep, of . . . . OVINE
sheep owner, Bibl. . . . NABAL
sheep pasture, old Eng. . HEAF
sheep, pert. to . . . . . . OVINE
sheep, Tibet . . . . . SHA, SNA,
    URIAL, BHARAL, NAHOOR,
    OORIAL
sheep tick . . . . . . KED, KADE
sheep, unshorn HOGG, HEDER
sheep walk: Scot. . . . . . SLAIT
sheep, wild . . . SHA, SNA, ARUI,
    UDAD, RASSE, BHARAL,
    NAHOOR, AOUDAD, AR-
    GALI, OORIAL
sheep, young . . . . . TAG, TEG
sheepfold . . . . REE, COTE
sheeplike . . . . OVINE
sheepskin leather . . . BOCK,
    ROAN, SKIVER
sheerly . . . . SOLELY
shekel, ¼, Hebrew . . . . REBA
shelf . . . . LEDGE
shelf above altar . . RETABLE
shell . . . . BOMB
shell   TEST, LORICA, TUNICA
shell beads . . . . PEAG
shell, large . . . . CONCH
shell, marine . . . . TRITON
shell money . . . . ULLO,
b   COWRY, UHLLO, COWRIE
shellfish, edible
    CRAB, ABALONE, SCALLOU
shelter . . . . . LEE, COTE,
    SHED, HAVEN, SCREEN
shelter, hillside . . . . . . ABRI
shelter: Scot. . BIELD, SHEAL
shelter, to . . . . ALEE
sheltered . . . . ALEE
Shem descendant . . . . SEMITE
Shem's brother . . . . HAM
Shem's son
    LUD, ARAM, ELAM, ASSHUR
Sheol . . . . HADES
shepherd prophet . . . . . AMOS
shepherd's crook PEDA, PEDUM
shepherd's pipe . OAT REED
shepherd's son . . . MADRIGAL
shepherdess, "Winter's Tale"
    MOPSA
sheriff substitute . . . . ELISOR
sheriff's men . . . . . . POSSE
Sherwood . . . . FOREST
Shetland court president FOUD
Shetland hill pasture . HOGA
shield   ECU, EGIS AEGIS,
    PAVIS, DEFEND, PROTECT
shield, Athena's . . . . AEGIS
shield, Austral. . . . . MULGA
shield-bearing or border ORLE

c
shield, medieval . . . . ECU
shield, Rom.
    SCUTA, SCUTUM, CLIPEUS
shield-shaped
    PELTATE, SCUTATE
shield, small . . . . ECU
shield strap . . . . . . ENARME
shield's corner: Her. . CANTON
shift . . . . VEER
shift position GIBE, GYBE, JIBE
shin . . . . CNEMIS
shine
    GLOW, GLISTEN, ERADICATE
shingle, wedge-shaped . SHIM
shingles . . . . ZONA
shining . . . . NITID
Shinto deity . . . . KAMI
Shinto temple . . . . SHA
Shinto temple gate . . . . TORII
ship . . . KEEL, SEND, LINER,
    TANKER, TENDER, VESSEL,
    CARAVEL
ship, back part . . . . . STERN
ship boat . . . . . . GIG, DORY
ship body or frame . . . . HULL
ship bow, curve of . . . . LOOF
ship canvas . . . . SAIL
ship clock . . . . NEF
d ship drainage hole . SCUPPER
ship employee . . . . STEWARD
ship, 1st Northwest Passage
    GJOA
ship, forward part BOW, PROW
ship, fur-hunting . . . SEALER
ship, ironclad . . . . MONITOR
ship: Jap. . . . . MARO, MARU
ship keel, rear part . . SKEG
ship, large . . . . TONNER
ship, lowest part . . . . BILGE
ship, Medit. . . SETEE, SETTEE
ship, middle part . . . . WAIST
ship mooring place
    DOCK, BERTH
ship, oar-propelled . . GALLEY
ship, part of
    RIB, DECK, HULL, KEEL
ship plank . . . . . . STRAKE
ship platform . . . . DECK
ship pole . . . . . MAST, SPAR
ship shaped clock . . . . NEF
ship side, opp. middle ABEAM
ship timber, bevel . . SNAPE
ship timber curve . . . . SNY
ship timber, extra . . . . RIDER
ship wheel . . . . HELM
ship, wrecked . . . . . . HULK
ship, 1-masted . . . . . SLOOP
ship, 2-masted . . BRIG, SNOW
ship's kitchen . . . . . . GALLEY
shipboard covering . . . CAPOT

144

a shipbuilding curve ...... SNY
shipbuilding piece
           SPALE, THWART
shipworm ... BORER, TEREDO
shipwreck, causing
           NAUFRAGEOUS
shirk ...... GOLDBRICK
SHIRT ... see also GARMENT
shirt ...... KAMIS, CAMISE
shirt, Oriental ...... CAMISE
shoal .... REEF
shoal water deposit ... CULM
shock .... STUN,
    APPAL, APPALL, TRAUMA
shock absorber .... SNUBBER
shod, as monks .. CALCED
shoe ...... GAITER, SANDAL
shoe form .... LAST
shoe front .... VAMP
shoe gripper .... CLEAT
shoe, heavy BROGAN, BROGUE
shoe latchet .... TAB
shoe, mule .... PLANCH
shoe part
   LAST, RAND, WELT, INSOLE
b shoe strip ..... RAND, WELT
shoe, wooden .. GETA, SABOT
shoe, wooden-soled ... CLOG
shoes .... SHOON
shoes, Mercury's winged
           TALARIA
shoelace .... LACET
shoemakers' saint .. CRISPIN
shoemaker's tool ...... AWL
shoot .... BAG, POT
shoot at from ambush . SNIPE
shoot at, marble to .... MIG
shoot, cotton ...... RATOON
shoot, plant .... BINE, CION,
      GEMMA, SPRIT,
           STOLO, STOLON
shoot, small .... SPRIG
shoot, sugar cane .. RATOON
shooter, hidden ..... SNIPER
shooter marble .... TAW,
           AGATE, AGGIE
shooting match .... TIR
shooting match: Fr. ...... TIR
shooting star .... LEONID
shop .... STORE
shop, Rom. wine .. TABERNA
shops, Rom. wine TABERNAE
shop's name plate .... FACIA
shore ...... COAST, STRAND
SHORE BIRD see BIRD, SHORE
short .... CURT,
    BRIEF, TERSE, STUBBY

e short-breathed ...... PURSY
short comedy sketch ... SKIT
short-spoken .. CURT, TERSE
short tail .... SCUT
shorten ... CUT, DELE, ELIDE
shortly
   ANON, SOON, PRESENTLY
Shoshonean .... UTE
shoulder blade .... SCAPULA
shoulder, of the
           ALAR, SCAPULAR
shoulder ornament
           EPAULET, EPAULETTE
shoulder, road .... BERM
shoulder wrap ...... SHAWL
shout CRY, CALL, ROAR, YELL
shove .... PUSH
shovel .... SPADE
show as false .... BELIE
show off .... FLAUNT
show place, Rom. ... CIRCUS
show, street .... RAREE
"Showboat" author ... FERBER
showy .... LOUD
shrew .... ERD, TARTAR
shrewd SAGE, CANNY, ASTUTE
shrike genus .... LANIUS
d shrill .... PIPY
shrill, to ...... STRIDULATE
shrimplike crustacean PRAWN
shrine .... ALTAR
shrink .... CONTRACT
shroud-stopper: naut. .. WAPP
SHRUB ..... see also TREE
shrub and tree ...... ALDER
shrub, Asia .... CHE
shrub, berry-bearing .. ELDER
shrub, berry, Pacific .. SALAL
shrub, Chin. .... TEA
shrub, Congo medical . BOCCA
shrub, desert
           RETEM, OCOTILLO
shrub, Eng. ... . HEATH
shrub, evergreen BOX, YEW,
    TITI, ERICA, HEATH, SAL-
    AL, OLEANDER
shrub, flowering ITEA, AZALEA,
    PRIVET, SPIREA, SPIRAEA,
    SYRINGA
shrub genus BIXA, INGA, ITEA,
    ROSA, ALDER, IXORA,
    AZALEA
shrub, Hawaiian .... OLONA
shrub, low spiny .... GORSE
shrub, Medit. .... CAPER
shrub, poisonous
           SUMAC, SUMACH
shrub, prickly .... CAPER

a

shrub, Rhus genus .... SUMAC, SUMACH
shrub, strong-scented . BATIS
shrub with grapelike fruit SALAL
shrub, yellow flowers OLEASTER
shun .... AVOID, DODGE
shut up .... IMMURE
shy .... JIB, BALK
SIAM . see also SPECIAL SECTION
Siamese .... THAI
Siam. coin .... ATT
Siam. garment ..... PANUNG
Siam. group ..... KUI, LAO
Siam. monetary unit ... BAHT
Siamese twin .. ENG, CHANG
SIBERIAN . see also RUSSIAN
Siberian .... TATAR
Siberian wild cat .... MANUL
Siberian squirrel .... MINIVER
sibilant sound .... HISS
Sicilian resort .... ENNA
sickle, curved like .. FALCATE
sickle: variant .... SIVE
side, jewel's .... FACET
side arm .... GUN, SWORD, PISTOL, REVOLVER

b

side: Lat. .... LATUS
side of head .. LORA, LORUM
side, pert. to COSTAL, LATERAL
side-post, door's ..... JAMB
sidetrack .... SHUNT
side street, Chin. .. HUTUNG
side timber: naut. .... BIBB
side, toward the ... LATERAD
sidereal .... ASTRAL
sidewalk .... PAVEMENT
sidewalk edge .. CURB, KERB
sidewinder ...... CROTALUS
sidle .... EDGE
Siegfried's murderer .. HAGEN
siesta .... NAP
sieve .. SIFT, PUREE, BOLTER
sieve for clay .... LAUN
Sif, son of ..... ULL, ULLR
sift .... SCREEN
sift: dialect .... REE
sift: old Eng. .... LUE
sift: Scot. .... SIE
sifter .... SIEVE
sigh .... SOUF, SOUGH
sight, come into ..... LOOM
sight, dimness of .... CALIGO
sight on gun .... BEAD
sight, pert. to ..... OCULAR
sign ... MARK, OMEN, TOKEN

c

sign, music .. PRESA, SEGNO
sign: old Eng. .... SEIN
sign, pert. to .... SEMIC
sign up .... ENROL, ENROLL
signal for attention ..... PST
signal for parley .. CHAMADE
signal to act .... CUE
signal to begin .... CUE
signature, affix SIGN, ENDORSE
signet .... SIGIL
signify .... MEAN, DENOTE
"Silas Marner" author .. ELIOT
silence ...... GAG, HUSH
silence: music .... TACET
silent .. MUM, MUTE, TACIT
silica .... SAND, SILEX
silica, rich in .... ACIOLIC
silicate .... MICA
silk-cotton tree CEIBA, KAPOK
silk-cotton tree fiber KAPOK, KUMBI
silk fabric .... GROS, MOFF, PEKIN, SATIN, TULLE
silk filament .... BRIN
silk, fine ...... CRIN, TULLE
silk, heavy .... GROS
silk in cocoon .... BAVE
silk, India .. ROMAL, RUMAL
silk, old heavy .... CAMACA

d

silk, raw .... GREGE
silk substitute .... NYLON, RAYON, ORLON, DACRON
silk thread .... FLOSS
silk, twilled .... ALMA
silk, unravel ...... SLEAVE
silken .... SERIC
silkworm, Assam. .. ERI, ERIA
silkworm, China ..... TASAR
silkworm disease ...... UJI
silly .... INANE
silver: Her. .... ARGENT
silver lactate ...... ACTOL
silver ore .... PACO
silver, uncoined, in ingots SYCEE
silverfish . TARPON, TARPUN
silverize .... PLATE
silvery .... ARGENT
silvery-white metal . COBALT
simian .... APE
similar ...... LIKE, SUCH
Simon .... PETER
simper .... SMIRK
simple .... EASY, MERE
simple sugar .... OSE
simpleton, ... ASS, DAW, OAF, BOOB, COOT, FOOL, GABY, GAWK, GOWK, SIMP, GOOSE
simulate APE, SHAM, FEIGN, PRETEND

a

sin	ERR, EVIL
sin, grief for	ATTRITION
Sinai	HOREB
Sinbad's bird	ROC
since	AGO
since: Scot.	SIN, SYNE
Sinclair Lewis character	CASS
sine — non	QUA
sine qua —	NON
sinew	TENDON
sinewy	WIRY
sing	LILT, CAROL
sing, as a round	TROLL
sing softly	CROON
sing, Swiss style	JODEL, YODEL, YODLE
singer, synagogue	CANTOR
singing bird	OSCINE
singing girl, Egyptian	ALMA, ALME, ALMAH, ALMAI, ALMEH
singing, suitable for	MELIC
single	ONE, BILL, MONO, ONLY, UNAL
single out	CHOOSE
single: prefix	MONO
single thing	ONE, UNIT
singleton	ACE
sink, as putt	HOLE
sink: geol.	DOLINA

b

sinuous	WAVY, SERPENTINE
sinus cavities	ANTRA
Sioux, Siouan	OTO, OTOE
sir: India	MIAN
sir: Malay	TUAN
siren, Rhine	LORELEI
Sisera's killer	JAEL
sister	NUN, SIB
"Sistine Madonna" painter	RAPHAEL
sitatunga, Afr.	NAKONG
sitting	POSING, SEANCE, SESSION
sitting on	ASTRIDE
situation, difficult	STRAIT
siva snake	COBRA
Siva, wife of	DEVI, KALI, SATI
six, group of	SENARY, SESTET, SEXTET
six-line verse	SESTET, SESTINA
six on a die	CISE, SICE, SISE
six, series of	HEXAD
six: Sp.	SEIS
sixpence: slang	SICE
sixteen annas	RUPEE
sixth: music	SEXT
sixth sense: abbr.	ESP
size of shot	BB, FF, TT
sizing	SEALER
skate	RAY
skate genus	RAIA

c

skating area	RINK
skegger	PARR
skein of yarn	RAP, HANK
skeletal	BONY
skeleton, sea animal	CORAL, SPONGE
skeptic	AGNOSTIC
sketch	DRAW, OUTLINE
ski, heel spring	AMSTUTZ
ski race	SLALOM
ski run	SCHUSS, SLALOM
ski wax	KLISTER
skier, mark of	SITZMARK
skiing position	VORLAGE
skiing, zigzag	SLALOM
skilled person	ADEPT
skillful	ABLE, DEFT, ADEPT, HABILE
skillfully	ABLY
skim over	SKIP
skin	FLAY, DERMA
skin, deeper layer	CUTIS
skin, design on	TATOO, TATTOO
skin disease	ACNE, MANGE, PSORA, TETTER
skin disease, horse's	CALORIS
skin disease, Peru	UTA
skin infection	LEPRA
skin layer	DERM, CUTIS, DERMA, CORIUM, ENDERON

d

skin of a beast	FELL
skin, pert. to	DERIC, DERMIC
skinflint	MISER
skink, Egypt.	ADDA
skip	OMIT
skip a stone	DAP
skip happily	CAPER
skipjack	ELATER
skirmish	MELEE
skirt, ballet	TUTU
skirt section	PANEL
skittle	PIN
skulk	LURK
skull, pert. to	INIAL, INION
skull protuberance	INION
skullcap, Arab.	CHECHIA
skunk	CHINCHA, CHINCHE
sky	FIRAMENT
sky god, Assyrian	ANAT
sky: Chin.	TIEN
sky god, Babyl.	ABU, ANU
sky god, Norse	TIU, TIW, TYR, ZIO, ZIU
sky, highest part	ZENITH
sky: Polyn.	LANGI
sky serpent, Vedic	AHI
slab, engraved	TABLET
slab, flooring, decorative	DALLE
slag	DROSS, SCORIA

147

a

slam .... BANG
slam in cards .... VOLE
slander ..... LIBEL, ASPERSE
slang .... ARGOT
slant .... BEVEL, SLOPE
slanted edge .... BEVEL
slanted: naut. .... ARAKE
slanting ...... SKEW, ASKEW
slanting type .... ITALIC
slantingly, drive ...... TOE
slap .... CUFF, SPANK
slash .... JAG, SLISH
slater's tool, same as slate-
          trimming tool
slate-trimming tool
          SAX, ZAT, ZAX
Slav .... SERB
Slav, ancient
     VEND, WEND, VENED
Slav, E. Ger. .... WEND
Slav in Saxony ...... SORB
slave ... ESNE, SERF, THRALL
slave, fugitive ..... MAROON
slave, Spartan .... HELOT
sled, Swiss .... LUGE
sled to haul logs ..... TODE
sleep ...... NAP, NOD, DOZE
sleep, deep .... SOPOR
sleep lightly .... DOZE

b

sleeping .... DORMANT
sleeping place
       BED, COT, BERTH
sleeping sickness fly . TSETSE
sleeve, large ...... DOLMAN
sleigh .... PUNG
sleight-of-hand ...... MAGIC
slender .... LANK, LEAN,
       SLIM, THIN, REEDY
slender woman ...... SYLPH
slice, bacon .... RASHER
slice of meat .... COLP
slice, thick .... SLAB
slick .... LOY
slide .... SKID, SLUE
sliding door, Jap. .. FUSUMA
sliding piece .... CAM
sliding valve .... PISTON
slight ... MERE, SLIM, FAINT
slight intentionally
          SLUR, SNUB
slimy .... COZY
sling around .... SLUE
slip
    ERR, BONER, GLIDE, LAPSE
slip by .... ELAPSE
slip out of course ..... SLUE
slip, plant ... CION, CUTTING
slipknot .... NOOSE
slipper .... MULE, MOYLE
slipper, P. I. ...... CHINELA
slope ..... RAMP, GRADIENT
slope: fort. .... GLACIS

e

slope of vein or lode ... HADE
slope of land ..... VERSANT
slope: Scot. .... BRAE
slope, steep .. SCARP, ESCARP
sloping edge
       BASIL, BEZEL, BEZIL
sloth, three-toed .... AI
sloth, two-toed .... UNAU
slouch: Scot. .... LOUCH
slow .... POKY
slow loris .... KOKAM
slow: music . TARDO, LARGO
      LENTO, ADAGIO, ANDANTE
slower: music .... RIT
sluggish .... DOPEY
sluice .... CLOW
slump .... RECESSION
slur over .... ELIDE
slushy mass .... FOSH
sly look ...... LEER, OGLE
sly: old Eng. ... SLEE, SLOAN
sly: Scot. .... SLEE
smack ..... BUSS, KISS, SLAP
small .... WEE, TINY,
       PETIT, PETTY, PETITE
small amount . DRAM, MINIM
small arachnid .... MITE
small bottle .... VIAL
small bunch .... WISP

d

small case .... ETUI
small cluster .... SPRIG
small coin .... MITE
small creature
       MITE, MINIMUS
small dog ...... POM, PUG
       PUP, PEKE, FEIST
small goby, Atlantic .. MAPO
small: law .... PETIT
small marine animal ... SALP
small monkey ...... LEMUR
small pearl .... PEARLET
small poem .... ODELET
small: Scot. .... SMA
small stream
       RUN, RILL, RILLET
small: suffix .... ING
small weight .. GRAM, MITE
smallest .... LEAST
smallest integer .... ONE
smallpox .... VARIOLA
smaragd .... EMERALD
smart .... STING
smart CHIC, ASTUTE, CLEVER
smartly dressed .. CHIC, TRIG
smear on .... DAUB
smell, disagreeable
       OLID, REEK, FETOR
smelting mixture .... MATTE
smelting waste . SLAG, DROSS
smirch .... SULLY
smith, aided Siegfried . MIME

smock .... CAMISE
smoke ...... FUME, REEK
smoke-colored ..... FUMOUS
smoke, wisp of ..... FLOC
smoked beef .... PASTRAMI
smokeless powder ..... FILITE
smoking .... AREEK
smoking pipe .. BRIAR, BRIER
smoking pipe, Oriental
　　　　HOOKAH, NARGILE
smoky .... FUMID
smooth
　EVEN, IRON, LEVEL, PREEN
smooth-breathing ..... LENE
smooth, make .... LEVIGATE
smooth: phonetics ..... LENE
smooth-spoken .... GLIB
smoothing tool .... PLANE
snail, large WHELK, ABALONE
snail, marine .... TRITON
snake .... ASP, BOA, ADDER,
　VIPER, PYTHON, REPTILE
snake, Amer. . ADDER, RACER
snake-bite antidote
　　　　GUACO, CEDRON
snake, black .... RACER
snake charmer's clarinet BEEN
snake-haired woman GORGON,
　MEDUSA, STHENO, EURYALE
snake, India .... COBRA,
　KRAIT, DABOIA, DABOYA
snake-like .... SINUOUS
snake, S. Amer. ..... ABOMA
snake, tree .... LORA
snake, venomous, Ind. BONGAR
snakebird .... DARTER
snakeroot, white ..... STEVIA
snakes, pert. to .... OPHIOID
snap up bargains ..... SNUP
snapper ...... SESI, PARGO
snapper fish: Maori . TAMURE
snapper: N. Z. ...... TAMURE
snare . GIN, NET, WEB, TRAP
snarl .... GNAR, GNARR
snatch .... GRAB, SEIZE
sneer
　GIBE, JIBE, FLEER, SCOFF
sniff .... NOSE
snipe, Europ. ...... BLEATER
snipe's cry .... SCAPE
snoring .... STERTOR
snow field, Alpine FIRN, NEVE
snow goose genus ... CHEN
snow, ground down ... LOLLY
snow house
　IGLU, IGLOE, IGLOO, IGLOU
snow leopard .... OUNCE
snow lily .... VIOLET
snow, living in ...... NIVAL
snow mouse .... VOLE

snow panther .... OUNCE
snow runner ...... SKI, SKEE
snow: Scot. .... SNA
SNOW WHITE
　　　see SEVEN DWARFS
snuff .... RAPPEE
snuffbox bean
　　CACOON, MACKAYBEAN
snug .... COSY, COZY
snuggery .... NEST
so .... THUS, TRUE, VERY
so be it! .... AMEN
so much: music ..... TANTO
so: Scot. .... SAE
soak .... RET, SOG, SOP, WET
soak flax .... RET
soap, fine .... CASTILE
soap-frame bar ...... SESS
soap: pharm. .... SAPO
soap plant .... AMOLE
soap substitute ..... AMOLE
soap vine .... GOGO
soapstone .... TALC
soapy mineral .... TALC
sober ...... GRAVE, STAID
social affair .... TEA
social division ...... CASTE
social unit or group ... SEPT
society, entrance into . DEBUT
society swell .... NOB
sock, Jap. .... TABI
sock, Rom. .... UDO
sod .... TURF
sodium alum ... MENDOZITE
sodium carbonate ... TRONA
sodium chloride ..... SALT
sodium chloride: pharm. . SAL
sodium compound ... SODA
sodium nitrate . NITER, NITRE
sofa .... DIVAN
soft
　LOW, EASY, WAXY, TENDER
soft area on bill .... CERE
soft drink
　ADE, POP, COLA, SODA
soft feathers .. DOWN, EIDER
soft ice from floes ... LOLLY
soft job .... SNAP, SINECURE
soft mass .... WAD
soft palate .... VELUM
soft palate lobe .... UVULA
soft palate, pert. to
　　　　VELAR, UVULAR
soft palates .... VELA
soft-spoken .... MEALY
soften in temper .... RELENT
softly: music ...... SOAVE
soil: comb. form ..... AGRO
soil, organic part ... HUMUS

149

Soil

soil, rich .... **LOAM**
soil, sticky . **GOMBO, GUMBO**
soil, type of ...... **PEDOCAL**
solar disc ..... **ATEN, ATON**
solar over lunar year,
   excess of .... **EPACT**
soldier: Am. Rev. . **BUCKSKIN**
soldier, Austral., N. Z. **ANZAC**
soldier, Brit. .... **ATKINS**
soldier, former ...... **LANCER**
soldier, Gr. .... **HOPLITE**
soldier, Indo-Brit. .... **SEPOY**
soldier, native India .. **SEPOY**
soldier's shelter .... **FOXHOLE**
sole .... **PELMA**
sole of foot .... **VOLA**
sole of plow .... **SLADE**
solemn declaration
   VOW, OATH
solicit .... **BEG, URGE,**
   COURT, CANVASS
solicitor's chamber ...... **INN**
solicitude .... **CARE**
solid ... **CONE, CUBE, PRISM**
solid, become
   GEL, SET, HARDEN
solid: comb. form ... **STEREO**
solidify .. **GEL, SET, HARDEN**
solitary .. **LONE, ONLY, SOLE**
solo .... **ARIA**
Solomon's aid giver .. **HIRAM**
Solomon's temple rebuilder
   HIRAM
solution .... **KEY**
solution, strength of
   TITER, TITRE
solvent .... **ACETONE**
solvent, treat with . **SOLUTIZE**
some .... **ANY**
somite .... **MEROSOME**
son: Fr. .... **FILS**
son-in-law .... **GENER**
son: Ir. .... **MAC**
son of .... **MAC**
son of Agrippina ...... **NERO**
son of Joktan .... **OPHIR**
son of Reuben .... **PALLU**
son of: Scot. .... **MAC**
song .... **LAY, ODE, DITE,**
   DITTY, MELOS, TROLL
song, Christmas
   NOEL, CAROL, WASSAIL
song for solo voices .... **GLEE**
song: Ger. .... **LIED**
song, Hawaiian .... **MELE**
song, Jap. .... **UTA**
song, morning: poet. .. **MATIN**
song, of a .... **MELIC**
song of praise, joy
   PEAN, PAEAN, ANTHEM
"Song of the South" Uncle
   REMUS

song, operatic .... **ARIA**
song, religious
   HYMN, CHANT, ANTHEM
song, sacred
   HYMN, CHANT, ANTHEM
song, sad .... **DIRGE**
song: Scot. .... **STROUD**
song, simple .... **DITTY**
song, Sp. .... **CANCION**
song thrush .. **MAVIE, MAVIS**
sonship .... **FILIETY**
soon .... **ANON**
sooner .... **ERE, ERER**
soot .... **COOM, SMUT**
soot: old Eng. .... **SOTE**
soothe .... **EASE, LULL**
soothing **ANODYNE, LENITIVE**
soothsayer .... **SEER**
Sophocles, play by .. **OEDIPUS**
soprano, prima donna . **ALDA,**
   BORI, PONS, RISE,
   RAISA, CALLAS, STEBER
sora bird .... **RAIL**
sorceress .... **CIRCE**
sorceress, Hindu ...... **USHA**
sorceress, myth. ...... **LAMIA**
sorceress, "Odyssey," Greek
   CIRCE
sorcery, W. Ind.
   OBE, OBI, OBEAH
sore, make .... **RANKLE**
sore: Scot. .... **SAIR**
sorghum variety ...... **MILO**
sorrow .... **DOLOR, REMORSE**
sorrow, feel
   RUE, LAMENT, REPENT
sorrowful **SAD, BLUE, DOLENT**
sort .... **KIND,**
   CLASS, GROUP, SPECIES
sortie .... **SALLY**
sortilege .... **LOT**
sorting machine .... **GRADER**
soul .... **ANIMA**
soul, Egyp. .... **BA, KA**
soul, Hindu **ATMA, ATMAN**
sound .. **TONE, NOISE, VALID**
sound, kind of ..... **PALATAL**
sound loudly . **BLARE, LARUM**
sound, monotonous
   HUM, DRONE
sound perception ...... **EAR**
sound, pert. to ..... **SONANT**
sound reasoning ...... **LOGIC**
sound, resemblance of
   ASSONANT
sound, solid .... **KLOP**
sound the ocean
   PLUMB, FATHOM

sound waves, of ..... AUDIO
sound, without .... ASONANT
sounding .... SONANT
soundless .... ASONANT
soup, heavy . PUREE, POTAGE
soup spoon .... LADLE
soup, thick .... BISK,
HOOSH, PUREE, BISQUE
soup vessel .... TUREEN
souffin shark .... TOPE
sour .... ACID, ACERB,
ACIDIC, ACETOSE
sour-curdled milk: Nor. SKYR
sour-leaved plant .... SORREL
sour milk drink LEBAN, LEBEN
source, mineral .... ORE
source, obsidian's ...... LAVA
soursop .... ANNONA
south: Sp. .... SUR
South African .... BOER
SOUTH AFRICA ... see also
SPECIAL SECTION
S. Afr. assembly ...... RAAD
S. Afr. dialect .... TAAL
S. Afr. Dutch ... BOER, TAAL
S. Afr. garter snake ... ELAPS
S. Afr. grass country ... VELD
S. Afr. greenhorn .... IKONA
S. Afr. gully .... DONGA
S. Afr. "out" .... UIT
S. Afr. town .... STAD
S. Afr. village ...... KRAAL
SOUTH AMERICA ... see also
SPECIAL SECTION
South American animal TAPIR
S. Amer. bird .. GUAN, JACU,
SYLPH, TURCO, SERIEMA
S. Amer. game bird TINAMOU
S. Amer. Indian group ... GES
S. Amer. lizard .... TEJU
S. Amer. tree
VERA, CEBIL, FOTUI
S. Amer. ungulate .... TAPIR
"South Pacific" hero .. EMILE
Southern Cross constellation
CRUX
Southern France ...... MIDI
Southern river ...... PEEDEE
Southern state: abbr. ... ALA
Southwest river .... RED
sovereign (coin) ...... SKIV
sovereignty .... EMPERY
SOVIET .. see also RUSSIAN
Soviet news agency ... TASS
Soviet newspaper ... PRAVDA
sow .... PIG, GILT
sow .... SEED, PLANT
sow: Prov. Eng. .... YELT
sow: Scot. .... SOO
sower .... SEEDER
sown: Her. .... SEME
soybean .... SOJA, SOYA

spa, Bohemian .... BILIN
spa, Eng. .... BATH
spa, Ger. ..... EMS, BADEN
space between bird's eye
and bill .... LORA, LORE,
LORUM
space between triglyphs
METOPE
space, small AREOLA, AREOLE
spaces on bird's face
LORAE, LORES
spade .... LOY, SHOVEL
spade, narrow ... LOY, SPUD
spade-shaped ... PALACEOUS
spade, turf .... SLANE
Spain, ancient ...... IBERIA
SPANISH see also SPAIN, SPE-
CIAL SECTION
SP. ARTIST
see SP. PAINTER
Sp. belle .... MAJA
Sp. cellist .... CASALS
Sp. coin, old ...... PISTOLE
Sp. dance .... JOTA, BOLERO
Sp. epic .... CID
Sp. explorer
CORTEZ, BALBOA, CORTES
Sp. fabric .... CREA
Sp. fortress commander CAID
Sp. game of ball ... PELOTA
Sp. general, dukes ALBA, AVA
Sp. hero .... CID
Sp. kettle .... OLLA
Sp. lady ... DONA, SENORA
Sp. length unit .... VARA
Sp. man ...... DON, SENOR
Sp. nun .... AVILA
Sp. painter
GOYA, MIRO, SERT, PICASSO
Sp. poet .... ENCINA
Sp. pot .... OLLA
Sp. title DON, SENOR, SENORA

SPANISH WORDS:
(tilde omitted throughout)
abbey .... ABADIA
afternoon .... TARDE
annatto seeds .. ACHIOTE
another .... OTRO
article .... EL, LA, LAS,
LOS, UNO
ass .... ASNO
aunt .... TIA
bay .... BAHIA
bean .... HABA
before .... ANTES
being .... ENTE
black .... NEGRA
blue .... AZUL
box canyon .... CAJON

a

boy	NINO
bravo!	OLE
bull	TORO
but	PERO
canal	CANO
chaperon	DUENA, DUENNA
chest	CAJETA
chief	JEFE, ADALID
child	NINO
church	IGLESIA
city	CIUDAD
clay building	ADOBE, TAPIA
cloak	CAPA
clothes	ROPA
corral	ATAJO
cut	TAJO
day	DIA
dining hall	SALA
dove	PALOMA
drawing room	SALA
estuary	RIA
evening	TARDE
evil	MALO
first	PRIMUS
for	POR
friend	AMIGO
funds	CAJA
girl	NINA
God	DIOS
gold	ORO
good-bye	ADIOS

b

grass fiber rope	SOGA
grille	REJA
gulch	ARROYO
gypsy	GITANO
hall	SALA
hamlet	ALDA
harbor entrance	BOCA
health	SANO
hello	HOLLA
hill	ALTO, CERRO, MORRO
hillside	FALDA
hotel	POSADA
house	CASA
Indian	INDIO
inlet	RIA, ESTERO
jail keeper	CAID
judge	JUEZ
king	REY
lady	DAMA
lake	LAGO
landmark	SENAL
latter	ESTE
lawsuit	ACTO
letter	CARTA
lime	LIMA
love	AMOR
man	HOMBRE
manservant	MOZO
mayor	ALCADE, ALCALDE

c

mouth	BOCA
movie house	CIN…
meadow	VEGA
my	MI…
of	D…
open space	COSO
other	OTRA
parish priest	CURA
peak	PICO
people	GENT…
pine	PINO
pole	PALO
pole, wooden	PALO
porridge	ATOL…
post office	CORREO
pot	OLLA
priest	CURA, PADR…
queen	REINA
ragged person	ROTO
raisin	PASA
red	ROJO
river	RIO
road	CAMINO
room	SALA
rum	RON
saint, feminine	SANTA
she	ELLA
silver	PLATA
six	SEIS
snake	CULEBRA
song	CANCION
south	SU…
street	CALLE, CALL…
sweet potato	CAMOT…
tall	ALTA
this	ESTA, EST…
three	TRES
to be	SER, EST…
tomorrow	MANANA
trench	TAJO
uncle	TIO
very	MU…
water	AGUA
wax	CERA
wit	SA…
with	D…
work	OBRA
yes	S…
you	T…

d

spar	BOX, BOOM, GAFF, MAST, YARD, SPRI…
spar for colors	GAF…
spar, heavy	BARIT…
spar, loading	STEEV…
spar, small	SPRI…
spare	LEAN, EXTRA, GAUNT, LENTE…
sparkle	GLITTE…
sparkling, as wine	MOUSSEU…
sparrow, hedge	DONE…

152

Sparta queen .... LEDA
Spartan army division . MORA
Spartan magistrate .. EPHOR
spasm .... FIT, TIC, JERK
spawning place .... REDD
speak
        UTTER, ORATE, DECLAIM
speak: comb. form .... LALO
speak, inability to .. ALALIA
speak theatrically .... EMOTE
speaker .. ORATOR, LOCUTOR
speaking tube, pilot's GOSPORT
spear .... DART, LANCE
spear, Afr. ASSAGAI, ASSEGAI
spear, fish ...... GIG, GAFF
spear-like weapon
        PIKE, LANCE
spear-shaped ...... HASTATE
spear, 3-prong .... TRIDENT
spear thrower, Austral.
        WOMERA
special: Moslem law
        KHAS, KHASS
species .... KIND, SORT
specific date .... DAY
specified time .... DATE
specimen .... SAMPLE
speck ... DOT, MOTE, FLECK
speckle ......DOT, STIPPLE
spectacle .... PAGEANT
specter ...... BOGY, BOGEY,
        GHOST, SHADE
speech .. LECTURE, ORATION
speech, art of .... RHETORIC
speech defect
        LISP, ALOGIA, STAMMER
speech goddess, Hindu
        VAC, DEVI, VACH
speech, local .... PATOIS
speech, long .... SPIEL
speech, loss of .... APHASIA
speech peculiarity .... IDIOM
speech, violent ...... TIRADE
speechless .... DUMB, MUTE
speed ...... HIE, RUN, PACE,
        RACE, HASTE, HASTEN,
        RAPIDITY
speed, at full .... AMAIN
spelt .... ADOR, EMMER
Spenser heroine ...... UNA
Spenser's name for Ireland
        IRENA
sphre .... ORB
sphere of action ..... ARENA
spice .... MACE
spice ball .. FAGOT, FAGGOT
spicknel .... MEU, MEW
spicy .... RACY
spider crab genus
        MAIA, MAJA
spider fluid: Pharm. ARANEIN

spider monkey
        QUATA, ATELES, COAITA
spider nest .... NIDUS
spigot .... TAP
spike ..... EAR, GAD, BROB
spikenard .... NARD
spin
        BIRL, REEL, TWIRL, ROTATE
spinal column .. AXIS, AXON
spinal cord .... MYELON
spinal membrane ..... DURA
spindle .... COP, AXLE
spindle, yarn .... HASP
spine .... AXIS, AXON
spine bones .... SACRA
spine, slender .... SETA
spineless cactus .... CHAUTE
spiniform .... SPINATE
spinning jenny .... MULE
spiny shrub genus .... ULEX
spiral formation .... VOLUTE
spire ornament .... EPI
spirit .. ELAN, SOUL, METAL
spirit: Egyp. myth ... BA, KA
spirit: Ger. .... GEIST
spirit, Ir. BANSHEE, BANSHIE
spirit lamp .... ETNA
spirit, Moslem ..... JIN, JINN,
        GENIE, GENII, JINNI, JINNEE
spirit of air .... ARIEL
spirit of evil . DEMON, DEVIL
spirit of man: Egypt .... AKH
spirit raiser . ELATER, ELATOR
spirited ... EAGER, CONMOTO
spirited horse .... STEED
spirits and water ..... GROG
spirits of the dead ... MANES
spiritual body: Egypt. .. SAHU
spiritual struggle .... PENIEL
spiritualist meeting .. SEANCE
splash .... LAP
spleen .... MILT
splendid .... GRAND
splendor .... ECLAT
splendor, goddess of: Hindu
        UMA
split ...... RIT, RENT, RIVE,
        CLEFT, RIVEN, CLEAVE
split pulse .... DAL
spoil .... ROT, BOTCH
spoil, as eggs .... ADDLE
spoils of war .... LOOT
spoken .... ORAL
spoken word ...... AGRAPH
spokes, having ...... RADIAL
sponge, calcareous .. LEUCON
sponge gourd .. LOOF, LOOFA
sponge on ... MUMP, LEACH
sponge spicule, bow-shaped
        OXEA, TOXA, PINULUS
sponge, young .... ASCON

153

spongewood .... SOLA
sponsor .... PATRON
sponsorship ..... EGIS, AEGIS
spool .... REEL
spore .... SEED
spore cluster .... SORUS
spore fruit of rust fungi
    AECIA, TELIA, AECIUM, TELIUM
spore sac, fungus ASCI, ASCUS
sport .... RUX, GAME, GOLF, PLAY, POLO
sports arena
    STADIA, STADIUM
sports center .. RINK, ARENA
sports hall .... GYM
spot in mineral ..... MACLE
spot on card .... PIP
spotted ...... PIED, PINTO, DAPPLED, MACULOSE
spotted cavy .... PACA
spotted deer KAKAR, CHITAL
spotted moth .... FORESTER
spotted sting-ray .... OBISPO
spotted, to make
    DAPPLE, STIPPLE
spouse .... MATE, WIFE
spray .... ATOMIZE
spray, sea .... LIPPER
spread .... TED
spread by peening .... RIVET
spread by report
    BRUIT, NORATE
spread out .... FAN
spread rumor ...... GOSSIP
spread the word ..... TELL
spread to dry, as hay ... TED
sprightly ..... PERT, PEART
spring .... SPA
spring back .... RESILE
spring: Bible .... AIN
spring-like .... VERNAL
spring: old Eng. ..... KELD
spring, mineral ...... SPA
spring rice, India .... BORO
spring, small .... SEEP
springboard .... BATULE
springs, warm ... THERMAE
sprinkle DEG, WATER, SPARGE
sprinkling: Her. ..... SEME
sprint .... RUN, RACE
sprite ELF, FAY, PIXY, PIXIE
sprite, tricksy ...... ARIEL
sprout . CION, GROW, SCION
spruce .. TRIG, TRIM, NATTY
spruce, Jap. .... YEDDO
spruce, white .... EPINETTE
spume .... FOAM
spun wool .... YARN
spur .. GAD, GOAD, CALCAR
spur of mountain .... ARETE

spur part .... ROWEL
spur wheel .... ROWEL
spurs, having .. CALCARATE
spurt .... JET, GUSH
spy, garment-trade slang KEEK
spy, British, Revolution ANDRE
squama .... ALULA
squander .... SPEND
square dance .... REEL
square-meshed net .... LACIS
squash .... PEPO, CRUSH, GOURD, FLATTEN
squash bug .... ANASA
squaw .... MAHALA
squawfish .... CHUB
squid genus ...... LOLIGO
squirrel fur, Siberian
    CALABAR, CALABER
squirrel, ground Europ. SISEL
squirrel-like animal DORMOUSE
squirrel skin .... VAIR
squirrel's nest .. DRAY, DREY
ST. .... see SAINT
stab .... GORE
stabilize .... STEADY
stable ...... FIRM, SOLID
stable compartment .. STALL
stable-keeper, royal . AVENER
stableman .... OSTLER
stables, royal ...... MEWS
stack of hay .... RICK
staff .... ROD, MACE
staff-bearer .... MACER
staff, bishop's ..... CROSIER
staff of office .... MACE
staff, royal SCEPTER, SCEPTRE
stag ... DEER, HART, MALE
stage direction
    MANET, SENET, EXEUNT
stage equipment .... PROPS
stage extra ... SUPE, SUPER
stage horn signal ... SENNET
stage setting .... SCENE
stage whisper ...... ASIDE
stagger .... REEL
stagger: Prov. Eng. ... STOT
stagnation .... STASIS
stagnation, blood .. STASIS
stain, DYE, SOIL, SPOT, TASH
stair part .... RISER, TREAD
stair post .... NEWEL
staircase spindle .... SPEEL
stake ...... ANTE, WAGER
stake, like a .... PALAR
stake, pointed .. PALISADE
stake, poker .... ANTE
stakes .... POT
stakes, —, Epsom Downs Race
    OAKS
stale .... TRITE
stalk .... STEM

154

a stalk, flower . SCAPE, PEDICEL
stalk, frond .... STIPE
stalk, plant .... CAULIS
stalk, short .... STIPE
stalk, sugarcane .... RATOON
stall in mud .... STOG
stammer .... HAW, HEM
stammering sound ...... ER
stamp .... MARK, SIGIL
stamp battery block ..... VOL
stamp of approval ...... OK
stamp-sheet part ...... PANE
stamping device .... DIE
stamping machine .... DATER
stanch .... STEM
stand .... RISE
stand . BEAR, ABIDE, ENDURE
stand, cuplike .... ZARF
stand in awe of ...... FEAR
stand, small
          TABORET, TAROURET
stand, 3-legged TRIPOD, TRIVET
standard PAR, FLAG, ENSIGN
standard NORM, TYPE, NORMA
standard of chemical strength
                        TITER
standard, Turk .... ALEM
standing .... STATUS
stannum .... TIN
b stanza, last .... ENVOY
stanza, Nor. .... STEV
stanza, part of ...... STAVE
star .... ASTRO
star, blue .... VEGA
star, brightest .... COR
star cluster, distant
          NEBULA, NEBULAE
star, day .... SUN
star, evening VENUS, HESPER,
          VESPER, HESPERUS
star facet .... PANE
star, fixed .... SUN, ALYA
star: Fr. .... ÉTOILE
star in Aquarius ...... SKAT
star in Aquilla ...... ALTAIR
star in Argo .... NAOS
star in Big Dipper .... PHAD
star in Bootes .... IZAR
star in Cetus .... MIRA
star in Cygenus SADR, DENEB
star in Draco .... ADIB, JUZA
star in Eridanus .. AZHA, BEID
star in Leo . DUHR, REGULUS
star in Lyra ... VEGA, WEGA
star in Orion .... RIGEL
star in Pegasus . ENIF, MATAR
star in Pleiades ...... MAIA
star in Perseus .... ATIK
star in Scorpio .... ANTARES

e star in Serpens ...... ALYA
star in Taurus NATH, PLEIAD
star in Virgo .... SPICA
star near Mizar ...... ALCOR
star, new .... NOVA
star-shaped ..... STELLATE
star-shaped spicule
          ACTER, ACTINE
star, temporary ...... NOVA
stars, dotted with .... SEME
stars, pert. to ..... ASTRAL
starch ...... AMYL, ARUM,
          SAGO, FARINA, CASSAVA
starchy rootstock ..... TARO
starfish .... ASTEROID
stark mad .... RAVING
starnose .... MOLE
— Starr, comic strip character
                        BRENDA
starred lizard AGAMA, HARDIM
start .. BEGIN, SALLY, ROUSE
starvation .... INEDIA
starwort .... ASTER
state .... AVER
STATE .. see also GAZETTEER
STATE FLOWERS see page 208
state, New England: abbr. . RI
state of affairs ...... PASS
state, pert. to CIVIL
d state of: suffix .... ERY
stat of being: suffix .... URE
state precisely ..... SPECIFY
stately home . DOME, ESTATE
statements, confused
          RIGMAROLE
statesman, Brit. ...... PITT
station . POST, DEPOT, PLACE
stationary .... FIXED, STATIC
stationary motor part STATOR
statistician .... STATIST
statute .... ACT, LAW
stave, barrel .... LAG
stay .... WAIT, TARRY
stay rope .... GUY
stays .... CORSET
stead .... LIEU, PLACE
steal
     COP, ROB, GLOM, SNITCH
steal cattle .... RUSTLE
steal: Eng. .... GLOM
steal, Eng. dialect ..... NIM
steel beam .... GIRDER
steel: Ger. .... STAHL
steel splint, armor skirt
          TACE, TASSE, TASSET
steep .... RET, SOP
steep .... SHEER
steep in lime .... BOWK
steer wildly .... YAW
steer, young: Prov. Eng. STOT

155

a steering, direct ship's
COND, CONN
steersman .... **COX**
stellar .... **ASTRAL, STARRY**
stem .... **CION,**
CORM, SCAPE, STALK
stem, fungus .... **STIPE**
stem, hollow .... **CANE**
stem, jointed .... **CULM**
stem of hop .... **BINE**
stem, rudimentary . **CAULICLE**
stem, ship's .... **PROW**
stench .... **ODOR, FETOR**
stentorian .... **LOUD**
step ...... **GRADE, PHASE**
step .... **PACE, STAIR, TREAD**
step, dance ..... **PAS, CHASSE**
step up to mark .... **TOE**
step, upright part of .. **RISER**
steppes, storm on ..... **BURAN**
steps, outdoor ..... **PERRON**
steps over fence ...... **STILE**
stern **GRIM, HARSH, AUSTERE**
steward: Scot .... **MORMAOR**
stick **BAR, BAT, ROD, CANE,**
WAND, BATON, MUNDLE
stick .... **GLUE,**
PASTE, ADHERE, CLEAVE
stick, conductor's .... **BATON**
stick together ..... **COHERE**
stick used in hurling . **CAMAN**
stickler for formality . **TAPIST**

b sticks, bundle of .... **FAGOT**
sticky substance .. **GOO, GUM**
stiffly nice .... **PRIM**
stigma .... **BRAND**
stigmatic point of mango **NAK**
still .... **BUT, YET**
stimulant, coffee
CAFFEIN, CAFFEINE
stimulant, tea **THEIN, THEINE**
stimulate . **FAN, WHET, ELATE**
sting .... **BITE, SMART**
stinging ant .... **KELEP**
stinging herb ...... **NETTLE**
stingy .... **MEAN**
stint .... **TASK**
stipend, church .... **PREBEND**
stipend: Scot. .... **ANNAT**
stipulation .... **CLAUSE**
stir . **ADO, MIX, TODO, ROUSE**
stir up .... **RILE, ROIL**
stitch .... **PUNTO**
stitchbird .... **IHI**
stitched fold .... **TUCK**
stithy .... **ANVIL**
stock .... **BREED**
stock .... **STORE**
stock exchange, membership in
SEAT
stock exchange, Paris **BOURSE**

c stock market crash ... **PANIC**
stockade: Russ. ...... **ETAPE**
stocking run .... **LADDER**
stockings .... **HOSE**
stocky .... **STUB**
stolen goods .... **SWAG**
stomach ..... **MAW, CRAW**
stomach division, ruminant's
OMASUM
stomach, first ...... **RUMEN**
stomach, ruminant's .. **TRIPE**
stone . **AGATE, LAPIS, SLATE**
Stone Age tool .... **CELT,**
EOLITH, NEOLITH
stone, aquamarine .... **BERYL**
stone, breastplate .. **JASPER**
stone chest .... **CIST**
stone chip .... **SPALL**
stone: comb. form .... **LITH**
stone-cutter's chisel .. **DROVE**
stone fruit .... **DRUPE**
stone, green **BERYL, OLIVINE**
stone hammer .... **MASH**
stone, hard ...... **ADAMANT**
stone heap .... **CARN, KARN,**
CAIRN, CARNE, CAIRNE
stone, hollow ...... **GEODE**
stone implement ..... **CELT,**
EOLITH, NEOLITH
stone, like a ...... **LITHOID**
stone, monument ... **MENHIR**

d stone paving block ..... **SETT**
stone pillar .... **STELE**
stone, red .... **SARD, SPINEL**
stone roller fish ..... **TOTER**
stone, rough ...... **RUBBLE**
stone: Scot. .. **STEAN, STEEN**
stone set .... **PAVER**
stone, squared ..... **ASHLAR**
stone to death ... **LAPIDATE**
stone, woman turned to **NIOBE**
stone worker .... **MASON**
stone, yellow ..**TOPAZ, CITRINE**
stonecrop
ORPIN, SEDUM, ORPINE
stonecutter **MASON, LAPICIDE**
stonecutter's chisel .. **DROVE**
stoneware: Fr. .... **GRES**
stool pigeon .... **NARK**
stop .... **DAM, BALK, HALT,**
STEM, WHOA, DESIST
stop, as engine . **CONK, STALL**
stop by accident ..... **STALL**
stop: naut. ..... **AVAST, BELAY**
stop short .... **BALK**
stoppage .... **JAM**
stopper .... **BUNG, PLUG**
storage battery plate .. **GRID**
storage place **BIN, BARN, SILO**
store, army ...... **CANTEEN**
store fodder .... **ENSILE**

156

Storehouse

storehouse .... ETAPE
storehouse, army .... DEPOT
storehouse, India ...... GOLA
storehouse, public .... ETAPE
stork .... MARABOU
storm FUME, FURY, RAGE, RAVE
storm, away from ..... ALEE
storm, dust .... SIMOON
storm: Fr. .... ORAGE
storm god, Babyl. ZU, ADAD,
.... ADDA, ADDU
story, Norse .... SAGA
story, short .... CONTE
stoss, opposite of ...... LEE
stout .... BURLY
stout, kind of ...... PORTER
stove .... ETNA, RANGE
"Stowe" character
.... EVA, TOM, TOPSY
straight .... DIRECT
straight-edge .... RULER
strain .... EXERT
strained .... TENSE
strainer .... SIEVE
strainer, wool cloth ... TAMIS
Straits Settlement region
.... PENANG
strange .... ODD
strap on falcon's leg ... JESS
strap-shaped ...... LORATE
strass .... PASTE
stratagem ...... RUSE, WILE
stratagem, sudden .... COUP
stratum .... LAYER
straw hat ..... BAKU, MILAN
stray .... ERR
stray .... WAIF
stray animal .... CAVY
streak .... ROE, LINE, VEIN,
.. STRIA, STRAKE, STRIAE
streaky .... LINY, ROWY
stream
FLOW, RILL, BOURN, RIVER
streamlet .... RILL, RUNNEL
street Arab .... GAMIN
street: It., Sp. .. CALLE, CALLI
street, narrow .... LANE
street roisterer .... MUN
street urchin .... ARAB
street, Venice water . RIO, RII
strength .... POWER
strengthening .... ROBORANT
stress .... ICTUS
stressed beat, syllable . ARSIS
stretch: Scot. .... STENT
stretched out ...... PROLATE
stretcher .... LITTER
stretching frame .... TENTER,
.... STENTER
strewn with flowers: Her. SEME

strife .... WAR
strife, civil .... STASIS
strike . BAT, HIT, RAP, CONK,
SLOG, SLUG, SOCK, SWAT,
WHAM, SMITE
strikebreaker .... FINK, SCAB
striking effect ...... ECLAT
string of mules ...... ATAJO
stringy .... ROPY
strip . BARE, DIVEST, STRAKE
strip of land .... DOAB, DUAB
strip of wood .... LATH
strip off skin .... FLAY
strip, oxhide, S. Afr. .. RIEM
strip, wood, metal .. SPLINE
stripe .... BAR, BAND, WALE,
.... WEAL, STREAK
stripe of color: zool. .. PLAGA
stripling .... BOY, LAD
strive .... AIM, VIE
strobile .... CONE
stroke .... FIT, ICTUS
stroke, brilliant ...... COUP
stroll .... AMBLE
strong-arm man ...... GOON
strong, as cigars ... MADURO
strong desire ...... HUNGER
strong man .... SAMSON
strong man, Gr. ...... ATLAS
strong point .... FORTE
strong-scented .. OLID, RANK
strongbox .... SAFE
stronghold FORT, SION, ZION
struck with horror .. AGHAST
structure, tall .... TOWER
struggle .... COPE
struggle helplessly FLOUNDER
struggled .... HOVE
stud .... BOSS
student in charge .. MONITOR
studio, art .... ATELIER
study .... CON, PORE, READ
study group .... SEMINAR
stuff ...... PAD, RAM, CRAM
stuffing .... KAPOK
stum .... MUST
stumble: prov. Eng. .... STOT
stump of branch ...... SKEG
stunted trees .... SCRUB
stupefied .... MAZED
stupefy .... DAZE, MAZE,
.... STUN, BESOT
stupid ...... CRASS, DENSE
stupid person ..... ASS, OAF,
CLOD, COOT, DOLT, LOON,
LOUT, LOWN, MOKE
stupor ...... COMA, SOPOR
sturgeon, small .... STERLET
style .... MODE, NAME
style of art .... DADA, GENRE

157

a
stylet, surgical	TROCAR
stymie	IMPEDE
Styx ferryman	CHARON
subbase	PLINTH
subdued shade	PASTEL
subject	TOPIC, VASSAL
subject in grammar	NOUN
subjoin	ADD
sublime	NOBLE
submarine	PIGBOAT, SNORKEL
submit	BOW, YIELD
subordinate	MINOR, DEPENDENT
subside	EBB, SINK, ABATE, RELAPSE
substance, lustrous	METAL
substances, class of	LIPIN
substantiate	VERIFY
substantive word	NOUN
substitute	VICE, PROXY, ERSATZ
substitute for: suffix	ETTE
subtle emanation	AURA
subtle variation	NUANCE
subtract	DEDUCT
subway, Eng.	TUBE
subway entrance	KIOSK
subway, Fr.	METRO
success	HIT, WOW

b
succession	LINE
successively	AROW
succinct	TERSE
succor	AID
succulent plant	ALOE, HERB
such	SO
sucking fish	PEGA, REMORA
Sudan lake	CHAD
Sudan native	FUL
Sudan Negroid	SERE
Sudan people	HAUSA
sudden attack: Med.	ICTUS
suet	TALLOW
suffer	LET, BIDE
suffer from hunger	CLEM, STARVE
suffer: Scot.	DREE
sufficient: poet.	ENOW

SUFFIXES:
act of	TION
action	ANCE
adjective	ENT, IAL, INE, ISH, IST, ITE, OUS
agent	URE
alcohol	OL
carbohydrate	OSE
chemical or chemistry	ANE, ENE, IDE, INE, OLE, ONE, ENOL, ITOL, OLIC

c
common ending	ENT, INE, ING, ION
common suffix	ES, ESE, ESS, INE, IVE, ETTE, YNONE
condition	ATE, ILE, ISE, ANCE, SION, STER
comparative	IER, IOR
compound	ICAL, ILITY
diminutive	ET, IE, ULA, ULE, ETTE
feminine	INA, INE, ELLA
feminine noun	ESS
follower	ISE, ITE
forming nouns from verbs	ER
full of	OSE
inflammation	ITIS
inhabitant of	ITE
into	EN
like	OID
little	ET
made of	EN
make	ISE
medical	IA, OMA
mineral	ITE, LITE
native of	ITE
noun	IA, OR, ATE, ENT, ERY, ESS, IER, ISE, IST, ITE, ANCY, ENCE, ENSE, STER

d
noun ending	STER
noun forming diminutive	CLE
number	TEEN
oil	OL, OLE
one who	IST, STER
one who does	IST
or ordinal number	ETH
order of animals	INI
ordinal	ETH
origin, denoting	OTE
participle	ING
person	ER
plural	(old EN), ES
quality	ANCE, ILITY
rocks, of	ITE, LITE
science of	ICS
skin	DERM
small	ING
state of	ERY, ANCE
state of being	URE
substitute for	ETTE
superlative	EST
sympathizer	ITE
town	TON
tumor	OMA
verb	ISE, ESCE
with mineral names	LITE
zoological	ATA
Sufi disciple	MURID
sugar	OSE, SUCROSE
sugar cane disease	ILIAU

sugar cane residue .. BAGASSE
sugar, crude .... GUR
sugar, fruit .... KETOSE
sugar, raw ..... CASSONADE
sugar, simple .... OSE
sugar source .... CANE
suggestion .... CUE, HINT
suit of mail .... ARMOR
suitable APT, FIT, PAT, PROPER
suitcase .. BAG, GRIP, VALISE
suitor .... SWAIN
sullen .DOUR, GLUM, MOROSE
sullen, act .... MOPE
sullen, be ...... POUT, SULK
sully .... SOIL, DIRTY
sultan, Turkish .... SELIM
sultan's order .... IRADE
sultan's residence .... SERAI
sultanate .... OMAN
sultry .... HUMID
Sulu Moslem .... MORO
"sum," infinitive following ESSE
sum paid as punishment .FINE
sumac genus .... RHUS
sumac, P. I. ... ANAM, ANAN
Sumatra squirrel shrew . TANA
Sumatra wildcat ...... BALU
Sumatran silk .... IKAT
"summa — laude" ..... CUM
summary
    DIGEST, PRECIS, EPITOME
summer: Fr. .... ETE
summer-house
    ARBOR, PERGOLA
summer, pert. to .... ESTIVAL
summit
    APEX, KNAP, PEAK, SPIRE
summits .... APICES
summon .... CALL, CITE,
    PAGE, CLEPE, EVOKE
sun .... SOL, HELIOS
sun apartments .... SOLARIA
sun bittern .... CAURALE
sun: comb. form ...... HELIO
sun disk .... ATEN, ATON
sun-dried brick
    DOBE, DOBY, ADOBE, DOBIE
sun god, Babyl. .. UTU, UTUG,
    BABBAR, SHAMASH
sun god, Egypt. .... RA, TEM,
    TUM, AMON, AMEN,
    AMUN, ATMU, ATUM
sun god, Gr., Rom. ..... SOL,
    APOLLO, HELIOS
sun god, Inca .... INTI
sun, halo around .. CORONA
sun, pert. to .... SOLAR
sun porches .... SOLARIA
sun tree, Jap. .... HINOKI

sunbaker building
    DOBE, DOBY, ADOBE, DOBIE
Sunday of Lent, 4th . LAETARE
sunder
    PART, REND, SPLIT, DIVIDE
sundial, style of .... GNOMON
sunfish .... BREAM
sunfish genus .... MOLA
sunken fence .... AHA, HAHA
sunset, occurring at
    ACRONICAL
sunspot center
    UMBRA, UMBRAE
supercilious person .... SNOB
superfluous: Fr. .... DE TROP
superintendent, office
    MANAGER
superior, most ... BEST, TOPS
superior quality: Fr. ... LUXE
superiority, belief in . RACISM
superlative, absolute .ELATIVE
superlative ending ...... EST
supernatural .... OCCULT
supernatural being, Melanesia
    ADARO
supernatural power, E. Afr.
    NGAI
supernatural power, Polyn.
    MANA
superscribe .... DIRECT
superstition, object of
    FETICH, FETISH
supper .... TEA
supplication, make .... PRAY
supply ...... STOCK, ENDUE
supply, fresh .... RELAY
supply of horses .... REMUDA
support ... LEG, RIB, ABET,
    BACK, PROP, BRACE
support, one-legged . UNIPOD
suppose .. ASSUME, IMAGINE
suppose: archaic ..... TROW
suppress ...... ELIDE, QUASH
Supreme Being, Hebrew IHVH,
    JHVH, JHWH, YHVH, YHWH
surety agreement ..... BOND
surf, roar of .... ROTE
surface, attractive .. VENEER
surface of gem ...... FACET
surface of a tool .... FACE
surfeit ... CLOY, GLUT, SATE
surfeited .... BLASE
surge .... TIDE, BILLOW
surgeon's instrument TREPAN,
    TROCAR, ABLATOR, LE-
    VATOR, SCALPEL
surgical thread ...... SETON
Surinam toad .... PIPA
surly .... GRUFF, SULLEN
surmise INFER, GUESS, OPINE
surnamed: Fr. .... DIT

159

surpass ..... CAP, TOP, BEST
surplice, chorister's ... COTTA
surplus ...... EXTRA, EXCESS
surrender
        CEDE, YIELD, DEDITION
surrender: law ...... REMISE
surround GIRD, BESET, INARM
surrounding area ...... ZONE
surtout .... COAT
survey .... MAP, POLL
surveyor's assistant RODMAN
surveyor's instrument
            ROD, ALIDADE
surveyor's rod, sight on
                TARGET
Susa inhabitant .... ELAMITE
suspend .... HANG
suspenders .... BRACES
suture .... SEAM
svelte .... SLIM, TRIM
swab .... MOP
swain .... LOVER
swallow BOLT, GULP, MARTIN
swallow, sea .... TERN
swamp ..... BOG, FEN, MARSH,
    MORASS, SLEW, SLOO, SLUE
swamp gas MIASM, MIASMA
swamp, S. Afr. .. VLEI, VLEY
swampy belt, India .... TERAI
swan, female .... PEN
swan genus .... OLOR
swan, male .... COB
swan, whistling ...... OLOR
swap .... TRADE
sward .... SOD, TURF
swarm ...... NEST, NORDE
swarthy ...... DUN, DARK
swastika .... FYLFOT
sway .... ROCK, ROLL
swear .... AVER, CURSE
sweat .... SUDOR, PERSPIRE
SWEDISH .. see also SPECIAL
        SECTION—SWEDEN
Swedish:
    beer .... OL
    tea .... TE
    toe .... TA
    you .... ER
Swedish coin .... ORE
Swedish county, district . LAN
Swedish explorer ... HEDIN
Swedish order of merit VASA
Swedish royal guard DRABANT
Swedish sculptor .... MILLES
sweep, scythe's .... SWATH
sweet flag SEDGE, CALAMUS
sweet gale .... GAGL
sweet liquid ...... NECTAR
sweet potato
        YAM, BATATA, OCARINA
sweet potato: Sp. ... CAMOTE

sweet red wine ... ALICANTE
sweet-smelling
        OLENT, REDOLENT
sweet spire .... ITEA
sweetfish .... AYU
sweetheart: Ir. .... GRA
sweetheart: Scot. .... JO
sweetmeat: Fr. ..... DRAGEE
sweetsop .... ATA,
    ATES, ATTA, ANNONA
swell .... DILATE
swell of water ...... WAVE
swelling LUMP, NODE, EDEMA
swelling on plants ... GALL
swerve .... SHY, SKEW
swift .... FAST, FLEET
swift, common .... CRAN
swift horse . ARAB, PACOLET
swiftly, run ... DART, SCUD
swimming .... NATANT
swimming bell . NECTOPHORE
swindle GIP, GYP, DUPE, SWIZ
swindler .... COZENER
swine HOG, PIG, SOW, BOAR
swine, feeding of .. PANNAGE
swine fever .... ROUGET
swine genus .... SUS
swing music .... JIVE
swing musician ..... HEPCAT
swinish .... PORCINE
swipe .... GLOM
swirl .... EDDY, GURGE
SWISS .see also SPECIAL SEC-
        TION—SWITZERLAND
Swiss capital .. BERN, BERNE
Swiss card game ...... JASS
Swiss critic .... AMIEL
Swiss patriot .... TELL
Swiss state .... CANTON
switch .... TOGGLE
swollen .... TURGID
swoon .... FAINT
swoon: old Eng. ..... SWEB
sword PATA, EPEE, BLADE,
    SABER, SABRE, RAPIER
sword, Arthur's
    EXCALIBAR, EXCALIBUR
sword, curved SABER, SABRE
sword, fencing ...... EPEE
sword, matador's .. ESTOQUE
sword, medieval ..... ESTOC
sword, Norse myth. .... GRAM
sword, put away .. SHEATHE
sword, St. George's
        ASCALON, ASKELON
sword-shaped ..... ENSATE
sword, Siegfried's .... GRAM
sword, slender ...... RAPIER
swordsman's dummy stake PEL
syllable, last .... ULTIMA

160

a syllable, scale ... **DO, FA, LA, MI, RE, SO, TI, SOL**
syllable, short **MORA, MORAE**
sylvan deity **PAN, FAUN, SATYR**
SYMBOL, CHEMICAL .. see **SPECIAL SECTION**
symbol .... **TOKEN**
symbol of authority ... **MACE**
symbol of Crusaders .. **CROSS**
symbol of protection ... **EGIS**
sympathizer: suffix ...... **ITE**
synagogue ... **SHUL, TEMPLE**
syncopated music ...... **RAG**
syncope ..... **FAINT, SWOON**
synod, Russian ...... **SOBOR**
syntax, give the ...... **PARSE**

c synthetic fabric or fiber **NYLON, ORLON, RAYON, DACRON**
synthetic rubber **BUNA, ELASTOMER**
Syria, ancient .... **ARAM**
Syrian, ancient port .. **SIDON**
Syrian bear .... **DUBB**
Syrian bishop's title ... **ABBA**
Syrian city, old ..... **ALEPPO**
system .... **ISM**
system of rule ...... **REGIME**
system of rules ...... **CODE**
system of weights ..... **TROY**
system of worship ..... **CULT**
systematic regulation .. **CODE**

T

T-shaped .... **TAU**
tab .... **FLAP, LABEL**
tabard .... **CAPE**
table mountain, Abyssin. **AMBA**
tableland .... **MESA**
tablet .... **PAD, SLATE**
taboo, opposite of ..... **NOA**
b tabor, Moorish **ATABAL, ATTABAL**
Tacoma's Sound ..... **PUGET**
tack: naut. .... **BUSK**
tact .... **FINESSE**
tackle, anchor .... **CAT**
tael, part of .... **LI**
tag .... **LABEL**
tag, metal ... **AGLET, AIGLET**
Tagalog for river .... **ILOG**
Tahitian national god ... **ORO**
Tai race branch ...... **LAO**
tail, of ... **CAUDAL, CAUDATE**
tail of coin .... **VERSO**
tail, rabbit's .... **SCUT**
tail: zool. .... **CAUDA**
tailor .... **SARTOR**
Taino fetish ..... **ZEME, ZEMI**
Tai Mahal site .... **AGRA**
take away by force .. **REAVE**
take away: law ...... **ADEEM**
take back .... **RECANT**
take effect again .... **REVEST**
take off .... **DOFF**
take one's ease ...... **REST**
take on cargo .. **LADE, LOAD**
take out ...... **DELE, ELIDE, EXPUNGE**
take part .... **SIDE**
take up again ...... **RESUME**
take up weapons ...... **ARM**
tale .... **SAGA, YARN, STORY**
tale, medieval Fr. .... **LAI**

tale, Norse .... **SAGA**
"Tale of Two Cities" girl **LUCIE**
"Tales of a Wayside —" **INN**
talent .... **FLAIR**
talented .... **SMART**
talisman .... **CHARM**
talisman, Afr. .... **GRIGRI**
talk ... **GAB, GAS, CHAT, PRATE, PALAVER**
d talk: slang .... **YAK**
talk freely .... **DESCANT**
talk pompously **ORATE, HARANGUE**
talk, rambling .. **RIGMAROLE**
talk wildly ..... **RANT, RAVE**
Tallinn .... **REVAL**
tallow tree .... **CERA**
tally .... **SCORE**
Talmud commentary .. **GEMARA**
talon .... **CLAW, NAIL**
tamarack .... **LARCH**
tamarisk .... **ATLE**
tame, as hawks ...... **MAN**
tan .... **BUFF, BEIGE**
tan skins .... **TAW**
tanager ..... **YENI, REDBIRD**
tanager, S. Am. **HABIA, LINDO**
tanbark .... **ROSS**
tangle ...... **SNARL, SLEAVE**
tangled mass .... **MAT, SHAG**
tanning gum .... **KINO**
tanning, plant for .... **ALDER**
tanning shrub **SUMAC, SUMACH**
tanning tree, India **AMLA, AMLI**
tantalize .... **TEASE**
Tantalus' daughter ... **NIOBE**
tantra .... **AGAMA**
tantrum .... **RAGE**
tap **PAT, COCK, SPIGOT, FAUCET**

161

a
tapering dagger .... ANLACE
tapering piece .... SHIM
tapestry
     ARRAS, TAPIS, DOSSER
tapestry center .... ARRAS
tapeworm .... TAENIA
tapeworm larva ..... MEASLE
tapioca-like food ..... SALEP
tapioca source
     CASAVA, CASSAVA
tapir, S. Amer. ...... DANTA
Tapuyan .... GE
tarboosh .... FEZ
target .... BUTT
Tariff Act writer ...... SMOOT
Tarkington character ... SAM
tarnish .... SPOT, SULLY
taro .. GABE, GABI, DASHEEN
taro paste .... POI
taro root .. EDO, EDDO, KALO
tarpaulin .... PAULIN
tarpon .... SABALO
tarradiddle .... FIB, LIE
tarry .... BIDE, WAIT,
          STAY, LINGER
tarsus .... ANKLE
tarsus, insect .... MANUS
tart .... ACID
tartar, crude . ARGAL, ARGOL
Tartini's B-flat .... ZA
b
task ...... DUTY, CHORE,
          STENT, STINT
task, punishing ..... PENSUM
taste ...... SIP, SUP, SAPOR,
          SNACK, PALATE
tasteful .... ELEGANT
tasty .... SAPID
Tatar .... HU
Tatar dynasty, China ... WEI
Tatar tribe, W. Siberia . SHOR
tattle .... BLAB
tattler, idle .... GOSSIP
Tattler publisher ..... STEELE
tau cross .... ANKH
taunt .... JEER, MOCK, TWIT
taut .... TENSE
taut, pull .... STRETCH
tavern .... INN
tax . CESS, GELD, LEVY, SCOT,
     SESS, STENT, ASSESS, EX-
     CISE, IMPOST
tax, church .... TITHE
tea .... CHA, CHAA
tea, black
     PECO, BOHEA, PEKOE
tea bowl .... CHAWAN
tea box
     CADDY, CALIN, CANISTER
tea, China .... BOHEA
tea, Chin. green ..... HYSON

c
tea genus .... THEA
tea-growing region ... ASSAM
tea, kind of
     OOPAK, OOLONG, OOPACK
tea, Labrador .... LEDUM
tea, marsh .... LEDUM
tea, medicinal PTISAN, TISANE
tea, oriental .... CHA
tea, Paraguay . MATE, YERBA
tea, rolled . CHA, TCHA, TSIA
tea tree .... TI
teacake ..... SCON, SCONE
teacher ... DOCENT, MENTOR
teacher, Hebrew ..... RABBI
teacher, Islam religious
     ALIM, MOLLA, MULLA
teacher, Jewish .... RAB, REB
teacher, Moslem
     ALIM, MOLLA, MULLA
teacher, Xenophan's
     ISOCRATES
teacher's association: abbr.
     NEA
team of horses .... SPAN
team, 3-horse ...... RANDEM
teamster's command GEE, HAW
tear .... RIP, REND, RENT
tear apart
     REND, TATTER, DIVULSE
tease .... TWIT, BOTHER
technical name: biol. .. ONYM
technique .... ART
tedious writer ...... PROSER
d
teem .... RAIN, POUR
teeth, false ...... DENTURES
teeth, incrustation .. TARTAR
Telamon's son .... AJAX
telegraph inventor ... MORSE
telegraph key ...... TAPPER
telegraph signal .. DOT, DASH
telegraph, underwater . CABLE
telegraphic speed unit . BAUD
telephone exchange CENTRAL
telephone inventor ..... BELL
telephone wire .... LINE
telescope part .... LENS
television .... VIDEO
television broadcast TELECAST
television cable ..... COAXIAL
television recording KINESCOPE
television tube
     MONOSCOPE, ICONSCOPE
tell IMPART, RELATE, NARRATE
tell in detail ...... RECOUNT
Tell, site of legend ..... URI
telling blow .... COUP, ONER
temper .... ANNEAL
temper, fit of .... PET
temperament: Ger. ... GEMUT
"Tempest" sprite .... ARIEL
"Tempest" slave ... CALIBAN
temple . FANE, RATH, RATHA
temple, Asian ...... PAGODA

162

temple chamber, Gr. ... NAOS
temple, inner part .... CELLA
temple: Siam. .... VAT, WAT
temple tower, India . SHIKARA
tempo: music .... TAKT
temporary decline .... SLUMP
temporary fashion .... FAD
temporary relief ... REPRIEVE
tempt .... LURE, TOLE
temptation .... ALLURE
ten .... DECAD
ten ares .... DECARE
Ten Commandments
DECALOG, DECALOGUE
"Ten Days that Shook the
World" author ... REED
ten million ergs ...... JOULE
tenant .... LESSEE
tenant, early Ir. ...... SAER
tend .... SERVE
tender .... SOFT, OFFER
tending toward .... FOR
tendril· bot. ...... CAPREOL
tennis score ... LOVE, DEUCE
tennis shoe ...... SNEAKER
tennis stroke ACE, LOB, LOBB
tennis term .... LET
Tennyson character ... ENID,
ARDEN
Tennyson heroine
ELAIN, ELAINE
Tennyson sailor ..... ENOCH
tenon .... COG
tenonlike piece . COAG, COAK
tenor, famous .... MELCHIOR
tense .... TAUT
tent dweller KEDAR, SCENITE
tent dwelling Arabs .. KEDAR
tent flap .... FLY
tentmaker, the ...... OMAR
tents .... CAMP
tentacle .... FEELER
tenth part ...... DECI, TITHE
tepid .... WARM
Tereus' son .... ITYS
term .... NAME
term .... SESSION
term: algebra .... NOME
TERM, GEOMETRY ...... see
GEOMETRY, GEOMETRIC
term in office ...... TENURE
term, math. .. SINE, COSINE
term of address ... SIR, SIRE,
MADAM
termagant .... SHREW
terminable .... ENDABLE
termite, P. I. .... ANAI, ANAY
tern .... SKIRR

tern, black .... DARR
tern genus .... STERNA
tern, Hawaii .... NOIO
terpene alcohol ..... NEROL
terpene compound TEREBENE
terrapin .... EMYD,
POTTER, SLIDER
terrapin, red-bellied
POTTER, SLIDER
terrestrial .... GEAL
terrible .... DIRE
terrier, kind of . SKYE, CAIRN
terrier, Scottish breed of SKYE
terrified .... AFRAID
territorial division ...... AMT
territory .... LAND, SOIL
territory, additional
LEBENSRAUM
territory, enclosed . ENCLAVE
terror .... PANIC
terrorist .... GOON
tessellated .... MOSAIC
tessera .... TILE
test .... ASSAY, TEMPT,
TRIAL, EXAMINE
test ground .... BOSE
testament .... WILL
testifier .... DEPONENT
testify .... DEPONE, DEPOSE
tetrachord, upper tone of .NETE
Teutonic, ancient ..... GOTH
Teutonic barbarian .... GOTH
Teutonic deity .... ER
Teut. Fate .... NORN, URTH
TEUTONIC GODS, GODDESSES,
DEITY see NORSE SPECIAL
SECTION
Teut. legendary hero ... OFFA
Teut. letter of alphabet . RUNE
Teut. people ...... GEPIDAE
Teut. sea goddess ...... RAN
Teut. sky god . TY, TIU, TIW,
TYR, ZIO, ZIU, TYRR
Texas shrine .... ÁLAMO
textile screw pine
ARA, PANDAN
texture .... WALE,
WOOF, GRAIN
Thailand .... SIAM
Thames estuary ...... NORE
than: Ger. .... ALS
than: Scot. .... NA
thankless person .. INGRATE
that is: abbr. ...... E.G., I.E.
that not .... LEST
that one: Lat. .... ILLE

a

that which follows .. SEQUEL
thatch, grass to .... NETI
thatching palm .... NIPA
the: Ger. .... DAS, DER
"The Ballad of Reading—"
.... GAOL
"The Jairite" .... IRA
"The Lion of God" ...... ALI
"The Red" .... ERIC
the same: Lat. .... IDEM
the squint .... SKEN
theatre ..... ODEA, ODEON,
.... ODEUM, STAGE
theatre box seat ...... LOGE
theatre district ...... RIALTO
theatre floor .... PIT
theatre, Grecian ...... ODEA,
.... ODEON, ODEUM
theatre group .... ANTA
theatre, part of Greek .SKENE,
...... SCENA, SCENAE, SKENAI
theatre sign .... SRO
"Theban Bard" ..... PINDAR
Thebes deity .. AMEN, AMON,
...... AMUN, MENT, AMENT,
.... MENTU
Thebes, king of
.... CREON, OEPIDUS
theme .... MOTIF
theme: music .... TEMA
then .... ANON

b

then: music .... POI
theoretical .... PLATONIC
there: Fr. .... VOILA
therefore .... ERGO
theseli veil .... TEMPE
Theseus' father ..... AEGEUS
thesis, opp. of ...... ARSIS
thespian .... ACTOR
Thessaly, king of ... AEOLUS
Thessaly mountain ..... OSSA
Thessaly valley ...... TEMPE
they: Fr. .... ILS
thick-lipped .... LABROSE
thicket . BOSK, SHAW, COPSE,
.... COPPICE, SPINNEY
thicket: dialect .... RONE
thicket, game .... COVERT
thickness .... PLY
thief, gypsy .... CHOR
thief: Yiddish .... GANEF,
.... GANOF, GONOF
thigh bone .... FEMUR
thigh, of the ..... FEMORAL
thin .... LANK, LEAN, RARE,
...... SHEER, DILUTE, PAPERY,
...... SPARSE, TENUOUS
thin cake .... WAFER
thin: comb. form ..... SERO
thin disk .... WAFER
thin layer .... FILM

c

"Thin Man" dog ...... ASTA
"Thin Man" wife ...... NORA
thin-toned .... REEDY
thin out .... ATTENUATE
thing: law (Latin) ...... RES
things added ..... ADDENDA
things done .... ACTA
things to be done
.... AGENDA, AGENDUM
think .. DEEM, TROW, OPINE
think: archaic .... WIS
think (over) .... MULL, MUSE
third: comb. form ..... TRIT
third day, every .... TERTIAN
third king of Judah ..... ASA
third: music .... TIERCE
Third Reich special police:
abbr. .... SS
thirst-tortured king: Gr. myth
.... TANTALUS
thirsty .... DRY, ADRY
thirty: Fr. .... TRENTE
thirty, series of .... TRENTAL
this: Fr. .... CE
this: Sp. ..... ESTA, ESTE
this one: Lat. ..., HIC, HAEC
thither .... THERE
Thomas Hardy heroine .. TESS
thong .... STRAP
thong, braided ...... ROMAL
thong-shaped ...... LORATE

d

thong, S. Afr. .... RIEM
thorax, crustacean's .. PEREION
Thor's stepson .... ULL, ULLR
Thor's wife .... SIF
thorn .. BRIAR, BRIER, SPINE
thorn apple .... METEL
thorn, bearing a .... SPINATE
thornback ray . DORN, ROKER
Thorne Smith character
.... TOPPER
thorny plant .. BRIAR, BRIER
thorny shrub ... NABK, NUBK
thoroughfare .... WAY, ROAD,
.... AVENUE, STREET
thoroughgoing ...... ARRANT
those .... YON, YOND
those in power or office .. INS
thou: Fr. .... TU
thought .... IDEA
thought: comb. form .... IDEO
thoughts, form ...... IDEATE
thousand .... MIL
thousand: comb. form . MILLE
Thrace, ancient people of
.... EDONI
thrall .... ESNE, SLAVE
thrash .... LAM, BEAT
thread: comb. form .. NEMA
thread, cotton .... LISLE
threaded fastener ..... NUT
thread, guiding ball of . CLEW
thread-like .... NEMALINE
thread-like process ..... HAIR

a
thread-like structure .. FILUM
thread, of a .... FILAR
threads, cross ..... RETICLE
threads crossed by woof WARP
threads crossing warp
.... WEFT, WOOF
threads, lengthwise .. WARP
threaten .. IMPEND, MENACE
three .... TER, TRIO, TRIAD
three: Ger. .... DREI
three: Ital. .... TRE
three-legged stand
.... TRIPOD, TRIVET
three-masted ship
.... XEBEC, FRIGATE
3 parts, divided into: Her.
.... TIERCE
3.1416 .... PI
three: Sp. .... TRES
three-spot .... TREY
threefold .... TRINE, TREBLE,
.... TERNARY, TERNATE
threefold: comb. form ... TER
threshold .... SILL
threshold, psychology .. LIMEN
thrice: music .... TER
thrifty .... FRUGAL, SAVING
thrive .... BATTEN, PROSPER
b
throat ..... GORGE, GULLET
throat: Lat. .... GULA
throat, pert. to .... GULAR
throb .BEAT, PULSE, PULSATE
throe .... PANG
throng .. MOB, HORDE, SWARM
through .... PER
through: prefix .... DIA
throw ...... CAST, PITCH
throw aside .... FLING
throw back .... REPEL
thrush ...... VEERY, MISSEL
thrush, Hawaiian ..... OMAO
thrush, India .... SHAMA
thrush, missel . MAVIE, MAVIS
thrust .... LUNGE
thrust back .... REPEL
thrust down ...... DETRUDE
thunderfish .... RAAD
thurible .... CENSER
Thuringian city ...... JENA
Thursday, source of name
.... THOR
thus .... SO, SIC
thus far .... YET
thwart .... FOIL
Tiber tributary .... NERA
Tibetan chief ...... POMBO
Tibetan ox .... YAK
Tibetan priest ...... LAMA
Tibetan tribe ...... CHAMPA

c
tibia .... CNEMIS
Tichborne Claimant .. ORTON
tick .... ACARID
tick genus .... ARGAS
tick, S. Amer. .... CARAPATO
tickets, sell illegally .. SCALP
tickle .... TITILLATE
Ticonderoga's commander
.... GATES
tidal flood .... BORE, EAGRE
tidal wave, flow or bore EAGRE
tidbit .... CATE
tide, lowest high ...... NEAP
tidings ...... NEWS, WORD
tidings, glad .... GOSPEL
.... EVANGEL, EVANGILE
tidy ..... NEAT, REDO, TRIM
tie .... BIND, BOND, LASH,
.... TRUSS, CRAVAT
tie-breaking game ... RUBBER
tie, kind of .... ASCOT
tie off .... LIGATE
tie, railroad .... SLEEPER
tier .... ROW
tiger cat, S. Amer. ... CHATI
tiger, Persian .... SHER, SHIR
tight .... SNUG, TAUT, TENSE
tight place .. FIX, JAM, MESS
tighten: naut. .... FRAP
tightly stretched ...... TENSE
til .... SESAME
d
tile, hexagonal .... FAVI
tile, roofing .... PANTILE
tilelike .... TEGULAR
till the earth .... FARM, PLOW
tilled land ... ARADA, ARADO
tiller .... HELM
tilt .... TIP, CANT, LIST
tilt .... JOUST
tilting: naut. .... ALIST
timber bend .... SNY
timber, flooring .... BATTEN
timber, nautical ..... KEVEL
timber, pine: Asia .. MATSU
timber rot .... DOAT, DOTE
timber truck .... WYNN
timber, wolf .... LOBO
timbrel .... TABOR, TABOUR
time .... ERA, TEMPI, TEMPO
time before .... EVE
time being .... NONCE
time gone by .... PAST
time out .... RECESS
time, space of ...... WHILE
time value, equalling in
.... DIMORIC
times, old ..... ELD, YORE
timetable .... SCHEDULE
timid .... SHY, PAVID
timorous .... TREPID
timothy .... HAY
Timothy's mother: Bib. .. LOIS

165

Tin

a
tin .... CAN, STANNUM
tin, containing ... STANNOUS
tin foil .... TAIN
tin plate .... TAIN
tin roofing .... TERNE
tinamou .... YUTU
tincture: Her. .... OR, GULES,
VERT, AZURE, SABLE,
ARGENT, PURPURE
tinder ...... PUNK, AMADOU
tine .... PRONG
tine of antler .... SNAG
tinge .... TAINT
tinge deeply .... IMBUE
tingle of feeling ... THRILL
tinkle .... TING
tiny bird, W. Ind. ..... TODY
tip ... END, FEE, APEX, KNAP
tip .... CANT, LEAN,
TILT, CAREEN
tipping .... ALIST, ATILT
tiptoe, on .... ATIP
tire .... FAG, JADE
tire casing .... SHOE
tire, face of .... TREAD
tire support .... RIM
tissue .... TELA
tissue, of a .... TELAR
tissue, pert. to ...... TELAR
TITAN. see SPECIAL SECTION,
GREEK MYTH, Page 200

b
Titania's husband .. OBERON
titanic iron-ore sand . ISERENE
titlark .... PIPIT
title ..... EARL, NAME, TERM
title, baronet's .... SIR
title, Benedictine ...... DOM
title, church ...... PRIMATE
title, East .... COJA, HOJA
title, Ethiopian .... RAS
title Hindu gives Moslem
MIAN
title, India ..... AYA, NAWAB,
SAHEB, SAHIB
title, Jewish .RAB, REB, RABBI
title, knight's .... SIR
title, king's .... SIRE
title, lady's .. DAME, MADAM
title, Moslem ...... AGA, ALI,
MOLLA, MULLA,
SHERIF, SHEREFF
title of address .. MME., MRS.,
SIR, MAAM, MADAM
title of honor, Moslem .SAYID,
SAIYID, SAYYID
title of kings of Edessa ABGAR
title of respect .... SIR, SIRE,
MADAME
title of respect, Afr. ..... SIDI

c
title of respect, India ... SRI,
SHRI, SAHIB, SHREE,
HUZOOR
title of respect, Malay .. TUAN
title, Oriental .... BABA
title, Persian MIR, AZAM, KHAN
title, Spanish
DOM, DON, SENOR
title to property or land . DEED
title, Turkish . PACHA, PASHA
titleholder .... TITLIST
titmice, genus of ..... PARUS
titmouse .... MAG, PARUS
tittle ...... JOT, IOTA, WHIT
Titus Andronicus' daughter
LAVINIA
Tiwaz .... ER, TIU
to .... FOR, UNTO
to: prefix .... AP
to: Scot. .... TAE
to be: Fr. .... ETRE
to be: Lat. .... ESSE
"to be," part of .... AM, IS,
ARE, WAS
to go: Fr. .... ALLER
to love: Fr. .... AIMER
to the point that ..... UNTIL
to use: Lat. .... UTOR
toad genus .... BUFO
toad, huge .... AGUA
toad, order of .... ANURA

d
toad, tree genus .... HYLA
toadfish .... SAPO
toast, bit of .... SIPPET
toasting word .... SALUD,
SKOAL, PROSIT
tobacco ash . DOTTEL, DOTTLE
tobacco, chewing ..... QUID
tobacco, coarse
SHAG, CAPORAL
tobacco, Cuban .... CAPA
tobacco, low grade .... SHAG
tobacco, Peru .... SANA
tobacco, roll .... CIGAR
toddy palm juice ...... SURA
toe .... DIGIT
toe, fifth .... MINIMUS
toe: Scot. .... TAE
togs .... DUDS
toilet case .... ETUI
Tokyo Bay City .... CHIBI
Tokyo, old name .. EDO, YEDO
tolerable .... SOSO
toll .... FEE, KNELL
Tolstoi heroine ...... ANNA
tomb, Moslem TABUT, TABOOT
tomboy ...... HOIDEN, HOYDEN
tomcat .... GIB
tone down ...... SOFTEN
tone, lack of .... ATONY
tone, of .... TONAL
tone quality .... TIMBRE

a
tone: Scot. .... TEAN
tones, series of ..... OCTAVE
tongue, gypsy .... CHIB
tongue of Agni .... KALI
tongue, pert. to .... GLOSSAL
tongue, using the .... APICAL
tongue, wagon .... NEAP
tonic .... ROBORANT
tonic, dried India
              CHIRATA, CHIRETTA
tonic herb ..... ALOE, TANSY
Tonkin native .... THO
too early ...... PREMATURE
too much: Fr. .... TROP
tool, boring .... AWL, BIT,
              AUGER, GIMLET
tool, cutting ..... AX, ADZ, AXE,
    HOB, SAW, SAX, SYE, ADZE
tool, engraver's
              BURIN, MATTOIR
tool, enlarging ...... REAMER
tool, grass-cutting .. SITHE,
              SCYTHE, SICKLE
tool, machine .... LATHE
tool, molding .... DIE
tool, pointed .... BROACH
tool, post hole digging .. LOY
tool shaper .... SWAGER
tool, splitting .. FROE, FROW
b
tool, stone, prehistoric
              CELT, EOLITH
tool, threading ...... CHASER
tool's biting edge ...... BIT
tooth ...... COG, TINE, MOLAR,
    CANINE, CUSPID, FANG
tooth-billed pigeon .. DODLET
tooth, canine ...... CUSPID
tooth: comb. form .... ODONT
tooth, gear .... COG
tooth: Lat. .... DENS
tooth-like ornament .. DENTIL
tooth, long FANG, TUSH, TUSK
tooth pulp .... NERVE
toothed formation .... SERRA
toothed margin, having
              DENTATE
toothed wheel .... GEAR
toothless .... EDENTATE
toothless mammals EDENTATA
top .... APEX, CAP, LID
top-notch .... AONE
top ornament .... EPI, FINIAL
topaz humming bird .. AVA
topee material .... SOLA
toper .... SOT, SOUSE
topic .... THEME
topmast crossbar support . FID
topsail .... RAFFE
torment .... BAIT, ANNOY,
    DEVIL, HARRY, TEASE
torn: archaic .... REFT

c
torn place .... RENT
torrid region or zone . TROPIC
tortoise .... GALAPAGO
tortoise, fresh water .. EMYD
tortoise, marsh genus .. EMYS
tortoise, order of .. CHELONIA
torturer .... RACKER
"Tosca" villain ..... SCARPIA
toss ..... CAST, FLIP, HURL,
              FLING, PITCH
tossspot .... SOT
total ..... ADD, SUM, UTTER
total abstinence . NEPHALISM
totalitarian ruler .. DICTATOR
totem pole .... XAT
toucan .... TOCO
toucan, S. Am. .... ARACARI
touch .... ABUT
touch lightly .... PAT
touch, organ of ...... PALP
touch, pert. to HAPTIC, TACTIC,
              TACTILE, TACTUAL
touch sense, pert. to .. HAPTIC
touchwood .... PUNK
tough .... WIRY, HARDY,
              ROWDY, CHEWY
tour: It. .... GIRO
tourmaline, colorless
              ACHROITE
d
tow .... PULL, DRAW
towai .... KAMAHI
toward: Lat. .... AD
toward stern ... AFT, ABAFF,
              ABAFT, ASTERN
towel .... WIPER
towel fabric ... HUCK, TERRY
tower, Bibl. .... BABEL
tower, India .... MINAR
tower, little .... TURRET
tower, mosque, slender
              MINARET
towering .... STEEP
towhead ... BLOND, BLONDE
town, Arcadia ancient .. ALEA
town: Cornish prefix ..... TRE
town: Dutch .... STAD
town: Ger. .... STADT
town, India pilgrimage SORON
town: It. ...... CASAL, CASALE
town: Jap. .... MACHI
town: suffix .... TON
township, ancient Attica DEME
townsman .... CIT
toxic protein .... ABRIN
toy with .... TRIFLE
trace .... TINGE, VESTIGE
track .... TRACE
track, animal .... RUN, SLOT,
              SPUR, SPOOR
track circuit .... LAP

167

a
track of ship .... WAKE
track, deer's .... SLOT
track, otter's ... SPUR, SPOOR
track, put off .... DERAIL
track, put on another
           SHUNT, SWITCH
tracker, India ...... PUGGI
tract .... LOT, AREA
tract of farm land ... FIELD
trade .... SWAP, SWOP,
           BARTER, TRAFFIC
trade .... METIER
trade agreement .... CARTEL
trader .... DEALER, MONGER
trader selling to soldiers
           SUTLER
trading exchange .... PIT
trading vessel of Ceylon
           DONI, DHONI
traditional story ...... SAGA
traduce ...... SLUR, DEFAME
traffic .... TRADE
trail ... SLOT, SPOOR, TRACK
train of attendants
           SUITE, RETINUE
train, overhead .... EL
train, slow, many-stops LOCAL
tramp .... BO, HOBO
trample .... TREAD
tranquil or tranquilize
b
           SERENE, SOOTHE
transaction ..... DEAL, SALE
transfer .... CEDE
transfer, property
           DEED, GRANT
transfer, sovereignty . DEMISE
transferer, property . ALIENOR
transform .... CONVERT
transgress .... ERR, SIN
transit coach .... BUS
"— transit gloria mundi" . SIC
translator of Freud, Amer.
           BRILL
transmit .... SEND
transom .... TRAVE
transpire ... OCCUR, HAPPEN,
           DEVELOP
transverse pin ...... TOGGLE
trap ..... SNARE, ENSNARE
trap door .... DROP
trap, mouse: dial. ...... TIPE
trap, rabbit: dial. ...... TIPE
trappings .... REGALIA
travel .... TREK
traveler .... PASSENGER
tray ...... SALVER, SERVER
tread softly ..... PAD, SNEAK
treasure ...... ROON, TROVE
treasurer, college ... BURSAR
treasury agents .... TMEN
treat .... USE

c
treat with acid ...... ACIDIZE
treat with malice ...... SPITE
treatment .... USE
tree .... (3 letters) ASH, ELM,
    FIR, LIN, OAK, YEW; (4 let-
    ters) AKEE, AMLA, AMLI,
    ANAM, ANDA, ARAR,
    ASAK, AULU, AUSU, AUZU,
    BARU, BIJA, BITO, BIWA,
    BOBO, BOGO, DALI, DILO,
    DOON, DOUM, DUKU,
    EBOE, EJOO, GOAI, GUAO,
    HINO, IFIL, IPIL, KINO,
    KIRI, KOPI, KOZO, LIME,
    LINN, MAKO, MYXA,
    NAIO, NEEM, NIOG, NIPA,
    ODUM, OHIA, PALM, PELU,
    PINE, PUKA, RATA, RIMU,
    ROKA, SAUL, SHEA, SUPA,
    TALA, TARA, TAWA, TEAK,
    TEIL, TEYL, TOON, TORO,
    TUNG, TUNO, TUWI, UPAS,
    WHAU, YATE, YAYA, YPIL;
    (5 letters) ASPEN; (6 let-
    ters) LINDEN
tree, African ... AKEE, BAKU,
        COLA, KOLA, ROKA,
        SHEA, AEGLE, ARTAR
d
tree, Afr. & Asia .... SIRIS
tree, Afr. gum ...... BUMBO
tree, Afr. tallow .... ROKA
TREE, AMER. TROPICAL .. see
    TREE, TROPICAL AMER.
tree, Argentine timber .. TALA
TREE, ASIATIC .. see ASIATIC
           TREE
tree, arrow poison ..... UPAS
TREE, AUSTRAL. .... see
        AUSTRAL. TREE
tree, Bengal quince ..... BEL
tree black gum ..... TUPELO
tree body of .... TRUNK
tree, boxwood yielding SERON
tree, buckwheat .... TITI
tree, butter .... SHEA
tree, caucho-yielding .... ULE
tree, chicle .... SAPOTA
tree, Chin. .. GINKO, GINKGO
tree clump, prairie ... MOTTE
tree cobra .... MAMBA
tree, coniferous (cone) . FIR,
        YEW, PINE, LARCH
TREE. E. IND. ... see E. IND.
    TREE and TREE, IND.
TREE, EVERGREEN ...... see
        EVERGREEN
tree, flowering ...... CATALPA
tree genus .... MABA
tree genus, Afr. ..... OCHNA

a   tree genus, elms .... ULMUS, CELTIS
tree genus, small .. CATALPA
tree, gum .... ICICA
tree, hardwood ASH, OAK, IPIL
tree, India ... DAR, MEE, SAJ, SAL, AMLA, AMLI, DHAK, MYXA, NEEM, SHOQ, MAHUA, BANYAN
tree knot .... BURL
tree, locust .... ACACIA
tree, maidenhair ..... GINKGO
tree, Malay .... TERAP
tree, Medit. .... CAROB
tree, mimosaceous .... SIRIS
tree moss .... USNEA
tree, N. Am...
     TAMARAC, TAMARACK
TREE, N. Z.
     see NEW ZEALAND TREE
tree, oak .... ENCINA
tree of olive family ..... ASH
tree, Pacific .... KOU
tree, palm .. GRIGRI, GRUGRU
tree, palm, Asiatic ... ARENG
TREE, P.I. ......see P. I. TREE
tree, pod .... CAROB
tree, resinous ..... FIR, PINE, BALSAM
tree, showy Asia .... ASAK
b   tree-snake .... LORA
tree, sun, Jap. ...... HINOKI
tree, swamp .... ALDER
tree, tamarisk salt ..... ATLE
tree, tea .... TI
tree, thorny .... ACACIA
tree tiger .... LEOPARD
tree toad genus ...... HYLA
tree, tropical ... EBOE, PALM, BALSA, MANGO, COLIMA, SAPOTA, LEBBEK
tree, tropical Amer. CEBA, DALI, GUAO, CEIBA, COLIMA, GUAMA, CEDRON
tree trunk .... BOLE
tree, W. Ind. .... GENIP, SAPOTE, LIBIDIBI
treeless plain .... PAMPAS, TUNDRA, STEPPES
trees of a region ..... SILVA
tremble ..... QUAKE, DIDDER
trembling .... ASPEN, TREPID
trench .... SAP
trench extension .... SAP
trench, rear wall of . PARADOS
trend .... TENOR
trespass . INFRINGE, INTRUDE

e   trespass for game ... POACH
trespass to recover goods
         TROVER
triad .... TRIO
trial .... TEST
triangle ... TRIGON, SCALENE
triangle, side of ...... LEG
triangular insert ...... GORE
tribal symbol .... TOTEM
TRIBE
    see also SPECIAL SECTION
tribe ..... CLAN, FOLK, RACE
TRIBE, BIBLICAL .... see
        SPECIAL SECTION
tribe: Bib. tent-dwellers.KEDAR
tribe division, Rom.
       CURIA, CURIAE
TRIBE, ISRAELITE .... see
      ISRAELITE TRIBE
TRIBESMAN .. see TRIBES in
      SPECIAL SECTION
tribulation .... TRIAL
tribunal .... BAR, FORUM
tribute .... SCAT, SCATT
tribute: Gaelic .... CAIN
trick FLAM, GAWD, JEST, RUSE, WILE, DODGE, FICELLE, STRATAGEM
tricks, game for no ... NULLO
tricks, win all .... CAPOT
d   Trieste measure . ORNA, ORNE
trifle ..... TOY, DOIT, FICO, STRAW, NIGGLE, PALTER
trifling ...... SMALL, SLIGHT
trig .... NEAT, TRIM
trigonometry function
      SINE, COSINE
trigonometry line .... SECANT
trill, bird's .... TIRALEE
trim .... NEAT, TRIG, ADORN, DECORATE
trimmed .... SNOD
trimming, dress . GIMP, RUCHE
trimmings, overlapping . FLOTS
Trinidad tree .... CYP
trinket .... GAUD
triple .... TRI, TREBLE
triplet .... TRIN
tripletail, P. R. .... SAMA
tripod, 6-footed .... CAT
Tripoli: measure, see page 188,
"Tristram Shandy" author
        STERNE
Tristram's beloved .. ISOLT, YSEUT, ISAUDE, ISAULT, ISEULT, ISOLDE, ISOLTA, ISOUDE, ISULTE
trite . BANAL, CORNY, STALE
triton ..... EFT, EVET, NEWT

troche ..... **PASTIL, ROTULA, PASTILE, PASTILLE**
TROJAN ...... see also TROY
Trojan hero .. **PARIS, ENEAS, AENEAS, AGENOR, DARDAN, HECTOR, HEKTOR, ACHILLES**
trolley .... **TRAM**
troop-carrying group: abbr. **ATS**
troop, division, Gr. .... **TAXIS**
troops .... **MEN**
troops, spread ...... **DEPLOY**
trophy .... **CUP**
tropic .... **SOLAR**
tropical Am. bird genus **CACICUS**
tropical disease **BUBA, BUBAS**
tropical fever ...... **DENGUE**
TROPICAL FRUIT ...... see **FRUIT, TROPICAL**
tropical plant .... **TARO**
tropical shrub genus **INGA, SIDA**
trot .... **JOG, AMBLE**
trouble ... **ADO, AIL, WORRY, EFFORT, MOLEST**
troubles .... **ILLS**
troublesome person **PEST, AGITATOR**
trough, inclined .... **CHUTE**
trough, mining ..... **SLUICE**
trout, British **SEWEN, SEWIN**
trout, brook .... **CHAR**
trowel, plasterers' .. **DARBY**
Troy .... **ILION, ILIUM**
Troy, founder of .... **ILUS**
Troy, land of .... **TROAS**
Troy, last king of .... **PARIS, PRIAM, PRIAMOS**
Troy, of ancient ..**ILIAC, ILIAN**
Troy: poetic .... **ILIUM**
truant, play: Scot. .. **TRONE**
truck .... **LORRY, CAMION**
trudge .... **PACE, PLOD, SLOG**
true copy: law .... **ESTREAT**
true olives .... **OLEA**
trumpet .... **HORN, CLARION**
trumpet call, reveille . **DIAN**
trumpet, mouth of ... **CODON**
trumpet shell .... **TRITON**
trumpeter perch ...... **MADO**
trumpeter, pigeon-like **AGAMI**
trundle, as ore .... **RULL**
trunk of body .... **TORSO**
trunkfish .... **CHAPIN**
truss up .... **TIE**
trust .... **RELY, TROW, RELIANCE**
trustee of a wakf.**MUTAWALLI**
trusting .... **RELIANT**
truth: Chin. .... **TAO**

truth drug ...... **PENTOTHAL**
Truth personified .... **UNA**
try ... **TEST, ESSAY, ATTEMPT**
try to equal ... **VIE, EMULATE**
tsetse fly .... **MAU, KIVU**
tsetse fly genus ... **GLOSSINA**
tub ...... **VAT, KNAP, KNOP**
tub, brewer's .... **KEEVE**
tub, brood .... **KEELER**
tub, wooden: dialect ..... **SOE**
tube .... **DUCT**
tube, glass ... **PIPET, PIPETTE**
tube, plane's .... **PITOT**
tuber delicacy ..... **TRUFFLE**
tuber, edible . **OCA, OKA, YAM, TARO, POTATO**
tuber, orchid .... **SALEP**
tuber, S. Amer. ... **OCA, OKA**
Tuesday, god who gave name to .... **TIU, TYR**
tuft .... **CREST**
tuft: bot. .... **COMA**
tufted plant .... **MOSS**
tulip tree .... **POPLAR**
TUMERIC ..... see TURMERIC
tumor .... **OMA, WEN**
tumor, skin .... **WEN**
tumult .... **RIOT**
tune .... **AIR, ARIA, SONG, MELODY**
tune, bagpipe .... **PORT**
tune: Scot. .... **PORT**
tungstite .... **OCHER, OCHRE**
tuning fork ...... **DIAPASON**
Tunis, ruler of ..... **BEY, DEY**
tunnel, train, Alps ... **CENIS**
tunny .... **AMIA, TUNA**
turban, Oriental ... **MANDIL**
turbid, make .... **ROIL**
turf .... **SOD**
turf, bit of: golf ...... **DIVOT**
Turkestan town dwellers **SART**
turkey buzzard ...... **AURA**
turkey red .... **MADDER**
turkeys, collection of **RAFTER**
Turkic person **TATAR, TARTAR**
Turkic person, 8th century **OGOR**
Turkish army corps .... **ORDU**
Turkish army officer .... **AGA**
Turkish caliph .... **ALI**
Turkish chamber . **ODA, ODAH**
Turkish chieftain ..... **AMIR, ZAIM, AMEER**
Turkish commander . **AGA, ALI**
Turkish copper coin ... **PARA**
Turkish decree ...... **IRADE**
Turkish flag .... **ALEM**
Turkish general .... **AGA**
Turkish gold coin ..... **LIRA, ALTUN, MAHBUB**

170

Turkish government ... **PORTE**
Turkish govt. summer residence
YALI
Turkish governor . **VALI, WALI**
Turkish hostelry .... **IMARET**
Turkish judge ... **CADI, KADI**
Turkish leader .... **AGA**
Turkish liquor ...... **MASTIC**
Turkish magistrate **CADI, KADI**
Turkish military district . **ORDO**
Turkish money of account
ASPER
Turkish officer ... **AGA, AGHA**
Turkish oxcart . **ARBA, ARABA**
Turkish palace .... **SERAI**
Turkish pavilion ..... **KIOSK**
Turkish president, former
INONU
Turkish regiment ...... **ALAI**
Turkish standard **ALEM, TOUG**
Turkish sultan ...... **SELIM**
Turkish title ..... **AGA, AGHA,
BABA, EMIR, EMEER,
PASHA, BASHAW**
Turkish tribesman .... **TATAR**
Turkish tribesman, Persia
GHUZ
Turkoman tribesman
SEID, SHIK
tumeric .... **REA, ANGO**
turmoil .... **WELTER**
turn .... **BEND, GYRE, VEER,
ROTATE, SWERVE**
turn aside **SKEW, VEER, SHUNT**
turn back to .... **REVERT**
turn direction .... **VERT**
turn inside out ...... **EVERT**
turn over: mus. ..... **VERTE**
turning point . **CRISES, CRISIS**
turning: prefix .... **ROTO**
turnover .... **PIE**
turnip . . **BAGA, NEEP, SWEDE**
turnip: Scot. .... **NEEP**
turpentine derivative
ROSIN, PINENE
turpentine distillate ... **ROSIN**
turpentine resin
ALK, GALLIPOT, GALIPOT
turtle, Amazon ...... **ARRAU**
turtle, edible
TERAPIN, TERRAPIN
turtle, edible part of **CALIPEE**
turtle enclosure ..... **CRAWL**
turtle genus .... **EMYS**
turtle, hawkbill ...... **CARET**
turtle, order of ... **CHELONIA**
Tuscany art city ...... **SIENA**
tusk, elephant ...... **IVORY**
tutelary god .... **LAR, LARES**
tutor .... **TUTE**

TV advertiser ..... **SPONSOR**
"Twelfth Night" clown . **FESTE**
"Twelfth Night" heroine
VIOLA
twelve and one-half cents . **BIT**
twenty-fourth part
CARAT, KARAT
twenty quires .... **REAM**
twice .... **BIS**
twice: prefix .... **BI**
twig, willow .. **WITHE, WITHY**
twilight .... **EVE, DUSK,
GLOAM, EVENTIDE**
twilled coth .... **REP**
twilled wool fabric .... **SERGE**
twin .... **GEMEL**
twin crystal .... **MACLE**
twin gods, Teut. ..... **ALCIS**
twine ..... **COIL, WIND, TWIST**
twining stem .... **BINE**
twist ...... **PLY, COIL, FEAK,
KINK, SKEW, GNARL,
WREATHE, CONTORT**
twist inwards .... **INTORT**
twist out of shape ..... **WARP**
twisted .... **AWRY, SKEW,
TORTILE**
twisted roll of fibers ... **SLUB**
twisted spirally ...... **TORSE**
twitch .... **TIC**
twitching .... **TIC**
two .... **DUO, DUAD, PAIR**
two ears, affecting the **DIOTIC**
two elements, having . **BINARY**
two feet, verse of ... **DIPODY**
two-footed .... **BIPED, BIPEDAL**
two-horse chariot ...... **BIGA**
two-hulled boat . **CATAMARAN**
two-masted ship . **YAWL, ZULU**
two-month period . **BIMESTER**
two, music for .... **DUET**
two notes, group of ... **DUOLE**
two-pronged, as sponges
DICELLATE
two-pronged weapon . **BIDENT**
two-spot .... **DEUCE**
two tenacles, having **DICEROUS**
two-toed sloth .... **UNAU**
two-wheeled vehicle **GIG, CART**
two-year-old sheep
TEG, TEGG, BIDENT
"Two Years Before the Mast"
author .... **DANA**
twofold .. **DUAL, TWIN, BINAL**
twofold: prefix .... **DI**
tycoon .... **NABOB**
tymp arch of furnace . **FAULD**
Tyndareus, wife of .... **LEDA**
type collection .... **FONT**

171

Type

type, conforming to	TYPICAL	type size	PICA, AGATE, BREVIER
type face	RUNIC, CASLON	type, slanting	ITALIC
type, 5½ point	AGATE	type square	EM
type, jumbled	PI, PIE	type tray	GALLEY
type, kind of	ELITE	typewriter roller	PLATEN
type measure	EM, EN	Tyr, Norse war god	ER
type metal piece	QUAD	tyrant	DESPOT
type, mixed	PI, PIE	tyrant of Rome	NERO
type of script	RONDE	Tyre, king of	HIRAM
type part	KERN	Tyre, princess of	DIDO
type set	FONT	tyro	NOVICE

U

Uganda native	KOPI	uncouth person	CAD, BOOR, YAHOO, GALOOT
ukase	EDICT	unction	BALM
Ukraine legislature	RADA	unctuous	OILY, SUAVE
"Ulalume" author	POE	under	INFRA, NEATH, SOTTO, NETHER
ulexite	TIZA	under: Fr.	SOUS
ultra-conservative	TORY	under: naut.	ALOW
ULYSSES .see also ODYSSEUS		under: prefix	SUB
Ulysses' swineherd	EUMAEUS	under side, pert. to	VENTRAL
Ulysses' voyages	ODYSSEY	undergo: obs.	DREE
umbrella	GAMP	underground bud	BULB
umbrella finial, Burma	TEE	underground reservoir, natural water	CENOTE
umbrella, India	CHATTA	underground stream, S. Afr.	AAR
umbrella part	RIB	underhand, throw	LOB
umpire	REFEREE	undersong	TIERCE
unaccented vowel sound	SCHWA	undershirts	SKIVVIES
unadulterated	PURE	undersized animal	RUNT
unaffected	SIMPLE, ARTLESS	understand	GRASP
Unalaskan	ALEUT	understanding	KEN, SENSE, ENTENTE
unaspirate	LENE	underwater box	CAISSON
unassuming	MODEST, NATURAL	underworld	HADES, SHEOL
unbeliever	HERETIC	underworld, Egypt.	DUAT, AMENTI
unbleached	ECRU, BEIGE	underworld god	DIS, PLUTO
unburnt brick	DOBE, ADOBE	underworld god, Egypt.	OSIRIS, SERAPIS
uncanny	EERY, EERIE, WEIRD	underworld goddess	HEL
Uncas' beloved	CORA	underwrite	ENSURE, INSURE
unceasing	ETERNAL, PERPETUAL	undeveloped	LATENT
uncinate	HAMATE	undraped	NUDE
uncivil	RUDE	undulant fever	BRUCELLOSIS
uncle, dial.	EME	undulating	WAVY
uncle: Scot.	EME	undulation	WAVE
"Uncle Remus" author	HARRIS	unequal	UNIQUE
"Uncle Remus" rabbit	BRER	unequal angled	SCALENE
unclean: Jewish law	TREF	unequal conditions	ODDS
unclose	OPE, OPEN	uneven	ODD, EROSE
uncommon	RARE, SPECIAL	unevenly shaped	EROSE
unconcerned	CALM, OPEN, SERENE		
unconscious state	COMA		
unconstrained	EASY		

172

a
unfadable .... FAST
unfair move .... FOUL
unfair shove in marbles . FULK
unfasten .... UNTIE, LOOSEN
unfavorable .... BAD, ILL
unfeeling .. HARSH, CALLOUS
unfermented grape juice
.... STUM
unfit to eat, make DENATURE
unfledged bird .... EYAS
unfold .... EVOLVE
unguent, Roman wrestlers'
.... CEROMA
ungula .. CLAW, HOOF, NAIL
ungulate, S. Am. ...... TAPIR
unhappy .... SAD, BLUE,
.... MOROSE, RUEFUL
unicorn fish .... LIJA, UNIE
uniform .... EVEN
uniform in hue .. FLAT, FLOT
uninteresting .... DULL
union .... MERGER
union, labor .. AFL, CIO, ILA,
.... ITA, ILGWU
union, political .... BLOC
union, Russ. workers' .. ARTEL
unique person .... ONER
unique thing: slang .... ONER
unit .... ACE, ONE

b
unit of capacity .... FARAD
unit of conductance .... MHO
unit of electrical intensity:
abbr. .... AMP
unit of electrical resistance or
reluctance .... REL
unit of electricity OHM, WATT,
.... FARAD, WEBER
unit of electromotive force
.... VOLT
unit of energy .... ERG,
.... RAD, ERGON
unit of fluidity .... RHE
unit of force .... DYNE
unit of heat .... CALORIE
unit of illumination .... PHOT
unit of jet propulsion ... JATO
unit of light ... PYR, LUMEN,
.... HEFNER
unit of power .... DYNE
unit of power, electric .. OHM,
.... WATT, FARAD, WEBER
unit of pressure BARAD, BARIE
unit of reluctance ...... REL
unit of resistance ...... OHM
unit of weight .... WEY
unit of work .... ERG, ERGON
unit, pert. to ..... MONADIC
unit, power ratio .... BEL

c
unite ..... WED, ALLY, JOIN,
KNIT, WELD, YOKE,
MERGE, INTEGRATE
unite edges .... RABBET
UNITED STATES
.... see AMERICAN
unity .... ONE
univalent element .... MONAD
universal . WORLD, GENERAL
universal language .. RO, IDO
universe .. WORLD, COSMOS
universe: Hindu .... LOKA
universe, pert. to .... COSMIC
university degree-holder
.... LICENTIATE
University in Conn. ..... YALE
unkeeled .... RATITE
unkind ILL
unknown Hindu god ..... KA
unless .... BUT, SAVE
unless: Lat. .... NISI
unlock .... OPE, OPEN
unmarried .... CELIBATE
unmatched .... ODD
unmixed ...... PURE, SHEER
unmusical clang ...... TONK
unnecessary ...... NEEDLESS
unplowed strip .... HADE
unpredictable ...... ERRATIC

d
unprincipled person ... CAD,
SCAMP, BOUNDER,
REPROBATE
unprofitable, as rents ... SECK
unrefined .... EARTHY
unrelenting . IRON, ADAMANT
unruffled .... CALM, SERENE
unruly outbreak .... RIOT
unruly person .... RANTIPOLE
unsophisticated ...... NAIVE
unsorted flour .... ATA, ATTA
unspoken .... TACIT
unstable .. ASTATIC, ERRATIC
unsuitable .... INAPT, INEPT
untamed ...... WILD, FERAL
untidiness ...... MESS, MUSS
untidy person .... SLOB
until .... TILL
untrained .... RAW
unusual ...... RARE, EXOTIC
unusual person or thing .ONER
unwavering .... SURE, STEADY
unwholesome ILL
unwieldly thing ...... HULK
unwilling .... LOTH, LOATH,
AVERSE
unwilling, be: archaic .... NILL
unyielding .. FIRM, ADAMANT
unyielding: naut. .... FAST

173

Up

up: comb. form .... ANO
Upanishad .... ISHA
upland plain .... WOLD
upbraid ..... CHIDE, SCOLD,
                        REPROACH
upon ...... EPI, ATOP, ONTO
upon: law .... SUR
Upper Nile Negro .... MADI
Upper Nile tribesman .. MADI
Upper Silurian ... ONTARIAN
uppermost part .... TOP
upright .. . ERECT, HONEST
upright column ...... STELE
upright piece ... JAMB, STUD
uprising .... REVOLT
uproar .... DIN
upward, heave: naut. .. SCEND
uraeus .... ASP
Uranus' satellite ..... ARIEL
urban office-holder .. MAYOR
urchin ... IMP, TAP, GAMIN
Urfa, modern ...... EDESSA
urge ..... EGG, PLY, YEN,
                      IMPEL, PRESS
urge: Scot. .... ERT

urial .... SHA
urticaria .... HIVES
urus .... TUR
us: Ger. .... UNS
usage .... WONT
use a divining rod ... DOWSE
use, be of .... AVAIL
use exertions .... STRIVE
use one's efforts ..... EXERT
used up ..... ATE, DEPLETED
useful .... UTILE, PRACTICAL
useless .... IDLE, FUTILE,
                    OTIOSE, INUTILE
usual .... NORMAL
Utah State flower ..... SEGO
utmost ...... LAST, FINAL,
                        GREATEST
utmost hyperbole ..... ELA
utter .... SAY, SHEER,
                    SPEAK, STARK
utter, as greeting ..... BID
utter loudly ... VOCIFERATE
uttered .. ORAL, SAID, SPOKE
utterly .... STARK
Uz, brother of .... ARAN

V

V-shaped piece ...... WEDGE
vacant .... IDLE, EMPTY
vacuum .... VOID
vacuum, opposite of . PLENUM
vacuum tube .... DIODE
vagabond VAG, HOBO, TRAMP
vogue .... HAZY, LOOSE
vainglory .... PRIDE
valance, short ...... PELMET
vale . DALE, DELL, VALLEY
Vali, mother of ...... RIND
valiant ... BRAVE, STALWART
Valkyrie .... DIS, NORN
valley .... DALE, DELL, VAIL,
                    VALE, GLADE
valley, deep .... COULEE
valley, Jordan ...... GHOR
value .... RATE, PRIZE,
                WORTH, APPRAISE
value, thing of little .. TRIFLE
valve .... COCK
vampire .... LAMIA
van .... FORE
vandal .... HUN
vanish .... EVANESCE
vanity .... PRIDE
vanity case .... ETUI
vantage, place of ..... COIGN
vapid .... INANE, STALE

vapor .... STEAM
vapor: comb. form ..... ATMO
vapor: dialect. .... ROKE
vapor in air ..... HAZE, MIST
Varangians .... ROS
variable .... PROTEAN
variable, most ... PROTEAN
variable star ... MIRA, NOVA
variation, small
                    SHADE, NUANCE
variegated .... SHOT
variegated in color
                    PIED, CALICO
variety .... KIND
variety of bean
            SOY, LIMA, PINTO
various: comb. form
                    VARI, VARIO
varnish ingredient
            LAC, COPAL, RESIN
varnish, kind of
            SHELLAC, SHELLACK
varnish material ..... ELEMI
vase .... URN
vat ..... BAC, TUB, CISTERN
vat, beer .. GAAL, GAIL, GYLE
vat, brewer's .. KIVE, KEEVE
vat, large ...... KEIR, KIER
vault .... SAFE

174

a

vault, church .... CRYPT
vaulted alcove .... APSE
vaunt .... BRAG, BOAST
vector, that which turns a
VERSOR
Vedic dialect .... PALI
VEDIC GODS
see SPECIAL SECTION
veer ...... SHY, TURN, SHIFT
veer off .... SHEER
vegetable .. PEA, BEAN, BEET,
KALE, OCRA, OKRA, OKRO,
CHARD, ENDIVE, TOMATO,
WOBBIE, CELTUCE
vegetable fuel .... PEAT
vegetables, pod .... PEASE
vehicle .... CAR, CART,
CYCLE, HANSOM
vehicle, Am. Ind.
TRAVOIS, TRAVOISE
vehicle 4-wheeled .... LANDAU
vehicle, light, India .. TONGA
vehicle, Near East .... ARABA
vehicle, Russ. .... TROIKA
vehicle, war .... TANK
veil, chalice .... AER
vein: Lat. .... VENA

b

vein of body .... CAVA
vein, ore ...... LODE, SCRIN
vein, ore: prov. Eng. ... ROKE
vein, ore beside ...... RIDER
vein, throat ...... JUGULAR
vellum .... PARCHMENT
velocity per second .... VELO
velum .... PALATE
velvet .... PANNE
velvet grass .... HOLCUS
vend .... SELL
vendetta .... FEUD
venerable ...... OLD, HOARY
"Venerable" monk ..... BEDE
venerate ... ESTEEM, REVERE
veneration .... AWE
Venetian nobleman ... DOGE
Venetian painter ..... TITIAN
Venetian red .... SIENA
Venetian resort .... LIDO
Venetian rose .... SIENA
Venetian traveler ..... POLO
Venezuela copper center AROA
Venezuela Ind. language PUME
vengeance goddess .... ARA
Venice marble bridge . RIALTO
Venice canals .... RII
Venice district ...... RIALTO
ventral .... HEMAD, HAEMAD
venture .... DARE

c

Venus, Island of ..... MELOS
Venus' son .... CUPID
Venus, youth loved by ADONIS
veranda, Dutch, S. Afr. . STOEP
veranda, Hawaii ...... LANAI
veranda, India .... PYAL
verb form ...... IS, AM, ARE,
WAS, TENSE
verbal .... ORAL
verbal ending .ED, ER, ES, ING
verbal noun .... GERUND
verbal rhythm .... METRE
verbally .... ALOUD
Verdi heroine .... AIDA
verily .... YEA, AMEN
verity .... TRUTH
versatile .... MOBILE
verse .... LINE, STICH
verse, Fr. .... RONDEL
verse, Ir. .... RANN
verse, pert. to kind of IAMBIC
version, Bible .... ITALA
vertebral bones
SACRA, SACRUM
verticle line, in a ..... APEAK
verticle timber: naut. ... BITT
vertigo .... DINUS
very .... SO
very abundant .. LUXURIANT
very: Fr. .... TRES
very: Scot. .... VERA
very: Span. .... MUY

d

Ve's brother .... ODIN
vesicle, skin .... BLISTER
VESSEL . see also BOAT, SHIP,
GALLEY
vessel .... ARK
vessel, anat. ...... VAS, VASA
vessel, Arab. .. DOW, DHOW
vessel, chemical ...... ETNA
vessel, coasting, E. Ind.
PATAMAR
vessel, cooking ... PAN, POT
vessel, drinking .... GOURD
vessel for liquors . DECANTER
vessel, glass .... BOCAL
vessel, Gr. . CADUS, AMPHORA
vessel, heating ...... ETNA
vessel, large .... TANK
vessel, liquor ..... FLAGON
vessel, Medit. ..SETEE, MISTIC
vessel, Rom. .... PATERA
vessel, sacred .... PIX, PYX
vessel, sailing ...... SAIC,
SETEE, XEBEC
vessel, shallow ...... BASIN
vessel, supply ..... COALER
vessel, 3-masted
XEBEC, FRIGATE
vessel, 2-masted . YAWL, ZULU

175

vessel with two handles, Gr. DIOTA
vessel's curved planking . SNY
vestal . . . . CHASTE
vestige . IOTA, RELIC, TRACE
vestment . ALB, COPE, AMICE, EPHOD, STOLE
vestment, white . . ALB, AMICE
vesuvianite, brown . . . EGERAN
vetch . . . . TARE
vetch, bitter . . . . ERS
vetch, India . . . . AKRA
vetiver, grass . . . . BENA
vex GALL, RILE, ROIL, HARRY
vex persistently . . . . . NETTLE
vex: Scot. . . . . FASH
vexed . . . . RILY
via . . . . PER
viands . . . . DIET
viands, dainty . . . . CATES
Viaud's pseudonym . . . . LOTI
vibrate . . . . THRILL
vibration: music . TREMOLO
vice . . . . SIN
viceroy . . . . VALI
Vichy Premier . . . . LAVAL
vicious man . . . . YAHOO
victim . . . . PREY
victorfish . . . . AKU
victor's crown . . . . . . LAUREL
victory, Eng. CRECY, CRESSY
victory trophy . . . . SCALP
victuals . . . . FOOD
"— victus," woe to the con-
    quered . . . . VAE
"— vide," "which see" QUAE
vie with . . . . EMULATE
Viennese park . . . . . . PRATER
view . . . . SCENE, VISTA
vigilant . . . . . . WARY, ALERT
vigor . . . . PEP, VIM, VIS, ZIP, FORCE
Viking . . ERIC, OLAF, ROLLO
Viking explorer . . . . ERIC
vilify . . . . REVILE
village . DORP, VILL, HAMLET
village, Afr. . . . . KRAAL
village Java . . . . DESSA
village Russ. . . . . MIR
village, Scot. . . . . REW
village, S. Afr. native . . . STAD
villain . . . . KNAVE
villein . . . . CEORL
vindicate . . . . AVENGE
vindication . . . . REVENGE
vine . . . . IVY, BINE
vine: comb. form . . . . . VITI
vine, N. Z. . . . . AKA
vine, P. I. . . . . IYO

vine, woody . . ABUTA, LIANA
"vin du —," wine of the
    country . . . . CRU
vinegar of ale . . . . . . ALEGAR
vinegar, pert. to . . . . . ACETIC
vinegar worm . . . . EEL, NEMA
vinous . . . . WINY
viol, ancient type . . . . . REBEC
viol, bass . . . . GAMBA
viol, Shetlands . . . . GUE
viola . . . . ALTO
violent . . . . HOT
violet-adored ketone . . IRONE
violin, bass . . . . CELLO
violin, early . . REBAB, REBEC
violin, famous . . . . STRAD
violin, It. . AMATI, CREMONA
violin, small . . . . KIT
violin, tenor . . . . ALTO, VIOLA
violinist . . . . . ELMAN, YSAYE
viper . . . . ASP, ADDER
viper genus . . . . ECHIS
viper, horned . . . . . CERASTES
Virgil's hero . ENEAS, AENEAS
Virgin Mary pictured mourning PIETA
virus-fighting substance ANTIVIRAL
visage . . . . FACE
viscous LIMY, ROPY, SIZY, SLIMY
viscous substance TAR, SLIME
Vishnu, Incarnation, 7th RAMA
Vishnu, soul of universe VASU
Vishnu's bow . . . . SARAN
Vishnu's serpent . . . . . . NAGA
visible juncture . . . . . . SEAM
Visigoth king ALARIC, ALARIK
vision, defective . . . ANOPIA
vision, pert. to . . . . . OPTIC
visionary . . . . . AIRY, IDEAL, DREAMY, UNREAL, IDEALIST
visit . . . . SEE, CALL, HAUNT
visit at sea . . . . GAM
visit between whalers . . GAM
vison . . . . MINK
vital energy . . . . HORME
vital fluid . . . . SAP
vital principle . . . . . . SOUL
vitalize . . . . ANIMATE
vitamin . . . CITRIN, ADERMIN, ANEURIN, TORULIN
vitamin B NIACIN, THIAMINE
vitamin B2 . . . . FLAVIN
vitamin H . . . . BIOTIN
vitiate . . . . . SPOIL, TAINT, POLLUTE, INVALIDATE
vitriol-infused earth . . . . SORY
vituperate . . . . SCOLD

a

vivacious ..... AIRY, BRIGHT
vivacity .... ELAN, LIFE
vocal flourish ..... ROULADE
vocation .... CAREER
"— voce" .... SOTTO
voice .... SAY
voice
   ALTO, BASS, VOCE, TENOR
voice: It. .... VOCE
voice: Lat. .... VOX
voice, loss of ..... APHONIA
voiced .... SONANT
voiced, not .... ASONANT
voiceless .... SPIRATE
voiceless consonant .. SURD
void .... NUL, NULL,
   ABYSS, SPACE, INVALID
void, to make ANNUL, CANCEL
void, to render: Scot. .. CASS
voided escutcheon ..... ORLE
volcanic cinder ..... SCORIA
volcanic islands, Atlantic
                  FAROE
volcanic rock
   TUFA, TUFF, LATITE
volcanic scoria-matter
            LAVA, SLAG
volcano . ETNA, AETNA, PELEE
volcano crater .... MAAR
volcano hole .... CRATER

c

volcano, Martinique Is. . PELEE
volcano mouth ...... CRATER
volcano, P. I. .... APO
volcano pit .... CRATER
volcano, Sicily . ETNA, AETNA
volcano, W. Indies .... PELEE
volition .... WILL
volt-ampere .... WATT
Voltaire .... AROUET
Voltaire play: Fr. ...... ZAIRE
voluble .... GLIB
volume .... MO, TOME
vomiting .... EMESIS
voodoo charm .... MOJO
voodoo snake deity ... ZOMBI
vote .... BALLOT
vote into office .... ELECT
vote, right to ... FRANCHISE
vote, take a .... POLL
votes .... AYES, NOES, YEAS
vouch for .... SPONSOR
voucher .... CHIT, NOTE
"vous —": Fr., you are ETES
vowel, line over .... MACRON
vowel suppression ... ELISION
voyaging .... ASEA
vulcanite .... EBONITE
Vulcan's wife .... MAIA
vulgar .... COARSE
vulture
   AURA, URUBU, CONDOR

b

"W", old English....... WEN
wade across .... FORD
wading birds .... IBIS, RAIL,
   CRANE, EGRET, HERON,
   STILT, AVOCET, AVOSET,
   JACANA, FLAMINGO
wag .... WIT
wages .... PAY
Wagner heroine . ELSA, SENTA,
            ISOLDA
Wagnerian role ...... ERDA
wagon ... CART, DRAY, WAIN
wagon pin .... CLEVIS
wagon, Russ. ...... TELEGA
wagon shaft .... THILL
wagon tongue ... NEAP, POLE
wagtail .... LARK
wahoo, fish .... PETO
wail ...... KEEN, LAMENT
waist ...... CAMISA, TAILLE
waistcoat
   VEST, GILET JERKIN
wait .... BIDE
waken ..... ROUSE, AROUSE

d

wale .... WELT
Wales emblem .... LEEK
walk .... PACE, STEP, TREAD
walk affectedly ..... MINCE
walk heavily .... PLOD, SLOG
walk, inability to .... ABASIA
walk lamely .... LIMP
walk stiffly .... STALK
walk, tree-lined .... ALAMEDA
walking stick ... CANE, STILT
wall, arena .... SPINA
wall around fortified place
        RAMPART
wall, divided by .... SEPTATE
wall: Fr. .... MUR
wall material .... COB
wall, of a .... MURAL
wall paneling .... WAINSCOT
wall piece TEMPLET, TEMPLATE
wall section . DADO, PANEL
wall, squeeze against . MURE
wallaba tree, Brazil ..... APA
walled city, Nigeria .... KANO

177

a wallflower .... KEIRI
wallop .... LAM
wallow .... WELTER
walls .... SEPTA
walrus .... MORSE
wampum
    PEAG, SEWAN, SEAWAN
wan .... ASHY, PALE, ASHEN
wand .... BATON
wander .. ERR, HAAK, ROAM,
  ROVE, RAMBLE, DIGRESS
wander idly .... GAD
wanderer ..... VAG, NOMAD
"Wandering Jew" author . SUE
wane .... EBB
want ... LACK, NEED, DESIRE
wapiti .... ELK
war-club, medieval .... MACE
war correspondent
    PYLE, BALDWIN
war cry, ancient Gr. .. ALALA
war god .... ARES, MARS
war god, Babyl. ... IRA, IRRA
war god, Norse TY, TYR, TYRR
war god, Teut. .... ER
war goddess, Gr. ...... ENYO
war horse .... CHARGER
war, religious ..... CRUSADE
war, Russ.-Eng. ..... CRIMEA
war vessel .... CRUISER
warble . SING, TRILL, YODEL
b ward off ...... FEND, AVERT,
  PARRY, REPEL, STAVE
ward politician ...... HEELER
warden, fire .... RANGER
warehouse .... DEPOT
warehouse room ...... LOFT
warm .... CALID, TEPID
warning of danger: biol.
    SEMATIC
warning signal .... SIREN
warning system, attack
    DEW, BMEWS
warp yarn .... ABB
warrant, from monarch BERAT
warrior, Samoa .... TOA
warship, sailing .... FRIGATE
wary .... CAGY
was not: dialect .... NAS
wash .... LAVE
wash leather .... LOSH
wash out .... ELUTE
washings: chem. ..... ELUATE
Washington Irving character
    RIP
wasp .... HORNET
wasps, the .... VESPA
waste .... LOSS
waste allowance ...... TRET
waste away GNAW, ATROPHY
waste fiber .... NOIL
waste land .... MOOR
waste matter .... DROSS
waste silk .... KNUB, FRISON

c waste time .... IDLE
wastes, growing in . RUDERAL
watch .... SEE, GLOM
watch chain .... FOB
watchdog, Hel's ...... GARM
watchful .... ALERT
watchful guardian ... ARGUS
watchful, name meaning . IRA
watchman, alert ..... ARGUS
watchman, night .... SERENO
watchtower .... MIRADOR
water .. SPRINKLE, IRRIGATE
water arum .... CALLA
water chestnut, Chin. ... LING
water cock .... KORA
water, covered by ... AWASH
water: Fr. .... EAU, EAUX
water: Lat. .... AQUA
water lily .... LOTUS
water passage SLUICE, STRAIT
water pipe
  HOOKA, HOOKAH, NARGILE
water-raising device
    TABUT, TABOOT
water reservoir, natural
    CENOTE
water scorpion genus .. NEPA
water, seek .... DOWSE
water, sound of ...... PLASH
water: Sp. .... AGUA
d water spirit
  ARIEL, SPRITE, UNDINE
water sprite ..... NIX, NIXIE
water sprite: Gaelic ... KELPIE
water surface .... RYME
water vessel, India
  LOTA, LOTO, LOTAH
water wheel
  NORIA, DANAIDE, TURBINE
water wheel, Persian . NORIA
water's surface: naut. .. RYME
watercourse .. LADE, BROOK,
  CANAL, RIVER, STREAM
watered appearance ... MOIRE
watered silk .... MOIRE
waterfall, Scot.
  LIN, LYN, LINN
watering place . SPA, BADEN
waterproof canvas .... TARP
waterskin .... MATARA
watertight, make
  CALK, CAULK
waterway ... BAYOU, CANAL
waterway, narrow ... STRAIT
watery .... SEROUS
watery: comb. form .... SERO
wattle tree .... BOREE
wattle honeyeater
    IAO, MANUAO
wave .... FLY, SEA
wave-crest comb. ..... COOM
wave: Fr. .... ONDE
wave, huge .... SEA

a
waver ...... FALTER, TEETER
wavy: Her.
UNDE, UNDY, NEBULE
wax .... CERE
wax ointment ...... CERATE
wax, pert. to .... CERAL
wax: Sp. .... CERA
wax, yellow or white CERESIN
waxy chemical .... CERIN
waxy substance .... CERIN
way .... VIA, MODE, ROUTE
way of walking .... GAIT
way out .... EGRESS
wayside — .... INN
wayside stop, India .. PARAO
we: Lat. .... NOS
weak ...... PUNY, FRAIL,
DEBILE, EFFETE, FEEBLE
weak cider .... PERKIN
weaken SAP, LABEFY, VITIATE,
ENERVATE, ENFEEBLE
weakfish, S. Am. ... ACOUPA
weakness .... ATONY
weal .... WALE
wealth, man of ...... NABOB
wealthy: Scot. .... BIEN

b
weapon .... LANCE,
SPEAR, SWORD, MUSKET
weapon, ancient ...... CELT
weapon, dagger-like .. BALAS
weapon: Fr. .... ARME
weapon, gaucho's
BOLA, BOLAS
weapon, Maori .... PATU
weapon, medieval .... ONCIN
weapon, N. Z. .... PATU
weapon, P. I. .... BOLO
weapon, S. Am. . BOLA, BOLAS
wear away
EAT, ERODE, ABRADE
wear away slowly .. CORRODE
wear by friction .... RUB
wear off .... ABRADE
wearing down .... ATTRITION
weary .... BORE, TIRE
weasel VARE, ERMINE, FERRET
weasel: Eng.
STOT, STOAT, STOTE
weather indicator BAROMETER
weathercock .... VANE
weaverbird .... BAYA, MAYA
weaverbird, S. Afr. .. TAHA
weaver's bobbin on shuttle
PIRN
weaver's reed .... SLEY
weaving frame .... LOOM
weaving term .... LISSE
weaving tool .... EVENER

c
web .... TELA
web-footed bird . DUCK, LOON,
GOOSE
web-like membrane .... TELA
web-spinning
RETIARY, TELARIAN
wed .... MARRY
wedding anniversaries   1st,
PAPER; 2nd, COTTON;
3rd, CANDY OR LEATHER;
4th, SILK, FRUIT, FLOW-
ERS, or LEATHER; 5th
WOODEN; 6th, IRON OR
CANDY; 7th, WOOL, COP-
PER, OR FLORAL; 8th,
WOOL, BRONZE, OR POT-
TERY; 9th, WILLOW OR
POTTERY; 10th, TIN; 11th,
STEEL; 12th, SILK OR LIN-
EN; 13th, LACE; 14th,
IVORY; 15th, CRYSTAL;
20th, CHINA; 25th, SIL-
VER; 30th, PEARL; 35th,
CORAL; 40th, RUBY OR
SAPPHIRE; 50th, GOLDEN;
55th, EMERALD; 75th,

d
DIAMOND
wedge, entering COIN, COIGN,
QUOIN, COIGNE
wedge-like piece ...... QUOIN
wedge-shaped ...... CUNEATE
wedge-shaped piece GIB, SHIM
wedge, steel .... FROE
Wednesday, source of name
WODEN
weed .... TARE, DARNEL
weed coarse .... DOCK
week .... SENNET, SENNIGHT
week day .... FERIA
weep
CRY, SOB, BOHO, LAMENT
weep, Scot. .... ORP
weeping statue ...... NIOBE
weeping woman, Gr. myth
NIOBE
weft .... WOOF
WEIGHT .. see also SPECIAL
SECTION
weight .... TON, HEFT
weight allowance TARE, TRET
weight, ancient MINA, TALENT
weight, ancient: var. ... MNA
weight, Asiatic ...... TAEL
weight, balance ...... RIDER

Weight

a weight, Danish .... ORT
   weight, India .... SER, TOLA
   weight machine: Scot.
                        TRON, TRONE
   weight, metric unit of . GRAM
   weight of England ... STONE
   weight of silk before
        degumming .... PARI
   weight, pert. to ...... BARIC
   weight system .... TROY
   weir .... DAM
   weird .... EERY, EERIE
   welcome .... GREET
   well, Bib. .... AIN
   well-bred people ... GENTRY
   "well done" .. EUGE, BRAVO
   well done: Eng. .... EUGE
   well: Fr. .... BIEN
   well: It. & Lat. .... BENE
   well: Scot. .... AWEEL
   Welsh dog .... CORGI
   Welsh god of sea ..... DYLAN
   Welshman .... CELT
   welt .... WALE
   wen .... TALPA
   Wend of Saxony ...... SORB
   wergeld .... CRO
   W. Australia capital .. PERTH
   W. Afr. timber tree ... ODUM
b W. Afr. tribe IBO, BUBE, BUBI
   W. Ind. bayberry AUSU, AUZU
   W. Ind. fish
               BOGA, CERO, TESTAR
   W. Ind. idol ..... ZEME, ZEMI
   W. Ind. isle .... CUBA, HAITI
   W. Ind. key .... CAY
   W. Ind. scrapper ..... CAJI
   W. Ind. shrub plant .... ANIL
   West Point mascot .... MULE
   West Pointer
               PLEB, CADET, PLEBE
   West Saxon king .... INE
   Western division of Osset DIGOR
   Western European CELT, KELT
   Western Indian .... UTE
   Western shrub .... SAGE
   "Western Star" author BENET
   Western state .... UTAH
   Westphalian city ..... HERNE
   wet: Scot. .... WAT
   wet .... ASOP, MOIST
   whale ...... CET, ORC, ORK,
        CETE, BELUGA, GRAMPUS
   whale carcass KRANG, KRENG
   whale hunter .... AHAB
   whale oil cask .... RIER
   whale-shark .... MHOR
   whale tail part ...... FLUKE
   whale, white .... BELUGA

c whale, white Caspian
                        HUSE, HUSO
   whalebone .... BALEEN
   whales .... CETE
   whales, herd of ... GAM, POD
   whales, pert. to ..... CETIC
   whales, school of .. GAM, POD
   wharf KEY, PIER, QUAI, QUAY
   what is it? obs. ...... ANAN
   whatnot .... ETAGERE
   wheal .... WALE, WEAL
   wheat disease .... BUNT
   wheat, German EMMER, SPELT
   wheat, India .... SUJI, SUJEE
   wheat, kind of EMMER, SPELT
   wheat middlings .. SEMOLINA
   wheedle ...... COG, COAX
   wheedling .... BUTTERY
   wheel .... ROTA
   wheel band .... STRAKE
   wheel center HOB, HUB, NAVE
   wheel, furniture .... CASTER
   wheel, grooved ..... SHEAVE
   wheel horse .... POLER
   wheel part ...... HUB, RIM,
                        FELLY, SPOKE
   wheel projection ...... CAM
   wheel shaft .... AXLE
   wheel-shaped ...... ROTATE
   wheel spindle . AXLE, ARBOR
d wheel tread .... TIRE
   wheels, pert. to ...... ROTAL
   where: Lat. .... UBI
   whetstone, fine . BUHR, HONE
   whey of milk .. SERA, SERUM
   which see: abbr. .... QV
   whiff .... PUFF
   while .... AS, WHEN
   whimper ...... MEWL, PULE
   whin .... GORSE
   whine .... PULE
   whinny .... NEIGH
   whip CAT, BEAT, FLOG, LASH
   whip, cowboy ..... CHICOTE
   whip mark .... WALE, WEAL
   whip, Russ. .... KNOUT
   whipsocket .... SNEAD
   whirl .... REEL, SPIN
   whirlpool .... EDDY, GURGE,
                        VORTEX
   whirlpool: Scot. .. WEEL, WIEL
   whirlwind in Atlantic ... OE
   whirring sound .... BIRR
   whiskers ... BEARD, GOATEE
   whiskey: Ir. .... POTEEN
   whiskey drink: Scot.
                    ATHOL, ATHOLE
   whist win .... SLAM
   whistle .... PIPE, SIREN
   whit .... BIT, JOT,
                    ATOM, DOIT, IOTA

180

a
white acid, pert. to .. TROPIC
white alkaline .... SODA
white, ant, P. I. .. ANAI, ANAY
white, bitter compound LININ
white: comb. form ... ALBO
"White Elephant" land SIAM
white ermine LASSET, MINIVER
white-flecked .... ROAN
White Friar ...... CARMELITE
white: Ir. .... BAWN
white man: P. I. ... CACHILA
white matter, brain .... ALBA
white oak .... ROBLE
white poplar .... ABELE
white spruce ...... EPINETTE
white with age .... HOAR
whitefish .... CISCO
whiten .... ETIOLATE
whitish .... HOARY
whitlow grass .... DRABA
Whittier heroine ...... MAUD
whiz ...... PIRR, WHIR, ZIZZ
whoa .... HOLLA
whole amount .... GROSS
whole: comb. form .... TOTO
wholesome .... SALUTARY
wholly .... ALL
wicked .... EVIL
wicker basket ...... CESTA,
KIPSY, PANNIER

b
wicker basket, Guiana PEGALL
wickerwork .... RATAN
wickerwork hut ..... JACAL
wicket, croquet ...... HOOP
wide-mouthed vessel
EWER, OLLA
widgeon .... SMEE
widgeon genus ..... MARECA
widow .... RELICT
widow in cards ...... SKAT
widow monkey .... TITI
widow's bit or coin ... MITE
widow's third: Scot. ... TERCE
wield .... PLY, USE
wife, Moroccan ruler's SHERIFA
wife .... FEME, FRAU, FEMME
wife's property ...... DOS
wig .... PERUKE
wigwam . TIPI, TEPEE, TEEPEE
wild ...... FERAL, SAVAGE
wild animals, collection of
ZOO, MENAGERIE
wild animal's trail
SLOT, SPUR, SPOOR
wild apple ... CRAB, DOUCIN
wild ass, Afr. ..... QUAGGA
wild ass, Asia ...... ONAGER
wild boar genus .... SUS
wild buffalo, India
ARNA, ARNI, ARNEE

c
wild buffalo, Malay .... GAUR,
SLADANG, SALADANG,
SELADANG
wild cat, Siberia, Tibet, steppes
MANUL
wild cattle, India GAUR, GOUR
wild cry .... EVOE
wild dog .... DHOLE
wild dog genus .... THOS
wild dog, Japan .... TANATE
"Wild Duck" author ... IBSEN
wild garlic .... MOLY
wild ginger ...... ASARUM
wild hog .... BOAR
wild honeybee, E. Ind. DINGAR
wild horse of Tartary TARPAN
wild lime .... COLIMA
wild olive tree .... OLEASTER
wild ox .... ANOA
wild ox, Malay. .... BANTENG
wild plum .... SLOE
wild plus, Calif. ..... ISLAY
wild sheep, Asia
RASSE, ARGALI
wild sheep, horned MOUFLON
wild sheep, India SHA, SNA,
URIAL, NAHOOR, OORIAL
wild sheep, N. Afr.
ARUI, UDAD, AOUDAD
wild sheep, Tibet ..... SHA,
SNA, BHARAL, NAHOOR

d
wild turnip .... NAVEW
wild vanilla .... LIATRIS
wildcat ...... BALU, LYNX
wildcat, Afr. & India . CHAUS
wildcat, S. Am. ...... EYRA
wildcat, Sumatra ...... BALU
wildebeest .... GNU
wile .... ART
will addition .... CODICIL
will, one inheriting from
DEVISEE
will, one making ... DEVISOR
will power, loss of .. ABULIA
William: Ir. .... LIAM
William I, half brother of ODO
William the Conqueror's
daughter .... ADELA
willingly .... LIEF
willow ...... ITEA, OSIER
willow, Europ. ..... SALLOW
willow genus, Virginia .. ITEA
Wilson's thrush ...... VEERY
wilt .... FADE, DROOP
wily .... FOXY
wimple .... GORGET
win .... GAIN
winch .... WHIN
wind .... GALE
wind, Adriatic .... BORA

181

Wind

a

wind, Andes ... **PUNA, PUNO**
wind, Austral. ...... **BUSTER**
wind, away from ...... **ALEE**
wind, cold Malta .. **GREGALE**
wind, cold Medit. ... **MISTRAL**
wind, cold Swiss Alps **BISE, BIZE**
wind: comb. form .... **ANEMO**
wind-deposited loam .. **LOESS**
wind, dry, from Sahara **LESTE**
wind, east .... **EURUS**
wind god, Babyl.
    ADAD, ADDA, ADDU
wind god, Hindus ...... **YAYU**
wind god, pert. to
    EOLIAN, AEOLIAN
wind, hot, dry .... **KAMSIN,**
  SIMOOM, SIMOON, SIROCCO
wind, hot, Medit. ... **SOLANO**
wind indicator .. **SOCK, VANE**
wind instrument
   HORN, OBOE, PIPE, BUGLE
wind, Levant ...... **ETESIAN**
wind, Madeira ...... **LESTE**
wind, Medit. ...... **ETESIAN**
wind, Medit., poet. .... **SIROC**
wind, Mesop. ...... **SHAMAL**
wind, north ...... **BOREAS**
wind off Faroe Islands ... **OE**
wind, Peru Andes **PUNA, PUNO**
wind, sand-laden
  SAMIEL, SIMOOM, SIMOON

b

wind, Sahara ...... **LESTE**
wind, South . **NOTUS, AUSTER**
wind, southeast ...... **EURUS**
wind, southwest ...... **AFER**
wind, Trieste, cold .... **BORA**
wind, warm dry **FOHN, FOEHN**
wind, west .... **AFER**
winds, south, Peru .... **SURES**
windborne .... **AEOLIAN**
windflower .... **ANEMONE**
windlass .... **CAPSTAN**
windmill sail .... **AWE**
window lead .... **CAME**
window ledge .... **SILL**
window part .... **SASH**
window, semipolygonal **ORIEL**
window setter ...... **GLAZIER**
windrow .... **SWATH**
windstorm
  OE, BURAN, TORNADO
windstorm, Asia **BURA, BURAN**
wine .... **VIN, HOCK, PORT,**
  SACK, VINO, MEDOC, TO-
  KAY, CLARET, MALAGA,
  MUSCAT, SHERRY, MO-
  SELLE
wine, Am. .... **CATAWBA**
wine, ancient ...... **MASSIC**
wine cask ...... **TUN, BUTT**
wine city, It. .... **ASTI**

c

wine cup .... **AMA**
wine, delicacy of: Fr. .. **SEVE**
wine disorder ...... **CASSE**
wine district, Calif. ... **NAPA**
wine drink .... **NEGUS**
wine, dry .... **SEC, BRUT**
wine, golden .... **BUAL**
wine, heavy .... **TOKAY**
wine, honey and ...... **MULSE**
wine, Madeira ...... **BUAL**
wine measure, Trieste
    ORNA, ORNE
wine merchant ... **VINTNER**
wine, new .... **MUST**
wine pitcher, Gr. ...... **OLPE**
wine, red **PORT, TINTA, CLARET**
wine, sweet ...... **MUSCAT**
wine, sweet: Fr. .... **MASDEU**
wine, to make .... **VINT**
wine vessel ...... **AMA, OLPE,**
   AMULA, CHALICE
wine, white .... **HOCK,**
  SHERRY, SAUTERNE
wineberry, N. Z. ...... **MAKO**
wing .... **ALA, PENNA,**
   PINNA, PINION
wing, bastard .... **ALULA**
wing, beetle ...... **TEGMAN,**
  TEGMINA, TEGUMEN
wing: Fr. .... **AILE**

d

wing-footed animal .. **ALIPED**
winglike .... **ALAR**
wing-like part ... **ALA, ALAE**
wing movement ...... **FLAP**
wing tip, pert. to .... **ALULAR**
wings .... **ALAE**
wings, divested of
  DEALATA, DEALATED
wings, having .. **ALAR, ALATE**
wings: Her. ...... **VOL, AILE**
winged figure, Gr.
  IDOLON, IDOLUM, EIDOLON
winged fruit, indehiscent
    SAMARA
winged god .... **EROS, CUPID**
winged seed ...... **SAMARA**
winged victory .... **NIKE**
wingless .... **APTERAL**
wingless invertebrates **APTERA**
wink rapidly .... **BAT**
winning at bridge ..... **SLAM**
winnow .... **FAN**
winter, pert. to .... **BRUMAL,**
  HIEMAL, HYEMAL, HIBERNAL
winter squash ...... **CUSHAW**
wipe out .... **ERASE**
wire measure .... **MIL**
wire service .... **AP, UP,**
   INS, UPI, REUTERS

wires, cross .... RETICLE
Wisconsin college .... RIPON
wisdom ..... LORE, GNOSIS
wisdom, god of: Babyl.
                    NABU, NEBO
wisdom, goddess of: Gr.
              ATHENA, PALLAS
wisdom, goddess of: Rom.
                      MINERVA
wise ...... SAGE, SENSIBLE
wise adviser .... MENTOR
wise man
     SAGE, SOLON, NESTOR
Wise Men .... MAGI, GASPAR,
     MELCHIOR, BALTHASAR
wise men, A-S .... WITAN
wisecrack .. GAG, JOKE, QUIP
wish for .... YEARN, DESIRE
wish undone .... RUE
wisp of hair .... TATE
wit .... WAG, HUMOR
wit: Sp. .... SAL
witless chatter .... GAB
witch ... HAG, HECAT, LAMIA,
     HECATE, HECCAT, HEKATE
witch city .... SALEM
witch doctor .... GOOFER
witch in "Faerie Queene"
                      DUESSA
witchcraft .... OBEAH
with: Fr. .... AVEC
with: Ger. .... MIT
with joy .... FAIN
with: prefix .... SYN
withdraw RECEDE, REMOVE,
     RETIRE, SECEDE, RETRACT
wither .... FADE
withered .... SERE
within .... INTO, INTERIOR
within: comb. form
     ESO, ENDO, ENSO, ENTO
within: prefix .... ENDO
without: comb. form .... ECT
without energy ...... ATONY
without: Fr. .... SANS
without: Ger. .... OHNE
without: Lat. .... SINE
without: poetic ...... SANS
without teeth, claws, lion
                      MORNE
without veins ..... AVENOUS
witness .... SEE
witness, law TESTE, DEPONENT
witness, to bear .... ATTEST
witty remark .... MOT, QUIP
witty reply ...... REPARTEE
wobble .... TEETER
Woden .... ODIN
woe .... MISERY
woe is me .... ALAS

wolf, gray .... LOBO
wolf, Ôdin's ..... GERE, GERI
wolf, timber .... LOBO
wolfhound .... ALAN
wolfish .... LUPINE
wolframite .... CAL
wolverine genus ...... GULO
woman diplomat, first U.S.
                       OWEN
woman: Gr. .... GYNE
woman, ill-tempered
              SHREW, VIRAGO
woman personified, Ir.
                EMER, EIMER
woman's name (3 letters) ADA,
     AMY, ANN, EVA, EVE, FAY,
     IDA, INA, MAE, MAY, NAN,
     RAE, UNA, ZOE, (4 let-
     ters) AFRA, ALIX, ALMA,
     ALYS, ANNA, ANNE, AVIS,
     BONA, CARA, CLOE, CORA,
     DORA, EDNA, ELLA, ELSA,
     EMMA, ENID, ERMA, ETTA,
     INEZ, JANE, JEAN, JOAN,
     JUNE, LEAH, LIDA, LILA,
     LOIS, LORA, LUCY, MARY,
     MAUD, MYRA, NONA,
     NORA, OLGA, RITA, ROSA,
     ROSE, RUTH, SARA, VERA,
     VIDA, (5 letters) ALICE,
     ANITA, CLARE, DELIA,
     DIANA, ELAIN, ELSIE,
     ERICA, FAITH, FLORA,
     GRACE, IRENE, SARAH,
     SELMA, (6 letters) AL-
     THEA, BERTHA, DAPHNE,
     EDWINA, ELAINE, EMILIA,
     PHOEBE, (7 leetters) ABI-
     GAIL, CELESTE, LAVINIA
woman's nickname CAT, DEB,
     HAT, KIT, LOU, MAB, MAG,
     MEG, SAL, SUE, ABBY,
     ADDY, BESS, BETH, CARO,
     DORA, GAIL, JILL, JOSY,
     JUDY, JULE, KATE, KATY,
     LINA, LISA, LULU, MART,
     MIMI, MINA, MOLL, NELL,
     NINA, ROXY, SUSY, TAVE,
     TAVY, TESS, TINA, XINA,
     SALLY, SALLIE
Wonderland girl ...... ALICE
wont .... HABIT
wood .... ALOE
wood apple, Ind. .... BEL
wood, black .... EBONY
wood, flexible ...... EDDER
wood, fragrant ALOES, CEDAR
wood: comb. form ..... XYLO
wood: Fr. .... BOIS
wood gum .... XYLAN

a
wood, light .... BALSA
wood, long piece ...... POLE
wood: obsolete ...... WOLD
wood, piece of ...... SLAT,
                 SPRAG, BILLET
wood pussy .... SKUNK
wood robin, N. Z. ...... MIRO
wood sorrel ...... OCA, OKA
wood, timber: P. I. ... CAHUY
woodchuck .... MARMOT
woodchuck: dialect MOONACK
wooden .... TREEN
wooden brick .... DOOK
wooden collar, convict's CANG
wooden pail .... SOE
wooden peg .... SKEG
wooden shoe .SABOT, PATTEN
woodland deity . FAUN, SATYR
woodland god .... PAN
woodpecker genus JYNX, YUNX
woodpecker, green HICKWALL
woodpecker group ...... PICI
woodpecker, red-bellied . CHAB
woodpecker, small ... PICULE
woodpeckers, of ..... PICINE
woodwind
     OBOE, BASSOON, CLARINET
woodworking tool .... SAPPER
woodworm .... TERMITE
woody fiber .... BAST

b
woody hill .... HOLT
woody plant .... TREE
woof .... WEFT
wool .... ANGORA, MERINO
wool cluster .... NEP
wool, coarse .... GARE
wool fat LANOLIN, LANOLINE
wool: Lat. .... LANA
wool measure .... HEER
wool package .... FADGE
wool, reclaimed ..... MUNGO
woolen cloth ...... ETAMINE
woolen cloth, coarse, twilled
                      KERSEY
woolen fabric .... FRISCA
woolen thread .... YARN
woolly .... LANATE, LANOSE
woolly pyrol .... URD
word by word ...... LITERAL
word expressing action . VERB
word meanings, pert. to
                   SEMANTIC
word of affirmation .... AMEN
word of choice .... OR
word of God .... LOGOS
word of honor, promise
               PAROL, PAROLE
word of mouth, by
               PAROL, PAROLE
word of ratification ... AMEN
word, scrambled .. ANAGRAM

c
work .... MOIL,
          TOIL, CHARE, LABOR
WORK see also COMPOSITION
work aimlessly ...... POTTER
work at steadily ...... PLY
work hard
     PEG, MOIL, TOIL, SLAVE
work, in terms of heat ERGON
work, musical
     OPUS, OPERA, ORATORIO
work persistently ...... PEG
work, piece of .... JOB, STINT
work: Sp. .... OBRA
work unit .... ERG, ERGON
workbasket .... CABA, CABAS
worker .... HAND,
          OPERANT, OPERATOR
worker ant .... ERGATE
worker: comb. form . ERGATE
worker's group, worldwide ILO
worker's union, Soviet . ARTEL
workhorse: Scot. ...... AVER
working boat, Chesapeake Bay
                      FLATTIE
workman, mine ...... CAGER
workman, S. Afr. ...... VOLK
workshop .... ATELIER
world: Hindu myth .... LOKA
world, holder of ...... ATLAS
World War I battle site

d
          MONS, MARNE
World War I group AEF, AMEX
World War II area ...... ETO
worm . ESS, TINEA, ANNELID
worm, African .... LOA
worm, bait .... LURG
worm, eye-infesting ..... LOA
worm, S-shaped .... ESS
work track, fossil .. NEREITE
worn, as rope ...... MAGGED
worn by friction ... ATTRITE
worn out .... EFFETE
worn-out horse
          NAG, HACK, PLUG
worry .... RUX, CARE, CARK,
               FRET, STEW
worship .... ADORE
worship, form of .... RITUAL
worship, house of .... BETHEL
worship, object of ..... IDOL
worship of saints ..... DULIA
worship, place of
          ALTAR, TEMPLE
worthless BAD, RACA, TRASHY
worthless bit from table ORT
worthless rock ..... GANGUE
wound: Her. .... VULN
wound mark .... SCAR
wrangle .... HAGGLE
wrap .... SWATHE, SWADDLE

184

a

wrapping .... PLIOFILM
wrath .... IRE
wrathful .... IRATE
wreath .... CHAPLET
wreath: Her. .... TORSE
wreathe ...... COIL, WIND
wrest .... REND
wrestle .... TUSSLE
wrestling throw .. HIPE, HYPE
wriggling .... EELY
wrinkle ...... RUCK, RUGA,
    SEAM, RUGAE, RIMPLE
wrinkled .. RUGATE, RUGOSE
wrist .... CARPUS
wrist bone .... CARPAL
wrist guard .... BRACER
wrists .... CARPI
writ of execution .... ELEGIT
writ, sheriff's .... VENIRE
writ to arrest .... CAPIAS

c

write .... PEN, SCRIVE
write comments ..... POSTIL
write music .... NOTATE
writer .... DITER, SCRIBE
writer, Ger. .... MANN
writing instrument ..... PEN
writing on the wall
    MENE, TEKEL
writing paper size ..... CAP
writing table ... ESCRITOIRE
writing well, art of . RHETORIC
wrong .... OUT, EVIL, AMISS
wrong: Lat. .. MALA, MALUM
wrong, legal .... TORT
wrong: prefix .... MIS
wrongdoing .... EVIL
wrongdoing, serious .. CRIME
wryneck .... LOXIA
Wyoming peak, highest
    GANNETT

b

Y, in Middle Eng. . YOK, YOGH
Y's .... WIES
yacht .... SAIL
yacht pennant ...... BURGEE
Yale .... ELI
yam, Hawaii .... HOI
yam, white
    UBE, UBI, UVE, UVI
Yang, opposite of ..... YIN
Yangtze tributary ..... HAN
Yap Island stone money . FEI
yarn .. GARN, TALE, CREWEL
yarn count .... TYPP
yarn for warp .... ABB
yarn measure .... LEA, HEER
yarn, projection . KNAP, KNOP
yarn, quantity of ..... SKEIN
Yarura language ..... PUME
yataghan .... BALAS
yaupon holly ...... CASSENA
yawn .... GAPE
yawn: obs. .... GANE
yearly .... ETESIAN
yearly church payment ANNAT
yearn .... ACHE, LONG
year's crops .... ANNONA
yeast .... BEES
yeast, brewer's ...... BARM
yeast, Jap. .... KOJI
yeast, wild .... ANAMITE
yell: Scot. .... GOWL
yellow ..... AMBER, OCHER,
    OCHRE, MELINE, CITRINE
yellow-brown .... TOPAZ
yellow bugle .... IVA

d

yellow dye plant ...... AMIL
yellow fish ...... ORF, ORFE
yellow Ide ...... ORF, ORFE
yellow iris .... SEDGE
yellow ocher .... SIL
yellow pigment .... SIL
yellow wood ...... AVODIRE
yellowhammer, Eur. .. AMMER
yellowish .... SALLOW
yelp .... KIYI, YOUP
Yemenite .... ARAB
Yemen's capital ...... SANA
yes: Sp. .... SI
yesterday: Fr. .... HIER
yesterday, pert. to HESTERNAL
yet .... E'EN, STILL
yew, pert. to .... TAXINE
yield CEDE, ACCEDE, CONCEDE
Yogi .... SWAMI
yoke bar, S. Afr. ..... SKEY
yokel ..... OAK, HICK, RUBE
yolk of egg .... VITELLUS
yolky .... EGGY
yon .... THERE
yorker: cricket .... TICE
Yorkshire city ...... LEEDS
Yorkshire river ... URE, OUSE
you: It. .... TU
you: Sp. .... TE
young animal
    CUB, PUP, COLT, WHELP
young female hog ..... GILT
young girl of Burma .. MIMA
young hog .... SHOAT, SHOTE
young kangaroo .... JOEY

185

young man, handsome ADONIS
young ox: Eng. .... STOT
young plant .... SET
young rowdy ..... HOODLUM
youngest son .... CADET
youngster
    KID, TAD, TOT, SHAVER
youth .... LAD
youth .... GOSSOON
youth shelter .... HOSTEL

youthful: zool. ...... NEANIC
Yucatan Indian .... MAYA
yucca-like plant ..... SOTOL
Yugoslav ..... SERB, CROAT
Yugoslav leader .... TITO
Yum-Yum's friend
    KOKO, NANKIPOO
Yutang .... LIN

Z

zeal .... ELAN, ARDOR
zealot .... BIGOT
zealous .... AVID
Zebedee, son of JOHN, JAMES
zebra, young .... COLT
zebrawood .... ARAROBA
zebu-yak hybrid ZO, ZOH, ZOBO
zenith ..... TOP, ACME, PEAK
zenith, opposite of .... NADIR
Zeno's follower .... STOIC
zeppelin .... BLIMP
Zeppelin .... GRAF
zero .... CIPHER
zest .... TANG
zetetic .... SEEKER
Zeus, epithet of ..... AMMON
Zeus, maiden loved by
    IO, LEDA, EUROPA
Zeus, mother of ...... RHEA
Zeus, old Doric name for ZAN
Zeus' daughter
    ATE, HEBE, IRENE
Zeus' sister .... HERA

Zeus' son ..... ARES, ARCAS
    MINOS, APOLLO
Zeus' wife ..... HERA, METIS
Zilpah's son .... GAD, ASHER
zinc in slabs ..... SPELTER
zinc ingot .... SPELTER
Zionist group .... ITO
zipper .... TALON
zodiac sign ...... LEO, ARIES,
    LIBRA, VIRGO, CANCER,
    PISCES, TAURUS, SCORPIO
Zola novel .... NANA
zone .... AREA
zone: Lat. .... ZONA
zoophyte, marine ..... CORAL
Zophah, son of ...... BEERA
Zoroastrian .. PARSI, PARSEE
Zoroastrian bible .... AVESTA
zounds .... OONS
Zulu headman ...... INDUNA
Zulu language .... BANTU

SPECIAL SECTION

READY REFERENCE WORD LISTS

In one compact section, here are lists of the most useful and widely-used word categories. Some of these words, having certain customary definitions, are also listed in the definitions' section of this book, but these complete word lists will be of greatest help when you are confronted with GENERALIZED definitions such as "Roman goddess," "South American Indian," "Heraldic term," or "African tribe."

All words in each separate listing are placed according to the number of their letters. This is a tremendous advantage to puzzle solvers, who are more concerned with the length of a word than with its alphabetical placement.

MEASURES

AREA MEASURES

AR, ARE, ACRE, DECARE (10
ARES), CENTIAR, CENTIARE
Annam .... MAU, QUO, SAO
Bengal .... BEGA
Czechoslovakia ... LAN, MIRA
Dutch E. Ind. .... BOUW
England, Old .... HYDE
Japan .... BU, SE, TAN
Norway .... MAL, MAAL
Paraguay .... LINO
Poland .... MORG
Rome, Ancient ...... CLIMA,
                   CLIMATA
Serbia .... RIF, RALO
Shetlands, Orkney ...... URE
Siam .... RAI, NGAN
Sweden .... MORGEN

DRY MEASURES

PECK, PINT, STERE
Algeria .... TARRI
Austria .... MUTH
Borneo .... GANTANG
Brazil .... MOIO
Burma .... TENG
Calcutta ..... KUNK, RAIK
Channel Is. .... CABOT
China .... HO, HU
Dutch .... KOP, ZAK
Egypt .... KADA, KILAH
Hebrew .... CAB, KAB, KOR,
     EPHA, OMER, SEAH, EPHAH
Italy .... SALM, SALMA
Japan .... SHO
Morocco .... SAHH
Netherlands ...... KOP, ZAK
Portugal .... MEIO, PIPA
Russia .... LOF
Tangier .... MUDD
Tunis ..... SAA, SAAH, UEBA

LENGTH, DISTANCE MEASURES

ELL, ROD, FOOT, HAND, INCH,
MILE, YARD, METER, METRE,
PERCH, MICRON, FURLONG
Annam .... LY, GON, NGU
Brazil .... PE
Calcutta ..... DHAN, JAOB
China ...... HU, LI, PU, TU,
         CH'IH, TCHI, TSUN
Czechoslovakia .. SAH, LATRO
Denmark FOD, MIL, MUL, ALEN
Domin. Repub. .... ONA
Dutch .... DUIM, VOET
D. E. Indies .... DEPA
Egypt . PIC, PIK, KHET, THEB
Eritrea .... CUBI
Estonia .... LIIN, SULD
France .... AUNE
Greece . PIC, PIK, BEMA, PIKI
         POUS, ACAENA
Hebrew .... EZBA
Iceland .... FET, ALIN, LINA
India .. GAZ, GEZ, GUZ, JOW,
         KOS, JAOB, KOSS
Italy .... CANNA
Japan . BU, JO, RI (marine),
    CHO, DJO, KEN, RIN, HIRO

Java .... PAAL
Libya ...... DRA, PIK, DRAH
Malabar .... ADY
Malacca .... ASTA
Netherlands .... DUIM, VOET
Norway .... FOT, ALEN
Persia .... GAZ, GEZ, GUZ
         ZAR, ZER
Poland .... MILA, PRET
Prussia .... RUTE
Rangoon .. LAN, DAIN, TAUN
Rome, ancient .... ACTUS,
   GRADUS, STADIA, STADIUM
Russia .... FUT, VERST
Siam .... WA, KUP, NIU, SEN,
    SOK, WAH, NIOU, SAWK
Spain .... BARA, CODO,
         DEDO, VARA
Sweden ..... FOT, REF, FAMN
Switzerland .... TOISE
Tripoli .... DRA, DRAA
Turkey .... PIC, PIK,
         KHAT, ZIRA

(liquid measures on page 189)

LIQUID MEASURES

TUN, DRAM, GILL, PINT, MINIM

Abyssinia ...... CUBA, KUBA	Hungary .... AKO
Annam .... TAO	Japan .... KOKU, SHO
Arabia .... SAA	Malaya .... PAU
Austria .... FASS	Netherlands . AAM, AUM, KAN
Brazil .... PIPA	Portugal .... BOTA, PIPA
Burma .... BYEE, SEIT	Rangoon ...... BYEE, SEIT
China .. KO, QUEI, SHIH	Rome, Ancient .... URNA
Cyprus .... CASS	Russia .. STOF, STOFF, STOOF
Dutch . (old) AAM, AUM, KAN	Somaliland .... CABA
Egypt .... HIN	Spain .... COPA
England ...... PIN, CRAN	Sweden .... AM, AMAR, KAPP
Ethiopia ..... see ABYSSINIA	Switzerland .... IMMI, SAUM
Germany ..... AAM, EIMER	Tangier .... KULA
Hebrew .... HIN	Trieste .... ORNA, ORNE
	Yugoslavia .... AKOV

WEIGHTS

KIP, TON, GRAM, KILO, CARAT, GRAIN, OUNCE, CENTRAL

Abyssinia ...... KASM, NATR, OKET, ALADA, NETER	Hebrew .... BEKA, REBA
Annam .... BINH	India .... SER, BHAR, PALA, RATI, TOLA, VISS, RATTI
Arabia .... KELA	Italian .... SALM, SALMA
Austria .... UNZE	Japan ..... KIN, SHI, MORIN
Bavaria .... GRAN	Malay .... CHEE
Brazil .... ONCA	Malta .... SALM, SALMA
Bulgaria .... OKA, OKE	Mexico .... LIBRA, ONZA
Burma .... VIS, KYAT, VISS	Mongolia .... LAN
Calcutta .. PANK, PAWA, RAIK	Morocco .... ARTEL
China .... LI, FEN, HAO, KIN SSU, TAN, YIN, TAEL	Moslem .... ROTL
Columbia .... SACO	Netherlands ...... ONS, LOOD
Denmark ES, ORT, VOG, ESER, PUND	Norway .... PUND
Dutch .... ONS, LOOD	ORIENT .... MANN, ROTL, TAEL, ARTAL
Dutch E. Ind. ..... TJI, HOEN, TALI, WANG	Palestine ...... ROTLA, ZUZA
Egypt .. KAT, KET, OKA, OKE, HEML, KHAR, OHIA, OKIEH	Persia .... SER
England .... STONE	Poland .... LUT
Estonia .... NAEL, PUUD	Portugal. GRAO, ONCA, LIBRA
Ethiopia ...... See Abyssinia	Rangoon .... RUAY
France .... GROS	Rome, Ancient ..... AS, BES, LIBRA, SOLIDUS
Germany .... LOT, LOTE, LOTH, STEIN	Russia .... LAN, PUD, DOLA, POOD, POUD
Greece .... MNA, MINA, OBOLE, OBOLUS	Siam .... PAI, KLAM KLOM, TICAL
Guinea .... AKEY, PISO UZAN, SERON	Shetland Island .. URE (ounce)
	Spain .... ONZA
	Sweden ASS, ORT, STEN, UNTZ
	Turkey ...... OCK, OKA, OKE, KILE, OCHA, KERAT

189

COINS, MONEY

Abyssinia ..... BESA, GIRSH, TALARI
Afghanistan .... AMANIA
Albania .... LEK
Anglo-Saxon ..... ORA, SCEAT
Annam .... QUAN
Austria .... DUCAT
Biblical .. BEKA, MITE (small), SHEKEL, TALENT
Brazil .... REI
Bulgaria ... LEV, LEW, DINAR
Chile .... COLON
China .. LI, CASH, TAEL, TIAO, YUAN, PU (early)
Colombia .... REAL
Costa Rica .... COLON
Czechoslovakia ..... DUCAT, KRONE (plural, KRONEN)
Denmark .. ORA, ORE, ORAS, KRONE (plural, KRONER)
Dutch OORD, DALER, GULDEN, STIVER
D. E. Indies ..... BONK, DUIT
Egypt .... GIRSH
England .. ORA, RIAL (gold), RYAL, RYEL, GROAT, PENCE, FLORIN, GUINEA
Equador .... SUCRE
Ethiopia ......see ABYSSINIA
Europe .. (old) GROS, DUCAT
France .. ECU (old), SOL, SOU, AGNEL (old), FRANC, LIARD (old), LOUIS, OBOLE, BESANT or BEZANT (old).
Genoa .... JANE (old)
Germany ..... MARK, KRONE (former), TALER, THALER
Ger. E. Africa .... PESA
Greece ..OBOL or OBOLI (old), STATER (old)
Hungary ...... GARA, PENGO
Iceland .... AURAR, EYRIR, KRONA
India LAC, PIE, ANNA, DAWM, FELS, HOON, LAKH, PICE, (small bronze), TARA, MOHUR (old), RUPEE
Iran .... see PERSIA
Iraq .... DINAR
Ireland .... RAP (old)

Italy .... LIRA, LIRE, SOLDO, TESTER, TESTON, TESTONE, TESTOON
Japan .... BU, RIN, SEN, YEN, OBAN
Latvia .... LAT, LATU
Lithuania .. LIT, LITAI, LITAS
Macao .... AVO
Malaya TRA (tin, pewter), TRAH
Mexico ... PESO, CENTAVO
Montenegro .... PARA
Morocco .... OKIA, RIAL
Nepal .... MOHAR
Netherlands ...... DAALDER
Norway .... ORE, KRONE, (KRONER)
Oman .... GAJ, GAZ, GOZ, GHAZI
Persia PUL, KRAN, POUL, RIAL DARIC, DINAR, MOHUR (old), TOMAN, STATER
Peru .... SOL, DINERO
Poland .... DUCAT
Portugal .... JOE, REI, PECA, DOBRA (former)
Rome, ancient SEMIS, DINDER
Roman ..... AS, AES, ASSES, SOLIDUS
Rumania .. LEU, LEY, BANI
Russia COPEC, KOPEK, RUBLE
Siam .... AT, ATT, BAHT, TICAL or TIKAL
Sicily .... TARI
Somaliland .... BESA
South Africa ..... DAALDER
Spain .... COB, DURO, PESO, REAL, DOBLA (old), PESETA, PISTOLE (old)
Sweden ORE, KRONA (KRONOR), KRONE (KRONER)
Switzerland .... BATZ
Thailand .... see SIAM
Timor .... AVO
Turkey .... LIRA (gold), PARA, ALTUN (gold), ASPER, MAHBUB (gold), PIASTER
United States .. CENT, DIME, EAGLE
Venice ... BETSO (old silver)
Yugoslavia .... DINAR

TRIBES (including peoples, natives)

EUROPE:

Albania .... GEG, CHAM, GHEG, TOSK
Balto-Slav .... LETT
Celtic on Danube ..... BOII
Finnish near Volga .... VEPS, VEPSA
Finnish, Ingria ... VOT, VOTE, VOTH, WOTE
Lithuania .... BALT
Syryenian .... KOMI
Teuton, ancient .... UBII

MIDDLE EAST:

Arab .... AUS, IBAD
Bedouin .... ABSI, HARB
Turkey .... KURD
East Turkey .... KURD
Persia .... see under ASIA

ASIA:

Afghanistan .... SAFI
Assam .... AO, AKA; AHOM, GARO, NAGA
Borneo . DYAK, IBAN; DAYAK
Burma ...... WA, LAI, KAW, MON, WAS; AKHA, CHIN, KADU, KUKI, TSIN; KAREN
Caucasus .. IMER, KURI, LASI, LAZE, LAZI, SVAN; OSSET, SVANE
Celebes, Malayan ...... BUGI
China, Miao .... HEH
China, Nord ... USUN, UZUN; USSUN
China, Tatar .... TOBA
India .... AWAN, BHIL, BHEEL, TURI
Kolarian (India) ...... BHAR
Japan, aborigine . AINO, AINU
Madagascar .... HOVA
Manchu .... DAUR
Mongol .... CHUD
Nepal .... AOUL, KHAS
Persia .... LUR, KURD, FARSI, IRANIAN
Tibet .... CHAMPA

AFRICA:

Abyssinian .... SHOA
Bantu .... KUA; BANE, BAYA, BIHE, BULE, FANG, FUNG, GOGO, GOLO, GOMA, GUHA, HAKU, HEHE, JAGA, LUBA, MAKA, NAMA, SOGA, SUKU, VIRA, YAKA,

ZULU (largest); KAFIR; KAFFIR
Bedouin .... ABSI
Berber DAZA, RIFF, TEDA, TIBU
Bushman .. SAN, SAAN, QUNG
Congo .... FIOT, SUSU
Central Africa .. ABO; BULO, DOMA, KALI, KURI, LURI, YAKO; LUREM
Dahomey ...... FON, FONG
East Africa .. JUR, LUR, YAO; AKKA, ALUR, ASHA, BARI, BONI, GOLO, MADI, NUER, VITI
Gold Coast ... AKAN, AKIM, AKRA
Hamitic .. AFAR, BEJA, BENI, BOGO, GALA, HIMA
Kaffir .... XOSA, ZULU
Kenya .... BONI
Lake Albert .... ALUR, LURI
Liberia .... GI, KRA, KRU, TOMA, VAI, VEI, KROO
Libya .... FUL, FULA, MZAB
Mozambique .... YAO
Nigeria .. ARO, EDO, IBO, IJO; BENI, BINI, EBOE, EKOI, IDJO, IDYO, IDZO, NUPE; BENIN
Nilotic .... SUK, BARI
Pygmy .... AKKA, DOKO
Slave Coast .... EGBA
Sudan.. FUL, FUR, VEI; FULA, GOLO, MABA, MEGE, NUBA, SUSU, TAMA
West Africa ... GA; AJA, EWE, IBO, KRU, KWA; AGNI, AKIM, APPA, BAGA, BINI, EFIK, EGBA, EKOI, GENG, GOLA, HABE, IKWE, JEBU, JOAT, JOLA, KETU, NALU, ONDO, REMO, SAPE, TCHI, TSHI, VACA, WARI

ALASKA:
Aleutians .... ATKA

GREENLAND .... ITA

AUSTRALIA .... KOKO

NEW GUINEA .... KARON

SOUTH AMERICA:
Fr. Guiana .... BONI

INDIANS, INDIAN TRIBES

Alaska .... ALEUT, SITKA

Algonquin or Algonkian
Indians   FOX, SAC, WEA;
     CREE, SAUK, MIAMI; LEN-
     APE, OTTAWA, PIEGAN;
     SHAWNEE

Amazon ...... (lower) MURA,
     (upper) ANDOA

Apache .... LIPAN

Araucanian .... AUCA

Arawak .... ARAUA, CAMPA,
     INERI

Arikara .... REE

Arizona . HANO, HOPI, MOKI,
     PIMA, TEWA, YUMA;
     MOQUI; APACHE

Athapascan Indians   DENE,
     HUPA, TAKU, LIPAN,
     TINNE, APACHE, NAV-
     AHO

Aymara .... COLLA

Bolivia .... ITE, URO, URU;
     ITEN, LECA, MOJO, MOXO,
     URAN; CHOLO

Brazil .... GE; YAO; CAME,
     DIAU, MAKU, MURA, PURI,
     PURU, TUPI; ACROA,
     ANDOA, ARAUA, CARIB,
     GUANA, SIUSI; ZAPARO

Caddoan Indians   REE; ADAI;
     IONI, CADDO, BIDAI;
     PAWNEE

California   HUPA, KOSO,
     MONO, NOZI, POMO, SERI,
     TATU, YANA; MAIDU,
     YANAN; SALINA

Canada . AHT, CREE, DENE,
     TAKU; NISKA, TINNE;
     SARCEE

Carib .... YAO, TRIO

Carolina .... CATAWBA

Chaco .... TOBA

Chile .... AUCA

Colorado .... UTE

Colombia ...... BORO, DUIT,
     MUSO, MUZO, TAMA,
     TAPA; CHOCO; COLIMA

Costa Rica .... BOTO VOTO

Cowichan Indians . NANAIMO

Dakotas . REE, SIOUX, TETON;
     MANDAN, . SANTEE;
     ARIKARA

Delaware .... LENAPE

Ecuador ..... CARA (extinct);
     ANDOA, ARDAN

Eskimo .... ATKA; ALEUT

Florida .... CALUSA

Fuegan .... ONA

Great Lakes ... ERIE; HURON

Guatemala .... MAM; CHOL,
     ITZA, IXIL, IXLI, MAYA,
     ULVA, VOTO; KICHE, PIPIL

Honduras .... PAYA

Iowa .... FOX, SAC; SAUK

Indiana ..... WEA; MIAMI

Iroquoian Indians,
     Irquois: .... ERIE, HURON,
          CAYUGA, MOHAWK,
          ONEIDA, SENECA

Jalisco .... CORA

Keresan Indians: SIA; ACOMA

Kusan .... COOS

Lesser Antilles .... INERI

Mayan Indians . MAM, CHOL

Mexico   MAM, CHOL, CORA,
     MAYA, MIXE, PIMA, PIME,
     SERI, TECA, TECO, WABI;
     AZTEC, OTOMI, SERIA;
     TOLTEC

Miami .... WEA

Mississippi .... TIOU, BILOXI

Montana ...... CROW, HOHE

Muskohegan Indians   CREEK,
     YAMASI, CHOCTAW,
     SEMINOLE

Nebraska .... KIOWA

Nevada .... PAIUTE

New Mexico   SIA, PIRO, TANO,
     TAOS, TEWA, ZUNI;
     ACOMA, KERES, PECOS

New York .... SENECA

Nicaragua MIXE, RAMA, ULVA

Oklahoma   KAW, OTO; LOUP,
     OTOE; CADDO, CREEK,
     KANSA, KIOWA, OSAGE,
     PONCA; PAWNEE

Oregon ...... COOS, KUSAN,
     MODOC, CHINOOK

192

Panamint .... KOSO
Panama ...... CUNA, CUEVA
Pawnee Indians .... LOUP
Payaguas .... AGAZ
Peru .... ANDE, ANTI, BORO,
   CANA, INCA, INKA, LAMA,
   PEBA, PIBA, PIRO, YNCA;
   CAMPA, CHIMU, CHOLO,
   COLAN, YUNCA; CHANCA;
   QUICHU
Peru South .... CANA, COLLA,
   CHANCA
Piman Indians .. CORA, JOVA,
   MAYO, PIMA, XOVA, YAKI,
   YAQUI
Plains Indians   CREE, CROW;
   KIOWA, OSAGE; PONCA,
   TETON, PAWNEE
Pueblo Indians   HOPI, MOKI,
   TANO, TAOS, ZUNI;
   KERES, MOQUI
Rio Grande .... TANO
Sacramento Valley .... YANA
Salishan Indians .... ATNAH,
   LUMMI
Shoshonean Indians .... UTE;
   HOPI, KOSO, MOKI,
   MONO; MOQUI, PIUTE;
   UINTA, PAIUTE

Siouan Indians .. KAW, OTO;
   CROW,   IOWA,   OTOE;
   KANSA, OMAHA, OSAGE,
   PONCA; BILOXI, DAKOTA,
   MANDAN; CATAWBA
Sonora .... JOVA, PIMI, SERI
South American (widely
   distributed) .   GES, ONA,
   YAO; LULE, MOXO, PANO,
   PIRO,   TOBA;   CARIB,
   INERI; ARAWAK
South Carolina .... CATAWBA
Tacanan Indians .... CAVINA
Tanoan .... TEWA
Tapuyan Indians .... GE, GES,
   GHES, ACROA
Texas .... LIPAN
Tierra del Fuego ...... ONA
Tlingit .... AUK, SITKA
Tupian .... ANTA
Utah .... UTE
Washington .. HOH, LUMMI,
   MAKAH
Yucatan .... MAYA
Yukian .... TATU
Yukon .... TAKU
Yuncan .... CHIMU

ARMOR

Head .... COIF, HELM; ARMET, VISOR; BEAVER, CAMAIL;
                                              BASINET, HAUBERK
Neck .... GORGET
Shoulder .... AILETTE, PAULDRON, EPAULIERE, PASSEGARDE
Body .... TACE; CULET, TASSE; CORIUM, GORGET, LORICA,
                    TASSET; CUIRASS, HAUBERK, SURCOAT; BRAGUETTE
Arm .... BRASSARD, PALLETTE, VAMBRACE;
                                              CUBITIERE, REREBRACE
Hand .... GAUNTLET
Thigh .... CUISH, TASSE, TUILE; CUISSE,
                                              TASSET, TUILLE
Leg, foot .... JAMB, JAMBE; GREAVE; CHAUSSE,
                                              PEDIEUX; SOLLERET
Complete suit .... BARD, MAIL; BARDE

HERALDRY—HERALDIC TERMS

Heraldic bearings: BEND, ENTE, FESS, ORLE, FESSE, GIRON, GYRON, LAVER, PHEON; SALTIRE

Heraldic tinctures:
gold, OR; fur, PEAN, VAIR, VAIRE; green, VERT; blue, AZURE; red, GULES; black, SABLE; orange, TENNE; silver, ARGENT; blood-red, MURREY; purple, PURPURE

attitude of animal .... SEJANT, GARDANT, PASSANT, RAMPANT
ball .... ROUNDEL
band .... FESS, ORLE, FESSE
barnacle .... BREY
bend .... COTISE
bird .... MARTLET
circle ... BEZANT, ANNULET
colter .... LAVER
creature .. LION, PARD; BISSE, WYVER; CANNET, WYVERN; GRIFFON, MARTLET
cross .... CRUX, NOWY, PATY; FLORY, FORMY, PATEE; PATTE; CLECHE; SALTIRE
curved in middle ...... NOWY
curves, made of .... NEBULE
division .... PALE, PALY
dog, short-eared ..... ALANT
drops, serne of ...... GUTTE
duck .... CANNET, CANNETTE
fillet .... ORLE
fish trap .... WEEL
flower strewn .... SEME

flying in air ...... FLOTANT
fountain .... SYKE
grafted .... ENTE
headless .... ETETE
horizonal band .... see band
leaves, having ...... POINTE
lines .... UNDE, UNDY, URDY, NEBULY
lozenge ..... FUSIL, MASCLE
manacle .... TIRRET
pointed .... URDE
powdered .... SEME
scattered .... SEME
sheaf of grain . GERB, GERBE
shield .... PAVIS
shield division ...... ENTE
shield's corner ...... CANTON
silver .... ARGENT
sitting .... ASSIS
snake .... BISSE
sown .... SEME
spangled .... SEME
star-strewn .... SEME
strewn .... SEME
three parts, divided into TIERCE
triangle ..... GIRON, GYRON
two-winged .... VOL
voided escutcheon ..... ORLE
walking .... PASSANT
wavy .. ONDE, UNDE, UNDY, UNDEE, NEBULE
winged .... VOL, AILE
wound .... VULN
wreath .... ORLE, TORSE

194

CHEMICAL ELEMENTS

METALLIC ELEMENTS	NON-METALLIC ELEMENTS	GASEOUS ELEMENTS
TIN	ARGON	ARGON
GOLD	BORON (inert)	CHLORINE
IRON	CARBON	FLUORINE
LEAD	HELIUM	HELIUM
ZINC	IODINE	HYDROGEN
CERIUM	NEON (inert)	KRYPTON
CESIUM	RADON-NITON	NEON (inert)
COBALT	SILICON	NITROGEN
COPPER	XENON	OXYGEN
ERBIUM		XENON
NICKEL		
RADIUM		
SILVER		
SODIUM		
YTTRIUM		

CHEMICAL SYMBOLS

Solver: Important Note—it is not necessary to list for you the chemical symbol of every element. The chemical symbol of any element not given below is found simply by writing down the first 2 letters of the names of the element. For example: Ruthenium's chemical symbol is simply RU.

alabamine, AB;	hafnium, HF;	samarium, SM;
antimony, SB;	iron, FE	silver, AG;
arsenic, AS;	lead, PB;	sodium, NA;
boron, B;	magnesium, MG;	strontium, SR;
cadmium, CD;	manganese, MN;	terbium, TB;
cesium, CD;	mercury, HG;	thallium, TL;
chlorine, CL;	neodymium, ND;	thulium, TM;
chromium, CR;	palladium, PD;	tin, SN;
columbium, CB;	protoactinium, PA;	ytterbium, YB;
copper, CU;	platinum, PT;	zinc, ZN;
curium, CM;	radon, RN;	zirconium, ZR;
gadolinium, GD;	rhenium, RE;	
gold, AU;	rubidium, RB;	

195

BIBLICAL REFERENCES

BOOKS OF THE BIBLE

Names and order of books of the:

OLD TESTAMENT

1 GENESIS	11 KINGS 1	21 ECCLESIASTES	30 AMOS
2 EXODUS	12 KINGS 2	22 SONG OF	31 OBADIAH
3 LEVITICUS	13 CHRONICLES 1	SOLOMON	32 JONAH
4 NUMBERS	14 CHRONICLES 2	23 ISAIAH	33 MICAH
5 DEUTERONOMY	15 EZRA	24 JEREMIAH	34 NAHUM
6 JOSHUA	16 NEHEMIAH	25 LAMENTATIONS	35 HABAKKUK
7 JUDGES	17 ESTHER	26 EZEKIEL	36 ZEPHANIAH
8 RUTH	18 JOB	27 DANIEL	37 HAGGAI
9 SAMUEL 1	19 PSALMS	28 HOSEA	38 ZECHARIAH
10 SAMUEL 2	20 PROVERBS	29 JOEL	39 MALACHI

Names and order of books of the:

NEW TESTAMENT

1 MATTHEW	9 GALATIANS	15 TIMOTHY 1	23 JOHN 1
2 MARK	10 EPHESIANS	16 TIMOTHY 2	24 JOHN 2
3 LUKE	11 PHILIPPIANS	17 TITUS	25 JOHN 3
4 JOHN	12 COLOSSIANS	18 PHILEMON	26 JUDE
5 THE ACTS	13 THESSALON-	19 HEBREWS	27 REVELATION
6 ROMANS	IANS 1	20 JAMES	
7 CORINTHIANS 1	14 THESSALON-	21 PETER 1	
8 CORINTHIANS 2	IANS 2	22 PETER 2	

BIBLICAL PROPHETS

AMOS (minor), ESAY, EZRA, JOEL (minor), HOSEA (minor), JONAH
(minor), MICAH (minor), MOSES, DANIEL (major), NAHUM (minor),
ELISHA, HAGGAI (minor), ISAIAH (major), EZEKIEL (major), JERE-
MIAH (major)

BIBLICAL PATRIARCHS

REU; ADAM, EBER, ENOS, NOAH, SETH, SHEM; ISAAC, JACOB,
JARED, NAHOR, PELEG, SERUG, TERAH; LAMECH

BIBLICAL RULERS

OG; ASA (Judah), GOG, IRA; AGAG, AHAB, AHAZ, AMON, ELAH, JEHU, OMRI, SAUL; CYRUS, DAVID, DEBIR, HEROD, HIRAM, JORAM, NADAB, PEKAH, PIRAM, REZIN, SIHON, ZIMRI; ABIJAH, BAASHA, CAESAR, DARIUS, HEZION, HOSHEA, JAPHIA, JOSHUA, JOSIAH, JOTHAM, UZZIAH

BIBLICAL PEOPLES—TRIBES

DAN, GOG; ANAK, ARAD, CUSH, EMIM, MOAB, PHUD, PHUT (o.t.); ARKITE, HAMITE, HIVITE, KENITE, SEMITE, SHELAH, SINITE; EDOMITE, HITTITE, LEHABIM, MOABITE, REPHAIM

BIBLICAL PLACES

City .. DAN, GATH, GAZA, ZOAR, BABEL, EKRON, SODOM; HEBRON

Mt. HOR, EBAL, NAIN, NEBO, PEOR; HOREB, SEIR, SINA, SINAI, TABOR; ARARAT, GILEAD, HERMON

Country .. EDOM, ENON, SEBA; SHEBA

Place .... ENON, AENON; JORDAN, SHILOH

Hill, Jerusalem's .... ZION

Pool .... SILOAM

Kingdom .... ELAM, MOAB; SAMARIA

Region . ARAM, EDAR; BASHAN

Town .... CANA (1st miracle), NAIN (miracle site); BETHEL

Land .... NOD

Land of plenty ...... GOSHEN

River .... ARNON, JORDAN

BIBLICAL MEN

OG, UZ; ARA, DAN, ELI, GOG, HAM, IRA, LOT, NUN, URI; ABEL, AMOS, BOAZ, CAIN, CUSH, DOEG, EBAL, ENON, ENOS, ESAU, HETH, IRAD, JADA, JEHU, JOAB, KISH, LEVI, MASH, MOAB, OBAL, OBED, OMAR, OREB, OZEM, SETH, SODI, ULAM, UNNI, URIA; AARON (high priest), ABIAH, ABIEL, AHIRA, AMASA, ANNAS, CALEB, CHUZA, ENOCH, HAMAN, HARAN, HIRAM, HOHAM, IBZAN, ISAAC, JACOB, JAMES, JARED, MASSA, MOREH, NABAL, NAHBI, NAHOR, OPHIR, REZON, SACAR, TERAH, URIAH, ZAHAM; SAMSON; ANANIAS, ISHMAEL

BIBLICAL WOMEN

EVE; ADAH, JAEL, LEAH, MARY, RUTH; DINAH, EGLAH, HAGAR, JULIA, JUNIA, LYDIA, MERAB, NAOMI, PHEBE, RAHAB, SARAH, SARAI, SHUAH, TAMAR; ABITAL, BILHAH, DORCAS, ESTHER, HANNAH, HOGLAH, MAACAH, MAHLAH, MICHAL, MILCAH, MIRIAM, PERSIS, RACHEL, RIZPAH, SALOME, VASHTI, ZILLAH, ZILPAH; ABIGAIL, HAMUTAL

BIBLICAL NAMES

ED, ER; IRI, NER, ONO, REI, TOI; ABIA, ADER, ANER, ANIM, ASOM, DARA, ELON, ENOS, IRAD, IVAH, REBA; ABIAM, AHIRA, AMASA, ASEAS

197

GODS (DEITIES), GODDESSES, AND MYTHOLOGY

ASSYRIAN GODS

ANAT (sky), ASUR or ASSUR (war)

BABYLONIAN GODS

Chief gods: EA, ABU or ANU, BEL
EA (chief), ZU (wind), ABU or ANU (chief, sky, sun), BEL (chief), HEA
(see EA), IRA (war), SIN (moon), UTU (sun), ADAD or ADDA or ADDU
(wind, storm), APSU (chaos), ENKI (see EA), ENZU (see SIN), IRRA
(war), NABU or NEBO (wisdom), UTUG (sun), DAGAN (earth), ETANA
(eagle rider), SIRIS (alcoholic drinks), BABBAR (sun), SHAMASH (sun)

BABYLONIAN GODDESSES

AI or AYA (consort of Shamash), ERUA (mother), NINA (watery
deep), NANAI (daughter of Anu), ISTAR or ISHTAR (chief, love)

BRYTHONIC GODDESS

DON (ancestress of gods)

CELTIC GODS—GODDESS

ANA, ANU, DANA, DANU (mother, queen), LER (sea), LUG, LUGH
(light, sun), DAGDA (chief)

CYMRIC GODS

GWYN, LLEU, LLEW (solar)

EGYPTIAN GODS

RA (sun), SU (solar deity), BES (evil, pleasure), GEB (earth), KEB
(earth), MIN (procreation), SEB (earth), SET (evil), SHU (see SU),
TEM or TUM (sun), AANI (dog-headed ape, sacred to Thoth), AMEN
(king), AMON (sun and king), AMUN (king), ATMU or ATUM (sun),
BESA (see BES), HAPI (the Nile as a god), KHEM (see MIN), MENT
(falcon-headed), PTAH (Memphis god), SETH (evil), SOBK (crocodile-
headed), AMMON (see AMEN), HORUS (hawk-headed), MENTU (see
MENT), SEBEK (see SOBK), THOTH (wisdom, magic), OSIRIS (underworld), SERAPIS (see OSIRIS)

EGYPTIAN GODDESSES

MA (same as MAAT), MUT (Amen's wife), NUT (heavens), ANTA,
APET (maternity), BAST (cat- or lion-headed), BUTO (serpent), ISIS
(cow-headed, Horus' mother), MAAT (truth, justice), SATI (queen),
ATHOR (see HATHOR), HATHOR (love, mirth, cow-headed)

EGYPTIAN MYTH

BA (soul of man), KA (body of man), NU (chaos), AKH (spirit of man), NUN (see NU), APIS (sacred bull), ATEN (solar disk), DUAT (see AMENTI), HAPI (Nile or Amenti's jinnee), AMENTI (underworld region)

GREEK GODS

DIS (underworld), PAN (field, flocks, forest), ZAN (old name for Zeus), ARES (war, Eris' brother), EROS (love), ZEUS (chief of Olympian gods), COMUS (mirth and revelry), EURUS (southeast wind), HADES (underworld), KOMOS (see COMUS), MOMUS (ridicule), PLUTO (underworld), AEOLUS (wind), APOLLO (sun, youth), AUSTER (south wind), BOREAS (north wind), CRONUS (a Titan, Rhea's spouse; harvest), HELIOS (sun), HERMES (herald), KRONOS (see CRONUS), NEREUS (sea), PLUTUS (wealth), TRITON (sea), BACCHUS (wine), POSEIDON (sea)

GREEK GODDESSES

GE (earth, mother of Titans), ARA (destruction, retribution, vengeance), ATE (discord, mischief, infatuation), EIR (healing), EOS (dawn), ALEA (ATHENA), CORA (see KORE), DICE or DIKE (one of Horae), ENYO (Ares' mother, war), ERIS (discord, sister of Ares), GAEA or GAIA (see GE), HEBE (youth), HERA (queen), HORA (one of Horae), KORE (vegetation), LEDA (Tyndareus' wife), NIKE (victory), RHEA (mother of gods, wife of Kronos), UPIS, ARTEMIS, HORAE (three goddesses of seasons), IRENE (peace), METIS (Zeus' first wife), MOIRA (fate of Fates), ATHENA (wisdom), CLOTHO (a Fate, thread spinner), CYBELE (nature), EIRENE (see IRENE), HECATE (moon, magic), MOERAE (see MOIRA), PALLAS (wisdom), SELENA and SELENE (moon), ARTEMIS (moon, woods, nature), ATROPOS (one of the Fates, thread cutter), DEMETER (grain, agriculture), CHLORIS (flowers), NEMESIS (revenge), LACHESIS (one of the Fates, thread length), APHRODITE (love)

GREEK MYTH

IO (Zeus' beloved changed to a heifer), INO (Cadmus' daughter), PAN (field, flocks, forest), ANAX (one of Dioscuri), AUGE (Arcadian princess), CEYX (Halcyone's husband turned into kingfisher), CLIO (Muse of History), FAUN (see PAN), IDAS (hero, killed Castor), IOLE (Hercules' captive), LETO (Apollo's mother), MAIA (Hermes' mother), OTUS (giant killed by Apollo), ALTIS (sacred grove, Olympic games), ATLAS (held up heavens), CREON (Oedipus' brother-in-law), DIONE (Aphrodite's mother), ENEAS (Troy's defender), ERATO (Clio's sister), HADES (underworld), HELLE (fell into Hellespont with golden fleece), HYDRA (9-headed monster), MINOS (king), NIOBE (weeping stone), SATYR (part-horse demigod), THEIA (Hyperion's sister, wife), ADONIS (beautiful youth), AENEAS (see ENEAS), AGENOR (Trojan warrior), ALECTO (a Fury), DAPHNE (Apollo's nymph turned into tree), EUROPA (carried off by Zeus in form of white bull), HECTOR (Trojan warrior), NEREID (see nymph to Poseidon), NESTOR (wise king, fought Troy), THETIS (Achilles' mother), TITHON (see TITHONUS), TRITON (sea demigod, Poseidon's son), URANIA (astronomy), ARIADNE (Theseus' love), ATHAMAS (Ino's husband), CENTAUR (half man, half horse), CYCLOPS (1-eyed giant), ERINYES, (avenging spirits), EUTERPE (Muse of Music), SILENUS (woodland deity, horse-goat-human), ATALANTA (picked up golden apples—lost the race), TARTARUS (infernal regions), TITHONUS (immortal king of Troy, Eos' favorite), TISIPHONE (one of Erinyes)

The Gorgons: MEDUSA, STHENO, EURYALE

The Graces: AGLAIA, THALIA

The Titans or Titanesses: primeval deities: GAEA or GE (mother of Titans). URANUS (father of Titans). Titans: RHEA, COEUS, CREUS, THEIA, CRONUS or KRONOS, PHOEBE, THEMIS

HINDU GODS

KA (unknown), AGNI (fire), AKAL (immortal), CIVA (see SIVA), DEVA or DEWA (divine being), KAMA (love), RAMA (incarnation of Vishnu), SIVA (supreme), VAYU (wind), YAMA (judge of dead), BHAGA (love), DYAUS (heaven, sky), VISHNU (supreme), KRISHNA (avatar of Vishnu)

HINDU GODDESSES

SRI (beauty, wealth, luck, Vishnu's wife), UMA (splendor), VAC (speech), DEVI (any divinity, Siva's consort), KALI (evil), SHRI (see SRI), USAS (dawn), VACH (see VAC), SHREE (see SRI), MATRIS (mothers), LAKSHMI (see SRI)

HINDU MYTH

BANA (1,000-arm giant), KALI (tongue of Agni), KETU (Rahu's tail), NAGA (Vishnu's serpent), RAHU (dragon, swallows sun), USHA (Bana's daughter)

INCA GOD

INTI (sun)

IRISH—see CELTIC

NORSE GODS

ER (war), TY (see TIU), VE (Odin's brother, slayed Ymir), EAR (see ER), LOK (see LOKI), TIU (sky, war, Tiwaz), TIW (see TIU), TYR (sky, war), ULL (bow skill), VAN (seal), ZIO (sky), ZIU (see ZIO), FREY fertility), HLER (sea), HOTH (blind god), LOKE or LOKI (discord, mischief), ODIN (chief god, war, wisdom, slayed Ymir), THOR (thunder), TYRR (war), ULLR (see ULL), VALE (see VALI), VALI (Odin's son), VANS (see VANIR), VILI (Odin's brother), AEGIR (sea), AESIR (chief), ALCIS (twin gods), BALDR (see BALDER), BRAGE or BRAGI (poetry), DONAR (see THOR), HODER or HOTHR (see HOTH), VANIR (early race of gods), WODAN or WODEN or WOTAN (see ODIN), BALDER or BALDUR (light)

The Aesir or chief gods: TIU, TYR, ULL, FREY, LOKI, ODIN, THOR, VALI, BRAGI, DONAR, WODEN, BALDER

NORSE GODDESSES

EIR (healing), HEL (Loki's daughter, underworld, dead), RAN (sea, death, wife of Aegir), SIF (Thor's wife), URD (destiny), VOR (betrothal), ERDA (earth), FREA or FRIA (see FRIGG), GERD (Frey's wife), HELA (see HEL), NORN (fate), RIND (Odin's wife, Vali's mother), SAGA (golden beaker), URTH (see URD), FREYA (love beauty), FRIGG (Odin's wife), NANNA (flowers), NORNA or NORNS (see NORN), FREYJA (see FREYA)

NORSE MYTH

ASK (see ASKR), DIS (female spirit), ASKR (first man), ATLI (king), EGIL (story hero), GARM (Hel's watchdog, slays Tyr), GERI (Odin's wolf), IDUN (Bragi's wife), MARA (nightmare demon), NATT or NOTT (night), WATE (giant), YMIR or YMER ("rime-cold giant"), EGILL (see EGIL), MIMIR (giant), ASGARD (abode of gods)

PHOENICIAN GODDESS

ASTARTE (fertility, love)

ROMAN GODS

DIS (underworld), SOL (sun), AMOR (love), FAUN (field, herds, half goat), JOVE (chief god), MARS (war), MORS (death), COMUS (mirth, joy), CUPID (love), EURUS (southeast wind), KOMOS (see COMUS), MANES (spirits of dead, gods of underworld), ORCUS (dead), APOLLO (sun, music), AUSTER (south wind), BOREAS (north wind), FAUNUS (rural deity), VULCAN (fire), NEPTUNE (sea)

ROMAN GODDESSES

NOX or NYX (night), OPS (harvest, plenty), DIAN (moon, chase, woods), IRIS (rainbow, Zeus' messenger), JUNO (queen), LUNA (moon), MAIA (Vulcan's consort), NONA (Fate), SPES (hope), CERES (earth, grain, agriculture, vegetation), DIANA (see DIAN), EPONA (horses), FIDES (faith), FAUNA (field), FLORA (flowers), MORTA (a Fate), PARCA (a Fate), SALUS (prosperity), TERRA (earth), VENUS (love), VESTA (hearth), ANNONA (crops), AURORA (dawn), DECUMA (a Fate), PARCAE (the Fates), VACUNA (Sabine huntress)
The Fates or Parcae: NONA, MORTA, DECUMA

TEUTONIC GODS—see NORSE GODS

TEUTONIC GODDESSES—see NORSE GODDESSES

VEDIC GODS—see HINDU GODS

VEDIC GODDESSES—see HINDU GODDESSES

WELSH GOD

DYLAN

201

Fournier .... ALAIN
Fra Filippo ... LIPPI
Frances ..... ALDA
Francesco .... NITTI
Francis ....BACON,
         DRAKE
Francis Scott . KEY
Franchot .... TONE
Franck ..... CESAR
Francoise .. SAGAN
Frank ...... BACON,
  BUCK, CAPRA,
  CRAVEN, FAY
Frankie .... CARLE,
        LAINE
Frans ...... HALS
Franz ...... LEHAR
Frome ...... ETHAN
Gabor EVA, MAGDA,
    ZSA ZSA
Gale .STORM, ZONA
Gam .... RITA
Gardner .. AVA, ERLE
Gavin ...... MUIR
George ...... ADE,
  BROWN, CLARK,
  CUSTER, DEWEY,
  ELIOT, GOBEL,
  OHM, PATTON,
  SAND
George Bernard
       SHAW
Geraldine .... PAGE
Gershwin .... IRA
Gertrude .... BERG,
      STEIN
Gil .... BLAS
Giuseppe.... BELLI
Glasgow ... ELLEN
Glenn ...... FORD
Gluck ...... ALMA
Gorin ...... IGOR
Gosden, F. F. AMOS
Gould ...... JAY
Graham .... BILLY
Grant ..... WOOD
Gray .... ASA, ZANE
Greco ...... JOSE
Gregor ... MENDEL
Griffith ... ANDY
Gueden ... HILDE
Guido ...... RENI
Guiseppe ... VERDI
Guitry .... SACHA
Gustavus ... SWIFT
Guy ...... MOLLET
Gypsy Rose . LEE
H.ST. .... TRUMAN
Hagen ...... UTA
Hal .... MARCH
Hale ...... ALAN

Hallstrom .... IVAR
Hals ...... FRANS
Halsey ..... BULL
Hansson .... OLA
Harold .TEEN, UREY
Harriet Beecher
     STOWE
Harris .. JOEL, PHIL
Hart ...... CRANE
Harte ..... BRET
Havoc ..... JUNE
Hayward ... SUSAN
Hayworth ... RITA
Hazel ..... SCOTT
Heifetz ... JASCHA
Heinrich .... HEINE
Held ...... ANNA
Henri ..... PETAIN
Henrik .... IBSEN
Henry .... HUDSON
Herbert .... ALAN
Herbert George
     WELLS
Hernando de . SOTO
Hess ...... MYRA
Heywood .. BROUN
Hobson .... LAURA
Hogan ..... BEN
Holt ...... TIM
Holtz ..... LOU
Horace .... MANN
Horne ..... LENA
Houston ... SAM
Howard .... PYLE
Howe ..... ELIAS
Hubbel .... CARL
Hugh ..... LAING
Hunter .. IAN, KIM,
  TAB, EVAN
Hus ...... JAN
Hyerdahl .. THOR
Ian ...... HUNTER
Ida Bailey . ALLEN
Igor ...... GORIN
Ilka ..... CHASE
Immanuel .. KANT
Ina ...... CLAIRE
Inonu ..... ISMET
Irene .. CASTLE,
  DUNNE, RICH
Iris ...... MANN
Irvin S. .... COBB
Irving .... BERLIN
Isaac ..... STERN
Ismet ..... INONU
Italo ..... TAJO
Ives ..... BURL
J. Carroll .. NAISH
Jack ... LONDON,
  OAKIE, PARR,
  WEBB

Jacob ...... RIIS
Jagger ..... DEAN
James ... BARRIE,
  BARTON, BEARD,
  FARLEY, HILL,
  AGEE, WATT
James Montgomery
     FLAGG
Jan .HUS, PEERCE,
  SMUTS, STEEN
Jane ..... AUSTEN,
  COWL, EYRE
Janet ..... BLAIR,
  GAYNOR, LEIGH
Janis ...... PAIGE
Jannings .... EMIL
Jay ...... GOULD
Jean-Paul .. MARAT
Jeanmaire .. RENEE
Jeanne .... CRAIN,
    EAGELS
Jeffreys .... ANNE
Jenkins .... ALLEN
Jenny ..... LIND
Jerome .... KERN
Jessica ... TANDY
Jimmy ..... SAVO
Joel Chandler
    HARRIS
Johan ..... SARS
Johann Sebastian
    BACH
John .AGAR, ALDEN,
  BROWN, DALY,
  DEWEY, DREW,
  GAY, GOLDEN,
  HAY, KEATS,
  LITEL, LODER,
  LUND, RAITT
John Godfrey . SAXE
John Philip . SOUSA
John Wilkes . BOOTH
Johnny ... MERCER
Johnnie .... RAY
Johnson . OSA, VAN
Jolson ...... AL
Jonas ..... SALK
Jonathan .. SWIFT
Jonson .... BEN
Johnston ... ALVA
Jose ...... GRECO
Jobal ..... EARLY
Juanita .... HALL
Juhani ..... AHO
Jules ..... VERNE
Julia Ward . HOWE
Julie ..... ADAMS
June ..... HAVER,
  HAVOC, LANG
Kaltenborn .. HANS

Karel ...... CAPEK
Karl .... MARX
Kay .... STARR
Kaye .... NORA
Kazan ...... ELIA
Keith .... IAN
Kelly .GENE, EMMET
Kenton ..... STAN
Khachaturian .ARAM
Khan .... AGA, ALI,
          ALY
Kibbee ...... GUY
Kiepura ..... JAN
Kim ...... HUNTER
Kitchell ...... IVA
Knight ...... ERIC
Koussevitzky SERGE
Kovacs ..... ERNIE
Kurt .... ADLER
Kyser .... KAY
Lafcadio ... HEARN
Lagerkvist ... PAR
Lagerlof .... SELMA
Lahr .... BERT
Laing ...... HUGH
Lanchester .. ELSA
Lange .... HOPE
Lanny ...... ROSS
Lardner ..... RING
Lauck, Chester LUM
Laura Hope .CREWS
Laurel ...... STAN
Laurence . STERNE,
          OLIVIER
Laurie ..... PIPER
Law .... BONAR
Lazarus .... EMMA
Learned .... HAND
Lee . OMA, CANADA
Le Gallienne ... EVA
Lehmann ... LOTTE
Lehr .... LEW
Lena ...... HORNE
Leslie ..... BANKS
Levant ..... OSCAR
Levene ..... SAM
Levenson .... SAM
Lew .AYRES, CODY
Lewin, Liliane .LILO
Lewis .. ADA, JOHN,
     LAWES, STONE,
          TED
"Light-horse Harry"
          LEE
Lillian . GISH, ROTH
Lillie ... BEA, PEEL
Lily ...... PONS
Linkletter .... ART
Linn ...... BAMBI
Liszt ...... FRANZ
Lollobrigida .. GINA

Lombardo .... GUY
Long .... HUEY
Loos .... ANITA
Loren .... SOPHIA
Lorre ..... PETER
Louise .... ANITA
Lowell ..... AMY
Lucas .FOSS, SCOTT
Lucrezia .... BORI
Ludwig ..... EMIL
Lugosi ..... BELA
Luise ..... RAINER
Lupescu .. MAGDA
Lupino ..... IDA
Lynn ...... BARI
Lyons ..... GENE
Mack ...... TED
MacMahon .. ALINE
Madame de . STAEL
Madge ..... EVANS
Magnani ... ANNA
Major .... BOWES
Malbin ... ELAINE
Mann IRIS, HORACE
Marco ..... POLO
Maria .... CALLAS
Marie ..... CURIE
Mario .... LANZA
Mark ..... CLARK
Markey ..... ENID
Marner .... SILAS
Marquette .. PERE
Marquis .... DON
Marshall ... ALAN
Martha HYER, RAYE
Martini .... NINO
Mary ..... ASTOR,
       GARDEN, URE
Mary Baker . EDDY
Marx ..... CHICO,
       HARPO, KARL
Masaryk JAN, TOMAS
Mason ..... JAMES,
          PAMELA
Massey CURT, ILONA
Mata ...... HARI
Maude .... ADAMS
Maurice .... RAVEL
Maxwell .... ELSA
Maynard .... KEN
McCarey .... LEO
McCoy ...... TIM
Meg ...... MUNDY
Mel .. ALLEN, OTT,
          TORME
Menken ADA, HELEN
Merimee . PROSPER
Meriwether .. LEWIS
Merkel ..... UNA
Merman .... ETHEL
Meyerson ... BESS

Milton ..... CROSS
Miranda .... ISA
Mischa .... AUER,
          ELMAN
Mitzi ..... GREEN
Mollet ..... GUY
Montague ... LOVE
Montez .... LOLA,
          MARIA
Moorhead .. AGNES
Morgana FATA, NINA
Morini ..... ERICA
Mostel ..... ZERO
Mowbray .... ALAN
Mundt ...... KARL
Munson ..... ONA
Murray . DON, JAN,
       KEN, MAE
Musial ..... STAN
Myra ...... HESS
Nahum ..... TATE
Nazimova ... ALLA
Ned ...... SPARKS
Neilson ..... ADA
Nelson .... GENE,
          MILES
Nethersole ... OLGA
Nicholas ... AMATI
Nicholas Murray
          BUTLER
Nikolaidi ... ELENA
Niels ..... BOHR
Noel ..... COWARD
Nora . BAYES, KAYE
Novello ..... IVOR
O. Henry .. PORTER
O'Casey ..... SEAN
O'Connor .... UNA
Ogden . NASH, REID
Oley ..... SPEAKS
Oliver ..... HARDY
Olsen ...... OLE
Oma .... LEE
Onegin .... EUGEN
O'Neill ..... OONA
Opie ...... READ
Oren ...... ROOT
Orlando ... LASSO
Oscar .... LEVANT,
          WILDE
Ott .... MEL
Page ...... PATTI
Paine ...... TOM
Palmer LILLI
Parker ..... FESS
Pasternak ... BORIS
Pastor ..... TONY
Paton ..... ALAN
Paul ..... DRAPER,
       MUNI, POTTER
Pauline ..... LORD

Pauling .... LINUS
Pavlova ...... ANNA
Peerce ...... JAN
"Peewee" .... REESE
Peggy ...... WOOD
Pendleton .... NAT
Peron . EVA, EVITA,
          JUAN
Peter ...... ARNO,
     LORRE, MUNCH
Petina ...... IRRA
Petri ...... EGON
Philip .. HALE, NERI
Picon ...... MOLLY
Pierre ..... CURIE,
          LOTI
Pieter ..... HOOCH
Pinky ...... LEE
Polo ...... MARCO
Ponce de .. LEON
Pons ...... LILY
Ponselle .... ROSA
Porter ...... COLE
Pound ...... EZRA
Preminger ... OTTO
Priscilla ... ALDEN,
     MULLEN
Proust .... MARCEL
Pyle ...... ERNIE
Rainer ...... LUISE
Raines ..... ELLA
Rains ..... CLAUDE
Ralph Adams CRAM
Rathbone ... BASIL
Ray ...... ALDO,
     BLOCH, NOBLE
Read ...... OPIE
Rebecca .... WEST
Red, the .... ERIC
Reed ALAN, DONNA
Reese .. "PEEWEE"
Regan ...... PHIL
Rehan ...... ADA
Reinhardt .... MAX
Rene ...... COTY
Rex ...... BEACH,
     BELL, STOUT
Rhodes .... CECIL
Richard .... BYRD,
     CONTE, DIX,
     HOWE, LONG
Rip ...... TORN
Rita ...... GAM
Robb ...... INEZ
Robert .... ALDA,
     BURNS, DONAT,
     FULTON, PEEL,
          TAFT
Rodzinski . ARTUR
Roger ..... BACON,
     PRYOR, RICO

Romain ..ROLLAND
Romero .... CESAR
Rooney ...... PAT
Root . ELIHU, OREN
Rosa ...... RAISA
Rubinstein . ANTON
Rudolf ...... BING
Ruth ...... DRAPER
Rutherford .... ANN
S.F.B. ...... MORSE
Saint, — Marie EVA
St. John .... ADELA
St. Vincent Millay
          EDNA
Salmon P. .. CHASE
Sam ...HOUSTON,
          SNEAD
Samuel .... LOVER,
          MORSE
Sand ..... GEORGE
Sande ...... EARL
Sandra ...... DEE
Sayao ...... BIDU
Scheffer .... ARY
Schipa ...... TITO
Shloem ..... ASCH
Seegar ..... ALAN
Segovia .. ANDRES
Seton ...... ANYA
Sevareid .... ERIC
Shaw ..... ARTIE
Shawn ...... TED
Sheldon .... HERB
Shelley ... PERCY
     BYSSHE, WINTERS
Short ...... ADAM
Shriner .... HERB
Shubert .... LEE
Siddons .... SARAH
Sidney ... LANIER
Signe ...... HASSO
Silvers .. PHIL, SID
Sinclair ... LEWIS
Skinner ..... OTIS
Slagle ..... SUSIE
Slavenska .... MIA
Smith . AL, ALFRED
Snead ...... SAM
Sonny .... TUFTS
Sophia ... LOREN
Sothern ..... ANN
Sparks ..... NED
Speaker .... TRIS
Speaks ..... OLEY
Spewack ... BELLA
Spitalny ..... PHIL
Stanford ... WHITE
Steen ...... JAN
Stephen ... CRANE,
          LONG
Stephen V... BENET

Sterling ...... JAN
Steve ..... BRODY
Stevens MARK, RISE
Stoker ..... BRAM
Storm ...... GALE
Stravinsky ... IGOR
Struthers ... BURT
Sullivan ...... ED
Sunday .... BILLY
Susan B. .ANTHONY
Syngman .... RHEE
Tab ...... HUNTER
Tajo ...... ITALO
Tamiroff .... AKIM
Tanguay ..... EVA
Tarbell ...... IDA
Tarkington . BOOTH
Taylor .... DEEMS
Teasdale .... SARA
Tegner ... ESAIAS
Templar ... SIMON
Templeton .. ALEC
Tennessee .. ERNIE
Teresa ... AVILA
Terry ...... ELLEN
Tex ...... RITTER
Theda ...... BARA
Thelma .... RITTER
Thomas ARNE, BATA,
     DYLAN, GRAY,
     HARDY, HICKS,
     HOOD, MANN,
     NAST, WOLFE
Thornton .. WILDER
Tilden ...... BILL
Tillstrom ... BURR
Tim ...... HOLT
"Tinker to —"
     EVERS, CHANCE
Tiselius .... ARNE
Tito ...... BROZ
Tolstoy ...... LEO
Tom ...... EWELL,
     MIX, PAINE
Torme ...... MEL
Torn ...... RIP
Truex ..... ERNIE
Truman ... CAPOTE
Trygve ...... LIE
Tse-tung ... MAO
Turpin ...... BEN
Twain .... MARK
Uriah ..... HEEP
Ulric ... LENORE
Vallee ..... RUDY
Van .... GUS
Vance ..... ETHEL
Velez ...... LUPE
Venerable, the BEDE
Verdon ..... GWEN
Verdugo .... ELENA

206

Verne ...... JULES	Weber and —	William Randolph
Vernon ...... CASTLE	FIELDS	HEARST
Victor BORGE, HUGO	Weill .... KURT	William Rose BENET
Vincent ..... PRICE	Wheeler ..... BERT	William Sidney
Vitus ..... BERING	White .... PEARL,	PORTER
Vivien ..... LEIGH	WILLIAM ALLEN	Williams ... ROGER,
Vivienne .... SEGAL	Whitelaw ..... REID	TED
Vladimir ... LENIN	Whitfield ..... MAL	Wills CHILL, HELEN
W.C. ...... FIELDS	Whitman .... WALT	Winslow ... HOMER
W. Mackenzie KING	Whitney ...... ELI	Winterhalter . HUGO
Wallace .... HENRY,	Wilbur ..... CROSS	Wolfert .... IRA
AGARD, LEW	Wilhelm von . OPEL	Wynn .... ED
Wallach .... ELI	Willa .... CATHER	Xavier ..... CUGAT
Wally .... PIP	William ... BOOTH,	Young .... CY, GIG,
Walter .... ABEL,	HANDY, HART,	ALAN
BRUNO, REED	HOLDEN, HULL,	Youskevitch .. IGOR
Warburg .... OTTO	INGE, PENN,	ZaSu ...... PITTS
Washington	PITT	Zebulon ..... PIKE
BOOKER	William Butler	Zernial ..... GUS
Waugh ...... ALEC	YEATS	Zetterling .... MAI
Webb .... ALAN	William Cullen	Zola ...... EMILE
	BRYANT	Zorina ...... VERA

PRESIDENTS OF THE UNITED STATES

(In Order)

1. GEORGE WASHINGTON
2. JOHN ADAMS
3. THOMAS JEFFERSON
4. JAMES MADISON
5. JAMES MONROE
6. JOHN QUINCY ADAMS
7. ANDREW JACKSON
8. MARTIN VAN BUREN
9. WILLIAM HENRY HARRISON
10. JOHN TYLER
11. JAMES KNOX POLK
12. ZACHARY TAYLOR
13. MILLARD FILLMORE
14. FRANKLIN PIERCE
15. JAMES BUCHANAN
16. ABRAHAM LINCOLN
17. ANDREW JOHNSON
18. ULYSSES SIMPSON GRANT
19. RUTHERFORD BIRCHARD
    HAYES

20. JAMES ABRAM GARFIELD
21. CHESTER ALAN ARTHUR
22. GROVER CLEVELAND
23. BENJAMIN HARRISON
24. GROVER CLEVELAND
25. WILLIAM McKINLEY
26. THEODORE ROOSEVELT
27. WILLIAM HOWARD TAFT
28. WOODROW WILSON
29. WARREN GAMALIEL HARDING
30. CALVIN COOLIDGE
31. HERBERT CLARK HOOVER
32. FRANKLIN DELANO ROOSEVELT
33. HARRY S. TRUMAN
34. DWIGHT DAVID EISENHOWER
35. JOHN FITZGERALD KENNEDY
36. LYNDON BAINES JOHNSON
37. RICHARD MILHOUS NIXON
38. GERALD RUDOLPH FORD
39. JAMES EARL CARTER

40. RONALD WILSON REAGAN

STATES INFORMATION TABLE

STATE	ABBREV.	RANK BY AREA	STATE CAPITAL	RANK BY POP.	STATE NICKNAME	STATE FLOWER
ALABAMA	Ala.	29	Montgomery	19	Yellow Hammer, Cotton, Heart of Dixie	Goldenrod
ALASKA	Alsk.	1	Juneau	50	The Last Frontier	Forget-Me-Not
ARIZONA	Ariz.	6	Phoenix	35	Grand Canyon, Sunset Land, Apache	Saguaro Cactus
ARKANSAS	Ark.	27	Little Rock	32	Wonder, Land of Opportunity, Bear	Apple Blossom
CALIFORNIA	Calif., Cal.	3	Sacramento	1	Golden, Grizzy Bear	Golden Poppy
COLORADO	Colo.	8	Denver	33	Centennial, Rover	Columbine
*CONNECTICUT	Conn.	48	Hartford	26	Constitution, Nutmeg	Mountain Laurel
*DELAWARE	Del., Dela.	49	Dover	46	First, Diamond, Blue Hen	Peach Blossom
†DISTRICT OF COLUMBIA	D.C.					American Beauty Rose
FLORIDA	Fla.	22	Tallahassee	12	Sunshine, Everglade, Live Oak, Peninsula	Orange Blossom
*GEORGIA	Ga.	21	Atlanta	16	Empire State of the South, Peach, Cracker	Cherokee Rose
HAWAII	Haw.	47	Honolulu	44	Paradise of the Pacific	Hibiscus
IDAHO	Id.	13	Boise	42	Gem, "Potato"	Lewis Mockorange
ILLINOIS	Ill.	24	Springfield	4	Prairie, Sucker	Violet
INDIANA	Ind.	38	Indianapolis	10	Hoosier	Peony
IOWA	Ia.	25	Des Moines	23	Hawkeye, "Corn"	Wild Rose
KANSAS	Kan., Kans.	14	Topeka	29	Sunflower, Corn Cracker, Garden, Jayhawk	Sunflower
KENTUCKY	Ky.	37	Frankfort	21	Blue Grass	Goldenrod
LOUISIANA	La.	31	Baton Rouge	20	Pelican, Creole, Sugar	Magnolia
MAINE	Me.	39	Augusta	36	Pine Tree, Lumber, Potato	Pine Cone and Tassel
*MARYLAND	Md.	42	Annapolis	22	Old Line, Free, Cockade	Black-Eyed Susan
*MASSACHUETTS	Mass.	45	Boston	9	Bay, Old Colony	Arbutus
MICHIGAN	Mich.	23	Lansing	7	Wolverine	Apple Blossom

*One of the Thirteen Original States

†District

208

STATE	ABBREV.	RANK BY AREA	STATE CAPITAL	RANK BY POP.	STATE NICKNAME	STATE FLOWER
MINNESOTA	Minn.	12	St. Paul	18	North Star, Gopher, Land of 10,000 Lakes	Moccasin Flower
MISSISSIPPI	Miss.	32	Jackson	28	Magnolia, Bayou	Magnolia
MISSOURI	Mo.	19	Jefferson City	13	Show Me, Bullion	Hawthorn
MONTANA	Mont.	4	Helena	41	Treasure, Bonanza	Bitterroot
NEBRASKA	Nebr.	15	Lincoln	34	Beef Cornhusker, Antelope	Goldenrod
NEVADA	Nev.	7	Carson City	49	Sagebrush, Silver, Battle-Born	Sagebrush
*NEW HAMPSHIRE	N.H.	44	Concord	45	Granite	Lilac
*NEW JERSEY	N.J.	46	Trenton	8	Garden	Violet
*NEW MEXICO	N.M.	5	Santa Fe	39	Sunshine	Yucca
*NEW YORK	N.Y.	30	Albany	2	Empire, Excelsior	Rose
*NORTH CAROLINA	N.C.	28	Raleigh	11	Tar Heel, Old North, Turpentine	Dogwood
NORTH DAKOTA	N.D.	17	Bismarck	43	Sioux, Flickertail	Wild Prairie Rose
OHIO		35	Columbus	6	Buckeye	Scarlet Carnation
OKLAHOMA	Okla.	18	Oklahoma City	27	Sooner	Mistletoe
OREGON	Ore.	10	Salem	31	Beaver, Webfooter	Oregon Grape
*PENNSYLVANIA	Penna., Pa., Penn.	33	Harrisburg	3	Keystone, Quaker	Mountain Laurel
*RHODE ISLAND	R.I.	50	Providence	37	Little Rhody, Gunflint	Violet
*SOUTH CAROLINA	S.C.	40	Columbia	25	Palmetto	Yellow Jessamine
SOUTH DAKOTA	S.D.	16	Pierre	40	Coyote, Sunshine	Pasque Flower
TENNESSEE	Tenn.	34	Nashville	17	Volunteer, Big Bend	Iris
TEXAS	Tex.	2	Austin	5	Lone Star	Bluebonnet
UTAH		11	Salt Lake City	38	Beehive, Mormon	Sego Lily
VERMONT	Vt.	43	Montpelier	47	Green Mountain, Granite	Red Clover
*VIRGINIA	Va.	36	Richmond	15	Old Dominion, Cavalier, "Mother of Presidents"	Dogwood
WASHINGTON	Wash.	20	Olympia	24	Evergreen, Chinook	Rhododendron
WEST VIRGINIA	W. Va.	41	Charleston	30	Mountain, Panhandle	Great Rhododendron
WISCONSIN	Wisc., Wis.	26	Madison	14	Badger, Cheese	Violet
WYOMING	Wyo.	9	Cheyenne	48	Equality	Indian Paintbrush

*One of the Thirteen Original States

†District

GAZETTEER

OR

GEOGRAPHICAL DICTIONARY

cities, states, countries, counties, provinces, towns, rivers, communes, ports and harbors, regions, lakes, mountains, islands, volcanoes, settlements, kingdoms, districts, divisions, peninsulas, mountain ranges, nomes, etc.; n = north; s = south

A

ABYSSINIA ... city, HARAR, GONDAR, HARRAR; town, ADOWA, (s) MEGA, province, TIGRE; river, OMO, ABBA; lake, TANA, TSANA

ADRIATIC ... port and harbor, FIUME; peninsula, ISTRIA; resort, LIDO

AEGEAN .... river, STRUMA; island, MELOS, SAMOS, TENOS; gulf, SAROS

AFGHANISTAN .. city, HERAT

AFRICA .... (see also SOUTH AFRICA page 216)

AFRICA .. (n) country, TUNIS, UGANDA, ALGERIA, TUNISIA, TUNISIE; lake, NYASA; province, LAGOS, NATAL; river, UMO, NILE, TANA, CONGO, NIGER; city (n) ORAN, DAKAR, TUNIS; mountains, ATLAS; region, CONGO, NUBIA, SUDAN, SOUDAN; port (w) DAKAR

ALABAMA ...... city, SELMA ANNISTON

ALASKA .. city, NOME, SITKA; island, ADAK, ATKA, ATTU; peninsula, UNGA; mountain, ADA; inlet, COOK; river, YUKON; highest peak in North Amer., McKINLEY; glacier, MUIR

ALBANIA ... capital, TIRANA; river, DRIN

ALEUTIANS ... islands, ADAK, ATKA, ATTU

ALGERIA .... city, port, ORAN

ALPS ..... mountain, BLANC, MATTERHORN

ANNAM .... capital, HUE

ANTARCTIC ...... sea, ROSS

ARABIA .. city, ADEN, BEDA, BERA, SANA; state, ASIR, OMAN, YEMEN; port, ADEN; district, TEMA; kingdom, NEJD; gulf, ADEN, OMAN

ARCTIC .. gulf, OB; sea, KARA

ARIZONA . city, MESA, YUMA; river, GILA

ARMENIA .... river, ARAS

ASIA . mountains, ALTAI; lake, ARAL; sea, ARAL; river, OB, ILI, AMUR, LENA, ONON, TIGRIS; kingdom, NEPAL, SIAM; country, ANAM, IRAK, IRAN, BURMA, CHINA, KOREA, SYRIA, TIBET, SITSANG; kingdom E. Asia, KOREA; desert, GOBI

ASIA MINOR .. district, IONIA; mountains, IDA

ASIATIC .... (see ASIA)

AUSTRIA .. city, GRAZ, WEIN, VIENNA; river, MUR, ENNS, RAAB, RABA

AUSTRALIA . peninsula, EYRE; river, SWAN; city PERTH

AZORES .... port and harbor, HORTA; island, PICO, FAYAL, FLORES; volcano, PICO, (ALTO)

B

BALEARIC ISLANDS .... port, PALMA; island, MAJORCA

BALTIC island, OSEL (opposite RIGA); gulf, RIGA; capital, RIGA; river, ODER

BAVARIA .. river, NAB, ISAR, NAAB

BELGIAN CONGO ..river, UELE

BELGIUM .. city, HUY, MONS, GHENT, LIEGE, MALINES; commune (town), ANS, ATH, SPA, LEDE, MONS, NIEL, ROUX, NAMUR; river, LYS, YSER, MEUSE, SENNE; port and harbor, OSTEND; province, LIEGE

BOHEMIA .. river, ELBE, ISER; mountains, ORE

BOMBAY .. city, POONA; district, SURAT; seaport and harbor, SURAT

BOTHNIA .... islands, ALAND

BRAZIL .... city, RIO, BELEM; port and harbor, PARA, BELEM, NATAL, SANTOS, PELOTAS; state, PARA, BAHIA; river, APA, ICA, PARA; capital, RIO

BRITISH WEST INDIES .island, NEVIS

BULGARIA .... capital, SOFIA

BURMA (see also INDIA).capital (former) AVA, (present) RANGOON; district, PROME

C

CALIFORNIA ..... city, LODI,

NAPA, POMONA, ALAMEDA, SALINAS; town, OJAI, county, NAPA, YOLO, MODOC, MADERA; lake, TAHOE; mountain peak, LASSEN, SHASTA; valley, NAPA

CANADA ..mountains, LOGAN, ROBSON; peninsula, GASPE; province, ALBERTA (ALTA.), BRITISH COLUMBIA (B.C.), MANITOBA (MAN.) NEW BRUNSWICK (N.B.), NEWFOUNDLAND (NEWF.), NOVA SCOTIA (N.S.), ONTARIO (ONT.), PRINCE EDWARD ISLAND (P.E.I.), QUEBEC (QUE.), SASKATCHEWAN (SASK.); national park, JASPER

CANAL ZONE .... city, ANCON, COLON; lake, GATUN

CARIBBEAN .... island, CUBA

CAROLINES .. island, PALAU (PELEW), PONAPE, TRUK, YAP

CAPE VERDE..... island, SAL, FOGO

CASPIAN .. seaport and harbor, BAKU

CENTRAL AFRICA .... region, SUDAN, SOUDAN

CENTRAL AMERICA .... river, LEMPA

CEYLON ...... province, UVA

CHANNEL ISLANDS
island, SARK

CHILE ...... river, LOA; port, harbor, town, ARICA

CHINA ..... city, AMOY, IPIN, CANTON; port and harbor, AMOY; kingdom old, WU, SHU, WEI; river, SI, HAN, KAN, PEI, AMUR, HWAI, CANTON; province, AMOY, AMUR, HONAN; mountains, OMEI; division, MIAO

COLORADO .... city, LAMAR, PUEBLO, DURANGO; park, ESTES; town, OURAY; range, RATON; mountain, OSO, EOLUS; peak, OSO; county, OTERO; resort, ASPEN

COLOMBIA .... river, MAGDALENA; city, CALI

CONGO .... river, UELE

CONNECTICUT town, DARIEN, ANSONIA, MERIDEN

CORSICA ... port and harbor, BASTIA

CRETE ...... port and harbor, CANDIA; capital, CANEA; mountain, IDA

CRIMEA .... port and harbor, KERCH; river, ALMA

CUBA .... town, GUINES

CYCLADES . island, IOS, NIOO, MILO, SYRA, DELOS, MELOS, TENOS, THERA

CZECHOSLOVAKIA ..... city, BRNO; BRUNN; river, EGER, GRAN, HRON, IPEL, ISER, ODER, OHRE, MOLDAU; region, SUDETEN; capital, PRAGUE (PRAHA); mountains, ORE

D

DENMARK ... island off, ALS, AERO; islands, FAROE

DOMINICAN REPUBLIC .. city, MOCA

DUTCH ..... see Netherlands

DUTCH EAST INDIES .. island, BALI, JAVA NIAS; island group, ARU, ALOR, LETI; gulf, BONI; capital, BATAVIA

E

EAST ASIA . kingdom, KOREA

EAST EUROPEAN . river, DRAU, TISA, DRAVA, DRAVE, TISZA, THEISS

EAST INDIES . see also (Dutch East Indies) island, BORNEO

ECUADOR ..... province, ORO

EGYPT .. city, SAIS, CAIRO; ancient city, THEBES; town, KISH; province, GIZA; river, NILE

ENGLAND .. city, ELY, BATH, YORK, LEEDS, COVENTRY; port and harbor, HULL, DOVER, POOLE; town, ETON; river, ALN, CAM, DEE, EXE, NEN, URE, AVON, NENE, OUSE, TEES, TYNE, TRENT; county, KENT, YORK, BERKS, BUCKS, DERBY, DEVON, ESSEX, HANTS, WILTS, DORSET, SURREY, SUSSEX

ESTONIA ..... island, SAARE; province, SAARE; capital, REVAL

ETHIOPIA ..... see Abyssinia

EUROPE .... river, ISAR, OISE, URAL, DANUBE; lake, BALATON (largest); peninsula, IBERIA; resort, LIDO

F

FIJI .... capital, SUVA

FINLAND .. port and harbor, ABO, KEM, PORI; town, northern, ENARE; lake, ENARE; islands, ALAND

FLORIDA .... county, DADE; resort, DELAND; city, OCALA; cape, SABLE

FRANCE .... city, AIX, DAX, PAU, AGEN, ALBI, CAEN, LAON, LYON, METZ, NICE, OPPY, VAUX, ARLES, ARRAS, BLOIS, DINAN, LILLE, (n) NESLE, PARIS, SEDAN, TULLE, CANNES, NANTES, SEVRES; colony, ALGERIA; commune, EU, AUX, AUBY, BRON, ISSY, LOOS, MERU, ORLY, SENS, VIMY, VIRE, CENON; port and harbor, CAEN, MEZE, (s) SETE, BREST; resort, PAU, NICE, CANNES; department, VAR, GARD, JURA, NORD, ORNE, MEUSE, VENDEE; river, AIN, LOT, LYS, AIRE, AUDE, CHER, EURE, LOIR, OISE, ORNE, RHIN, SAAR, YSER, AISNE, ISERE, LOIRE (largest), MARNE, MEUSE, SAONE, SARRE, SEINE, SELLE (small), (n) VESLE, MOSELLE; Mount, BLANC; mountains, JURA; region, ANJOU, ALSACE

212

FRENCH EQUATORIAL AFRICA
river, SHARI

FRENCH INDO-CHINA
see Indo China

FRENCH MOROCCO .. capital,
RABAT; city, RABAT

FRENCH WEST AFRICA
city, DAKAR

FRIENDLY ISLANDS .. TONGA

G

GEORGIA ..... city, MACON,
SPARTA, AUGUSTA

GERMANY ... city, EMS, ULM,
BONN (capital W. Germany),
GERA, JENA, LAHR, LINZ,
EMDEN, ESSEN, NEUSS; com-
mune town, AUE, WALD; spa,
AIX, BADEN; canal, KIEL;
river, EMS, ALLE, EDER, EGER,
ELBE, ISAR, MAIN, ODER,
PRUT, REMS, RUHR, SAAR,
LIPPE, MOSEL, REGEN, RHINE,
SAONE, WESER; mountain,
ORE, HARZ; state, HESSE; dis-
trict, ALSACE; region, SUDE-
TEN

GOLD COAST port and harbor,
KETA

GREAT BARRIER ISLAND OTEA

GREECE .... city, ELIS,
SPARTA, SPARTE; colony, an-
cient, IONIA; island, COS, IOS,
KOS, NIO, MILO, SCIO, SERO,
CRETE, DELOS, MELOS, PAROS,
SAMOS, IONIAN; mountain,
OETA, OSSA, HELICON; nome,
ELIS; river, ARTA; peninsula,
MOREA; region, DORIS; dis-
trict, ancient, ATTICA

GREENLAND .... town, settlement, base, ETAH

GUAM .. city, capital, AGANA;
port and harbor, APRA

GUATEMALA . volcano, AGUA

H

HAWAII .. chief city, HILO;
island, MAUI, OAHU; district,

HANA; islet, KURE

HEBRIDES, INNER ... island,
IONA, SKYE, UIST

HOLLAND see NETHERLANDS

HONDURAS ...... port, TELA

HONSHU .... bay, ISE; port
and harbor, KOBE

HUNGARY ..... city, BUDA,
PECS; commune, town, ERLAU;
river, RAAB

HYOGO .... capital, KOBE

I

IDAHO ...... capital, BOISE;
town, ARCO

ILLINOIS . city, PANA, ALEDO,
ELGIN, PEKIN, CANTON, MO-
LINE, PEORIA, SPARTA

INDIA ..... capital, MADRAS;
city, AGRA, DELHI, POONA,
SIMLA, MADRAS, BENARES;
commune, town, ARCOT, SOR-
ON; kingdom (n) NEPAL; state,
DHAR, JATH, JIND, ASSAM,
MYSORE, GWALIOR; province,
SIND, SWAT, ASSAM, BERAR,
DELHI, MADRAS; Portuguese
possession, GOA; river, SIND,
SWAT, GANGA, INDUS, KABUL,
GANGES; district, SIMLA, SA-
TARA

INDIA, NORTH
see NORTH INDIA

INDIANA .... city, GARY,
PERU, MARION

INDOCHINA . country, ANAM,
ANNAM; kingdom, ANAM,
ANNAM; city, HUE, HANOI,
SAIGON; region, LAOS; state,
ANAM, LAOS; port and harbor,
ANNAM

INDONESIA .... island, AROE,
BALI, JAVA, TERNATE,
CELEBES; island group, KAI,
OBI

IOWA .. city AMES (college);
county, IDA

IRAQ ..... capital, BAGDAD, BAGHDAD; port and harbor, BASRA

IRAN .... see PERSIA

IRELAND .. old capital, TARA; port and harbor, COBH, TRALEE; county, MAYO, CLARE; island, ARAN; river, LEE, BANN, ERNE, NORE; lake, REE, ERNE; town, TARA

ISLE OF WIGHT .... port and harbor, COWES

ISRAEL ..... port and harbor, ACRE, HAIFA; plain, SHARON; desert, NEGEB

ITALY . capital, ROMA, ROME; city, BARI, COMO, PISA, ROMA, ROME, MILAN, PARMA, SIENA, TRENT, NAPLES, SIENNA, VENICE, (s) CASERTA; commune or town, BRA, ARCO, ASTI, ATRI, DEGO, ESTE, LARI, NOLA, SAVA, TODI, ADRIA, ASOLA, PADUA, TURIN, EMPOLI; resort, LIDO; port and harbor, OSTIA, TRANI; province, ALBA, CONI, POLA, ROMA, ZARA, UDINE; river, PO, ADDA, ARNO, NERA, RENO, PIAVE, TIBER; lake, COMO, ISEO, NEMI; strait, OTRANTO; gulf, SALERNO

J

JALAUN ...... capital, ORAI

JAPAN ...... capital, TOKIO, TOKYO (old name EDO); resort city, HONSHU; capital, NARA; city, KOBE, KOFU, CHIBA, OSAKA, OTARU, TOKIO, TOKYO; harbor or port or seaport, OSAKA, OTARU; island, HONDO (largest), SADO; volcano, ASO, FUJI; bay, ISE; province, old, ISE, IYO, YAMATO; mountain, FUJI

K

KANSAS .. city, ARMA, IOLA, SALINA; county, OSAGE; river, OSAGE

KOREA ... city, KEIJO, SEOUL

KASHMIR ...... river, INDUS

KENTUCKY .. county, ADAIR LA RUE

KENYA . (Africa) river, TANA

L

LATVIA .. capital, port, RIGA; river, AA

LEBANON ...... port, SIDON

LIBYA ..... port and harbor, DERNA; capital, TRIPOLI

LITHUANIA .. seaport, VILNA

LITTLE AMERICA .. sea, ROSS

LUZON ...... province, ABRA river, ABRA, AGNO

M

MAINE .. bay, CASCO; town, BATH, (University) ORONO; city, SACO

MALAYA ..... state, PERAK, JOHORE; region, PENANG; island, BALI, JAVA, TIMOR; port, PEKAN

MALAY ARCHIPELAGO island, CELEBES

MALTA .... island, GOZO

MARTINQUE . volcano, PELEE

MASSACHUSETTS ...... city, SALEM, NEWTON; cape, ANN, COD; mountain, TOM

MEDITERRANEAN island, IOS, GOZO, RODI, CAPRI, CRETE, MALTA; gulf, TUNIS; resort, LIDO, NICE

MESOPOTAMIA .. river, TIGRIS

MEXICO .... town, TULA; state, COLIMA; lake, CHAPALA

MICHIGAN ..... city, ALMA, CLARE, FLINT, SPARTA; county, EATON

214

MINDANAO ... volcano, APO; gulf, DAVAO

MISSISSIPPI ... city, BILOXI; river, YAZOO

MISSOURI .... city, SEDALIA; resort, AVA; river, SAC

MOLUCCA ...... island, OBI, TERNATE

MONGOLIA ..... desert, GOBI

MONTANA ..... city, BUTTE; river, TETON

MOROCCO . region, RIF, RIFF; mountains, ANTI, ATLAS; province, SUS; port and harbor, RABAT; town, IFNI

MOZAMBIQUE ... town, IBA; port and harbor, BEIRA

N

NEBRASKA .. city, ORD; river, LOUP, PLATTE; county, OTOE; capital, LINCOLN

NEPAL .... mountain, API

NETHERLANDS .. city, EDAM, UTRECHT; commune or town, EDE, EPE, BEEK, ECHT, ELST, OLST, UDEN, GEMERT; port and harbor, EDAM; river, EEM, MAAS (Dutch Meuse), MAES, RIJN, WAAL; island, SUMATRA

NEVADA ... city, ELY, ELKO, RENO; lake, TAHOE

NEW GUINEA .. city, port and harbor, LAE; island, PAPUA

NEW HAMPSHIRE ..... lake, OSSIPEE; city, KEENE, NASHUA, LACONIA; county, COOS

NEW HEBRIDES .... port and harbor, VILA; island, EPI, TANA, EFATE, TANNA

NEW JERSEY . city, TRENTON; river, RARITAN

NEW MEXICO .. town, TAOS; river, GILA; resort, TAOS

NEW YORK ..... city, town, ROME, TROY, OLEAN, UTICA, ELMIRA, MALONE, OSWEGO; island, STATEN; county, TIOGA; village, ILION

NEWFOUNDLAND
          peninsula, AVALON

NEW ZEALAND ...... lake, TAUPO; island, reef, OTEA

NIGERIA .. town, ABA, IWO, LERE; region, BENIN

NICARAGUA ..... city, LEON

NORMANDY .... town, ST. LO

NORTH CAROLINA .... river, HAW, TAR, PEE DEE (Yadkin); cape, FEAR; county, ASHE

NORTH DAKOTA city, MINOT

NORTHUMBERLAND river,
                    TYNE

NORTH INDIA kingdom, NEPAL

NORTH VIETNAM
          capital, HANOI

NORWAY .... capital, OSLO; river, TANA; city, HAMAR

O

OHIO .... county, ROSS; city, ADA (college town Ohio Northern), KENT, LIMA, BEREA, ELIDA, NILES, XENIA, CANTON, FOSTORIA

OKINAWA .. port and harbor, NAWA, NAHA

OKLAHOMA ...... city, ADA, ENID, SHAWNEE

OREGON ...... city, SALEM, ASTORIA; peak, HOOD

ORKNEYS ...... island, HOY

P

PACIFIC ISLANDS ... island, LAU, YAP, FIJI, GUAM, SULU, TRUK, WAKE, LEYTE, SAMOA, TAHITI; island group, PELEW

PAKISTAN ... city, **LAHORE**; river, **INDUS**

PALESTINE (see also separate Biblical lists on page 197); mountain, **EBAL, SION, ZION, TABOR, HERMON** (highest); valley, **GHOR**; plain, **ONO**; area, **BEISAN**; port, **ACRE, GAZA**; town, **GAZA**

PANAMA .... port, **COLON**

PARAGUAY ...... city, **ITA**; river, **APA**

PENNSYLVANIA .. city, **ERIE, EASTON, CHESTER, TYRONE**; port, **ERIE**

PERSIA ... city, **NIRIZ, SUSA, RESHT**

PERU ...... department, **ICA**; capital, **LIMA**; city, **ICA**; cold district, **PUNO**; port and harbor, (s) **ILO, CALLAO**; river, **ICA**

PHILIPPINE ISLANDS (see also Luzon and Mindanao); city, **IBA, CEBU, NAGA, ILOILO**; mountain or peak, **IBA, APO**; volcano, **APO**; port and harbor, **ILOILO, BATANGAS**; province, **DAPA**; island, **CEBU, SULU, BATAN SAMAR, PANAY**

POLAND .. city, **LIDA, LODZ, LWOW, POSEN, SRODA**; river, **SAN, STYR, BIALA, VISLA, STRYPA, VISTULA**

PORTUGAL ..... cape, **ROCA**

PUNJAB .... river, **INDUS**

Q

QUEBEC ... peninsula, **GASPE**; district and town, **LEVIS**

R

RAJPUTANA ... district, **ABU**

ROUMANIA ..... city, **ARAD, IASI**; department, **ALBA**; river, **OLT**

RUSSIA .... city, **KIEF, OMSK, OREL**; port and harbor, **OREL, ODESSA**; commune, town, **KOLA**; river, **OB, OM, DON, ILI, OKA, ROS, UFA, DUNA, LENA, NEVA, ONON, SEIM, URAL, TEREK**; lake, **ONEGA**; sea, **ARAL, AZOF, AZOV**; mountains, **ALAI, URAL, ALTAI**; peninsula, **KOLA, KRIM, CRIMEA**; lake in European Russia, **SEG**; state in Dagestan, **AVAR**; region, **OMSK**

S

SAMOA port, capital and harbor, **APIA**

SAVAGE ISLAND island, **NIUE**

SAXONY commune, town, **AUE**

SCOTLAND .. port and harbor, **OBAN**; seaport, **AYR**; county, **AYR, BUTE**; river, **DEE, TAY** (largest), **DOON, SPEY, TYNE, AFTON**; city, **AYR**; mountains, **IME**; lake, **AWE, LOCH**; district, **ATHOLE, ATHOLL**; island off. **ARRAN**

SERBIA ...... department or capital, **NIS, NISH**

SIBERIA .... (see also Russia) river, **OB, ENISEI, YENISEI**

SICILY ...... volcano, **ETNA, AETNA**; commune, town, **RAGUSA**; city, **ENNA**; province, **ENNA**; resort, **ENNA**

SOCIETY ISLANDS island, **TAHITI**

SOUTH AFRICA district, **RAND**; river, **VAAL**

SOUTHEAST AFRICA district, **NIASSA, NYASSA**

SOUTHWEST AFRICA port and harbor, **DAKAR**

SOUTH AMERICA river, **BENI, PLATA, YAPURA**; district, **CHACO**; mountains, **ANDES**

SOUTH CAROLINA river, **SANTEE**

SOUTH DAKOTA capital, **PIERRE**

216

SOUTH PACIFIC .... isle, FIJI, BALI, COOK, SAMOA

SOUTHWEST .... river, PECOS

SPAIN .... city, JACA, JAEN, LEON, AVILA; province, ADRA, JAEN, LEON, LUGO, AVILA, MALAGA; port and harbor, ADRA, NOYA, VIGO, PALOS, MALAGA; river, EBRO, MINHO, TAGUS; kingdom, LEON, CASTILE; commune, town, ORIA

SPANISH MOROCCO (see also Morocco) port and harbor, CEUTA; district, IFNI

SUMATRA .... district, DELI

SWEDEN .. river, UME, LULE; island off ALAND; port and harbor, MALMO, OREBRO; strait, ORESUND

SWITZERLAND .... city, BEX, BALE, BERN, GENF, SION, BASLE, BERNE, LOCARNO; commune, town, AY, BAAR, BIEL, CHUR, RUTI, WALD, AARAU, MORAT; canton, URI ZUG, BERN, VAUD, ZOUG, BASLE, BERNE; river, AAR, AARE; lake, ZUG, JOUY, LUCERNE; mountain, TODI, VISO, MATTERHORN; resort, DAVOS; capital, BERN, BERNE; town, see commune

SYRIA .... city, ALEP, HOMS, ALEPPO; port and harbor, SIDON

T

TAHITI .... capital, PAPEETE

TEXAS .... county, CLAY, CARSON; city, WACO, LAREDO, ABILENE

TIBET capital, LASSA, LHASA; river, INDUS

TRANS-JORDAN .. mountain, HOR; mountain range, SEIR

TUNISIA ..... capital, TUNIS

TURKEY .... city, ADANA, ANGORA; river, ARAS; vilayet, ORDU, URFA; island, TENEDOS

TUSCANY ...... river, ARNO

U

UTAH .... city, HEBER, LOGAN; mountains, UINTA

V

VENEZUELA .... state, LARA; island, ARUBA; river, PAO

VERMONT ...... city, BARRE

VIRGINIA .... river, DAN, RAPIDAN

VIRGIN ISLANDS capital, CHARLOTTE AMALIE

W

WALES .... river, DEE, USK; lake, BALA

WASHINGTON .. city, TACOMA

WEST AUSTRALIA capital, PERTH

WEST INDIES .... isle, island, CUBA, HAITI, NEVIS

WISCONSIN .... city, RIPON, RACINE

WYOMING .... city, CASPER, LARAMIE; highest mountain peak, GANNETT; range, TETON

Y

YEMEN .... capital, SANA

YORKSHIRE ..... river, OUSE; city, LEEDS

YUGOSLAVIA .... island, RAB, ARBE, SOLTA; city, NIS; river, SAVA, DRINA, NARENTA; district and province, BANAT

YUKON .... city, DAWSON; river, HESS, PEEL, ROSS

217

WORD-FINDER

with CROSS-REFERENCES

FOR THE SOLVER

You can complete any unfinished 2-, 3-, or 4-letter word in the crossword you are working by using this WORD-FINDER. Even though you are at first unable to locate it in the Definitions Section for some reason, if you have just two letters of your wanted word (just one if it's a 2-letter word) you can find it here.

The WORD-FINDER words are listed according to the following Letter-Combination system:

      XX - -   (for cases when the first two letters are known)
      - XX -   (when the second and third letters are known)
      - - XX   (when the last two letters are known)
      X - - X   (when the first and last letters are known)

Let us say that you need to complete a word that is four letters long.

STEP ONE: Find the Letter-Combination that is the same as the letters which you have written into the crossword puzzle. Have you, for example, found "ON" as the end of a 4-letter word? Then turn to the "- - ON" Letter-Combination. Of course, since the WORD-FINDER is thorough-going, a number of words, all containing the same letter combination, are listed under this Letter-Combination.

- - ON	Acon,	agon,	Amon,	anon,
	Avon,	axon,	azon,	bion,
	boon,	cian,	coon,	Dion,
	doon,	ebon,	Enon,	Eton,
	faon,	Gaon,	hoon,	icon,
	iron,	Leon,	lion,	loon,
	moon,	neon,	etc.	

STEP TWO: You may know, after looking through the words listed under your Letter-Combination, the word which is the only correct possibility. If not, you now begin to eliminate words in the list by working with the words in the crossword puzzle which CROSS your unfinished word. You do this by experimentally inserting words from the Letter-Combination list. When the experimental insert produces such impossible-looking combinations with the crossing word as "bv", "pv" etc. it can be discarded.

STEP THREE: After eliminating the words that make highly unlikely or "impossible" combinations with the crossing words, you still may not be sure how to complete your unfinished puzzle. Here you make use of the invaluable CROSS-REFERENCE listings following the words in the WORD-FINDER. Each number following a word is the number of the page of the Definitions Section on which the word and one of its definitions will be found. The alphabetical letters a, b, c, d indicate in exactly which section of the definition page you will be able to locate the word with its meaning.

Example: adat (90b,95d)

On page 90 of this Dictionary, in section b of the page, you will find the word ADAT in bold face type. The definition is "law, D. E. Ind". On page 95, section d, you will find another cross-reference to ADAT. The definition reads "Malay law."

STEP FOUR: Now re-examine the definition in your puzzle. Eliminate words in the WORD-FINDER by comparing definitions until you arrive at the "logical candidate" word for which you have been looking. Definitions in this dictionary and those in your puzzle will not always agree in exact wording. In that case, let the general meaning of the definitions be your guide. Everyday words are not always cross-referenced in this WORD-FINDER, nor are some words of exceptional terminology. Only some of the words listed in the Special Section are cross-referenced. If your definition calls for a word likely to be found in the Special Section, it is recommended that you look there first.

TWO-LETTER WORDS

A · Aa (47a), aa (90b), Ab (48d,75b,102a), ab (63d), AC (39d), ad (90a,112d,167d), ae ((42b,43c,d,122b,139a), Ae (82c,115b), ah (52c), al (143c,148c), al (8c,80c,102c,104b), am (166c,175c), an (11b,13b), Ao (13d,88b,c,116c), AP (107a,182d), ap (122d,166c), ar (88b,91c,98a,99b,110c), as (51b,67b,92b,126a,133a,b,180d), at (25c,32c,106a,123a,128a), au (63a,69c), aw (44a), ax (40c, 139a,167a), ay (7c,8b,9b,28d,55a,60a)

· **A** Aa (47a), aa (90b), BA (42a), Ba (150d,153c), ba (139a), da (9b,37a,56a,133d,135d), DA (124d), ea (43c), EA (15b,68a), fa (108b,138a,161a), Ga (69c), ha (52c), ia (43d,158c), Ja (66d), ka (68c,77b,150d,153c,173c), la (13b,61a,83a,108b,138a,151d,161a), ma, MA (42a), Ma (69a,b,85d), na (140c,163d), NA (36c), oa (143c,d), pa (60b,106d), ra (108b), Ra (159b), SA (36c), ta (112d,139a,160b), VA (83a), va (105a), wa (188), Wa (24c,d,88c), ya, za (162a)

B · BA (42a), ba (139a,150d,153c), bb (147b), be, bi (122d,171c), bo (23d,24c,136a,168a), bu (190), by (18b,32c,106a)

· **B** ab (63d), Ab (48d,75b,102a), bb (147b), FB (59c), HB (59c), eb (122b), QB (59c)

C · ce (62d,164c), CE (42a)

· **C** DC (39d), ec (122c)

D · da (9b,37a,56a,133d,135d), DA (124d), DC (39d), DD (42a), de (63d,89b,122b,122c,124a,152c,d), di (68c,89b,108b,122b,122c, 122d,171d), dm (131cc), do (108b,138a,161a)

· **D** ad, (90a,112d,167d), DD (42a), ed (175c), Ed (18d), id (26d, 40c,51c,57a,b,d), od (8d,59d,79c), td (32a)

E · ea (43c), EA (115b,68a), ec (122c), ed (175c), Ed (18d), ee (139c,) EE (42a), ef (91c), eg (59d,163d), eh (52c), ei (13b,42a, 47a,99b,151d,168a), El (68a,108a), em (91c,98a,123d,172a,c), en (15b,29c,50a,91c,98a,119d,123d,158c,d,172a), eo (34a), er (35b,76c,137d,155a,158c,d,160b,175c), Er (18d,68c,85c,163d, 166c,172c,178a), es (49b,50a,66c,119d,158c,d,175c), et (10b,61a, b,89a,158c), ex (60b,91c,122c)

· **E** ae (42b,43c,122b,139a), Ae (82c,115b), be, CE (42a), Ce (62d), ce (164c), de (63d,89b,122b,c,124a,152c,d) ee (139c), EE (42a), Ge (47d,69a), he (91c), le (74c,158c,163d), LE (59c), le (13b, 61a,108b), me (108b,124b), Me. (124d), ne (35b,106b), oe (43c, 54d,82d,180d,182a,b), pe (91c), Pe. (124d), re (6b,10b,35d,108b, 122b,129b,138a,161a), RE (59c), se (35b,108b), te (43a,62d, 108b,131c,152d,160b,185d), Ve (63c,109c), we (48c,124b), We (92b), ye (124b)

F · fa (108b,138a,161a), FB (59c), ff (147b), Fi (108b), Fo (23d), fu (42c,84c), Fu (30b)

· **F** ef (91c), ff (147b), if (35d,125a), LF (16d), of (6b), RF (16d)

G - Ga (69c), Ge (47d,69a), Gj (91d), go (64c,90d)

- G eg (59d,163d), Og (16d,18c)

H - ha (52c), HB (59c), he (91c), hi (52c), ho (39b,79a), Ho (87c), Hu (101c,108a,162b)

- H ah (52c), eh (52c), oh (52c), Rh (20c), sh (17b,43c,79c,126d), th (43c)

I - ia (43d,158c), id (26d,40c,51c,57a,b,d), ie (74c,158c,163d), if (35d,125a), Il (122c), im (122c), in (9d,123a), io (74b,74c,103c, 115b), Io (25a,85d,95c,186b), Ir (99d,122c), is (51a,166c,175c), Is (15b,23c,86c), it (124b)

- I ai (143c,148c), bi (122d,171c), di (68c,89b,108b,122b,c,d,171d), fi (108b), GI (91d), hi (52c), Ii (130a,b,37b,98a,108b,161b), mi (43b,108b,138a,161a), pi (71b,85d,91c,165a,172a), ri (84c,96d, 98a,108b), RI (106c), si (108b,152d,185d), ti (92b,108b,113a,b, 120d,138a,161a,162c,169b), xi (91c)

J - ja (66d) jo (140c,160c), Jo (8c,94b), ju (121a)

K - ka (45c), Ka (68c,77b,150d,153c,173c), ko (22c,87c,121a)

- K OK (155a)

L - la (13b,61a,83a,108b,138a,151d,161a), le (13b,61a,108b), LE (59c), Lf (16d), li (30a,b,37b,98a,108b,161b), Lt (143c), LT (59c), lu (65a), lo (17d,93d)

- L al (8c,80c,102c,104b), Al (96b), el (13b,42a,47a,99b,151d,168a), El (68a,108a), il (122c), ol (29c,158b,d,160b)

M - ma, Ma (69a,b,85d), MA (42a), me (108b,124b), Me. (124b), mi (43b,108b,138a,161a), mo (21d,81c,101c), Mo (88c,177c), mu (10a,30a,60c,71a,91c), my (52c,124c)

- M am (166c,175c), em (91c,98a,123d,172a,c), dm (131c), im (122c), om (49a,77a,77b,105c,136a), um (52c,76c)

N - na (140c,163d), NA (36c), ne (35b,106b), no (42b,106b), No (84b), nu (71b,91c), Nu (29a,49a)

- N an (11b,13b), en (15b,29c,50a,91c,98a,119d,123d,158c,d,172a), in (9d,123a), on (8b,9a,60c,106a,123a), un (34c,122c)

O - oa (43c,d), ob (122b), od (8d,59d,79c), oe (43c,54d,82d,180d), 182a,b), of (6b), Og (16d,18c), oh (52c), OK (155a), ol (29c, 158b,d,160b), om (49a,77a,b,105c,136a), on (8b,9a,60c,106a, 123a), oo (34a,74b), or (9b,36a,37b,69c,158c,166a,184b), os (21d,67b,104a,131b), ow (52c), ox (10c,22c), oy (139c)

- O Ao (13d,88b,c,116c), bo (23d,24c,136a,168a), do (108b,138a, 161a), eo (34a), Fo (23d), go (64c,90d), ho (39b,79a), Ho (87c), io (74b,c,103c,115b), Io (25a,85d,95c,186b), jo (140c,160c), Jo (8c,94b), ko (22c,87c,121a), lo (17d,93d), mo (21d,81c,101c), Mo (88c,177c), no (42b,106b), No (84b), oo (34a,74b), Ro (13c, 81d,88c,131c,173c), so (76a,108b,125a,138a,158b,161a,165b, 175c), to (10b,13c), uo (43d), vo (91a), yo, zo (13d,186b)

P - pa (60b,106d), pe (91c), Pe (124d), pi (71b,85d,91c,165a,172a), pu (30b,140a)

- P ap (122d,166c), AP (107a,182d), up (123a), UP (107a,182d)

Q - QB (59c), q.v. (180d)

221

R - ra (108b), Ra (159b), re (6b,10b,35d,108b,122b,129b,138a,161a), RE (59c), RF (16d), Rh (20c), ri (84c,96d,98a,108b), RI (106c), Ro (13c,81d,88c,131c,173c), RT (59c)

- R ar (88b,91c,98a,99b,110c), er (35b,76c,137d,155a,158c,d,160b, 175c), Er (18d,68c,85c,163d,166c,172c,178a), Ir (99d,122c), Ir (10a,28a,82b), or (9b,36a,37b,69c,158c,166a,184b), Ur (6b,28d, 94a,100d)

S - SA (36c), se (35b,108b), Se, sh (17b,43c,79c,126d), si (108b, 152d,185d), so (76a,108b,125a,138a,158b,161a,165b,175c), SS (16d,164c), Su (127a), Sw (35b), Sy (141a)

- S as (51b,67b,92b,126a,133a,b,180d), es (49b,50a,66c,119d,158c, d,175c), is (51a,166c,175c), Is (15b,23c,86c), os (21d,67b,104a, 131b), S.S. (16d,164c), us (124b)

T - ta (112d,139a,169b), td (32a), te (43a,62d,108b,131c,152d,160b, 185d), th (43c), tl (92b,108b,113a,120d,138a,161a,162c,169b), to (10b,13c), tt (147b), tu (83c,164d,185d), Ty (68c,109c,163d, 178a)

- T at (25c,32c,106a,123a,128a), et (10b,61a,b,89a,158c) It (124b), Lt (143c), LT (59c), RT (59c), tt (147b), ut (72b,180b), Ut (67a)

U - um (52c,76c), un (34c,122c), Uo (43d), up (123a), Ur (6b,28d, 94a,100d), UP (107a,182d), us (124b), ut (72b,108b), Ut (67a), Ux (48c)

- U au (63a,69c), bu (190), fu (49c,84c), Fu (30b), Hu (101c,108a, 162b), ju (121a), lu (65a), mu (10a,30a,60c,71a,91c), nu (71b, 91c), Nu (29a,49a), pu (30b,140a), Su (127a), tu (83c,164d, 185d), Wu (30b), Zu (68c,157a)

V - va (105a), Va (83a), Ve (63c,109c), vo (91a)

- V q.v. (180d)

W - wa (188), Wa (24c,88c), we (48c,124b), We (92b), Wu (30b), wy (91c)

- W aw (44a), ow (52c), sw (35b)

X - xi (91c)

- X ax (40c,139a,167a), ex (60b,91c,122c), ox (10c,22c)

Y - ya, ye (124b), yo

- Y ay (7c,8b,9b,28d,55a,60a), by (18b,32c,106a), my (52c,124c), sy (141a), oy (139c), Ty (68c,109c,163d,178a), wy (91c)

Z - za (162a), zo (13d,186a), Zu (68c,157a)

- Z Ux (48c)

THREE-LETTER WORDS

AA - aal (47c,80c,104b), aam (47a,49d,93a), aar (172d), Aar (131a)
A - A aba (12a,25d,32b,33a,65b), Ada (110a,112c,183c), aea (25a,36d), aga (35a,39a,48b,102d,103a,b,111c,166b,170d,171a), aha (52c, 55c,159c), aka (188b,c,176b), Aka (13d), ala (6d,13a,15c,61a,

222

133d,182c,d), **Ala** (151b), **ama** (26a,28d,31a,35b,39c,95b,108d, 111c,117b,182c), **ana** (10b,33c,60d,93a,98c,122b,d,140d,142b), **Ana** (28a,68d,100c), **apa** (23a,177d), **ara** (33a,114a,116a,118b, 163d), **Ara** (9b,18c,36b,c,68d,69b,c,85a,95a,175b), **Asa** (6a,18c, 71a,84d,86d,164c), **ata** (58d,97d,158d,160c,173d), **Ata** (79c,80d, 94d,95d,100a,106b,117a), **ava** (78d,86a,116a,120d,139a,167b), **Ava** (24c), **awa** (100a,139a), **aya** (77b,166b)

- **AA**   **baa** (143d), **maa** (97d,143d), **saa** (98a), **taa** (112d)

AB -   **aba** (12a,25d,32b,33a,65b), **abb** (58b,178b,185b), **ABC** (134d), **Abe** (71a,96a,123a), **Abi** (76c), **Abo** (25d), **Abt** (34c), **abu** (17a), **Abu** (15b,42a,55a,68a,147d)

A - B   **abb** (58b,178b,185b), **alb** (65b,176a)

- **AB**   **Bab** (15a), **cab** (75c), **dab** (46a,57b,58b,d,114d,115c), **gab** (29b, 78a,116c,122a,161c,183a), **jab** (120b,125c), **kab** (75c), **lab**, **Mab** (54b,126b,183d), **nab** (13b,26c,27b,142a), **pab** (139c), **rab** (17c, 75c,85b,102d,162c,166b), **Rab** (45a), **tab** (29b,39c,58b,86a,128d, 145a)

AC -   **ace** (7a,26c,52d,57a,77d,110c,114c,120b,147a,163a,173a), **ach** (8b,48a,52c,66b,80c), **aci** (29c), **act** (41d,55b,119c,155d), **acu** (34c), **acy** (34c)

A - C   **ABC** (134d), **arc** (31b,39d,92a,126a,127c,142a)

- **AC**   **bac** (31b,55c,174d), **fac** (41c), **lac** (53c,99d,130c,135d,174d), **Mac** (96a,140b,150b), **pac** (73b,94c,100d), **sac** (15d,121d), **Sac** (80c), **tac** (34d,130a), **Vac** (153b), **zac** (27c)

AD -   **Ada** (110a,112c,183c), **add** (10d,11d,14c,158a,167c), **ade** (18c, 149d), **Ade** (9c,53b), **ado** (22b,24d,35b,64c,78d,121d,156b,170a), **ady** (188), **adz** (40c,167a)

A - D   **aid** (14a,15b,64c,75d,158b), **add** (10d,11d,14c,158a,167c), **and** (36a,119d)

- **AD**   **bad** (55a,173a,184d), **cad** (22b,23b,75c,172c,173d), **dad, fad** (38b,108c,163a), **gad** (58c,100a,b,127d,132b,153c,154b,178a), **Gad** (84a,186d), **had, lad** (22c,25b,55b,157c,186a), **mad** (10c, 82b), **pad** (39d,59c,76c,157d,161a,168b), **rad** (50b,138d,173b), **sad** (29c,42c,94c,98c,104a,150d,173a), **tad** (22c,174a,186a), **wad** (94d,97b,109c,112b,149d)

AE -   **aea** (26a,36d), **AEF** (184d), **aer** (8b,28d,34a,b,175a), **aes** (23c, 89a,101c,132d,133a,b), **aet** (89a,109d), **Aex** (46d)

A - E   **Abe** (71a,96a,123a), **ace** (7a,26c,52d,57a,77d,110c,114c,120b, 147a,163a,173a), **ade** (18c,149d), **Ade** (9c,53b), **age** (51d,66a, 92a,97c,98c,116b,141c), **ake** (60a,107a), **ale** (17c,18c,50c,55d, 92d,104c), **ame** (37a,62d,131b), **ane** (61c,140a,158b), **ape** (36d, 79d,100a,101d,146d), **are** (51a,88b,98a,99b,110c,166c,175c), **ase** (51a,139a), **Ase** (79b,115d), **ate** (81a,108c,158c,174c), **Ate** (20c, 68b,d,69a,b,116c,186b), **ave** (54c,71d,73a,122a,134c,136d), **awe** (81d,100a,130d,175b,182b), **axe** (30c,40c,167a), **aye** (7c,9b,55a, 60a)

- **AE**   **dae** (139b), **eae** (34b), **hae** (139c), **kae** (84a,140b), **Mae** (183c), **nae** (139d), **rae** (136b,138d,140b), **Rae** (183c), **sae** (140b,149c), **tae** (138d,140c,166c,d), **vae** (176b)

AF -   **AFL** (173a), **Afr.** (36c), **aft** (14a,15b,17d,128b,167d)

223

A - F AEF (184d), Alf (96a)

- AF gaf (12b), kaf (12b), Kaf (104a), oaf (22a,45b,146d,157d,185d), Qaf (104a)

AG - aga (35a,39a,48b,102d,103a,b,111c,166b,170d,171a), age (51d, 66a,92a,97c,98c,116b,141c), ago (25a,69d,114d,147a)

- AG bag (26c,139a,145b,159a), cag (91d,109d), dag (11b,118c,139c), Dag (108c), fag (55a,166a), gag (146c,183a), hag (140a,183a), jag (124d,148a), lag (93c,155d), mag (73b,95b,166c), Mag (183d), nag (73d,78b,138c,184d), rag (59b,77c,100c,133c,161a), sag (46b), tag (45a,54c,65a,87b,144a), vag (174b,178a), wag (85b,104a,183a), zag (84a)

AH - aha (52c,55c,159c), Ahi (32c,147d), ahu (24c,41d,65d,103d,120d)

A - H ach (8b,48a,52c,66b,80c), akh (153d), ash (24d,33c,49c,73d, 134b,168c,169a), auh (52c)

- AH bah (52c), dah (24c,87a), hah (52c), Jah (84d), Mah (10b,57c, 102b), pah (52c,60b,106d), rah (29b), sah (188), wah (113c), yah (52c)

AI - aid (14a,15b,64c,75d,158b), aik (139d), ail (170a), aim (42d,43d, 67d,109b,125d,157c), ain (18d,91c,110c,124b,140a,154b,180a), air (11c,12c,42b,44c,53a,96b,98c,99d,125c,170c), ait (82d,132a), Aix (46d)

A - I Abi (76c), aci (29c), Ahi (32c,147d), Ali (7b,12a,25c,48b,55a,60c, 92d,101a,103a,164a,166b,170d), ami (61d), ani (19b,d,20b,39b), api (34a,76d), Ari (18d), asi (137a), ati (106d,107a), Ati (45d, 106b,113c,117a)

- AI hai (55c), kai (59c), Kai (14d,84c), lai (98b,161b), Lai (24c,d, 88c), mai (62a), rai (188), sai (101d), tai (84b,111c,121b), Tai (80d), Vai (91d)

- AJ gaj (190), raj (129c), saj (48a,169a), taj (75a,97d)

AK - aka (176b), Aka (13d,88b,c), ake (60a,170a), akh (153d), ako (189), aku (57c,176a)

A - K aik (139d), alk (171b), ark (21a,29d,38a,58b,60d,175d), ask (38b, 82a,126c), auk (19b)

- AK dak (95c), hak (46d), iak (38a), nak (156b), oak (73d,168c,169a), sak (37c), Sak (88c), yak (112c,161d,165b), zak (188)

AL - ala (6d,13a,15c,61a,133d,182c,d), Ala. (151b), alb (65b,176b), ale (17c,18c,50c,55d,92d,104c), Alf (96a), Ali (7b,12a,25c,48b, 55a,60c,92d,101a,103a,164a,166b,170d), alk (171b), all (35c, 118a,126d,181a), alp (24b,103d,115c), als (66d,163d), alt (66c, 76c,109c), aly (95d)

A - L aal (47c,80c,104b), AFL (173a), ail (170a), all (35c,118a,126d, 181a), awl (145b,167a)

- AL aal (47c,80c,104b), bal (9d,37b,61a,61b), cal (183c), Cal (123a), dal (117d,153d), gal, Hal (69d), lal (158b), mal (34a,b,44a,52b, 62c,122b), Mal (94b), pal (35b,38d), sal (29c,48a,136d,149d, 152d,169a,183a), Sal (183d), tal (40c,77a,113c), Zal (135d)

AM - ama (26a,28d,31a,35b,39c,95b,108d,111c,117b,182c), ame (37a, 62d,131b), ami (61d), amo (79a,89c), amp (49b,173b), amt (37d,40d,108a,163c), amy (63c), Amy (8c,94b,183c)

A - M   aam (47a,49d,93a), aim (42d,43d,67d,109b,125d,157c), arm (22d,60c,81b,92b,124b,161b), aum (189)

- AM   aam (47a,49d,93a), bam (29b), cam (48b,65d,95a,98b,134a, 139b,148b,180c), dam (30c,49c,55b,156d,180a), gam (76b,176d, 180c), ham (98a,144b), Ham (18d,107c), jam (123a,156b,165c), lam (51b,58b,93d,164d,178a), Mam (192), pam (26c,65a,87a, 105b), Ram (36b), ram (17a,45b,50b,79c,112b,121d,143d,157d), Sam (96a,162a), tam (74d), yam (48c,121d,160b,170c)

AN -   ana (10b,33c,60d,93a,98c,122b,d,140d,142b), Ana (28a,68d, 100c), and (36a,119d), ane (61c,140a,158b), ani (19b,d,20b, 39b), Ann (183c), ano (19d,20b,34d,122d,174a), Ans (92a), ant (49d,60b,81b,118c), Anu (15b,28a,68a,d,75b,88c,147d), any (14b,150b)

A - N   ain (18d,91c,110c,124b,140a,154b,180a), Ann (183c), arn (8c, 139a), awn (12c,17b,140a)

- AN   ban (81d,97a,124a), can (24c,36c,123a,166a), dan (24c,97c), Dan (18c,39c,77d,83a,84a,141b), ean (17d,23b,88a), fan (43a, 154b, 156b,182d), Gan (132d), Han (16c,30b,185b), ian (85b, 96a,139d), kan (93a), lan (37b,37d,160b), man (29c,60c,64c, 65a,142d,161d), Nan (183c), pan (34a,61a,104a,175d), Pan (56a, 68a,68b,76b,120c,135b,161a,184a), ran (73d), Ran (7c,107d, 141a,163d), san (91c), San (24d), tan (23d,33c,46a,72d,90d), van (7b,59d,60a,63d,90c), wan (113a), Zan (186b)

A - O   Abo (25d), ado (22b,24d,35b,64c,78d,121d,156b,170a), ago (25a, 69d,114d,147a), ako (189), amo (79a,89c), ano (19d,20b,34d, 122d,174a), Apo (122b,177c), Aro (107a,111c), Aso (84c), azo (107c)

- AO   dao (117a), hao (189), iao (78a,96c,178d), Lao (80d,88c,146a, 161b), mao (115b), Mao (30b), sao (141b), Sao (113c), tao (10d, 131c,170b), Tao (117a), Yao (30a,c,104b)

AP -   apa (23a,177d), ape (36d,79d,100a,101d,146b), api (34a,76d), apo (122b), Apo (177c), apt (11d,23b,32b,58a,80b,92b,114d, 116d,124b,159a)

A - P   alp (24b,103d,115c), amp (49b,173b), asp (7b,32b,149a,174a, 176c)

- AP   bap (93b,132d), Bap (124d), cap (19d,39a,43a,53a,74d,160a, 167b 185c), dap (43b,c,46b,91b,147d), gap (11b,23a,29b,76c, 110d 128a), hap (17d,28d), Jap, lap (31b,37d,59b,127a,131d, 153d, 167d), map (27a,29b,54a,98d,160a), nap (65a,117d,146b, 148a), pap (59c), rap (90d,110a,147c,157c), sap (45d,52d,85c, 169b, 176d,179a), tap (55a,114d,153c), yap (16c,29b,122a)

AR -   ara (33a,114a,116a,118b,163d), Ara (8c,9b,36b,c,68d,69b,c,85a, 95a, 175b), arc (31b,39d,92a,126a,127c,142a), are (51a,88b, 98a,99b,110c,166c,175c), Ari (18d), ark (21a,29d,38a,58b,60d, 175d), arm (22d,60c,81b,92b,124b,161b), arn (8c,139a), Aro (107a, 111c), ars (13b,89a), Ars (112c), art (22d,38b,39c,43b, 56c,124a, 162c,181d), aru (80c,82b), Aru (82d)

A - R   aar (172d), Aar (131a), aer (8b,28d,34a.b,175a), Afr. (36c), air (11c,12c,42b,44c,53a,96b,98c,99d,125b,170c)

- AR   aar (172d), Aar (131a), bar (37c,39a,46a,52c,76d,78b,91a,124a,

137a,156a,157c,169c), **car** (16a,61d,93b,175a), **dar** (65c,111b,
169a), **ear** (14c,d,28c,63d,64a,73c,111b,116a,124b,137d,150d,
153c), **far** (44c), **gar** (57b,c,d,106b), **har** (139c), **jar** (31d,70d,
143b), **lar** (24c,51d,67a,78d,95d,101d,171b), **mar** (40b,44a,79a,
d,81a,140d), **Mar** (93d), **nar** (139d), **oar** (20b,124c,134b), **par**
(15a,51a,51b,c,69d,107c,135b,155a), **sar** (57d), **tar** (8c,68a,94d,
111c,118c,136a,c,176d), **war** (157c), **yar** (72a), **zar** (188)

AS -   **Asa** (6a,18c,71a,84d,86d,164c), **ase** (51a,139a), **Ase** (79b,115d),
ash (24d,33c,49c,73d,134b,168c,169a), **asi** (137a), **ask** (38b,82a,
126c),. **Aso** (84c), **asp** (7b,32b,149a,174a,176c), **ass** (17b,20c,
45b,c,59c,110c,112b,146d,157d)

A - S   **aes** (23c,89a,101c,132d,133a,b), **als** (66d, 163d), **Ans** (92a), **ars**
(13b,89a), **Ars** (112c), **ass** (17b,20c,45b,c,59c,110c,112b,146d,
157d), **aus** (66c), **Aus** (98b)

- AS   **bas** (62a,d,129d,134b), **das** (13b,15d,36d,66b,d,164a), **fas** (44d,
89d,129d), **gas** (10b,29b,59a,116d,161c), **has**, **kas** (32c,47a), **las**
(13b,151d), **mas** (34b,55b,119a), **nas** (74a,89c,178b), **pas** (40d,
156a), **ras** (6c,26b,48b,51d,53d,61c,75a,111c,123c,166b), **vas**
(46d,89d,119c,133b,175d), **was** (166c,175c), **Was** (24d)

AT -   **ata** (58d,97d,158d,160c,173d), **Ata** (79c,80d,94d,95d,100a,106b,
117a), **ate** (81a,108c,158c,174c), **Ate** (20c,68b,d,69a,b,116c,
186b), **atl** (106d,107a), **Ati** (45d,106b,113c,117a), **att** (146a)

A - T   **Abt** (35c), **act** (41d,55b,119c,155d), **aet** (89a,109d), **aft** (14a,15b,
17d,128b,167d), **ait** (82d,132a), **alt** (66c,76c,109c), **amt** (37d,
40d,108a,163c), **ant** (49d,60b,81b,118c), **apt** (11d,23b,32b,58a,
80b,92b,114d,116d,124b,159a), **art** (22d,38b,39c,43b,56c,124a,
162c,181d), **att** (146a), **aut** (34d,89d)

- AT   **bat** (39c,107c,156a,157c,182d), **cat** (10a,45b,55b,71d,161b,169d,
180d,183d), **eat** (37b,96b,135d,179b), **fat** (110a,124a), **gat** (28d,
72c,131a), **hat** (74d), **Hat** (183d), **Jat** (80d,125c), **kat** (105d), **lat**
(24a,33d,106b,118a), **mat** (46d,50d,94d,117c,161d), **Mat** (96a),
nat (7a,24c,24d,106a), **oat** (15a,28b,70b,144b), **pat** (11d,116d,
159a,161d,167c), **Pat** (96a), **rat** (16a,42d,73b,132c), **sat** (13d),
tat (48c,72d,87c), **Tat** (82a), **vat** (31b,36c,163a,170c), **wat** (73d,
140d,163a,180b), **xat** (167c), **zat** (148a)

AU -   **auh** (52c), **auk** (19b), **aum** (189), **aus** (66c), **Aus** (98b), **aut** (34d,
89d), **aux** (6d,61a)

A - U   **abu** (17a), **Abu** (15b,42a,55a,68a,c,147d), **acu** (34c), **ahu** (24c,
41d,65d,103d,120d), **aku** (57c,176a), **Anu** (15b,28a,68a,d,75b,
88c,147d), **aru** (80c,82b), **Aru** (82d), **ayu** (160c)

- AU   **eau** (63a,178c), **gau** (66d,67a), **mau** (170c,188), **pau** (130c),
Pau (48c,76a), **tau** (71b,91c,136c,161a), **vau** (91c), **Yau** (30c)

AV -   **ava** (78d,86a,116a,120d,139a,167b), **Ava** (24c), **ave** (54c,71d,
73a, 122a,134a,136d)

- AV   **gav** (72d), **lav** (72d), **tav** (91c)

AW -   **awa** (100a,139a), **awe** (81d,100a,130d,175b,182b), **awl** (145b,
167a), **awn** (12c,17b,140a)

- AW   **baw** (52c), **caw** (19b,d), **daw** (39a,70b,84a,1646d), **gaw** (140c),
haw (35a,52c,74d,91a,155a,162c), **jaw** (97d,138c), **law** (26b,33a,

226

40a,48c,60b,85d,91a,111b,134d,155d), **maw** (38b,d,72c,111a, 121a,142a,156c), **paw** (32d,59c,73c), **raw** (20c,39a,105d,173d), **saw** (7a,11b,40c,54c,97d,125a,137d,167a), **taw** (90d,91c,96c,d, 145b,161d), **waw** (12b,91c), **yaw** (43a,155d)

AX -   axe (30c,40c,167a)

A - X   Aex (46d), Aix (46d), aux (6d,61a)

- AX   lax (93d,130a), Max (96a), pax (89d,115b), sax (40c,148a,167a), tax (13a,14a,80a,91d), wax (28b,72a,80b,120c), zax (148a)

AY -   aya (77b,143c,166b), aye (7c,9b,55a,60a), ayu (160c)

A - Y   acy (34c), ady (188), aly (95d), amy (63c), Amy (8c,94b,183c), any (14b,150b)

- AY   bay (12d,16c,33c,73d,78b,81b,90a,128d), cay (82d,180b), day (153a), fay (32c,54b,154b), Fay (183c), gay, Gay (17d), hay (52c,55c,165d), jay (19b,91c), kay (82d), Kay (13b,134b), lay (16a,25c,80a,98b,107d,141d,150b), may (74d), May (183c), nay (42b,106b), pay (35b,128c,130a,d,177b), ray (38a,49a,57b,58b, 147b), Ray (96a), say (131c,174c,177a), way (37d,96b,134b, 164d)

AZ -   azo (107c)

A - Z   adz (40c,167a)

- AZ   gaz (188,190), Laz (27d)

BA -   baa (143d), Bab (15a), bac (31b,55c,174d), bad (55a,173a, 184d), bag (26c,139a,145b,159a), bah (52c), bal (9d,37b,61a,b), bam (29b), ban (81d,97a,124a), bap (93b,132d), Bap. (124d), bar (37c,39a,46a,52c,76d,78b,91a,124a,137a,156a,157c,169c), bas (62a,d,129d,134b), bat (39c,107c,156a,157c,182d), baw (52c), bay (12d,16c,33c,73d,78b,81b,90a,128d)

B - A   bass (143d), boa (36c,55b,106a,125d,138b,142d,149a)

- BA   aba (12a,25d,32b,33a,65b), iba (117a)

B - B   Bab (15a), bib, bob (57c,115d), Bob (96a), bub (22c)

- BB   abb (58b,178b,185), ebb (6a,15b,41c,43c,104a,128c,158a,178a)

B - C   bac (31b,55c,174d), BSC (42a)

- BC   ABC (134d)

B - D   bad (55a,173a,184d), bed (60c,148b), bid (35a,82a,109d,111b, 174c), bud (22c)

BE -   bed (60c,148b), bee (46b,81b,91c,108c), beg (38b,150a), bel (64a,93c,168d,173b,183d), Bel (15b,68a,126d), ben (78c,81b, 102c,115c), Ben (12d,77c,96a,106c,139d,140a), ber (85c), Bes (68b,119c), bet, bey (70b,170d)

B - E   bee (46b,81b,91c), bye (38c,141d)

- BE   Abe (71a,96a,123a), obe (31d,87d,150b), ube (185b)

B - G   bag (26c,139a,145b,159a), beg (38b,150a), big, bog (97a,160a), bug (24b,66b,81b)

B - H   bah (52c), boh (24c)

BI -   bib, bid (35a,82a,109d,111b,174c), big, Bim (16c), bin (22c, 59a,78a,128c,156d), bis (50a,90a,102c,130b,171c), bit (46a,86b, 114c,167a,b,171c,180d), biz

227

- BI   Abi (76c), obi (55d,67b,84c,137b,150d), ubi (90a,180d,185b)

B - K   Bok (9c)

B - L   bal (9d,37b,61a,61b), bel (64a,93c,168d,173b,183d), Bel (15b, 68a,126d), Bul (25d,102a)

B - M   bam (29b), Bim (16c), bum (21b)

B - N   ban (81d,97a,124a), ben (78c,81b,102c,115c,139d,140a), Ben (12d,77c,96a,106c), bin (22a,59a,78a,128c,156d), bon (30a,61d, 86b,88c), Bon (84b), bun (25b,73b)

BO -   boa (36c,55b,106a,125d,138b,142d,149a), bob (57c,115c), Bob (96a), bog (97a,160a), boh (24c), Bok (9c), bon (30a,61d,86b, 88c), Bon (84b), boo, Bor (120c), Bos (27c), bot (59a,88d), bow (11c,21b,39d,60a,107c,109a,125a,144d,158a),   box   (36a,128c, 145d, 152d), boy (142d,157c), Boz (43b,115d)

B - O   boo

- BO   Abo (25d), ebo (28b,110a), Ibo (107a,180a)

B - P   Bap. (124d), bap (93b,132d)

B - R   bar (37c,39a,46a,52c,76d,78b,91a,124a,137a,156a,157c,169c), ber (85c), Bor (120c), bur (123b)

BS -   BSC (42a)

B - S   bas (62a,d,129d,134b), Bes (68b,119c), bis (50a,90a,102c,130b, 171c), Bos (27c), bus (125b,168)

B - T   bat (39c,107c,156a,157c,182d), bet, bit (46a,86b,114c,167a,b, 171c,180d), bot (59a,88d), but (36a,52b,156b,173c)

- BT   Abt (35c)

BU -   bub (22c), bud (22c), bug (24b,66b,81b), Bul (25d,102a), bum (21b), bun (25b,73b), bur (123b), bus (125b,168b), but (36a, 52b,156b,173c), buy

- BU   abu (17a), Abu (15b,42a,55a,68a,c,147d)

B - W   baw (52c), bow (11c,21b,39d,60a,107c,109a,125a,144d,158a)

B - X   box (36a,c,128c,145d,152d)

BY -   bye (38c,141d)

B - Y   bay (12d,16c,33c,73d,78b,81b,90a,128c), bey (70b,170d), boy (142d,157c), buy

B - Z   biz, Box (43b,115d)

CA -   cab (75c), cad (22b,23b,75c,172c,173d), cag (81d,109d), cal (183c), Cal (123a), cam (48b,65d,95a,98b,134a,139b,148b,180c), can (24c,36c,123a,166a), cap (19d,39a,43a,53a,74d,160a,167b, 185c), car (16a,61d,93b,175a), cat (10a,45b,55b,71d,161b,169d, 180d), Cat (183d), caw (19b,d), cay (82d,180b)

C - A   cha (162b,c)

- CA   ECA (8a), oca (48c,112c,116d,133d,170c,184a), Uca (56a)

C - B   cab (75c), cob (28c,78b,95d,160b,177d), cub (92d,185d)

C - D   cad (22b,23b,75c,172c,173d), Cid (151c,d), cad (57b,c), cud (126c,135a)

CE -   cee (91c), cept (63a), ces (62b), cet (62d,180b)

C - E   cee (91c), che (145d), cie (61b,63b), cle (158d), coe (143d),

228

Coe (33c), cue (7a,27b,92c,117d,124b,132c,146c,159a)

- **CE** ace (7a,26c,52d,57a,77d,110c,114c,120b,147a,163a,173a), ice (30a,36d,42d,63d)

C - G cag (81d,109d), cig, cog (33a,65d,163b,167b,180c)

CH - cha (162b,c), che (145d), chi (91c), Chi (69c), cho (188)

- **CH** ach (8b,48a,52c,66b,80c), ich (66c), och (8b), tch (52c)

CI - Cid (151c,d), cie (61b,63b), cig, CIO (173a), cis (34c,122c), cit (81a,167d)

C - I chi (91c), Chi (69c)

- **CI** aci (29c), ici (61d), ici (9b), LCI (21b)

- **CK** ock (189), tck (52c)

CL - cle (158d)

C - L cal (183c), Cal (123a), col (103d,114c)

C - M cam (48b,65d,95a,98b,134a,139b,148b,180c), com (122d), cum (159b), cwm (31b,37b,103d)

C - N can (24c,36c,123a,166a), con (7d,29b,83c,116c,157d)

CO - cob (28c,78b,95d,160b,177d), cod (57b,c), coe (143d), Coe (33c), cog (33a,65d,163b,167b,180c), col (103d,114c), com (122d), con (7d,29b,83c,116c,157d), coo (19b), Coo (82d), cop (36a, 120c,126d,153c,155d), cor (36c,75b,155b), cos (91d,132d), cot (129b,148b), cow (22c,45b,81d), cox (156a), coy (16d), coz

C - O cho (188), CIO (173a), coo (19b), Coo (82d), cro (104c),115b, 180a)

C - P Cap (19d,39a,43a,53a,74d,160a,167b,185c), cep (63a), cop (36a, 120c,126d,153c,155d), cup (46b,69d,118b,170a), cyp (169d)

CR - cro (104c),115b,180a), cru (63a,176c), cry (25c,124a,145c,179d)

C - R car (16a,61d,93b,175a), cor (36c,75b,155b), cur (101d)

C - S ces (62b), cis (34c,122c), cos (91d,132d)

- **CS** ics (158d)

C - T cat (10a,45b,55b,71d,161b,169d,180d,183d), cet (62d,180b), cit (81a,167d), cot (148b), cut (30c,32b,145c)

- **CT** act (41d,55b,119c,155d), ect (35a,122d,183b), oct (34a,122c)

CU - cub (92d,185d), cud (126c,135a), cue (7a,27b,92c,117d,124b, 132c,146c,159a), cum (159b), cup (46b,69d,118b,170a), cur (101d), cut (30c,32b,145c)

C - U cru (63a,176c)

- **CU** acu (34c), ecu (58a,144b,c)

CW - cwm (31b,37b,103d)

C - W caw (19b,d), cow (22c,45b,81d)

C - X cox (156a)

CY - cyp (169d)

C - Y cay (82d,180b), coy (16d), cry (25c,124a,145c,179d)

- **CY** acy (34c), icy (65d)

C - Z coz

DA - dab (46a,57b,58b,d,114d,115c), dad, dae (139b), dag (11b,118c,

229

139c), **Dag** (108c), **dah** (24c,87a), **dak** (95c), **dal** (117d,153d), **dam** (30c,49c,55b,156d,180a), **dan** (24c,97c), **Dan** (18c,39c,77d, 83a,84a,141b), **dao** (117a), **dap** (43b,c,46b,91b,147d), **dar** (65c, 111b,169a), **das** (13b,15d,36d,66b,d,164a), **daw** (39a,70b,84a, 146d), **day** (153a)

D - A   **dea** (68d,89b), **dha** (99d), **dia** (122b,d,152a,165b), **dra** (188), **dua** (122d)

- DA   **Ada** (110a,112c,183c), **ida** (183d,183c), **oda** (74a,170d)

D - B   **dab** (46a,57b,58b,114d,115c), **deb, Deb** (183d), **dib** (21b,43b,c, 120d,140a), **dub** (25c,46a,c,87a,105b,121a,140a)

D - C   **dec** (122d), **doc** (143a), **duc** (61c)

DD -   **DDS** (42a)

D - D   **dad, did, dod** (11a,32a,43b,140c), **dud** (21c,54a)

- DD   **add** (10d,11d,14c,158a,167c), **odd** (46b,53a,109b,157a,172d, 173c)

DE -   **dea** (68d,89b), **deb, Deb** (183d), **dec** (122d), **dee** (91c), **Dee** (131d,139b), **deg** (154b), **dei** (68d), **den** (38b,44d,74b,130d,133c, 140d), **der** (13b,66b,d,164a), **des** (13b,61a,62b,d), **dev** (42a,b), **dew** (41a), **dey** (8d,84a,114c135a,139b,170d)

D - E   **dae** (139b), **dee** (91c), **Dee** (131d,139b), **die** (27b,54a,65a,155a, 167a), **doe** (41d,55b,127a), **due** (7b,115b,124c), **dye** (33c,154d)

- DE   **ade** (18c,149d), **Ade** (9c,53b), **Ede** (35b,65d), **ide** (40c,57a,b,d, 158b), **ode** (26b,79c,94d,118a,119d,120a,150b)

D - G   **dag** (11b,118c), **Dag** (108c,139c), **deg** (154b), **dig** (52b), **dog** (10b,45b,59b), **dug**

DH -   **dha** (99d), **dhu** (40b), **Dhu** (28a,87d)

D - H   **dah** (24c,87a), **doh** (113b)

- DH   **edh** (91c)

DI -   **dia** (122b,d,152a,165b), **dib** (21b,43b,c,120d,140a), **did, die** (27b,54a,65a,155a,167a) **dig** (52b), **dii** (68d), **dim** (47a,48b,54a, 74d,94d,109b), **din** (31c,130b,174a), **dip** (26a,79d,117c,138c), **dis** (122b,d), **Dis** (68b,73a,119d,172d,174b), **dit** (62b,d,120a,159d), **div** (42b,139b), **dix** (118b), **Dix** (60b)

D - I   **dei** (68d), **dii** (68d), **dui** (46d)

- DI   **Udi** (108a)

DJ -   **djo** (188)

D - K   **dak** (95c)

D - L   **dal** (117d,153d)

D - M   **dam** 30c,49c,55b,156d,180a), **dim** (47a,48b,54a,74d,94d,109b), **dom** (121c,166b,c), **Dom** (94b) **dum** (45c,67b,113a)

D - N   **dan** (24c,97c), **Dan** (18c,39c,77d,83a,84a,141b), **den** (38b,44d, 74b,130d,133c,140d), **din** (130b,174a), **don** (151d,166c), **Don** (96a), **dun** (19a,39d,46d,71a,97d,115b,160b)

DO -   **Doc** (143a), **dod** (11a,32a,43b,140c), **doe** (41d,55b,127a), **dog** (10b,45b,59b), **doh** (113b), **dom** (121c,166b,c), **Dom** (94b), **don** (151d,166c), **Don** (96a), **dop** (39c,43b), **dor** (17d,24b,32b,46b, 47a,81b,85d), **dos** (45d,61a,97a,181b),**dot** (45d,97a,104d,105a, 116b,153a,162d), **dow** (17d,87a,88d,175d)

D - O   dao (117a), djo (188), DSO (99d), duo (46d,113a,171d)

- DO   ado (22b,24d,35b,64c,121d,156b,170a), edo (162a), Edo (107a, 166d), Ido (13c,81d,88c,173c), Odo (181d), udo (28a,30c,48c, 84b,c,d,136c,149d)

D - P   dap (43b,c,46b,91b,147d), dip (26a,79d,117c,138c), dop (39c, 43b)

DR -   dra (188), dry (46d,85a,137c,164c)

D - R   dar (111b,169a), der (13b,66b,d,164a), dor (17d,24b,32b,46b, 47a,81b,85d), dur (95c)

DS -   DSO (99d)

D - S   das (13b,15d,36d,66b,d,164a), DDS (42a), des (13b,61a,62b,d), dis (122b,d), Dis (68b,73a,119d,172d,174b), dos (45d,61a,97a 181b)

- DS   DDS (42a), ods (109a)

D - T   dit (62b,d,120a,159d), dot (45d,97a,104d,105a,116b,153a,162d)

DU -   dua (122d), dub (25c,46a,c,87a,105b,121a,140a), duc (61c), dud (21c,54a), due (7b,115b,124c), dug (46d), dui (46d), dum (45c,67b, 113a), dun (19a,39d,46d,71a,97d,115b,160b), duo (46d,113a, 171d), dur (95c), dux (31d,64a,90c)

D - U   dhu (40b), Dhu (28a,87d)

D - V   dev (42a,b), div (42b,139b)

D - W   daw (39a,70b,84a), dew (41a), dow (17d,87a,88d,175d)

D - X   dix (118b), Dix (60b), dux (31d,64a,90c)

DY -   dye (33c,154d)

D - Y   day (153a), dey (8d,84a,114c,135a,189b,170a), dry (46d,85a, 137c,164c)

- DY   ady (188)

- DZ   adz (40c,167a)

EA -   eae (34b), ean (17d,23b,88a), ear (14c,d,28c,63d,64a,73c,111b, 116a,124b,137d,150d,153c), eat (37b,96b,135d,179b), eau (63a, 178c)

E - A   ECA (8a), ela (21c,53c,72b,76c,108b,174c), Ena (8c,126), era (8a,51a,116b,165d), ESA (8a), eta (71a,84c,91c), Eva (157a, 183c)

- EA   aea (26a,36d), dea (68d,89b), Hea (15b), kea (114a,b), lea (56a, 97d,114d,185b), Lea (22d), N.E.A. (162c), pea (32d,91b,142a, 175a), rea (9c,171a), sea (19a,52d,58c,112c,178d), tea (13d, 18c,79c,81a,145d,149c,159d), Wea (192), yea (7c,175c), zea (95c)

EB -   ebb (6a,15b,41c,43c,104a,128c,158a,178a), ebo (28b,110a)

E - B   ebb (6a,15b,41c,43c,104a,128c,158a,178a), elb (85c)

- EB   deb, Deb (183d), Geb (47d), Keb (47d), neb (17b,19a,d,115d), reb (35d,75c,85b,162c,166b), Seb (47d), web (50d,70a,98c,99a, 106c,149b)

EC -   ECA (8a), ect (35a,122d,183b), ecu (58a,144b,c)

E - C   etc (10b)

- EC   dec (122d), sec (46c,182c), tec (43a)

ED · Ede (35b,65d), edh (91c), edo (162a), Edo (107a,166d)

E · D Eed (102d), eld (10b,93c,110b,165d), end (8b,67d,120a,125d, 130a,166a), erd (47d,119d,145c)

· **ED** bed (60c,148b), Eed (102d), fed, ged (100a,140a), ked (140b, 144a), led, Ned (96a), ped (16d,34b), red (33c,38d,59a,127b, 134c,135b), Red (151b), sed (89a), ted (74d,138b,154b), Ted (96b), wed (97a,173c), zed (91c)

EE · Eed (102d), eel (36a,49c,57a,b,88a,102c,176c), een (52a,139c, 185d), eer (9b,52a), ees (139c)

E · E eae (34b), Ede (35b,65d), eke (14c,117c), ele (48c), eme (38d, 70a,140c,172b), ene (35b,158b,c), ere (17d,150c), ese (35b, 158c), ete (36c,62d,141c,159b), eve (47a,131a,143a,165d,171c), Eve (183c), ewe (88a,143d), Exe (43a), eye (93d,111b,140d)

· **EE** bee (46b,81b,91c,108c), cee (91c), dee (91c), Dee (131d,139b), fee (29a,58a,70d,166a,d), gee (35a,91c,100a,131c,139c,162c), lee (74b,144b), Lee (9c,31c,96a), mee (169a), nee (19d,22b,25c, 60b,95c), pee (91c), ree (12c,50a,80c,134d,137a,140b,144a, 146b), Ree (25a), see (20a,43c,44a,51c,53c,93d,109b,113c,116a, 176d,178c,183b), tee (39d,52b,69d,91c,112d,115d,118b,172a), vee (58a,91c,106a), wee (52c,100a,148c), zee (81b,91c)

EF · eft (93b,107a,136c,169d)

E · F elf (54b,154b)

· **EF** AEF (184d), kef (12a,46c,75d,88c), nef (32b,144c,d), ref

EG · egg (32d,80b,81c,112c,174a), ego (51a,79a,142b)

E · G egg (32d,80b,81c,112c,174a), eng (48a,146a), erg (50b,173b), 184c)

· **EG** beg (38b,150a), deg (154b), Geg (8c), keg (27a,105b), leg (37d, 92b,141d,159d,169c), Meg (8c,183d), peg (38c,46b,54d,98a, 118a,184c), teg (45a,54b,171d)

E · H edh (91c), eth (91c,158d)

· **EH** Heh (191), reh (8d)

EI · ein (66b,c), Eir (69a,75a), eis (66c)

E · I Ell (18c,d,76c,96a,137a,185a), epi (56c,61c,d,111c,112d,122d, 133c,153c,167b,174a), eri (13d,21c,146c), Eri (18c)

· **EI** dei (68d), fei (16a,185b), hei (65a), lei (65b,74c), rei (89b,121c), Rei (18d), Vei (91d), Wei (30b,162b)

EK · eke (14c,117c)

E · K elk (22c,90d,178a)

· **EK** lek (65c)

EL · ela (21c,53c,72b,76c,108b,174c), elb (85c), eld (10b,93c,110b, 165d), ele (48c), elf (54b,154b), Ell (18c,d,76c,96a,137a,185a), elk (22c,90d,178a), ell (10d,24b,32c,98a), elm (168c), els (140a), elt (87a,117c,139d), Ely (27c,50b)

E · L eel (36a,49c,57a,b,88a,102c,176c), ell (10d,24b,32c,98a)

· **EL** bel (64a,93c,168d,173b,183d) Bel (15b,68a,126b), eel (36a,49c, 57a,b,88a,102c,176c), gel (32d,73d,150a), Hel (68d,93c,172d), mel (77d), pel (55c,160d), rel (49b,173b), sel (62c,140b), tel (34a,b,122c), zel (40c)

232

EM - eme (38d,70a,140c,172b), Ems (125a,151c), emu (19b,58c,111d)

E - M elm (168c)

· EM gem (104b), hem (22a,36a,48b,52c,155a), mem (91c), Sem (107c), Tem (143a,159b)

EN - Ena (8c,126b), end (8b,67d,120a,125d,130a,166a), ene (35b, 158b,c), eng (48a,146a), ens (17d,18a,51a,52d), ent (34d,158b,c)

E - N ean (17d,23b,88a), een (52a,139c,185d), ein (66b,c), eon (8a, 37b,51d,116b), ern (19c,d,47b,54b,141a)

· EN ben (78c,81b,102c,115c), Ben (12d,77c,96a,106c,139d,140a), den (38b,44d,74b,130d,133c,140d), een (52a,139c,185d), fen (21c, 97a,160a), gen (31d,76b), hen (19a,60c,114c,136c), ken (60b, 87c,122b,172d), men (38c,116a,117b,170a), Men (94d), pen (36a,50a,80d,118b,126d,160a,185c), sen (190), ten (19a,26c,41c, 42b), wen (40c,72a110a,170c,177b), yen (33b,42d,93c,174a), Zen (24a)

EO - eon (8a,37b,51d,116b), Eos (14d,41a,68d)

E - O ebo (28b,110a), edo (162a), Edo (107a,166d), ego (51a,79a, 142b), eso (34d,183b), ETO (184d), exo (122d)

· EO geo (34a,47d), Leo (36b,c,92d,186d), Meo (27b,80c), neo (34a,b, c,100d,106d,108c,122c,d,128c), Reo (26c)

EP - epi (56c,61c,d,111c,112d,122d,133c,153c,167b,174a)

E - P e.s.p. (147b)

· EP cep (63a), hep (52c), kep (139b), nep (27c,32d,56a,87c,184b), pep (50b,176b), rep (53b,d,131a,171c), yep, Zep

ER - era (8a,51a,116b,165d), erd (47d,119d,145c), ere (17c,150c), erg (50b,173b,184c), erl (13d,21c,146d), Erl (18c), ern (19c,d,47b, 54b,141a), err (21a,43a,67d,100c,d,147a,148b,157b,168b,178a), ers (20a,176a), ert (140c,174a), ery (155d,158c,d)

E - R ear (14c,d,28c,63d,64a,73c,111b,116a,124b,137d,150d,153c), eer (9b,52a), Eir (69a,75a), err (21a,43a,67d,100c,d,147a,148b,157b, 168b,178a), Eur. (36c)

· ER aer (8b,28d,34a,b,175a), ber (85c), der (13b,66b,d,164a), eer (9b, 52a), ger (8d,36d,75c,124d), her (124b,c), ier (50a,158c), Ker (71b,95d), Ler (23d,28a,b,64b,106c,141a), mer (62c,141a), ner (137c), o'er (6b,112a), per (25c,122d,165b,176a), ser (80d,83b, d,116c,152d,180a), ter (34d,122d,165a), xer (34a), zer (188)

ES - ESA (8a), ese (35b,158c), eso (34d,183b), esp (147b), ess (39d, 78a,91c,158c,184d), est (50a,61c,62a,79b,89c,158d,159c)

E - S ees (139c), eis (66c), els (140a), Ems (125a,151c), ens (17d,18a, 51a,52d), Eos (14d,41a,68d), ers (20a,176a), ess (39d,78a,91c, 158c,184d)

· ES aes (23c,89a,101c,132d,133a,b), Bes (68b,119c), ces (62b), des (13b,61a,62b,d), ees (139c), Ges (151b), les (13b,61a), mes (62b), nes (26b), oes (109a), pes (59d), res (80a,89d,91a,97c, 164c), ses (61d), yes (7c,55a)

ET - eta (71a,84c,91c), etc (10b), ete (36c,62d,141a,159b), eth (91c, 158d), ETO (184d)

E - T eat (37b,96b,135d,179b), ect (35a,122d,183b), eft (93b,107a, 136c,169d), eit (87a,117c,139d), ent (34d,158b,c), ert (140c, 174a), est (50a,62a,79b,89c,158d,159c)

233

· ET aet (89a,109d), bet, cet (62d,180b), get (44d,64b,109b,141d), jet (20b,35a,154c), ket (189), let (9a,76d,77c,116b,130a,158b,163a), met (28d), net (26c,32a,50d,53b,60d,99a,124a,142a,149b), pet (26d,37c,55a,59b,162d), ret (58b,95a,149c,155d), set (7b,11d, 13a,23c,32b,33c,37c,58a,73d,109b,118c, 121c, 142c,150a, 186a), Set (52b,68a,b,111d), vet (40d,46a,101a,124a,127c,149c), yet (18b,24d,64c,77c,80a,108c,156b,165b)

EU · Eur. (136c)

E · U eau (63a,178c), ecu (58a,144b,c), emu (19b,58c,111d)

· EU feu (55d,61c,88b), heu (8b,30c,52c), jeu (61d), leu (190), meu (153b), peu (62a), Reu (115d)

EV · Eva (157a,183c), eve (47a,131a,143a,165d,171c), Eve (183c)

· EV dev (42a,b), lev (33b), rev

EW · ewe (88a,143d)

· EW dew (41a), few, hew (40a), Jew, lew (190), Lew (96a), mew (25b,27b,50a,55b,72c,74d,101b,141b,153b), new (11a,63c,88d, 111c,128c), pew (30d,52c,57d,120b,141c), rew (75c,140c,176b), sew, yew (36a,52a,b,145d,168c,d)

EX · Exe (43a), exo (122d)

· EX Aex (46d), hex (18c), lex (90b), rex (86c,96a), sex, vex (7c,10d, 44c,82c)

EY · eye (93d,111b,140d)

E · Y Ely (27c,50b), ery (155d,158c,d)

· EY bey (70b,170d), dey (8d,84a,114c,135a,139b,170d), fey (49c), gey (140a), hey (25c,52c), key (14c,82d,88b,117c,118c,150b, 180c), ley (190), Ney (63b,97b,105d), rey (86c,152b), sey (120c), wey (173b)

· EZ fez (75a,162a), gez (188), nez (62b), tez (125c), yez

FA · fac (41c), fad (38b,108c,163a), fag (55a,166a), fan (43a,154b, 156b,182d), far (44c), fas (44d,89d,129d), fat (110a,124a), fay (32c,54b,154b), Fay (183c)

F · A Fha (8a), fra (23c,63c,101d,123b,129d)

· FA MFA (42a)

F · B fib (162a), fob (29b,59b,113b,178c), fub (29b,119d)

F · C fac (41c)

F · D fad (38b,108c,163a), fed, fid (16b,54d,118a,167b), fod (188)

FE · fed, fee (29a,58a,70d,166a,d), fei (16a,185b), fen (21c,97a, 160a), feu (55d,61c,88b), few, fey (49c), fez (75a,162a)

F · E fee (29a,58a,70d,166a,d), fie (52c,59d), foe (111a)

· FE ife (22c,75d)

· FF off (6b,15c,44c,76a)

F · G fag (55a,166a), fig, fog (109b), fug (129a)

FH · FHA (8a)

F · H foh (52c)

FI · fib (162a), fid (16b,54d,118a,167b), fie (52c,59d), fig. fin (86a), fir (16a,36a,52a,168c,d,169a), fit (7a,11d,51b,75a,114a,123a, 124c,126a,153a,157c,159a), fix (7b,10a,13a,14c,43a,c,141d,165c)

234

F - I   fel (16a,185b)

FL -   flo, flu, fly (58c,81b,163b,178d)

F - L   Ful (158b)

- FL   AFL (173a)

F - N   fan (43a,154b,156b,182d), fen (21c,97a,160a), fin (86a), Fon (40b), fun

FO -   fob (29b,59b,113b,178c), fod (188), foe (111a), fog (109b), foh (52c), Fon (40b), foo (42c), fop (38a,40d,46d), for (123d,163a, 166c), fot (188), fou (139a), fox 134a)

F - O   Flo, foo (42c), fro (15b)

- FO   Ufo (59a)

F - P   fop (38a,40d,46d)

FR -   fra (23c,63c,101d,123b,129d), fro (15b), fry (57d)

F - R   far (44c), fir (16a,36a,52a,168c,d,169a), for (123d,163a,166c), fur

- FR   Afr. (36c)

F - S   fas (44d,89d,129d)

F - T   fat (110a,124a), fit (7a,11d,51b,75a,114a,123a,124c,126a,153a, 157c,159a), fot (188), fut (188)

- FT   aft (14a,15b,17d,128b,167d), eft (93b,107a,136c,169d), oft (63c)

FU -   fub (29b,119d), fug (129a), Ful (158b), fun, fur, fut (188)

F - U   feu (55d,61c,88b), flu, fou (139a)

F - W   few

F - X   fix (7b,10a,13a,14c,43a,c,141d,165c), fox (134a)

F - Y   fay (32c,54b,154b), Fay (183c), fey (49c), fly (58c,81b,163b, 178d), fry (57d)

F - Z   fez (75a,162a)

GA -   gab (29b,78a,116c,122a,161c,183a), gad (58c,100a,127d,132b, 153c,154b,178a), Gad (84a,186d), gaf (12b), gag (146c,183a), gaj (190), gal, gam (76b,176d,180c), Gan (132d), gap (11b,23a, 29b,76c,110d,128a), gar (57b,c,106b), gas (10b,29b,59a,116d, 161c), gat (28d,72c,131a), gau (66d,67a), gav (72d), gaw (140c), gay, Gay (17d), gaz (188,190)

G - A   goa (65d,104b,126c), Goa (121c), gra (59b,94b,160c)

- GA   aga (35a,39a,48b,102d,103a,b,111c,166b,170d,171a)

G - B   gab (29b,78a,116c,122a,161c,183a), Geb (47d), gib (17b,38b, 95d,166d,179d), gob (97b,136c)

G - D   gad (58c,100a,b,127d,132b,153c,154b,178a), Gad (84a,286d), ged (140a), Ged (100a), gid (143d), god (42a), God (84d)

GE -   Geb (47d), Ged (100a,140a), gee (35a,91c,100a,131c,139c,162c), Geg (8c), gel (32d,73d,150a), gem (104b), gen (31d,76b), geo (34a,47d), ger (8d,36d,75c,124d), Ges (151b), get (44d,64b,109c, 141d), gey (140a), gez (188)

G - E   gee (35a,91c,100a,131c,139c,162c), gie (139c,140a), gue (176c)

- GE   age (51d,66a,92a,97c,98c,116b,141c)

G - F   gaf (12b)

G - G	gag (146c,183a), Geg (8c), gig (26d,28d,57c,105b,127a,144c, 153a,171d), gog (95b)
- GG	egg (32d,80b,81c,112c,174a)
GH -	ghi (24d)
- GH	ugh (52c)
GI -	gib (17b,38b,95d,166d,179d), gid (143d), gie (139c,140a), gig (26d,28d,57c,105b,127a,144c,153a,171d), gin (37c,92d,139a, 142a,149b), gip (29b,160c), git (101a)
G - I	ghi (24d), goi (107c), gri (75c,78b)
G - J	gaj (190)
G - L	gal, gel (32d,73d,150a), gul (134a)
G - M	gam (76b,176d,180c), gem (104b), gum (7b,53c,80b,130c,156b), gym (154a)
GN -	gnu (11a,181d)
G - N	gan (132d), gen (31d,76b), gin (37c,92d,139a,142a,149b), gon (188), gun (56d,131a,146a)
GO -	goa (65d,104b,126c), Goa (121c), gob (97b,136c), god (42a), God (84d), gog (95b), goi (107c), gon (188), goo (156b), Gor (81a), got, goy (107c), goz (190)
G - O	geo (34a,47d), goo (156b)
- GO	ago (25a,69d,114d,147a), ego (51a,79a,142b)
G - P	gap (11b,23a,29b,76c,110d,128a), gip (29b,160c), gup (70a), gyp (29b,42a,160c)
GR -	gra (59b,94b,160c), gri (75c,78b), grr (52b), gry (78b)
G - R	gar (57b,c,d,106b), ger (8d,36d,75c,124d), Gor (81a), grr (52c), gur (159a)
G - S	gas (10b,29b,59a,116d,161c), Ges (151b), Gus (96a)
G - T	gat (28d,72c,131a), get (44d,64b,109b,141d), git (101a), got, gut (114d,130a)
GU -	gue (176c), gul (134a), gum (7b,53c,80b,130c,156b), gun (56d, 131a,146a), gup (70a), gur (159a), Gus (96a), gut (114d,130a), guy (55b,131b,155d), Guy (96a), gux (188)
G - U	gau (66d,67a), gnu (11a,181d)
- GU	ngu (188)
G - V	gav (72d)
G - W	gaw (140c)
GY -	gym (154a), gyp (29b,42a,160c)
G - Y	gay, Gay (17d), gey (140a), goy (107c), gry (78b), guy (55b, 131b,155d), Guy (96a)
G - Z	gaz (188,190), gez (188), goz (190), guz (188)
HA -	had, hae (139c), hag (140a,183a), hah (52c), hai (55c), hak (46d), Hal (69d), ham (98a,144b), Ham (18d,107c), Han (16c, 30b,185b), hao (189), hap (17d,28d), har (139c), has, hat (74d), Hat (183d), haw (35a,52c,74d,91a,155a,162c), hay (52c,55c, 165d)
H - A	Hea (15b), hia (114b), hoa (39b)

- HA	aha (52c,55c,159c), cha (162b,c), dha (99c), FHA (8a), Kha (88d,106b), sha (110c,143d,144a,c,174c,181c)
H - B	hob (40c,56d,100c,124b,167a,180c), hub (28b,118b,180c)
H - C	hic (52c,90a,164c)
H - D	had, hid, hod (23b,32b,102d,141a)
HE -	Hea (15b), Heh (191), hei (65a), Hel (68d,93c,172d), hem (22a, 36a,48b,52c,155a), hen (19a,60c,114c,136c), hep (52c), her (124b,c), heu (8b,30c,52c), hew (40a), hex (39c), hey (25c,52c)
H - E	hae (139c), hie (79a,153b), hoe (39c), hue (33c,143b)
- HE	che (145d), rhe (59a), she (124b), She (73a), the (13b)
H - G	hag (140a,183a), hog (45b,117c,160c), hug (32c,49d)
H - H	hah (52c), Heh (191), Hoh (80d), hsh (79c), huh (52c)
HI -	hia (114b), hic (52c,90a,164c), hid; hie (79a,153b), him (124b), hin (189), hip (52c,54b,85b,133c,134a), hir (76a), his (124c), hit (32d,157c,158a)
H - I	hal (55c), hei (65a), hoi (52c,74b,185b), hui (14a,30b,56d,114c)
- HI	Ahi (32c,147c), chi (91c), Chi (69c), ghi (24d), ihi (57c,156b), phi (91c)
H - K	hak (46d)
H - L	Hal (69d), Hel (68d,93c,172d)
H - M	ham (98a,114b), Ham (18d,107c), hem (22a,36a,48b,52c,155a), him (124b), hum (24d,46b,150d)
- HM	ohm (49b,67a,173b)
H - N	Han (16c,30b,185b), hen (19a,60c,114c,136c), hin (189), Hun (16c,21d,174b)
HO -	hoa (39b), hob (40c,56d,100c,124b,167a,180c), hod (23b,32d, 102d,141a), hoe (39c), hog (45b,117c,160c), Hoh (80d), hoi (52c, 74b,185b), hop (40b), Hor (103d), hot (10c,176c), how, hoy (16c,52c)
H - O	hao (189)
- HO	cho (188), mho (49b,173b), oho (52c), Rho (71b,91c), sho (188), tho (52a), Tho (167a), who (129c)
H - P	hap (17d,28d), hep (52c), hip (52c,54b,85b,133c,134a), hop (40b), hup (35a), hyp
H - R	har (139c), her (124b,c), hir (76a), Hor (103d), Hur (91d)
- HR	ihr (66d)
HS -	hsh (79c)
H - S	has, his (124c)
H - T	hat (74d), Hat (183d), hit (32d,157c,158a), hot (10c,176c), hut (143c)
HU -	hub (28b,118b,180c), hue (33c,143b), hug (32c,49d), huh (52c), hui (14a,30b,56d,114c), hum (24d,46b,150d), Hun (16c,21d, 174b), hup (35a), Hur (91d), hut (143c)
H - U	heu (8b,30c,52c)
- HU	ahu (24c,41d,65d,103d,120d), dhu (40b), Dhu (28a,87d), phu (38c), Shu (30b,127a)

237

H - W	haw (35a,52c,74d,91a,155a,162c), hew (40a), how
H - X	hex (18c)
HY -	hyp
H - Y	hay (52c,55c,165d), hey (25c,52c), hoy (16c,52c)
- HY	shy (16d,99d,128c,160c,165d,175a), thy, why (52c)
IA -	ial (158b), ian (85b,96a,139d), iao (78a,96c,178d)
I - A	iba (117a), Ida (103d,183c), Ila (16b), ILA (173a), Ina (158c), Ina (183c), Ira (18c,d,41a,68c,82c,96a,164a,178a,c), Ita (51b, 71d,94d,95d,106b,117a), ITA (173a), iva (76a,97b,127d,185b), Iwa (63c), Iya (95b,108d,111c)
- IA	dia (122b,d,152a,165b), hia (114b), Lia (82b), mia (83c), pia (13b,22d,48a,120d), ria (38c,51d,81b,152a,b), Sia (80c), tia (151d), via (132a,133a,b,179a)
IB -	iba (117a), Ibo (107a,180b)
- IB	bib, dib (21b,43b,c,120d,140a), fib (162a), gib (17b,38b,95d, 166d,179d), jib (38b,136b,146a), mib (8d,96c), nib (17b,19d, 115d), rib (37c,85b,90c,98a,144d,159d,172a), sib (86b,129c, 139d,147b)
IC -	ice (30a,36d,42d,63d), ich (66c), ici (61d), ici (9b), ics (158d), icy (65d)
- IC	hic (52c,90a,164c), pic (188), sic (90a,165b,168b), tic (104d, 153a,171c,d)
ID -	Ida (103d,183c), ide (40c,57a,b,d,158b), Ido (13c,81d,88c,173d)
I - D	Ind (80c)
- ID	aid (14a,15b,64c,75d,158b), bid (35a,82a,109d,111b,174c), Cid (151c,d), did, fid (16b,54d,118a,167b), gid (143d), hid, kid (67d, 85b,90d,186a), lid (167b), mid (9d,28b,73b), nid (72a,106b,c, 116d), old (158c), rid (32a,44a,60d), Sid (96a)
IE -	ier (50a,158c)
I - E	ice (30a,36d,42d,63d), ide (40c,57a,b,d,158b), ife (22c,75d), ike (123a), ile (62a,63b,158c), ine (29c,158b,c), Ine (10c,137d,180b), ire (10c,30c,52b,64c,125a,130b,185a), ise (40d,158c,d), Ise (78a, 84c), ite (59b,81a,105d,130c,158b,c,d,161a), ive (158c)
- IE	cie (61b,63b), die (27b,54a,65a,155a,167a), fie (52c,59d), gie (139c,140a), hie (79a,153b), lie (53a,69d,162a), nie (53c), pie (42d,85d,95b,114d,171b,172a), rie (28c,70d,97d), sie (46c,66d, 139b,140b,146b), tie (10a,14c,38b,45d,51a,88d,109b,127c,138b, 170b), vie (36c,157c,170c)
IF -	ife (22c,75d)
- IF	Lif (107d), rif (188), Sif (164d), vif (62a), Zif (102a)
I - G	Ing (114b,d,148d,158c,d,175c), Ing (10c,115b)
- IG	big, cig, dig (52b), fig, gig (26d,28d,57c,105b,127a,144c,153a, 171d), jig (40b,d), mig (8d,96c,145b), Mig (118d), nig (33b,40a, 46a), pig (27a,45b,99a,151b,160c), rig (51b,112a), tig (46b), wig (73b), zig (84a)
IH -	ihi (57c,156b), ihr (66d)
I - H	ich (66c), ish (158b), Ith (10a,28a,82b,99d)

238

239

I - R   ier (50a,158c), ihr (66d), ior (50a,158c)

- IR   air (11c,12c,42b,44c,53a,96b,98c,99d,125b,170c), Eir (69a,75a), fir (16a,36a,52a,168c,d,169a), hir (76a), mir (29d,135c,d,166c, 176b), pir (103a,b,136c), sir (163b,166b), tir (61d,62c,87a,145b), vir (89c)

IS -   ise (40d,158c,d), Ise (78a,84c), -ish (158b), ism (45a,79b,161c), iso (34a,122c,d), ist (7b,34b,43a,59b,66c,158c,d)

I - S   ics (158d), ifs (62b,d,164b), ins (164d), INS (107a,182d), ios (74d), its (124c)

- IS   bis 50a,90a,102c,130b,171c), cis (34c,122c), dis (122b,d), Dis (68b,73a,119d,172d,174b), eis (66c), his (124c), lis (54b,58b, 60c,62a,92b), Lis (47a), mis (122b,c,d,185c), nis (23d,67d,68a, 87c), Nis (19d), ris (131d), sis (67b,129c), tis, vis (59d,89b,d, 90b,176b), wis (79d,164c)

IT -   ita (51b,71d,94d,95d,106b,117a), ITA (173a), ite (59b,81a,105d, 130c,158b,c,d,161a), Ite (130c), ith (10a,28a,82b,99d), ito (84a, c,186d), its (124c)

I - T   ist (7b,34b,43a,59b,66c,158c,d)

- IT   ait (82d,132a), bit (46a,86b,114c,167a,b,171c,180d), cit (81a, 167d), dit (62b,d,120a,159d), fit (7a,11d,51b,75a,114a,123a, 124c,126a,153a,157c,159a), git (101a), hit (32d,157c,158a), kit (112a,176c), Kit (96a,183d), lit, mit (56c,66d,183b), nit (48d), pit (52b,142a,164a,168a), rit (148c,140b,153d), sit (98c,116a, 121c,130c,142d), tit (19c,130d), uit (47a,111d,151a), wit (78d, 85b,177b)

I - U   imu (15d), I.O.U. (124b)

- IU   piu (102c), Tiu (7c,68c,147d,163d,166c,170c), Ziu (147d,163d)

IV -   iva (76a,97b,127b,185b), ive (158c), ivy (32b,38c,176b)

- IV   div (42b,139b), Liv (93b)

IW -   iwa (63c)

- IW   Tiw (68c,147d,163d)

- IX   Aix (46b), dix (118b), Dix (60b), fix (7b,10a,13a,14c,43a,c,141d, 165c), mix (156b), nix (23d,108c,178d), pix (31a,51d,175d), six (26c), vix (89d,138b)

IY -   iya (95b,108d,111c), iyo (7d,176b)

I - Y   icy (65d), ivy (32b,38c,176b)

- IZ   biz, viz (105b)

JA -   jab (120b,125c), jag (124d,148a), Jah (84d), jam (123a,156d, 165c), Jap, jar (31d,70d,143b), Jat (90d,125c), jaw (97d,138c), jay (19b,91c)

J - B   jab (120b,125c), jib (38b,136b,146a), Job (30d,184c), Job (96a)

JE -   jet (20b,35a,154c), jeu (61d), Jew

J - E   Joe (96a)

J - G   jag (124d,148a), jig (40b,d), jog (82c,85c,170a), jug (118c,123d)

J - H   Jah (84d)

JI -   jib (38b,136b,146a), jig (40b,d), Jim (96a), jin (42b,153c)

- JI   tji (189), uji (146d)

J - M   **jam** (123a,156d,165c), **Jim** (96a), **jum** (39c)

J - N   **jin** (42b,153c)

JO -   **job** (30d,184c), **Job** (96a), **Joe** (96a), **jog** (82c,85c,170a), **jot** (82a,114c,166c,180d), **jow** (188), **joy**

- JO   **djo** (188), **Ijo** (107a)

J - P   **Jap**

J - R   **jar** (31d,70d,143b), **Jur** (107b)

J - S   **jus** (61d,90b)

J - T   **Jat** (90d,125c), **jet** (20b,35a,154c), **jot** (82a,114c,166c,180d), **jut** (53a,124a)

JU -   **jug** (118c,123d), **jum** (39c), **Jur** (107b), **jus** (61d,90b), **jut** (53a,124a)

J - U   **jeu** (61d)

J - W   **jaw** (97d,138c), **Jew**, **jow** (188)

J - Y   **jay** (19b,91c), **joy**

KA -   **kab** (75c), **kae** (84a,104b), **kaf** (12b), **Kaf** (104a), **kai** (59c), **Kai** (14d,84c), **kan** (93a), **kas** (32c,47a), **kat** (105d), **kay** (82d), **Kay** (13b,134b)

K - A   **kea** (114a,b), **Kha** (88d,106b), **koa** (74c), **Kra** (11b,91b), **Kua** (95c)

- KA   **aka** (176b), **Aka** (13d,88b,c), **oka** (170c,184a,189)

K - B   **kab** (75c), **Keb** (47d), **kob** (11a)

K - D   **ked** (140b,144a), **kid** (67d,85b,90d,186a)

KE -   **kea** (114a,b), **Keb** (47d), **ked** (140b,144a), **kef** (12a,46c,75d,88c), **keg** (27a,105b), **ken** (60b,87c,122b,172d), **kep** (139b), **Ker** (71b, 95d), **ket** (189), **key** (14c,82d,88b,117c,118c,150b,180c)

K - E   **kae** (84a,140b)

- KE   **ake** (60a,107a), **eke** (14c,117c), **Ike** (123a), **oke** (189)

K - F   **kaf** (12b), **Kaf** (104a), **kef** (12a,46c,75d,88c)

K - G   **keg** (27a,105b)

KH -   **Kha** (88d,106b)

- KH   **akh** (153d)

KI -   **kid** (67d,85b,90d,186a), **kil** (82b), **Kim** (86d), **kin** (30b,81c, 129d), **Kin** (30b), **kip** (17c,72d,76c,189), **kit** (112a,176c), **Kit** (96a,183d)

K - I   **kai** (59c), **Kai** (14d,84c), **koi** (26d), **kri** (75c,96d), **Kri** (75c), **kui** (86a,88c,146a)

- KI   **ski** (149c)

K - L   **kil** (82b), **Kol** (18b), **kyl** (76d,79b)

K - M   **Kim** (86d)

K - N   **kan** (93a), **ken** (60b,87c,122b), **kin** (30b,81c), **Kin** (30b)

KO -   **koa** (74c), **kob** (11a), **koi** (26d), **Kol** (18b), **kop** (76d), **kor** (75c), **Kos** (77c,82d), **kou** (169a)

- KO   **ako** (189), **TKO** (22c)

K - P   **kep** (139b), **kip** (17c,72d,76c,189), **kop** (76d), **kup** (188)

KR - Kra (11b,91d), kri (75c,96d), Kru (91d)

K - R Ker (71b,95d), kor (75c)

K - S kas (32c,47a), Kos (77c,82d)

K - T kat (105d), ket (189), kit (112a,176c), Kit (96a,183d)

KU - Kua (95c), Kui (86a,88c,146a), kup (188)

K - U kou (169a), Kru (91d)

- KU aku (57c,176a)

KY - kyl (76d,79b)

K - Y kay (82d), Kay (13b,134b), key (14c,82d,88b,117c,118c,150b, 180c)

- KY sky (56d)

LA - lab, lac (53c,99d,130c,135b,174d), lad (22c,25b,55b,157c,186a), lag (93c,155d), Lai (24c,d,88c), lai (98b,161b), lak (38a), lam (51b,58b,93d,164d,178a), lan (37b,d,160b), Lao (80d,88c,146a, 161b), lap (31b,37d,59b,127a,131d,153d,167d), lar (24c,51d,67a, 78d,95d,101d,171b), las (13b,151d), lat (24a,33d,106b,118a), lav (72d), law (26b,33a,40a,48c,60b,85d,91a,111b,134d,155d), lax (93d,130a), lay (16a,25c,80a,98b,107d,141d,150b), Laz (27d)

L - A lea (56a,97d,114d,185b), Lea (22d), Lia (82b), loa (7d,53c,97d, 184d)

- LA ala (6d,13a,15c,61a,133d,182c,d), Ala. (151b), ela (21c,53c,72b, 76c,108b,174c), lla (16b), ILA (173a), ola (113b), ula (72c,158c)

L - B lab, LLB (42a), lob (15d,23b,94c,100b,163a,172d)

- LB alb (65b,176a), elb (85c), LLB (42a)

LC - LCI (21b)

L - C lac (53c,99d,130c,135b,174d)

L - D lad (22c,25b,55b,157c,186a), led, lid (167b), LLD (42a), lud (100a), Lud (23c,144b)

- LD eld (10b,93c,110b,165d), LLD (42a), old (8a,71a,77c,123c,175b)

LE - lea (56a,97d,114d,185b), Lea (22d), led, lee (74b,144b), Lee (9c, 31c,96a), leg (37d,92b,141d,159d,169c), lei (65b,74c), lek (65c), Leo (36b,c,92d,186d), Ler (23d,28a,b,64b,106c,141a), les (13b, 61a), let (9a,76d,77c,116b,130a,158b,163a), leu (190), lev (33b), lew (190), Lew (96a), lex (90b), ley (190)

L - E lee (74b,144b), Lee (9c,31c,96a), lie (53a,69d,162a), loe (139d), lue (146b), lye (8d,27d,93b)

- LE ale (17c,18c,50c,55d,92d,104c), cle (158d), ele (48c), ile (62a, 63b,158c), ole (24b,29b,113b,152a,158b,d), ule (23a,27d,134c, 158c,168d)

L - F Lif (107d), lof (188)

- LF Alf (96a), elf (54b,154b)

L - G lag (93c,155d), leg (37d,92b,141d,159d,169c), log (64a,128d), lug (27a,45d,47b,73c,136b), Lug (28b)

LI - Lia (82b), lid (167b), lie (53a,69d,162a), Lif (107d), lll (72d), lim (21a), lin (92c,140c,168c,178d), Lin (115d,186c), lip (48b,58b, 80a,131c), lis (54b,58b,60c,62a,92b), Lis (47a), lit, Liv (93b)

242

L - I	**Iai** (98b,161b), **Lai** (24c,d,88c), **LCI** (21b), **lei** (65b,74c), **loi** (62a)
- LI	**Ali** (7b,12a,25c,48b,55a,60c,92d,101a,103a,164a,166a,170d), **Eli** (18c,d,76c,96a,137a,185a)
L - K	**Iak** (38a), **Iek** (65c), **Lok** (15d,68b)
- LK	**alk** (171b), **elk** (22c,90d,178a), **ilk** (31d,54c,86b,136d,139c,140b)
LL -	**LLB** (42a), **LLD** (42a)
L - L	**lil** (72d)
- LL	**all** (35c,118a,126d,181a), **ell** (10d,24b,32c,98a), **ill** (43d,121a, 173a,c,d), **Ull** (7c,68c,146b,164d)
L - M	**Iam** (51b,58b,93d,164d,178a), **lim** (21a), **lum** (30a)
- LM	**elm** (168c), **olm** (48c), **ulm** (49c), **Ulm** (40d)
L - N	**Ian** (37b,d,160b), **lin** (140c,168c,178a), **Lin** (115d,186c), **Lon** (86c,96a), **lyn** (140c,178d)
LO -	**loa** (7d,53c,97d,184d), **lob** (15d,23b,94c,100b,163a,172d), **loe** (139d), **lof** (188), **log** (64a,128d), **loi** (62a), **Lok** (15d,68b), **Lon** (86c,96a), **loo** (65a), **lop** (30c,40a,46b,143a), **los** (13b,151d), **lot** (24b,28d,55a,65d,114a,119c,143c,150d,168a), **Lot** (6b,73d), **Lou** (96a,183d), **low** (16c,149d), **loy** (121c,148b,151c,167a)
L - O	**Iao** (80d,88c,146a,161b), **Leo** (36b,c,92d,186d), **loo** (65a), **Luo** (107b), **Lwo** (107b)
- LO	**Flo**, **ILO** (184c), **ulo** (34b,80d)
L - P	**Iap** (31b,37d,59b,127a,131d,153d,167d), **lip** (48b,58b,80a,131c), **lop** (30c,40a,46b,143a)
- LP	**alp** (24b,103d,115c)
L - R	**Iar** (24c,51d,67a,78d,95d,101d,171b), **Ler** (23d,28a,28b,64b,106c, 141a), **Lur** (116c)
LS -	**Lst** (21a,b,88b)
L - S	**Ias** (13b,151d), **les** (13b,61a), **lis** (54b,58b,60c,62a,92b), **Lis** (47a), **los** (13b,151d), **lys** (58b,92b)
- LS	**als** (66d,163d), **els** (140a), **ils** (62b,d,164d)
L - T	**Iat** (24a,33d,106b,118a), **let** (9a,76d,77c,116b,130a,158b,163a), **lit**, **lot** (24b,28d,55a,65d,114a,119c,143c,150d,168a), **Lot** (6b, 73d), **Lst** (21a,b,88b), **lut** (189)
- LT	**alt** (66c,76c,109c), **elt** (87a,117c,139d), **Olt** (41a)
LU -	**lud** (100a), **Lud** (23c,144b), **lue** (146b), **lug** (27a,45d,47b,73c, 136b), **Lug** (28b), **lum** (30a), **Luo** (107b), **Lur** (116c), **lut** (189), **lux** (79d)
L - U	**leu** (190), **Lou** (96a,183d)
- LU	**flu**, **ulu** (87a)
L - V	**Iav** (72d), **lev** (33b), **Liv** (93b)
LW -	**Lwo** (107b)
L - W	**Iaw** (26b,33a,40a,48c,60b,85d,91a,111b,134d,155d), **lew** (190), **Lew** (96a), **low** (16c,149d)
L - X	**Iax** (93d,130a), **lex** (90b), **lux** (79d)
LY -	**lye** (8d,27d,93b), **lyn** (140c,178d), **lys** (58b,92b)
L - Y	**Iay** (98b,107d,141d,150b), **ley** (190), **loy** (121c,148b,151c,167a)

243

- **LY** aly (95d), Ely (27c,50b), fly (58c,81b,163b,178d), ply (59b,90b, 118d,164b,171c,174a,181b,184c), sly (13b,38b,64c,81b,132c)

L - Z Laz (27d)

MA - maa (97d,143d), Mab (54b,126b,183d), Mac (96a,140b,150b), mad (10c,82b), Mae (183c), mag (73b,95b,166c), Mag (183d), Mah (10b,57c,102b), mai (62a), mal (34a,b,44a,52b,62c,122b), Mal (94b), Mam (192), man (29c,60c,64c,65a,142d,161d), mao (115b), Mao (30b), map (27a,29b,54a,98d,160a), mar (40b,44a, 79a,d,81a,140d), Mar (93d), mas (34b,55b,119a), mat (46d,50d, 94d,117c,161d), Mat (96a), mau (170c,188), maw (38b,d,72c, 111a,121a,142a,156c), Max (96a), may (74d), May (183c)

M - A maa (97d,143d), MFA (42a), mia (83c), mna (71d,179d), moa (19b), Myra (31c)

- **MA** ama (26a,28d,31a,35b,39c,95b,108d,111c,117b,182c), oma (158c, d,170c), sma (140b,148d), Uma (43a,69b,153d)

M - B Mab (54b,126b,183d), mib (8d,96c), mob (39a,127a,165b)

M - C mac (96a,140b,150b)

M - D mad (10c,82b), mid (9d,28b,73b), Mod (138d), mud (6c)

ME - mee (169a), Meg (8c,183d), mel (77d), mem (91c), men (38c, 116a,117b,170a), Men (94d), Meo (27b,80c), mer (62c,141a), mes (62b), met (28d), meu (153b), mew (25b,27b,50a,55b,72c, 74d,101b,141b,153b)

M - E Mae (183c), mee (169a), Mme. (166b), Moe (96a)

- **ME** ame (37a,62d,131b), eme (38d,70a,140c,172b), Mme. (166b), ume (11d)

MF - MFA (42a)

M - G mag (73b,95b,166c), Mag (183d), Meg (8c,183d), mig (8d,96c, 145b), Mig (118d), mug (46b,54a,65a)

MH - mho (49b,173b)

M - H Mah (10b,57c,102b)

MI - mia (83c), mib (8d,96c), mid (9d,28b,73b), mig (8d,96c,145b), Mig (118d), mil (80b,110c,164d,182d), Mil (10a,82b), mim (12b), Min (29d,68b,113c), mio (152c), mir (29d,135c,d,166c,176b), mis (122b,c,d,185c), mit (56c,66d,183b), mix (156b)

M - I mai (62a), Moi (80d)

- **MI** ami (61d)

M - L mal (34a,b,44a,52b,62c,122b), Mal (94b), mel (77d), mil (80b, 110c,164d,182d), Mil (10a,82b), mol (58b,70c), mul (188)

MM - Mme. (166b)

M - M Mam (192), mem (91c), mim (12b), mom, mum (30d,95a,146c)

MN - mna (71d,179d)

M - N man (29c,60c,64c,65a,142d,161d), men (38c,116a,117b,170a), Men (94d), Min (29d,68b,113c), mon (15d,84b), Mon (24c), mun (157b)

MO - moa (19b), mob (39a,127a,165b), Mod (138d), Moe (96a), Moi (80d), mol (58b,70c), mom, mon (15d,84b), Mon (24c), moo (94b), mop (160a), mos (59b), mot (126d,130a,137d,183b), mow (32b,40a)

244

M - O   mao (115b), Mao (30b), Meo (27b,80c), mho (49b,173b), mio (152c), moo (94b), Mro (88c)

- MO   amo (79a,89c), omo (34d)

M - P   map (27a,29b,54a,98d,160a), mop (160a)

- MP   amp (49b,173b), imp (42b,127d,174a)

MR -   Mro (88c), Mrs. (166b), Mru (80d,88c)

M - R   mar (40b,44a,79a,d,81a,140d), Mar (93d), mer (62c,141a), mir (29d,135c,d,166c,176b), mur (63a,177d)

M - S   mas (34b,55b,119a), mes (62b), mis (122b,c,d,185c), mos (59b), Mrs. (166b), Mus (104a,132c)

- MS   Ems (125a,151c)

M - T   mat (46d,50d,94d,117c,161d), Mat (96a), met (28d), mit (56c, 66d,183b), mot (126d,130a,137d,183b), mut (39c), Mut (9b, 127a)

- MT   amt (37d,40d,108a,163c)

MU -   mud (6c), mug (46b,54a,65a), mul (188), mum (30d,95a,146c), mun (157b), mur (63a,177d), Mus (104a,132c), mut (39c), Mut (9b,127a), muy (152d,175d)

M - U   mau (170c,188), meu (153b), Mru (80d,88c)

- MU   emu (19b,58c,111d), imu (15d), SMU (40b), umu (112a)

M - W   maw (38b,d,72c,111a,121a,142a,156c), mew (25b,27b,50a,55b, 72c,74d,101b,141b,153b), mow (32b,40a)

M - X   Max (96a), mix (156b)

MY -   Mya (31c)

M - Y   may (74d), May (183c), muy (152d,175d)

- MY   amy (63c), Amy (8c,94b,183c)

NA -   nab (13b,26c,27b,142a), nae (139d), nag (73d,78b,138c,184d), nak (156b), Nan (183c), nap (65a,117d,146b,148a), nar (139d), nas (74a,89c,178b), nat (7a,24c,d,106a), nay (42b,106b)

N - A   NEA (162c), noa (35b,124a,161a), NRA (8a,20d)

- NA   ana (10b,33c,60d,93a,98c,122b,d,140d,142b), Ana (28a,68d, 100c), Ena (8c,126b), ina (158c), Ina (183c), mna (71d,179d), Ona (26b,64a), sna (105b,140b,143d,144a,149c,181c,d), Una (54a,153b,170c,183c)

N - B   nab (13b,26c,27b,142a), neb (17b,19a,d,115d), nib (17b,19d, 115d), nob (38c,74d,84a,149d), nub (67b,94d,95c,118c,124d)

N - D   Ned (96a), nid (72a,106c,116d), nod (17c,46c), Nod (18d,25b)

- ND   and (36a), end (8b,67d,120a,125d,130a,166a), ind (80c), und (66b)

NE -   N.E.A. (162c), neb (17b,19a,d,115d), Ned (96a), nee (19d,22b, 25c,60b,95c), nef (32b,144c,d), neo (34a,b,c,100d,106d,108c, 122c,d,128c), nep (27c,32d,56a,87c,184b), ner (137c), nes (26b), net (26c,32a,50d,53b,60d,99a,124a,142a,149b), new (11a,63c, 88d,111c,128c), Ney (63b,97b,105d), nez (62b)

N - E   nae (139d), nee (19d,22b,25c,60b,95c), nie (53c,66c), NNE (35b), nye (72a,116d), Nye (9c,18b)

245

- NE ane (61c,140a,158b), ene (35b,158b,c), ine (29c,158b,c), Ine (10c,137d,180b), NNE (35b), one (79a,b,80b,d,124b,147a,148d, 173a,c), une (13b,61a,62b,95c)

N - F nef (32b,144c,d)

NG - ngu (188)

N - G nag (73d,78b,138c,184d), nig (33b,40a,46a), nog (20c,46a,48d, 54d,100b,115d,118a)

- NG eng (48a,146a), ing (114b,d,148d,158c,d,175c), Ing (10c,115b)

N - H nth (42a)

NI - nib (17b,19d,115d), nid (72a,106c,116d), nie (53c,66c), nig (33b, 40a,46a), nil (108c), nim (96d,155d), nin (107d), nip (20c,29b, 45d,46a,b,115c,118a), nis (23d,67d,68a,87c), Nis (19d), nit (48d), nix (23d,108c,178d)

- NI ani (19b,d,20b,39b), ini (158d), oni (11b), uni (34c,118d,122c), Uni (51d)

N - K nak (156b)

- NK ink (20b,40c)

N - L nil (108c), nul (108c,177a)

N - M nim (96d,155d), nom (62b,125a), Nym (54c,76a)

NN - NNE (35b), NNW (35b)

N - N Nan (183c), nin (107d), non (34c,62b,89c,106b,122c,147a), nun (24c,91c,117d,147b), Nun (29a,85c)

- NN Ann (183c), inn (72b,73b,78c,150a,161c,162b,179a), Inn (41a)

NO - noa (35b,124a,161a), nob (38c,74d,84a,149d), nod (17c,46c, 148a), Nod (18d,25b), nog (20c,46a,48d,54d,100b,115d,118a), nom (62b,125a), non (34c,62b,89c,106b,122c,147a), noo (108c, 139d), nor (10b,36a,37b,92b), nos (62b,90a,179a), not (78b, 106b), now (60b,79d), Nox (69b)

N - O neo (34a,b,c,100d,106d,108c,122c,d,128c), noo (108c,139d)

- NO ano (19d,20b,34d,122d,174a), Ino (14b,25b), ono (34a), Ono (18d,118d), uno (83c,151d)

N - P nap (65a,117d,146b,148a), nep (27c,32d,56a,87c,184b), nip (20c,29b,45d,46a,b,115c,118a)

NR - NRA (8a,20d)

N - R nar (139d), ner (137c), nor (10b,36a,37b,92b), nur (67d)

N - S nas (74a,89c,178b), nes (26b), nis (23d,67d,87c), Nis (19d), nos (62b,90a,179a)

- NS Ans (92a), ens (17d,18a,51a,52d), ins (164d), INS (107a,182d), ons (38c), uns (66d,174c)

NT - nth (42a)

N - T nat (7a,24c,d,106a), net (26c,32a,50b,53d,60d,99a,124a,142a, 149b), nit (48d), not (78b,106b), nut (24c,32d,38b,54d,64a,65d, 86b,141c,165a), Nut (69a)

- NT ant (49d,60b,81b,118c), ent (34d,158b,c), TNT (53a)

NU - nub (67b,94d,95c,118c,124d), nul (108c,177a), nun (24c,91c, 117d, 147b), Nun (29a,85c,129d), nur (67d), nut (24c,32d,38b, 54d,64a,65d,86b,141c,165a), Nut (69a)

246

N - U	**ngu** (188)
- NU	**Anu** (15b,28a,68a,d,75b,88c,147d), **gnu** (11a,181d), **Unu** (24d)
N - W	**new** (11a,63c,88d,111c,128c), **NNW** (35b), **now** (60b,79d)
- NW	**NNW** (35b), **WNW** (35b)
N - X	**nix** (23d,108c,178d), **Nox** (69b), **Nyx** (69b)
NY -	**nye** (72a,116d), **Nye** (9c,18b), **Nym** (54c,76a), **Nyx** (69b)
N - Y	**nay** (42b,106b), **Ney** (63b,97b,105d)
- NY	**any** (14b,150b), **ony** (139a), **sny** (18a,39d,43d,87a,119a,144d, 145a,165d,176a)
N - Z	**nez** (62b)
OA -	**oaf** (22a,45b,146d,157d,185d), **oak** (73d,168c,169a), **oar** (20b, 124c,134b), **oat** (15a,28b,70b,144b)
O - A	**oca** (48c,112c,116c,133d,170c,184a), **oda** (74a,170d), **oka** (170c, 184a,189), **ola** (113b), **oma** (158c,d,170c), **Ona** (26b,64a), **OPA** (8a), **ora** (10c,40d,41b,45b,83a,c,101c,104a,122d,123d), **ova** (48d), **oxa** (29c)
- OA	**boa** (36c,55b,106a,125d,138b,142d,149a), **goa** (65d,104b,126c), **Goa** (121c), **hoa** (39b), **koa** (74c), **loa** (7d,53c,184d), **Loa** (97d), **moa** (19b), **noa** (35b,124a,161a), **poa** (20d,70d,97d), **roa** (23d, 87a), **toa** (17c,178b), **Zoa** (20b)
OB -	**obe** (31d,87d,150d), **obi** (55d,67b,84c,137b,150d)
O - B	**orb** (50a,53c,67d,153b)
- OB	**bob** (57c,115d), **Bob** (96a), **cob** (28c,78b,95d,160b,177d), **fob** (29b,59b,113b,178c), **gob** (97b,136c), **hob** (40c,56d,100c,124b, 167a,180c), **job** (30d,184c), **Job** (96a), **kob** (11a), **lob** (15d,23b, 94c,100b,163a,172d), **mob** (39a,127a,165b), **nob** (38c,74d,84a, 149d), **pob** (121b,129b,139c), **rob** (119d,155d), **Rob** (96a), **sob** (39b,179d)
OC -	**oca** (48c,112c,116c,133d,170c,184a), **och** (8b), **ock** (189), **oct** (34a,122c)
O - C	**orc** (28c,70c,180c)
- OC	**Doc** (143a), **roc** (19c,53b,54a,147a), **soc** (44c,85d)
OD -	**oda** (74a,170d), **odd** (46b,53a,109b,157a,172d,173c), **ode** (26b, 79c,94d,118a,119d,120a,150b), **Odo** (181d), **ods** (109a)
O - D	**odd** (46b,53a,109b,157a,172d,173c), **oid** (158c), **old** (8a,71a,77c, 123c,175b), **Ord** (25b,60b)
- OD	**cod** (57b,c), **dod** (11a,32a,43b,140c), **fod** (188), **god** (42a), **God** (84d), **hod** (23b,32d,102d,141a), **Mod** (138d), **nod** (17c,46c), **Nod** (18d,25b), **pod** (76b,78d,91b,141b,180c), **rod** (6a,72d,88b,131a, 154d,156a,160a), **sod** (160b,170d), **tod** (24d,60c,83d), **Vod** (16a)
OE -	**o'er** (6b,112a), **oes** (109a)
O - E	**obe** (31d,87d,150d), **ode** (26b,79c,94d,118a,119d,120a,150b), **oke** (189), **ole** (24b,29b,113b,152a,158b,d), **one** (79a,b,80d,124b, 147a,148d,173a,c) **ope** (172b,173c), **ore** (39a,99b,108a,115b, 141c,151a,160b), **ose** (102a,146d,158b,c,d,159a), **owe** (25b), **ote** (158d), **oye** (139c)
- OE	**coe** (143d), **Coe** (33c), **doe** (41d,55b,127a), **foe** (111a), **hoe** (39c), **Joe** (96a), **loe** (139d), **Moe** (96a), **poe** (114b), **Poe** (9c,d, 128a,172a), **roe** (27d,41d,48d,57b,76d,95b,157b), **soe** (170c, 184a), **toe** (43c,69d,148a,156a), **voe** (17a,81b), **woe** (25b), **Zoe** (36b,183c)

OF - off (6b,15c,44c,76a), oft (63c)

O - F oaf (22a,45b,146d,157d,185d), off (6b,15c,44c,76a), orf (57b, 185c), ouf (52c)

- OF lof (188)

- OG bog (97a,160a), cog (33a,65d,163b,167b,180c), dog (10b,45b, 59b), fog (109b), gog (95b), hog (45b,117c,160c), jog (82c,85c, 170a), log (64a,128d), nog (20c,46a,48d,54a,100b,115d,118a), sog (149c), tog (46a), vog (189)

OH - ohm (49b,67a,173b), oho (52c)

O - H och (8b)

- OH boh (24c), doh (113b), foh (52c), Hoh (80d), poh (52c), soh (52c,72d), zoh (13d,186b)

OI - oid (158c), oil (105c), oil (11a,71a)

O - I obi (55d,67b,84c,137b,150d), oii (105c), oni (11b), ori (34a), ovi (34a)

- OI goi (107c), hoi (52c,74b,185b), koi (26d), loi (62a), Moi (80d), pol (44a,59c,74c,117a,162a,164b), roi (55c,62a,133d), toi (62b, d,63a), Toi (18d), yoi (52c,79a)

OK - oka (170c,184a,189), oke (189)

O - K oak (73d,168c,169a), ock (189), ork (180b), ouk (140c)

- OK Bok (9c), Lok (15d,68b), Rok (87c), sok (188), yok (10c,185a)

OL - ola (113b), old (8a,71a,77c,123c,175b), ole (24b,29b,113b,152a, 158b,d), olm (48c), Olt (41a)

O - L oil (11a,71a), owl

- OL col (103d,114c), Kol (18b), mol (58b,70c), sol (108b), Sol (117b, 159b), tol (137b), vol (155a,182d)

OM - oma (158c,d,170c), omo (34d)

O - M ohm (49b,67a,173b), olm (48c)

- OM com (122d), dom (121c,166b,c), Dom (94b), mom, nom (62b, 125a), pom (45a,148d), rom (72d), tom (95d), Tom (96b,157a), yom (41a)

ON - Ona (26b,64a), one (79a,b,80b,d,124b,147a,148d,173a,c), oni (11b), ono (34a), Ono (18d,118d), ons (38c), ony (139a)

O - N own (6d)

- ON bon (30a,61d,86b,88c), Bon (84b), con (7d,29b,83c,116d,157d), don (151d,166c), Don (96a), eon (8a,37b,51d,116b), Fon (40b), gon (188), ion (11c,29a,49b,101b,114c,158c), Lon (86c,96a), mon (15d,84b), Mon (24c), non (34c,62b,89c,106b,122c,147a), ron (152c), Ron (86c,88a), son (42d,75d), ton (158d,167d,179d), von (66d,67a), won, yon (44c,112a,164d)

OO - oop (139a), oot (140a)

O - O Odo (181d), oho (52c), omo (34d), ono (34a), Ono (18d,118d), oro (34c,122c,152a), Oro (161b), oto (34a), Oto (147b)

- OO boo, coo (19b), Coo (82d), foo (42c), goo (156b), loo (65a), moo (94b), noo (108c,139d), roo (140a), soo (127d,140b,151b), Soo (137c), too (18b,102c), woo, zoo (181b)

OP - OPA (8a), ope (172b,173c), Ops (28c,69a,b,74a,137c), opt (30c)

248

O - P oop (139a), orp (140c,179d)

- OP cop (36a,120c,126d,153c,155d), dop (39c,43b), fop (38a,40d, 46d), hop (40b), kop (76d), lop (30c,40a,46b,143a), mop (160a), oop (139a), pop (52d,53a,130b,149d), sop (23b,35d,149c,155d), top (38c,52b,118b,123d,160a,174a,186b), wop

OR - ora (10c,40d,41b,45b,83a,c,101c,104a,122d,123d), orb (50a,53c, 67d,153b), orc (28c,70c,180c), Ord (25b,60b), ore (39a,99b, 108a,115b,141c,151a,160b), orf (57b,185c), ori (34a), ork (180b), oro (34c,122c,152a), Oro (161b), orp (140c,179d), orr (77c), ort (59b,90d,91a,102c,129b,140d,180a,184d), ory (36c)

O - R oar (20b,124c,134b), oer (6b,112a), orr (77c), our (124c)

- OR Bor (120c), cor (36c,75b,155b), dor (17d,24b,32b,46b,47a,81b, 85d), for (123d,163a,166c), Gor (81a), Hor (103d), ior (50a, 158c), kor (75c), nor (10b,36a,37b,92b), por (152a), tor (38b, 76d,85d,115c,124b,132b,c), Vor (69a)

OS - ose (102a,146d,158b,c,d,159a), ost (15d,86b)

O - S ods (109a), oes (109a), ons (38c), Ops (28c,69a,b,74a,137c), ous (158b)

- OS Bos (27c), cos (91d,132d), dos (45d,61a,97a,181b), Eos (14d, 41a,68d), ios (74d), Kos (77c,82d), los (13b,151d), mos (59b), nos (62b,90a,179a), ros (37b), Ros (138a,174d), SOS

OT - ote (158d), oto (34a), Oto (147b)

O - T oat (15a,28b,70b,144b), oct (34a,122c), oft (63c), Olt (41a), oot (140a), opt (30c), ort (59b,90d,91a,102c,129b,140d,180a,184d), ost (15d,86b), out (6b,14b,60b,69d,80a,108b,185c)

- OT bot (59a,88d), cot (129b,148b), dot (45d,97a,104d,105a,116b, 153a,162d), fot (188), got (188), hot (10c,176c), Jot (82a,114c,166c, 180d), lot (24b,28d,55a,65d,114a,119c,143c,150d,168a), Lot (6b, 73d), mot (126d,130a,137d,183b), not (78b,106b), oot (140a), pot (120b,145d,154d,175d), rot (22b,134c,143c,153d), sot (46c, 167b,c), tot (186a), Vot (56d)

OU - ouf (52c), ouk (140c), our (124c), ous (158b), out (6b,14b,60b, 69d,80a,108b,185c)

- OU fou (139a), IOU (124b), kou (169a), Lou (96a,183d), sou (63b), you

OV - ova (48d), ovi (34a)

OW - owe, owl, own (6d)

- OW bow (11c,21b,39d,60a,107c,109a,125a,144d,158a), cow (22c,45b, 81d), dow (17d,87a,88d,175d), how, Jow (188), low (16c,149d), mow (32b,40a), now (60b,79d), pow (188), row (44c,56b,92c,109a, 126b,127d,165c), sow (45b,117c,119a,138b,160c), tow (45d,58b, 75d,125b), vow (119c,150a), wow (52c,158a), yow (52c)

OX - oxa (29c)

- OX box (36a,c,128c,145d,152d), cox (156a), fox (134a), Nox (69b), pox (44a), vox (90a, 177a)

OY - oye (139c)

O - Y ony (139a), ory (36c)

- OY boy (142d,157c), coy (16d), goy (107c), hoy (16c,52c), Joy (169d), joy, loy (121c,148b,151c,167a), Roy, soy (17b,137c,74d), toy (169d)

249

- OZ   Boz (43b,115d), coz, goz (190)

PA -   pab (139c), pac (73b,94c,100d), pad (39d,59c,76c,157d,161a, 168b), pah (52c,60b,106d), pal (35b,38d), pam (26c,65a,87a, 105b), pan (34a,61a,104a,175d), Pan (56a,68a,b,76b,120c,135b, 161a,184a), pap (59c), par (15a,51a,b,c,69d,107c,135b,155a), pas (40d,156a), pat (11d,116d,159a,161d,167c), Pat (96a), Pau (48c,76a,130c), paw (32d,59c,73c), pax (89d,115b), pay (35b, 128c,130a,d,177b)

P - A   pea (32d,91b,142a,175a), pia (13b,22d,48a,120d), poa (20d,70d, 97d), pta (6a), pua (74c,76a)

- PA   apa (23a,177d), OPA (8a), spa (75b,100b,130c,154b,178d)

P - B   pab (139c), pob (121b,129b,139c)

P - C   pac (73b,94c,100d), pic (188)

P - D   pad (39d,59c,76c,157d,161a,168b), ped (16d,34b), pod (76b, 78d,91b,141b,180c), pud (59d,73c,115a)

PE -   pea (32d,91b,142a,175a), ped (16d,34b), pee (91c), peg (38c, 46b,54d,98a,118a,184c), pel (55c,160d), pen (36a,50a,80d,118b, 126d,160a,185c), pep (50b,176b), per (25c,122d,165b,176a), pes (59d), pet (26d,37c,55a,59b,162d), peu (62a), pew (30d, 52c,57d,120b,141c)

P - E   pee (91c), pie (42d,85d,95b,114d,171b,172a), poe (114b), Poe (9c,d,128a,172a), pre (17d,122b,c), pue (52c), Pye (50d,55a)

- PE   ape (36d,79d,100a,101d,146d), ope (172b,173c)

P - G   peg (38c,46b,54d,98a,118a,184c), pig (27a,45b,99a,151b,160c), pug (45a,101a,108a,148d)

PH -   phi (91c), phu (38c)

P - H   pah (52c,60b,106d), poh (52c)

PI -   pia (13b,22d,48a,120d), pic (188), pie (42d,85d,95b,114d,117b, 172a), pig (27a,45b,99a,151b,160c), pik (188), pil (34b), pin (45d,54d,141d,147d), pip (11d,44a,121d,142a,154a), Pip (43b), pir (103a,b,136c), pit (52b,142a,164a,168a), piu (102c), pix (31a,51d,175d)

P - I   phi (91c), poi (44a,59c,74c,117a,162a,164b), psi (91c)

- PI   api (34a,76d), epi (56c,61c,d,111c,112d,122d,133c,153c,167b, 174a), UPI (107a,182d)

P - K   pik (188)

PL -   ply (59b,90b,118d,164b,171c,174a,181b,184c)

P - L   pal (35b,38d), pel (55c,160d), pil (34b), pul (190), Pul (14a)

P - M   pam (26b,65a,87a,105b), pom (45a,148d)

P - N   pan (34a,61a,104a,175d), Pan (56a,68a,b,76b,120c,135b,161a, 184a), pen (36a,50a,80d,118b,126d,160a,185c), pin (45d,54d, 141d,147d), pun (119c)

PO -   poa (20d,70d,97d), pob (121b,129b,139c), pod (76b,78d,91b, 141b,180c), poe (114b), Poe (9c,d,128a,172a), poh (52c), poi (44a,59c,74c,117a,162a,164b), pom (45a,148d), pop (52d,53a, 130b,149d), por (152a), pot (120b,145b,154d,175d), pow, pox (44a)

P - O   pro (59d,126d), Pwo (88c)

250

- PO apo (122b), Apo (177c)

P - P pap (59c), pep (59b,176b), pip (11d,44a,121d,154a), Pip (43b), pop (52d,53a,130b,149d), pup (141b,148d,185d)

PR - pre (17d,122b,c), pro (59d,126d), pry (52b,91d,98b,123d)

P - R par (15a,51a,b,c,69d,107c,135b,155a), per (25c,122d,165b,176a), pir (103a,c,136c) por (152a), pur, pyr (92a,b,122c,173b)

PS - psi (91c), pst (25c,126d,146c)

P - S pas (40d,156a), pes (59d), pus

- PS Ops (28c,69a,b,74a,137c)

PT - Pta (6a)

P - T pat (11d,116d,159a,161d,167c), Pat (96a), pet (26d,37c,55a,59b, 162d), pit (52b,142a,164a,168a), pot (120b,145b,154d,175d), pst (25c,126d,146c), put (65a,69d,90b)

- PT apt (11d,23b,32b,58a,80b,92b,114d,116d,124b,159a), opt (30c)

PU - pua (74c,76a), pud (59d,73c,115a), pue (52c), pug (45a,101a, 108a,148d), pul (190), Pul (14a), pun (119c), pup (141b,148d, 185d), pur, pus, put (65a,69d,90b), puy (61d)

P - U Pau (48c,76a,130c), peu (62a), phu (38c), piu (102c)

PW - Pwo (88c)

P - W paw (32d,59c,73c), pew (30d,52c,57d,120b,141c), pow

P - X pax (89d,115b), pix (31a,51d,175d), pox (44a), pyx (31a,51d, 175d)

PY - Pye (50d,55a), pyr (92a,b,122c,173b), pyx (31a,51d,175d)

P - Y pay (35b,128c,130a,d,177b), ply (59b,90b,118d,164b,171c,174a, 181b,184c), pry (52b,91d,98b,123d), puy (61d)

- PY spy (44a,51c,52b,141d)

QA - Qaf (104a)

Q - A qua (13c,80a,89c,147a)

Q - E que (62d)

Q - F Qaf (104a)

Q - I qui (62d)

Q - O quo (188)

QU - qua (13c,80a,89c,147a), que (62d), qui (62d), quo (188)

RA - rab (17c,75c,85b,102d,162c,166b), Rab (45a), rad (50b,138d, 173b), rae (136b,138d,140b), Rae (183c), rag (59b,77c,100c, 133c,161a), rai (29b), raj (129c), ram (17a,45b,50b, 79c,112b,121d,143d,157d), Ram (36b), ran (73d), Ran (7c,107d, 141a,163d), rap (90d,110a,147c,157c), ras (6c,26b,48b,51d,53d, 61c,75a,111c,123c166b), rat (16a,42d,73b,132c), raw (20c,39a, 105d,173d), ray (38a,49a,57b,58b,147b), Ray (96a)

R - A rea (9c,171a), ria (38c,51d,81b,152a,b), roa (23d,87a), rua (118c), Rua (16b)

- RA ara (33a,114a,116a,118b,163d), Ara (9b,18c,36b,c,68d,69b,c,85a, 95a,175b), dra (188), era (8a,51a,116b,165d), fra (23c,63c,101d, 123b,129d), gra (59b,94b,160c), Ira (18c,d,41a,68c,82c,96a, 164a,178a,c), Kra (11b,91d), NRA (8a,20d), ora (10c,40d,41b, 45b,83a,c,101c,104a,122d,123d), tra (33b)

R - B   rab (17c,75c,85b,102d,162c,166b), Rab (45a), reb (35d,75c,85b, 162c,166b), rib (37c,85b,90c,98a,144d,159d,172a), rob (119d, 155d), Rob (96a), rub (6b,24d,28c,43c,120c,179b)

- RB   orb (50a,53c,67d,153b)

R - C   roc (19c,53b,54a,147a)

- RC   arc (31b,39d,92a,126a,127a,142a), orc (28c,70c,180b)

R - D   rad (50b,138d,173b), red (33c,38d,59a,127b,134c,135b), Red (151b), rid (32a,44a,60d), rod (6a,72d,88b,131a,154d,156a, 160a), rud (26d,57b)

- RD   erd (47d,119d,145c), Ord (25b,60b), urd (17b,184b), Urd (68d, 107d)

RE -   rea (9c,171a), reb (35d,75c,85b,162c,166b), red (33c,38d,59a, 127b,134c,135b), Red (151b), ree (12c,50a,80c,134d,137a,140b, 144a,146b), Ree (25a), ref, reh (8d), rei (89b,121c), Rei (18d), rel (49b,173b), Reo (26c), rep (53b,d,131a,171c), res (80a,89d, 91a,97c), ret (58b,95a,149c,155d), Reu (115d), rev, rew (75c, 140c,176b), rex (86c,96a), rey (86c,152b)

R - E   rae (136b,138b,140b), Rae (183c), ree (12c,50a,80c,134d,137a, 140b,144a,146b), Ree (25a), rhe (59a,173b), rie (28c,70d,97d), roe (27d,41c,48d,57b,76d,95b,157b), rue (76a,b,129c,150d,183a), rye (28b,70b,72d,92d)

- RE   are (51a,88b,98a,99b,110c,166c,175c), ere (17d,150c), Ire (10c, 52d,30c,64c,125a,130b,185a), ore (39a,99b,108a,115b,141c,151a, 160b), pre (17d,122b,c), tre (37b,83c,122d,165a,167d), ure (40a, 139d,155d,158b,d), Ure (138d,185d)

R - F   ref, rif (188)

- RF   orf (57b,185c)

R - G   rag (59b,77c,100c,133c,161a), rig (51b,112a), rug

- RG   erg (50b,173b,184c)

RH -   rhe (59a,173b), rho (71b,91c)

R - H   rah (29b), reh (8d)

RI -   ria (38c,51d,81b,152a,b), rib (37c85b,90c,98a,144d,159d,172a), rid (32a,44a,60d), rie (28c,70d,97d), rif (188), rig (51b,112a), rii (157b,175b), rim (22a,48b,96d,116b,124b,166a,180c), rin (33b, 142b), rio (33a,131d,132a,152c,157b), Rio (23a), rip (87b,130a, 162c), Rip (178b), ris (131d), rit (140b,148c,153d)

R - I   rai (188), rei (89b,121c), Rei (18d), rii (157b,175b), roi (55c, 62a,133d)

- RI   Ari (18d), eri (13d,21c,146d), Eri (18c), gri (75c,78b), Iri (18a,d, 75a), kri (75c,96d), ori (34a), sri (60c,77b,166c), Sri (17c), tri (122d,169d), Uri (162d)

R - J   raj (129c)

R - K   Rok (87c)

- RK   ark (21a,29d,38a,58b,60d,175d), irk (10d), ork (180b)

R - L   rel (49b,173b)

R - M   ram (17a,45b,50b,79c,112b,121d,143d,157d), Ram (36b), rim (22a,48b,96d,116b,124b,166a,180c), rom (72d), rum (8c,92d)

252

- RM   **arm** (22d,60c,81b,92b,124b,161b)

R - N   **ran** (73d), **Ran** (7c,107d,141a,163d), **rin** (33b,142b), **ron** (152c), **Ron** (86c,88a), **run** (10d,23c,58d,110d,148d,153b,154b,167d)

- RN   **arn** (8c,139a), **ern** (19c,d,47b,54b,141a), **urn** (36c,174d)

RO -   **roa** (23d,87a), **rob** (119d,155d), **Rob** (96a), **roc** (19c,53b,54a, 147a), **rod** (6a,72d,88b,131a,154d,156a,160a), **roe** (27d,41d,48d, 57b,76d,95b,157b), **rol** (55c,62a,133d), **Rok** (87c), **rom** (72d), **ron** (152c), **Ron** (86c,88a), **roo** (140a), **ros** (37b), **Ros** (138a, 174d), **rot** (22b,134c,143d,153d), **row** (44c,56b,92c,109a,126b, 165c), **Roy**

R - O   **Reo** (26c), **rho** (71b,91c), **rio** (33a,131d,132a,152c,157b), **Rio** (23a), **roo** (140a)

- RO   **Aro** (107a,111c), **cro** (104c,115b,180a), **fro** (15b), **Mro** (88c), **oro** (34c,122c,152a), **Oro** (161b), **pro** (59d,126d), **S.R.O.** (16a164a), **Uro** (192)

R - P   **rap** (90d,110a,147c,157c), **rep** (53b,d,131a,171c), **rip** (87b,130a, 162c), **Rip** (178b)

- RP   **orp** (140c,179d)

R - R   **rur** (132b)

- RR   **err** (21a,43a,67d,100c,d,147a,148b,157b,168b,178a), **grr** (52c), **orr** (77c)

R - S   **ras** (6c,26b,48b,51d,53d,61c,75a,111c,123c,166b), **res** (80a,89d, 91a,97c,164c), **ris** (131d), **ros** (37b), **Ros** (138a,174d), **rus** (89b), **Rus** (138a)

- RS   **ars** (13b,89a), **Ars** (112c), **ers** (20a,176a), **Mrs.** (166b)

R - T   **rat** (16a,42d,73b,132c), **ret** (58b,95a,149c,155d), **rit** (140b,148c, 153d), **rot** (22b,134c,143d,153d), **rut** (73a)

- RT   **art** (22d,38b,39c,43b,56c,124a,162c,181d), **ert** (140c,174a), **ort** (59b,90d,91a,102c,129b,140d,180a,184d)

RU -   **rua** (118c), **Rua** (16b), **rub** (6b,24d,28c,43c,120c,179b), **rud** (26d, 57b), **rue** (76a,b,129c,150d,183a), **rug**, **rum** (8c,92d), **run** (10d, 23c,58d,110d,148d,153b,154b,167d), **rur** (132b), **rus** (89b), **Rus** (138a), **rut** (73a), **rux** (154a,184d)

R - U   **Reu** (115d)

- RU   **aru** (80c,82b), **Aru** (82d), **cru** (63a,176c), **Kru** (91d), **Mru** (80d, 88c), **Uru** (192)

R - V   **rev**

R - W   **raw** (20c,39a,105d,173d), **rew** (75c,140c,176b), **row** (44c,56b, 92c,109a,126b,127d,165c)

R - X   **rex** (86c,96a), **rux** (154a,184d)

RY -   **rye** (28b,70b,72d,92d)

R - Y   **ray** (38a,49a,57b,58b,147b), **Ray** (96a), **rey** (86c,152b), **Roy**

- RY   **cry** (25c,124a,145c,179d), **dry** (46d,85a,137c,164c), **ery** (155d, 158c,d), **fry** (57d), **gry** (78b), **ory** (36c), **pry** (52b,91d,98b,123d), **try** (7c,10d,14c,50a,51c,130a), **wry** (13d)

SA -   **saa** (98a), **sac** (15d,121d), **Sac** (80c), **sad** (29c,42d,94c,98c,104a,

253

150d,173a), sae (140b,149c), sag (46b), sah (188), sai (101d), saj (48a,169a), sak (37c), Sak (88c), sal (29c,48a,136d,149d, 152d,169a,183a), Sal (183d), Sam (96a,162a), san (91c), San (24d), sao (141b), Sao (113c), sap (45d,52d,85c,169b,176d, 179a), sar (57d), sat (13d), saw (7a,11b,40c,54c,97d,125a,137d, 167a), sax (40c,148a,167a), say (131c,174a,177a)

S - A   saa (98a), sea (19a,52d,58c,112c,178d), sha (110c,143d,144a,c, 174c,181c), sia (80c), sma (140b,148d), sna (105b,140b,143d, 144a,149c,181c,d), spa (75b,100b,130c,154b,178d), sta (13c, 91b,104d,105a), sua (89d)

- SA   Asa (6a,18c,71a,84d,86d,164c), ESA (8a)

S - B   Seb (47d), sib (86b,129c,139d,147b), sob (39b,179d), sub (90a, 122d,172c)

S - C   sac (15d,121d), Sac (80c), sec (46c,182c), sic (90a,165b,168b), soc (44c,85d)

- SC   BSC (42a)

S - D   sad (29c,42c,94c,98c,104a,150d,173a), sed (89a), Sid (96a), sod (160b,170d), sud (59a)

SE -   sea (19a,52d,58c,112c,178d), Seb (47d), sec (46c,182c), sed (89a), see (20a,43c,44a,51c,53c,93d,109b,113c,116a,176d,178c, 183b), sel (62c,140b), Sem (107c), sen (190), ser (80d,83b,d, 116c,152d,180a), ses (61d), set (7b,11d,13a,23c,32b,33c,58a, 73d,109b,118c,121c,142c,150a,186a), Set (52b,68a,b,111d), sew, sex, sey (120c)

S - E   sae (140b,149c), see (20a,43c,44a,51c,53c,109b,113c,116a,176d, 178c,183b), she (124b), She (73a), sie (46c,66d,139b,140b, 146b), soe (170c,184a), SSE (35b), ste (62c,136c), sue (119c), Sue (63a,178a,183d), sye (40c,46c,139b,141a,167a)

- SE   ase (51a,139a), Ase (79b,115d), ese (35b,158c), Ise (40d,158c,d), lse (78a,84c), ose (102a,146d,158b,c,d,159a), SSE (35b), use (7b,47a,49d,64c,109b,168b,c,181b)

S - F   Sif (164d)

S - G   sag (46b), sog (149c)

SH -   sha (110c,143d,144a,c,174c,181c), she (124b), She (73a), sho (188), Shu (30b,127a), shy (16d,99d,128c,160c,165d,175a)

S - H   sah (188), soh (52c,72d)

- SH   ash (24d,33c,49c,73d,134b,168c,169a), hsh (79c), ish (158b), ush

SI -   Sia (80c), sib (86b,129c,139d,147b), sic (90a,165b,168b), Sid (96a), sie (46c,66d,139b,140b,146b), Sif (164d), sil (30c,185c,d), Sim (96b), sin (91c,140b,147a,168b,176a), Sin (102b), sip (46b, 79c,104a,162b), sir (87a,163b,166b), sis (67b,129c), sit (98c, 116a,121c,130c,142d), six (26c)

S - I   sai (101d), Sia (80c), ski (149c), sri (60c,77b,166c), Sri (17c), sui (30b)

- SI   asi (137a), psi (91c)

S - J   saj (48a,169a)

254

SK -   ski (149c), sky (56d)

S - K   sak (37c), Sak (88c), sok (188), Suk (107b)

- SK   ask (38b,82a,126c)

SL -   sly (13b,38b,64c,81b,132c)

S - L   sal (29c,48a,136d,149d,152d,169a,183a), Sal (183d), sel (62c, 140b), sil (30c,185c,d), sol (108b), Sol (117b,159b)

SM -   sma (140b,148d), SMU (40b)

S - M   Sam (96a,162a), sem (107c), Sim (96b), sum (8a,123a,167c)

- SM   ism (45a,79b,161c)

SN -   sna (105b,140b,143d,144a,149c,181c), sny (18a,39d,43d,87a, 119a,144d,145a,165d,176a)

S - N   san (91c) San (24d), sen (190), sin (91c,140b,147a,168b,176a), Sin (102b), son (42d,75d), sun (75d,111a,117b,155b), syn (122d, 183b)

SO -   sob (39b,179d), soc (44c,85d), sod (160b,170d), soe (170c,184a), sog (149c), soh (52c,72d), sok (188), sol (108b), Sol (117b, 159b), son (42d,75d), soo (127d,140b,151b), Soo (137c), sop (23b,35d,149c,155d), SOS, sot (46c,167b,c), sou (63b), sow (45b,117c,119a,138b,160c), soy (17b,137c,174d)

S - O   sao (141b), Sao (113c), sho (188), soo (127d,140b,151b), Soo (137c), S.R.O. (6a,164a)

- SO   Aso (84c), DSO (99d), eso (34d,183b), Iso (34a,122c,d)

SP -   spa (75b,100b,130c,154b,178d), spy (44a,51c,52b,141d)

S - P   sap (45d,52d,85c,169b,176d,179a), sip (46b,79d,104a,162b), sop (23b,35d,149c,155d), sup (46b,104a,162b)

- SP   asp (7b,32b,149a,174a,176c), e.s.p. (147b)

S - Q   suq (22a,97a)

SR -   sri (60c,77b,166c), Sri (17c), S.R.O. (6a,164a)

S - R   sar (57c), ser (80d,83b,d,116c,152d,180a), sir (87a,163b,166b), sur (34a,62b,d,104b,151a,152d,174a)

SS -   SSE (35b), ssu (189), SSW (35b)

S - S   ses (61d), sis (67b,129c), SOS, sus (117c), Sus (160c,181b)

- SS   ass (17b,20c,45b,c,59c,110c,112b,146d,157d), ess (39d,78a,91c, 158c,184d)

ST -   sta (13c,91b,104d,105a), ste (62c,136c), sty (50a,53c)

S - T   sat (13d), set (7b,11d,13a,23c,32b,33c,37c,58a,73d,109b,118c, 121c,142c,150a,186a), Set (52b,68a,b,111d), sit (98c,116a,121c, 130c,142d), sot (46c,167b,c)

- ST   est (50a,61c,62a,79b,89c,158d,159c), Ist (7b,34b,43a,59b,66c, 158b,c,d), LST (21a,88b), ost (15d,86b), pst (25c,126d,146c), tst (81d,126d)

SU -   sua (89d), sub (90a,122d,172c), sud (59a), sue (119c), Sue (63a, 178a,183d), Sui (30b), Suk (107b), sum (8a,123a,167c), sun (75d,111a,117b,155b), sup (46b,104a,162b), suq (22a,97a), sur (34a,62b,d,104b,151a,152d,174a), sus (117c), Sus (160c,181b)

S - U   Shu (30b,127a), SMU (40b), sou (63b), ssu (189)

- SU   ssu (189)

S - W saw (7a,11b,40c,54c,97d,125a,137d,167a), sew, sow (45b,117c, 119a,138b,160c), SSW (35b)

- SW SSW (35b), WSW (35b)

S - X sax (40c,148a,167a), sex, six (26c)

SY - sye (40c,46c,139b,141a,167a), syn (122d,183b)

S - Y say (131c,174c,177a), sey (120c), shy (16d,99d,128c,160c,165d, 175a), sky (56d), sly (13b,38b,64c,81b,132c), sny (18a,39d,43d, 87a, 119a,144d,145a, 165d,176a), soy (17b,137c,174d), spy (44a, 51c,52b,141d), sty (50a,53c)

TA - taa (112d), tab (29b,39c,58b,86a,128d,145a), tac (34d,130a), tad (22c,174a,186a), tae (138d,140c,166c,d), tag (45a,54c,65a, 87b,144a), tai (84b,111c,121b), Tai (80d), taj (75a,97d), tal (40c, 77a,113b), tam (74d), tan (23d,33c,46a,72d,90d), tao (10d,131c, 170b), Tao (117a), tap (55a,114d,153c), tar (8c,68a,94d,111c, 118c,136a,c,176d), tat (43b,48c,72d,87c), Tat (82a), tau (71b, 91c,136c,161a), tav (91c), taw (90d,91c,96c,d,145b,161a), tax (13a,14a,80a,91d)

T - A taa (112d), tea (13d,18c,79c,81a,145c,149c,159d), tia (151d), toa (17c,178b), tra (33b), tua (117a)

- TA ata (58d,97d,158d,160c,173d), Ata (79c,80d,94d,95d,100a,106b, 117a), eta (71a,84c,91c), Ita (51b,71d,94d,95d,106b,117a), ITA (173a), Pta (6a), sta (13c,91b,104d,105a), uta (53c,84d,93b, 147c,150b)

T - B tab (29b,39c,58b,86a,128d,145a), tub (21a,27a,36c,174d)

TC - tch (52c), tck (52c)

T - C tac (34d,130a), tec (43a), tic (104d,153a,171c,d)

- TC etc (10b)

T - D tad (174a,186a), ted (74d,138b,154b), Ted (96b), tod (24d,60c, 83d)

TE - tea (13d,18c,79c,81a,145d,149c,159d), tec (43a), ted (74d,138b, 154b), Ted (96b), tee (39d,52b,69d,91c,112d,115d,118b,172a), teg (45a,54b,143d,144a,171d), tel (34a,b,122c), Tem (143a, 159b), ten (19a,26c,41c,42b), ter (34d,122d,165a), tez (125c)

T - E tae (138d,140c,166c,d), tee (39d,52b,69d,91c,112d,115d,118b, 172a), the (13b), tie (10a,14c,38b,45d,51a,88d,109b,127c,138b, 170b), toe (43c,69d,148a,156a), tre (37b,83c,122d,165a,167d), tue (114b), tye (28c,134a)

- TE ate (81a,108c,158c,174c), Ate (20c,68b,d,69a,b,116c,186b), ete (36c,62d,141c,159b), Ite (59b,81a,105d,130c,158b,c,d,161a) ote (158d), ste (62c,136c), Ute (145c,180b)

T - G tag (45a,54c,65a,87b,144a), teg (45a,54b,143d,144a,171c), tig (46b), tog (46a), tug (45d,125b), tyg (46b)

TH - the (13b), tho (52a), Tho (167a), thy

T - H tch (52c)

- TH eth (91c,158d), ith (10a,28a,82b,99d), nth (42a)

TI - tia (151d), tic (104d,153a,171c,d), tie (10a,14c,38b,45d,51a,88d, 109b,127c,138b,170b), tig (46b), til (142d), Tim (43b), tin (36c, 99a,b,108b,155a,179c), tio (152d), tip (26b,d,50a,70d,77d,78a,

120a,165d), tir (61d,62c,145b), tis, tit (19c,130d), Tiu (7c,68c, 147d,163d,166c,170c), Tiw (68c,147d,163d)

T - I   tai (84b,111c,121b), Tai (80d), tji (189), toi (62b,d,63a), Toi (18d), tri (122d,169d), tui (47c,114b,117a), Twi (69c)

- TI   ati (106d,107a), Ati (45d,106b,113c,117a)

TJ -   tji (189)

T - J   taj (75a,97d)

TK -   TKO (22c)

T - K   tck (52c)

T - L   tai (40c,77a,113b), tei (34a,b,122c), til (142d), toi (137b)

T - M   tam (74d), Tem (143a,159b), Tim (43b), tom (95d), Tom (96b), 157a), tum (26d), Tum (143a,159b)

TN -   TNT (53a)

T - N   tan (23d,33c,46a,72d,90d), ten (19a,26c,41c,42b), tin (36c,99a,b, 108b,155a,179c), ton (158d,167d,179d), tun (23b,27a,182b)

TO -   toa (17c,178b), tod (24d,60c,83d), toe (43c,69d,148a,156a), tog (46a), toi (62b,d,63a), Toi (18d), tol (137b), tom (95d), Tom (96b,157a), ton (158d,167d,179d), too (18b,102c), top (38c,52b, 118b,123d,160a 174a,186b), tor (38b,76d,85d,115c,124b,132b,c), tot (186a), tow (45d,58b,75d,125b), toy (169d)

T - O   tao (10d,131c,170b), Tao (117a), tho (52a), Tho (167a), tio (152d), TKO (22c), too (18b,102c), two 26c,37d,80a,93a)

- TO   ETO (184d), Ito (84a,c,186d), oto (34a), Oto (147b)

T - P   tap (55a,114d,153c), tip (26b,d,50a,70d,77b,78a,120a,165d), top (38c,52b,118b,123d,160a174a,186b), tup (115a,117d,127d,143d)

TR -   tra (33b), tre (37b,83c,122d,165a,167d), tri (122d,169d), try (7c, 10d,14c,50a,51c,130a)

T - R   tar (8c,68a,94d,111c,118c,136a,c,176d), ter (34d,122c,165a), tir (61d,62c,145b), tor (38b,76d,85d,115c,124b,132b,c), tur (14d, 27c,68a,79b,117d,174c), tyr (7c,68c,147d,163d,170c,178a)

TS -   tst (81d,126d)

T - S   tis

- TS   its (124c)

T - T   tat (43b,48c,72d,87c), Tat (82a), tit (19c,130d), TNT (53a), tot (186a), tst (81d,126d), tut (52c)

- TT   att (146a)

TU -   tua (117a), tub (21a,27a,36c,174d), tue (114b), tug (45d,125b), tui (47c,114b,117a), tum (26d), Tum (143a,159b), tun (23b,27a, 182b), tup (115a,117d,127d,143d), tur (14d,27c,68a,79b,117d, 174c), tut (52c)

T - U   tau (71b,91c,136c,161a), Tiu (7c,68c,147d,163d,166c,170c)

- TU   utu (35b,137c), Utu (96c,107a,159b)

T - V   tav (91c)

TW -   Twi (69c), two (26c,37d,80a,93a)

T - W   taw (90d,91c,96c,d,145b,161d), Tiw (68c,147d,163d), tow (45d, 58b,75d,125b)

257

T - X   tax (13a,14a,80a,91d)

TY -   tye (28c,134a), tyg (46b), Tyr (7c,68c,109c,147d,163d,170c, 178a)

T - Y   thy, toy (169d), try (7c,10d,14c,50a,51c,130a)

- TY   sty (50a,53c)

T - Z   tez (125c)

U - A   Uca (56a), ula (72c,158c), Uma (43a,69b,153d), Una (54a,153b, 170c,183c), uta (53c,84d,93b,147c,150b), uva (64a,70c)

- UA   dua (122d), Kua (95c), pua (74c,76a), qua (13c,80a,89c,147a), rua (118c), Rua (16b), sua (89d), tua (117a)

UB -   ube (185b), ubi (90a,180d,185b)

- UB   bub (22c), cub (92d,185d), dub (25c,46a,c,87a,105b,121a,140a), fub (29b,119d), hub (28b,118b,180c), nub (67b,94d,95c,118c, 124d), rub (6b,24d,28c,43c,120c,179b), sub (90a,122d,172c), tub (21a,27a,36c,174d)

UC -   Uca (56a)

- UC   duc (61c)

UD -   Udi (108a), udo (28a,30c,48c,84b,c,d,136c,149d)

U - D   und (66b), urd (17b,184b), Urd (68d,107d)

- UD   bud (22c), cud (126c,135a), dud (21c,54a), lud (100a), Lud (23c, 144b), mud (6c), pud (59d,73c,115a), rud (26d,57b), sud (59a)

U - E   ube (185b), ule (23a,27d,134c,158c,168d), ume (11d), une (13b, 61a,62b,95c), ure (40a,139d,155d,158b,d), Ure (138d,185d), use (7b,47a,49d,64c,109b,168b,c,181b), Ute (145c,180b), uve (185b)

· UE   cue (7a,27b,92c,117d,124b,132c,146c,159a), due (7b,115b,124c), gue (176c), hue (33c,143b), lue (146b), pue (52c), que (62d), rue (76a,b,129c,150d,183a), sue (119c), Sue (63a,178a,183d), tue (114b)

UF -   ufo (59a)

· UF   ouf (52c)

UG -   ugh (52c)

· UG   bug (24b,66b,81b), dug, fug (129a), hug (32c,49d), jug (118c, 123d), lug (27a,45d,47b,73c,136b), Lug (28b), mug (46b,54a, 65a), pug (45a,101a,108a,148d), rug, tug (45d,125b), vug (28a, 66a)

U - H   ugh (52c), ush

· UH   auh (52c), huh (52c)

UI -   uit (47a,111d,151a)

U - I   ubi (90a,180d,185b), Udi (108a), uji (146d), uni (34c,118c,122c), Uni (51d), UPI (107a,182d), Uri (162d), uvi (185b)

· UI   dui (46d), hui (14a,30b,56d,114c), Kui (86a,88c,146a), qui (62d), Sui (30b), tui (47c,114b,117a)

UJ -   uji (146d)

· UK   auk (19b), ouk (140c), Suk (107b)

UL -   ula (72c,158c), ule (23a,27d,134c,158c,168d), Ull (7c,68c,146b, 164d), ulm (49c), Ulm (40d), ulo (34b,80d), ulu (87a)

U - L   Ull (7c,68c,146b,164d)

- UL   Bul (25d,102a), Ful (158b), gul (134a), mul (188), nul (108c, 177a), pul (190), Pul (14a)

UM -   Uma (43a,69b,153d), ume (11d), umu (112a)

U - M   ulm (49c), Ulm (40d)

- UM   aum (189), bum (21b), cum (159b), dum (45c,67b,113a), gum (7b,53c,80b,130c,156b), hum (24d,46b,150d), Jum (39c), lum (30a), mum (30d,95a,146c), rum (8c,92d), sum (8a,123a,167c), tum (26d), Tum (143a,159b)

UN -   Una (54a,153b,170c,183c), und (66b), une (13b,61a,62b,95c), uni (34c,118d,122c), Uni (51d), uno (83c,151d), uns (66d,174c), Unu (24d)

U - N   urn (36c,174d)

- UN   bun (25b,73b), dun (19a,39d,46d,71a,97d,115b,160b), fun, gun (56d,131a,146a), Hun (16c,21d,174b), mun (157b), nun (24c, 91c,117d,129d,147b), Nun (29a,85c), pun (119c), run (10d,23c, 58d,110d,148d,153b,154b,167d), sun (75d,111a,117b,155b), tun (23b,27a,182b), wun (24c), Yun (88d)

U - O   udo (28a,30c,48c,84b,c,d,136c,149d), ufo (59a), ulo (34b,80d), uno (83c,151d), Uro (192)

- UO   duo (46d,113a,171d), Luo (107b), quo (188)

UP -   UPI (107a,182d)

- UP   cup (46b,69d,118b,170a), gup (70a), hup (35a), kup (188), pup (141b,148d,185d), sup (46b,104a,162b), tup (115a,117d,127d, 143d)

- UQ   suq (22a,97a)

UR -   urd (17b,184b), Urd (68d,107d), ure (40a,139d,155d,158b,d), Ure (138d,185d), Uri (162d), urn (36c,174d), Uro (192), Uru (192)

- UR   bur (123b), cur (101d), dur (95c), Eur. (36c), fur, gur (159a), Hur (91d), Jur (107b), Lur (116c), mur (63a,177d), nur (67d), our (124c), pur, rur (132b), sur (34a,62b,d,104b,151a,152d, 174a), tur (14d,27c,68a,79b,117d,174c)

US -   use (7b,47a,49d,64c,109b,168b,c,181b), ush

U - S   uns (66d,174c)

- US   aus (66c), Aus (98b), bus (125b,168b), Gus (96a), jus (61d,90b); Mus (104a,132c), ous (158b), pus, rus (89b,138a), sus (117c), Sus (160c,181b)

UT -   uta (53a,84d,93b,147c,150b), Ute (145c,180b), utu (35b,137c), Utu (96c,107a,159b)

U - T   uit (47a,111d,151a)

- UT   aut (34d,89d), but (36a,52b,156b,173c), cut (30c,32b,145c), fut (188), gut (114d,130a), hut (143c), jut (53a,124a), lut (189), mut (39c), Mut (9b,127a), nut (24c,32d,38b,54d,64a,65d,86b, 141c,165a), Nut (69a), out (6b,14b,60b,69d,80a,108b,185c), put (65a,69d,90b), rut (73a), tut (52c)

U - U   ulu (87a), umu (112a), Unu (24d), Uru (192), utu (35b,137c), Utu (96c,107a,159b)

UV -   uva (64a,70c), uve (185b), uvi (185b)

259

- **UX**   **aux** (6d,61a), **dux** (31d,64a,90c), **lux** (79d), **rux** (154a,184d)
- **UY**   **buy, guy** (55b,131b,155d), **Guy** (96a), **muy** (152d,175d), **puy** (61d)
- **UZ**   **guz** (188)
VA -   **Vac** (153b), **vae** (176b), **vag** (174b,178a), **Vai** (91d), **van** (7b,59d, 60a,63d,90c), **vas** (46d,89d,119c,133b,175d), **vat** (31b,36c,163a, 170c), **vau** (91c)
V - A   **via** (132a,133a,b,179a)
- **VA**   **ava** (78d,86a,116a,120d,139a,167b), **Ava** (24c), **Eva** (157a,183c), **iva** (76a,97b,127b,185b), **ova** (48d), **uva** (64a,70c)
V - C   **Vac** (153b)
V - D   **Vod** (16a)
VE -   **vee** (58a,91c,106a), **Vei** (91d), **vet, vex** (7c,10d,44c,82c)
V - E   **vae** (176b), **vee** (58a,91c,106a), **vie** (36c,157c,170c), **voe** (17a, 81b)
- **VE**   **ave** (54c,71d,73a,122a,134a,136d), **eve** (47a,131a,143a,165d, 171c), **Eve** (183c), **ive** (158c), **uve** (185b)
V - F   **vif** (62a)
V - G   **vag** (174b,178a), **vog** (189), **vug** (28a,66a)
VI -   **via** (132a,133a,179a), **vie** (36c,157c,170c), **vim** (50b, 176b), **vin** (63a,182b), **vir** (89c), **vis** (59d,89b,d,90b,176b), **vix,** (89d,138b), **viz** (105b)
V - I   **Vai** (91d), **Vei** (91d)
- **VI**   **ovi** (34a), **uvi** (185b)
V - L   **vol** (155a,182d)
V - M   **vim** (50b,176b)
V - N   **van** (7b,59d,60a,63d,90c), **vin** (63a,182b), **von** (66d,67a)
VO -   **Vod** (16a), **voe** (17a,81b), **vog** (189), **vol** (155a,182d), **von** (66d, 67a), **Vor** (68d), **Vot** (56d), **vow** (119c,150a), **vox** (90a,177a)
V - R   **vir** (89c), **Vor** (68d)
V - S   **vas** (46d,89d,119c,133b,175d), **vis** (59d,89b,d,90b,176b)
V - T   **vat** (31b,36c,163a,170c), **vet, Vot** (56d)
VU -   **vug** (28a,66a)
V - U   **Vau** (91c)
V - W   **vow** (119c,150a)
V - X   **vex** (7c,10d,44c,82c), **vix** (89d,138b), **vox** (90a,177a)
V - Z   **viz** (105b)
- **VY**   **ivy** (32b,38c,176b)
WA -   **wad** (94d,97b,109c,112b,149d), **wag** (85b,104a,183a), **wah** (113c), **wan** (113a), **war** (157c), **was** (166c,175d), **Was** (24d), **wat** (73d, 140d,163a,180b), **waw** (12b,91c), **wax** (28b,72a,80b,120c), **way** (37d,96b,134b,164d)
W - A   **Wea** (192)
- **WA**   **awa** (100a,139a), **iwa** (63c)
W - B   **web** (50d,70a,98c,99a,106c,149b)

W - D **wad** (94d,97b,109c,112b,149d), **wed** (97a,173c)

WE - **Wea** (192), **web** (50d,70a,98c,99a,106c,149b), **wed** (97a,173c), **wee** (52c,100c,148c), **Wei** (30b,162b), **wen** (40c,72a,110a,170c, 177b), **wet** (40d,46a,101a,124a,127c,149c), **wey** (173b)

W - E **wee** (52c,100c,148c), **woe** (25b), **wye** (91c)

- WE **awe** (81d,100a,130d,175b,182b), **ewe** (88a,143d), **owe**

W - G **wag** (85b,104a,183a), **wig** (73b)

WH - **who** (129c), **why** (52c)

W - H **wah** (113c)

WI - **wig** (73b), **win** (7a,17b,64b,123b), **wis** (79d,164c), **wit** (78d,85b, 177b)

W - I **Wei** (30b,162b)

- WI **Twi** (69c)

- WL **awl** (145b,167a), **owl**

- WM **cwm** (31b,37b,103d)

WN - **WNW** (35b)

W - N **wan** (113a), **wen** (40c,72a,110a,170c,177b), **win** (7a,17b,64b, 123b, **won**, **wun** (24c), **wyn** (110a)

- WN **awn** (12c,17b,140a), **own** (6d)

WO - **woe** (25b), **won**, **woo**, **wop**, **wow** (52c, 158a)

W - O **who** (129c), **woo**

- WO **Lwo** (107b), **Pwo** (88c), **two** (26c,37d,80a,93a)

W - P **wop**

WR - **wry** (13d)

W - R **war** (157c)

WS - **WSW** (35b)

W - S **was** (166c,175c), **Was** (24d), **wis** (79d,164c)

W - T **wat** (73d,140d,163a,180b), **wet** (40d,46a,101a,124a,127c), **wit** (78d,85b,177b)

WU - **wun** (24c)

W - W **waw** (12b,91c), **WNW** (35b), **wow** (52c,158a), **WSW** (35b)

W - X **wax** (28b,72a,80b,120c)

WY - **wye** (91c), **wyn** (110a)

W - Y **way** (37d,96b,134b,164d), **wey** (173b), **why** (52c), **wry** (13d)

XA - **xat** (167c)

- XA **oxa** (29c)

XE - **xer** (34a)

- XE **axe** (30c,40c,167a), **Exe** (43a)

- XO **exo** (122d)

X - R **xer** (34a)

X - T **xat** (167c)

YA - **yah** (52c), **yak** (112c,161d,165b), **yam** (48c,121d,160b,170c), **Yao** (30a,c,104b), **yap** (16c,29b,122a), **yar** (72a), **Yau** (30c), **yaw** (43a,155d)

Y - A yea (7c,175c)

- YA aya (77b,166b), **Aya** (143c), **Iya** (95b,108d,111c), **Mya** (31c)

YE - yea (7c,175c), yen (33b,42d,93c,174a), yep, yes (7c,55a), yet (18b,24d,64c,77c,80a,108c,156b,165b), yew (36a,52a,b,145d, 168c,d), yez

- YE aye (7c,9b,55a,60a), bye (38c,141d), dye (33c,154d), eye (93d, 111b,140d), lye (8d,27d,93b), nye (72a,116d), **Nye** (9c,18b), oye. (139c), **Pye** (50d,55a), rye (28b,70b,72d), **sye** (40c,46c, 139b,141a,167a), tye (28c,134a), wye (91c)

- YG tyg (46b)

Y - H yah (52c)

YI - yin (140a), **Yin** (30b,143c,185b), yip (16c)

Y - I yol (52c,79a)

Y - K yak (112c,161d,165b), yok (10c,185a)

- YL kyl (76d,79b)

Y - M yam (48c,121d,160d,170c), yom (41a)

- YM gym (154a), **Nym** (54c,76a)

Y - N yen (33b,42d,93c,174a), yin (140a), **Yin** (30b,143c,185b), yon (44c,112a,164d), **Yun** (88d)

- YN lyn (140c,178d), syn (122d,183b), wyn (110a)

YO - yol (52c,79a), yok (10c,185a), yom (41a), yon (44c,112a,164d), you, yow (52c)

Y - O **Yao** (30a,c,104b)

- YO lyo (7d,176b)

Y - P yap (16c,29b,122a), yep, yip (16c)

- YP cyp (169d), gyp (29b,42a,160c), hyp

Y - R yar (72a)

- YR pyr (92a,b,122c,173b), **Tyr** (7c,68c,109c,147d,163d,170c,178a)

Y - S yes (7c,55a)

- YS lys (58b,92b)

Y - T yet (18b,24d,64c,77c,80a,108c,156b,165b)

YU - **Yun** (88d)

Y - U **Yau** (30c), you

- YU ayu (160c)

Y - W yaw (43a,155d), yew (36a,52a,b,145d,168c,d), yow (52c)

- YX **Nyx** (69b), pyx (31a,51d,75d)

Y - Z yez

ZA - zac (27c), zag (84a), zak (188), **Zal** (135d), **Zan** (186b), zar (188), zat (148a), zax (148a)

Z - A zea (95c), **Zoa** (20b)

Z - C zav (27c)

Z - D zed (91c)

ZE - zea (95c), zed (91c), zee (81b,91c), zel (40c), **Zen** (24a), **Zep**, zer (188)

Z - E   zee (81b,91c), Zoe (36b,183c)
Z - F   Zif (102a)
Z - G   zag (84a), zig (84a)
Z - H   zoh (13d,186b)
ZI -   Zif (102a), zig (84a), Zio (147d,163d), zip (24b,50b,176b), Ziu (147d,163d)
Z - K   zak (188)
Z - L   Zal (135d), zel (40c)
Z - N   Zan (186b), Zen (24a)
ZO -   zoa (20b), Zoe (36b,183c), zoh (13d,186b), zoo (181b)
Z - O   zio (147d,163d), zoo (181b)
- ZO   azo (107c)
Z - P   Zep, zip (24b,50b,176b)
Z - R   zar (188), zer (188)
Z - T   zat (148a)
Z - U   Ziu (147d,163d)
Z - X   zax (148a)

FOUR-LETTER WORDS

AA - -   Aalu (6b,48d), Aani (45a,48d), Aare, Aaru (6b,48d)
- AA -   baal (142b), baas (97c), caam (93d), Faam (111a), gaal (23b, 174d), Haab (97d), haaf (57d), haak (57b,178a), haar (139c), kaan (93d,116c), kaat (105d), laap (51d,91b,141d), maal (188), ma'am (95a,166b), maar (177a), Maas (132a), Maat (69a,b,85d), Naab, naam (44c), Naam (105b), paal (188), paar (28c,137a), raab (32d), raad (14a,49b,151a,165b), Raad (151a), raas (91b), Saad (12b), saah (188), saal (66c,73b), Saan (24d), Saar (63b, 102d,132a), Taal (7d,88c,151a), taar (12b), Waac, waag (71d, 101d)
- - AA   blaa (162b), chaa (162b), draa (188)
A - - A   Abba (20a,55a,161c), Abfa (76b), Abia (18d,137a), abra (26b), Abra, acca (53b,d), acta (41d,123d,128d,164c), adda (147d), Adda (68c,119d,157a,182a), aera (8a), Aeta (94d,100a,106b, 117a), Afra (183c), agha (35a,171a), agla (7a), agra (26d,34d), Agra (161b), agua (152d,166c,178c), Aida (110d,175c), Aira (70d), Akha (86a,c), akia (74c), Akka (125d), akra (176a), Akra (191), akua (120d), alba (98b,181a), Alba (151d), Alca (14c, 128b), alda (152b), Alda (110d,150c), Alea (14b,31c,167d), alfa (70d), alga (141b,c), alia (89d), alla (6d), alma (40d,53d,146d, 147a), Alma (38d,183c), alta (89c,152d), Alva (151d), Alya (155b,c), amba (161a), amia (22c,170d), amia (48a,161d,168c, 169a), amma (6a), amra (77c), anba (36d), anda (23a,168c), anna (190), Anna (110c,166d,183c), anoa (28a,60a,112c,181c), ansa (73c,93d,137c), anta (83d,117c,d,121a), Anta (164a), apia (121b), aqua (90a,178c), arba (135d,171a), arca (9a,22c,29d, 115a,130a), Arca (101b), area (37d,38a,44c,53a,93b,110d,127d, 138c,168a,186d), aria (8b,98c,150a,c,170c), arna (24a,181b),

263

Aroa (175b), arpa (83b), arra (47d,52c,82b), Arta (72b), Arya (80d), asea (39b,177c), Asha (191), Asia (48a), asta (188), Asta (107a,164c), Atka (11a), atma (150d), atta (58d,90c,97d,160c, 173d), Atta (94d,95d,100a,160b,117a), atua (120d), Auca (192), aula (66c,73b), aura (44c,49c,66a,96b,158a,170d,177c), Ausa, Azha (155b)

AB · · abas (61c), Abba (20a,55a,161c), abbe (32b,63b,123b), Abby (183d), ABC's (57a), abed (130c), Abel (7a,25b), abet (8b,15b, 50a,59b,75d,81c,141d,159d), Abfa (76b), Abia (18d,137a), Abib (102a,b), Abie (96b,107a), abir (129a), able (26b,35b,126a,147c), ably (147c), aboo (17a), Abot (100c), Abou (48b,55a), abox (22d), abra (26b), Abra, abri (61c,62c,144b), Absi (191), abut (22a,167c)

· AB · baba (108d,120c,166c,171a), babe, Babi (116c), babu (77a), baby (108d,120c), caba (184c), Faba, gabe (162a), gabi (162a), gaby (59c, 146d), haba (151d), habe (191), Maba (103a,168d), mabi (58d), nabk (30d,164d), nabo (117a), Nabu (68c,183d, Raba, rabi (38d, 74a), Rabi (14b,117b), saba (56a,117a), Saba (143d), sabe, tabi (84c,149d), tabu (59d,111d), Wabi (192)

· · AB Ahab (18c,26c,85b,86d,100d,116a,180b), Arab (30a,78b,c,106a, 107c,157c,160c,185d), blab (162b), brab (113b), chab (184a), crab (39b,144b,181b), doab (157c), drab (23d,29c,33d,46d,53b, d), duab (157c), frab (138c), grab (105b,142a,149b), Haab (97d), Joab (41a), knab (107a), Moab (18d,85a,86d,94a), Naab, raab (32d), scab (80b,107d,157c), slab (148b), snab (23c,139a), stab (14c,87a,117c), swab (102b)

A · · B Abib (102a,b), Adib (155b), Agib (12a,42d), Ahab (18c,26c,85b, 86d,100d,116a,180b), Arab (30a,78b,c,106a,107c,157b,160c, 185d)

AC · · acca (53b,d), Acer (96c), ache (79a,112d,185b), acht (66c), achy, acid (151a,162a), Acis (64b), acle (13d,82c,115d), acme (39c,115c,186b), acne (147c), acon (62c,140d), acor (6d), acre (39b,56a,88b), Acre, acta (41d,123d,128d,164c), acth (13b), acto (152b), Acts, actu (7a,89a), acus (89d,118a), acyl (6d)

· AC · Bach (35c), back (75d,76d,159d), Caca (67a), caco (73b), dace (57a,b), each, face (159d,176c), fact (7a,128b), hack (40a,77c, 184d), jaca (84a), jack (26c,58a,127c), Jack (96b), jacu (19a, 151b), lace (58b,179c), lack (178a), lact (34c), lacy, mace (49d, 108d,153b,154d,161a,178a), mack, nach, paca (132c,154a), pace (64b,98a,153b,156a,170b,177d), pack (24b,140d), paco (9b, 146d), pacs (94c), pact (8a), raca (19a,59c,130b,184d), race (116a,153b,154b,169c), rack (32c,64b), racy (153b), sack (43d, 118a,119d,182b), saco (189), tace (13a,155d), tack (28d,37d, 54d), tact (43c,d,116a), Vach (153b), Waco, Zach (96b)

· · AC utac (22d), Waac

A · · C aesc (12d,64d), alec (10a,57c,d,76c,137c), amic (9d), avec (63a, 183a)

AD · · adad (52c,56a), Adad (68c,157a,182a), Adah (25b,51b), Adam (26b,96a,111c), adan (102d), Adar (85c,102a), adat (90b,95d), adda (147d), Adda (68c,119d,157a,182a), Addu (68c,157a,182a), Addy (183d), aden (34b), Aden, Ader (18d), Ades (73a), Adib

264

(155b), **adit** (51a,100a,114d), **admi** (65d), **ador** (153b), **adry** (164c), **adze** (40c,167a)

- AD - **Badb** (82b), **bade, cade** (25c,27a,76c,85d,116d), **Cade** (50c), **cadi** (12a,103a,171a), **cady** (69d), **Dada** (13b,63a,157d), **dado** (41c,111c,115c,177d), **Eads** (23b,24b,50b,82a), **fade** (181d,183b), **fado** (121c), **fady, gade, hade** (66a,148c,173c), **hadj** (98b,118a), **jade** (33c,65d,71d,166a), **jadu** (95a), **jady, kada** (188), **kade** (144a), **kadi** (103a,171a), **Kadu** (91), **lade** (24c,26d,43c,93b, 100a,132a,139d,161b,178d), **Ladd** (143c), **lady, made, Madi** (174a), **mado** (14d,57a,170b), **padi** (131b), **rada** (135c,172a), **rade** (138d), **sadd** (33a,40b,58c,107b), **sade** (91d), **sadh** (77a), **sado** (26d,84d), **sadr** (94a), **Sadr** (155b), **vade** (42c,67d,89b), **wadd** (109c), **wade, wadi** (46c,106a,109a,128a,132a), **wady** (109a,128a,132a)

- - AD **adad** (52c,56a), **Adad** (68c,157a,182a), **arad** (13a,c,84a), **bead** (17a,122a,146b), **brad** (54d,67c,105b), **Chad** (158b), **ciad** (46a, 82a), **dead, diad** (113a), **duad** (113a,171d), **dyad** (113a), **ecad** (73a,119b), **egad** (100a,109a), **Fuad** (54d), **glad** (85c), **goad** (80b,154b), **grad** (28b), **head** (29d), **Ibad** (191), **Irad** (18d), **Joad** (50c), **lead** (35d,43d,72b,74d,81a), **load** (24c,26d,161b), **mead** (46a,78a,97d,99b), **Mead** (78a), **orad** (104a), **Phad** (155b), **quad** (33c,172a), **raad** (14a,49b,151a,165b), **read** (116d,157d), **road** (37d,164d), **Saad** (12b), **scad** (31a,57a,78b,88d,137c), **shad** (27d, 57a,b,c), **spad** (105b), **Spad** (118d), **stad** (151b,167d,176b), **swad** (94d), **toad** (10a,17a,63d,126d), **udad** (143d,144a,181c), **woad** (20d,47c)

A - - D **abed** (130c), **acid** (151a,162a), **adad** (52c,56a), **Adad** (68c,157a, 182a), **aged** (110a), **alod** (51c,55d,88a,124c), **amid** (9d,50a), **apod** (59d), **arad** (13a,c,84a), **arid** (46c,85a), **Arnd** (67a), **Arod** (86c), **avid** (47b,71a,186b)

AE - - **aera** (8a), **aeri** (34a), **aero** (8b,34a,b,58c,59a), **aery** (47b,51d, 106c), **aesc** (12d,64d), **Aeta** (94d,95d,100a,106b,117a)

- AE - **Caen, daer** (22b), **daez, faex** (46a), **Gaea** (47d,69a), **Gael** (28a, 96c,138d), **haec** (90a,164c), **haem** (122b), **Jael** (147b), **laet** (60d), **nael** (189), **saer** (163a), **tael** (91d,179d), **waeg** (19b,72c, 87a), **waer** (40b)

- - AE **alae** (182d), **blae** (93b), **brae** (76d,139a,c,140b,148c), **Irae** (43c), **koae** (74b), **quae** (176b), **spae** (139c)

A - - E **Aare, abbe** (32b,63b,123b), **Able** (96b,107a), **able** (26b,35b,126a, 147c), **ache** (79a,112d,185b), **acle** (13d,82c,115d), **acme** (39c, 115c,186b), **acne** (147c), **acre** (39b,56a,88b), **Acre, adze** (40c, 167a), **agee** (13d,15c,38d), **ague** (30a,55d,95c,137b), **aide** (7b, 14a,75d), **aile** (62b,63a,182c,d), **aine** (49b,62c,142c), **aire** (82c), **Aire, ajee** (15c,139a), **akee** (168c), **alae** (182d), **albe** (133a), **alee** (15c,75d,144b,157a,182a), **Alle** (14c), **alme** (40d,147a), **aloe** (7d,20a,76a,b,92b,98b,119b,158b,167a,183d), **amie** (61d), **ance** (158b,c,d), **Ande** (193), **ange** (61a), **Anne** (50c,84a,143b,183c), **ante** (87a,89a,115b,120b,122b,125d,154d), **a-one** (52b,167b), **apse** (9b,20a,31a,128c,130a,142b,175a), **arme** (63a,179b), **Arne** (35c,50c,134d), **asse** (25a,60d,74a), **atle** (136d,161d,169b), **Aude, auge** (123c,132b), **aune** (188), **axle** (153c,180c)

AF - - **afar** (44c), **Afar** (6c), **afer** (48a,182b), **affy** (18b), **Afra** (183c)

265

- AF - baff (69d), baft (14a,53b), cafe daff (125d), daft (59c), gaff (57c, d,152d,153a), haft (76d), Kafa (6c), raft (75b), raft (27b,33c,58c, 75b), safe (141d,157d,174d), Safi (191), Taft (29d), Wafd (49a), waft (20d,58c)

- - AF deaf, goaf (104b), Graf (37c,66b,67a,107c,186b), haaf (57d), heaf (144a), leaf (55c,73c,119b), loaf (79b,94b), neaf (58a,73c), Olaf (108a,176b), Plaf (63c), Wraf

A - - F alef (91c), alif (12b), arif (127d), atef (39a,48d), Azof (20b,135d)

AG - - Agag (18c,86c,137a), agal (17c,36d), Agao (6c,73c), agar (7d, 28c,39c,103c,141c), Agau (73c), Agaz (193), aged (110a), agee (13d,15c,38d), ager (47c,56a,89b,c,131d,133b), agha (35a,171a), Agib (12a,42d), agio (52c,60a,101c,123a), Agis (86d), agla (7a), agni (88a,89c), Agni (56d,68b), agog (47b,52c,86b), agon (12c, 36c,41b,55d,71b), agra (26d,34d), Agra (161b), agri (89b), agro (149d), agua (152d,166c,178c), ague (30a,55d,95c,137b)

- AG - baga (171b), bago (13d), cage (36a), cagy (178a), dagg (118c), dagh (76d), Dago, gage (28d,98a,119c,d), gagi (160b), hagg, hagi (84b), lago (54b,111d,143c), Jaga (191), jagg, kago (113a), kagu (106c), lago (83b,152b), mage (95b), magg (95b), Magh (102a), magi (123c), Magi (95b,116c,183a), naga (13d,33a,55b, 127c), Naga (24c,77a,88c,176d), Nagy (78d), Paga (117a), page (51b,59b,142d,159b), raga (56d,105a), rage (10c,30c,157a,161d), ragi (28b), saga (79b,91a,138a,157a,161b,c,168a), Saga, sage (13a,90d,100c,141c,145c,180b,183a), sago (54c,59b,113b,125b, 155c), sagy, vagi (38b), wage (27a,115b), yage (23a)

- - AG Agag (18c,86c,137a), brag (21a,175a), coag (45d,118a,163b), crag (132c), drag (74a,125b), flag (16b,50d,82b,88c,115a,155a), knag (115d,139c), krag (131c), peag (144a,178a), quag (21c, 102c), shag (73b,105b,161d,166d), skag (7d,46d), slag (46c,99a, 138c,148d,177a), snag (11b,27b,35c,87c,124b,166a), stag (65a, 98d), swag (22a,156c), waag (71d,101d)

A - - G Agag (18c,86c,137a), agog (47b,52c,86b), ajog, areg (116a,137a)

AH - - Ahab (18c,26c,85b,86d,100d,116a,180b), Ahaz (86d), ahem, Ahet (49a,102a), ahey (52c), Ahir (27b), Ahom (88c), ahoy (106a), ahum

- AH - bahi (60c), baho (122a), baht (146a), haha (55c,159c), kaha (123d), kahu (14d, maha (28c,88c,136d), mahr (103a), Oahu, paha (67b), pahi (21b,26a), paho (122a), Rahu (42b,48b), saha, sahh (188), Saho (6c), sahu (153d), taha (179a), tahr (68a,76d)

- - AH Adah (25b,51b), Amah (95b,108d,111c), arah (52c), ayah (108d), blah, drah (188), Elah (18c,86d), Etah (51c,71d), eyah (95b,108d,111c), ivah (18d), kyah (19a), Leah (19a,84a,87b, 183c), Noah (88a,99b), odah (170d), opah (23b,57a,b,86d), prah (21b,26a,95c,d), Ptah (48d,98c), saah (188), seah (188), shah (116c), Utah (180b), yeah

A - - H acth (13b), Adah (25b,51b), aich (9a), Alph (132a), amah (95b, 108d,111c), ankh (38b,162b), arah (52c), arch (29d,38b,39d, 123d,132c), ayah (108d)

AI - - aich (9a), Aida (110d,175c), aide (7b,14a,75d), aile (62b,63a, 182c,d), aine (49b,62c,142c), Aino (84a,c), aint, Ainu (84a,c),

266

aipi (27a), **Aira** (70d), **aire** (82c), **Aire, airs** (123b), **airy** (177a, 176d)

- Al -   **bail** (43c), **bain** (61a), **bait** (15d,51a,94d,167b), **caid** (35a,151d, 152b), **cain** (169c), **Cain** (6a,7a,50d,88a,104c,143a), **Dail** (49a, 82b,c), **dain** (188), **dats** (119b), **fail, fain** (42d,67c,183b), **fair** (17a,55d), **fait** (6d,61b), **Gaia** (47d,69a), **gail** (23b,174d), **Gail** (183d), **gain** (7a,b,124a,181d), **gait** (96b,179a), **haik** (57b,65b, 108a), **hail** (6d,15a,71d), **hair** (56b,164d), **jail** (123d), **Jain** (77b), **kaid** (29d,66a), **kaif** (88c), **kaik** (96c), **kail** (18c,22a,25a,79b), **kain, kair, laic** (32b,90b,107d,124a,141d), **laid, lain, lair** (37c, 42b), **Lais** (17c), **lait** (62a), **Maia** (76b,109a,153b,155b,177c), **maid** (45b,142d), **mail** (12d,99b,121c), **maim** (43d,81a,105c), **main** (29d,35d,123d), **mais** (61b), **Nala** (33a), **naid** (63c), **naif** (74b,105d), **naik, nail** (31d,54d,141d,161d,173a), **naio** (107a, 168c), **Nair** (45d), **nais** (63c,132a), **paid** (129c), **pail, pain** (7c), **pair** (22d,37d,85b,171d), **pais** (37d), **qaid** (35a), **raia** (107d), **Raia** (147b), **raid** (59d,80c), **raik** (188,189), **rail** (16b,19b,c,37a, 97b,138c,150c,177b), **rain** (121d,162d), **raip** (36d), **rais** (26c, 29d,75a,103b), **Rais** (106b), **saic** (86b,91d,175d), **said** (174c), **Said** (42d,101a,121b), **sail** (144c,185a), **sain** (20c,38d,48a), **sair** (140b,150d), **sais** (48d,71d), **tail** (11d,27d,59b,143b), **tain** (166a), **tair** (68a,76d), **tait** (14d), **vail** (94b,124a,174b), **vain** (81a), **vair** (64c,154c), **waif** (157b), **wail** (39b,88a), **wain** (177b), **Wain wait** (26d,42b,92c,155d,162a), **zain** (170d), **zain** (41a)

- - Al   **aiai** (171a), **Alai** (135c), **anai** (163b,181a), **chai** (72d), **goai** (106d,168c), **ngai** (48a,159c), **peai** (98b), **quai** (88b,117c,180c), **Thai** (146a)

A - - I   **Aani** (45a,48d), **abri** (61c,62c,144b), **Absi** (191), **admi** (65d), **aeri** (34a), **agni** (88a,89c), **Agni** (56d,68b), **agri** (89b), **aipi** (27a), **alai** (171a), **Alai** (135c), **Aibi** (58a), **alli** (74c,134c), **ambi** (34a,122c), **amii** (48a,161d,168c,169a), **ammi** (98c), **amoi** (62a), **anai** (163b, 181a), **Andi** (27d), **anti** (7d,111a,122b), **Anti** (193), **apii** (74c), **arni** (24a,181b), **arui** (11b,143d,144a,181c), **asci** (154a), **assi** (77d), **Asti** (83d,182b), **Atli** (14c,72b,79a,107d), **Atri, auri** (34a)

AJ - -   **ajar** (110c), **Ajax** (71b,162d), **ajee** (15c,139a), **ajog**

- AJ -   **baju** (84a), **caja** (152a), **caji** (180b), **gajo** (107c), **haje** (33a,48d), **maja** (151c), **Maja** (153b), **majo** (33a), **Naja** (33a), **pajo** (122a), **raja** (77a,123c), **Raja, tajo** (152a,d), **yaje** (23a)

AK - -   **Akal** (56d), **Akan** (191), **akee** (168c), **akey** (189), **Akha** (86a,c), **akia** (74c), **Akim** (135d,191), **akin** (8b,92b,129c), **Akka** (125d), **akov** (189), **akra** (176a), **Akra** (191), **akua** (120d)

- AK -   **baka** (52b), **bake** (139a), **baku** (26d,157b,168c), **cake, caky, fake** (123a,143c), **faky, hake** (57a,b), **hakh** (46d), **hako** (115b), **haku** (86d), **jake** (40d), **Jake** (96b), **jako** (71a), **kaka** (114b), **kaki** (84c, 106d), **lake** (117d), **lakh** (110c), **laky, make** (35b,36d,54a,123a), **maki** (91b), **mako** (18a,19a,20d,143c,168c,182c), **Maku** (192), **oaks** (154c), **oaky, rake** (41b,44c,134c,140d), **Saka** (10a), **sake** (84b,125d), **saki** (39c,84b,102a), **take, takt** (105a,163a), **Taku** (80c), **taky, waka** (26a), **wake** (134b,168a), **wakf** (103a), **waky, Yaka** (191), **Yaki** (193)

- - AK   **Anak** (67a), **asak** (13d,168c,169a), **beak** (19a), **coak** (45d,118a, 163b), **dhak** (48a,169a), **Dyak** (22b), **feak** (39d,171c), **flak** (11a), haak (57b,178a), irak (99a,d), kiak (51c), kyak (51c), leak (110c), peak (9a,38c,159b,186b), siak (72d), soak (46c,137c), teak (41a,48a,168c), weak (55b)

A · · K   amok (18b,63c), Anak (67a), asak (13d,168c,169a), asok (13d), Atik (155b)

AL · ·   alae (182d), alai (171a), Alai (135c), alan (45a,79a,183), Alan, alar (15c,145c,182d), alas (52c,136b,183b), alat (136d), alay (96c), alba (98b,181a), Alba (151d), albe (133a), Albi (58a), albo (34d,181a), Alca (14c,128b), alco (45b), alda (152b), Alda (110d, 150c), Alea (14b,31c,167d), alec (10a,57c,d,76c,137c), alee (15c, 75d,144b,157a,182a), alef (91c), alem (98b,155a,170d,171a), alen (40d,138a), alfa (70d), alga (141b,c), Algy (96b), alia (89d), alif (12b), alii (74c,134c), alim (103b,162c), alin (188), alit (44b, 143a), Alix (183c), alky, alla (6d), Alle (14c), allo (34c), ally (14a,35c,d,173c), alma (40d,53d,146d,147a), Alma (38d,183c), alme (40d,147a), alms (29a), alod (51c,55d,88a,124c), aloe (7d, 20a,76a,b,92b,98b,119b,158b,167a,183d), alop (13d,46b,93d), alow (18a,172c), Alph (132a), Alps (85d), also (10b,18b,80a), alta (89c,152d), alto (152b,176c,177a), alum (14a,45c), Alur (191), Alva (151d), Alya (155b,c), Alys (183c)

· AL ·   Aalu (6b,48d), Bala (26c,66a), bald (16c), bale (24b,74a), bali, Bali, balk (118c,146a,156d), ball, balm (110a,172c), Balt (93a), balu (104b,159a,181d), cale (72d), calf, calk (78c,109a,141c), 178d), call (145c,159b,176d), calm (8d,11d,112b,118d,126c,d, 172b,173d), calo (72d), calp (92b), calx (23c,75c,112c), dale (43c,128a,174b), dali (168c,169b), fala (129b), fall (46b,141c), falx (133b), gala (55d), Gala (191), gale (181d), gali (6c), gall (19a,28c,29b,82c,160c,176a), galt, hala (112b), hale (125b), Hale (9d,131a), half (101a), hali (37b,114d), halm, halo (14d, 31b,92a,107b,131d), Hals (47a), halt (13b,28a,38d,156d), lalu (48d), kala (19a), kale (22a,25a,119b,175a), kali (26d,67c,136d, 167a), Kali (147b), kalo (162a), lala (129b), lalo (16b,34d,153a), Lalo (35c), mala (89b,c,90a,94b,97d,109d,185c), male (154d), Male (45d), mali (27b), mall (95d,124b,143b), malm (32a,92b), malo (23a,74c,152a), malt (17c), Nala (77a), pala (189), Pala (88b), pale (113a,117c,178a), pali (122b), Pali (23d,24a,137b, 175a), pall (32d,81b,112a), palm (59b,168c,169b), palo (152c), palp (11a,55b,58b,167c), paly (194), rale (7c,23a,29d,41b), ralo (188), sala (152a,b,c), Sala (50c), sale (14c,61c,62b,c,168b), salp (109c,148d), salt (35d,105b,123a,136c,141c,149d), tala (16d,113a,168c,d), talc (28d,63b,99c,100b,122a,149c), tale (91a, 185b), tall (189), talk, tall (118d), vale (54c,128a,174b), Vale (7c,109c), vali (171a,176a), Vali (7c,109c), wale (70b,131b,157c, 163d,179a,180a,c,d), wall (171a), walk, wall, Walt (96b), Yale (173c), yali (171a)

· · AL   agal (17c,36d), Akal (56d), Aral (135d), aval (70c), axal (120b), Baal (142b), beal (139d), bual (182c), coal (49c,64a), cral, deal (11d,16c,36c,44c,81a,168b), dhal (12b), dial (25c), dual (45c, 171d), eral (51a), etal (89a), foal (78c), gaal (23b,174d), geal (47d,163c), goal (8b,109b,120b,125d), heal, ical (158c), keal (25a), kral, leal (54b,94c,139d), maal (188), meal (72a,130b), Neal odal (48a,88b,112c), opal (20a,65d,67b,82b), oral (114a, 153d,174c,175c), oval (48d,49c,127a), paal (188), peal (131c,d),

268

pyal (175c), real (7a), rial (190), ryal (110a,190), saal (66c, 73b), seal (10c,d,54d,64c,96a,118b,128a), sial (112a), Taal (7d, 88c,151a), teal (19b,20d,46c,d), udal (76b,88b,131c), unal (147a), ural, Ural (135c), uval (70c), veal, vial (148c), weal (124d,157c,180c,d), zeal (12c,55d)

269

anay (72b,163b,181a), **anba** (36d), **ance** (158b,c,d), **ancy** (158c), anda (23a,168c), **Ande** (193), **Andi** (27d), **Andy** (96b), **Aner** (18d, 96b), **anes** (110c,140a), **anet** (43c), **anew** (7c), **ange** (61a), **ango** (171a), **anil** (47c,80d,180b), **Anim** (18d), **anis** (55c), **ankh** (38d, 162b), **anna** (190), **Anna** (110c,166d,183c), **Anne** (50c,84a, 143b,183c), **anoa** (28a,60a,112c,181c), **anon** (7d,14d,79d,80b, 123a,145c,150c,164a), **ansa** (73c,93d,137c), **anse** (61d), **ansu** (11d), **anta** (83d,117c,d,121a), **Anta** (164a), **ante** (87a,89a,115b, 120b,122b,125d,154d), **anti** (7d,111a,122b), **Anti** (193), **anzu** (11 d)

- **AN** - **Aani** (45a,48d), **Bana** (67a), **banc** (61a,85c), **band** (72a,157c), **bane** (74a,106b,120b,139a), **bang** (75d,105d,148a), **bani** (190), **bank** (18a,58c), **bans, bant** (43c), **Cana** (57a,64b,100c), **cane** (17b,128a,156a,159a,177d), **Cane, cang** (184a), **cano** (152a), **cant** (28d,81b,84d,90c,109b,136c,165d,166a), **Dana** (28a,96a, 171d), **Dane** (85d),107d,138a), **dang, dank** (40b,101a), **dans** (62a), **Danu** (28a), **fana, fane** (30d,137a,162d), **fang** (167b), **Fano** (51d,96b,113c,d), **gane** (185b), **gang** (38c), **Gano** (132d), **hand** (60c,114c,115d,184c), **hang** (160a), **hank** (147c), **Hano** (125b), **Hans** (66d,96a), **hant** (67a), **jane** (190), **Jane** (183c), **Jann** (102d), **kana** (84d), **Kane** (74c), **k'ang** (30a), **Kano** (84c, 177d), **kant** (28d), **Kant** (67a), **lana** (58a,66a,90a,184b), **land** (44 a,163c), **lane** (134b,157b), **lank** (148b,164b), **lanx** (133a,b), **mana** (30a,120d,122a,159c), **mand** (28b), **mane, mani** (115c), **mann** (189), **Mann** (9c,48c,185c), **mano** (71d,73d,74b,83b), **Mans** (30a), **Manu** (10a,76d,77a,b), **Manx** (27b,28a,82d), **many** (108d), **nana** (118b), **Nana** (15c,105d,116d,186d), **nane** (139d), **Pana, pane** (113c,155a,b), **pang** (165b), **Pani** (120c), **pank** (189), **pant, rana** (77a,123c), **Rana** (63d), **rand** (16d,22a,131b,145a,b), **Rand** (69c), **rang, rani** (72d,77b,123c,127c), **rank** (31d,55d,70b,92c,94d, 157d), **rann** (175c), **rant** (41c,127b,128a,161d), **sana** (56a,166d), **Sana** (185d), **sand** (71d,146c), **sane** (128a), **sang, sank, sano** (152b), **sans** (63a,183b), **tana** (159a), **Tana** (87d), **Tane** (120d), **tang** (30b,58b 186b), **tanh** (97c), **tank** (175a,d), **Tano** (192), **uang** (131a), **vane** (179b,182a), **vang** (72d,134a,140b), **Vans** (107d), **wand** (120b),132c,156a), **wane** (41c,43c), **wang** (189), **want** (41b,42d,87b,106b,122a), **wany, Yana** (192,193), **yang** (30b,70a), **yank, Yank,** zany (24a,32d,59c)

- - **AN** **adan** (102d), **Akan** (191), **alan** (45a,79a,183c), **Alan** (96a), **anan** (49a,159a,180c), **Aran** (18c,48c,64d,82d,174c), **Awan** (191), **azan** (102d), **bean** (91b,142a,175a), **bran** (23c,39a,72a,79c,70b), **Bran** (23c,50c), **chan** (26c,130c), **clan** (169c), **Coan** (37b), **cran** (160c), **cyan, dean** (33c,109d), **dhan** (124c), **dian** (46c,130d,170b), **Dian** (68d,69a,c,102b), **duan** (64b), **elan** (12c,41a,50d,62a,153c,177a, 186b), **Eoan** (41a,85b), **Evan** (96a), **Ewan, flan** (39d,40a,114d), **gean** (29c), **Goan, gran, guan** (151b), **Iban** (47c), **Iran** (6a,48c, 116b), **Ivan,** (40c,85b,96a), **Jean** (37c), **jean** (183c), **Joan** (183c), **juan** (113a), **Juan** (96a), **kaan** (93d,116c), **khan** (7c,26c,81b,93d, 116c,123c,130c,166c), **kran** (190), **kuan** (30b,c), **Kuan, kwan** (30b), **lean** (128a,148b,152d,164b,166a), **loan, mean** (15a,42b, 146c,156b), **mian** (97c147b,166b), **moan, ngan, oban** (190), **Olan** (115c), **Oman** (159a), **Onan** (18c,85c), **Oran, oxan, pean** (65c), **plan** (99b,124a,138b), **quan** (190), **roan** (78b,c,114c,128d, 144a,181a), **Saan** (24d), **Sean** (85b,96a), **Shan** (13c,80d,88c,

270

101d), **scan** (52b,93d,98a,116d,128b,c,140d), **span** (23b,107b, 113a,128b,162c), **Svan** (27d), **swan** (19b,33a), **tean** (140c,167a), **than** (35b), **tran** (7a), **tuan** (95d,147b,166c), **ulan** (27d,88a), **uran** (101d), **Uran, uzan** (189), **wean** (8d,42d), **yean** (88a), **yuan** (190), **Yuan** (30b,101d)

A - - N **acon** (62c,140d), **adan** (102d), **aden** (34b), **Aden, agon** (12c,36c, 41b,55d,71b), **Akan** (191), **akin** (8b,92b,129c), **alan** 45a,79a, 183c), **Alan** (96a), **alen** (40d,138a), **alin** (188), **amen** (14a, 80b,94a,137a,149c,175c,184b), **Amen** (86d,127d,159b,164a), **amin** (9d), **Amon** (86d,96b,127d,159b,164a), **Amun** (86d,127d, 159b,164a, **anan** (49a,159a,180c), **anon** (7d,14d,79d,80b,123a, 145c,150c,164a), **Aran** (18c,48c,64d,82d,174c), **Asin** (102a), **aten** (150a,159b), **aton** (150a,159b), **Avon** (143b), **Awan** (191) **axon** (106c,153c), **ayin** (91c), **azan** (102d), **azon** (127b)

AO - - **aone** (52b,167b), **Aoul** (191)

- AO - **faon** (33c,55a), **gaol** (123d), **Gaol** (164a), **Gaon** (85b), **jaob, Laos** (80d,129c), **naos** (28a,71c,137a,163a), **Naos** (155b), **paon** (115b), **Taos** (192), **Yaou** (30c)

- - AO **Agao** (6c,73c), **dhao** (24c), **grao** (189), **guao** (168c,169b), **Miao** (30a,b), **omao** (165b), **prao** (21b,26a,95c,d), **tlao**

A - - O **aboo** (17c), **acto** (152b), **aero** (8b,34a,b,58c,59a), **Agao** (6c,73c), **agio** (52c,60a,1101c,123a), **agro** (149d), **Aino** (84a,c), **albo** (34d, 181a), **alco** (45b), **allo** (34c), **also** (10b,18b,80a), **alto** (152b, 176c,177a), **ambo** (125b,128b), **ammo** (9d), **ango** (171a), **apio** (125b), **areo** (34c), **Argo** (12c,36b,c), **Arno** (27a), **aroo** (80c,82b), **arro** (52c), **arto** (34a), **asno** (151d), **Ateo** (120d), **atmo** (34d, 174d), **auto** (34d)

AP - - **Apap** (102a), **apar** (12d), **aper** (32d), **Apet** (97c), **apex** (39c,76c, 115c,118b,159b,166a,167b), **apia** (121b), **apil** (74c), **apio** (125b), **Apis** (17c,24b,49a,125a,136a), **apod** (59d), **apse** (9b,20a,31a, 128c,130a,142b,175a), **Apsu** (29a), **Apus** (36b,c)

- AP - **capa** (152a,166d), **cape** (75a,96c,124b,161a), **caph** (91c), **capp** (27a), **gape** (185b), **gapo** (60a), **gapy, Hapi** (66a,107b,136a), **hapu** (106d), **jape** (85a,b), **kapa** (74b), **kaph** (91d), **kapp, Lapp** (108a), **mapo** (68a,148d), **napa** (25c,67d,90d), **Napa** (182c), **nape** (15b,108c,d), **napu** (29d,80d), **papa, pape** (19b,113a), **rapt** (6c, 27a,50d), **sapa** (70c), **sapo** (149c,166d), **tapa** (16c,32c,53b,56a, 74b,104b,112b,113d,120d), **tape** (16a,19a,128d), **tapu, wapp** (54b,133d,145d), **yapa** (113b), **Yapp** (22a)

- - AP **Apap** (102a), **atap** (113b), **chap** (55b), **clap** (58b), **drap** (61b,c, 62a), **flap** (17b,59a,104a,118d,161a,182d), **frap** (45d,165c), **heap** (117d), **knap** (76d,107a,139b,159b,166a,170c,185b), **laap** (51d, 91b,141d), **leap** (26c), **neap** (165c,167a,177b), **plap** (54b), **reap** (7a,40a,74a), **shap, slap** (24a,128c,148c), **snap** (23a,36d,38b, 48b,54d,56c,58c,149d), **soap, swap** (168a), **trap** (27b,67b,132b, 149b), **wrap** (32b,51a)

A - - P **alop** (13d,46b,93d), **Apap** (102a), **asop** (180b), **tap** (113b), **atip** (14b,166a), **atop** (112a,174a)

AQ - - **aqua** (90a,178c)

- AQ - **waqf** (103a)

- - AQ **Iraq** (99a,d)

271

AR · ·   **Arab** (30a,78b,c,106a,107c,157b,160c,185d), **arad** (13a,c,84a), **arah** (52c), **Aral** (135d), **Aram** (18d,50c,105c,144b,161c), **Aran** (18c,48c,64d,82d,174c), **arar** (137a,168c), **Aras**, **arba** (135d, 171a), **arca** (9a,22c,29d,115a,130a), **Arca** (101b), **arch** (29d,38b, 39d,123d,132c), **area** (37d,38a,44c,53a,93b,110d,127d,138c,186a, 186d), **areg** (116a,137a), **areo** (34c), **Ares** (49b,51b,68c,76a,97a, 105c,110b,178a,186d), **aret** (128c), **Argo** (12c,36b,c), **aria** (8b, 98c,150a,c,170c), **arid** (46c,85a), **arif** (127d), **aril** (142a), **aris** (101b), **arme** (63a,179b), **arms**, **army** (78c), **arna** (24a,181b), **Arnd** (67a), **Arne** (35c,50c,134d), **arni** (24a,181b), **Arno** (27a), **arn't**, **Aroa** (175b), **Arod** (80c,82b), **arow** (92c,158b), **arpa** (83b), **arra** (47d,52c,82b), **arro** (52c), **Arta** (72b), **arto** (34a), **arts** (138c), **arty**, **arui** (11b,143d,144a,181c), **arum** (13a, 39b,58d,92b,155c), **Arum** (66a), **Arya** (80d)

· AR ·   **Aare, Aaru** (6b,48d), **bara** (188), **barb** (20b,57d,78b,117d,120a,b, 124b), **bard** (12d,120a), **bare** (43d,157c), **bari** (79c), **Bari** (37c, 83d), **bark** (115c), **barm** (185b), **barn** (156d), **baro** (71a,122c), **barr** (49b), **Bart** (96b), **baru** (168c), **cara** (83a), **Cara** (48b,183c), **card** (33d,114d), **care** (11b,14c,35d,150a,184d), **cark** (26d,184d), **carl** (115c,135d), **Carl** (96a), **carn** (156c), **caro** (83a,183d), **carp** (27d,38d,40c,55a,56c,57a), **carr** (120d,140a), **cart** (171d,175a, 177b), **Dara** (18d), **Dard**, **dare** (28d,41b 42a,74d,175b), **Dare** (57a), **dari** (38a,70b), **dark** (47a,67d,109b,160b), **darn** (130b), **darr** (163c), **dart** (13b,88a,100c,120b,153a,160c), **Dart** (100c), **earl** (107c), **earn** (42d,64b,99a), **fard** (112d), **fare** (43c,59b,67d, 123b), **farl** (138c,140b), **farm** (165d), **faro** (65a), **gara** (190), **garb** (32c,46a), **gare** (61b,c,62c,127c,184b), **Garm** (178c), **garn** (67d,185b), **Garo** (88c), **Harb** (191), **hard** (109b), **hare** (91b, 132c), **hark** (92d), **harl** (16b,56b,59a), **harm** (40b,81a), **harp** (105a,129a), **hart** (41d,154d), **Jarl** (40d,107d), **kara** (132a), **Kari** (14d), **Karl** (96a), **karn** (156c), **karo** (106d), **Lara** (25c), **lard** (54d,61a,71a,110a), **lari** (78a,101c), **Lari** (72c), **lark** (19a,63d, 177b), **larp** (51d), **Lars** (51d,121b), **mara** (114d), **Mara** (24a,d, 105b,107b), **marc** (70c), **Marc** (96a), **mare** (78b,108b), **mari** (16a,61d), **mark**, **Mark** (52a,96a,146b,155a), **marl** (32a,42c,55d), **maro** (144d), **Mars** (68c,118d,119a,178a), **mart** (49d,97a), **Mart** (96b,183d), **maru** (84c,144d), **Mary** (50c,126b,183c), **nard** (13a, 97c,102b,110a,153c), **Nare** (93c), **nark** (81a,156d), **nary** (108b), **oary**, **para** (134c,170d), **Para** (18a,51d), **parc** (62b,112c), **pard** (27b,91b), **pare** (115c,129a), **pari** (34a,180a), **park**, **parr** (136d, 147c), **pars** (89d), **part** (44d,60d,121c,159c), **paru** (57a), **rara** (119a), **rare** (138b,164b,172b,173d), **Sara** (24d,183c), **sard** (26d, 28d,65d,111a,142b,156d), **Sarg** (96d,125c), **sarl** (48b,65b,77b), **Sark** (28d), **Sart** (82b,103b,170d), **tart** (22a 55c,113a,168c), **Tara** (82b,c,138b), **tare** (9a,18d,41a,176a,179d), **tarl** (47d,69a), **tarn** (87d,103d,120d), **taro** (13c,48c,49b,64b,112b,120a,133d,155c, 170a,c), **tarp** (26b,178d), **tart** (114d), **vara** (151d), **vare** (179b), **vari** (34d,91b,134d,174d), **vary** (28d,43c), **ward** (31c,55c,86b), **ware** (27d,35a), **warf**, **warm** (7c,75b,163b), **warn** (7b), **warp** (36c,165a,171c), **wart** (124d), **wary** (27d,176b), **yard** (152d), **yare** (96b,124b,128b), **yark** (22c), **yarl** (40d,107d), **yarn** (154b, 161b,184b), **yarr** (72a), **Yaru** (48d), **zarf** (39c,155a), **zarp** (120c)

· · AR   **Adar** (85c,102a), **afar** (44c), **Afar** (6c), **agar** (7d,28c,39c,103c,

141c), ajar (110c), alar (15c,145c,182d), amar (189), apar (12d), arar (137a,168c), asar (67b), atar (58d,116b,134a), Avar (27d, 108a), bear (27a,50b,113c,155a), Bhar (191), boar (77c,117c, 160c,181c), char (24d,138c,170b), czar (42d,49d,60b,135c), dear, Dhar, duar, Edar (18d), fear (113c,155a), gear (32c,112a, 167b), gnar (72a), guar (46c,59d), haar (139c), hear (75b,92d), hoar (63d,71a,181a), inar (65b), isar (41a,104c,132a), iyar (102b), izar (65b,103b,155b), joar (100a), juar (100a), khar (189), knar (87c,134b), kuar (102a), kyar (33a), lear (139d), Lear (37a,143b), liar (98d), maar (177a), near (11d,32c,107b), omar (103b), Omar (48c,51b,163b), osar (51b,67b,131b), paar (28c), pear (64a), rear (15b,23a,b,24a,51b,76d,127c), roar (145c), Saar (63b,102d,132a), scar (31a,184d), sear (23d,27d,72d,138c), soar (59a), spar (22c,24c,64b,97b,100b,144d), star (14a,21c, 94c,100c), taar (12b), tear (57c,87b,130a), thar (68a,76d), tiar (39a,75a,121a), tsar (42d,49d,60b,135c), tzar (42d,49d,60b, 135c), usar (8d,16c), wear (50b), year, Zoar

A - - R   Abir (129a), Acer (96c), acor (6d), Adar (85c,102a), Ader (18d), ador (153b), afar (44c), Afar (6c), afer (48a,182b), agar (7d,28c, 39c,103c,141c), ager (47,56a,89b,c,131d,133b), Ahir (27b), ajar (110c), alar (15c,145c,182d), Alur (191), amar (189), amer (61b), amir (7c,12a,103a,b,123c,170d), amor (152b), Amor (39c,68b), Aner (18d,96b), apar (12d), aper (32d), arar (137a,168c), asar (67b), Aser (84a), Askr (107d), asor (75c,105a), Asur (68c), atar (58d,116b,134a), Ater (18c), Auer (79a), Avar (27d,108a), aver (7c,14a,15c,41c,95c,140d,155c,160b,184c)

AS - -   asak (13d,168c,169a), asar (67b), asci (154a), asea (39b,177c), asem (9a,49a,69c), Aser (84a), Asha (191), ashy (113a,178a), Asia (48a), Asin (102a), Askr (107d), asno (151d), asok (13d), Asom (18d), asop (180b), asor (75c,105a), asse (25a,60d,74a), assi (77d), asta (188), Asta (107a,164c), Asti (83d,182b), Asur (68c)

- AS -   base (6a,43b,44b,51c,60c,79b,94b,122b), bash, bask (94b), bass (57b,c,177a), best (16c,56a,117b,184a), Bast (27b), casa (152b), case (22c,36c,81c,91a,108c), cash (101c), cask, Caso (82d), cass (140c,177a), Cass (147a), cast (165b,167c), dash (125c,162d), dasi (77a), ease (7c,8d,35a,100d,129d,130b,c,150c), East (111b), easy (54a,146d,149d,172b), fash (140c,176a), fass (189), fast (56d,126c,141d,160c,173a,d), gash (40a), gasp (113c), hase (74d), nash, hasp (31d,54d,153c), hast, iass (160d), kasa (48a), kasi (116b), kasm (189), lash (58c,87b,165c,180d), Lasi (191), lass (95b), last (16c,50b,145a,174c), masa (37a), mash (39b, 156c), mask (44a,45c), mass (8a,24b,35b,142d), mast (17c, 108d,120b,144d,152d), masu (57a,84c), nase (26b,75a,124b), Nash (9c), nasi (34c,108a,115a), Nast (9c,27a), oast (15d,86b, 112a), pasa (46a,127c,152c), pasi (94b), pass (110b,155c), past (25c,69d,165d), rasa (51c), rase (42b d 91d), rash (75a), rasp (56b,70d,140d), sasa (55c), sash (18a,45c,67b,182b), sass (154d), task (156b), Tass (107a,135d,151b), vasa (46d,114a,160b, 175d), Vasa, vase, vast (78d,79d), vasu (106c), Vasu (176d), wash, wasp, wast

- - AS   abas (61c), alas (52c,136b,183b), Anas (46c,d), Aras, baas (97c), bias (43b,123a), blas (6c,49c), Blas (67b), bras (61a), Dyas

273

(66a), ELAS (71c), eyas (106c,173a), gras (78b), Idas (27b,71c), Iras (11b,32a), khas (153a), kras (76d), kvas (135c), Lias (66a), Lyas (66a), Maas (132a), mias (111a), Nias (82d), oras (40d), quas (135c), upas (84d,120b,168c,d), Usas (68d), utas (49a, 109c), Xmas, yeas (177c), Zoas (20b)

A · · S   abas (61c), ABC's (57a), Acis (64b), Acts, acus (89d,118a), Ades (73a), Agis (86d), Alas, Airs (123b), alas (52c,136b,183b), alms (29a), Alps (85d), Alys (183c), Ames (9c,82a), Amos (96a,144b), Anas (46c,d), Anes (110c,140a), anis (55c), Apis (17c,24b,49a, 125a,136a), Apus (36b,c), Aras, Ares (49b,51b,68c,76a,97a,105c, 110b,178a,186d), aris (101b), arms, arts (138c), ates (160c), atis (76d,102a), Aves (19d), Avis (89a,183c), avus (89b), axis (28b, 41d,77c,153c), ayes (177c)

AT · ·   atap (113b), atar (58d,116b,134a), atef (39a,48d), aten (150a, 159b), Ateo (120d), Ater (18c), ates (160c), Atik (155b), atip (14b,166a), atis (76d,102a), Atka (11a), atle (136d,161d,169b), Atli (14c,72b,79a,107d), atma (150d), atmo (34d,174d), Atmu (143a,159b), atom (101c,114c,180d), aton (150a,159b), atop (112a,174a), Atri, atry (141b), atta (58d,90c,97d,160c,173d), Atta (94d,95d,100a,106b,117a), Attu, atua (120d), Atum (143a, 159b)

· AT ·   bata (30a,142d), bate (43c,91b,100d), bath, Bath (50d,151c), batt (37c), batz (190), cata (122c), cate (165c), Cato (132d, 133b), data (54a), date (64a,153a), dato (95c,102c,117a), datu (95c,102c,117a), eats, fate (42d,52a,87a,94a), gata (143c), gate (51a,121b), Gath (117a), hate (6a,43a), hath, Hati (48d), jati (27b), Jato (173b), Kate (143c,183d), kath (14a), Katy (183d), lata (85d,95d), late (128c), lath (157c), latu (190), mate (18c, 35b,41d,113a,154a,162c), math (77a), Matt, maty (80c), Nata (15c,47c), Nate (22b), Nath (155c), Nato (6a,8d), natr (189), Natt (107b), oath (119c,150a), pata (32c,160d), pate (39a,74d), path (132a,134b), pato (46d), patu (179b), rata (29d,56b,89d, 96c,106d,120c,168c), rate (11d,14a,31d,36b,51d,52a,70b,85c, 112b,123b,127d,128a,138c,143a,174b), rath (29a,76d,162d), rati (189), rats, sate (32d,52c,67d,70d,137c,159d), sati, Sati (49a, 126b,147b), tate (183a), tatt (87c), tatu (12d), Tatu, Wate (141a), watt, Watt (82a,173b,177c), yate (51d,168c), yati (76d), zati (21d)

· · AT   adat (90b,95d), alat (136d), Anat (138c,147d), beat (58c,87b, 131a,164d,165b,180d), bhat (80c), blat (25b), boat (27b,106a), brat, chat (9b,19c,161c), coat (160a), doat (17a,94b,112a,165d), drat (100a), Duat (172d), erat (89c), etat (62d), feat (7a,52d), fiat (35a,41d,48c,111b,137a), Fiat (83c), flat (41b,124b,173a), frat, geat (77d,101a), Geat (138a), ghat (32d,88b,103d,132a), gnat (59a,81b,99c), goat (135a), heat, Ikat (53b,159a), kaat (105d), khat (105d), kyat (189), Maat (69a,85d), meat (59b), moat (44d), neat (165c,169d), peat (64a,b,173a), piat (11a), plat (22d,96c,114a,119c,133d), pyat (95b), scat (26b,67a,d,126c, 169c), seat (98c,156b), shat (87d), skat (181b), Skat (155b), slat (58b,89a,117c,184a), spat (112c,126b,134b), stat (72d), swat (15d,20d,32d,157c), Swat (103a), that (42b,124b,129c), what (129c)

274

A - - T abet (8b,15b,50a,59b,75d,81c,141d,159d), **Abot** (100c), **abut** (22a,167c), **acht** (66c), **adat** (90b,95d), **adit** (51a,100a,114d), **Ahet** (49a,102a), **aint, alat** (136d), **alit** (44b,143a), **amit** (94a), **Anat** (138c,147d), **anet** (43c), **Apet** (97c), **aret** (128c), **arn't, aunt** (129c)

AU - - **Auca** (192), **Aude, Auer** (79a), **auge** (123c,132b), **aula** (66c,73b), **aulu** (74c,168c), **aune** (188), **aunt** (129c), **aura** (44c,49c,66a,96b, 158a,170d,177c), **auri** (34a), **Ausa, ausu** (168c,180b), **auto** (34d), **auza** (168c,180b)

- AU - baud (162d), baul (18b), **Baum** (9c,112c), cauk (139b), caul (16d,74d), caur (139a), daub (148d), dauk (95c), **Daur** (139b), dauw (24c), eaux (178c), faun (56a,68b,137c,161a,184a), gaub (116c), gaud (169d), gaue (67a), **Gaul** (10a,60d,63c), gaup, gaur (112c,181c), gaus (67d), gaut (88b,103d,132a), haul (27b,45d), jaun (113a), kaun (93d), laud (122a), laun (146b), maud (53d, 136d,143c), **Maud** (181a,183c), **Maul** (120d), maul (73c), maun (139d), naut (141b), **Paul** (96a), paun (18b), paut (140a), **Sauk** (192), saul (48a,168c), **Saul** (18c,86d,115a), saum (189), taun (188), taut (163b,165c), **Vaux** (63b), yaup

- - AU Agau (73c), beau, Diau (192), Drau, Esau (82c,84a,128c), frau (181b), miau (27b,99b), prau (21b,26a,95c,d), sgau (88c), unau (148c,171d), whau (107a,168c)

A - - U Aalu (6b,48d), Aaru (6b,48d), Abou (48b,55a), actu (7a,89a), Addu (68c,157a,182a), Agau (73c), Ainu (84a,84c), ammu (9d), ansu (11d), anzu (11d), Apsu (29a), Atmu (143a,159b), Attu, aulu (74c,168c), ausu (168c,180b), auzu (168c,180b)

AV - - aval (70c), **Avar** (27d,108a), avec (63a,183a), aver (7c,14a,15c, 41c,95c,140d,155c,160b,184c), **Aves** (19d), avid (47b,71a,186b), avis (89a), **Avis** (183c), **Avon** (143b), avow (6d,36a,41c,112c), avus (89b)

- AV - bave (61d,146c), cava (116a,175b), cave (27d), cavy (72b,120d, 132c,157b), **Dave** (96b), **Davy** (96b,136b), eave (133c), favi (138a,165d), gave, have, **Java** (33a), **Jave** (84d), kava (18c, 116a), **Kavi** (84d), lava (101c,132b,151a,177a), lave (16d,178b), nave (30d,31a,78d,114b,180c), navy (33c,58b), pave (85a), pavo (115b), **Pavo** (36b,c), pavy (115b), rave (41c,157a,161d), ravi, **Ravi** (16b), save (52b,110c,123a,173c), **Tave** (183d), **Tavy** (183d), wave (19a,59a,111c,131d,160c,172d), wavy (147b,172d), yava

- - AV **Muav** (66a), **Slav** (13c,40c,48b,52a,120b,135b)

A - - V akov (189), **Azov** (20b,135d)

AW - - **Awan** (191), away (6b,69d,76a,109d,111d), awry (13d,38d,171c)

- AW - bawl, bawn (181a), cawk (133c), dawk (95c), dawm (190), dawn (14d,41b), fawn (33c) gawd (169d), gawk (146d), gawp, hawk (19c,115c), jawy, kawa (188), **Kawi** (84d), kawn (93d), lawn (20a,37c,53c,92c), pawa (189), pawl (43a,95a), pawn (29c,119c), sawk (188), sawn, tawa (106d,168c), yawl (136b,171d,175d), yawn, yawp

- - AW chaw (97c), claw (29c,105b,161d,173a), craw (38d,72c,156c), dhaw (125a), draw (42c,53a,92b,117c,121c,167d), flaw, gnaw (20a,107a,178b), miaw (27b,99b), shaw (164b), **Shaw** (50c,53b), slaw, thaw

A - - W Alow (18a,172c), anew (7c), arow (92c,158b), avow (6d,36a,41c, 112c)

AX - - Axal (120b), axil (10c), axis (28b,41d,77c,153c), axle (153c, 180c), axon (106c,153c)

- AX - saxe (20d,33c), taxi (13a,125b), taxo (13a), waxy (119c,149d)

- - AX Ajax (71b,162d), Anax (43c,120c), coax (180c), Crax (19b,39d), flax, hoax (41c,122a), Odax (132c), Olax (52b)

A - - X abox (22d), Ajax (71b,162d), Alix (183c), Amex (184d), Anax (43d,120c), apex (39c,76c,115c,118b,159b,166a,167b)

AY - - ayah (108d), ayes (177c), ayin (91c)

- AY - baya (179b), Baya (191), cayo (123d), Daye (191), days, hayz, kayo (87c), maya (179b), Maya (23d,186c), Mayo (193), raya (19b, 23c,76d,107d), saya (117a), Vayu (68c,182a), ways, yaya (113c, 168c)

- - AY alay (96c), anay (72b), away (6b,69d,76a,109d,111d), blay (57d), bray, chay (48a,128d), Clay (9d), dray (27a,154c,177b), esay, flay (147c,157c), fray (56b,60d), gray (33c,77c), Gray (50c), okay (8d), olay (113b), play (98b), play (63d,154a), pray (18b, 51a),159d), quay (88b,117c,180c), ruay (189), shay (110c), slay, stay (72d,124c,130a,134a,162a), sway (104a)

A - - Y Abby (183d), ably (147c), achy, Addy (183d), adry, (164c), aery (47b,51d,106c), affy (18b), ahey (52c), ahoy (106a), airy (176d, 177a), akey (189), alay (96c), Algy (96b), alky, ally (14a,35c,d, 173c), Amoy (88c), anay (72b,163b,181a), ancy (158c), Andy (96b), army, arty, ashy (113a,178a), atry (141b), away (6b,69d, 76a,109d,111d), awry (13d,38d,171c)

AZ - - Azam (166c), azan (102d), Azha (155b), Azof (20b,135d), azon (127b), Azov (20b,135d), azul (151d)

- AZ - caza, cazi (103a), cazy (103a), Daza (191), daze (157d), dazy, faze (43d), Gaza (117a), gaze, gazi, gazy, haze (100c,174d), hazy (174b), jazz, Kazi (103a), kazy (103a), laze (79b), Laze (191), Lazi (191), lazo (88d,128b,133d), lazy, maze (87b,157d), naze (26b,124b), Nazi, raze (42b,d,91d), razz (131b), vaza (114a)

- - AZ Agaz (193), Ahaz (86d), Boaz (135d)

A - - Z Agaz (193), Ahaz (86d)

BA - - Baal (142b), baas (97c), baba (108d,120c,166c,171a), babe, Babi (116c), babu (77a), baby, Bach (35c), back (75d,76d,159d), Badb (82b), bade (43d), baff (69d), baft (14a,53b), baga (171b), bago (13d), bahi (60c), baho (122a), baht (146a, bail (43c), bain (61a), bait (15d,51a,94d,167b), baju (84a), baka (52b), bake (139a), baku (26d,157b,168c), Bala (26c,66a), bald (16c), bale (24b,74a), balk (118c,146a,156d), ball, balm (110a,172c), Balt (93a), balu (104b, 159a,181d), Bana (67a), banc (61a,85c), band (72a,157c), bane (74a,106b,120b,139a), bang (75d,105d,148a), bani (190), bank (18a,58c), bans, bant (43c), bara (188), barb (20b,57d,78b,117d, 120a,b,124b), bard (12d,120a), bare (43d,157c), bari (37c,79c), Bari (83d), bark (115c), barm (185b), barn (156d), baro (71a, 122c), barr (49b), Bart (96b), baru (168c), base (6a,43b,44b,51c, 60c,79b,94b,122b), bash (94b), bask (94b), bass (57b,c,177a), bast (16c,56a,117b,184a), Bast (27b), bata (30a,142d), bate (43c,

276

91b,100d), bath, Bath (50d,151c), batt (37c), batz (190), baud
(162d), baul (18b), Baum (9c,112c), bave (61d,146c), bawl, bawn
(181a), baya (179b), Baya (191)

- BA - abas (61c), ibad (191), iban (47c), oban (190)
- - BA Abba (20a,55a,161c), alba (98a,181a), Alba (151d), amba (161a),
anba (36d), arba (135d,171a), baba (108d,120c,166c,171a), boba
(29d), buba (170a), caba (184c), ceba (169b), cuba (189), Cuba
(180b), Egba (191), Elba (105d), ezba (188), Faba, haba (151d),
isba (135c), juba (106b), koba (11a), kuba (26d,189), Luba
(191), Maba (103a,168d), Nuba (108c), peba (12d), Peba (193),
Raba, reba (144a), Reba (18d,86c), saba (56a,117a), Saba
(143d,) Seba (18c,39d), Toba (80c), tuba (105a,137d), ueba (188)
B - - A baba (108d,120c,166c,171a), baga (171b), baka (52b), Bala (26c,
66a), Bana (67a), bara (188), bata (30a,142d), baya (179b),
Baya (191), Beda (101d), bega (188), Beja (6c,191), beka (189),
bela (12a), Bela (18b,48c), bema (28d,31a,114b,119b,125b,137a),
bena (176a), Bera (86d), Besa (68b,119c), beta (71a,91c,141d),
biga (171d), bija (168c), bina (77a), bisa (11a), biwa (93d,168c),
Bixa (145d), blaa, boba (29d), boca (152b,c), boga (57d,180b),
bola (16a,179b), boma (7d), bona (89d,183c), Bona, bora (181d,
182b), bosa (12a), bota (189), boza (12a), brea (100b), buba
(170a), buda (83d), buna (161c), bura (182b)
- BB - Abba (20a,55a,161c), abbe (32b,63b,123b), Abby (183d)
- - BB bibb (97c,146b), Cobb (9c), dubb (161c), hobb (124b), hubb
(118b), jibb, lobb (23b,94c,163a)
B - - B Badb (82b), barb (20b,57d,78b,117d,120a,b,124b), bibb (97c,
146b), blab (162b), bleb (20c,23d,67c), blob, blub, Bodb (82b),
bomb (144a), boob (146d), brab (113b), brob (153c), bulb (37a,
172c)
- BC - ABC's (57a)
B - - C banc (61a,85c), bloc (173a), Bosc (115c)
B - - D bald (16c), band (72a,157c), bard (12d,120a), baud (162d),
bead (17a,122a,146b), Beid (155b), bend (39d,171b), bind (33b,
165c), biod (59d,79c), bird, bled, bold (41a), bond (92a,101c,
141d,143b,159b,165c), bord (100b), brad (54d,67c,105b), bred
(23c,48c,127c), bund (49c,66c,90c), Byrd (9c,120b)
BE - - bead (17a,122a,146b), beak (19a), beal (139d), beam, bean
(91b,142a,175a), bear (27a,50b,113c,155a), beat (58c,87b,131a,
164a,165b,180d), beau, beck (107c), Beda (101d), Bede (48c,
50c,101d,175b), beef, been (149a), beer (18c), bees (185b), beet
(175a), bega (188), behn (137d), Beid (155b), Beja (6c,191),
beka (189), bela (12a), Bela (18b,48c,78d), bell (24c), bell (24c,
39d), Bell (162d), belt (16a,31a), bema (28d,31a,114b,119b,
125b,137a), bena (176a), bend (39d,171b), bene (18a,83c,90a,
106d,122a,180a), beng (43a), beni (116a,142d), Beni (191), beno
(113b,117a), bent (80b), benu (49a), Bera (86d), berg (79b),
berm (25d,90d,145c), Bern (160d), Bert (96c), Besa (68b,119c),
Bess (76c,183d), best (41d,159c,160a), beta (71a,91c,141d), bete
(61a,107c), beth (91c), Beth (8c,183d), bevy (38a,58c)
- BE - abed (130c), Abel (7a,25b), abet (8b,15b,50a,59b,75d,81c,141d,
159d), Eben (96a), Eber (51a,75c,99d), ibex (67d,68a), obex
(22d), obey (35c,75c), Obed (135d), uber (66b)

277

· · BE   abbe (32b,63b,123b), aIbe (133a), babe, Bube (180b), cube (66b, 150a), dobe (159b,c,172b), Elbe (108a), gabe (162a), gibe (8a, 42c,84d,100d,138c,144c,149b), gybe (144c), Habe (191), Heb (39c,69c,186b), imbe (37a,56a,133d), jibe (8a,33b,35d,37b,42c, 100d,138c,144c,149b), jube (28d), klbe, Kobe (78a), lobe (90c, 134b),lube (110a), ribe (139a), robe (65b), rube (37d,135d,185d), Rube (96b), sabe, tobe (7d,137b), tube (118b,158a)

B · · E   babe, bade, bake (139a), bale (24b,74a), bane (74a,106b,120b, 139a), bare (43d,157c), base (6a,43b,44b,51c,60c,79b,94b, 122b), bate (43c,91b,100d), bave (61d,146c), Bede (48c,50c, 101d,175b), bene (18a,83c,90a,106d,122a,180a), bete (61a,107c), bice (20d,117d), Bice (27b), bide (47c,50b,130a,158b), bike, bile (30c), bine (145b,156a,171c,176b), bise (182a), bite (29d,156b), bize (182a), blae (93b), blue (33c,98c,102c,150d,173a), boce (23b,52a,57b), bode (14c,60a,110b,121b), bole (31d,32a,169b), bone, bore (14c,25b,46a,116a,165c,179b), bose (163c), bra (76d,139a,c,140b,148c), bree (139a), Brie (29c), Bube (180b), bure (61b), byee (189), byre (38a)

· BF ·   Abfa (76b)

B · · F   baff (69d), beef, biff, buff (134c,161d)

B · · G   bang (75d,105d,148a), beng (43a), berg (79b), bing, bong, borg (40d), brag (21a,175a), brig (72b,106a,144d), bung (119d,156d), burg (22b,73c)

BH · ·   Bhar (191), bhat (80c), bhel (126d), Bhil (191), b'hoy (134b), bhut (67a)

· · BH   Cobh (37a)

B · · H   Bach (35c), bash, bath, Bath (50d,151c), beth (91c), Beth (8c, 183d), bikh (120b), binh (189), bish (120b), blah, booh (52c), bosh, both, bruh (95a), bukh (122a), bush

BI · ·   bias (43b,123a), bibb (97c,146b), bibi (87d), bice (20d,117d), Bice (27b), bide (47c,50b,130a,158b,162a,177b), bien (63a,140c, 179a,180a), bier (33b,66b), biff, biga (171d), bija (168c), bike, bikh (120b), bile (30c), bilk (29b,41c,42a), bill (17b,147a), Bill (96b), bilo (131b), bina (77a), bind (33b,165c), bine (145b, 156a,171c,176b), bing, binh (189), Bini (191), binn (22c), bino (113b,117a), biod (59d,79c), bion (117b), bios (92a), bird, bird (93c,131a,153c), birn (31d,139a), birr (180c), bisa (11a), bise (182a), bish (120b), bisk (120b,151a), bite (29d,156b), biti (20b), bito (7d,57d,168c), bitt (54d,175c), biur (35a), biwa (93d,168c), Bixa (145d), bize (182a), bizz

· BI ·   Abia (18d,137a), Abib (102a,b), Able (96b,107a), abir (129a), ibid (80a,117a,137a), ibis (48d,49a,177b), ibit (117a), obia (55d), obit (41b,64c), Ubii (191)

· · BI   Albi (58a), ambi (34a,122c), Babi (116c), bibi (87d), Bubi (180b), cubi (188), gabi (162a), gobi, Gobi (42d), kobi (84b), mabi (58d), rabi (38d,74a), Rabi (14b,117b), sebi (34b), tabi (84c,149d), Tybi (102a), Wabi (192), Yobi

B · · I   Babi (116c), bahi (60c), Bali, bani (190), bari (79c), Bari (37c, 83d), Bell (23c), beni (116a,142d), Beni (191), bibi (87d), Bini (191), biti (20b), Boil (191), Boni (63b), Bori (110d,150c), Bubi (180b), Bugi (191), buri (56b)

· · BK   nabk (30d,164d), nubk (30d,164d, Sobk (38d)

B · · K   back (75d,76d,159d), balk (118c,146a,156d), bank (18a,58c), bark (115c), bask (94d), beak (19a), beck (107c), bilk (29b,41c, 42a), bisk (120b,151a), bock (17c,90d,144a), bonk (190), book, bosk (164b), bowk (155d), buck (122a), bukk (97b), bunk, busk (17b,37b,55d,161b)

BL · ·   blaa, blab (162b), blae (93b), blah (6c,49c), Blas (67b), blat (25b), blay (57d), bleb (20c,23d,67c), bled (64a), blet (61b), blew, blob (173a), bloc (173a), blot, blow, blub, blue (33c,98c, 102c,150d,173a), blup, blur, blut (66b)

· BL ·   able (26b,35b,126a,147c), ably (147c)

B · · L   baal (142b), bail (43c), ball, baul (18b), bawl, beal (139d), bell (24c,39d), Bell (162d), bhel (126d), Bhil (191), bill (17b,147a), Bill (96b), birl (93c,131a,153c), boil, boll (119b,d), bool (39d), bowl, bual (182d), buhl (81a), bull (113c), burl (87c,169a)

B · · M   balm (110a,172c), barm (185b), Baum (9c,112c), beam, berm (25d,90d,145c), boom (152d), Bram (96a), brim

B · · N   bain (61a), barn (156d), bawn (181a), bean (91b,142a,175a), been (149a), behn (137d), Bern (160d), bien (63a,140c,179a, 180a), binn (22c), blon (117b), birn (31d,139a), Bonn (17d), boon (18b,20c,55a), born, bran (23c,39a,70b,72a,79c), Bran (23c,50c), bren (72d,95a), brin (32c,54c,146c), bunn (25b), burn

BO · ·   boar (77c,117c,160c,181c), boat (27b,106a), Boaz (135d), boba (29d), bobo (112c,168c), boca (152b,c), boce (23b,52a,57b), bock (17c,90d,144a), Bodb (82b), bode (14c,60a,110b,121b), Bodo (88c), body (72a), Boer (151a), boga (57d,180b), bogo (117a, 168c), Bogo (191), bogy (153a), boho (117a,179d), Bohr (14b, 40d,138c), Boil (191), boll, bois (62b,63a,183d), bojo (117a), boko (52b), bola (16a,179b), bold (41a), bole (31d,32a,169b), boll (119b,d), bolo (87a,179b), bolt (13b,54d,58b,132d,160a), boma (7d), bomb (144a), bona (89d), Bona (183c), bond (92a, 101c,141d,143b,159d,165c), bone, bong (63b), bonk (190), Bonn (17d), bony (147c), Bony (96b), boob (146d), booh (52c), book, bool (39d), boom (152d), boon (18b,20c,55a), boor (47a, 135d,172c), boot (128d), bora (181d,182b), bord (100b), bore (14c,25b,46a,116a,165c,179b), borg (40d), Bori (110d,150c), born, boro (154b), Boro (193), Bors (70b,134b), bort (43b), Bort (134b), bosa (12a), Bosc (115c), bose (163c), bosh (146d), bosk (164b), boss (49d,157d), bota (189), both, Boto (192), bott (32a,88d), bout (36c), bouw (188), bowk (155d), bowl, boxy, boza (12a), bozo (55b)

· BO ·   aboo (17a), Abot (100c), Abou (48b,55a), abox (22d), eboe (28b, 110a,168c,169b), Eboe, ebon (20b), oboe (74b,104d,105a,182a, 184a), obol (29b,110a)

· · BO   albo (34d,181a), ambo (125b,128b), bobo (112c,168c), bubo (112c), Egbo (141d), Gobo (84d), hobo (168a,174b), jobo (77c), lobo (165d,183c), nabo (117a), Nebo (68c,102d,103d,183a), umbo (22b), zobo (186b)

B · · O   bago (13d), baho (122a), baro (71a,122a), beno (113b,117a), bilo (131b), bino (113b,117a), bito (7d,52d,168c), bobo (112c,168c), Bodo (88c), bogo (117a,168c), Bogo (191), boho (117a,179d),

279

bojo (117a), boko (52b), bolo (87a,179b), boro (154b), Boro (193), Boto (192), bozo (55b), broo (139a), bubo (112c), Bufo (166c), Buto (142d), buyo (18b), bygo (114c)

B - - P   blup, bump

BR - -   brab (113b), brad (54d,67c,105b), brae (76d,139a,c,140b,148c), brag (21a,175a), Bram (96a), bran (23c,39a,70b,72a,79c), Bran (23c,50c), bras (61a), brat, bray, brea (100b), bred (23c,48c, 127c), bree (139a), bren (72d,95a), Brer (172b), Bres, brew (35d), brey (194), Brie (29c), brig (72b,106a,144d), brim, brin (32c,54c,146c), brit (76c), brob (153c), broo (139a), brow, bruh (95a), brut (182c), Brut (23c)

- BR -   abra (26b), Abra, abri (61c,62c,144b), Ebro (132a), obra (152d, 184c)

B - - R   barr (49b), bear (27a,50b,113c,155a), beer (18c), Bhar (191), bier (33b,66b), birr (180d), biur (35a), blur, boar (77c,117c, 160c,181c), Boer (151a), Bohr (14b,40d,138c), boor (47a,135d, 172c), Brer (172b), buhr (180d), burr (123b)

- BS -   Absi (191)

- - BS   dibs (70c), Lubs (94c), nibs (116c), nobs (38c,87a)

B - - S   baas (97c), bans, bass (57b,c,177a), bees (185b), Bess (76c, 183d), bias (43b,123a), bios (92a), blas (6c,49c), Blas (67b), bois (62b,63a,183d), Bors (70b,134b), boss (49d,157d), bras (61a), Bres, buss (87a,148c)

- - BT   debt (91d,109b)

B - - T   baft (14a,53b), baht (146a), bait (15d,51a,94d,167b), Balt (93a), bant (43c), Bart (96b), bast (16c,56a,117c,184a), Bast (27b), batt (37c), beat (58c,87b,131a,164d,165b,180d), beet (175a), belt (16a,31a), bent (80b), Bert (96b), best (41d,159c,160a), bhat (80c), bhut (67a), bitt (54d,175c), blat (25b), blet (64a), blot, blut (66b), boat (27b,106a), bolt (13b,54d,58b,132d,160a), boot (128d), bort (43b), Bort (134b), bott (32a,88d), bout (36c), brat, brit (76c), brut (182c), Brut (23c), bult (76d), bunt (15d, 180c), bust, butt (27a,77b,127d,162a,182b)

BU - -   bual (182c), buba (170a), Bube (180b), Bubi (180b), bubo (112c), buck, buda (83b), buff (134c,161d), Bufo (166c), Bugi (191), buhl (81a), buhr (180d), bukh (122a), bukk (122a), bulb (37a,172c), bulk (97b), bull (113c), bult (76d), bump, buna (161c), bund (49c,66c,90c), bung (119d,156b), bunk, bunn (25b), bunt (15d,180c), buoy (28d,58c), bura (182b), bure (61b), burg (22b,73c), burl (56b), burl (87c,169a), burn, burr (123b), bury (81d), bush, busk (17b,37b,55d,161b), buss (87a,148c), bust, busy, Buto (142d), butt (27a,77b,127d,162a,182b), buxy (115b), buyo (18b), buzz

- BU -   abut (22a,167c), ebur (89c)

- - BU   babu (77a), kobu (84b), Nabu (68c,183a), tabu (59d,111d), Tibu (191), zebu (22d,80d,112c)

B - - U   babu (77a), baju (84a), baku (26d,157b168c), balu (104b,159a, 187d), baru (168c), beau, benu (49a), bleu (61b)

B - - W   blew, blow, bouw (188), brew (35d), brow

BY - -   byee (189), bygo (114c), Byrd (9c,120b), byre (38a)

281

C - - C   chic (148d), circ (31a), cric (131c), croc (13a,74a)

C - - D   caid (35a,151d,152b), card (33d,114d), Chad (158b), chid, Chud (191), clad (46a,82a), clod (22a,45b,157d), coed, cold (65d), cond (156a), cord (39b,131a) curd (99d)

CE - -   ceba (169b), cede (67b,70c,129d,160a,168b,185d), ceil (92c, 112a), cela (62d), cell (39b), celt (30c,123a,156c,167b,179b), Celt (10a,180a,b), cena (88d,133a), cene (34c), cens (115b), cent (36d), cepa (110c), cepe (48c), cera (152d,161d,179a), cere (19a,114b,149d,179a), cern (41c), cero (57b,c,d,180b), cess (91d, 94c,162b), cest (18a,67b), cete (180b,c), ceto (34a), Ceyx (73b)

- CE -   Acer (96c), icer

- - CE   ance (158b,c,d), bice (20d,117d), Bice (27b), boce (23b,52a, 57b), dace (57a,b), dice (65a), duce (29d), ecce (17d,89a,c), ence (158c), esce (158d), face (159d,176c), lace (58b,179c), luce (58c,117d), Luce (7b,35a), mace (49d,108d,153b,154d,161a, 178a), nice (54d,119c,130c), Nice (98c), once (60b,79b), pace (64b,98a,153b,156a,170b,177d), pice (190), puce (33c,d, 52a), race (116a,153b,154b), Rice (46a), sice (71d,147b), syce (71d), tace (13a,155d), tice (9a,38c,51a,185d), vice (31d,158a), voce (83c,177a)

C - - E   cade (25c,27a,76c,85d,116d), Cade (50c), cafe, cage (36a), cake, cale (72d), came (182b), Came (192), cane (17b,128a,156a,159a, 177d), Cane, cape (75a,96c,124b,161a), care (11b,14c,35d,150a, 184d), case (22c,36c,81c,91a,108c), cate (165c), cave (27d), cede (67b,70c,129d,160a,168b,185d), cene (34c), cepe (48c), cere (19a,114b,149d,179a), cete (180b,c), chee (189), cine (104b,152c), cise (147b), cite (15a,98d,126d,159b), cive (110c), clee (19a,129a), Cloe (183c), clue (58d), code (21c,31a,40c,161c), coke (32d,64a), cole (25a), Cole, come, cone (66b,150a,157c), cope (12b,26b,36c,65b,157d,176a), core (28b,51c,75b,81b), cose (29b), cote (19b,143d,144a,b), cove (17a,73d,107d), coze (29b), Cree (192), cube (66b,150a), cuke (39b), cure (123b,d), cute (39c), cyke (40c), cyme (58d,69c)

C - - F   calf, chef, clef (104d,105a), coif (73a), cuff (148a), culf (139a,d, 140c)

C - - G   cang (184a), chug (53a), clog (30c,145b), coag (45d,118a,163b), crag (132c), crig (20d)

CH - -   chaa (162b), chab (184a), Chad (158b), chai (72d), cham (20a, 29d), Cham (8c), chan (26c,130c), chap (55b), char (24d,138c, 170b), chat (9b,19c,161c), chaw (97c), chay (48a,128d), chee (189), chef, chek (59c), Chen (149b), cher (61b), chew (97c), chez (14b,61a), chia (136d), chib (167a), chic (148d), chid ch'ih (188), chil, chin, Chin (30b), chip (69d), chir (29b,116d), chit (67b,98c,108b,116c,177c), chiv (87a), chob (23c), chol (118d), Chol (192), chop (98a), chor (164b), chou (61b), Chou (30b), chow (45a), choy (48a,128d), chub (40c,154c), Chud (191), chug (53a), chum (38d), Chun (30c), chut!

- CH -   ache (79a,112d,185b), acht (66c), achy, echo (130b,d), Echo (105d), icho (67b), ichu (10b,70d), ocha (189), tcha (162c), tche (13d,30b,105a), tchi, Tchi, tchu

282

- - CH   **alch** (9a), **arch** (29d,38b,39d,123d,132c), **bach, Bach** (35c), **each, etch, Foch** (63b), **hoch** (52c,66c), **Hoch, inch, itch, Koch** (66d), **lech** (102b), **loch** (88a,139d), **much, nach, ouch, rich, Roch** (136c), **sech** (97c), **such** (146d), **Tech, Vach** (153b), **Zach** (96b)

C - - H   **caph** (91c), **Caph, cash** (101c), **ch'ih** (188), **Cobh** (37a), **cosh** (35a,97c), **cush** (101c), **Cush** (51d,73c)

CI - -   **cima** (83b,c), **cine** (104b,152c), **cinq** (61d), **cion** (42d,70b,145b, 148b,154b,156a), **cipo** (91d), **circ** (31a), **cirl** (24c), **cise** (147b), **cist** (22c,29d,156c), **cite** (15a,98d,126d,159b), **cito** (89d,126c), **cits, city, Civa** (56d), **cive** (110c)

- CI -   **acid** (151a,162a), **Acis** (64b), **Scio**

- - CI   **asci** (154a), **deci** (163b), **foci** (28b), **fuci** (132c), **loci** (66b,118c), **Pici** (19c,184a), **unci** (31d)

C - - I   **cadi** (12a,103a,171a), **Cadi, caji** (180b), **cazi** (103a), **chai** (72d), **coli, Coni, Cori** (138c), **cubi** (188)

- - CK   **back** (75d,76d,159d), **beck** (107c), **bock** (17c,90d,144a), **buck, cock** (19a,29a,55a,133d,136d,161d,174b), **deck** (13b,41c,144d), **dick** (43a,55b), **Dick** (96b), **dock** (40a,117c,144d,179d), **duck** (26b,53b,179c), **hack** (40a,77c,184d), **heck** (100a), **hick** (185d), **hock** (91a,115b,182b,c), **huck** (167d), **jack** (26c,58a,127c), **Jack** (96b), **jock** (96b), **Jock, juck** (114c), **kick, lack** (178a), **lick lock** (54d), **luck** (28d), **mack, mick** (82c), **mock** (131b,162b), **muck, neck** (83a), **nick** (30c,108b), **nock** (13b,108b), **pack** (24b, 140d), **peck** (24d), **pick, puck** (44b,68a,77c,100c), **Puck** (99d, 143b), **rack** (32c,64b), **reck** (26d,75c), **rick** (74d,117d), **rock** (160b), **ruck** (39a,185a), **sack** (43d,118a,119d,182b), **seck** (173d), **sick, sock** (157c,182a), **suck, tack** (28d,37d,54d), **teck** (128b), **tick** (12b,20d,97c), **tock** (7d,19b), **tuck** (156b), **wick**

C - - K   **calk** (78c,109a,141c,178d), **cark** (26d,184d), **cask, cauk** (139b), **cawk** (133c), **chek** (59c), **coak** (45d,118a,163b), **cock** (19a,29a, 55a,133d,136d), **conk** (41c,108a,156d,157c), **cook** (137b), **cork** (119d), **cusk** (57b)

CL - -   **clad** (46a,82a), **clam** (20b,101b), **clan** (169c), **clap** (58b), **claw** (29c,105b,161d,173a), **clay, Clay** (9d), **clee** (19a,129a), **clef** (104d,105a), **clem** (56b,158b), **Cleo** (126b), **clew** (16a,33a,77b, 136b,164d), **Clim** (12b), **Clio** (104d), **clip** (54d,143b), **clod** (22a, 45b,157d), **Cloe** (183c), **clog** (30c,145b), **clop, clot** (32d,94d), **clou** (62b), **clow** (58c,148c), **cloy** (61b,137c,159d), **club** (39c), **clue, Clym** (12b)

- CL -   **acle** (13d,82c,115d)

C - - L   **call** (145c,159b,176d), **carl** (115c,135d), **Carl** (96a), **caul** (16d, 74d), **ceil** (92c,112a), **cell** (39b), **chil, chol** (118d), **Chol** (192), **cirl** (24c), **coal** (49c,64a), **coel** (39b), **coil** (39d,171c,185a), **cool** (25c,107d), **cowl** (101d), **cral, cull** (117c), **curl** (38d,73b,93b, 131d)

- CM -   **acme** (39c,115c,186b)

C - - M   **caam** (93d), **calm** (8d,11d,112b,118d,126c,d,172b), **cham** (20a, 29d), **Cham** (8c), **chum** (38d), **clam** (20b,101b), **clem** (56b,158b), **Clim** (12b), **Clym** (12b), **coom** (32d,150c,178d), **corm** (24b,38d, 156a), **cram** (157d), **Crom, culm** (11a,32d,70d,145a,156a)

CN - - Cnut (40d,50c)

- CN - acne (147c)

C - - N Caen, cain (169c), **Cain** (6a,7a,50d,88a,104c,143a), carn (156c), cern (41c), chan (26c,130c), Chen (149b), chin, Chin (30b), Chun (30c), cion (42d,70~; 15b,148b,154b,156a), cian (169c), Coan (37b), coin (19b,37a,100c,101c,179d), conn (43d,156a), coon (121c), corn (39d,95c,123a), coyn (37a), cran (160c), crin (146c), cyan

CO - - coag (45d,118a,163b), coak (45d,118a,163b), coal (49c,64a), Coan (37b), coat (160a), coax (180c), Cobb (9c), Cobh (37a), coca (29d,33a,105d,113a), cock (19a,29a,55a,133d,136d,161d, 174b), coco (113a), coda (32c,35d,56c), code (21c,31a,40c,161c), codo (188), coed, coel (39b), coho (136d), colf (73a), coil (39d, 171c,185a), coin (19b,37a,100c,101c,179d), coir (33a,37a,56a, 133d), Coix (70d,85b), coja (103b,166b), coke (32d,64a), coky, cola (25b,108d,149d,168c), cold (65d), cole (25a), Cole, coll, colp (28a,148b), colt (78c,131a,185d,186b), Colt, coly (104a), coma (91c,157d,170c,172b), comb (38c), come, Como, cond (156a), cone (66b,150a,157c), Coni, conk (41c,108a,156d,157c), conn (43d,156a), cony (127a), cook (137b), cool (25c,107d), coom (32d,150c,178d), coon (121c), coop, Coos, (192), coot (19b,46d,72b,138d,141a,146d,157d), copa (88b,113c), cope (12b, 26b,36c,65b,157d,176a), copt (48d), copy, cora (65d), Cora (42b,69c,80c,116b,124d,172b,183c), cord (39b,139a), core (28b, 51c,75b,81b), Corl (138c), cork (119d), corm (24b,38d,156a), corn (39d,95c,123a), cose (29b), cosh (35a,97c), coso (152c), coss (98a), cost (29a), cosy (149c), cota (117a), cote (19b,143d, 144a,b), coto (16c,90b), Coty (63c), coup (20d,97c,157b,c,162d), cous (38a), cove (17a,73d,107d), cowl (101d), coxa (77b), coyn (37a), coyo (15a,30c), coze (29b), cozy (149c)

- CO - acon (62c,140d), acor (6d), icon (79d,92b,136a), scob (42a), scon (162c), scop (120a), scot (14a,162b), Scot (64b,132c), scow (21a,58b)

- - CO alco (45b), caco (73b), coco (113a), Duco, fico (169d), loco (38b,119b,120b), mico (97a), paco (9b,146d), peco (162b), pico (65a,152c), poco (83b,93a), saco (189), soco (22d), Teco (192), toco (19b,167c), unco (140c), Waco

C - - O caco (73b), caio (72d), cano (152a), caro (83a), Caro (183d), Caso (82d), Cato (132d,133b), cayo (15a), cero (57b,c,d,180c), ceto (34a), cipo (91d), cito (89d,126c), Cleo (126b), Cllo (104d), coco, (113a), codo (188), coho (136d), Como, coso (152d), coto (16c, 90b), coyo (15a,30c)

C - - P calp (92b), camp (163b), Capp (27a), carp (27d,38d,40c,55a, 56c,57a), caup, chap (55b), chip (69d), chop (98a), clap (58b), clip (54d,143d), clop, colp (28a,148b), coop, coup (20d,97c, 157b,c,162d), crop (38b), cusp (38c,78b,119a,120a,b)

C - - Q cinq (61d)

CR - - crab (39b,144b,181b), crag (132c), cral, cram (157d), cran (160c), craw (38d,72c,156c), Crax (19b,39d), crea (92c,151d), Cree (192), crew (72a,160a), Crex (37a), crib (96b,120d), cric (131c), crig (20d), crin (146c), cris (40b,95d), croc (13a,74a), Crom, crop (38b), crow (19a), crus (91a,143c), crux (39a,151b)

284

acre (39b,56a,88b), **Acre, ecru** (17d,23d,172b), ocra (72c,175a)

C · · R carr (120d,140a), caur (139a), char (24d,138c,170b), cher (61b), chir (29b,116d), chor (164b), colr (33a,37a,56a,133d), cuir (45c, 62a), curr (104c), **Czar** (42d,49d,60b,135c)

· · CS ABC's (57a), pacs (94c)

C · · S cass (140c,177a), **Cass** (147a), cens (115b), cess (91d,94c,162b), cits, **Coos** (192), coss (98a), cous (38a), cris (40b,95d), crus (91a,143c), cuss

· CT · acta (41d,123d,128d,164c), acth (13b), acto (152b), **Acts, actu** (7a,89a), ecto (34c,122d), octa (122c), octo (34a,89b,122c)

· · CT duct (170c), fact (7a,128b), lact (34c), pact (8a), **Pict** (23c,47d), rect (117b), sect (42b,54a,114c), tact (43c,d,116a)

C · · T cant (28d,81b,84d,90c,109b,136c,165d,166a), cart (171d,175a, 177b), cast (165b,167c), **Catt** (9d), celt (30c,82c,123a,156c,167b, 179b), **Celt** (10a,180a,b), cent (36d), cest (18a,67b), chat (9b, 19c,161c), chit (67b,98c,108b,116c,177c), chutl, cist (22c,29d, 156c), clot (32d,94d), coat (160a), colt (78c,131a,185d,186b), **Colt** (131a), coot (19b,46d,72b,138d,141a,146d,157d), **Copt** (48d), cost (29a), cult (141d,161c), curt (145b,c), cyst

CU · · cuba (189), **Cuba** (180b), cube (66b,150a), cubi (188), cuca (33a,105d), cuff (148a), culf (139a,d,140c), cuir (45c,62a), cuke (39b), cull (117c), culm (11a,32d,70d,145a,156a), cult (141d, 161c), **Cuna** (193), cura (152c), curb (130c,146b), curd (99d), cure (123b), curl (38d,73b,93b,131d), curr (104c), curt (145b,c), cush (101c), **Cush** (51d,73c), cusk (57b), cusp (38c,78b,119a, 120a,b), cuss, cute (39c), cuvy (141a), cuya (39b)

· CU · acus (89d,118a), scud (32c,126c,135b,160c), scum (129b), scup (57a,121b), scur (78b), scut (145c,161b)

· · CU jacu (19a,151b), jocu (45b,57a)

C · · U chou (61b), **Chou** (30b), clou (62b)

C · · V chiv (87a)

C · · W chaw (97c), chew (97c), chow (45a), claw (29c,105b,161d,173a), clew (16a,33a,77b,136b,164d), clow (58c,148b), craw (38d,72c, 156c), crew (72a,106a), crow (19a)

C · · X calx (23c,75c,112c), **Ceyx** (73b), coax (180c), **Coix** (70d,85b), **Crax** (19b,39d), **Crex** (37a), crux (39a,151b)

CY · · cyan (40c), cyke (40c), cyma (101a,b), cyme (58d,69c), cyst

· CY · acyl (6d)

· · CY ancy (158c), lacy, **Lucy** (183c), racy (153b)

C · · Y cady (69d), cagy (178b), caky, cavy (72b,120d,132c,157b), cazy (103a), chay (48a,128d), choy (48a,128d), city, clay, **Clay** (9d), cloy (61b,137c,159d), coky, coly (104a), cony (127a), copy, cosy (149c), **Coty** (63c), cozy (149c), cuvy (141a)

CZ · · czar (42d,49d,60b,135c)

C · · Z chez (14b,61a)

DA · · dace (57a,b), **Dada** (13b,63a,157d), dado (41c,111c,115c,177d), daer (22b), daez, daff (125d), daft (59c), dagg (118c), dagh (76d), **Dago, Dail** (49a,82b,c), dain (188), dais (119b), dale (43c, 128a,174b), dali (168c,169b), dama (65d,152b), dame (67b,87c,

166b), **damn, damp** (101a), **Dana** (28a,96a,171d), **Dane** (85d, 107d,138a), **dang, dank** (40b,101a), **dans** (62a), **Danu** (28a), **Dara** (18d), **Dard, dare** (28d,41b,42a,74d,175b), **Dare** (57a), **dari** (38a,70b), **dark** (47a,67d,109b,160b), **darn** (130b), **darr** (163c), **dart** (13b,88a,100c,120b,153a,160c), **dash** (125c,162d), **dasi** (77a), **data** (54a), **date** (64a,153a), **dato** (95c,102c,117a), **datu** (95c,102c,117a), **daub** (148d), **dauk** (95c), **Daur** (139b), **dauw** (24c), **Dave** (96b), **Davy** (96b,136b), **dawk** (95c), **dawm** (190), **dawn** (14d,41b), **Daye** (123d), **days, Daza** (191), **daze** (157d), **dazy**

- **DA** - **adad** (52c,56a), **Adad** (68c,157a,182a), **Adah** (25b,51b), **Adam** (26b,96a,111c), **adan** (102d), **Adar** (85c,102a), **adat** (90b,95d), **Edam** (29c), **Edar** (18d), **Idas** (27b,71c), **odah** (170d), **odal** (48a, 88b,112c), **Odax** (132c), **udad** (143d,144a,181c), **udal** (76b,88b, 131c)

- - **DA** **adda** (147d), **Adda** (68c,119d), **Aida** (110d,175c), **aida** (152b), **Alda** (110d,150c), **anda** (23a,168c), **Beda** (101d), **Buda** (83d), **coda** (32c,35d,56c), **Dada** (13b,63a,157d), **Edda** (76b,79b,107d), **Erda** (23d,41a,47d,68d,69a,131d,177b), **Juda, kada** (188), **Leda** (27b,75d,120c,153a,171d,186b), **Lida** (183c), **meda** (110a), **nuda** (39b), **peda** (114d,144b), **rada** (135c,172a), **Roda** (107b), **sida** (37a,126c,170a), **soda** (19a,149d,181a), **Teda** (191), **Toda** (45d, 76d), **Veda** (77a,b), **Vida** (183c)

D - - A **Dada** (13b,63a,157d), **dama** (65d,152b), **Dana** (28a,96a,171d), **Dara** (18d), **data** (54a), **Daza** (191), **deca** (34d,122d), **depa** (188), **dera** (34c), **deva** (23d,42a,b,56d,77a), **dewa, dika** (23a), **Disa** (111a), **dita** (117a), **diva** (110d,123c), **dola** (189), **dona** (83d,121c,151d), **dopa** (117d), **dora** (70b), **Dora** (36d,41a,43b), **dosa** (74b), **doxa** (48b), **draa** (188), **Duma** (135c), **dura** (153c), **dyna** (34c)

- - **DB** **Badh** (82b), **Bodh** (82b), **Medb**

D - - B **daub** (148d), **dieb** (84a), **doab** (157c), **doob** (18b), **doub** (18b), **drab** (23d,29c,33d,46d,53b,d), **drib** (46b), **drub** (17b,39c), **duab** (157c), **dubb** (161c), **dumb** (153b)

D - - C **disc** (31b), **douc** (101d)

DD - - **DDSC** (42a)

- **DD** - **adda** (147d), **Adda** (68c,119d,157a,182a), **Addu** (68c,157a,182a), **Addy** (183d), **Edda** (76b,79b), **eddo** (162a), **eddy** (37d,39d,160d, 180d), **odds** (28d,172d)

- - **DD** **dodd** (139c,140c), **gedd** (140a), **Ladd** (143c), **ludd** (23c), **mudd** (188), **Nudd** (23c), **Redd** (153a), **Ridd** (94a), **rodd** (38d), **rudd** (26d,57a,b), **sadd** (33a,40b,58c,107b), **sudd** (40b,58c,107b), **wadd** (109c)

D - - D **dard, dead, deed** (7a,52d,91a,166c,168b), **diad** (113a), **dord** (42c), **dowd** (143b), **duad** (113a,171d), **dyad** (113a)

DE - - **dead, deaf, deal** (11d,16c,36c,44c,81a,168b), **dean** (33c,109d), **dear, debt** (91d,109b), **deca** (34d,122d), **deci** (163b), **deck** (13b,41c,144d), **dedo** (188), **deed** (7a,52d,91a,166c,168b), **deem** (36b,85c,164c), **deep** (124a), **deer** (28c,135a,154d), **defi** (61b), **deft** (147c), **defy** (28d), **degu** (132c), **deil** (139b), **dein** (66d), **deie** (26a,49c,51b,53a,110b,123c,124c,130a,145c,161b), **deli**

286

(43c,174b), **deme** (71b,c,167d), **demi** (34b,122c), **demo** (122d),
demy (113d), **dene** (137a), **Dene** (192), **dens** (90a,167b), **dent**
(42c,77d), **deny** (36d,43d,129b), **depa** (188), **dera** (34c), **dere**
(74a,79c), **derm** (147c,158d), **desi** (85d), **desk, deul** (77b), **deus**
(68a,89b), **Deva** (23d,42a,b,56d,77a), **Devi** (147b,153b), **dewa,**
dewy (101a)

· **DE** ·   **aden** (34b), **Aden, Ader** (18d), **Ades** (73a), **edel** (66c), **Eden** (6b,
50d,107c,113d,123c), **Eder, EDES** (71c), **idea** (54c,108c,124a,
164d), **idee** (61d), **idem** (89d,164a), **Iden** (76a), **ideo** (34b,d),
Ides (41a,b,133a), **odea** (105a,164a), **odel** (48a,112c), **Oder**
(132a)

· · **DE**   **aide** (7b,14a,75d), **Ande** (193), **Aude, bade, Bede** (48c,50c,101d,
175b), **bide** (47c,50b,130a,158b,162a), **bode** (14c,60a,110b,
121b), **cade** (25c,27a,76c,85d,116d), **Cade** (50c), **cede** (67b,70c,
129d,160a,168b,185d), **code** (21c,31a,40c,161c), **Dode** (96b),
dude (40d), **eide** (119c), **fade** (181d,183b), **fide, gade, Gide**
(63a), **hade** (66a,148c,173c), **hide** (53a), **hyde** (188), **Hyde** (45a),
inde, jade (33c,65d,71d,166a), **Jude** (11c,96a), **kade** (144a),
lade (24c,26d,43c,93b,100a,132a,139d,161b,178d), **lode** (42c,
99a,111b,175b), **made, Mede** (10a,b,13c), **mide** (110a), **mode**
(54d,96b,157d,179a), **nide** (23c,72a,106c,116d), **node** (35c,85b,
87c,94d,120a,124d,160c), **nude** (16c), **onde** (63a,178d), **rede**
(37c,81d,138d), **ride** (46b,85c), **rode** (46c), **rude** (134b,172b),
sade (91d), **side** (13d,22a,b,54a,58a,89a,161b), **tide** (39d,75d,
109c,141c,159d), **Tide, tode** (80a,148a), **unde** (179a), **urde** (86b),
vade (42c,67d,89b), **vide** (89d,126a,142a), **wade, wide** (133d)

D · · E   **dace** (57a,b), **dale** (43c,128a,174b), **dame** (67b,87c,166b), **Dane**
(85d,107d,138a), **dare** (28d,41b,42a,74d,175b), **Dare** (57a), **dade**
(64a,153a), **Dave** (96b), **Daye** (123d), **daze** (157d), **dele** (26a,
49c,51b,53a,110b,123d,124c,130a,145c,161b),   **deme**   (71b,c,
167d), **dene** (137a), **Dene** (192), **dere** (74a,79c), **dice** (65a), **dike**
(49c,91d), **Dike** (78a), **dime, dine, dire** (45d,55a,104a,163c), **dite**
(150b), **dive** (42b,74b,119d), **dobe** (159b,c,172b), **Dode** (96b),
doge (95b), **dole** (44c,118c,121c,129d), **Dole** (74c), **dome** (39c,
133c,155d), **done, dope** (46c,105d), **dore** (61d,67b,69d,117d),
Dore (50d,63a,b), **dose** (123a), **dote** (17a,90b,94b,97a,112a,
139d,165d), **dove** (19a,117d), **doze** (148a), **dree** (139b,140c,
158b,172c), **duce** (29d), **dude** (40d), **duff** (125b), **duke** (107c),
dune (137a), **dupe** (27c,41c,72c,160c), **duse** (83c), **dyke** (49c,
91d), **dyne** (59d)

D · · F   **daff** (125d), **deaf, doff** (130a,161b), **duff** (125b)

· **DG** ·   **edge** (22a,96d,131c,143c,146b), **edgy** (106c)

D · · G   **dagg** (118c), **dang, ding** (130b), **Doeg** (137c), **dong, drag** (74a,
125b), **dreg, drug** (105d)

DH · ·   **dhak** (48a,169a), **dhal** (12b), **dhan** (124c), **dhao** (24c), **Dhar,**
dhaw (125a), **dhow** (88d,111c,175d)

· · **DH**   **sadh** (77a), **Sadh, yodh** (91d)

D · · H   **dagh** (76d), **Dagh, dash** (125c,162d), **dish, doth, drah** (188)

DI · ·   **diad** (113a), **dial** (25c), **dian** (46c,130d,170b), **Dian** (68d,69a,c,
102b), **Diau** (192), **dibs** (70c), **dice** (65a), **dick** (43a,55b), **Dick**
(96b), **dido** (11b,26c,65a,122a), **Dido** (27a,172c), **dieb** (84a),

287

diem (89b,116a), dier, dies (41b,89b), diet (14a,54c,84c,91b, 176a), Dieu (61d), dika (23a), dike (49c,91d), Dike (78a), dill (13a,117c), dilo (120d,168c), dime, dine, ding (130b), dino (34b), dint (48c,59d,122a), Dion (96a,152a), dipt, dire (45d,55a, 104a,163c), dirk (40b), dirt, Disa (111a), disc (31b), dish, disk (31b), diss (98b), dita (117a), dite (150b), diva (110d,123c), dive (42b,74b,119d), divi, dixi

- DI - Adib (155b), adit (51a,100a,114d), edit (20d,49d,123a,129a, 131a), idic (79b), idio (34b,c), odic (79c,120a), Odin (7c,29d, 63c,68c,175d,183b), odio (83b), udic (108a)

- - DI Andi (27d), cadi (12a,103a), kadi (103a,171a), Lodi (105d), ludi (133b), Madi (174a), medi (34c), Midi (151b), nidi (106c), nodi (35c,87c), padi (131b), pedi (34b), rodi (98c), sidi (103b), wadi (46c,106a,109a,128a,132a)

D - - I dali (168c,169b), dari (38a,70b), dasi (77a), deci (163b), defi (61b), demi (34b,122c), desi (85d), Devi (147b,153b), divi, dixi, doni (21a,28c,168a), drei (66d,165a)

- DJ - Idjo (191)

- - DJ hadj (98b,118a)

D - - K dank (40b,101a), dark (47a,67d,109b,160b), dauk (95c), dawk (95c), deck (13b,41c,144d), desk, dhak (48a,169a), dick (43a, 55b), Dick (96b), dirk (40b), disk (31b), dock (40a,117c,144d, 179d), dook (184a), duck (26b,53b,179c), dunk (43c,79d), dusk (171c), Dyak (22b)

- DL - idle (174b,c,178c), idly

D - - L Dail (49a,82b,c), deal (11d,16c,36c,44c,81a,168b), dell (139b), dell (43c,174b), deul (77b), dhal (12b), dial (25c), dill (13a, 117c), doll (125c), dowl, dual (45c,171d), duel, dull (21a,32c, 173a, Dull (94b)

- DM - adml (65d)

D - - M dawm (190), deem (36b,85c,164c), derm (147c,158d), diem (89b,116a), doom (42d,55a,134d), dorm, doum (168c), dram (46b,110c,121d,148c), drum (105a), duim (188)

- DN - Edna (183c)

D - - N dain (188), darn, damn, dawn (14d,41b), dean (33c,109d), dein (66d), dhan (124c), dian (46c,130d,170b), Dian (68d,69a,c, 102b), Dion (96a,152a), Domn (135a), doon (140b,168c), dorn (164d), down (149d), duan (64b)

DO - - doab (157c), doat (17a,94b,112a,165d), dobe (159b,c,172b), doby (159b,c), dock (40a,117c,144d,179d), dodd (139c,140c), Dode (96b), dodo (19b) Doeg (137c), doer (8a,116b), does, doff (130a,161b), doge (25b,175b), dogy (46d,103c), doit (47a,169d, 180d), Doko (191), dola (189), dole (44c,118c,121c,129d), Dole (74c), doll, doll (125c), dolt (20c,59c,157d), dome (39c,133c, 155d), Domn (135a), domy, dona (83d,121c,151d), done, dong, doni (21a,28c,168a), don't, doob (18b), dook (184a), doom (42d, 55a,134d), doon (140b,168c), door (51a,121b), dopa (117d), dope (46c,105d), dopp (43c), dora (70b), Dora (36d,41a,43b,183 c,d), dord (42c), dore (61d,67b,69d,117d), Dore (50d,63a,b), dorm, dorn (164d), dorp (73c,176b), dorr (32b), dory (21b,58b, 144c), dosa (74b), dose (123a), doss (17c), dost, dote (17a,90b,

288

94b,97a,112a,139d,165d), doth, Doto (141b), doty (43d), doub (18b), douc (101d), doum (168c), dour (67d,159a), dove (19a, 117d), dowd (143b), dowl, down (149d), doxa (48b), doxy (129d), doze (148a), dozy

- DO - ador (153b), Edom (18c,51b,79b,82c,84a), idol (48c,54c,55a, 75b,79d,112d,130b,184d), odor (138b,156a)

- - DO Bodo (88c), codo (188), dado (41c,111c,115c,177d), dedo (188), dido (11b,26c,65a,122a), Dido (27a,172c), dodo (19b), eddo (162a), endo (34d,122d,183b), fado (121c), Jodo (113d), judo (84b,85c,142b), Lido (83d,175b), ludo (65a,112b), mado (14d, 57a,170b), ordo (22a,30d,122a,171a), pedo (34b), redo (165c), sado (26d,84d), todo (22b,24d,35b,64c,156b), undo (11a,93d), Yedo (166d)

D - - O dado (41c,111c,115c,177d), Dago, dato (95c,102c,117a), dedo (188), demo (122d), dhao (24c), dido (11b,26c,65a,122a), Dido (27a,172c), dilo (120d,168c), dino (34b), dodo (19b), Doko (191), Doto (141b), Duco, duro (190)

D - - P damp (101a), deep (124a), dopp (43c), dorp (73c,176b), drap (61b,c,62a), drip, drop (43d,54b,100b,114c,168b), dump

DR - - draa (188), drab (23d,29c,33d,46d,53b,d), drag (74a,125b), drah (188), dram (46b,110c,121d,148c), drap (61b,c,62a), drat (100a), Drau, draw (42c,53a,92b,117c,121c,167d), dray (27a,154c,177b), dree (139b,140c,158b,172c), dreg, drei (66d,165a), drew, drey (154c), drib (46b), Drin, drip, drop (43d,54b,100b,114c,168b), drub (17b,39c), drug (105d), drum (105a), drun (132b)

- DR - adry (164c)

- - DR sadr (94a), Sadr (155b)

D - - R daer (22b), darr (163c), Daur (139b), dear, deer (28c,135a, 154d), Dhar, dier, doer (8a,116b), door (51a,121b), dorr (32b), dour (67d,159a), duar, Duhr (155b), durr (70b), dyer

- DS - DDSC (42a)

- - DS duds (32c,166d), Eads (23b,24b,50b,82a), odds (28d,172c), suds (59a)

D - - S dais (119b), dans (62a), days, dens (90a,167b), deus (68a,89b), dibs (70c), dies (41b,89b), diss (98b), does, doss (17c), duds (32c,166d), Duns, Dyas (66a)

D - - T daft (59c), dart (13b,88a,100c,120b,153a,160c), debt (91d,109b), deft (147c), dent (42c,77d), diet (14a,54c,84c,91b,176a), dint (48c,59d,122a), dipt, dirt, doat (17a,94b,112a,165d), doit (47a, 169d,180d), dolt (20c,59c,157d), don't, dost, drat (100a), Duat (172d), duct (170c), duet (104d,171d), duit (190), Duit (192), dunt, dust

DU - - duab (157c), duad (113a,171d), dual (45c,171d), duan (64b), duar, Duat (172d), dubb (161c), duce (29d), duck (26b,53b, 179c), Duco, duct (170c), dude (40d), duds (32c,166d), duel, duet (104d,171d), duff (125b), Dufy (63a), Duhr (155b), duim (188), duit (190), Duit (192), duke (107c), duku (95d,168c), dull (21a,32c,173a), Dull (94b), Duma (135c), dumb (153b), dump, dune (137a), dunk (43c,79d), Duns, dunt, dupe (27c,41c,72c, 160c), dura (153c), duro (190), durr (70b), duse (83c), dusk (171c), dust, duty (109b,162b)

289

- **DU** - idun (107d), odum (168c,180a)
- - **DU** Addu (68c,157a,182a), Jadu (95a), Kadu (191), kudu (11a), ordu (170d), pudu (41d), Urdu (77b), widu (102d), wudu (102d)
- **D - - U** Danu (28a), datu (95c,102c,117a), degu (132c), Diau (192), Dieu (61d), Drau, duku (95d,168c)
- **D - - W** dauw (24c), dhaw (125a), dhow (88d,111c,175d), draw (42c,53a, 92b,117c,121c,167d), drew
- **DY - -** dyad (113a), Dyak (22b), Dyas (66a), dyer, dyke (49c,91d), dyna (34c), dyne (59d,173b)
- - **DY** - idyl (114d), Idyo (191), odyl (59d,79c)
- - - **DY** Addy (183d), Andy (96b), body (72a), cady (69d), eddy (37d, 39d,160d,180d), fady, jady Judy (125c,183d), lady, sidy (123b), tidy (106a,111b), tody (19b,d,59a,166a), undy (179a), urdy (86b), wady (109a,128a,132a)
- **D - - Y** Davy (96b,136b), dazy, defy (28d), demy (113d), deny (36d,43d, 129b), dewy (101a), doby (159b,c), dogy (46d,103c), domy, dory (21b,58b,144c), doty (43d), doxy (129d), dozy (dray (27a,154c, 177b), drey (154c), Dufy (63a), duty (109b,162b)
- - **DZ** - adze (40c,167a), Idzo (191)
- - - **DZ** Lodz
- **D - - Z** Daez
- **EA - -** each, Eads (23b,24b,50b,82a), eard (139b), earl (107c,166b), earn (42d,64b,99a), ease (7c,8d,35a,100d,129d,130b,c,150c), east, East (111b), easy (54a,146d,149d,172b), eats, eaux (178c), eave (133c),
- - **EA** - bead (17a,122a,146b), beak (19a), beal (139d), beam, bean (91b,142a,175a), bear (27a,50b,113c,155a), beat (58c,87b,131a, 164d,165b,180d), beau, dead, deaf, deal (11d,16c,36c,44c,81a, 168b), dean (33c,109d), dear, feak (39d,171c), fear (113c,155a), feat (7a,52d), geal (47d,163c), gean (29c), gear (32c,112a,167b), geat (77d,101a), Geat (138a), head (29d), heaf (144a), heal, heap (117d), hear (75b,c,92d), heat, jean, (37c), Jean (183c), keal (25a), lead (35d,43d,72b,74d,81a), leaf (55c,73c,119b), Leah (19a,84a,87b,183c), leak (110c), leal (54b,94c,139d), lean (128a,148b,152d,164b,166a), leap (26c), lear (139d), Lear (37a, 143b), mead (46a,78a,97d,99b), Mead (78a), meal (72a,130b), mean (15a,42b,146c,156b), meat (59b), neaf (58a,73c), Neal, neap (165c,167a,177b), near (11d,32c,107b), neat (165c,169d), peag (144a,178a), peal (98b), peak (9a,38c,159b,186b), peal (131c,d), pean (64c,150b), pear (64a), peat (64a,175a), read (116d,157d), real (7a), ream (18c,37d,50d,113d,171c), reap (7a, 40a,74a), rear (15b,23a,b,24a,51b,76d,127c), seah (188), seal (10c,d,54d,64c,96a,118b,128a), seam (85b,d,160a,176d,185a), Sean (85b,96a), sear (23d,27d,72a,138c), seat (98c,156b), teak (41a,48a,168c), teal (19b,20d,46c,d), team (38c,72a,113a), tean (140c,167a), tear (67c,87b,130a), veal, weak (55b), weal (124d, 157c,180c,d), wean (8d,42d), wear (50b), yeah, Yean (88a), year, yeas (177c), zeal (12c,55d)
- - - **EA** Alea (14b,31c,167d), area (37d,38a,44c,53a,93b,110d,127d,138c, 168a,186d), asea (39b,177c), brea (100b), crea (92c,151d), evea (82a), Evea (95a), flea (81b), Frea, Gaea (47d,69a), idea (54c,

290

108c,124a,164d), **Itea** (145d,160c,181d), **odea** (105a,164a), **olea** (170b), **Olea** (110b), **Otea** (71a,82d), **oxea** (153d), **plea** (51a,52d, 122a,130b), **rhea** (37a,56a,111d,133d), **Rhea** (19b,68d,87c,103c, 186b), **shea** (25a,168c,d), **Thea** (162c), **uvea** (53c,82b)

E - - A **Ecca**, (66a), **Edda** (76b,79b,107d,136b), **Edna** (183c), **Egba** (191), **Ekka** (26d), **Elba** (105d), **Elia** (88a,115d), **ella** (152c, 158c), **Ella** (183c), **Elsa** (70a,93c,110d,177b,183c), **Emma** (183c), **Enna** (146a), **epha** (75c), **Erda** (23d,41a,47d,68d,69a,131d,177b), **eria** (13d,146d), **Erma** (183c), **Erua** (103c), **esca** (11c,44a,70c), **esta** (152d,164c), **etna** (75b,153c,157a,175d,177a,c), **Etta** (183c), **evea** (82a,95a), **eyra** (181d), **ezba** (188), **Ezra** (96a)

EB - - **Eben** (96a), **Eber** (51a,75c,99d), **Ebro** (132a), **eboe** (28b,110a, 168c,169b), **Eboe, ebon** (20b), **ebur** (89c)

- EB - **ceba** (169b), **debt** (91d,109b), **Hebe** (39c,69c,186b), **Nebo** (68c, 102d,103d,183a), **peba** (12d), **Peba** (193), **Reba** (18d,86c,144a), **Seba** (18c,39d), **sebl** (34b), **ueba** (188), **zebu** (22d,80d,112c)

- - EB **bleb** (20c,23d,67c), **dieb** (84a), **pleb** (10d,35b,180b), **Sleb** (12a), **sweb** (160d), **theb** (188)

EC - - **ecad** (73a,119b), **Ecca** (66a), **ecce** (17c,89a,c), **echo** (130b,d), **Echo** (105d), **ecru** (17d,23d,172c), **ecto** (34c,122d)

- EC - **beck** (107c), **deca** (14d,122d), **decl** (163b), **deck** (13b,41c,144d), **heck** (100a), **lech** (102b), **neck** (83c), **peca** (190), **peck** (24d), **peco** (162b), **reck** (26d,75c), **rect** (117b), **sech** (97c), **seck** (173d), **sect** (42b,54a,114c), **teca, Teca** (192), **Tech, teck** (128b), **Teco** (192)

- - EC **alec** (10a,57c,d,76c), **Alec** (137a), **avec** (63a,183a), **haec** (90a, 164c), **spec**

E - - C **epic** (76b,120a), **eric** (115b), **Eric** (71d,96a,107d,138a,164a, 176b), **eruc** (37a,56a)

ED - - **Edam** (29c), **Edar** (18d), **Edda** (76b,79b,107d,136b), **eddo** (162a), **eddy** (37d,39d,160d,180d), **edel** (66c), **Eden** (6b,50d,107c,113d, 123c), **Eder, Edes** (71c), **edge** (22a,96d,131c,143c,146b), **edgy** (106c), **edit** (20d,49d,123a,129a,131a), **Edna** (183c), **Edom** (18c, 51b,79b,82c,84a)

- ED - **Beda** (101d), **Bede** (48c,50c,101d,175b), **cede** (67b,70c,129d, 160a,168b,185d), **dedo** (188), **gedd** (140a), **Leda** (27b,75d,120c, 153a,171d,186b), **meda** (110a), **Medb, Mede** (10a,b,13c), **medi** (34c), **peda** (114d,144a), **pedi** (34b), **pedo** (34b), **redd** (153a), **rede** (37c,81d,138d), **redo** (165c), **Teda** (191), **Veda** (77a,b), **Yedo** (166d)

- - ED **abed** (130c), **aged** (110a), **bled, bred** (23c,48c,127c), **coed, deed** (7a,52d,91a,166c,168b), **feed** (108c), **fled, Fred** (96b), **gled** (19a, 52a,87a), **heed** (14c,75b,109b), **hued, lied** (66d,150b), **meed** (128c,131a), **Moed** (100c), **need** (42b,52d,87b,122a,178a), **Obed** (135d), **pied** (96c,103c,114b,117c,154a,174d), **reed** (16a,70d,97b, 105a,111b,118b,144b), **Reed** (163a), **roed, seed** (70b,111c,112c, 119b,151b,154a), **shed** (27a,90c,101b,144b), **sled** (40a), **sned** (93d,125a,140a), **sped, syed** (103b), **tied, toed, used** (6d,73a), **weed**

E - - D **eard** (139b), **ecad** (73a,119b), **egad** (100a,109a), **eild** (138d, 140a), **elod** (49b,59d,79c), **emyd** (163c,167c), **Enid** (13b,25d, 66b,163a,183c)

291

EE - - eely (185a), eery (172b,180a)

- EE beef, been (149a), beer (18c), bees (185b), beet (175a), deed (7a,52d,166c,168b), deem (36b,85c,164c), deep (124a), deer (28c,135a,154d), feed (108c), feel (72a,142c), fees (128c), Geez (6c,51d), heed (14c,75b,109b), heel, Heep (41a,43b), heer (47a, 184b,185b), jeel, jeep, Jeer (138c,162b), keef (75d), keek (154c), keel (128d,134d,144c,d), keen (15a,88a,177b), keep (123a,130d), keet (72b), leek (58b,76a,110c,177d), leer (9d,58a,67c,93d,112a, 148c), lees (46a,142a), leet (26a,38a,139d), meed (128c,131a), meek (93d,99d), meer, meet (11d,13d,36a,50a,81d,142d), need (42b,52d,87b,122a,178a), neem (96d,168c,169a), neep (140c, 171b), neer (14b,86b,108b), peek (93d), peel (53a,114a), peen (73c), peep (93d,115c), peer (51a,107c), peet (64a), reed (16a, 70d,97b,105a,111b,118b,144b), Reed (163a), reef (129a,137a, 145a), reek (49d,53c,64a,148d,149a), reel (21b,40b,d,153c,154a, c,d,180d), reem (18d), seed (70b,111c,112c,119a,151b,154a), seek (141c), seel (20c,32c,143b), seem (11c), seen, seep (110c, 116a,154b), seer (60a,124c,150c), teel (142d), teem (6b,121d), teen (139b,c,140b,158d), teer (25b,69d), Tees (108a), veer (28d, 144c,171b), weed, week, weel (16d,57d,140d,180d), weep (39b, 88a,104a), weet (19d)

- - EE agee (13d,15c,38d), ajee (15c,139a), akee (168c), alee (15c,75d, 144b,157a,182a), bree (139a), byee (189), chee (189), clee (19a, 129a), Cree (192), dree (139b,140c,158b,172c), epee (55c,160d), flee, free (44a,70d,131b), ghee (24d), giee (99a,150b), idee (61d), inee (120b), Klee (113a), knee (85b), ogee (40c,101a,b, 120b), pree (139d), Rhee (87c), shee (82b), skee (149c), slee (140b,148c), smee (19b,46c,d,118b,119d,141b,181b), Smee (116d), snee (40a,b,43d,87a), Spee (66d,70b), thee (124b), tree (11d,37a,66a,184b), twee, tyee (29d), usee, whee

E - - E ease (7c,8d,35a,100d,129d,130b,c,150c), eave (133c), eboe (28b, 110a,168c,169b), Eboe, ecce (17d,89a,c), edge (22a,96d,131c, 143c,146b), elde (119c), eine (66c), Eire (82b), Elbe (108a), elle (62b,c), else (18b,79b,111d), ence (158c), enne (34c), ense (139b,158c), ente (70b,151d), epee (55c,160d), Erie (82c,87d), erne (19c,d,47b,54b,141a), Erse (28a,64b,82b), esce (158d), esne (10c,45b,142c,148a,164d), esse (7a,18a,52d,89a,90a,159a,166c), este (152b,d,164c), Este (55c,83c,112d), etre (61a,c,62d,166c), ette (158a,c,d), euge (180a), evoe (15b,130d,181c), eyre (23c, 31b,85c), Eyre

EF - - Efik (191)

- EF defi (61b), deft (147c), defy (28d), heft (179d), Heft, Jefe (152a), Jeff (133c), left (42c), reft (32a,42c,44d,167b), teff (6c), weft (39a,165a,184b)

- - EF alef (91c), atef (39a,48d), beef, chef, clef (104d,105a), elef (91c), fief (55d), keef (75d), kief (75d), lief (181d), reef (129a, 137a,145a), tref (172b)

E - - F elef (91c), Enif (155b)

EG - - egad (100a,109a), Egba (191), Egbo (141d), Eger (49a), eggs (112a), eggy (185d), Egil (107d), egis (14b,d,115a,124d,144b, 154a,161a), egol (11b)

- EG - bega (188), degu (132c), hegh, mega (34b,c), pega (57a,130a,

292

158b), **Pegu** (24c,102a,127d), **sego** (24b,25a,92b,174c), **tegg** (143d,171d), **vega** (110d,152c), **Vega** (155b), **Wega** (155b), **Wegg** (111d), **yegg** (24c)

- - **EG** areg (116a,137a), **Areg, Doeg** (137c), **dreg, Gheg** (8c), **skeg** (7d, 86a,144d,157d,184a), **sneg** (139b), **waeg** (19b,72c,87a)

EH - - eheu (52c)

- **EH** - behn (137d), **Hehe** (191), **jehu** (46b), **Jehu** (18c), **lehr** (67c, 112a), **peho** (19b,102c,106d), **sehr** (66d), **tehr** (27c,68a)

- - **EH** okeh (8d,37b)

E - - **H** each, **Elah** (18c,86d), **Esth** (16a,51d), **Etah** (51c,71d), **etch, eyah** (95b,108d,111c)

EI - - eide (119c), **eild** (138d,140a), **eine** (66c), **Eire** (82b)

- **EI** - **Beid** (155b), **ceil** (92c,112a), **deil** (139b), **dein** (66d), **feis** (82b), **gein** (67d), **heil** (74b), **hein** (52c,61c), **heir, keif** (75d), **keir** (20c), 174d), **Leif** (107d), **Leir, mein** (30b), **nein** (66c), **meio** (188), **Neil** (96a), **reim** (112c), **rein** (29b,130c), **reis** (26c,29d,75a,103b), **seid** (103b), **Seld** (42d,101a,171a), **Selk** (77b), **Selm** (120c), **sein** (146c), **selp** (110c, **Seir** (51b,94a,103d), **seis** (147b,152c), **seit** (189), **Telg** (96a), **teil** (92b,c,168c), **veil** (74d,76c), **vein** (20d, 157b), **weir** (40b,57d), **zein**

- - **EI** drei (66d,165a), **kuei** (44a), **kwei** (44a), **Omei** (24a), **quei** (189), **viel** (38c,160a)

E - - **I** Ekoi (191), **Enki** (15b), **equi** (122d), **etui** (27a,29b,62c,106b, 148d,166d,174b)

EJ - - ejoo (55b,168c)

- **EJ** - Beja (6c,191), **Nejd, reja** (152b), **Sejm** (120c), **teju** (151b)

EK - - Ekka (26d), **Ekoi** (191)

- **EK** - beka (189), **feke, Peke** (45a,148d), **Reki** (16a), **weka** (58c,106d, 107a,127b), **weki** (55c), **Zeke** (96b)

- - **EK** chek (59c), **esek** (18d), **hoek** (39d), **keek** (154c), **leek** (58b,76a, 110c,177d), **meek** (93d,99d), **peek** (93d,115c), **reek** (49d,53c, 64a,148d,149a), **seek** (141c), **trek** (85c,93c,99d,168b)

E - - **K** Efik (191), **esek** (18d)

EL - - Elah (18c,86d), **Elam** (18d,37d,82a,116c,144b), **elan** (12c,41a, 50d,62a,153c,177a,186b), **ELAS** (71c), **Elba** (105d), **Elbe** (108a), **elef** (91c), **Elia** (88a,115d), **Elis** (22c,37d,71b,107c), **ella** (152c, 158c, **Ella** (183c), **elle** (62b,c), **elmy, elod** (49b,59d,79c), **Elon** (18c,51b,108a), **Elsa** (70a,93c,110d,177b,183c), **else** (18b,79b, 111d), **Elul** (102b)

- **EL** - bela (12a), **Bela** (18b,48c,78d), **Bell** (23c), **bell** (24c,39d), **Bell** (162d), **belt** (16a,31a), **cela** (62d), **cell** (39b), **celt** (30c,82c,123a, 156c,167b,179b), **Celt** (10a,180a,b), **dele** (26a,49c,51b,53a,110b, 123d,124c,130a,145c,161b), **dell** (43c,174b), **eely** (185a), **fell** (40a,58b,76c,115d,147d), **fels** (190), **felt, geld** (162b), **gelt** (101c), **Hela** (93c), **held, helm** (144d,165d), **help** (14a), **kela** (189), **keld** (154b), **kelp** (82a,141c), **Kelt** (180b), **Lely** (47a), **mele** (74b,150b), **melt, Nell** (110a,183d), **pela** (30c), **Pele** (69c,74c), **pelf** (131b), **pelo** (83b), **pelt** (53a), **pelu** (30a,106d,168c), **rely** (16b,170b), **self** (48d,80d), **sell** (97a,115c,175b), **tela** (22d,98c,

293

121b,166a,179c), tele (34b,122c), teli (94b), tell (105d,129c,
154b), Tell (160d), vela (98c,136b,149d), Vela (36b,c), veld
(151a), velo (175b), weld (47c,85b,173c), Welf (67a), welk (65c,
96d,141b), well, welt (36d,131b,145a,b,177b,d), yell (145c),
yelp, yelt (151b)

185c), **Ment** (54b,164a), **menu** (19a,27a), **Menu, nene** (19b,74c), **pend, pene, pent** (36a), **rena** (25b,132c), **rend** (32a,159c,162c, 185a), **Reni** (83d), **Reno, rent** (58a,91b,138b,153d,162c,167c), **send** (42c,44b,95c,121c,130a,144c,168b), **senn** (76b), **Sens** (63b), **sent, tend** (26d,80b,93d,100a), **tene** (34d,131b), **teng** (188), **tent** (26b,115a), **vena** (90a,175a), **vend** (97a,115c,142b), **Vend** (10b, 148a), **vent** (8b,11b,110d,112a), **wend** (67d,123d), **Wend** (10b, 148a), **went** (42c), **xeno** (34d), **yeni** (19b,161d), **Zend, Zeno** (71b), **zenu** (143d)

- - **EN**   **aden** (34b), **Aden, aien** (40d,138a), **amen** (14a,80b,94a,137a, 149c,175c,184b), **Amen** (86d,127d,164a), **aten** (150a,159b), **been** (149a), **bien** (63a,140c,179a,180a), **bren** (72d,95a), **Caen, Chen** (149b), **Eben** (96a), **Eden** (6b,50d,107c,113d,123c), **even** (51a, 58b,79d,91d,149a,173a), **glen** (43c), **hien** (30b), **hoen** (189), **iden** (76a), **iren** (127c), **iten** (192), **keen** (15a,88a,177b), **lien** (65c,91a,124c), **mien** (11c,17b,26d,44c,96b), **omen** (14c,59d, 60a,121c,123a,146b), **open** (26a,60d,81a,109b,112c,125b,172b, 173c), **oven** (15d,78c,86b), **Owen** (96a,183c), **oxen** (10c), **peen** (73c), **pien** (13b), **rien** (62b), **seen** (68a), **Shen** (68a), **sken** (164a), **sten** (72c,95a), **teen** (139b,c,140b,158d), **then** (147d), **T-men** (168b), **when** (180d), **wren** (19b,c), **Wren** (50b)

E - - N   **earn** (42d,64b,99a), **Eben** (96a), **ebon** (20b), **Eden** (6b,50d,107c, 113d,123c), **elan** (12c,41a,50d,62a,153c,177a,186b), **Elon** (18c, 51b), **enin** (20d), **Enon** (18c,d), **Eoan** (41a,85b), **Eoin** (85b), **Erin** (82b), **Eton** (33b,50c,84a), **Evan** (96a), **even** (51a,58b,79d,91d, 149a,173a), **Ewan**

EO - -   **Eoan** (41a,85b), **Eoin** (85b)

- **EO -**   **feod** (55d), **Leon** (96a), **meou, meow, neon** (65c), **peon** (28c,59c, 99c), **Teos** (82a)

- - **EO**   **areo** (34c), **Ateo** (120d), **Cleo** (126b), **Ideo** (34b,d,164d), **oleo** (34c), **skeo** (57d)

E - - O   **Ebro** (132a), **echo** (130b,d), **Echo** (105d), **ecto** (34c,122d), **eddo** (162a), **Egbo** (141d), **ejoo** (55b,168c), **endo** (34d,122d,183b), **enso** (34d,183b), **ento** (34b,d,183b), **Enyo** (12c,69c,178a), **ergo** (164b)

EP - -   **epee** (55c,160d), **epha** (75c), **epic** (76b,120a), **epos** (51a,76b, 120a)

- **EP -**   **cepa** (110c), **cepe** (48c), **depa** (188), **kepi** (99d), **kept, Nepa** (106b,178c), **pepo** (39b,64a,70a,98c,125c,154c), **repp** (53b,131a), **seps** (93b,142d), **sept** (31d,82b,143a,149c), **Sept** (45b), **Veps** (191), **wept**

- - **EP**   **deep** (124a), **Heep** (41a,43b), **jeep, keep** (123a,130d), **neep** (140c,171b), **peep** (93d,115c), **prep** (138b), **seep** (110c,116a, 154b), **skep** (16d,17c,77c), **step** (70b,112b,177b,d), **weep** (39b, 88a,104a)

EQ - -   **equi** (122d)

ER - -   **eral** (51a), **erat** (89c), **Erda** (23d,41a,47d,68d,69a,131d,177b), **erer** (17d,150c), **ergo** (164b), **eria** (13d,146d), **eric** (115b), **Eric** (71d,96a,107d,138a,164a,176b), **Erie** (82c,87d), **Erin** (82b), **Eris** (12c,68d,109c), **Erma** (183c), **erne** (19c,d,47b,54b,141a), **Eros**

(11c,39c,68b,97c,182d), **Erse** (28a,64b,82b), **erst** (60b), **Erua** (103c), **eruc** (37a,56a), **eryx** (137a)

297

Jeux (61d), meum (27a,89c), **Meum, neue** (66c), peur (61c), **Zeus** (135a)

- - EU   **bleu** (61b), **Dieu** (61d), **eheu** (52c), **emeu** (111d), **lieu** (118c, 155d)

E - - U   **ecru** (17d,23d,172b), **eheu** (52c), **emeu** (111d), **Enzu** (102b), **Esau** (82c,84a,128c)

EV - -   **Evan** (96a), **even** (51a,58b,79d,91d,149a,173a), **evea** (82a,95a), **ever** (9b,14b,80b), **evet** (48d,107a,136c,169d), **evil** (79c,95d,147a, 181a,185c), **evoe** (15b,130d,181c)

- EV -   **bevy** (38a,58c), **Deva** (23d,42a,b,56d,77a), **Devi** (147b,153b), **hevi** (111d), **Leve** (62a), **Levi** (84a,90c), **levo** (91a), **levy** (14a, 162b), **Neva** (91b,132a), **neve** (56d,67c,70c,149b), **peva** (12d), **pevy** (91d,94c), **reve** (61c,104d), **revs** (131a), **seve** (63a,182c)

- - EV   **Kiev, Stev** (155b)

EW - -   **Ewan, ewer** (84d,85c,118c,181b), **ewry** (133c)

- EW -   **dewa, dewy** (101a), **hewn, mewl** (180d), **mews** (154c), **news** (165c), **newt** (48d,136c,169d), **sewn, Tewa** (193)

- - EW   **anew** (7c), **blew, brew** (35d), **chew** (97c), **clew** (16a,33a,77b, 136b,164d), **crew** (72a,106a), **drew, flew, grew, knew, Llew** (40c), **phew** (52c), **plew** (17c), **shew** (44c), **skew** (148a,160c, 171c), **slew** (160a), **smew** (19b,46d,99a,137d), **spew** (35a,49a), **stew** (21c,44b,184d), **thew** (104c), **view** (93d,138b), **whew**

E - - W   **enow** (50d,123a,158b)

EX - -   **exam, exit** (114d)

- EX -   **next** (106a), **sext** (26b,111b,147b), **text** (21c,140d),

- - EX   **Amex** (184d), **apex** (39c,76c,115c,118b,159b,166a,167b), **Crex** (37a), **faex** (46a), **flex** (18a), **ibex** (67d,68a), **ilex** (77d), **obex** (22d), **plex** (60b), **spex, Ulex** (153c)

E - - X   **eaux** (178c), **eryx** (137a), **esox** (57b)

EY - -   **eyah** (95b,108d,111c), **eyas** (106c,173a), **eyer, eyey** (74b), **eyot** (82d), **eyra** (181d), **eyre** (23c,31b,85c), **Eyre, eyry** (47b,106c)

- EY -   **Ceyx** (73b), **teyl** (92b,c,168c)

- - EY   **shey** (52c), **akey** (189), **brey** (194), **drey** (154c), **eyey** (74b), **fley** (63d), **Frey** (7c,68b,124d), **grey** (33c), **hoey** (114c), **Joey** (86a, 185d), **Joey** (96b,109c), **obey** (35c,75c), **prey** (119d,176a), **roey** (103d), **skey** (185d), **sley** (179b), **Spey, they** (124b), **trey** (26c, 165a), **Urey** (14b,107c,138c), **whey** (100a)

E - - Y   **easy** (54a), **eddy** (37d,39d,160d,180d), **edgy** (106c), **eely** (185a), **eery** (172b,180a), **eggy** (185d), **elmy, envy** (41b), **esay, espy** (44a,142a), **ewry** (133c), **eyey** (74b), **eyry** (47b,106c)

EZ - -   **ezba** (188), **ezel** (47a,85d), **Ezra** (96a)

- - EZ   **chez** (14b,61a), **daez, Geez** (6c,51d), **Inez** (45c,183c), **Juez** (152b), **knez** (123c), **oyez** (38a,39b,75b)

FA - -   **Faam** (111a), **Faba, face** (159d,176c), **fact** (7a,128b), **fade** (181d, 183b), **fado** (121c), **fady, faex** (46a), **fail, fain** (42d,67c,183b), **fair** (17a,55d), **fait** (6d,61b), **fake** (123a,143c), **faky, fala** (129b), **fall** (46b,141c), **falx** (133b), **Fama** (135a), **fame** (130a), **famn** (188), **fana, fane** (30d,137a,162d), **fang** (167b), **fano** (51d,96b, 113c,d), **faon** (33c,55a), **fard** (112d), **fare** (43c,59b,67d,123b), farl (138c,140b), farm (165d), faro (65a), fash (140c,176a), fass (189), fast (56d,126c,141d,160c,173a,d), fate (42d,52a,87a,94a), faun (56a,68b,137c,161a,184a), favi (138a,165d), fawn (33c), faze (43d)

- **FA -**   afar (44c), Afar (6c)
- **- - FA**   Abfa (76b), alfa (70d), gufa (21b,99a), Kafa (6c), kufa (21b, 99a), Offa (163d), sofa (44d), tufa (121b,177a), Urfa (99a)
- **F - - A**   Faba, fala (129b), Fama (135a), fana, flea (81b), fora (133a), Frea, Fria, fuga
- **F - - B**   flub (22b), frab (138c), frib (43d)
- **F - - C**   fisc (52c,134c), floc (149a)
- **- - FD**   Wafd (49a)
- **F - - D**   fard (112d), feed (108c), fend (114b,178b), feod (55d), feud (55d,126b,175b), find (44a), fled, fold, fond (7c,94b), food (109a, 176b), ford (177b), foud (54d,144b), Fred (96b), Fuad (54d), fund (6d,101c,130c), fyrd (110a),
- **FE - -**   feak (39d,171c), fear (113c,155a), feat (7a,52d), feed (108c), feel (72a,142c), fees (128c), feis (82b), feke (123a), fell (40a,58b,76c, 115d,147d), fels (190), felt, feme (181b), fend (114b,178b), feod (55d), fern (142a), feru (37a,56a,133d), fess (23c,51b), fest, fete (55d,129b), feud (55d,126b,175b)
- **- FE -**   afer (48a,182b)
- **- - FE**   cafe, fife (59a,105a), jefe (152a), life (19a,177a), nife (37a), orfe (57a,b,185c), rife (6b,c,39d,123b), safe (141d,157d,174d), wife (154a)
- **F - - E**   face (159d,176c), fade (181d,183b), fake (123a,143c), fame (130a), fane (30d,137a,162d), fare (43c,59b,67d,123b), fate (42d, 52a,87a,94a), faze (43d), feke, feme (181b), fete (55d,129b), fide, fife (59a,105a), fike (139c), file (13a,127d), fine (49b,50a, 104b,115d,159a), fire (13a,43d,44b), five, flee, floe (79b), flue (8b,30a), fore (63d,174b), free (44a,70d,131b), froe (32a,167a, 179d), fume (129a,149a,157a), fuse (98c), fute (51c), fuze (98c), fyke (15d)
- **- FF -**   affy (18b), offa, Offa (163d), offs (38c)
- **- - FF**   baff (69d), biff, buff (134c,161d), cuff (148a), daff (125d), doff (130a,161b), duff (125b), gaff (57c,d,152d,153a), goff (32d), guff, huff (58a), jeff (133d), Jeff, jiff (101c), kiff (88c), koff (47a), luff (136b), miff (44c), moff (53b,146c), muff (24b), puff (180d), raff (75b), riff (131d), Riff (18b,102c), ruff (19b, 33b,63d,137a), teff (6c), tiff (126b), toff (40d), tuff (121b,177a)
- **F - - F**   fief (55d)
- **F - - G**   fang (167b), flag (16b,50d,82b,88c,115a,155a), flog (180d), Fong (40b), frog (10a,17a,126d), Fung (191)
- **F - - H**   fash (140c,176a), fish, Foch (63b)
- **FI - -**   fiat (35a,41d,48c,111b,137a), Flat (83c), fico (169d), fide, fief (55d), fife (59a,105a), fike (139c), file (13a,127d), fili (109b), film (164b), filo (62d,150b), fils (62d,150b), find (44a), fine (49b,50a,104b), 115d,159a), fink (19a,56c,157c), Finn (107d), Fiot (191), fire (13a,43d,44b), firm (154c,173d), firn (67c,70c,106c,149b), fisc (52c,134c), fish, fisk (24d,52c,134c), fist (80c), five

- Fl - Efik (191), Ifil (117a,168c)
- - Fl defi (61b), Safi (191), sufi (103a,116c)
F - - I favi (138a,165d), fili, foci (28b), fuci (132c), fuji (84b), Fuji (84d)

F - - J Funj

F - - K feak (39d,171c), fink (19a,56c,157c), fisk (24d,52c,134c), flak (11a), folk (116a,169c), fork, fulk (173a), funk (63d,113c)

FL - - flag (16b,50d,82b,88c,115a,155a), flak (11a), flam (169c), flan (39d,40a,114d), flap (17b,59a,104a,118d,161a,182d), flat (41b, 124b,173a), flaw, flax, flay (147c,157c), flea (81b), fled, flee, flew, flex (18a), fley (63d), flip (167c), flit (41a), flix, floc (149a,) floe (79b), flog (180d), flop (54a), flot (173a), flow (157b), flub (22b), flue (8b,30a), flux (28d,58d)

F - - L fail, fall (46b,141c), farl (138a,140b), feel (72a,142c), fell (40a, 58b,76c,115d,147d), fill (109b), foal (78c), foil (15d,55c,165b), fool (24a,41c,47a,146d), foul (173a), fowl, fuel (65c), full (7b, 130b), furl (132d)

F - - M Faam (111a), farm (165d), film (164b), firm (154c,173d), flam (169c), foam (63d,154b), form (54d,143c), frim (58d), from

F - - N fain (42d,67c,183b), famn (188), faon (33c,55a), faun (56a,68b, 137c,161a,184a), fawn (33c), fern (142a), Finn (107d), firn (67c, 70c,106c,149b), flan (39d,40a,114d), fohn (182b)

FO - - foal (78c), foam (63d,154b), Foch (63b), foci (28b), fogy, fohn (182b), foil (15d,55c,165b), fold, folk (116a,169c), fond (7c,94b), Fong (40b), fono (137a), fons (60c), font (16b,171d,172a), food (109a,176b), fool (24a,41c,47a,146d), foot (115a), fora (133a), ford (177b), fore (63d,174b), fork, form (54d,143c), fort (63d, 157d), foss (44d,100d), foud (54d,144b), foul (173a), four (26c), fowl, foxy (38b,39c,181d)

- - FO Bufo (166c)

F - - O fado (121c), fano (51d,96b,113c,d), faro (65a), fico (169d), filo, fono (137a)

F - - P flap (17b,59a,104a,118d,161a,182d), flip (167c), flop (54a), frap (45d,165c)

FR - - frab (138c), frap (45d,165c), frat, frau (181b), fray (56b,60d), Frea, Fred (96b), free (44a,70d,131b), fret (28c,35b,111c,184d), Frey (7c,68b,124d), Fria, frib (43d), frim (58d), frit (64c,67c), friz (39d), froe (32a,167a,179d), frog (10a,17a,126c), from, frot (28c), frow (47a,167a)

- FR - Afra (183c)

F - - R fair (17a,55d), fear (113c,155a), four (26c)

- - FS offs (38c)

F - - S fass (189), fees (128c), feis (82b), feis (190), fess (23c,51b), fils (62d,150b), fons (60c), foss (44d,100d), fuss (22b,35b)

- - FT baft (14a,53b), daft (59c), deft (147c), gift (123a), haft (76d), heft (179d), Heft, left (42c), lift (49b), loft (14c,69d,104b,178b), raft (27b,33c,58c,75b), reft (32a,42c,44d,167b), rift (30c,32a, 58a,110d), sift (140d,142c,146b), soft (48b,95d,99d,163a), Taft (29d), tuft (24b,32d,38c), waft (20d,58c), weft (39a,165a,184b), yuft (135c)

F - - T fact (7a,128b), fait (6d,61b), fast (56d,126c,141d,160c,173a,d), feat (7a,52d), feit, fest, Fiat (83c), fiat (35a,41d,48c,111b,137a), Fiot (191), fist (80c), flat (41b,124b,173a), flit (41a), flot (173a), font (16b,171d,172a), foot (115a), fort (63d,157d), frat, fret (28c, 35b,111c,184d), frit (64c,67c), frot (28c), fust (105c,143b)

FU - - Fuad (54d), fuci (132c), fuel (65c), fuga, fugu (84b), fuji (84b), Fuji (84d), fulk (173a), full (7b,130b), fume (129a,149a,157a), fumy, fund (6d,101c,130c), Fung (191), funk (63d,113c), furl (132d), fury (157a), fuse (98c), fuss (22b,35b), fust (105c,143b), fute (51c), fuze (98c), fuzz (45d)

F - - U feru (37a,56a,133d), frau (181b), fugu (84b)

F - - W flaw, flew, flow (157b), frow (47a,167a)

F - - X faex (46a), faix (133b), flax, flex (18a), flix (28d,52d)

FY - - fyke (15d), fyrd (110a)

- - FY affy (18b), defy (28d), Dufy (63a)

F - - Y fady, faky, flay (147c,157c), fley (63d), fogy, foxy (38b,39c, 181d), fray (56b,60d), Frey (7c,68b,124d), fumy, fury (157a)

F - - Z friz (39d), fuzz (45d)

GA - - gaal (23b,174d), gabe (162a), gabl (162a), gaby (59c,146d), gade, Gaea (47d,69a), Gael (28a,96c,138d), gaff (57c,d,152d, 153a), gage (28d,98a,119c,d), gagi (160b), Gaia (47d,69a), gail (23b,174d), Gail (183d), gain (7a,b,124a,181d), gait (96b,179a), gajo (107c), gala (55d), Gala (191), gale (181d), gali (6c), gall (19a,28c,29b,82c,160c,176a), galt, Gama (121c), game (64d, 154a), gamp (172a), gane (185b), gang (38c), Gano (132d), gaol (123d), Gaol (164a), Gaon (85b), gape (185b), gapo (60a), gapy, gara (190), garb (32c,46a), gare (61b,c,62c,127c,184b), Garm (178c), garn (67d,185b), Garo (88c), Gary, gash (40a), gasp (113c), gata (143c), gate (51a,121b), Gath (117a), gaub (116c), gaud (169d), gaue (67a), Gaul (10a,60d,63c), gaup, gaur (112c,181c), gaus (67a), gaut (88b,103d,132a), gave, gawd (169c), gawk (146d), gawp, Gaza (117a), gaze, gazi, gazy

- GA - Agag (18c,86c,137a), agal (17c,36d), Agao (6c,73c), agar (7d, 28c,39c,103c,141c), Agau (73c), Agaz (193), egad (100a,109a), ngai (48a,159c), ngan, ogam (82b,c), Sgau (88c)

- - GA alga (141b,c), baga (171b), bega (188), biga (171d), boga (57d, 180b), fuga, giga (56a,105a), goga (24a), hoga (144b), inga (145d,170a), Jaga (191), juga (27a), mega (34b,c), muga, naga (13d,33a,55b,127c), Naga (24c,77a,88c,176d), Olga (135c,183c), paga (117a), pega (57a,130a,158b), raga (56d,105a), riga (118b), ruga (59b,185a), saga (79b,91a,138a,157a,161b,c,168a), Saga, soga (70d,152b), Soga (191), toga (132d,133a,b), vega (152c), Vega (155b), Wega (155b), yoga (10b,13c,77a), Yuga (76d), zyga (134b)

G - - A Gaea (47d,69a), Gaia (47d,69a), gala (55d), Gala (191), Gama (121c), gara (190), gata (143c), Gaza (117a), gena, (29b), geta (84b,145a), giga (56a,105a), glia (93b), Gita, Gjoa (144d), glia (106c), goga (24a), gola (27b,40c,70c,157a), Goma (191), Gona (106d), gora (81c), Goya (151d), gufa (21b,99a), Guha (191), gula (90a,101a,165b), guna (106a,137b)

301

- GB -   Egba (191), Egbo (141d)

G - - B   garb (32c,46a), gaub (116c), gerb (56d,143d), glib (58d,149a, 177c), glub, grab (105b,142a,149b), grub (88d), guib (11a)

G - - D   gaud (169d), gawd (169c), gedd (162b), Gerd (63c), gild (14a,49c,69c,98b), gird (32c,50a,123a,160a), glad (85c), gled (19a,52a,87a), goad (80b,154b), gold, Gond, good, grad (28b), grid (17a,70d,119b,156d)

GE - -   geal (47d,163c), gean (29c), gear (32c,112a,167b), geat (77d, 101a), Geat (138a), gedd (140a), Geez (6c,51d), gein (67d), geld (162b), gelt (101c), gena (29b), gene (54a,76b), Gene (96b), gens (42d,132d), gent, genu (6b,18a,87a,89c), gerb (56d,143d), Gerd (63c), Gere (183c), Geri (183c), germ (17d,99c,134d), gest (7c, 41d,52d,133c), geta (84b,145a), gett (44d), Geum (76b)

- GE -   aged (110a), agee (13d,15c,38d), ager (47c,56a,89b,c,131d, 133b), Eger (49a), ogee (101a,b,120b)

- - GE   ange (61a), auge (123c,132b), cage (36a), doge (95b,175b), edge (22a,96d,131c,143c,146b), euge (180a), gage (28d,98a, 119c,d), huge, Inge (24d,67d,117c,199c), kuge (84c), loge (164a), luge (148a), mage (95b), page (51b,59b,142d,159b), rage (10c,30c,157a,161d), sage (13a,90d,100c,141c,145c,180b,183a), tige (118a), urge (42d,46b,79d,80a,b,81c,124a,150a), wage (27a, 115b), yage (23a)

G - - E   gabe (162a), gade, gage (28d,98a,119c,d), gale (181d), game (64d,154a), gane (185b), gape (185b), gare (61b,c,62c,127c, 184b), gate (51a,121b), gaue (67a), gave, gaze, gene (54a,76b), Gene (96b), ghee (24d), gibe (8a,42c,84d,100d,138c,144c,149b), Gide (63a), gime (77d), gite (62a,118d), give (79d,123a), glee (99a,150b), glue (7b,156a), gone (6b,15c,42c,44c,114d), gore (115d,117c,154c,169c), guze (128d), gybe (144c), gyle (23b, 174d), gyne (34b,55b,183c), gyre (31b,171b), gyve (55d,143b)

G - - F   gaff (57c,d,152d,153a), goaf (104b), goff (32d), golf (154a), goof, Graf (37c,66b,67a,107c,186b), guff, gulf (6c)

- GG -   eggs (112a), eggy (185d)

- - GG   dagg (118c), hagg, hogg (144a), jagg, magg (95b), migg (96c), nogg (48d), tegg (143d,171d), vugg (28a,66a,132b), Wegg (111d), wigg, yegg (24c)

G - - G   gang (38c), Gheg (8c), glug, gong, grig (38c,70d,93a), grog (92d,153d)

GH - -   ghat (32d,88b,103d,132a), ghee (24d), Gheg (8c), Ghes (193), ghor (174b), ghos (30b), Ghux (171a)

- GH -   agha (35a,171a)

- - GH   dagh (76d), hegh, high, Hugh (96a), Lugh (28b), Magh (102a), nigh (106a), ough, pugh, sigh, vugh (28a,66a,136a), yogh (10c, 185a)

G - - H   gash (40a), Gath (117a), gish (102c), gosh, Goth (16c), gush (35a,154c)

GI - -   gibe (8a,42c,84d,100d,138c,144c,149b), Gide (63a), gier (47b), gift (123a), giga (56a,105a), gila (93b), gild (14a,49c,69c,98b), gill (22d), gilo (48a), gilt (69c,77c,151b,185d), gime (77d), gimp (169d), gink (48b), gird (32c,50a,123a,160a), girl, giro (38c,83c,

302

167c), **girt** (50a), **gish** (102c), **gist** (95c,118c), **Gita, gite** (62a, 118d), **give** (79d,12a)

- GI - **Agib** (12a,42d), **agio** (52c,60a,101c,123a), **Agis** (86d), **Egil** (107d), **egis** (14b,d,115a,124d,144b,154a,161a)

- - GI **Bugi** (191), **hagi** (84b), **jogi** (76d), **magi** (123c), **Magi** (95b,116c, 183a), **ragi** (28b), **sugi** (84b), **vagi** (38b), **yogi** (76d)

G - - I **gabi** (162a), **gali** (6c), **gazi, Geri** (183c), **goal** (106d,168c), **gobi, Gobi** (42d), **goli** (105c), **Guti, gyri** (22d,131b)

GJ - - **Gjoa** (144d)

G - - J **gunj** (70c)

G - - K **gawk** (146d), **gink** (48b), **gowk** (146d)

GL - - **glad** (85c), **gled** (19a,52a,87a), **glee** (99a,150b), **glen** (43c), **glia** (106c), **glib** (58d,149a,177c), **glim** (45c), **glom** (155d,160d, 178c), **glow** (144c), **glub, glue** (7b,156a), **glug, glum** (102c, 159a), **glut** (52c,70a,137c,159d)

- GL - **agla** (7a), **iglu** (51c,149b), **ogle** (9d,53c,91a,93d,148c)

- - GL **gagl** (160b)

G - - L **gaal** (23b,174d), **Gael** (28a,96c,138d), **gagl** (160b), **gall** (23b, 174d), **Gail** (183d), **gall** (19a,28c,29b,82c,160c,176a), **gaol** (123d), **Gaol** (164a), **Gaul** (10a,60d,63c), **geal** (47d,163c), **gill** (22d), **girl, goal** (8b,109b,120b,125d), **goel** (15a,75c), **Goll, goul** (102a), **gowl** (102a,140d,185b), **gull** (32d,41c,42a,72c,99b,141a)

G - - M **Garm** (178c), **germ** (99c,134d), **Geum** (76b), **glim, glom** (155d, 160d,178c), **glum** (102c,159a), **gram** (29d,99b,148d,160d,180a), **Gram, grim** (156a), **grum** (102c), **Guam**

GN - - **gnar** (72a), **gnat** (59a,81b,99c), **gnaw** (120a,107a,178b)

- GN - **agni** (88a,89c), **Agni** (56d,68b)

- - GN **sign** (121c,146c)

G - - N **gain** (7a,b,124a,181d), **Gaon** (85b), **garn** (67d,185b), **gean** (29c), **gein** (67d), **glen** (43c), **Goan, goon** (157c,163c), **gown, gran, grin, guan** (151b), **Gwyn** (40c,50b)

GO - - **goad** (80b,154b), **goaf** (104b), **goai** (106d,168c), **goal** (8b,109b, 120b,125d), **Goan, goat** (135a), **gobi, Gobi** (42d), **gobo** (84d), **goby** (57d), **goel** (15a,75c), **goer, goff** (32d), **goga** (24a), **gogo** (16b,24a,149c), **Gogo** (191), **gola** (27b,40c,70c,157a), **gold, golf** (154a), **goll** (105c, **Goll, Golo** (191), **Goma** (191), **Gona** (106d), **Gond, gone** (6b,15c,42c,44c,114d), **gong, good, goof, goon** (157c, 163c), **Goop** (107d), **goor, gora** (81c), **gore** (115d,117c,154c, 169c), **gory, gosh, Goth** (16c,163d), **goul** (102a), **gour** (112c, 181c), **gout, gowk** (146d), **gowl** (102a,140d,185b), **gown, Goya** (151d)

- GO - **agog** (47b,52c,86b), **agon** (12c,36c,41b,55d,71b), **egol** (11b), **Igor** (135d), **Ogor** (170d)

- - GO **ango** (171a), **Argo** (12c,36b,c), **bago** (13d), **bogo** (117a, 168c), **Bogo** (191), **bygo** (114c), **Dago, ergo** (164b), **gogo** (16b,24a, 149c), **Gogo** (191), **Hugo** (63a,96a), **Iago** (54b,111d,143c), **kago** (113a), **lago** (83b,152b), **mogo** (74b), **Pogo** (121c), **sago** (54c, 59b,113b,125b,155c), **sego** (24b,25a,92b,174c), **upgo** (13c), **zogo** (136a)

303

G - - O gajo (107c), Gajo, Gano (132d), gapo (60a), Garo (88c), gilo (48a), giro (38c,83c,167c), gobo (84d), gogo (16b,24a,149c), Gogo (191), Golo (191), grao (189), guao (168c,169b), Gulo (183c), gyro (34d)

- GP - Ogpu (135d)

G - - P gamp (172a), gasp (113c), gaup, gawp, gimp (169d), Goop (107d), gulp (46a,79d,160a), Gump (43b), grip (159a)

GR - - grab (105b,142a,149b), grad (28b), Graf (37c,66b,67a,107c, 186b), gram (29d,99b,148d,160d,180a), grao (189), gras (78b), gray (33c,77c), Gray (50c), gres (156d), grew, grey (33c), grid (17a,70d,119b,156d), grig (38c,70d,93a), grim (156a), grin, grip (159a), gris (61d), grit (137a,b), grog (92d,153d), gros (47a,53d, 146c), Gros (63a), grot (27d), grow (154b), grub (43c,88d), grum (102c), Grus (36b,c,38b)

- GR - agra (26d,34c), Agra (161b), agri (89b), agro (149d), ogre (67a, 102a)

G - - R gaur (112c,181c), gear (32c,167b), Ghor (174b), gier (47b), gnar (72a), goer, goor, gour (112c,181c), guar (46c,59d), guhr (47d)

- - GS eggs (112a), togs (32c)

G - - S gaus (67a), gens (42d,132d), Gens, Ghes (193), ghos (30b), glis (45c), Glis, gras (78b), gres (156d), gris (61d), gros (47a,53d, 146c), Gros (63a), Grus (36b,c,38b), gyps, Gyps (71d)

- - GT togt (77c), Vogt

G - - T gait (96b,179a), gait, gaut (88b,103d,132a), geat (77d,101a), Geat (138a), gelt (101c), gent, gest (7c,41d,52d,133c), gett (44d), ghat (32b,88b,103d,132a), gilt (69c,77c,151b), girt (50a), gist (95c,118c), giut (52c,70a,137c,159d), gnat (59a, 81b,99c), goat (135a), grit (137a,b), grot (27d), gust

GU - - Guam, guan (151b), guao (168c,169b), guar (46c,59d), gufa (21b,99a), guff, gugu, Guha (191), guhr (47d), guib (11a), gula (90a,101a,165b), gulf (6c), gull (32d,41c,42a,72c,99b,141a), Gulo (183c), gulp (46a,79d,160a), Gump (43b), guna (106a, 137b), gunj (70c), guru (77b), gush (35a,154c), gust, Guti, guze (128d)

- GU - agua (152d,166c,178c), ague (30a,55d,95c), ogum (82b)

- - GU degu (132c), fugu (84b), gugu, kagu (106c), Pegu (24c,102a, 127d)

G - - U genu (6b,18a,87a,89c), gugu, guru (77b)

GW - - Gwyn (40c,50b)

G - - W glow (144c), gnaw (20a,107a,178b), grew, grow (154b)

GY - - gybe (144c), gyle (23b,174d), gyne (34b,55b,183c), gyps, Gyps (71d), gyre (31b,171b), gyri (22d,131b), gyro (34d), gyve (55d, 143b)

- - GY algy, Algy (96b), bogy (153a), cagy (178b), dogy (46d,103c), edgy (106c), eggy (185d), fogy, logy (46b), Nagy (78d), orgy (26d,130d,137c), pogy (57a,88a,98d,103c), sagy

G - - Y gaby (59c,146d), Gaby, gapy, Gary (57d), gazy (96c), goby (57d), gory, gray (33c,77c), Gray (50c), grey (33c)

G - - Z Geez (6c,51d), Ghuz (171a)

HA · ·   Haab (97d), haaf (57d), haak (57b,178a), haar (139c), haba (151d), Habe (191), hack (40a,77c,184d), hade (66a,148c,173c), hadj (98b,118a), haec (90a,164c), haem (122b), haft (76d), hagg, hagi (84b), haha (55c,159c), haik (57b,65b,108a), hail (6d,15a,71d), hair (56b,164d), haje (33a,48d), hake (57a,b), hakh (46d), hako (115b), haku (86d), hala (112b), hale (125b), Hale (9d,131a), half (101a), hall (37b,114d, haim, halo (14d,31b,92a, 107b,131d), Hals (47a), halt (13b,28a,38d,156d), haml (78a), hand (60c,114c,115d,184c), hang (160a), hank (147c), Hano (125b), Hans (66d,96a), hant (67a), Hapi (66a,107b,136a), hapu (106d), Harb (191), hard (109b), hare (91b,132c), hark (92d), harl (16b,56b,59a), harm (40b,81a), harp (105a,129a), hart (41d, 154d), hase (74d), hash, hasp (31d,54d,153c), hast, hate (6a, 43a), hath, Hatl (48d), haul (27b,45d), have, hawk (19c,115c), hayz, haze (100c,174d), hazy (174b)

· HA ·   Ahab (18c,26c,85b,86d,100d,116a,180b), Ahaz (86d), Bhar (191), bhat (80c), chaa (162b), chab (184a), Chad (158b), chai (72d), cham (20a,29d), Cham (8c), chan (26c,130c), chap (55b), char (24d,26c,170b), chat (9b,19c,161c), chaw (97c), chay (48a,128d), dhak (48a,169a), dhal (12b), dhan (124c), dhao (24c), Dhar, dhaw (125a), ghat (32d,88b,103d,132a), khan (7c,26c,81b,93d, 116c,123c,130c,166c), khar (189), khas (153a), khat (105d), Phad (155b), shad (27d,57a,b,c), shag (73b,105b,161d,166d), shah (116c), sham (41c,55b,60d,80a,123a,b,146d), Shan (13c, 80d,88c,101d), shap, shat (87d), shaw (164b), Shaw (50c,53b), shay (110c), Thal (146a), than (35b), thar (68a,76d), that (42b, 124b,129c), thaw, wham (157c), what (129c), whau (107a,168c)

· · HA   agha (35a,171a), Akha (86a,c), Asha (191), Azha (155b), epha (75c), Guha (191), haha (55c,159c), isha (174a), kaha (123d), maha (28c,88c,136d), moha (42b,83d), ocha (189), paha (67b), poha (74c), saha, taha (179b), tcha (162c), Usha (16a,150c)

H · · A   haba (151d), Haba, haha (55c,159c), hala (112b), Hela (93c), Hera (69c,85d,110b,126b,186b,d), hila (53c), Hima (191), hoga (144b), hoja (166b), hola (74c,152b), hora (22a,40b), Hova (95a), Hoya (14d), Hsia (30b,47c), hula (19a,106d), hula (74b), Hupa (192), hura (20a,137a), Hura, Hyla (10a,166d,169b)

H · · B   Haab (97d), Harb (191), herb (58b,158b), hobb (124b), hubb (118b)

H · · C   haec (90a,164c)

H · · D   hand (60c,114c,115d,184c), hard (109b), head (29d), heed (14c, 75b,109b), held, herd (39a,46c,72a), Hild, hind (15b,41d,45a), hold (95c,124c,130d), hood (38a,74d), hued

HE · ·   head (29d), heaf (144a), heal (heap (117d), hear (75b,c,92d), heat, Hebe (39c,69c,186b), heck (100a), heed (14c,75b,109b), heel, Heep (41a,43b), heer (47a,184b,185b), heft (179d), Heft, hegh, Hehe (191), hell (74b), hein (52c,61c), heir, Hela (93c), held, helm (144d,165d), help (14a), hemi (122c), hemo (34a, 122b), hemp (26a,37a,56a,133d), hens (121d), Hera (69c,85d, 110b,126b,186b,d), herb (58b,158b), herd (39a,46c,72a), here, herl (16b,59a), hero (42b,124d,137b), Hero (90c), Herr (66c), hers (124c), hest (35a), Heth (77c), hevi (111c), hewn

· HE ·   ahem, Ahet (49a,102a), ahey (52c), bhel (126d), chee (189), chef, chek (59c), **Chen** (149b), cher (61b), chew (97c), chez (14b,61a), **eheu** (52c), ghee (24d), **Gheg** (8c), **Ghes** (193), **Hehe** (191), **Khem** (113c), khet (188), phew (52c), **rhea** (37a,56a, 111d), **Rhea** (19b,68d,87c,103c,186b), **Rhee** (87c), shea (25a, 168c,d), shed (27a,90c,101b,144b), shee (82b), **Shem** (107c), **Shen** (68a), sher (65d,165c), shew (44c), **Thea** (162c), theb (188), thee (124b), **them** (124b), then, thew (104c), they (124b), whee, when (180d), whet (143c,156b), whew, whey (100a)

· · HE   ache (79a,112d,185b), **Hehe** (191), **Hohe** (192), ache (13d,30b, 105a)

H · · E   **Habe** (191), hade (66a,148c,173c), haje (33a,48d), hake (57a,b), hale (125b), **Hale** (9d,131a), hare (91b,132c), hase (74d), hate (6a,43a), have, haze (100c,174d), **Hebe** (39c,69c,186b), **Hehe** (191), here, hide (53a), hike (185a), hipe (185a), hire (49d,50b,91b, 130a), hive (17c), **Hohe** (192), hole (6c,11b,110d,118c,147a), home, hone (110a,143c,180d), hope (13d,52d), hose (156c), hove (92a,157d), howe (77d), **Howe** (17a,82a), huge, hule (23a,134c), **Hume** (50c), huse (180c), hyde (188), **Hyde** (45a), hyke, hyle (97c), hype (185a)

H · · F   heaf (57d), half (101a), heaf (144a), hoof (173a), huff (58a)

H · · G   hagg (160a), hang (160a), hing (13c), hogg (144a), hong (30b), hung (188)

· · HH   sahh (188)

H · · H   hakh (46d), hash, hath, hegh, **Heth** (77c), high, hish, hoch (52c, 66c), **Hoc**, hoth, **Hoth** (20c), **Hugh** (96a), hunh?, hush (17b, 146c)

HI · ·   hick (185d), hide (53a), hien (30b), hier (63a,185d), high, hike, hiku (57a,106d,138a), hila (53c), **Hild**, hill, hilo (74c), hilt (73c), **Hima** (191), hind (15b,41d,45a), hing (13c), hino (106d,168c), hint (9a,39c,159a), hipe (185a), hire (49d,50b,91b,130a), hiro, hish, hiss (146a), hist (25c,93d), hive (17c)

· HI ·   **Ahir** (27b), **Bhil** (191), chia (136d), chib (167a), chic (148d), chid, **ch'ih** (188), chil, chin, **Chin** (30b), chip (69d), chir (29b, 116d), chit (67b,98c,108b,116c,177c), chiv (87a), jhil, ohia (74c, 168c), **Ohio**, **Phil** (96b), phit (24b), phix (54a), **Rhin**, shih (189), **Shik** (171a), shim (91d,144c,162a,179d), shin (91a,d,140b,143c), ship, shir (36d,65d,165c), thin (43b,c,148b), this (42b,124b), **Whig**, whim (26c,54c,108c), whin (64c,70a,132b,181d), whip (58c,88d), whir (25c,181a), whit (166c), whiz (25c)

· · HI   bahi (60c), **Bahi**, pahi (21b,26a), tchi, **Tchi**, tshi, **Tshi** (69c)

H · · I   hagi (84b), hami (78a), **Hapi** (66a,107b,136a), **Hati** (48d), heil (74b), hemi (122c), hevi (111d), **Hoii** (77a), hopi (33c), **Hopi** (12c,102c,125b), hoti

H · · J   hadj (98b,118a)

H · · K   haak (57b,178a), hack (40a,77c,184d), haik 57b,65b,108a), hank (147c), hark (92d), hawk (19c,115c), heck (100a), hick (185d), hock (91a,115b,182b,c), hoek (39d), honk (70a), hook (27b,39d), howk (139b), huck (167d), hulk (144d,173d), hunk, husk (53a, 78d,142a)

HL · ·   **Hler** (141a)

· · HL   buhl (81a), kohl (53c), kuhl (53c)

H - - L   hail (6d,15a,71d), hall (37b,114d), harl (16b,56b,59a), haul (27b,45d), heal, heel, herl (16b,59a), hill, howl (39b), hull (141d,142a,144c,d), hurl (167c)

H - - M   haem (122b), haim, harm (40b,81a), helm (144d,165d), holm (77d,82d,109a)

- HN -   ohne (66d,183b)

- - HN   behn (137d), fohn (182b), John (11c,96a,121a,186b)

H - - N   hein (52c,61c), hewn, hien (30b), hoen (189), hoon (190), horn (11a,105a,170b,182a), hymn (150c)

HO - -   hoar (63d,71a,181a), hoax (41c,122a), hobb (124b), hobo (168a, 174b), hoch (52c,66c), hock (91a,115b,182b,c), hoek (39d), hoen (189), hoer, hoey (114c), hoga (144b), hogg (144a), Hohe (192), hoja (166b), hoju (84b), hola (74c,152b), hold (95c,124c, 130d), hole (6c,11b,110d,118c,147a), Holi (77a), holm (77d,82d, 109a), holt (36d,119b,184d), holy, home, homo (122d), horny (38b), hone (110a,143c,180d), hong (30b), honk (70a), hood (38a,74d), hoof (173a), hook (27b,39d), hoon (190), hoop (181b), hoot (112c), hope (13d,52d), hopi (33c), Hopi (12c,102c,125b), hops (17c), hora (22a 40b), horn (11a,105a,170b,182a), hors (62b), hose (156c), host (13a,51d,104c), Hoth (20c), hotl, hour, Hova (95a), hove (92a,157d), howe (77d), Howe (17a,82a), howk (139b), howl (39b), Hoya (14d)

- HO -   Ahom (88c), ahoy (106a), b'hoy (134b), chob (23c), chol (118d), Chol (192), chop (98a), chor (164b), chou (61b), Chou (30b), chow (45a), choy (48a,128d), dhow (88d,111c,175d), Ghor (174b), ghos (30b,) khot, mhor (180b), ohoy (106a), phon (94a), phoo, phos, phot (173b), rhob (64a,95c), Shoa (6c), shod, shoe (166a), shoo (46b,67a,138b), shop, shoq (169a), shor (136d), Shor (162b), shot (9d,43d,90c,174d), shou (41d), show (42b, 44c,96b), thob (128a), Thor (7c,68c,99c,100c,109c,165b), Thos (84a,181c), thou (124b), whoa (156c), whom (42b), whoo

- - HO   baho (122a), boho (117a,179d), coho (136c), echo (130b,d), Echo (105d), icho (67b), kiho (82a), moho (19a,78a), otho (133a), paho (122a), peho (19b,102c,106d), Saho (6c), sohol, Soho (93c), toho (79a)

H - - O   hako (115b), halo (14d,31b,92a,107b,131d), Hano (125b), hemo (34a,122b), hero (42b,124d,137b), Hero (90c), hilo (74c), hfno (106d,168c), hiro (74c), hobo (168a,174b), homo (168a,174b), Hugo (63a,96a), huso (180c), hypo (117b)

H - - P   harp (105a,129a), hasp (31d,54d,153c), heap (117d), Heep (41a, 43b), help (14a), hemp (26a,37a,56a,133d), hoop (181b), hump (124d)

- HR -   Shri (17c,166c)

- - HR   Bohr (14b,40d,138c), buhr (180d), Duhr (155b), guhr (47d), lehr (67c,112a), mahr (103a), mohr (65d), rohr (72d), Ruhr, sehr (66d), tahr (68a,76d), tehr (27c,68a)

H - - R   haar (139c), hair (56b,164d), hear (75b,c,92d), heer (47a,184b, 185b), heir, Herr (66c), hier (63a,185d), Hier (141a), hoar (63d), 71a,181a), hoer, hour

HS - -   Hsia (30b,47c)

H - - S   Hals (47a), Hans (66d,96a), hens (121d), hers (124c), hiss (146a), hops (17c), hors (62b), hyps

- - HT   acht (66c), baht (146a)

H - - T   haft (76d), halt (13b,28a,38d,156d), hant (67a), hart (41d,154d), hast (76d), heat, heft (179d), Heft, hest (35a), hilt (73c), hint (9a,39c, 159a), hist (25c,93d), holt (36d,119b,184b), hoot (112c), host (13a,51d,104c), hunt (141c), hurt

HU - -   hubb (118b), huck (167d), hued (83a), huff (58a), huge, Hugh (96a), Hugo (63a,96a), huia (19a,106d), hula (74b), hule (23a,134c), hulk (144d,173d), hull (141d,142a,144c,d), hulu (55b), Hume (50c), hump (124d), hung, hunh?, hunk, hunt (141c), Hupa (192), hura (20a,137a), Hura, hurl (167c), hurt, huse (180c), hush (17b,146c), husk (53a,78d,142a), huso (180c), huzz

- HU -   ahum, bhut (67a), chub (40c,154c), Chud (191), chug (53a), chum, (38d), Chun (30c), chutl, Ghuz (171a), jhum, Phud (110b), phut (24b), Phut (110b), rhum (8c), Rhus (159a), shul (161a), shun (15a,51b,52a), shut, thud, thug (65a), thus (149c), whun (64c,70a)

- - HU   ichu (10b,70d), jehu (46b), Jehu (18c), kahu (14d), Oahu, Rahu (42b,48b), sahu (153d), tchu

H - - U   haku (86d), hapu (106d), hiku (57a,106d,138a), hoju (84b), hulu (55b)

- HV -   IHVH (159d), JHVH (159d), YHVH (159d)

- HW -   JHWH (159d), YHWH (159d)

H - - X   hoax (41c,122c)

HY - -   hyde (188), Hyde (45a), hyke, Hyla (10a,166d,169b), hyle (97c), hymn (150c), hype (185a), hypo (117b), hyps

- HY -   whyo (59d,65a)

- - HY   achy, ashy (113a,178a)

H - - Y   hazy (174b), hoey (114c), holy, homy (38b)

H - - Z   Hayz, huzz

IA - -   Iago (54b,111d,143c), Ialu (48d), Iamb (59c)

- IA -   bias (43b,123a), diad (113a), dial (25c), dian (46c,130d,170b), Dian (68d,69a,c,102b), Diau (192), fiat (35a,41d,48c,111b,137a), Fiat (83c), kiak (51c), Liam (181d), liar (98d), Lias (66a), miam (14d), mian (97c,147b,166b), Miao (30a,b), mias (111a), Mias, miau (27b,99b), miaw (27b,99b), Nias (82d), Piaf (63c), piat (11a), piay (98b), rial (190), siak (72d), sial (112a), Siam (163d, 181a), Tiam, tiao, tiar (39a,75a,121a), vial (148c)

- - IA   Abia (18d,137a), akia (74c), amia (22c,170d), apia (121b), aria (8b,98c,150a,c), Asia (48a), chia (136d), Elia (88a,115d), eria (13d,146d), Fria, Gaia (47d,69a), glia (106c), Hsia (30b,47c), huia (19a,106d), Ilia (21d,77b,115d), inia (9b,109b), Inia (28c, 45b), ixia (37a), Maia (76b,109a,153b,155b,177c), Naia (33a), obia (55d), ohia (74c,168c), okia (190), raia (107d), Raia (147b), Soia, tsia (162c), Uria (14c,16d)

I - - A   idea (54c,108c,124a,164d), Ijma (103b), Ikra (27d), Ilia (21d,77b, 115d), Inca (14b,30a), Inga (145d), inia (9b,109b), Inia (28c, 45b), Inka (193), iola, Iona (28a,82d), iota (71a,85c,91c,114c,

308

Dieu (61d), fief (55d), gier (47b), hien (30b), hier (63a,185d), kief (75d), kiel (128d,134d), Kiel (25d), kier (20c,174d), Kiev, lied (66d,150b), lief (181d), lien (65c,91a,124c), lieu (118c, 155d), mien (11c,17b,26d,44c,96b), pied (96c,103c,114b,117c, 154a,174d), pien (13b), pier (23a,88b,180c), piet (28b,95b), Riel (129a), riem (76c,112c,157c,164d), rien (62b), rier (180b), sier (57a,118b), tied, tien (147d), tier (118a,134b), vier (66c), view (93d,138b), wiel (140d,180d), wies (185a)

- - IE   Abie (96b,107a), Amie (61d), Brie (29c), Erie (82c,87d), Okie (99d), Opie (50c), plie (32c,59b), soie (62c), unie (173a)

I - - E   idee (61d), idle (174b,c,178c), ille (89b,d,163d), imbe (37a,56a, 133d), inde, inee (120b), Inge (24d,67d,117c,119c), inre (35d, 80a), iole (52a,76b,123c), Ione (24b,88d,94d), ipse (44d,89c), Irae (43c), isle (8b,53c,81d,82d,86b,88a), ixie (56a)

IF - -   ifil (117a,168c)

- IF -   biff, fife (59a,105a), gift (123a), jiff (101c), kiff (88c), life (19a, 177a), lift (49b), miff (44c), nife (37a), piff (24b), rife (6b,c,39d, 123b), riff (131d), Riff (18b,102c), rift (30c,32a,58a,110d), sift (140d,142c,146b), tiff (126b), wife (154a)

- - IF   alif (12b), arif (127d), coif (73a), culf (139a,d,140c), Enif (155b), kaif (88c), keif (75d), Leif (107d), luif, naif (74b,105d), waif (157b)

IG - -   iglu (51c,149b), Igor (135d)

- IG -   biga (171d), giga (56a,105a), high, migg (96c), nigh (106a), riga (118b), Riga, sigh, sign (121c,146c), tige (118a), wigg

- - IG   brig (72b,106a,144d), crig (20d), grig (38c,70d,93a), prig (112a, 116c), snig (45d), swig (46a,72c), Teig (96a), trig (106a,148d, 154b,169d), twig, Whig

I - - G   ilog (132a,161b)

IH - -   IHVH (159d)

- IH -   kiho (82a)

- - IH   ch'ih (188), shih (189)

I - - H   IHVH (159d), inch, itch, Ivah (18d)

II - -   liwi (19a,74b)

- II -   liin (188), Riis (9d)

- - II   alii (74c,134c), apli (74c), Boli (191), heii (74b), Ubii (191)

I - - I   iiwi (19a,74b), immi (189), impi (86a), Inti (159b), Ioni (192)

IJ - -   ijma (103b)

- IJ -   bija (168c), lija (57a,90d,173a)

IK - -   ikat (53b,159a), ikmo (18b), ikon (79d,136a), ikra (27d)

- IK -   bike, bikh (120b), dika (23a), dike (49c,91d), Dike (78a), fike (139c), hike, hiku (57a,106d,138a), kiki (27b), kiku (30d), like (13c,37d,146d), mike, Mike (96b), Nike (69c,100c,182d), pika (93a,128a,132c), pike (57a,b,76c,120b,153a), piki (95c), piky, rikk (49a), sika (41d,84b), Sikh (77b), tike (29d), Tiki (120c)

- - IK   Atik (155b), Efik (191), haik (57b,65b,108a), kaik (96c), naik, raik (188,189), Seik, (77b), Shik (171a)

I - - K   Irak (99a,d), irok (55b)

IL - -   ilex (77d), illa (21d,77b,115d), ille (89b,d,163d), ills (170a), llog (132a,161b), ilot (82d), ilus (88d,170b)

- IL -   aile (62b,63a,182c,d), bile (30c), bilk (29b,41c,42a), bill (17b, 147a), Bill, bilo (131b), dill (13a,117c), dilo (120d,168c), eild (138d,140a), file (13a,127d), fifi, fill (109b),film (164b), filo, fils (62d,150b), gila (93b), gild (14a,49c,69c,98b), gill (22d), gilo (48a), gilt (69c,77c,151b,185d), hila (53c), Hild, hill, hilo (74c), hilt (73c), Jill (183d), jilt, kile (189), kill (38c), kiln (15d,112a), kilo (99b,122d), kilt, Lila (183c), lill (15d,118a), lilt (93a,131a, 147a), lily, mila (188), mild (32a,66a), mile (64c), milk, mill (126c), milo (70b,87c,150d), Milo, milt (153d), nile (33c,71d), Nile (106b), nill (173d), oily (110b,172c), pile (45d,75b,117c), pill (34b,108d), pili, pily, rile (10c,d,82c,125a,156b,176a), rill (23c,102b,132a,148d,157b), rily (176a), silk (53b,179c), sill (45c, 76c,165a,182b), silo (59a,156d), silt (104b), tile (31d,56d,72b, 95b,133c,163c), till (39c,101c,173d), tilt (26b,d,166a), vila (56b), vile (16c,56c), vill (54b), Vill (109c), vilt (176b), vily (54b), wild (38b,173d), wile (13b,41c,157b,169c), wilk (65c,96d,141b), will (18b,43a,163c,177c), wilt (46b), wily (13b,38b,39c)

- - IL   amil (45a,48a,185c), anil (47c,80d,180b), aril (142a), axil (10c), bail (43c), Bhil (191), boil, ceil (92c,112a), chil, coil (39d,171c, 185a), Dail (49a,82b,c), deil (139b), Egil (107d), Emil (96a), evil (79c,95d,147a,181a,185c), fail, foil (15d,55c,165b), gail (23b, 174d), Gail (183d), hail (6d,15a,71d), ifil (117a,168c), ipil (117a, 168c,169a), ixil (192), jail (123d), jhil, kail (8c,22a,25a,79b), mail (12d,99b,121c), moil (46c,184c), nail (31d,54d,141d,161d, 173a), Neil (96a), noil (87c,178b), pail, Phil (96b), rail (16b, 19b,c,37a,97b,138c,150c,177b), roil (44c,104b,156b,170d,176a), sail (144c,185a), skil (57a), soil (154d,159a,163c), tail (11d,27d, 59b,143b), teil (92b,c,168c), toil (46c,184c), vail (94b,124a,174b), veil (74d,76c), wall (39b,88a), ypil (117a,168c)

I - - L   ical (158c), idol (48c,54c,55a,75b,79d,112d,130b,184d), idyl (114d), ifil (117a,168c), ipil (117a,168c,169a), itol (158b), ixil (192)

IM - -   imam (25c,102d,103a), imbe (37a,56a,133d), imer, imid (29c), immi (189), impi (86a)

- IM -   cima (83b,c), dime, gime (77d), gimp (169d), Hima (191), iima (17b,152b,174d), Lima (31b), limb (12d,22d), lime (25b,27d,31b, 33c,102d,168c), limn (45d,121c), limp (58a,81a,177d), limu (141c), limy (176d), mima (185d), mime (24a,71b,85a,100a), Mime (131d,148d), mimi (14d), Mimi (87b,110d,125b,183d), nimb (31b,73b,92a,107b,131d), oime (8b), pima (37c), Pima (192), rima (23a,30c,32a,58a,110d), rime (30c,36a,58a,63d,77c), rimu (79d,106d,129a,168c), rimy (63d), sima (132b), sime (101d), Simi (82d), simp (59c,146d), time (47a,131a), Yima (84a,116b,c), Zimb (6c)

- - IM   Anim (18d), Akim (135d,191), alim (103b,162c), brim, Clim (12b), duim (188), Emim (67a,100d), frim (58d), glim, grim (156a), maim (43d,81a,105c), prim (156b), Seim (120c), shim (91d,144c,162a,179d), skim (67c), slim (148b,160a), swim (58c), trim (40a,106a,154b,160a,165c,169d), urim (18d,23a,110a), whim (26c,54c,108c), zaim (170d)

311

312

niog (33a,168c), niou (188), pion (43c,52b), piot (95b), riot (44c, 111d,170c,173d), siol (82c), sion (125c,158c), Sion (75b,c,83a, 157d), tion (158b), Tiou (192), viol (105a), Zion (75b,c,83a,157d)

- - IO   agio (52c,60a,101c,123a), apio (125b), Clio (104d), idio (34b,c), meio (188), moio (188), naio (107a,168c), noio (107c,163c), odio (83b), Ohio, olio (44b,77c,98c,100d,121d), Scio, skio (57d), trio (104d,165a,169c), Unio (105c)

I - - O   Iago (54b,111d,143c), icho (67b), ideo (34b,d,164d), idio (34b,c), idjo (191), idyo (191), idzo (191), ikmo (18b), inro (84b,c,106c), into (123a), ipso (89c, itmo (18b)

IP - -   ipil (117a,168c,169a), ipse (44d,89c), ipso (89c)

- IP -   aipl (27a), cipo (91d), dipt, hipe (185a), kipp, lipa (54d), nipa (14b,46b,48a,164a,168c), pipa (159d), pipe (105a,180d,182a), pipi (106d,119d), pipy (145d), ripa (16b,131d), ripe (58a,97c, 98c), Sipe (101a,110c,140b), tipe (168b), tipi (181b), wipe, Xipe (15c), Zipa (29d), zipp, Zips (40c)

- - IP   atip (14b,166a), chip (69d), clip (54d,143d), drip, flip (167c), grip (159a), knip (115c), quip (183a,b), ralp (36d), seip (110c), ship (110b,114c,147c), slip (67c,119a), snip (32b,40a), trip (85c), whip (58c,88d)

I - - Q   Iraq (99a,d)

IR - -   Irad (18d), Irae (43c), Irak (99a,d), Iran (6a,48c,116b), Iraq (99 a,d), Iras (11b,32a), Iren (127c), Irid (38d,67c), Iris (53c,58a, 111c), Iris (127c), Irma (96d), Irok (55b), Iron (55c,d,69d,81a, 97b,143b,149a,173d,179c), Irra (68c,178a), Irus (109d)

- IR -   Aira (70d), aire (82c), Aire, airs (123b), airy (176d,177a), bird, birl (93c,131a,153c), birn (31d,139a), birr (180d), cirl (24c), circ (31a), dire (45d,55a,104a,163c), dirk (40b), dirt, Eire (82b), fire (13a,43d,44b), firm (154c,173d), firn (67c,70c,106c,149b), gird (32c,50a,123a,160a), girl, giro (38c,83c,167c), girt (50a), hire (49d,50b,91b,130a), hiro, kiri (86a,87c,115a,168c), kirk (31a, 139b), lira (28b,79a,170d), lire (62c), Mira (155b,174d), mire (21c,104b), mirk (41a,67d), miro (19a,106d,184a), Miro (113a, 151d), miry, pirn (21b,129a,179b), Piro (192), pirr (181a), rire (62a), sire (17d,55a,59d,124a,163b,166b), siri (18b), tire (15a, 22a,52d,55a,179b,180d), tiro (9b,17d,108c), Vira (191), vire (11a, 13b), wire, wiry (147a,167c), zira (188)

- - IR   Abir (129a), Ahir (27b), amir (7c,12a,103a,b,123c,170d), chir (29d,116d), coir (33a,37a,56a,133d), cuir (45c,62a), emir (12a, 103a,b,123c,134d,135a,171a), fair (17a,55d), hair (56b,164d), heir, kair, keir (20c,174d), koir (33a), lair (37c,42b), Leir, loir (45c), Loir, Muir (8b,142c), Nair (45d), noir (61b,134b), pair (22d,37d,85b,171d), sair (140b,150d), Seir (51b,94a,103d), shir (36d,65d,165c), skir, soir (61c), spir (97c), stir (8a,13a,35b, 78d,100d), tair (68a,76d), vair (64c,154c), weir (40b,57d), whir (25c,181a), Ymir (67a,131c)

I - - R   icer, igor (135d), imer, inar (65b), Isar (41a,104c,132a), Iser (49a), iter (22d,76c,85c,89c,114d,132a,b,133a,b), Iyar (102b), Izar (65b,103b), Izar (155b)

IS - -   Isar (41a,104c,132a), isba (135c), Iser (49a), Isha (174a), Isis (68d,78c,111d), isle (8b,53c,81d,82d,86b,88a), ismy (45a)

314

I - - T ibit (117a), ikat (53b,159a), ilot (82d)

- IU - biur (35a), Niue (137d), Pius (121a)

I - - U lalu (48d), lchu (10b,70d), iglu (51c,149b)

IV - - Ivah (18d), Ivan (40c,85b,96a), Ives (9c,90b)

- IV - Civa (56d), cive (110c), diva (110d,123c), dive (42b,74b,119d), divi, five, give (79d,123a), hive (17c), Jiva (77a), jive (160c), kiva (28c,125b), kive (174d), kivu (170c), live (47c), Livy (132d, 133a), rive (32a,153d), siva (67a,120d), Siva (56d,77a), sive (146a), viva (93d), vive (93d), vivo (93a), wive (97a)

- - IV chiv (87a), skiv (151b)

- IW - Biwa (93d,168c), iiwi (19a,74b), kiwi (11d,19a,58c)

IX - - ixia (37a), Ixil (192), ixie (56a)

- IX - Bixa (145d), dixi, Mixe (192), mixy, pixy (154b)

- - IX Alix (183c), Coix (70d,85b), flix, nolx (67c)

IY - - Iyar (102b)

- IY - kiyi (185d)

I - - Y idly, inky (20b), inly, Ismy (45a)

IZ - - izar (65b,103b), Izar (155b)

- IZ - bize (182a), bizz, size, sizy (176d), sizz, tiza (172a), zizz (181a)

- - IZ friz (39d), phiz (54a), swiz (160c), whiz (25c)

I - - Z Inez (45c,183c)

JA - - jaca (84a), jack (26c,58a,127c), Jack (96b), Jacu (19a,151b), jade (33c,65d,71d,166a), jadu (95a), jady, Jael (147b), Jaga (191), jagg, Jail (123d), Jain (77b), jake (40d), Jake (96b), jako (71a), jama (103b), Jamb (12d,45c,118a,146b,174a), Jami (103b), Jane (190), Jane (183c), jann (102d), jaob, jape (85a,b), jari (40d,107d), jass (160d), jati (27b), jato (173b), jaun (113a), Java (33a), Jave (84d), jawy, jazz

- JA - ajar (110c), Ajax (71b,162d)

- - JA Beja (6c,191), bija (168c), caja (152a), coja (103b,166b), hoja (166b), lija (57a,90d,173a), maja (151c), Maja (153b), Naja (33a), puja (77a), raja (77a,123c), reja (152b), soja (151b)

J - - A jaca (84a), Jaca, Jaga (191), jama (103b), Java (33a), Jena (105d,165b), Jiva (77a), jota (151c), Jova (193), juba (106b), juca (27a), Juda, juga (27a), Jula, jura, Juza (155b)

J - - B jamb (12d,45c,118a,146b,174a), jaob, jibb, Joab (41a)

- - JD Nejd

J - - D Joad (50c)

JE - - jean (37c), Jean (183c), jeel, jeep, jeer (138c,162b), jefe (152a), jeff (133d), Jeff, jehu (46b), Jehu (18c), Jena (105d,165b), jerk (153a), jess (157a), jest (169c), Jesu, jete (16a), Jeth (102a), jeux (61d)

- JE - ajee (15c,139a)

315

- - JE   haje (33a,48d), yaje (23a)

J - - E   jade (33c,65d,71d,166a), Jake (40d), Jake (96b), Jane (190), Jane (183c), Jape (85a,b), Jave (84d), jefe (152a), jete (16a), jibe (8a,33b,35d,37b,42c,100d,138c,144c,149b), jive (160c), joke (183a), jole (29b), Jose (96a), Jove (85d), jube (28d), Jude (11c, 96a), juke (114c), Jule (183d), June (183c), jupe (62b,84a), jure (90b), jute (37a,48a,56a,133d,136a), Jute

J - - F   jeff (133d), Jeff, jiff (101c)

J - - G   jagg, joug (138d), Jung (125a)

JH - -   Jhil, jhum, JHVH (159d), JHWH (159d)

J - - H   Jeth (102a), josh (85b), JHVH (159d), JHWH (159d)

JI - -   jibb, jibe (8a,33b,35d,37b,42c,100d,138c,144c,149b), jiff (101c), Jill (183d), jilt, jink, jinn (42b,103b,153c), jinx (78a), jitl, jiva (77a), jive (160c)

- - JI   caji (180b), Caji, fuji (84b), Fuji (84d), koji (185b), suji (180c)

J - - I   jami (103b), jati (27b), Jati, jiti, jogi (76d), joli (62b), joti

J - - K   jack (26c,58a,127c), Jack (96b), jerk (153a), jink, jock, Jock (96b), jonk, juck (114c), junk (30a,134c)

J - - L   Jael (147b), jail (123d), jarl (40d,170d), jeel, Jhil, Jill (183d), Joel (96a), jowl (29b)

- JM -   ijma (103b)

- - JM   Sejm (120c)

J - - M   jhum, joom (39c)

J - - N   Jain (77b), jann, Jann (102d), jaun (113a), jean (37c), Jean (183c), jinn (42b,103b,153c), Joan (183c), John (11c,96a,121a, 186b), join (36a,173c), juan (113a), Juan (96a)

JO - -   Joab (41a), Joad (50c), Joan (183c), joar (100a), jobo (77c), jock, Jock (96b), jocu (45b,57a), Jodo (113d), Joel (96a), joey (86a, 185d), Joey (96b,109c), jogi (76d), John (11c,96a,121a,186b), join (36a,173c), joke (183a), joky, jole (29b), joli (62b), jolt (143b), jonk, joom (39c), Jose (96a), josh (85b), joss (30b) Josy (183d), jota (151c), joti, joug (138d), Jova (193), Jove (85d), jowl (29b), Jozy

- JO -   ajog, ejoo (55b,168c), Gjoa (144d)

- - JO   bojo (117a), gajo (107c), Idjo (191), majo, mojo (177c), pajo (122a), rojo (129a,152c), tajo (152a,d)

J - - O   jako (71a), Jako, jato (173b), jobo (77c), Jodo (113d), judo (84b,85c,142b), Juno (69c,85d,100c,126b)

J - - P   jeep, jump

J - - R   jeer (162b), joar (100a), juar (100a)

J - - S   jass (160d), jess (157a), joss (30b)

J - - T   jest (169c), jilt, jolt (143b), just (51b,54b)

JU - -   juan (113a), Juan (96a), juar (100a), juba (106b), jube (28d), juca (27a), juck (114c), Juda, Jude (11c,96a), judo (84b,85c,

142b), **Judy** (125c,183d), **juez** (152b), **juga** (27a), **juju** (29b,55d), **juke** (114c), **jula, Jule** (183d), **jump, June** (183c), **Jung** (125a), **junk** (30a,134c), **Juno** (69c,85d,100c,126b), **jupe** (62b,84a), **Jura, Jura, jure** (90b), **jury** (38a), **just** (51b,54b), **jute** (37a,48a,56a, 133d,136a), **Jute, Juza** (155b)

- - JU **baju** (84a), **hoju** (84b), **juju** (29b,55d), **teju** (151b)

J - - U **jacu** (19a,151b), **Jadu** (95a), **jehu** (46b), **Jehu** (18c), **Jesu, Jocu** (45b,57a), **juju** (29b,55d)

J - - X **jeux** (61d), **jinx** (78a), **jynx** (78a), **Jynx** (184a)

JY - - **jynx** (78a), **Jynx** (184a)

J - - Y **jady, jawy, joey** (86a,185d), **Joey** (96b,109c), **joky, Josy** (183d), **Jozy, Judy** (125c,183d), **July, jury** (38a)

J - - Z **jazz, juez** (152b)

KA - - **kaan** (93d,116c), **kaat** (105d), **kada** (188), **kade** (144a), **kadi** (103a,171a), **Kadu** (191), **Kafa** (6c), **kago** (113a), **kagu** (106c), **kaha** (123d), **kahu** (14d), **kaid** (29d,66a), **kaif** (88c), **kaik** (96c), **kail** (18c,22a,25a,79b), **Kain, kair, kaka** (114b), **kaki** (84c,106d), **kala** (19a), **kale** (22a,25a,119b,175a), **kali** (26d,67c,136d,167a), **Kali** (147b), **kalo** (162a), **Kama** (56d), **kame** (67b,139b), **Kami** (68a,84b,88c,107c,144c), **kana** (84d), **Kane** (74c), **k'ang** (30a), **Kano** (84c,177d), **kant** (28d), **Kant** (67a), **kapa** (74b), **kaph** (91d), **Kapp, Kara** (132a), **Karl** (14d), **Karl** (96a), **karn** (156c), **karo** (106d), **kasa** (48a), **kasi** (116b), **kasm** (189), **Kate** (143c,183d), **kath** (14a), **Katy** (183d), **kaun** (93d), **kava** (18c,116a), **Kavi** (84d), **kawa** (18c,116a), **Kawi** (84d), **kawn** (93d), **kayo** (87c), **kazi** (103a), **kazy** (103a)

- KA - **Akal** (56d), **Akan** (191), **ikat** (53b,159a), **okay** (8d), **skag** (7d, 46d), **skat** (181b), **Skat** (155b)

- - KA **Akka** (125d), **Atka** (11a), **baka** (52b), **beka** (189), **dika** (23a), **Ekka** (26d), **inka** (193), **kaka** (114b), **loka** (173c,184c), **plka** (93a, 128a,132c), **puka** (107a,168c), **roka** (95a,168c,d), **Saka** (10a), **sika** (41d,84b), **soka** (20c), **waka** (26a), **weka** (58c,106d,107a, 127b), **Yaka** (191)

K - - A **kada** (188), **Kafa** (6c), **kaha** (123d), **kaka** (114b), **kala** (19a), **Kama** (56d), **kana** (84d), **kapa** (74b), **kara** (132a), **kasa** (48a), **kava** (18c,116a), **kawa** (18c,116a), **kela** (189), **keta** (45a), **kina** (126d), **kiva** (28c,125b), **koba** (11a), **kola** (25b,84a,108d), **Kola** (135b,c,d), **kona** (74c), **kora** (19a,178c), **kota** (117a), **Kota** (45d), **kuba** (26d,189), **kufa** (21b,99a), **kula** (189), **kusa**

K - - B **kerb** (146b), **knab** (107a), **knob** (73c,107c,124d), **knub** (178b)

K - - D **kaid** (29d,66a), **keld** (154b), **kind** (150d,153a,174d), **Kurd** (48b, 82a)

KE - - **keal** (25a), **keef** (75d), **keek** (154c), **keel** (128d,134d,144c,d), **keen** (15a,88a,177b), **keep** (123a,130d), **keet** (72b), **keif** (75d), **keir** (20c,174d), **kela** (189), **keld** (154b), **kelp** (82a,141c), **Kelt** (180b), **kemp** (139b), **keno, Kent** (90d), **kepi** (99d), **kept, kerb** (146b), **kere** (75c,128b), **kerf** (40a,108b), **keri** (75c,128b), **kern** (59c,172a), **Kern** (132b), **Kerr, keta** (45a), **Ketu** (48b)

- KE - **akee** (168c), **akey** (189), **okeh** (8d,37b), **oket** (189), **skee** (149c), skeg (7d,86a,144d,157d,184a), sken (164a), skeo (57d), skep (16d,17c,77c), skew (148a,160c,171b,c), skey (185d)

- - KE bake (139a), bike, cake, coke (32d,64a), cuke (39b), cyke (40c), dike (49c,91d), Dike (78a), duke (107c), dyke (49c,91d), fake (123a,143c), feke, fike (139c), fyke (15d), hake (57a,b), hike, hykel, jake (40d), Jake (96b), joke (183a), juke (114c), lake (117d), like (13c,37d,146d), Loke (15d,68b), luke, Luke (52a, 96a), make (35b,36d,54a,123a), mike, Mike (96b), moke (45c, 157d), Nike (69c,100c,182d), Peke (45a,148d), pike (57a,b,76c, 120b,153a), poke (108c), rake (41b,44c,134b,140d), roke (174d, 175b), sake (84b,125d), soke (44c,85d), syke (194), take, tike (29d), tuke (26b,53b), tyke (29d), wake (134b,168a), woke, yoke (85b,92d,173c), Zeke (96b)

K - - E kade (144a), kale (22a,25a,119b,175a), kame (67b,139b), Kane (74c), Kate (143c,183d), kere (75c,128b), kibe kile (189), kine (38a,112c), kite (19c,49a,74c,d), kive (174d), Klee (113a), knee (85b), koae (74b), Kobe (78a), Kome (71d), kore (107b), Kore (29a,42b,116b,124d), kuge (84c), Kure (84c), kyle (57a,139c)

- - KF wakf (103a), wukf (103a)

K - - F kaif (88c), keef (75d), kelf (75d), kerf (40a,108b), kief (75d), kiff (88c), koff (47a)

K - - G k'ang (30a), king (26c,29c), knag (115d,139c), krag (131c), kung (125b)

KH - - khan (7c,26c,81b,93d,116c,123c,130c,166c), khar (189), khas (153a), khat (105d), Khem (113c), khet (188), khot

- KH - Akha (86a,c)

- - KH ankh (38d,162b), bikh (120b), bukh (122a), hakh (46d), iakh (110c), rukh (53b,54a), Sikh (77b)

K - - H kaph (91d), kath (14a), kish (16d,70c), Kish (137c), kith (63c), Koch (66d), koph (91d), Kush, kyah (19a)

KI - - kiak (51c), kibe, kiby (29a), kick, kief (75d), kiel (128d,134d), Kiel (25d), kier (20c,174d), Kiev, kiff (88c), kiho (82a), kiki (27b), kiku (30d), kile (189), kill (38c), kiln (15d,112a), kilo (99b,122b), kilt, kina (126d), kind (150d,153a,174d), kine (38a, 112c), king (26c,29c), kink (38b,171c), kino (27c,34c,47c,72c, 98b,161d,168c), kipp, kiri (86a,87c,115a,168c), kirk (31a,139b), kish (16d,70c), Kish (137c), kiss (148c), kist (29d,58a,139b), kite (19c,49a,74c,d), kith (63c), kiva (28c,125b), kive (174d), kivu (170c), kiwi (11d,19a,58c), kiyi (185d)

- KI - akia (74c), Akim (135d,191), akin (8b,92b,129c), okia (190), Okie (99d), skid (148b), skii (57a), skim (67c), skin (53a,76c, 115c,d), skio (57d), skip (110b,114c,147c), skir, skit (145c), skiv (151b)

- - KI Enki (15b), kaki (84c,106d), kiki (27b), Kuki (191), Loki (7c,15d, 68b), maki (91b), moki (127b), piki (95c), Reki (16a), saki (39c, 84b,102a), Tiki (120c), weki (55c), yaki (193)

K - - I kadi (103a,171a), kaki (84c,106d), kali (26d,67c,136d,167a), Kali (147b), Kami (68a,84b,88c,107c,144c), Kari (14d), kasi (116b), Kavi (84d), Kawi (84d), kazi (103a), kepi (99d), keri (75c,128b), kiki (27b), kiri (86a,87c,115a,168c), kiwi (11d,19a,58c), kiyi

318

(185d), **kobi** (84b), **koji** (185b), **Koli** (27b), **Komi** (191), **kopi** (107a,168c), **Kopi** (172a), **kori** (7d,77a), **kuei** (44a), **Kuki** (191), **Kuli** (27b), **Kuri** (191), **kwei** (44a)

· KK ·   **Akka** (125d), **Ekka** (26d)

· · KK   **bukk** (122a), **rikk** (49a)

K · · K   **kaik** (96c), **kiak** (51c), **keek** (154c), **kick, kink** (38b,171c), **kirk** (31a,139b), **konk** (41c), **kunk** (188), **kurk** (31a,139b), **kyak** (51c)

KL · ·   **klam** (189), **Klee** (113a), **klom** (189), **klop** (150d)

K · · L   **kail** (18c,22a,25a,79b), **Karl** (96a), **keal** (25a), **keel** (128d,134d, 144c,d), **kiel** (128d,134d), **Kiel** (25d), **kill** (38c), **koel** (19a,b,39b), **kohl** (53c), **kral, kuhl** (53c)

· KM ·   **ikmo** (18b)

K · · M   **kasm** (189), **Khem** (113c), **klam** (189), **klom** (189)

KN · ·   **Knab** (107a), **knag** (115d,139c), **knap** (76d,107a,139b,159b,166a, 170c,185b), **knar** (87c,134b), **knee** (85b), **knew, knez** (123c), **knip** (115c), **knit** (173c,179b), **knob** (73c,107c,124d), **knop** (124b, 170c,185b), **knor** (87c), **knot** (43c,99d,107c,124d,137b), **knub** (178b), **knur** (67d,87c,107c), **knut, Knut** (40d,50c,96a)

K · · N   **kaan** (93d,116c), **Kaln, karn** (156c), **kaun** (93d), **kawn** (93d), **keen** (15a,88a,177b), **kern** (172a), **Kern** (132b), **khan** (7c,26c, 81b,93d,116c,123c,130c,166c), **kiln** (15d,112a), **kran** (190), **kuan** (30b), **Kuan** (30c), **kwan** (30b)

KO · ·   **koae** (74b), **koba** (11a), **Kobe** (78a), **kobi** (84b), **kobu** (84b), **Koch** (66d), **koel** (19a,b,39b), **koff** (47a), **kohl** (53c), **koir** (33a), **koji** (185b), **koko** (106d,114b), **Koko** (93d,186c), **koku** (189), **kola** (25b,84a,108d,168c), **Kola** (135b,c,d), **Koli** (27b), **kolo** (59b,135c), **Kome** (71d), **Komi** (191), **kona** (74c), **konk** (41c), **koop** (16c), **koph** (91d), **kopi** (107a,168c), **Kopi** (172a), **kora** (19a,178c), **Kora, kore** (107b), **Kore** (29a,42b,116b,124d), **kori** (7d,77a), **koso** (6c,80d), **Koso** (192,193), **koss** (188), **kota** (117a), **Kota** (45d), **koto** (84b), **kozo** (113d,168c)

· KO ·   **akov** (189), **Ekol** (191), **Ikon** (79d,136a)

· · KO   **boko** (52b), **Doko** (191), **hako** (115b), **Jako** (71a), **koko** (106d, 114b), **Koko** (93d,186c), **mako** (18a,19a,20d,143c,168c,182c), **moko** (96c), **toko** (30c)

K · · O   **kago** (113a), **kalo** (162a), **Kano** (84c,177d), **karo** (106d), **kayo** (87c), **keno, kiho** (82a), **kilo** (99b,122d), **kino** (27c,34c,47c,72c, 98b,161d,168c), **koko** (106d,114b), **Koko** (93d,186c), **kolo** (59b, 135c), **koso** (6c,80d), **Koso** (192,193), **koto** (84b), **kozo** (113d, 168c), **Kroo** (191)

K · · P   **Kapp, keep** (123a,130d), **kelp** (82a,141c), **kemp** (139b), **kipp, klop** (150d), **knap** (76d,107a,139b,159b,166a,170c,185b), **knip** (115c), **knop** (124b,170c,185b), **koop** (16c)

KR · ·   **krag** (131c), **kral, kran** (190), **kras** (76d), **kris** (40b,95d), **Kroo** (191)

· KR ·   **akra** (176a), **Akra** (191), **ikra** (27d), **okra** (72c,175a), **okro** (72c, 175a)

· · KR   **Askr** (107d)

319

K - - R kair, keir (20c,174d), Kerr, khar (189), kier (20c,174d), knar (87c,134b), knor (87c), knur (67d,87c,107c), koir (33a), Kuar (102a), kyar (33a)

- - KS oaks (154d)

K - - S khas (153a), kiss (148c), koss (188), kras (76d), kris (40b,95d), kvas (135c)

- - KT takt (105a,163a)

K - - T kaat (105d), kant (28d), Kant (67a), keet (72b), Kelt (180b), Kent (90d), kept, khat (105d), khet (188), khot, kilt, kist (29d, 58a,139b), knit (173c,179b), knot (43c,99d,107c,124d,137b), knut, Knut (40d,50c,96a), kyat (189)

KU - - Kuan (30c), kuan (30b), Kuar (102a), kuba (26d,189), kudu (11a), kuei (44a), kufa (21b,99a), kuge (84c), kuhl (53c), Kuki (191), kuku (19a,106d), kula (189), Kuli (27b), kung (125b), kunk (188), Kurd (48b,82a), Kure (84c), Kuri (191), kurk (31a, 139b), kusa, Kush

- KU - - akua (120d), skua (19b,72c,84a,141a)

- - KU baku (26d,157b,168c), duku (95d,168c), haku (86d), hiku (57a, 106d,138a), kiku (30d), koku (189), kuku (19a,106d), Maku (192), poku (11a), puku (11a), Suku (191), Taku (80c)

K - - U Kadu (191), kagu (106c), kahu (14d), Ketu (48b), kiku (30d), kivu (170c), kobu (84b), koku (189), kudu (11a), kuku (19a,106d)

KV - - kvas (135c)

- KV - NKVD (135d)

K - - V Kiev

KW - - kwan (30b), kwei (44a)

K - - W knew, know

KY - - kyah (19a), kyak (51c), kyar (33a), kyat (189), kyle (57a,139c)

- KY - Skye (163c), skyr (21d,151a), skyt (138c,140b)

- - KY alky, caky, coky, faky, inky (20b), joky, laky, oaky, piky, poky (148c), taky, waky

K - - Y Katy (183d), kazy (103a), kiby (29a)

K - - Z knez (123c)

LA - - laap (51d,91b,141d), lace (58b,179c), lack (178a), lact (34c), lacy, Ladd (143c), lade (24c,26d,43c,93b,100a,132a,139d,161b, 178d), lady, laet (60d), lago (83b,152b), laic (32b,90b,107d, 124a,141d), laid, lain, lair (37c,42b), Lais (17c), lait (62a), lake (117d), lakh (110c), laky, lala (129b), lalo (16b,34d,153a), Lalo (35c), lama (23d,24a,91d,165b), lamb, Lamb (49c), lame (38d, 43d,73b), lamp (92a,94c), lana (58a,66a,90a,184b), land (44a, 163c), lane (134b,157b), lank (148b,164b), lant, lanx (133a,b), Laos (80d,129c), Lapp (108a), Lara (25c), lard (54d,61a,71a, 110a), lari (78a,101c), Lari (72c), lark (19a,63d,177b), larp (51d), Lars (51d,121b), lash (58c,87b,165c,180d), Lasi (191), lass (95b), last (36c,50b,145a,174c), lata (85d,95d), late (128c), lath (157c), latu (190), laud (122a), laun (146b), lava (101c, 132b,151a,177a), lave (16d,178b), lawn (20a,37c,53b,92c), laze (79b), Laze (191), Lazi (191), lazo (88d,128b,133d), lazy

320

130d), **Keld** (154b), **meld** (26a,41c,99a,118b), **mild** (32a,66a), **mold** (54d),143c), **sold, suld** (188), **told** (129c), **veld** (151a), **weld** (47c,85b,173c), **wild** (38b,173d), **wold** (47c,60a,118d,174a, 184a)

L - - D **Ladd** (143c), **laid, land** (44a,163c), **lard** (54d,61a,71a,110a), **laud** (122a), **lead** (35d,43d,72b,74d,81a), **lend** (6d,79d), **lied** (66d,150b), **load** (24c,26d,161b), **lood** (189), **lord** (107c), **loud** (156a), **Ludd** (23c)

LE - - **lead** (35d,43d,72b,74d,81a), **leaf** (55c,73c,119b), **Leah** (19a,84a, 87b,183c), **leak** (110c), **leal** (54b,94c,139d), **lean** (128a,148b, 152d,164b,166a), **leap** (26c), **lear** (139d), **Lear** (37a,143b), **lech** (102b), **Leda** (27b,75d,120c,153a,171d,186b), **leek** (58b,76a,110c, 177d), **leer** (9d,58a,67c,93d,112a,148c), **lees** (46a,142a), **leet** (26a,38a,139d), **left** (42c), **lehr** (67c,112a), **Leif** (107d), **Leir, Lely** (47a), **lena** (56d), **Lena** (36b), **lend** (6d,79d), **lene** (36b, 149a,172b), **leno** (37c,53b), **lens** (67c,95b,111a,129b,162d), **lent** (54d), **Lent** (115d,141c), **Leon** (96a), **Lero** (82d), **lerp** (51d,141d), **less** (100c,108b,141d), **lest** (59d,163d), **lete, Leti** (82d), **Leto** (11c), **Lett** (16a,90a,93a), **leve** (62a), **Levi** (84a,90c), **levo** (91a), **levy** (14a,162b)

- LE - **Alea** (14b,31c,167d), **alec** (10a,57c,d,76c,137c), **alee** (15c,75d, 144b,157a,182a), **alef** (91c), **alem** (98b,155a,170d,171a), **alen** (40d,138a), **bleb** (20c,23d,67c), **bled, blet** (64a), **bleu** (61b), **blew, clee** (19a,129a), **clef** (104d,105a), **clem** (56b,158b), **clew** (16a,33a,77b,136b,164d), **elef** (91c), **flea** (81b), **fled, flee, flew, flex** (18a), **fley** (63d), **gled** (19a,52a,87a), **glee** (99a,150b), **glen** (43c), **Hier** (141a), **ilex** (77d), **Klee** (113a), **Lieu** (40c), **Llew** (40c), **olea** (170b), **Olea** (110b), **oleo** (34c), **plea** (51a,52d,122a, 130b), **pleb** (10d,35b,180b), **plet** (135d), **plew** (17c), **plex** (60b), **Sieb** (12a), **sled** (40a), **slee** (140b,148c), **slew** (160a), **sley** (179b), **Ulex** (153c), **vlei** (38c,160a), **vley** (160a)

- - LE **able** (26b,35b,126a,147c), **acle** (13d,82c,115d), **aile** (62b,63a, 182c,d), **Aile** (14c), **atle** (136d,161d,169b), **axle** (153c,180c), **bale** (24b,74a), **bile** (30c), **bole** (31d,32a,169b), **cale** (72d), **cole** (25a), **Cole, dale** (43c,128a,174b), **dele** (26a,49c,51b,53a, 110b,123d,124c,130a,145c,161b), **dole** (44c,118c,121c,129d), **Dole** (74c), **elle** (62b,c), **file** (13a,127d), **gale** (181d), **gyle** (23b, 174d), **hale** (125b), **Hale** (9d,131a), **hole** (6c,11b,110d,118c, 147a), **hule** (23a,134c), **hyle** (97c), **idle** (174b,c,178c), **ille** (89b, d,163d), **loie** (52a,76b,123c), **Isle** (8b,53c,81d,82d,86b,88a), **ixle** (56a), **jole** (29b), **Jule** (183d), **kale** (22a,25a,119b,175a), **kile** (189), **kyle** (57a,139c), **male** (154d), **Male** (45d), **mele** (74b, 150b), **mile** (64c), **mole** (19d,23a,24d,85a,117c,155c), **Mole** (88c), **mule** (45b,148b,153c,180b), **nile** (33c,71d), **Nile** (106b), **ogle** (9d,53c,91a,93d,148c), **orle** (17b,56b,76a,144b,177a), **pale** (113a, 117c,178a), **Pele** (69c,74c), **pile** (45d,75b,117c), **pole** (132c,143b, 177b,184a), **Pole** (52a), **pule** (180d), **pyle** (34b), **Pyle** (9c,178a), **rale** (7c,23a,29d,41b), **rile** (10c,d,82c,125a,156b,176a), **role** (114b), **rule** (11b,26b,90b), **sale** (14c,61c,62b,c,168b), **sole** (52c, 57a,b,58b,d,110c,115d,150a), **taie** (91a,185b), **tele** (34b,122c), **tile** (31d,56d,72b,95b,133c,163c), **tole** (9a,51a,99b,163a), **tule** (24b, 27c), **vale** (54c,128a,174b), **Vale** (7c,109c), **vile** (16c,56c), **vole**

322

(97d,104a), **wale** (70b,131b,157c,163d,179a,180a,c,d), **wile** (13b, 41c,157b,169c), **Yale** (173c), **Yule** (30d)

L - - E **lace** (58b,179c), **lade** (24c,26d,43c,93b,100a,132a,139d,161b, 178d), **lake** (117d), **lame** (38d,43d,73b), **lane** (134b,157b), **late** (128c), **lave** (16d,178b), **laze** (79b), **Laze** (191) **lene** (36b,149a, 172b), **lete**, **leve** (62a), **life** (19a,177a), **like** (13c,37d,146d), **lime** (25b,27d,31b,33c,102d,168c), **line** (12b,22b,36d,38a,126c,134b, 157b,158b,162d,175c), **lire** (62c), **lite** (158c,d), **live** (47c), **lobe** (90c,134b), **lode** (42c,99a,111b,175b), **loge** (164a), **Loke** (15d, 68b), **Lome**, **lone** (150a), **lope** (48b,64b,d), **lore** (77c,87c,90d, 151c,183a), **lose** (60a,100c), **lote** (24c,94a), **love** (163a), **lube** (110a), **luce** (58c,117d), **Luce** (7b,35a), **luge** 148a), **luke**, **Luke** (52a,96a), **lune** (38c,73b,74d), **lupe** (19a,64a), **lure** (41c,51a,54b, 163a), **lute** (11c,28b,84d,105a,131d), **luxe** (61c,62d,159c), **lyre** (11c,81c,105a,111c), **lyse**

- LF - **alfa** (70d),

- - LF **calf**, **golf** (154a), **gulf** (6c), **half** (101a), **pelf** (22a,56c,131b), **self** (48d,80d), **Welf** (67a), **wolf**

L - - F **leaf** (55c,73c,119b), **Leif** (107d), **lief** (81d), **loaf** (49b,94b), **loof** (144c,153d), **luff** (136b), **luif**

- LG - **alga** (141b,c), **Algy** (96b), **Olga** (135c,183c)

L - - G **ling** (24c,57a,b,75b,178c), **long** (38b,185b), **lung**, **lurg** (96d,141b, 184d)

L - - H **lakh** (110c), **lash** (58c,87b,165c,180d), **lath** (157c), **Leah** (19a, 84a,87b,183c), **lech** (102b), **lith** (34d,156c), **loch** (88a,139d), **losh** (178b), **loth** (15a,173d), **Lugh** (28b), **lush** (94d)

LI - - **Liam** (181d), **liar** (98d), **Lias** (66a), **lick**, **Lida** (183c), **Lido** (83d, 175b), **lied** (66d,150b), **lief** (181d), **lien** (65c,91a,124c), **lieu** (118c,155d), **life** (19a,177a), **lift** (49b), **liin** (188), **lija** (57a,90d, 173a), **like** (13c,37d,146d), **Lila** (183c), **lill** (15d,118a),**lilt** (93a, 131a,147a), **lily**, **lima** (17b,152b,174d), **Lima** (31b), **limb** (12d, 22d), **lime** (25b,27d,31b,33c,102d,168c), **limn** (45d,121c), **limp** (58a,81a,177d), **limu** (141c), **limy** (176d), **lina** (188), **Lina** (183d), **line** (12b,22b,36d,38a,126c,134b,157b,158b,162d,175c), **ling** (24c,57a,b,75b,178c), **link** (36a,81d,85b), **linn** (120d,140a,c, 168c,178d), **lino**, **lint** (46a,58d), **liny** (157b), **Linz** (40d), **lion** (55b,86c), **lipa** (54d), **lira** (28b,79a,170d), **lire** (62c), **Lisa** (183d), **lisp** (153b), **liss** (54d), **lira** (28b,79a,170d), **lire** (62c), **Lisa** (183 d), **lisp** (153b), **liss** (54b,58b,60c,129d,140a), **list** (26d,27b,75b, 83d,134a,138b,165d), **lite** (158c,d), **lith** (34d,156c), **liti** (60d), **litz** (127b), **live** (47c), **Livy** (132c,133a)

- LI - **alia** (89d), **alif** (12b), **alii** (74c,134c), **alim** (103b,162c), **alin** (188), **alit** (44b,143a), **Alix** (183c), **Clim** (12b), **Clio** (104d), **clip** (54d,143d), **Elia** (88a,115d), **Elis** (22c,37d,71b,107c), **flip** (167c), **flit** (41a), **flix**, **glia** (106c), **glib** (58d,149a,177c), **glim**, **glis** (45c), **Ilia** (21d,77b,115d), **ille** (89b,d), **olic** (158b), **olid** (55d,60c,148d, 157d), **olio** (44b,77c,98c,100d,121d), **plie** (32c,59b), **slid**, **slim** (148b,160a), **slip** (67c,119a), **slit** (40a)

- - LI **amli** (48a,161d,168c,169a), **Atli** (14c,72b,79a,107d), **Bali**, **Beli** (23c), **coli**, **dali** (168c,169b), **doli**, **fili**, **gali** (6c), **goli** (105c), **Holi** (77a), **joli** (62b), **kali** (26d,67c,136d,167a), **Kali** (147b), **Koli** (27b),

323

Kuli (27b), mali (27b), pali (122b), Pali (23d,24a,137b,175a), pili (34b,108d), puli (45a,78d), soli (12c,110c), tali (189), teli (94b), vali (171a,176a), Vali (7c,109c), vili (54b), Vili (109c), wali (171a), yali (171a)

L - - I Lari (72c), lari (78a,101c), Lasi (191), Lazi (191), Leti- (82d), Levi (84a,90c), liti (60d), loci (66b,118c), Lodi (105d), Loki, (7c, 15d,68b), lori (91b), Loti (63a,176a), ludi (133b), Luri (191)

- LK - alky

- - LK balk (118c,146a,156d), bilk (29b,41c,42a), bulk (97b), calk (78c, 109a,141c,178d), folk (116a,169c), fulk (173a), hulk (144d,173d), milk, mulk (60d), polk (37c), pulk (37c,88d), silk (53b,179c), sulk (159a), talk, volk (66c,105d,116a), Volk, walk, welk (65c, 96d,141b), yolk

L - - K lack (178a), lank (148b,164b), lark (19a,63d,177b), leak (110c), leek (58b,76a,110c,177d), lick, link (36a,81d,85b), lock (54d), lonk (143d), look (11c,53c,142a), luck (28d), lurk (92a,147b)

LL - - llyn (120d,140a), Lleu (40c), Llew (40c)

- LL - alla (6d), Alle (14c), allo (34c), ally (14a,35c,d,173c), ella (152c, 158c), Ella (183c), elle (62b,c), ille (89b,d,163d), ills (170a), olla (36d,44b,84d,113b,121d,151d,152c,181b), ullo (6a,144a), Ullr (146b,164d)

- - LL ball, bell (24c,39d), Bell (162d), bill (17b,147a), Bill (96b), boll (119b,d), bull (113c), call (145c,159b,176d), cell (39b), cull (117c), dell (43c,174b), dill (13a,117c), doll (125c), dull (21a, 32c,173a), Dull (94b), fall (46b,141c), fell (40a,58b,76c,115d, 147d), fill (109b), full (7b,130b), gall (19a,28c,29b,82c,160c, 176a), gill (22d), Goll, gull (32d,41c,42a,72c,99b,141a), hall (37b,114d),hill, hull (141d,142a,144c,d), Jill (183d), kill (38c), lill (15d,118a), loll (94b,128c), lull (126d,150c), mall (95d,124b, 143b), mill (126c), moll, Moll (183d), mull (53b,135a,164c), Nell (110a,183d), nill (173d), Noll (96b,110b), null (108c,177a), pall (32d,81b,112a), pill, poll (74d,160a,177c), pull (45d,167d), rill (23c,102b,132a,148d,157b), roll (134a,160b), rull (170b), sell (97a,115c,175b), sill (45c,76c,165a,182b), tall (118d), tell (105d, 129c, 154b), Tell (160d), till (39c,101c,173d), toll (131c), vill (176b), wall, well, will (18b,43a,163c,177c), yell (145c)

L - - L leal (54b,94c,139d), lill (15d,118a), loll (94b,128c), lull (25c, 126d,150c)

- LM - alma (40d,53d,146d,147a), Alma (38d,183c), alme (40d,147a), alms (29a), elmy, ulme (49c)

- - LM balm (110a,172c), calm (8d,11d,112b,118d,126c,d,172b,173d), culm (11a,32d,70d,145a,156a), film (164b), halm, helm (144d, 165d), holm (77d,82d,109a), malm (32a,92b), palm (59b,168a, 169b)

L - - M Liam (181d), loam (47d), loom (11c,146b,179b), lyam (139a)

- LN - ulna (21d,39b)

- - LN kiln (15d,112a), vuln (184d)

L - - N Lain, laun (146b), lawn (20a,37c,53b,92c), lean (128a,148b, 152d,164b,166a), Leon (96a), lien (65c,91a,124c), liin (188), limn (45d,121c), linn (120d,140a,c,168c,178d), lion (55b,86c),

324

llyn (120d,140a), loan, loin (40a,98a), loon (19a,b,c,157d,179c), lorn (42d,60b), loun (19a,b), lown (157d)

LO - - load (24c,26d,161b), loaf (79b,94b), loam (47d,150a), loan, lobb (23b,94c,163a), lobe (90c,134b), lobo (165d,183c), loch (88a, 139d), loci (66b,118c), lock (54d), loco (38b,119b,120b), lode (42c,99a,111b,175b), Lodi (105d), Lodz (189), loft (14c,69d,104b, 178b), loge (164a), logy (46d), loin (40a,98a), loir (45c), Loir, Lois (165d,183c), loka (173c,184c), Loke (7c,15d,68b), Loki (7c, 15d,68b), Lola (27d,97b), loll (94b,128c), Lolo (27d,30a), loma (58b,63d), Lome, lone (150a), long (38b,185b), Lonk (143d), lood (189), loof (144c,153d), look (11c,53c,142a), loom (11c,146b, 179b), loon (19a,b,c,157d,179c), loop (31b,107d), Loos, loot (22a,118a,119d,136a,153d), lope (48b,64b,d), lora (146b,149b, 151c,169b), Lora (183c), lord (107c), lore (77c,87c,90d,151c, 183a), lorl (91b), lorn (42d,60b), loro (19a,114b), lory (19a, 114a), lose (60a,100c), losh (178b), loss (42c,123d,178b), lost, lota (24c,121d,178d), lote (24c,94a), loth (15a,173d), Loti (63a, 176a), loto (65a,121d,178d), lots, loud (156a), loun (19a,b), loup (61d,62a,90c,139d), Loup (193), lour (13d,63d), lout (15c,22a, 24b,45b,109a,157d), love (163a), lowa (19a), lown (157d), lowp (90c,139d)

- LO - alod (51c,55d,88a,124c), aloe (7d,20a,76a,b,92b,98b,119b,158b, 167a,183d), alop (13d,46b,93d), alow (18a,172c), blob, bloc (173a), blot, blow, clod (22a,45b,157d), Cloe (183c), clog (30c, 145b), clop, clot (32d,94d), clou (62b), clow (58c,148c), cloy (61b,137c,159d), elod (49b,59d,79c), Elon (18c,51b,108a), floc (149a), floe (79b), flog (180d), flop (54a), flot (173a), flow (157b), glom (155d,160d,178c), glow (144c), ilog (132a,161b), ilot (82d), klom (189), klop (150d), Olor (160a,b), plod (170b), plop (54b), plot (25a,36b,118d,138b), plow (39c,165d), ploy (43c), slob (173d), sloe (14a,20b,64a,119b,181c), slog (157c, 170b,177d), sloo (160a), slop, slot (10d,11b,41d,110d,167d,168a, 181b), slow (43c)

- - LO allo (34c), bilo (131b), bolo (87a), calo (72d), dilo (120c,168c), filo, gilo (48a), Golo (191), Gulo (183c), halo (14d,31b,92a), hilo (74c), kalo (162a), kilo (99b,122d), kolo (59b,135c), lalo (16b, 34d), Lalo (35c), Lolo (27d,30a), malo (23a,74c,152a), milo (70b,87c), Milo, nolo (42a), orlo (56b,119c), Oslo, palo (152c), pelo (83b), polo (154a), Polo (175b), ralo (188), silo (59a), solo (12c,89a,110c), ullo (6a,144a), velo (175b)

L - - O iago (83b,152b), ialo (16b,34d), Lalo (35c), lazo (88d,128b,133d), leno (37c,53b), Lero (82d), Leto (11c), levo (91a), Lido (83d, 175b), lino (165d,183c), loco (38b,119b,120b), Lolo (27d, 30a), loro (19a,114b), loto (65a,121d), ludo (65a,112b)

- LP - Alph (132a), Alps (85d), olpe (90d,182c)

- - LP calp (92b), colp (28a,148b), gulp (46a,79d,160a), help (14a), kelp (82a,141c), palp (11a,55b,58b,167c), pulp, salp (148d), yelp

L - - P laap (151d,91b,141d), lamp (92a,94c), Lapp (108a), larp (51d), leap (26c), lerp (51d,141d), limp (58a,81a,177d), lisp (153b), loop (31b,107d), loup (61d,62a,90c,139d), Loup (193), lowp (90c,139d), lump (45a,160c)

- - LR Ullr (146b,164d)

325

L - - R	lair (37c,42b), lear (139d), Lear (37a,143b), leer (9d,58a,67c, 93d,112a,148c), lehr (67c,112a), Leir, liar (98d), loir (45c), Loir, lour (13d,63d)
- LS -	also (10b,18b,80a), Elsa (70a,93c,110d,177b,183c), else (18b, 79b,111d)
- - LS	fels (190), fils (62d,150b), Hals (47a), Ills (170a)
L - - S	Lais (17c), Laos (80d,129c), Lars (51d,121b), lass (95b), lees (46a,142a), lens (95b,111a,129b,162d), less (100c,108b,141d), Lias (66a), liss (54b,58b,60c,129d,140a), Lois (165d,183c), Loos, loss (42c,123d,178b), lots, Lubs (94c), Lyas (66a)
- LT -	alta (89c,152d), alto (152b,176c,177a)
- - LT	Balt (93a), belt (16a,31a), bolt (13b,54d,58b,132d,160a), bult (76d), celt (30c,82c,123a,156c,167b,179b), Celt (10a,180a,b), colt (78c,131a,185d,186b), Colt, cult (141d,161c), dolt (20c,59c, 157d), felt, gait, gelt (101c), guilt (69c,77c,151d,185d), halt (13b, 28a,38d,156d), hilt (73c), holt (36d,119b,184b), jilt, jolt (143b), Kelt (180b), kilt, lilt (93a,131a,147a), malt (17c), melt, milt (153d), molt (27a,143d), pelt (53a), salt (35d,105b,123a,136c, 141c,149d), silt (104b,142a), tilt (26b,d,166a), tolt, volt (49b, 78c), Walt (96b), welt (36d,131b,145a,b,177b,d), wilt (46b), yelt (151b)
L - - T	lact (34c), laet (60d), lait (62a), lant, last (36c,50b,145a,174c), leet (26a,38a,139d), left (42c), lent (54d), Lent (115d,141c), lest (59d,163d), Lett (16a,90a,93a), lift (49b), lilt (93a,131a,147a), lint (46a,58d), list (26d,27b,75b,83d,134a,138b,165d), loft (14c, 69d,104b,178b), loot (22a,118a,119d,136a,153d), lost, lout (15c, 22a,24b,45b,109a,157d), lust (41b)
LU - -	Luba (191), lube (110a), Lubs (94c), luce (58c,117d), Luce (7b, 35a), luck (28d), lucy, Lucy (183c), Ludd (23c), ludi (133b), ludo (65a,112b), luff (136b), luge (148a), Lugh (28b), luif, luke, Luke (52a,96a), lull (25c,126d,150c), lulu (19a,57b,112c), Lulu (183d), lump (45a,160c), luna (103c), Luna (102b), lune (38c,73b,74d), lung, luny (38b), lupe (19a,64a), lura (22d,82a), lure (41c,51a, 54b,163a), lurg (96d,141b,184d), Luri (191), lurk (92a,147d), lush (94d), lust (41b), lute (11c,28b,84d,105a,131d), luxe (61c, 62d,159c)
- LU -	alum (14a,45c), Alur (191), blub, blue (33c,98c,102c,150d,173a), blup, blur, blut (66b), club (39c), clue, Elul (102b), flub (22b), flue (8b,30a), flux (28d,58d), glub, glue (7b,156a), glug, glum (102c,159a), glut (52c,70a,137c,159d), Ilus (88d,170b), plug (156d,184d), plum, plup, plus (10b,102c), slub (171c), slue (97b, 148b,160a), slug (46b,99b,157c), slum (44b,124c,148b, 168a), ulua (57a,74c), Ulua (141b)
- - LU	Aalu (6b,48d), aulu (74c,168c), balu (104b,159a,181d), hulu (55b), Ialu (48d), iglu (51c,149b), lulu (19a,57b,112c), Lulu (183d), pelu (30a,106d,168c), pulu (74c), Sulu (102c), tolu (16a), Tulu (45d), zulu (171d,175d), Zulu (86a)
L - - U	Iatu (190), lieu (118c,155d), limu (141c), Lleu (40c), lulu (19a, 57b,112c), Lulu (183d)
- LV -	Alva (151d), Ulva (141b)

LW - - Lwow

L - - W Llew (40c), Lwow

- - LX calx (23c,75c,112c), falx (133b)

L - - X lanx (133a,b), lynx (26c,181d), Lynx (36b)

LY - - lyam (139a), Lyas (66a), lynx (26c,181d), Lynx (36b), Lyra (36b, 74a), lyre (11c,81c,105a,111c), lyse

- LY - Alya (155b,c), Alys (183c), Clym (12b), Ilyn (120d,140a)

- - LY ably (147c), ally (14a,35c,d,173c), coly (104a), eely (185a), hofy, idly, inly, July, Lely (47a), lily, moly (76a,181c), oily (110b, 172c), only (24d,52c,98d,147a,150a), Orly (8b), paly (194), pily, poly (34c,76b), puly, rely (16b,170b), rily (176a), ugly, vily (54b), wily (13b,38b,39c)

L - - Y Lacy, lady, laky, lazy, Lely (47a), levy (14a,162b), lily, limy (176d), liny (157b), livy (132d,133a), logy (46d), lory (19a,114a), lucy, Lucy (183c), luny (38b)

L - - Z Linz (40d), litz (127b), Lodz

MA - - maal (188), ma'am (95a,166b), maar (177a), Maas (132a), Maat (69a,b,85d), Maba (103a,168d), mabi (58d), mace (49d,108d, 153b,154d,161a,178a), mack, made, Madi (174a), mado (14d, 57a,170b), mage (95b), magg (95b), Magh (102a), magi (123c), Magi (95b,116c,183a), maha (28c,88c,136d), mahr (103a), Maia (76b,109a,153b,155b,177c), maid (45b,142d), mail (12d,99b, 121c), maim (43d,81a,105c), main (29d,35d,123d), mais (61b), maja (151c), Maja (153b), majo, make (35b,36d,54a,123a), maki (91b), mako (18a,19a,20d,143c,168c,182c), Maku (192), mala (89b,c,90a,94b,97d,109d,185c), male (154d), Male (45d), mali (27b), mali (95d,124b,143b), malm (32a,92b), malo (23a,74c, 152a), malt (17c), mama, Mama (116d), mamo (19a,74b), mana (30a,120d,122a,159c), mand (28b), mane, mani (115c), mann (189), Mann (9c,48c,185c), mano (71d,73d,74b,83b), Mans (30a), Manu (10a,76d,77a,b), Manx (27b,28a,82d), many (108d), mapo (68a,148d), mara (114d), Mara (24a,d,105b,107b), marc (70c), Marc (96a), mare (78b), Mare (108b), mari (61d), Mari (16a), mark (146b,155a), Mark (52a,96a), marl (32a,42c,55d), maro (144d), Mars (68c,118d,119a,129a,178a), mart (49d,97a), Mart (96b,183d), maru (84c,144d), Mary (50c,126b,183c), masa (37a), mash (39b,156c), mask (44a,45c), mass (8a,24b,35b, 142d), mast (17c,108d,120b,144d,152d), masu (57a,84c), mate (18c,35b,41d,113a,154a,162c), math (77a), Matt, maty (80c), maud (53d,71a,136d,143c), Maud (181a,183c), Maui (120d), maul (73c,96b), maun (139d), maya (77a,179b), Maya (23d, 186c), Mayo (193), maze (87b,157d)

- MA - amah (95b,108d,111c), amar (189), imam (25c,102d,103a), Oman (159a), omao (165b), omar (103b), Omar (48c,51b,116c, 163b), Xmas

- - MA alma (40d,53d,146d,147a), Alma (38d,183c), amma (6a), atma (150d), bema (28d,31a,114b,119b,125b,137a), boma (7d), cima (83b,c), coma (91c,157d,170c,172b), cyma (101a,b), dama (65d, 152b), Duma (135c), Emma (183c), Erma (183c), Fama (135a), Gama (121c), Goma (191), Hima (191), ijma (103b), Irma (96d), jama (103b), Kama (56d), lama (23d,24a,91d,165b), lima (17b,

152b,174d), **Lima** (31b), **loma** (58b,63d), **mama, Mama** (116d), **mima** (185d), **Nama** (78c), **Nema** (34d,48c,134b,164d,176c), **Numa** (133a), **pima** (37c), **Pima** (192), **puma** (27b,37c,55b, 103d), **Rama** (77a,80b,176d), **rima** (23a,30c,32a,58a,110d), **Roma** (83c,d), **sama** (105c,169d), **sima** (132b), **soma** (10c,21c, 34a,48a,81d,136b), **Tama** (192), **tema** (12a,164a), **Toma** (191), **xema** (72c), **Xema** (12c), **Yama** (57a,68a), **Yima** (84a,116b,c), **Yuma, Zama** (73d,141d)

M - - A   **Maba** (103a,168d), **maha** (28c,88c,136d), **Maia** (76b,109a,153b, 155b,177c), **maja** (151c), **Maja** (153b), **mala** (89b,c,90a,94b,97d, 109d,185c), **mama, Mama** (116d), **mana** (30a,120d,122a,159c), **mara** (114d), **Mara** (24a,d,105b,107b), **masa** (37a), **maya** (77a, 179b), **Maya** (23d,186c), **meda** (110a), **mega** (34b,c), **mela** (34a, 129d), **mesa** (49b,76d,119b,161a), **meta** (132d,133a), **Meta, mica** (82c,100b,146c), **mila** (188), **mima** (185d), **mina** (10b,70b, 71d,179d), **Mina** (23a,183d), **mira** (174d), **Mira** (155b), **moha** (42b,83d), **Mola** (159c), **mona** (72b,101d), **mora** (42b,65a,72b, 83d,99b,153a,161a), **mota** (103a), **moxa** (27d,30c), **muga, mura** (84d), **Mura** (192), **Musa** (16a), **muta** (28d,103a), **myna** (19a,c, 70b), **Myra** (10a,31b,183c), **myxa** (168c,169a)

- MB   **amba** (161a), **ambi** (34a,122c), **ambo** (125b,128b), **imbe** (37a, 56a,133d), **umbo** (22b)

- - MB   **bomb** (144a), **comb** (38c), **dumb** (153b), **lamb** (59c), **jamb** (12d, 45c,118a,146b,174a), **lamb, Lamb** (49c), **limb** (12d,22d), **nimb** (31b,73b,92a,107b,131d), **numb** (124d), **rumb** (120b), **tomb, Zimb** (6c)

M - - B   **medb, Moab** (18d,85a,86d,94a)

M - - C   **marc** (70c), **Marc** (96a)

M - - D   **maid** (45b,142d), **mand** (28b), **maud** (53d,71a,136d,143c), **Maud** (181a,183c), **mead** (46a,78a,97d,99b), **Mead** (78a), **meed** (128c, 131a), **meld** (26a,41c,99a,118b), **mend** (130b), **mild** (32a,66a), **mind** (75c,81d,93d,109b), **Moed** (100c), **mold** (54d,143c), **mood** (44c), **mudd** (188), **mund** (124d)

ME - -   **mead** (46a,78a,97d,99b), **Mead** (78a), **meal** (72a,130b), **mean** (15a,42b,146c,156b), **meat** (59b), **meda** (110a), **Medb, Mede** (10a,b,13c), **medi** (34c), **meed** (128c,131a), **meek** (93d,99d), **meer, meet** (11d,13d,36a,50a,81d,142d), **mega** (34b,c), **mein** (30b), **meio** (188), **mela** (34a,129d), **meld** (26a,41c,99a,118b), **mele** (74b,150b), **melt, memo** (108b), **mend** (130b), **mene** (19a, 73d,108d,185c), **Ment** (54b,164a), **menu** (19a,27a), **Menu, meou, meow, mere** (16c,22b,62a,78b,87d,96c,110c,120d,146b,148b), **merl** (20b), **mero** (72a), **Meru** (77a,103d), **mesa** (49b,76d,119b, 161a), **mese** (71c), **mesh** (50d,106c), **mess** (22b,44b,77c,85d, 104b,165c,173d), **meta** (132d,133a), **meta, mete** (9a,11d,22b, 44c,45b,98a,121c), **meum** (27a,89c), **Meum, mewl** (180d), **mews** (154c)

- ME -   **amen** (14a,80b,94a,137a,149c,175c,184b), **Amen** (86d,127d,159b, 164a), **amer** (61b), **Ames** (9c,82a), **Amex** (184d), **Emer** (39b, 183c), **emeu** (111d), **Imer, Omei** (24a), **omen** (14c,59d,60a,121c, 123a,146b), **omer** (51a,75c), **smee** (19b,46c,d,118b,119b,141b, 181b), **Smee** (116d), **smew** (19b,46d,99a,137d), **T-men** (168b), **Ymer** (67a,131c)

- - ME acme (39c,115c,186b), **aime** (40d), **arme** (63a,179b), **came** (182b), **Came** (192), **come**, **cyme** (58d,69c), **dame** (67b,87c, 166b), **deme** (71b,c,167d), **dime**, **dome** (39c,133c,155d), **fame** (130a), **feme** (181b), **fume** (129a,149a,157a), **game** (64d,154a), **gime** (77d), **home**, **Hume** (50c), **kame** (67b,139b), **Kome** (71d), **lame** (38d,43d,73b), **lime** (25b,27d,31b,102d,168c), **Lome**, **mime** (24a,71b,85a,100a), **Mime** (131d,148d), **name** (8a,11b,d,25c,46c, 107c,130b,157d,163b,166b), **nome** (71c,163b), **Nome**, **oime** (8b), **pome** (11d), **Pume** (137b,175b,185b), **rame** (22d), **rime** (30c, 36a,58a,63d,77c), **Rome** (31c,51d), **ryme** (178d), **same** (44d, 79b), **seme** (45c,138b,151b,154b,155c,157b), **sime** (101d), **some** (114b,121c,126a), **tame** (45a,66a), **Tame** (192), **time** (47a,131a), **tome** (21d,177c), **ulme** (49c), **zeme** (55d,161b,180b), **zyme** (55c)

M - - E mace (49d,108d,153b,154d,161a,178a), **made**, **mage** (95b), **make** (35b,36d,54a,123a), **male** (154d), **Male** (45d), **mane**, **mare** (78b), **Mare** (108b), **mate** (18c,35b,41d,113a,154a,162c), **maze** (87b, 157d), **Mede** (10a,b,13c), **mele** (74b,150b), **mene** (19a,73d,108d, 185c), **mere** (16c,22b,62a,78b,87d,96c,110c,120d,146d,148b), **mese** (71c), **mete** (9a,11d,22b,44c,45b,98a,121c), **mice**, **mide** (110a), **mike**, **Mike** (96b), **mile** (64c), **mime** (24a,71b,85a,100a), **Mime** (131d,148d), **mine** (69c,79d,111b,124c), **mire** (21c,104b), **mise** (8a,10a,70c), **mite** (12b,81b,82a,114a,148c,d,181b), **Mixe** (192), **mode** (54d,96b,157d,179a), **moke** (45c,157d), **mole** (19d, 23a,24d,85a,117c,155c), **Mole** (88c), **mope** (92d,159a), **more** (71a), **More** (50b), **Mose** (96b), **mote** (114c,153a), **moue** (61d, 62b), **move**, **mule** (45b,148b,153c,180b), **mure** (177d), **muse** (65b,93d,120d,164c), **Muse** (68d), **mute** (146c,153b)

M - - F miff (44c), **moff** (53b,146c), **muff**

M - - G magg (95b), **migg** (96c), **Ming** (30b,c), **morg** (188), **mung** (70d)

MH - - mhor (180b)

- - MH samh (56b)

M - - H Magh (102a), **mash** (39b,156c), **math** (77a), **mesh** (50d,106c), **moth**, **Moth** (112d), **much**, **mush** (97d), **muth** (188), **myth** (8b, 91a)

MI - - miam (14d), **mian** (97c,147b,166b), **Miao** (30a,b), **mias** (111a), **miau** (27b,99b), **miaw** (27b,99b), **mica** (82c,100b,146c), **mice**, **mick** (82c), **mico** (97a), **mide** (110a), **Midi** (151b), **mien** (11c, 17b,26d,44c,96b), **miff** (44c), **migg** (96c), **mike**, **Mike** (96b), **mila** (188), **mild** (32a,66a), **mile** (64c), **milk**, **mill** (126c), **milo** (70b, 87c,150d), **Milo**, **milt** (153d), **mime** (24a,71b,85a, 100a), **Mime** (131d,148d), **mimi** (14d), **Mimi** (87b,110d,125b, 183d), **mina** (10b,70b,71d,179d), **Mina** (23a,183d), **mind** (75c, 81d,93d,109b), **mine** (69c,79d,111b,124c), **ming** (30b,c), **mink** (176c), **mino** (84c), **mint** (13a,33b,58b,76a), **minx** (116c), **miny**, **Mira** (155b,174d), **mire** (21c,104b), **mirk** (41a,67d), **miro** (19a, 106d,184a), **Miro** (113a,151d), **miry**, **mise** (8a,10a,70c), **miss**, **mist** (46b,59b,174d), **mite** (12b,81b,82a,114a,c,148c,d,181b), **mitt** (56c), **mitu** (39d), **mity**, **Mixe** (192), **mixy**

- MI - amia (22c,170d), **amid** (9d,50a), **amie** (61d), **amil** (45a,48a,185c), **amin** (9d), **amir** (7c,12a,103a,b,123c,170d), **amit** (94a), **Emil** (96a), **Emim** (67a,100d), **emir** (12a,103a,b,123c,134d,

135a,171a), **emit** (43d,49a,53c,58d,83a,142c), **imid** (29c), **omit** (49c,52c,106b,114c,147d)

- - MI **admi** (65d), **ammi** (98c), **demi** (34b,122c), **hami** (78a), **hemi** (122c), **immi** (189), **jami** (103b), **kami** (68a,84b), **Kami** (88c, 107c,144c), **Komi** (191), **mimi** (14d), **Mimi** (87b,110d,125b,183d), **rami** (22d), **Remi** (10b), **romi** (72d), **semi** (34b,80b,122c,d), **Simi** (82d), **zemi** (55d,161b,180b)

M - - I **Mabi** (58d), **Madi** (174a), **magi** (123c), **Magi** (95b,116c,183a), **maki** (91b), **mali** (27b), **mani** (115c), **mari** (61d), **Mari** (16a), **Maui** (120d), **medi** (34c), **Midi** (151b, **mimi** (14d), **Mimi** (87b, 110d,125b,183d), **moki** (127b), **Moki**

M - - J **munj** (70d)

M - - K **Mack**, **mark** (146b,155a), **Mark** (52a,96a), **mask** (44a,45c), **meek** (93d,9d), **mick** (82c), **milk**, **mink** (176d), **mirk** (41a,67d), **mock** (131b,162b), **monk** (28b,63c,129d), **mosk** (97b,103b), **muck**, **mulk** (60d), **murk** (41a,67d), **musk** (116b)

- ML - **amla** (48a,161d,168c,168a), **amli** (48a,161d,168c,169a)

M - - L **maal** (188), **mail** (12d,99b,121c), **mall** (95d,124b,143b), **marl** (32a,42c,55d), **maul** (73c,96b), **meal** (72a,130b), **merl** (20b), **mewl** (180d), **mill** (126c), **moil** (46c,184c), **moll**, **Moll** (183d), **mull** (53b,135a,164c)

- MM - **amma** (6a), **ammi** (98c), **ammo** (9d), **ammu** (9d), **Emma** (183c), **immi** (189)

M - - M **ma'am** (95a,166b), **maim** (43d,81a,105c), **maim** (32a,92b), **meum** (27a,89c), **Meum**, **miam** (14d)

- MN - **omni** (34a)

- - MN **damn**, **Domn** (135a), **famn** (188), **hymn** (150c), **limn** (45d,121c)

M - - N **main** (29d,35d,123d), **mann** (189), **Mann** (9c,48c,185c), **maun** (139d), **mean** (15a,42b,146c,156b), **mein** (30b), **mian** (97c,147b, 166b), **mien** (11c,17b,26d,44c,96b), **moan**, **moon** (40b,132c, 137c), **morn**, **mown**

MO - - **Moab** (18d,85a,86d,94a), **moan**, **moat** (44d), **mock** (131b,162b), **mode** (54d,96b,157d,179a), **Moed** (100c), **moff** (53b,146c), **mogo** (74b), **moha** (42b,83d), **moho** (19a,78a), **mohr** (65d), **moil** (46c, 184c), **moio** (188), **mojo** (177c), **moke** (45c,157d), **moki** (127b), **moko** (96c), **Mola** (159c), **mold** (54d,143c), **mole** (19d,23a,24d, 85a,117c,155c), **Mole** (88c), **moll**, **Moll** (183d), **molt** (27a,143d), **moly** (76a,181c), **mona** (72b,101d), **monk** (28b,63c,129d), **mono** (34c,78d,122d,147a), **Mono** (193), **mons** (89c), **Mons** (184d), **mont** (62b), **mood** (44c), **moon** (40b,132c,137c), **moor** (10a,75b, 137b,141d,178b), **Moor** (102c,d,111d), **moot** (41b,44c), **mope** (92d,159a), **mora** (42b,65a,72b,83d,99b,153a,161a), **more** (71a), **More** (50b), **morg** (188), **morn**, **moro** (19a,56c), **Moro** (100a, 103a,117a,159a), **Mors** (41b), **mort** (41b,47a,78b,136d), **Mose** (96b), **mosk** (97b,103b), **moss** (91d,104c,114a,170c), **most**, **mosy** (67d), **mota** (103a), **mote** (114c,153a), **moth**, **Moth** (112d), **moto** (104b), **moue** (61d,62b), **move**, **mown**, **moxa** (27d,30c), **Moxo** (192), **mozo** (152b)

- MO - **amoi** (62a), **amok** (18b,63c), **Amon** (86d,96b,127d,159b,164a), **amor** (152b), **Amor** (39c,68b), **Amos** (96a,144b), **Amoy** (88c)

- **- MO**   ammo (9d), atmo (34d,174d), Como, demo (122d), hemo (34a, 122b), homo (122d), ikmo (18b), itmo (18b), mamo (19a,b,74b), memo (108b), nemo (34b), Nemo (56a,85c), Pomo (192), Sumo
- **M - - O**   mado (14d,57a,170b), majo, mako (18a,19a,20d,143c,168c,182c), malo (23a,74c,152a), mamo (19a,74b), mano (71d,73d,74b,83b), mapo (68a,148d), maro (144d), Mayo (193), meio (188), memo (108b), mero (72a), Miao (30a,b), mico (97a), milo (70b,87c, 150d), Milo, mino (84c), miro (19a,106d,184a), Miro (113a,151d), mogo (74b), moho (19a,78a), moio (188), mojo (177c), moko (96c), mono (34c,78d,122d,147a), Mono (193), moro (19a,56c), Moro (100a,103a,117a,159a), moto (104b), Moxo (192), mozo (152b), Muso (192), Muzo (192), myxo
- **- MP -**   impi (86a), umph
- **- - MP**   bump, camp (163b), damp (101a), dump, gamp (172a), gimp (169d), Gump (43b), hemp (26a,37a,56a,133d), hump (124d), jump, kemp (139b), lamp (92a,94c), limp (58a,81a,177d), lump (45a,160c), mump (29b,153d), pomp (111d,112d), pump, ramp (65a,80b,127b,148b), romp (63d), rump, samp (70b,77d,121b), simp (59c,146d), sump (28c,45d,100b), tamp (46b,112b,121d), tump (60a,76d,103d), tymp (20c), vamp (80a,145a)
- **M - - P**   mump (29b,153d)
- **- MR -**   amra (77c), Omri (18c,86d)
- **M - - R**   maar (177a), mahr (103a), meer, mhor (180b), mohr (65d), moor (10a,75b,137d,141d,178b), Moor (102c,d,111d), Muir (8b, 142c), murr (72b,128b)
- **- MS -**   Omsk
- **- - MS**   alms (29a), arms, Rems
- **M - - S**   Maas (132a), Mais (61b), Mans (30a), Mars (68c,118d,119a, 129a,178a), mass (8a,24b,35b,142d), mess (22b,44b,77c,85d, 104b,165c,173d), mews (154c), mias (111a), miss, moss (89c), Mons (184d), Mors (41b), moss (91d,104c,114a,170c), muss (135b,173d)
- **M - - T**   Maat (69a,b,85d), mait (17c), mart (49d,97a), Mart (96b,183d), mast (17c,108d,120b,144d,152d), Matt, meat (59b), meet (11d, 13d,36a,50a,81d,142d), melt, Ment (54b,164a), milt (153d), mint (13a,33b,58b,76a), mist (46b,59b,174d), mitt (56c), moat (44d), molt (27a,143d), mont (62b), moot (41b,44c), mort (41b, 47a,78b,136d), most, must (70c,101a,106d,157d,182c), mutt (39c,101d), myst (71c,123b)
- **MU - -**   Muav (66a), much, muck, mudd (188), muff, muga, Muir (8b, 142c), mule (45b,148b,153c,180b), mulk (60d), mull (53b,135a, 164c), mump (29b,153d), mund (124d), mung (170d), munj (70d), mura (84d), Mura (192), mure (177d), murk (41a,67d), murr (72b,128b), Musa (16a), muse (65b,93d,120d,164c), Muse (68d), mush (97d), musk (116b), Muso (192), muss (135b,173d), must (70c,101a,106d,157d,182c), muta (28d,103a), mute (146c, 153b), muth (188), mutt (39c,101d), Muzo (192)
- **- MU -**   Amun (86d,127d,159b,164a), smug, smur (32c,46b,100c), smut (32d,44a,119a,150c)
- **- - MU**   ammu (9d), Atmu (143a,159b), limu (141c), rimu (79d,106d, 129a,168c)

331

M • • U Maku (192), Manu (10a,76d,77a,b), maru (84c,144d), masu (57a,84c), menu (19a,27a), Menu, meou, Meru (77a,103d), miau (99b), mitu (39d), Mitu

M • • V Muav (66a)

M • • W meow, miaw (27b,99b)

M • • X Manx (27b,28a,82d), minx (116c)

MY • • myna (19a,c,70b), Myra (10a,31b,183c), myst (71c,123b), myth (8b,91a), myxa (168c,169a), myxo

• MY • amyl (155c), emyd (163c,167c), Emys (167c,171b)

• • MY army (78c), demy (113d), domy, elmy fumy, homy (38b), ismy (45a), limy (176d), rimy (63d)

M • • Y many (108d), Mary (50c,126b,183c), maty (80c), miny, miry, mity, mixy, moly (76a,181c), mosy (67d)

NA • • Naab, naam (44c,150b), nabk (30d,164d), nabo (117a), Nabu (68c,183a), nach, nael (189), naga (13d,33a,55b,127c), Naga (24c,77a,88c,176d), Nagy (78d), Naia (33a), naid (63c), naif (74b,105d), naik, nail (31d,54d,141d,161d,173a), naio (107a, 168c), Nair (45d), nais (63c,132a), Naja (33a), Nais (77a), Nama (78c), name (8a,11b,25c,46c,107c,130b,157d,163b,166b), nana (118b), Nana (15c,105d,116d,186d), nane (139d), naos (28a,71c, 137a,163a), Naos (155b), napa (25c,67d,90d), Napa (182c), nape (15b,108c,d), napu (29d,80d), nard (13a,97c,102b,110a, 153c), Nare (93c), nark (81a,156d), nary (108b), nase (26b,75a, 124b), Nash (9c), nasi (34c,108a,115a), Nast (9c,27a), nata (47c), Nata (15c), Nate (22b), Nath (155c), Nato (6a,8d), natr (189), Natt (107b), naut (141b), nave (30d,31a,78d,114b,180c), navy (33c,58b), naze (26b,124b), Nazi

• NA • anai (163b,181a), Anak (67a), anam (159a,168c), Anam, anan (49a,159a,180c), Anas (46c,d), Anat (138c,147d), Anax (43c, 120c), anay (72b,163b,181a), enam (70c,77a), Enam (85c), gnar (72a), gnat (59a,81b,99c), gnaw (20a,107a,178b), inar (65b), knab (107a), knag (139d), knap (76d,107a,139b,159b,166a,170c, 185b), knar (87c,134b), Onan (18c,85c), snab (23c,139a), snag (11b,27b,35c,87c,124b,166a), snap (23a,36d,38b,48b,54d,56c, 58c,149d), unai (147a), unau (148c,171d)

• • NA anna (190), Anna (110c,166d), arna (24a,181b), Bana (67a), bena (176a), bina (77a), bona (89d), Bona (183c), buna (161c), Cana (57a,64b,100c), cena (88d,133a), Cuna (193), Dana (28a, 96a,171d), dona (83d,121c,151d), dyna (34c), Edna (183c), Enna (146a), etna (75b,153c,157a,175d,177a,c), fana (29b), gena (29b), Gona (106d), guna (106a,137b), Iona (28a,82d), Jena (105d, 165b), kana (84d), kina (126d), kona (74c), lana (58a,66a,90a, 184b), Iena (56d), Lena (36b), lina (188), Lina (183d), luna (103c), Luna (102b), mana (30a,120d,122a,159c), mina (10b, 70b,71d,179d), Mina (23a,183d), mona (72b,101d), myna (19a, c,70b), nana (118b), Nana (15c,105d,116d,186d), nina (152a), Nina (26c,33d,68d,183d), nona (89b,107b), Nona (69a,114a, 183c), orna (169d,182c), Pana, pina (35d,118b), puna (10b,33b, 104a,119b,182a), rana (77a,123c), Rana (63d), rena (132c), sana (56a,166d), Sana (185d), sina (46c), Sina (102d,103d), tana (159a), Tana (87d), Tina (183d), tuna (57a,b,123b,170d), ulna

(21d,39b), **urna** (133a), **vena** (90a,175a), **vina** (77a,105a), **Xina** (183d), **Yana** (192,193), **zona** (144c,186d)

N - - A   **naga** (13d,33a,55b,127c), **Naga** (24c,77a,88c,176d), **Naia** (33a), **Naja** (33a), **Nala** (77a), **Nama** (78c), **nana** (118b), **Nana** (15c, 105d,116d,186d), **napa** (25c,67d,90d), **Napa** (182c), **nata** (47c), **Nata** (15c), **nema** (34d,48c,134b,164d,176c), **Nepa** (106b,178c), **Nera** (165b), **Neva** (91b,132a), **Nina** (26c,33d,68d,183d), **nipa** (14b,46b,48a,164a,168c), **Nola**, **nona** (89b,107b), **Nona** (69a, 114a,183c), **Nora** (79b,107a,164c,183c), **nota** (15c,89c), **nova** (20c,106d,155c,174d), **noxa**, **Nuba** (108c), **Nuda** (39b), **Numa** (133a)

- NB -   **anba** (36d)

N - - B   **Naab**, **nimb** (31b,73b,92a,107b,131d), **numb**

- NC -   **ance** (158b,c,d), **ancy** (158c), **ence** (158c), **Inca** (14b,30a), **inch**, **onca** (189), **once** (60b,79b), **unca** (49a), **unci** (31d), **unco** (140c), **Ynca** (193)

- - NC   **banc** (61a,85c), **zinc** (21a)

- ND -   **anda** (23a,168c), **Ande** (193), **Andi** (27d), **Andy** (96b), **endo** (34d, 122d,183b), **inde**, **onde** (63a,178d), **unde** (179a), **undo** (11a,93d), **undy** (179a)

- - ND   **Arnd** (67a), **band** (72a,157c), **bend** (39d,171b), **bind** (33b,165c), **bond** (92a,101c,141d,143b,159d,165c), **bund** (49c,66c,90c), **cond** (156a), **fend** (114b,178b), **find** (44a), **fond** (7c,94b), **fund** (6d, 101c,130c), **Gond**, **hand** (60c,114c,115d,184c), **hind** (15b,41d, 45a), **kind** (150d,153a,174d), **land** (44a,163c), **lend** (6d,79d), **mand** (28b), **mend** (130b), **mind** (75c,81d,93d,109b), **mund** (124d), **pend**, **pond**, **pund** (189), **rand** (16d,22a,131b,145a,b), **Rand** (69c), **rend** (32a,159c,162c,185a), **rind** (53a,115c), **Rind** (109c,174b), **rynd** (100a), **sand** (71d,146c), **send** (42c,44b,95c, 121c,130a,144c,168b), **Sind**, **tend** (26d,80b,93a,100a), **tind** (86b), **tund** (121d), **vend** (97a,115c,142b), **Vend** (10b,148a), **wand** (120b,132c,156a), **wend** (67d,123d), **Wend** (10b,148a), **wind** (33b, 39d,171c,185a), **yond** (164d), **Zend**

N - - D   **naid** (63c), **nard** (13a,97c,102b,110a,153c), **need** (42b,52d,87b, 122a,178a), **Nejd**, **NKVD** (135d), **Nudd** (23c)

NE - -   **neaf** (58a,73c), **Neal**, **neap** (165c,167a,177b), **near** (11d,32c, 107b), **neat** (165c,169d), **Nebo** (68c,102d,103d,183a), **neck** (83a), **need** (42b,52d,87b,122a,178a), **neem** (96d,168c,169a), **neep** (140c,171b), **neer** (14b,86b,108b), **Neil** (96a), **nein** (66c), **Nejd**, **Nell** (110a,183d), **nema** (34d,48c,134b,164d,176c), **nemo** (34b), **Nemo** (56a,85c), **nene** (19b,74c), **neon** (65c), **Nepa** (106b, 178c), **Nera** (165b), **Neri**, **Nero** (8a,126d,133a,150b,172c), **ness** (26b,75a,124b), **nest** (38b,74b,130d,149c,160b), **nete** (71c,108b, 163d), **neti** (164a), **nett**, **neue** (66c), **Neva** (91b,132a), **neve** (56d,67c,70c,149b), **news** (165c), **newt** (48d,136c,169d), **next** (106a)

- NE -   **Aner** (18d,96b), **anes** (110c,140a), **anet** (43c), **anew** (7c), **inee** (120b), **Inez** (45c,183c), **knee** (85b), **knew**, **knez** (123c), **oner** (20d,53a,75c,162d,172a,d), **ones** (116a), **sned** (93d,125a,140a), **snee** (40a,43d,87a), **sneg** (139b)

333

· · NE acne (147c), aine (49b,62c,142c), Anne (50c,84a,143b,183c), a-one (52b,167b), Arne (35c,50c,134d), aune (188), bane (74a, 106b,120b,139a), bene (18a,83c,90a,106d,122a,180a), bine (145b,156a,171c,176b), bone, cane (17b,128a,156a,159a,177d), Cane, cene (34c), cine (104b,152c), cone (66b,150a,157c), Dane (85d,107d,138a), dene (137a), Dene (192), dine, done, dune (137a), dyne (59d,173b), eine (66c), enne (34c), erne (19c,d,47b, 54b,141a), esne (10c,45b,142c,148a,164d), fane (30d,137a, 162d), fine (49b,50a,104b,115d,159a), gane (185b), gene (54a), Gene (96b), gone (6b,15c,42c,44c,114d), gyne (34b,55b,183c), hone (110a,143c,180d), lone (24b,88d,94d), jane (190), Jane (183c), June (183c), kane (74c), kine (38a,112c), lane (134b), 157b), lene (36b,149a,172b), line (12b,22b,36d,38a,126c,134b, 157b,158b,162d,175c), lone (150a), lune (38c,73b,74d), mane, mine (69c,79d,111b,124c), mene (19a,73d,108d,185c), nene (19b,74c), nine (26c,104d), none (108b), ohne (66d,183b), orne (169d,182c), Orne (25b), pane (113c,155a,b), pene, pine (36a, 52a,88c,93c,168c,d,169a), pone (37a,85b), rine (44d,75d,135c), rone (127c,164b), rune (9b,67a,94a,95a,105c,107d,120a,141d, 163d), sane (128a), sine (64c,66b,90a,97c,126a,163b,169d,183b), syne (140b,147a), Tane (120d), tene (34d,131b), tine (11b,124b, 167b), tone (6c,118c,150d), tune (8b,12c,98c), tyne, Tyne (108a), vane (179b,182a), vine (32b), wane (41c,43c), wine, zone (44c, 50a,160a)

N · · E name (8a,11b,d,25c,46c,107c,130b,157d,163b), nane (139d), nape (15b,108c,d), Nare (93c), nase (26b,75a,124b), Nate (22b), nave (30d,31a,78d,114b,180c), naze (26b,124b), nene (19b,74c), nete (71c,108b,163d), neue (66c), neve (56d,67c,70c,149b), nice (54d,119c,130c), Nice (98c), nide (23c,72a,106c,116d), nife (37a), Nike (69c,100c,182d), nile (33c,71d), Nile (106b), nine (26c,104d), Niue (137d), node (35c,85b,87c,94d,120a,124d,160c), nome (71c,163b), Nome, none (108b), Nore (163d), nose (118d, 125a,149b), note (98c,109b,124b,128d,130a,177c), nove (83b), noze (75a), nude (16c,172d), Nupe (191)

N · · F naif (74b,105d), neaf (58a,73c)

NG · · ngai (48a,159c), ngan

· NG · ange (61a), ango (171a), inga (145d,170a), Inge (24d,67d,117c, 119c)

· · NG bang (75d,105d,148a), beng (43a), bing, bong, bung (119d, 156d), cang (184a), dang, ding (130b), dong, fang (167b), Fong (40b), Fung (191), gang (38c), gong, hang (160a), hing (13c), hong (30b), hung, Jung (125a), k'ang (30a), king (26c,29c), kung (125b), ling (24c,57a,b,75b,178c), long (38b), lung, Ming (30b,c), mung (70d), pang (165b), ping, pong, pung (22c,148b), Qung (191), rang, ring (50a), Rong (88c), rung (28c,39a), sang, sing (26d,178a), song (12c,170c), sung, Sung (30b), tang (30b, 58b,186b), teng (188), ting (166a), Ting (30c), tong (30a,c), tung (110a,168c), uang (131a), vang (72d,134a,140b), wang (189), wing (10d,58c,59a,118b,d), wong (56a), yang (30b,70a), zing

N · · G niog (33a,168c), nogg (48d)

· · NH binh (189), hunh?, sinh (97c), tanh (97c)

334

N - - H Nach, Nash (9c), Nath (155c), nigh (106a), Nish (19d), Noah (88a,99b)

NI - - Nias (82d), nibs (116c), nice (54d,119c,130c), Nice (98c), nick (30c,108b), nide (23c,72a,106c,116d), nidi (106c), nife (37a), nigh (106a), Nike (69c,100c,182d), nile (33c,71d), Nile (106b), nill (173d), nimb (31b,73b,92a,107b,131d), nina (152a), Nina (26c,33d,68d,183d), nine (26c,104d), nino (152a), niog (33a, 168c), niou (188), nipa (14b,46b,48a,164a,168c), Nish (19d), nisi (90a,173c), nito (55c), Niue (137d)

- NI - anil (47c,80d,180b), Anim (18d), anis (55c), Enid (13b,25d,66b, 163a,183c), Enif (155b), enin (20d), inia (9b,109b), inia (28c, 45b), knip (115c), knit (173c,179b), snib (54d,93c), snig (45d), snip (32b,40a), unie (173a), Unio (105c), unis (91b), unit (101c, 110c,147a)

- - NI Aani (45a,48d), agni (88a,89c), Agni (56d,68b), arni (24a,181b), bani (190), beni (116a,142d), Beni (191), Bini (191), Boni (63b), Coni, doni (21a,28c,168a), Ioni (192), mani (115c), omni (34a), Pani (120c), rani (72d,77b,123c,127c), Reni (83d), yeni (19b, 161d), Zuni (125b)

N - - I nasi (34c,108a,115a), Nazi, Neri, neti (164a), ngai (48a,159c), nidi (106c), nisi (90a,173c), nodi (35c,87c), nori (8c,141c)

- - NJ Funj, gunj (70c), munj (70d)

NK - - NKVD (135d)

- NK - ankh (38d,162b), Enki (15b), Inka (193), inky (20b)

- - NK bank (18a,58c), bonk (190), bunk, conk (41c,108a,156d,157c), dank (40b,101a), dunk (43c,79d), fink (19a,56c,157c), funk (63d, 113c), gink (48b), hank (147c), honk (70a), hunk, jink, jonk, junk (30a,134c), kink (38b,171c), konk (41c), kunk (188), lank (148b,164b), link (36a,81d,85b), lonk (143d), mink (176d), monk (28b,63c,129d), pank (189), pink (26d,33c,60c,138a), punk (9b, 166a,167c), rank (31d,55d,70b,92c,94d,157d), rink (147c,154a), sank (41c,43c,46b,158a), sink (41c,43c,46b,158a), sunk, tank (175a), tonk (173c), wink (107a), yank, Yank

N - - K nabk (30d,164d), naik, nark (81a,156d), neck (83a), nick (30c, 108b), nock (13b,108b), nook (37a,130d), nubk (30d,164d)

- NL - inly, only (24d,52c,98d,147a,150a)

N - - L nael (189), nail (31d,54d,141d,161d,173a), Neal, Neil (96a), Nell (110a,183d), nili (173d), noel (26d,150b), Noel (30d,96a), noil (87c,178b), Noll (96b,110b), noyl (87c), null (108c,177a), nurl (33b,87c)

N - - M naam (44c,105b), Naam, neem (96d,168c,169a), norm (15a, 115a,128a,155a)

- NN - Anna (110c,166d,183c), anna (190), Anne (50c,84a,143b,183c), Enna (146a), enne (34c), Enns

- - NN binn (22c), Bonn (17d), bunn (25b), conn (43d,156a), Finn (107d), Jann (102d), jinn (42b,103b,153c), linn (120d,140a,c, 168c,178d), mann (189), Mann (9c,48c,185c), rann (175c), senn (76b), sunn (56a), wynn (165d)

N - - N nein (66c), neon (65c), ngan, noon, Norn (69a,163d,174b), noun (114b,158a)

NO · · Noah (88a,99b), nobs (38c,87a), nock (13b,108b), node (35c, 85b, 87c,94d,120a,124d,160c), nodi (35c,87c), noel (26d,150b), Noel (30d,96a), noes (177c), nogg (48d), noil (87c,178b), noio (107c,163c), noir (61b,134b), noix (67c), Nola, Noll (96b,110b), nolo (42a), nome (71c,163b), Nome, nona (89b,107b), Nona (69a,114a,183c), none (108b), nono (83b), nook (37a,130d), noon, Nora (79b,107a,164c,183c), Nore (163d), nori (8c,141c), norm (15a,115a,128a,155a), Norn (69a,163d,174b), nose (118d, 125a,149b), Nosu (27d), nosy, nota (15c,89c), note (98c,109b, 124b,128d,130a,177c), Nott (107b), noun (114b,158a), noup (124b), nous (81d,100a,128b), nova (20c,106d,155c,174d), nove (83b), nowt (106a,139a), nowy (194), noxa, noyl (87c), noze (75a)

· NO · anoa (28a,60a,112c,181c), anon (7d,14d,79d,80b,123a,145c,150c, 164a), enol (29c,158b), Enon (18c,d), Enos (7a,18d,52a,70c,96a, 143a), enow (50d,123a,158b), knob (73c), knop (124b,170c, 185b), knor (87c), knot (43c,99d,107c,124d,137b), know, snob (159c), snod (169d), snow

· · NO Aino (84a,c), Arno (27a), asno (151d), beno (113b,117a), cano (152a), dino (34b), fano (51d,96b,113c,d), fono (137a), Gano (132d), Hano (125b), hino (106d,168c), Juno (69c,85d,100c, 126b), Kano (84c,177d), keno (161d,168c), kino (27c,34c,47c, 72c,98b), leno (37c,53b), lino, mano (71d,73d,74b,83b), mino (84c), mono (34c,78d,122d,147a), Mono (193), nino (152a), nono (83b), pino (152c), puno (182a), Reno, sano (152b), sino (34a), Tano (192), Tino (136d), tuno (28b,168c), vino (92d,182b), xeno (34d), Zeno (71b)

N · · O nabo (117a), naio (107a,168c), Nato (6a,8d), Nebo (68c,102d, 103d,183a), nemo (34b), Nemo (56a,85c), Nero (8a,126d,133a, 150b,172c), nino (152a), nito (55c), noio (107c,163c), nolo (42a), nono (83b)

N · · P neap (165c,167a,177b), neep (140c,171b), noup (124b)

· · NQ cinq (61d)

· NR · inre (35d,80a), inro (84b,c,106c)

N · · R Nair (45d), natr (189), near (11d,32c,107b), neer (14b,86b, 108b), noir (61b,134b), nurr (67d)

· NS · ansa (73c,93d,137c), anse (61d), ansu (11d), ense (139b,158c), enso (34d,183b)

· · NS bans, cens (115b), dans (62a), dens (90a,167b), Duns, Enns, fons (60c), gens (42d,132d), Hans (66d,96a), hens (121d), lens (67c,95b,111a,129b,162d), Mans (30a), mons (89c), Mons (184d), oons (100a,186d), Pons (13d,63c,110d,150c), sans (63a, 183b), Sens (63b), sons (98d,109d), Vans (107d)

N · · S nais (63c,132a), naos (28a,71c,137a,163a), Naos (155b), ness (26b,75a,124b), news (165c), Nias (82d), nibs (116c), nobs (38c,87a), noes (177c), nous (81d,100a,128b)

· NT · anta (83d,117c,d,121a), Anta (164a), ante (87a,89a,115b,120b, 122b,125d,154d), anti (7d,111a,122b), Anti (193), ente (70b, 151d), ento (34b,d,183b), Inti (159b), into (123a,183b), onto (76a,174a), unto (166c), untz (189)

· · NT aint, arn't, aunt (129c), bant (43c), bent (80b), bunt (15d,180c), cant (28d,81b,84d,90c,109b,136c,165d,166a), cent (36d), dent (42c,77d), dint (48c,59d,122a), dont, dunt, font (16b,171d,172a), gent, hant (67a), hint (9a,39c,159a), hunt (141c), kant (28d), Kant (67a), Kent (90d), lant, lent (54d), Lent (115d,141c), lint (46a,58d), Ment (54b,164a), mint (13a,33b,58b,76a), mont (62b), oont (25d), pant, pent (36a), pint (67b), pont (55d,61b), punt (21a,58b), rant (41c,127b,128a,161d), rent (58a,77c,91b,138b, 153d,162c,167c), runt (47a,172d), sent, tent (26b,115a), tint (33c,d,114d), vent (8b,11b,110d,112a), vint (26c,182c), want (38b,41b,74b,106b,122a), went (42c), wont (6d,40a,73a,174c)

N · · T Nast (9c,27a), Natt (107b), naut (141b), neat (165c,169d), nest (38b,74b,130d,149c,160b), nett, newt (48d,136c,169d), next (106a), Nott (107b), nowt (106a,139a), nuit (62b)

NU · · Nuba (108c), nubk (30d,164d), nuda (39b), Nudd (23c), nude (16c,172d), nuit (62b), null (108c,177a), Numa (133a), numb, Nupe (191), nurl (33b,87c), nurr (67d)

· NU · Cnut (40d,50c), knub (178b), knur (67d,87c,107c), knut, Knut (40d,50c,96a), onus (24c,93b,109b), snub (128c,148b), snug (35a,38b,165c), Snug (99d), snup (149b)

· · NU Ainu (84a,c), benu (49a), Danu (28a), genu (6b,18a,87a,89c), Manu (10a,76d,77a,b), menu (19a,27a), Menu, tunu (28b), zenu (143d)

N · · U Nabu (68c,183a), napu (29d,80d), niou (188), Nosu (27d)

· NV · envy (41b)

· · NX jinx (78a), jynx (78a), Jynx (184a), lanx (133a,b), lynx (26c, 181d), Lynx (36b), Manx (27b,28a,82d), minx (116c), Yunx (184a)

N · · X noix (67c)

· NY · Enyo (12c,69c,178a), onym (162c), onyx (25d,28d,65d,142c), Pnyx (71c)

· · NY bony (147c), Bony (96b), cony (127a), deny (36d,43d,129b), liny (157b), luny (38b), many (108d), miny, piny, pony, puny (55b, 179a), tiny (100c,148c), tony, Tony (96b), tuny, viny, wany, winy (176c), zany (24a,32d,59c)

N · · Y Nagy (78d), nary (108b), navy (33c,58b), nosy, nowy (194)

· NZ · anzu (11d), Enzu (102b), onza (189), unze (189)

· · NZ Linz (40d)

OA · · Oahu, oaks (154d), oaky, oary, oast (15d,86b,112a), oath (119c, 150a)

· OA · boar (77c,117c,160c,181c), boat (27b,106a), Boaz (135d), coag (45d,118a,163b), coak (45d,118a,163b), coal (49c,64a), Coan (37b), coat (160a), coax (180c), doab (157c), doat (17a,94b, 112a,165d), Eoan (41a,85b), foal (78c), foam (63d,154b), goad (80b,154b), goaf (104b), goai (106d,168c), goal (8b,109b,120b, 125d), Goan, goat (135a), hoar (63d,71a,181a), hoax (41c,122a), Joab (41a), Joad (50c), Joan (183c), joar (100a), koae (74b), load (24c,26d,161b), loaf (79b,94b), loam (47d,150a), loan, Moab (18d,85a,86d,94a), moan, moat (44d), Noah (88a,99b), road (37d,164d), roam (178a), roan (78b,c,114c,128a,144a, 181a), roar (145c), soak (46c,137c), soap, soar (59a), toad (10a, 17a,63d,126d), woad (20d,47c), Zoar, Zoas (20b)

337

· · OA   anoa (28a,60a,112c,181c), Aroa (175b), Gjoa (144d), pooa (76a, 125b), proa (21b,26a,95c,d), Shoa (6c), stoa (33c,121a,c), tooa (17c), whoa (156d)

O · · A   obia (55d), obra (152d,184c), ocha (189), ocra (72c,175a), octa (122c), odea (105d,164a), Offa (163d), ohia (74c,168c), okia (190), okra (72c,175a), olea (170b), Olea (110b), Olga (135c, 183c), olla (36d,44b,84d,113b,121d,151d,152c,181b), onca (189), onza (189), orca (86b), orna (169d,182c), orra (139c,d,140a), ossa (21d), Ossa (103d,110b,164b), Otea (71a,82d), otra (152c), oxea (153d)

OB · ·   oban (190), Obed (135d), obex (22d), obey (35c,75c), obia (55d), obit (41b,64c), oboe (74b,104d,105a,182a,184a), obol (29b, 110a), obra (152d,184c)

· OB ·   boba (29d), bobo (112c,168c), Cobb (9c), Cobh (37a), dobe (159b,c,172b), doby (159b,c), gobi, Gobi (42d), gobo (84d), goby (57d), hobb (124b), hobo (168a,174b), Jobo (77c), Koba (11a), Kobe (78a), kobi (84b), kobu (84b), lobb (23b,94c,163a), lobe (90c,134b), lobo (165d,183c), nobs (38c,87a), nobe (65b), Sobk (38d), Toba (80c), tobe (7d,137b), toby (8c,85c,104b), Toby (96b,125c), Yobi, zobo (186b)

· · OB   blob, boob (146d), brob (153c), chob (23c), doob (18b), jaob, knob (73c,107c,124d), rhob (64a,85c), scob (42a), slob (173d), snob (159c), swob (102b), thob (128a),

OC · ·   ocha (189), ocra (72c,175a), octa (122c), octo (34a,89b,122c)

· OC ·   boca (152b,c), boce (23b,52a,57b), bock (17c,90d,144a), coca (29d,33a,105d,113a), cock (19a,29a,55a,133d,136d,161d,174b), coco, dock (40a,117c,144d,179d), Foch (63b), foci (28b), hoch (52c,66c), hock (91a,115b,182b,c), jock, Jock (96b), jacu (45b, 57a), Koch (66d), loch (88a,139d), loci (66b,118c), lock (54d), loco (38b,119b,120b), mock (131b,162b), nock (13b,108b), poco (83b,93a), Roch (136c), rock (160b), sock (157c,182a), soco (22d), tock (7d,19b), toco (19b,167c), voce (83c,177a)

· · OC   bloc (173a), croc (13a,74a), floc (149a)

O · · C   odic (79c,120a), olic (158b), otic (14c,d,47b)

OD · ·   odah (170d), odal (48a,88b,112c), Odax (132c), odds (28d,172d), Odea (105a,164a), odel (48a,112c), Oder (132a), odic (79c, 120a), Odin (7c,29d,63c,68c,175d,183b), odio (83b), odor (138b, 156a), odum (168c,180a), odyl (59d,79c)

· OD ·   Bodb (82b), bode (14c,60a,110b,121b), Bodo (88c), body (72a), coda (32c,35d,56c), code (21c,31a,40c,161c), codo (188), dodd (139c,140c), Dode (96b), dodo (19b), Jodo (113d), lode (42c,99a, 111b,175b), Lodi (105d), Lodz, mode (54d,96b,157d,179a), node (35c,85b,87c,94d,120a,124d,160c), nodi (35c,87c), Roda (107b), rodd (38d), rode (46c), rodi (98c), soda (19a,149d,181a), Toda (45d,76d), tode (80a,148a), todo (22b,24d,35b,64c,156b), tody (19b,d,59a,166a), yodh (91d)

· · OD   alod (51c,55d,88a,124c), apod (59d), Arod (86c), biod (59d, 79c), clod (22a,45b,157d), elod (49b,59d,79c), feod (55d), food (109a,176b), good, hood (38a,74d), iood (189), mood (44c), plod (170b,177d), pood (189), prod (67d,80b,106b,120d), quod (123d), rood (38d,39a,88b), shod, snod (169d), stod (40d,67d), trod, wood

338

O - - D obed (135d), olid (55d,60c,148d,157d), ooid (48d), oord (190), orad (104a), Ovid (132d,133b), oxid (112c)

OE - - oese (15d,119c)

- OE - Boer (151a), coed, coel (39b), Doeg (137c), doer (8a,116b), does, goel (15a,75c), goer, hoek (39d), hoen (189), hoer, hoey (114c), Joel (96a), joey (86a,185d), Joey (96b,109c), koel (19a, b,39b), Moed (100c), noel (26d,150b), Noel (30d,96a), noes (177c), poem (51a), poet (49b), roed, roer (72d), roey (103d), toed, voet (188)

- - OE aloe (7d,20a,76a,b,92b,98b,119b,158b,167a,183d), Cloe (183c), eboe (28b,110a,168c,169b), evoe (15b,130d,181c), floe (79b), froe (32a,167a,179d), oboe (74b,104d,105a,182a,184a), Otoe (147b), shoe (166a), sloe (14a,20b,64a,119d,181c)

O - - E oboe (74b,104d,105a,182a,184a), oese (15d,119c), ogee (40c, 101a,b,120b), ogle (9d,53c,91a,93d,148c), ogre (67a,102a), ohne (66d,183b), Oime (8b), Oise, Okie (99d), olpe (90d,182c), once (60b,79b), onde (63a,178d), ooze (53c,104b,116a), orfe (57a,b, 185c), orle (17b,56b,76a,144b,177a), orne (169d,182c), Orne (25b), oste (21d,83b), Otoe (147b), Ouse (132a,185d), owse

OF - - Offa (163d), offs (38c)

- OF - doff (130a,161b), goff (32d), koff (47a), loft (14c,69d,104b,178b), moff (53b,146c), sofa (44d), soft (48b,95d,99d,163a), toff (40d)

- - OF Azof (20b,135d), goof (173a), hoof (173a), loof (144c,153d), poof, roof (78d), stof (135c), woof (39a,163d,165a,179d)

O - - F Olaf (108a,176b)

OG - - ogam (82b,c), ogee (40c,101a,b,120b), ogle (9d,53c,91a,93d, 148c), Ogor (170d), Ogpu (135d), ogre (67a,102a), ogum (82b)

- OG - boga (57d,180b), bogo (117a,168c), Bogo (191), bogy (153a), doge (95b,175b), dogy (46d,103c), fogy, goga (24a), gogo (16b, 24a,149c), Gogo (191), hoga (144b), hogg (144a), jogi (76d), loge (164a), logy (46d), mogo (74b), nogg (48d), Pogo (121c), pogy (57a,88a,98d,103c), soga (70d,152b), Soga (191), toga (132d,133a,b), togs (32c), togt (77c), Vogt, yoga (10b,13c,77a), yogh (10c,185a), yogi (76d), zogo (136a)

- - OG agog (47b,52c,86b), ajog, clog (30c,145b), flog (180d), frog (10a, 17a,126d), grog (92d,153d), llog (132a,161b), niog (33a,168c), slog (157c,170b,177d), stog (155a), voog (28a,66a,132b)

OH - - ohia (74c,168c), Ohio, ohne (66d,183b), ohoy (106a)

- OH - boho (117a,179d), Bohr (14b,40d,138c), coho (136d), fohn (182b), Hohe (192), John (11c,96a,121a,186b), kohl (53c), moha (42b,83d), moho (19a,78a), mohr (65d), poha (74c), rohr (72d), sohol, Soho (93c); toho (79a)

- - OH booh (52c), pooh (22b,107d)

O - - H oath (119c,150a), odah (170d), okeh (8d,37b), opah (23b,57a,b, 86d), ouch!, ough

OI - - oily (110b,172c), oime (8b), Oise

- OI - Boii (191), boil (62b,63a,183d), coif (73a), coil (39d,171c, 185a), coin (19b,37a,100c,101c,179d), coir (33a,37a,56a,133d), Coix (70d,85b), doit (47a,169d,180d), Eoin (85b), foil (15d,55c,

339

165b), **join** (36a,173c), **koir** (33a), **loin** (40a,98a), **loir** (45c), **Loir,**
Lois (165d,183c), **moll** (46c,184c), **moio** (188), **noil** (87c,178b),
noio (107c,163c), **noir** (61b,134b), **noix** (67c), **ooid** (48d), **roil**
(44c,104b,156b,170d,176a), **Soia, soie** (62c), **soil** (154d,159a,
163c), **soir** (61c), **toil** (46c,184c), **void** (11a,49d,108d,174b), **zoid**
(62a), **zoii**

- - **OI** **amoi** (62a), **Ekoi** (191)

O - - **I** **Omei** (24a), **omni** (34a), **Omri** (18c,86d)

- **OJ** - **bojo** (117a), **coja** (103b,166b), **hoja** (166b), **hoju** (84b), **koji**
(185b), **mojo** (177c), **rojo** (129a,152c), **soja** (151b)

OK - - **okay** (8d), **okeh** (8d,37b), **oket** (189), **okla** (190), **Okie** (99d),
okra (72c,175a), **okro** (72c,175a)

- **OK** - **boko** (52b), **coke** (32d,64a), **coky, Doko** (191), **joke** (183a), **joky,**
koko (106d,114b), **Koko** (93d,186c), **koku** (189), **loka** (173c,
184c), **Loke** (15d,68b), **Lokl** (7c,15d,68b), **moke** (45c,157d),
moki (127b), **Mokl, moko** (96c), **poke** (108c), **poku** (11a), **poky**
(148c), **roka** (95a,168c,d), **roke** (174d,175b), **soka** (20c), **soke**
(44c,85d), **toko** (30c), **woke, yoke** (85b,92d,173c)

- - **OK** **amok** (18b,63c), **asok** (13d), **book, cook** (137b), **dook** (184a),
hook (27b,39d), **irok** (55b), **look** (11c,53c,142a), **nook** (37a,
130d), **pook** (68a), **rook** (19b,29c,39a), **sook** (22a,25c,97a), **took**

O - - **K** **Omsk**

OL - - **Olaf** (108a,176b), **olam** (51a,d,75c,81a), **Olan** (115c), **Olax** (52b),
olay (113b), **Olea** (110b,170b), **oleo** (34c), **Olga** (135c,183c), **olic**
(158b), **olid** (55d,60c,148d,157d), **olio** (44b,77c,98c,100d,121d),
olla (36d,44b,84d,113b,121d,151d,152c,181b), **Olor** (160a,b), **olpe**
(90d,182c)

- **OL** - **bola** (16a), **bold** (41a), **bole** (31d,32a,169b), **boll** (119b,d), **bolo**
(87a,179b), **bolt** (13b,54d,58b,132d,160a), **cola** (25b,108d,149d,
168c), **cold** (65d), **cole** (25a), **Cole, coli, colp** (28a,148b), **colt**
(78c,131a,185d,186b), **Colt, coly** (104a), **dola** (189), **dole** (44c,
118c,121c,129d), **Dole** (74c), **doli, doll** (125c), **dolt** (20c,59c,
157d), **fold, folk** (116a,169c), **gola** (27b,40c,70c,157a), **gold, golf**
(154a), **goll** (105c), **Goll, Golo** (191), **hola** (74c,152b), **hold** (95c,
124c,130d), **hole** (6c,11b,110d,118c,147a), **Holi** (77a), **holm**
(77d,82d,109a), **holt** (36d,119b,184b), **holy, lola, lole** (52a,76b,
123c), **jole** (29b), **joli** (62b), **jolt** (143b), **kola** (25b,84a,108d,
168c), **Kola** (135b,c,d), **Kolo** (59b,135c), **Lola** (27d,
97b), **loll** (94b,128c), **Lolo** (27d,30a), **Mola** (159c), **mold** (54d,
143c), **mole** (19d,23a,24d,85a,117c,155c), **Mole** (88c), **moll, Moll**
(183d), **molt** (27a,143d), **moly** (76a,181c), **Nola, Noll** (96b,
110b), **nolo** (42a), **Pola, pole** 132c,143b,177b,184a), **Pole**
(52a), **polk** (37c), **poll** (74d,160a,177c), **polo** (154a), **Polo** (175b),
poly (34c,76b), **role** (114b), **roll** (134a,160b), **sola** (9a,48a,74b,
118c,154a,167), **sold, sole** (52c,57a,b,58b,d,110c,115d,150a), **soli**
(12c,110c), **solo** (12c,89a,110c), **tola** (48a,80d), **Tola** (85b,180a),
told (129c), **tole** (9a,51a,99b,163a), **toll** (131c), **tolt, tolu** (16a),
vola (89d,150a), **vole** (97d,104a,148a,149b), **volk** (66c,105d,
116a,184c), **Volk, volt** (49b,78c,173b), **wold** (47c,60a,118d,174a,
184a), **wolf, yolk, Zola** (63a)

- - **OL** **bool** (39d), **chol** (118d), **Chol** (192), **cool** (25c,107d), **egol** (11b),
enol (29c,158b), **fool** (24a,41c,47a,146b), **gaol** (123d), **Gaol**

340

(164a), **idol** (48c,54c,55a,75b,79d,112d,130b,184d), **itol** (158b),
obol (29b,110a), **pool** (65a,119d,120d), **siol** (82c), **tool** (27c), **viol**
(105a), **wool** (58b,179c)

O - - L   **obol** (29b,110a), **odal** (48a,88b,112c), **odel** (48a,112c), **odyl**
(59d,79c), **opal** (20a,65d,67b,82b), **oral** (114a,153d,174c,175c),
Orel, **oval** (48d,49c), **oxyl** (112c)

OM - -   **Oman** (159a), **omao** (165b), **omar** (103b), **Omar** (48c,51b,116c,
163b), **Omei** (24a), **omen** (14c,59d,60a,121c,123a,146b), **omer**
(51a,75c), **omit** (49c,52c,106b,114c,147d), **omni** (34a), **Omri**
(18c,86d), **Omsk**

- OM -   **boma** (7d), **bomb** (144a), **coma** (91c,157d,170c,172b), **comb**
(38c), **come**, **Como**, **dome** (39c,133c,155d), **Domn** (135a), **domy**,
Goma (191), **home**, **homo** (122b), **homy** (38b), **Kome** (71d),
Komi (191), **loma** (58b,63d), **Lome**, **nome** (71c,163b), **Nome**,
pome (11d), **Pomo** (192), **pomp** (111d,112b), **Roma** (83c,d),
Rome (31c,51d), **romi** (72d), **romp** (63d), **soma** (10c,21d,34a,
48a,81d,136b), **some** (114b,121c,126a), **Toma** (191), **tomb**, **tome**
(21d,177c)

- - OM   **Ahom** (88c), **asom** (18d), **atom** (101c,114c,180d), **boom** (152d),
coom (32d,150c,178d), **Crom**, **doom** (42d,55a,134d), **Edom** (18c,
51b,79b,82c,84a), **from**, **glom** (155d,160d,178c), **joom** (39c),
klom (189), **loom** (11c,146b,179b), **room** (28d), **stom** (34c), **toom**
(139b), **whom** (42b), **zoom**

O - - M   **odum** (168c,180a), **ogam** (82b,c), **ogum** (82b), **olam** (51a,d,75c,
81a), **onym** (162c), **ovum** (48d)

ON - -   **Onan** (18c,85c), **onca** (189), **once** (60b,79b), **onde** (63a,178d),
oner (20d,53a,75c,162d,173a,d), **ones** (116a), **only** (24d,52c,98d,
147a,150a), **onto** (76a,174a), **onus** (24c,93b,109b), **onym** (162c),
onyx (25d,28d,65d,142b), **onza** (189)

- ON -   **a-one** (52b,167b), **bona** (89d), **Bona** (183c), **bond** (92a,101c,
141d,143b,159b,165c), **bone**, **bong**, **Boni** (63b), **bonk** (190),
Bonn (17d), **bony** (147c), **Bony** (96b), **cond** (156a), **cone** (66b,
150a,157c), **Coni**, **conk** (41c,108a,156d,157c), **conn** (43d,156a),
cony (127a), **dona** (83d,121c,151d), **done**, **dong**, **doni** (21a,28c,
168a), **don't**, **fond** (7c,94b), **Fong** (40b), **fono** (137a), **fons** (60c),
font (16b,171d,172a), **Gona** (106d), **Gond**, **gone** (6b,15c,42c,
44c,114d), **gong**, **hone** (110a,143c,180d), **hong** (30b), **honk**
(70a), **Iona** (28a,82d), **ione** (24b,88d,94d), **Ioni** (192), **jonk**, **kona**
(74c), **konk** (41c), **lone** (150a), **long** (38b,185b), **lonk** (143d),
mona (72b,101d), **monk** (28b,63c,129d), **mono** (34c,78d,122d,
147a), **Mono** (193), **mons** (89c), **Mons** (184d), **mont** (62b), **nona**
(89b,107b), **Nona** (69a,183c), **none** (108b), **nono** (83b), **oons**
(100a,186d), **oont** (25d), **pond**, **pone** (37a,85b), **pong**, **Pons** (13d,
63c,110d,150c), **pont** (55d,61b), **pony**, **rone** (127c,164b), **Rong**
(88c), **song** (12c,170c), **sons** (98d,109d), **tone** (6c,118c), **tong**
(30a,c), **tonk** (173c), **tony**, **Tony** (96b), **wong** (56a), **wont** (6d,40a,
73a), **yond** (164a), **zona** (144c,186d), **zone** (44c,50a,160a)

- - ON   **acon** (62c,140d), **agon** (12c,36c,41b,55d,71b), **Amon** (86d,96b,
127d,159b,164a), **anon** (7d,14d,79d,80b,123a,145c,150c,164a),
aton (150a,159b), **Avon** (143b), **axon** (106c,153c), **azon** (127b),
bion (117b), **boon** (18b,20c,55a), **cion** (42d,70b,145b,148b,154b,
156a), **coon** (121c), **Dion** (96a,152a), **doon** (140b,168c), **ebon**

341

(20b), **Elon** (18c,51b,108a), **Enon** (18c,d), **Eton** (33b,50c,84a), **faon** (33c,55a), **Gaon** (85b), **goon** (157c,163c), **hoon** (190), **Icon** (79d,92b,136a), **ikon** (79d,136a), **iron** (55c,d,69d,81a,97b,143b, 149a,173d,179c), **Leon** (96a), **lion** (55b,86c), **loon** (19a,b,c,157d, 179c), **moon** (40b,132c,137c), **neon** (65c), **paon** (115b), **peon** (28c,59c,99c), **phon** (94a), **pion** (43c,52b), **poon** (97c), **roon** (41a,168b), **scon** (162c), **sion** (125c,158c), **Sion** (75b,c,83a,157d), **soon** (123a), **tion** (158b), **toon** (80c,95b,168c), **tron** (180a), **upon** (6b), **woon** (24c), **Zion** (75b,c,83a,157d), **zoon** (43a)

O - - N   **oban** (190), **Odin** (7c,29d,63c,68c,175d,183b), **Olan** (115c), **Oman** (159a), **omen** (14c,59d,60a,121c,123a,146b), **onan** (18c), **Onan** (85c), **open** (26a,60d,81a,109b,112c,125b,172b,173c), **Oran**, **oven** (15d,78c,86b), **Owen** (96a,183c), **oxan** (65c), **oxen** (10c)

OO - -   **ooid** (48d), **oons** (100a,186d), **oont** (25d), **oord** (190), **ooze** (53c, 104b,116a), **oozy** (148b)

- OO -   **boob** (146d), **booh** (52c), **book, bool** (39d), **boom** (152d), **boon** (18b,20c,55a), **boor** (47a,135d,172c), **boot** (128d), **cook** (137b), **cool** (25c,107d), **coom** (32d,150c,178d), **coon** (121c), **coop, Coos** (192), **coot** (19b,46d,72b,138d,141a,146d,157d), **doob** (18b), **dook** (184a), **doom** (42d,55a,134d), **doon** (140b,168c), **door** (51a, 121b), **food** (109a,176b), **fool** (24a,41c,47a,146d), **foot** (115a), **good, goof, goon** (157c,163c), **Goop** (107d), **goor, hood** (38a, 74d), **hoof** (173a), **hook** (27b,39d), **hoon** (190), **hoop** (181b), **hoot** (112c), **joom** (39c), **koop** (16c), **lood** (189), **loof** (144c, 153d), **look** (11c,53c,142a), **loom** (11c,146b,179b), **loon** (19a,b,c, 157d,179c), **loop** (31b,107d), **Loos, loot** (22a,118a,119d,153d), **mood** (44c), **moon** (40b,132c,137c), **moor** (10a,75b,137b,141d, 178b), **Moor** (102c,d,111d), **moot** (41b,44c), **nook** (37a,130d), **noon, pooa** (76a,125b), **pood** (189), **poof, pooh** (22b,107d), **pook** (68a), **pool** (65a,119d,120d), **poon** (97c), **poop** (41c), **poor** (33a), **pootl, rood** (38d,39a,88b), **roof** (78d), **rook** (19b,29c,39a), **room** (28d), **roon** (41a,168b), **root** (53a), **Roos** (67a), **sook** (22a,25c, 97a), **soon** (123a,145c), **soot** (20b,26c,88a), **tooa** (17c), **took, tool** (27c), **toom** (139b), **toon** (80c,95b,168c), **toot** (17c), **voog** (28a, 66a,132b), **wood, woof** (39a,163d,165a,179d), **wool** (58b,179c), **woon** (24c), **yoop, zoon** (43a)

- - OO   **aboo** (17a), **aroo** (80c,82b), **broo** (139a), **ejoo** (55b,168c), **Kroo** (191), **phoo, shoo** (46b,67a,138b), **sloo** (160a), **whoo**

O - - O   **octo** (34a,89b,122c), **odio** (83b), **Ohio, okro** (72c,175a), **oleo** (34c), **olio** (44b,77c,98c,100d,121d), **omao** (165b), **onto** (76a, 174a), **ordo** (22a,30d,122a,171a), **orlo** (56b,119c), **Oslo, otho** (133a), **otro** (151d), **otto** (58d,116b,134a), **Otto** (14c,66d,67a,96a)

OP - -   **opah** (23b,57a,b,86d), **opal** (20a,65d,67b,82b), **open** (26a,60d, 81a,109b,112c,125b,172b,173c), **Opie** (50c), **opus** (35c,105a, 184c)

- OP -   **copa** (88b,113c), **cope** (12b,26b,36c,65b,157d,176a), **Copt** (48d), **copy, dopa** (117d), **dope** (46c,105d), **dopp** (43c), **hope** (13d,52d), **hopi** (33c), **Hopi** (12c,102c,125b), **hops** (17c), **koph** (91d), **kopi** (107a,168c), **Kopi** (172a), **lope** (48b,64b,d), **mope** (92d,159a), **pope** (20a,30d,31c,120d), **qoph** (91d), **rope** (36d,88d,128b), **ropy**

342

(157c,176d), **soph, Sopt** (45b), **tope** (24a,46b,57a,143c,151a), **toph** (75c), **topi** (37a,75a,118c), **tops** (159c)

· · OP **alop** (13d,46b,93d), **asop** (180b), **atop** (112a,174a), **chop** (98a), **clop, coop, crop** (38b), **drop** (43d,54b,100b,114c,168b), **Esop** (53b,54a), **flop** (54a), **Goop** (107d), **hoop** (181b), **klop** (150d), **knop** (124b,170c,185b), **koop** (16c), **loop** (31b,107d), **plop** (54b), **poop** (41c), **prop** (159d), **scop** (120a), **shop, slop, stop** (73b, 111b), **swop** (168a), **trop** (62d,167a), **yoop**

· · OQ **shoq** (169a)

OR · · **orad** (104a), **oral** (114a,153d,174c,175c), **Oran, oras** (40d), **orca** (86b), **ordo** (22a,30d,122a,171a), **ordu** (170d), **Orel, orfe** (57a,b, 185c), **orgy** (26d,130d,137c), **orle** (17b,56b,76a,144b,177a), **orlo** (56b,119c), **Orly** (8b), **orna** (169d,182c), **orne** (169d,182c), **Orne** (25b), **orra** (139c,d,140a), **orts** (60d), **oryx** (11a)

· OR · **bora** (181d,182b), **bord** (110b), **bore** (14c,25b,46a,116a,165c, 179b), **borg** (40d), **Bori** (110d,150c), **born, boro** (154b), **Boro** (193), **Bors** (70b,134b), **bort** (43b), **Bort** (134b), **cora** (65d), **Cora** (42b,69c,80c,116b,124d,172b,183c), **cord** (39b,131a), **core** (28b, 51c,75b,81c), **cork** (119d), **Cori** (138c), **corm** (24b,38d,156a), **corn** (39d,95c,123a), **dora** (70b), **Dora** (36d,41a,43b,183c,d), **dord** (42c), **dore** (61d,67b,69d,117d), **Dore** (50d,63a,b), **dorm, dorn** (164d), **dorp** (73c,176b), **dorr** (32b), **dory** (21b,58b,144c), **fora** (133a), **ford** (177b), **fore** (63d,174b), **fork, form** (54d,143c), **fort** (63d,157d), **gora** (81c), **gore** (115d,117c,154c,169c), **gory, hora** (22a,40b), **horn** (11a,105a,170b,182a), **hors** (62b), **kora** (178c), **Kora, kore** (107b), **Kore** (29a,42b,116b,124d), **kori** (7d, 77a), **lora** (146b,149b,151c,169b), **Lora** (183c), **lord** (107c), **lore** (77c,87c,90d,151c,183a), **lori** (91b), **lorn** (42d,60b), **loro** (19a, 114b), **lory** (19a,114a), **mora** (42b,65a,72b,83d,99b,153a,161a), **more** (71a), **More** (50b), **morg** (188), **morn, moro** (19a,56c), **Moro** (100a,103a,117a,159a), **Mors** (41b), **mort** (41b,47a,78b, 136d), **Nora** (79b,107a,164c,183c), **Nore** (163d), **nori** (8c,141c), **norm** (15a,115a,128a,155a), **Norn** (69a,163d,174b), **oord** (190), **pore** (59d,110d,111c,120d,157d), **pork, Poro** (141d), **port** (73d, 136b,140c,170c,d,182b,c), **Rori** (16b), **sora** (19b,c,127b), **sorb** (11d,103d,134b,142d), **Sorb** (148a,180a), **sore** (23d,142c), **sori** (55c,64a), **sorn** (139a,d), **sors** (44d,89b), **sort** (31d,39c,70b), 86b,153a), **sory** (176d), **tora** (11a,44d,74a,75c,85c,90b,102d, 115d), **tore, tori** (101b), **torn** (130a), **toro** (38a,107a,152a,168c), **torp** (54c), **tort** (31c,91a,185c), **Tory** (23c,36b,94c,172a), **word** (124b,165c), **wore, work** (64c,76b), **worm, worn** (143b), **wort** (76a,95d,121d), **yore** (10b,69d,93c,110b,165d), **york** (38c), **York** (50b,c)

· · OR **acor** (6d), **ador** (153b), **amor** (152b), **Amor** (39c,68b), **asor** (75c, 105a), **boor** (47a,135d,172c), **chor** (164b), **door** (51a,121b), **Ghor** (174b), **goor, Igor** (135d), **knor** (87c), **mhor** (180b), **moor** (10a, 75b,137b,141d,178b), **Moor** (102c,d,111d), **odor** (138b,156a), **Ogor** (170b), **Olor** (160a,b), **poor** (33a), **shor** (136d), **Shor** (162b), **Thor** (7c,68c,99c,100c,109c,165b), **utor** (90a,166c)

O · · R **Oder** (132a), **odor** (138b,156a), **Ogor** (170d), **Olor** (160a,b), **omar** (103b), **Omar** (48c,51b,116c), **omer** (51a,75c), **oner** (20d,53a, 75c,162d,173a,d), **osar** (51b,67b,131b), **oser** (61b), **over** (6b,38c, 80a,114d), **oxer** (55c), **oyer** (38a,75b,119c)

OS · · osar (51b,67b,131b), oser (61b), Oslo, ossa (21d), Ossa (103d, 110b,164b), oste (21d,83b)

· OS · bosa (12a), Bosa, Bosc (115c), bose (163c), bosh, bosk (164b), boss (49d,157d), cose (29b), cosh (35a,97c), coso (152c), coss (98a), cost (29a), cosy (149c), dosa (74b), dose (123a), doss (17c), dost, foss (44d,100d), gosh, hose (156c), host (13a,51d, 104c), Jose (96a), josh (85b), joss (30b), Josy (183d), koso (6c, 80d), Koso (192,193), koss (188), lose (60a,100c), losh (178b), loss (42c,123d,178b), lost, Mose (96b), mosk (97b,103b), moss (91d,104c,114a,170c), most, mosy (67d), nose (118d,125a,149b), Nosu (27d), nosy, pose (14c,15d), posh (49b,148c), post (89a, 95c,155d), Rosa (58d,134a,145d,183c), rose (33c), Rose (6a,50c, 183c), ross (16c,161d), Ross (50c), rosy (21a,111a), sosh (81d), soso (99c,114c,166d), tosh (106a), Tosk (8c), toss (24a,132d), Xosa (86a)

· · OS Amos (96a,144b), bios (92a), Coos (192), Enos (7a,18d,52a,70c, 96a,143a), epos (51a,76b,120a), Eros (11c,39c,68b,97c,182d), ghos (30b), gros (47a,53d,146c), Gros (63a), Laos (80d,129c), Loos, naos (28a,71c,137a,163a), Naos (155b), phos, Taos (192), Teos (82a), Thos (84a,181c)

O · · S oaks (154d), odds (28d,172d), offs (38c), ones (116a), onus (24c, 93b,109b), oons (100a,186d), opus (35c,105a,184c), oras (40d), orts (60d), Otis (9c,d,24d,82a,111a), Otus (67a), ours (124c), Ovis (143d), oyes (38a,39b,75b)

OT · · Otea (71a,82d), Otho (133a), otic (14c,d,47b), Otis (9c,d,24d, 82a,111a), Otoe (147b), otra (152c), otro (151d), otto (58d, 116b,134a), Otto (14c,66d,67a,96a), Otus (67a)

· OT · bota (189), both, Boto (192), bott (32a,88d), cota (117a), cote (19b,143d,144a,b), coto (16c,90b), Coty (63c), dote (17a,90b, 94b,97a,112a,139d,165d), doth, Doto (141b), doty (43d), Goth (16c,163d), Hoth (20c), hoti, iota (71a,85c,91c,114c,166c,176a, 180d), jota (151c), joti, kota (117a), Kota (45d), koto (84b), lota (24c,121d,178d), loth (15a,173d), lote (24c,94a), Loti (63a, 176a), loto (65a,121d,178d), lots, mota (103a), mote (114c, 153a), moth, Moth (112d), moto (104b), nota (15c,89c), note (98c,109b,124b,128d,130a,177c), Nott (107b), pott (113d), rota (27c,30d,38a,79a,92d,133a,134a,b,180c), rote (130b,134b,143a, 159d), roti (62c), roto (30a,122d,127b,152c, 171b), sote (150c), tota (71d), tote (27a,73c), toto (8d,15a,34d, 89a,181a), toty (87b), vota (133b), vote (60b), Vote (56d), Voth (191), Voto (192), Wote (191

· · OT Abot (100c), blot, boot (128d), clot (32d,94d), coot (19b,46d, 72b,138d,141a,146d,157d), eyot (82d), Flot (191), flot (173a), foot (115a), frot (28c), grot (27d), hoot (112c), ilot (82d), khot, knot (43c,99d,107c,124d,137b), loot (22a,118a,119d,136a,153d), moot (41b,44c), phot (173b), piot (95b), plot (25a,36b,118d, 138b), poott, riot (44c,111d,170c,173d), root (53a), ryot (115c), scot (14a,162b), Scot (64b,132c), shot (9d,43d,90c,174d), slot (10d,11b,41d,110d,167d,168a,181b), soot (20b,26c,88a), spot (93b,118c,154d,162a), stot (154d,155d,157d,179b,186a), swot, toot, trot (85b,93d,112d)

344

O · · T   oast (15d,86b,112a), obit (41b,64c), oket (189), omit (49c,52c, 106b,114c,147d), oont (25d), oust (44c,49a,52b,125d)

OU · ·   ouch!, ough!, ours (124c), Ouse (132a,185d), oust (44c,49a,52b, 125d)

· OU ·   Aoul (191), bout (36c), bouw (188), coup (20d,97c,157b,c,162d), cous (38a), doub (18b), douc (101d), doum (168c), dour (67d, 159a), foud (54d,144b), foul (173a), four (26c), goul (102a), gour (112c,181c), gout, hour, Joug (138d), loud (156a), loun (19a,b), loup (61d,62a,90c,139d), Loup (193), lour (13d,63d), lout (15c, 22a,24b,45b,109a,157d), moue (61d,62b), noun (114b,158a), noup (124b), nous (81d,100a,128b), pouf (190), poul (190), pour (162d), pous (188), pout (159a), roud (57a,b), roue (41b,44c, 127c,134b), roup (44a,121d), rout (41d,44b,46b), souf (146b), souk (22a,97a), soul (10d,125a,153c,176d), soup, sour, sous (62d,172c), toug (171a), toup (95d), tour (31b,85c), tout (61a, 127a), youp (185d), your (124c)

· · OU   Abou (48b,55a), chou (61b), Chou (30b), ciou (67b), meou, niou (188), shou (41d), thou (124b), Tiou (192), Yaou (30c)

O · · U   Oahu, Ogpu (135d), ordu (170d)

OV · ·   oval (48d,49c,127a), oven (15d,78c,86b), over (6b,38c,80a,114d, 130a), Ovid (132d,133b), Ovis (143d), ovum (48d)

· OV ·   cove (17a,73d,107d), dove (19a,117d), Hova (95a), hove (92a, 157d), Jova (193), Jove (85d), love (163a), move, nova (20c, 106d,155c,174d), nove (83b), rove (127d,132b,178a), wove, Xova (193)

· · OV   akov (189), Azov (20b)

OW · ·   Owen (96a,183c), owse

· OW ·   bowk (155d), bowl, cowl (101d), dowd (143b), dowl, down (149d), fowl, gowk (146d), gowl (102a,140d,185b), gown, howe (77d), Howe (17a,82a), howl (39b), howk (139b), Iowa (193), jowl (29b), Iowa (19a), Iown (157d), lowp (90c,139d), mown, nowt (106a,139a), nowy (194), powe, rowy (157b), town (73c), towy (58b), yowl, yowt (139c)

· · OW   alow (18a,172c), arow (92c,158b), avow (6d,36a,41c,112c), blow, brow, chow (45a), clow (58c,148c), crow (19a), dhow (88d,111c, 175d), enow (50d,123a,158b), flow (157b), frow (47a,167a), glow (144c), grow (154b), know, Lwow, meow, plow (39c,165d), prow (21b,22c,144d,156a), scow (21a,58b), show (42b,44c,96b), slow (43c), snow, stow (112b), swow (100a), trow (18a,21a,159d,164c, (170b)

OX · ·   oxan (65c), oxea (153d), oxen (10c), oxer (55c), oxid (112c), oxyl (112c)

· OX ·   boxy, coxa (77b), doxa (48b), doxy (129d), foxy (38b,39c,181d), moxa (27d,30c), Moxo (192), noxa, Roxy (183), toxa (153d)

· · OX   abox (22d), esox (57b)

O · · X   obex (22d), Odax (132c), Olax (52b), onyx (25d,28d,65d,142b), oryx (11a)

OY · ·   oyer (38a,75b,119c), oyes (38a,39b,75b), oyez (38a,39b,75b)

· OY ·   coyn (37a), coyo (15a,30c), Goya (151d), Hoya (14d), noyl (87c), soya (151b)

· · OY ahoy (106a), Amoy (88c), b'hoy (134b), buoy (28d,58c), choy (48a,128d), cloy (61b,137c,159d), ohoy (106a), ploy (43c), troy (161c,180a), Troy

O · · Y oaky, oary, obey (35c,75c), ohoy (106a), oily (110b,172c), okay (8d), olay (113b), only (24d,52c,98d,147a,150a), oozy (148b), orgy (26d,130d,137c), Orly (8b)

· OZ · boza (12a), bozo (55b), coze (29b), cozy (149c), doze (148a), dozy, Jozy, kozo (113d,168c), mozo (152b), noze (75a), ooze (53c,104b,116a), oozy (148b)

O · · Z oyez (38a,39b,75b)

PA · · paal (188), paar (28c), paca (132c,154a), pace (64b,98a,153b, 156a,170b,177d), pack (24b,140d), paco (9b,146d), pacs (94c), pact (8a), padi (131b), page (51b,59b,142d,159b), paha (67b), pahi (21b,26a), paho (122a), paid (129c), pail, pain (7c), pair (22d,37d,85b,171d), pais (37d), pajo (122a), pala (189), Pala (88b), pale (113a,117c,178a), pall (122b), Pall (23d, 24a,137b,175a), pall (32d,81b,112a), palm (59b,168c,169b), palo (152c), palp (11a,55b,58b,167c), paly (194), Pana, pane (113c, 155a,b), pang (165b), Pani (120c), pank (189), pant, paon (115b), papa, pape (19b,113a), para (134c,170d), Para (18a,51d), parc (62b,112c), pard (27b,91b), pare (115c,129a), pari (34a, 180a), park, parr (136d,137a,147c), pars (89d), part (44d,60d, 121c,159c), paru (57a), pasa (46a,127c,152c), pasi (94b), pass (110b,155c), past (25c,69d,165d), pata (25c,160d), pate (39a, 74d), path (132a,134b), pato (46d), patu (179b), paul, Paul (96a), paun (18b), paut (140a), pave (85a), pavo (115b), Pavo (36b,c), pavy (115b), pawa (189), pawl (43a,95a), pawn (29c, 119c)

· PA · Apap (102a), apar (12d), opah (23b,57a,b,86d), opal (20a,65d, 67b,82b), spad (105b), Spad (118d), spae (139c), span (23b, 107b,113a,128b,162c), spar (22c,24c,64b,97b,100b,144d), spat (112c,126b,134b), upas (84d,120b,168c,d)

· · PA arpa (83b), capa (152a,166d), cepa (110c), copa (88b,113c), depa (188), dopa (117d), Hupa (192), kapa (74b), lipa (54d), napa (25c,67d,90d), Napa (182c), Nepa, (106b,178c), nipa (14b, 46b,48a,164a,168c), papa (159d), pupa (30d,81b,c), ripa (16b,131d), ropa (152a), rupa (60b), sapa (70c), supa (168c), tapa (16c,32c,53b,56a,74b,104b,112b,113d,120d), yapa (113b), Zipa (29d)

P · · A paca (132c,154a), paga (117a), paha (67b), pala (189), Pala (88b), Pana, papa, para (134c,170d), Para (18a,51d), pasa (46a, 127c,152c), pata (32c,160d), pawa (189), peba (12d), Peba (193), peca (190), peda (114d,144b), pega (57a,130a), pela (30c), Pera (60a), pesa (190), peva (12d), pica (66b,95b,172c), pika (93a,128a,132c), pima (37c), Pima (192), pina (35d,118b), pipa (159d), Pisa (90c), pita (9c,28b,56a,83a), plea (51a,52d, 122a,130b), poha (74c), pola (189), pooa (76a,125b), proa (21b,26a, 95c,d), puca (68a), puja (77a), puka (107a,168c), puma (27b, 37c,55b,103d), puna (10b,33b,104a,119b,182a), pupa (30d,81b, c), Puya (118b), pyla (22d)

P · · B pleb (10d,35b,180b)

P - - C parc (62b,112c)

P - - D paid (129c), pard (27b,91b), **pend, Phad** (155b), **Phud** (110b), pied (96c,103c,114b,117c,154a,174d), piod (170b,177d), pond, pood (189), prod (67d,80b,106b,120b), pund (189), puud (189)

PE - - peag (144a,178a), peai (98b), peak (9a,38c,159b,186b), peal (131c,d), pean (64c,150b), pear (64a), peat (64a,175a), peba (12d), Peba (193), peca (190), peck (24d), peco (162b), peda (114d,144b), pedi (34b), **pedo** (34b), peek (93d,115c), peel (53a, 114a), peen (73c), peep (93d,115c), peer (51a,93d,107c), peet (64a), pega (57a,130a,158b), Pegu (24c,102a,127d), peho (19b, 102c,106d), Peke (45a,148d), pela (30c), Pele (69c,74c), pelf (22a,56c,131b), pelo (83b), pelt (53a), pelu (30a,106d,168c), pend, pene, pent (36a), peon (28c,59c,99c), pepo (39b,64a,70a, 98c,125c,154c), Pera (60a), pere (61c,63b), peri (54b,116b,c, 122b), perk (84d,93a), perm (49b,97d), pern (78a), pero (152a), pert (80a,93a,137c,154b), Peru, pesa (190), peso (99c), pest (108c,116b,118d,170a), pete (136b), Pete (96b), peto (57a,177b), Peto (76a), peur (61c), peva (12d), pevy (91d,94c)

- PE - aper (32d), Apet (97c), apex (39c,76c,115c,118b,159b,166a, 167b), epee (55c,160d), open (26a,60d,81a,109b,112c,125b, 172b,173c), spec, sped, Spee (66d,70b), spes, Spes (69a,78a), spet (16c,57a,142c), spew (35a,49a), spex, Spey

- - PE cape (75a,96c,124b,161a), cepe (48c), cope (12b,26b,36c,65b, 157d,176a), dope (46c,105d), dupe (27c,41c,72c,160c), gape (185b), hipe (185a), hope (13d), hype (185a), jape (85a,b), jupe (62b,84a), lope (48b,64b,d), lupe (19a,64a), mope (92d), nape (15b,108c,d), Nupe (191), olpe (90d), pape (19b,113a), pipe (105a,180d,182a), pope (20a,30d,31c,120d), ripe (58a,97c,98c), rope (36d,88d,128b), rype (19b,125a), sipe (101a,110c,140b), supe (53a,154d), sype (110c), tape (16a,19a,128d), tipe (168b), tope (24a,46b,57a,143c,151a), type (31d,115a,155a), wipe, Xipe (15c)

P - - E pace (64b,98a,153b,156a,170b,177d), page (51b,59b,142d,159b), pale (113a,117c,178a), pane (113c,155a,b), pape (19b,113a), pare (115c,129a), pate (39a,47d), pave (85a), Peke (45a,148d), Pele (69c,74c), pene, pere (61c,63b), pete (136b), Pete (96b), pice (190), pike (57a,b,76c,120b,153a), pile (45d,75b,117c), pine (36a,52a,88c,93c,168c,d,169a), pipe (105a,180d,182a), pise (127d), plie (32c,59b), poke (108c), pole (132c,143b,177b,184a), Pole (52a), pome (11d), pone (37a,85b), pope (20a,30d,31c, 120d), pore (59d,110d,111c,120d,157d), pose (14c,15d), powe, pree (139d), puce (33c,d,52a), pule (180d), pume (137b), Pume (175b,185b), pure (29b,172b,173c), pyle (34b), Pyle (9c,178a), pyre (64c)

P - - F pelf (22a,56c,131b), Piaf (63c), piff (24b), poor, pouf, puff (180d)

- PG - upgo (13c)

P - - G pang (165b), peag (144a,178a), ping, plug (156d,184d), pong, prig (112a,116c), pung (22c,148b)

PH - - Phad (155b), phew (52c), Phil (96b), phit (24b), phiz (54a), phon (94a), phoo, phos, phot (173b), Phud (110b), phut (24b), Phut (110b)

- PH - epha (75c)

- - PH - Alph (132a), caph (91c), kaph (91d), koph (91d), qoph (91d), soph (75c), toph (75c), umph

P - - H path (132a,134b), pish (36c,107d), pith (37a,51c,67b,95c,97a, 119b,126d), pooh (22b,107d), posh (49b,148c), prah (21b, 26a,95c,d), Ptah (48d,98c), pugh!, push (145c)

PI - - Piaf (63c), piat (11a), piay (98b), pica (66b,95b,172c), pice (190), Pici (19c,184a), pick, pico (65a,152c), Pict (23c,47d), pied (96c,103c,114b,117c,154a,174d), pien (13b), pier (23a,88b,180c), piet (29b,95b), piff (24b), pike (93a,128a,132c), pike (57a,b,76c, 120b,153a), piki (95c), piky, pile (45d,75b,117c), pili (34b,108d), pill, pily, pima (37c), Pima (192), pina (35d,118b), pine (36a, 52a,88c,93c,168c,d,169a), ping, pink (26d,33c,60c,138a), pino (152c), pint (67b), piny, pion (43c,52b), piot (95b), pipa (159d), pipe (105a,180d,182a), pipi (106d,119d), pipy (145d), pirn (21b, 129a,179b), Piro (192), pirr (181a), Pisa (90c), pise (127d), pish (36c,107d), pisk (9c,19b), piso (189), pist (25c), pita (9c,28b, 56a,83a), pith (37a,51c,67b,95c,97a,119b,126d), pito (9c,28b, 83a), Pitt (50d,155d), pity (35b), Pius (121a), pixy (154b)

- PI - apia (121b), apii (74c), apio (125b), Apis (17c,24b,49a,125a, 136a), epic (76b,120a), ipil (117a,168c,169a), Opie (50c), spin (131a,180d), spir (97c), spit (120a,132b,c), Upis (13b), ypil (117a,168c)

- - PI - aipi (27a), Hapi (66a,107b,136a), Hopi (12c,102c,125b), hopi (33c), impi (86a), kepi (99d), kopi (107a,168c), Kopi (172a), pipi (106d,119d), tipi (181b), topi (37a,75a,118c), Tupi (192)

P - - I padi (131b), pahi (21b,26a), pali (122b), Pali (23d,24a,137b, 175a), Pani (120c), pari (34a,180a), pasi (94b), peai (98b), pedi (34b), peri (54b,116b,c,122b), Pici (19c,184a), piki (95c), pili (34b,108d), pipi (106d,119d), puli (45a,78d), puri (80d)

P - - K pack (24b,140d), pank (189), park, peak (9a,38c,159b,186b), peck (24d), peek (93d,115c), perk (84d,93a), pick, pink (26d, 33c,60c,138a), pisk (9c,19b), polk (37c), pook (68a), pork, puck (44b,68a,77c,100c), Puck (99d,143b), pulk (37c,88d), punk (9b, 166a,167c)

PL - - plan (99b,124a,138b), plap (54b), plat (22d,96c,114a,119c,133d), play (63d,154a), plea (51a,52d,122a,130b), pleb (10d,35b,180b), plet (135d), plew (17c), plex (60b), plie (32c,59b), plod (170b, 177d), plop (54b), plot (25a,36b,118d,138b), plow (39c,165d), ploy (43c), plug (156d,184d), plum, plup, plus (10b,102c)

- PL - upla

P - - L paal (188), pall, pail (32d,81b,112a), paul, Paul (95a), pawl (43a,95a), peal (131c,d), peel (53a,114a), Phil (96b), pill, poll (74d,160a,177d), pool (65a,119d,120c), poul (190), pull (45d, 167d), purl (87c,104d), pyal (175c)

P - - M palm (59b,168c,169b), perm (49b,97d), plum (51a), poem (51a), pram (15a), prim (156b)

PN - - Pnyx (71c)

P - - N pain (7c), paon (115b), paun (18b), pawn (29c,119c), pean (64c, 150b), peen (73c), peon (28c,59c,99c), pern (78a), phon (94a),

348

plen (13b), **pion** (43c,52b), **pirn** (21b,129a,179b), **plan** (99b, 124a,138b), **poon** (97c)

PO - -   **poco** (83b,93a), **poem** (51a), **poet** (49b), **Pogo** (121c), **pogy** (57a, 88a,98d,103c), **poha** (74c), **poke** (108c), **poku** (11a), **poky** (148c), **pola, pole** (132c,143b,177b,184a), **Pole** (52a), **polk** (37c), **poll** (74d,160a,177c), **polo** (154a), **Polo** (175b), **poly** (34c,76b), **pome** (11d), **Pomo** (192), **pomp** (111d,112d), **pond, pone** (37a,85b), **pong, Pons** (13d,63c,110d,150c), **pont** (55d,61b), **pony, pooa** (76a,125b), **pood** (189), **poof, poof** (22b,107d), **pook** (68a), **poot** 65a,119d,120d), **poon** (97c), **poop** (41c), **poor** (33a), **poot!, pope** (20a,30d,31c,120d), **pore** (59d,110d,111c,120d,157d), **pork, Poro** (141d), **port** (73d,136d,140c,170c,d,182b,c), **pose** (14c,15d), **posh** (49b,148c), **post** (89a,95c,155d), **pott** (113d), **pouf, poul** (190), **pour** (162d), **pous** (188), **pout** (159a), **powe**

- PO -   **apod** (59d), **epos** (51a,76b,120a), **spot** (93b,118c,154d,162a), **upon** (6b)

- - PO   **cipo** (91d), **gapo** (60a), **hypo** (117b), **mapo** (68a,148d), **pepo** (39b,64a,70a,98c,125c,154c), **sapo** (149c,166d), **typo** (35c,51b)

P - - O   **paco** (9b,146d), **paho** (122a), **pajo** (122a), **palo** (152c), **pato** (46d), **pavo** (115b), **Pavo** (36b,c), **peco** (162b), **pedo** (34b), **peho** (19b,102c,106d), **pelo** (83b), **pepo** (39b,64a,70a,98c,125c,154c), **pero** (152a), **peso** (99c), **peto** (57a,177b), **Peto** (76a), **phoo, pico** (65a,152c), **pino** (152c), **Piro** (192), **piso** (189), **pito** (9c,28b,83a), **poco** (83b,93a), **Pogo** (121c), **polo** (154a), **Polo** (175b), **Pomo** (192), **Poro** (141d), **prao** (21b,26a,95c,d), **puno** (182a), **pyro**

- - PP   **Capp** (27a), **dopp** (43c), **kapp, kipp, Lapp** (108a), **repp** (53b, 131a), **typp** (185b), **wapp** (54b,133d,145d), **Yapp** (22a), **zipp**

P - - P   **palp** (11a,55b,58b), **peep** (93d,115c), **plap** (54b), **plop** (54b), **plup, pomp** (111d,112d), **poop** (41c), **prep** (138b), **prop** (159d), **pulp, pump**

PR - -   **prah** (21b,26a,95c,d), **pram** (15a), **prao** (21b,26a,95c,d), **prau** (21b,26a,95c,d), **pray** (18b,51a,159d), **pree** (139d), **prep** (138b), **pres** (62b), **pret** (188), **prey** (119d,176a), **prig** (112a,116c), **prim** (156b), **proa** (21b,26a,95c,d), **prod** (67d,80b,106b,120b), **prop** 159d), **prow** (21b,22c,144d,156a), **prutl, Prut** (41a)

- PR -   **spry** (7a,107b)

P - - R   **paar** (28c), **pair** (22d,37d,85b,171d), **parr** (136d,137a,147c), **pear** (64a), **peer** (51a,93d,107c), **peur** (61c), **pier** (23a,88b,180c), **pirr** (181a), **poor** (33a), **pour** (162d), **purr** (104c)

- PS -   **apse** (9b,20a,31a,128c,130a,142b,175a), **Apsu** (29a), **ipse** (44d, 89c), **ipso** (89c)

- - PS   **Alps** (85d), **gyps, Gyps** (71d), **hops** (17c), **hyps, seps** (93b,142d), **tops** (159c), **Veps** (191), **Zips** (40c)

P - - S   **pacs** (94c), **pais** (37d), **pars** (89d), **pass** (110b,155c), **phos, Pius** (121a), **plus** (10b,102c), **Pons** (13d,63c,110d,150c), **pous** (188), **pres** (62b), **puss**

PT - -   **Ptah** (48d,98c)

- - PT   **Copt** (48d), **dipt, kept, rapt** (6c,27a,50d), **sept** (31d,82b,143a, 149c), **Sept** (45b), **Sopt** (45b), **wept**

P - - T pact (8a), pant, part (44d,60d,121c,159c), past (25c,69d,165d), paut (140a), peat (64a,175a), peet (64a). pelt (53a), pent (36a), pert (80a,93a,137c,154b), pest (108c.116b,118d,170a), phit (24b), phot (173b), phut (24b), Phut (110b), piat (11a), Pict (23c, 47d), piet (29b,95b), pint (67b), piot (95b), pist (25c), Pitt (50d, 155d), plat (22d,96c,114a,119c,133d), plet (135d), plot (25a, 36b,118d,138b), poet (49b), pont (55d,61b), pootl, port (73d, 136b,140c,170c,d,182b,c), post (89a,95c,155d), pott (113d), pout (159a), pret (188), prutl, Prut (41a), punt (21a,58b), putt (69d), pyat (95b), pyet (95b)

PU - - puca (68a), puce (33c,d,52a), puck (44b,68a,77c,100c), Puck (99d,143b), pudu (41d), puff (180d), pughl, puja (77a), puka (107a,168c), puku (11a), pule (180d), pull (45a,78d), pulk (37c, 88d), pull (45d,167d), pulp, pulu (74c), puly, puma (27b,37c, 55b,103d), pume (137b), Pume (175b,185b), pump, puna (10b, 33b,104a,119b,182a), pund (189), pung (22c,148b), punk (9b, 166a,167c), puno (182a), punt (21a,58b), puny (55b,179a), pupa (30d,81b,c), pure (29b,172b,173c), puri (80d), purl (87c,104c), purr (104c), Puru (192), push (145c), puss, putt (69d), puud (189), puxy, Puya (118b)

- PU - Apus (36b,c), opus (35c,105a,184c), spud (121d,151c), spun, spur (10d,67d,167d,168a,181b), sput (21c)

- - PU hapu (106d), napu (29d,80d), Ogpu (135d), tapu

P - - U paru (57a), patu (179b), Pegu (24c,102d,127d), pelu (30a,106d, 168c), Peru (81a), poku (11a), prau (21b,26a,95c,d), pudu (41d), puku (11a), pulu (74c), Puru (192)

P - - W phew (52c), plew (17c), plow (39c,165d), prow (21b,22c,144d, 156a)

P - - X plex (60b), Pnyx (71c)

PY - - pyal (175c), pyat (95b), pyet (95b), pyla (22d), pyle (34b), Pyle (9c,178a), pyre (64c), pyro

- - PY copy, espy (44a,142a), gapy, pipy (145d), ropy (157c,176d), typy

P - - Y paly (194), pavy (115b), pevy (91d,94c), play (98b), piky, pily, piny, pipy (145d), pity (35b), pixy (154c), play (63d,154a), ploy (43c), pogy (57a,88a,98d,103c), poky (148c), poly (34c,76b), pony, pray (18b,51a,159d), prey (119d,176a), puly, puny (55b, 179a), puxy

P - - Z phiz (54a)

QA - - Qaid (35a)

Q - - D Qaid (35a), quad (33c,172a), quid (39b,166d), quod (123d)

QE - - qere (75c), qeri (75c)

Q - - E qere (75c), quae (176b)

- - QF waqf (103a)

Q - - G quag (21c,102c), Qung (191)

Q - - H qoph (91d)

Q - - I qeri (75c), quai (88b,117c,180c), quei (189)

Q - - N quan (190)

QO - - qoph (91d)

Q - - P	quip (183a,b)
Q - - S	quas (135c)
Q - - T	quit (90d,130c)
QU - -	quad (33c,172a), quae (176b), quag (21c,102c), quai (88b,117c, 180c), quan (190), quas (135c), quay (88b,117c,180c), quei (189), quid (39b,166d), quip (183a,b), quit (90d,130c), quiz, Qung (191), quod (123d)
- QU -	aqua (90a,178c), equi (122d)
Q - - Y	quay (88b,117c,180c)
Q - - Z	quiz
RA - -	raab (32d), raad (14a,49b,151a,165b), raas (91b), Raba, rabi (38d,74a), Rabi (14b,117b), raca (19a,59c,130b,184d), race (116a, 153b,154b,169c), rack (32c,64b), racy (153b), rada (135c, 172a), rade (138d), raff (75b), raft (27b,33c,58c,75b), raga (56d, 105a, rage (10c,30c,157a,161d), ragi (28b), Rahu (42b,48b), Raia (107d,147b), raid (59d,80c), raik (188,189), rail (16b,19b,c, 37a,97b,138c,150c,177b), rain (121d,162d), raip (36d), rais (26c, 29d,75a,103b), Rais (106b), raja (77a,123c), rake (41b,44c,134b, 140d), rale (7c,23a,29d,41b), ralo (188), Rama (77a,80b,176d), rame (22d), rami (22d), ramp (65a,80b,127b,148b), rana (77a, 123c), Rana (63d), rand (16d,22a,131b,145a,b), Rand (69c), rang, rani (72d,77b,123c,127c), rank (31d,55d,70b,92c,94d,157d), rann (175c), rant (41c,127b,128a,161d), rapt (6c,27a,50d), rara (119a), rare (138b,164b,172b,173d), rasa (51c), rase (42b,91d), rash (75a), rasp (56b,70d,140d), rata (92d,56b,89d,96c,106d, 120c,168c), rate (11d,14a,31d,36b,51d,52a,70b,85c,112b,123b, 127d,128a,138c,143a,174b), rath (29a,76d,162d), rati (189), rats, rave (41c,157a,161d), ravi (61b), Ravi (16b), raya (19b, 23c, 76d,107d), raze (42d,91d), razz (131b)
- RA -	Arab (30a,78b,c,106a,107c,157b,160c,185d), arad (13a,c,84a), arah (52c), Aral (135c), Aram (18d,50c,105c,144b,161c), Aran (18c,48c,64d,82d,174c), arar 137a,168c), Aras, brab (113b), brad (54d,67c,105b), brae (76d,139a,c,140b,148c), brag (21a, 175a), Bram (96a), bran (23c,39a,70b,72a,79c), Bran (23c,50c), bras (61a), brat, bray, crab (39b,144b,181b), crag (132c), cral, cram (157d), cran (160c), craw (38d,72c,156c), Crax (19b,39d), draa, drab (23d,29c,33d,46d,53d), drag (74a,125b), drah (188), dram (46b,110c,121d,148c), drap (61b,c,62a), drat (100a), Drau, draw (42c,53a,92b,117c,121c,167d), dray (27a,154c), eral (51a), erat (89c), frab (138c), frap (45d,165c), frat, frau (181b), fray (56b,60d), grab (105b,142a,149b), grad (28b), Graf (37c,66b, 67a,107c,186b), gram (29d,99b,148d,160d,180a), grao (189), gras (78b), gray (33c,77c), Gray (50c), irad (18d), Irae (43c), Irak (99a,d), Iran (6a,48c,116b), Iraq (99a,d), Iras (11b,32a), krag (131c), kral, kran (190), kras (76d), orad (104a), oral (114a, 153d,174c,175c), Oran, oras (40d), prah (21b,26a,95c,d), pram (15a), prao (21b,26a,95c,d), prau (21b,26a,95c,d), pray (18b, 51a,159d), tram (170a), tran (7a), trap (27b,67b,132b,149b), tray (128c,136d,142d,143c), ural, Ural (135c), uran (101d), Wraf, wrap (32b,51a)
- - RA	abra (26b), Abra, aera (8a), Afra (183c), agra (26d,34a), Agra (161b), Aira (70d), akra (176a), Akra (191), amra (77c), arra

351

(47d,52c,82b), **aura** (44c,49c,66a,96b,158a,170d,177c), **bara** (188), **Bera** (86d), **bora** (181d,182b), **bura** (182b), **cara** (83a), **Cara** (48b,183c), **cora** (65d), **Cora** (42b,69c,80c,116b,124d,172b, 183c), **cura** (152c), **Dara** (18d), **dera** (34c), **dora** (70b), **Dora** (36d,41a,43b,183c,d), **dura** (153c), **eyra** (181d), **Ezra** (96a), **fora** (133a), **gara** (19c), **gora** (81c), **Hera** (69c,85d,110b,126b,186b,d), **hora** (22a,40b), **hura** (20a,137a), **Hura, ikra** (27d), **irra** (68c, 178a), **jura, Jura, Kara** (132a), **kora** (19a,178c), **Kora, Lara** (25c), **lira** (28b,79a,170d), **lora** (146b,149b,151c,169b), **Lora** (183c), **lura** (22d,82a), **Lyra** (36b,74a), **mara** (114d), **Mara** (24a, d,105b,107b), **mira** (174d), **Mira** (155b), **mora** (42b,65a,72b,83d, 99b,153a,161a), **mura** (84d), **Mura** (192), **Myra** (10a,31b,183c), **Nera** (165b), **Nora** (79b,107a,164c,183c), **ocra** (72c,175a), **okra** (72c, 175a), **orra** (139c,d,140a), **otra** (152c), **para** (134c,170d), **Para** (18a,51d), **Pera** (60a), **Sara** (24d,183c), **sera** (11b,20d,59a, 83a,180d), **sora** (19b,c,127b), **sura** (87c,113b,166d), **Syra, tara** (22a,55c,113a,168c), **Tara** (82b,c,138b), **tera** (23d,84c), **tora** (11a,44d,74a,75c,85c,90b,102d,115d), **vara** (151d), **vera** (140c, 151b,175c), **Vera** (183c), **Vira** (191), **zira** (188)

R - - A   **Raba, raca** (19a,59c,130b,184d), **rada** (135c,172a), **raga** (56d, 105a), **Raia** (107d,147b), **raja** (77a,123c), **Rama** (77a,176d), **rana** (77a,123c), **Rana** (63d), **rara** (119a), **rasa** (51c), **rata** (29d,56b, 89d,96c,106d,120c,168c), **raya** (19b,23c,76d,107d), **reba** (144a), **Reba** (18d,86c), **rede** (37c,81d), **reja** (152b), **rena** (25b,132c), **rhea** (37a,56a,111d,133d), **Rhea** (19b,68d,87c,103c,186b), **riga** (118b), **Riga, rima** (23a,30c,32a,58a,110d), **ripa** (16b,131d), **rita, Rita** (37b,78d 183c), **Roda** (107b), **roka** (95a,168c,d), **Roma** (83c,d), **ropa** (152a), **Rosa** (58d,134a,145d,183c), **rota** (27c,30d, 38a,79a,92d,133a,134a,b,180c), **ruga** (59b,185a), **rupa** (60b), **rusa, Rusa** (41d,136d), **Ruta** (76b,134d)

  - RB   **arba** (135d,171a)

  - - RB   **barb** (20b,57d,78b,117d,120a,b,124b), **curb** (130c,146b), **garb** (32c,46a), **gerb** (56d,143d), **Harb** (191), **herb** (58b,158b), **kerb** (146b), **Serb** (15d,148a,186c), **sorb** (11d,103d,134b,142b), **Sorb** (148a,180a), **verb** (7a,114b,184b)

R - - B   **raab** (32d), **rhob** (64a,85c), **rumb** (120b)

  - RC -   **arca** (9a,22c,29d,115a,130a), **Arca** (101b), **arch** (29d,38b,39d, 123d,132c), **orca** (86b)

  - - RC   **circ** (31a), **marc** (70c), **Marc** (96a), **parc** (62b,112c)

  - RD -   **Erda** (23d,41a,47d,68d,69a,131d,177b), **ordo** (22a,30d,122a, 171a), **ordu** (170d), **urde** (86b), **Urdu** (77b), **urdy** (86b)

  - - RD   **bard** (12d,120a), **bird, bord** (100b), **Byrd** (9c,120b), **card** (33d, 114d), **cord** (39b,131a), **curd** (99d), **Dard, dord** (42c), **eard** (139b), **fard** (112d), **ford** (177b), **fyrd** (110a), **Gerd** (63c), **gird** (32c,50a,123a,160a), **hard** (109b), **herd** (39a,46c,72a), **Kurd** (48b,82a), **lard** (54d,61a,71a,110a), **lord** (107c), **nard** (13a,97c, 102b,110a,153c), **oord** (190), **pard** (27b,91b), **sard** (26d,28d,65d, 111a,142b,156d), **Sard, surd** (82c,177a), **verd** (71d), **ward** (31c, 55c,86b), **word** (124b,165c), **Wurd, Wyrd** (107d), **yard** (152d)

R - - D   **raad** (14a,49b,151a,165b), **Raad** (151a), **raid** (59d,80c), **rand** (16d,22a,131b,145a,b), **Rand** (69c), **read** (116d,157d), **redd** (153a), **reed** (16a,70d,97b,105a,111b,118b,144b), **Reed** (163a),

352

rend (32a,159c,162c,185a), Ridd (94a), rind (53a,115c), Rind (109c,174b), road (37d,164d), rodd (38d), roed, rood (38d,39a, 88b), roud (57a,b), rudd (26d,57a,b), rynd (100a)

RE - - read (116d,157d), real (7a), ream (18c,37d,50d,113d,171c), reap (7a,40a,74a), rear (15b,23a,b,24a,51b,76d,127c), reba (144a), Reba (18d,86c), reck (26d,75c), rect (117b), redd (153a), rede (37c,81d,138d), redo (165c), reed (16a,70d,97b,105a,111b,118b, 144b), Reed (163a), reef (129a,137a,145a), reek (49d,53c,64a, 148d,149a), reel (21b,40b,d,153c,154a,c,d,180d), reem (18d), reft (32a,42c,44d,167b), reim (112c), rein (29b,130c), reis (26c, 29d,75a,103b), reja (152b), Reki (16a), rely (16b,170b), Remi (10b), Rems, rena (25b,132c), rend (32a,159c,162c,185a), Reni (83d), Reno, rent (58a,77c,91b,138b,153d,162c,167c), repp (53b, 131a), rese (127b), resh (91d), rest (15d,91b,104d,105a,115a,b, 130a,b,161b), rete (106c,119c), reve (61c,104d), revs (131a)

- RE - area (37d,38a,44c,53a,93b,110d,127d,138c,168a,186d), areg (116a,137a), areo (34c), Ares (49b,51b,68c,76a,97a,105c,110b), aret (128c), brea (100b), bred (23c,48c,127c), bree (139a), bren (72d,95a), Brer (172b), Bres, brew (35d), brey (194), crea (92c), Cree (192), crew (72a,106a), Crex (37a), dree (139b,140c,158b, 172c), drei (65d,165a), dreg, drew, drey (154c), erer, (17d,150c), Frea, Fred (96b), free (44a,70d,131b), fret (28c,35b,111c,184d), Frey (7c,68b,124d), gres (156d), grew, grey (33c), Iren (127c), Orel, pree (139d), prep (138b), pres (62b), pret (188), prey (119d), tree (11d,37a,66a,184b), tref (172b), trek (85c,93c,99d, 168b), tres (19a,52b,63a,152d,165a,175c), tret (9a,178b,179d), trey (26c,165a), Urey (107c,138c), wren (19b,c), Wren (50b)

- - RE Aare, acre (39b,56a,88b), Acre, aire (82c), Aire, bare (43d,157c), bore (14c,25b,46a,116a,165c,179b), bure (61b), byre (38a), care (11b,14c.35d,150a,184d), cere (19a,149d,179a), core (28b,51c, 75b,81b), cure (123b), dare (28d,41b,42a,74d,175b), Dare (57a), dere (74a,79c), dire (45d,55a,104a,163c), dore (61d,67b,69d, 117d), Dore (50d,63a,b), Eire (82b), etre (61a,c,62d,166c), eyre (23c,31b,85c), Eyre, fare (43c,59b,67d,123b), fire (13a,43d,44b), fore (63d,174b), gare (61b,c,62c,127c), Gere (183c), gore (115d, 117c.154c,169c), gyre (31b,171b), hare (91b,132c), here, hire (49d,50b,91b,130a), inre (35d,80a), Jure (90b), kere (75c,128b), kore (107b), Kore (29a,42b,116b,124d), Kure (84c), lire (62c), lore (77c,87c,90d,151c,183a), lure (41c,51a,54b,163a), lyre (11c, 81c,105a,111c), mare (78b), Mare (108b), mere (16c,22b,62a, 78b,87d,96c,110c,120d,146d,148b), mire (21c,104b), more (71a), More (50b), mure (177d), Nare (93c), Nore (163d), ogre (67a, 102a), pare (115c,129a), pere (61c,63b), pore (59d,110d,111c, 120d,157d), pure (29b,172b,173c), pyre (64c), qere (75c), rare (138b,164b,172b,173d), rire (62a), sere (24d 46a,c,138c,183b), Sere (158b), sire (17d,55a,59d,124a,163b,166b), sore (23d,142c), sure (173d), tare (9a,18d,41a,176a,179d), tire (15a,22a,52d,55a, 179b,180d), tore, tyre (15a), Tyre (31b,90d,117b), vare (179b), vire (11a,13b), ware (27d,35a), were (139b), wire, wore, yare (96b,124b,128b), yore (10b,69d,93c,110b,165d)

R - - E race (116a,153b,154b,169c), rade (138d), rage (10c,30c,157c, 161d), rake (41b,44c,134b,140d), rale (7c,23a,29d,41b), rame (22d), rare (138b,164b,172b,173d), rase (42b,d,91d), rate (11d,

14a,31d,36b,51d,52a, 70b,85c,112b,123b, 127d, 128a,138c, 143a, 174b), rave (41c,157a,161d), raze (42b,d,91d), rede (37c,81d, 138d), rese (127b), rete (106c,119c), reve (61c,104d), ribe (139a), Rice (46a), ride (46b,85c), rife (6b,c,39d,123b), rile (10c, d,82c,125a,156b,176a), rime (30c,36a,58a,63d,77c), rine (44d, 75d,135c), ripe (58a,97c,98c), rire (62a), rise (49d,80b,155a), Rise (110d,150c), rite (93a,131d), rive (32a,153d), robe (65b), rode (46c), role (114b), Rome (31c,51d), rone (127c,164b), rope (36d,88d,128b), rose (33c), Rose (6a,50c,183c), rote (130b,134b, 143a,159d), roue (41b,44c,127c,134b), rove (127d,132b,178a), rube (37d,135d,185d), Rube (96b), rude (134b,172b), rule (11b, 26b,90b), rune (9b,67a,94a,95a,105c,107d,120a,141d,163d), ruse (13b,77c,157b,169c), rute (188), ryme (178d), rype (19b,125a)

- RF - orfe (57a,b,185c), Urfa (99a)

- - RF kerf (40a,108b), serf (21d,148a), surf (23a), turf (115c,149d, 160b), warf, werf (54d), zarf (39c,155a)

R - - F raff (75b), reef (129a,137a,145a), riff (131d), Riff (18b,102c), roof (78d), ruff (19b,33b,63d,137a)

- RG - Argo (12c,36b,c), ergo (164b), orgy (26d,130d,137c), urge (42d, 46b,79d,80a,b,81c,124a,150a)

- - RG berg (79b), borg (40d), burg (22b,73c), lurg (96d,141b,184d), morg (188), Sarg (96d,125c)

R - - G rang, ring (50a), Rong (88c), rung (28c,39a)

RH - - rhea (37a,56a,111d,133d), Rhea (19b,68d,87c,103c,186b), Rhee (87c), Rhin, rhob (64a,85c), rhum (8c), Rhus (159a)

R - - H rash (75a), rath (29a,76d,162c), resh (91d), rich, Roch (136c), rukh (53b,54a), rush, ruth (35b,118c), Ruth (105b,183c)

RI - - rial (190), ribe (139a), rice, Rice (46a), rich, rick (74d,117d, 154d), Ridd (94a), ride (46b,85c), Riel (129a), riem (76c,112c, 157c,164d), rien (62b), rier (180b), rife (6b,c,39d,123b), riff (131d), Riff (18b,102c), rift (30c,32a,58a,110d), riga (118b), Riga, Riis (9d), rikk (49a), rile (10c,d,82c,125a,156b,176a), rill (23c,102b,132a,148d,157b), rily (176a), rima (23a,30c,32a,58a, 110d), rime (30c,36a,58a,63d,77c), rimu (79d,106d,129a,168c), rimy (63d), rind (53a,115c), Rind (109c,174b), rine (44d,75d, 135c), ring (50a), rink (147c,154a), riot (44c,111d,170c,173d), ripa (16b,131d), ripe (58a,97c,98c), rire (62a), rise (49d,80b, 155a), Rise (110d,150c), risk (74d), risp (99a), Riss (66a), rita, Rita (37b,78d,183c), rite (93a,131d), rive (32a,153d)

- RI - aria (8b,98c,150a,c,170c), arid (46c,85a), arif (127d), aril (142a), aris (101b), Brie (29c), brig (72b,106a,144d), brim, brin (32c, 54c,146c), brit (76c), crib (96b,120d), cric (131c), crig (20d), crin (146c), cris (40b,95d), drib (46b), Drin, drip, eria (13d, 146d), eric (115b), Eric (71d,96a,107d,138a,164a,176b), Erie (82c,87d), Erin (82b), Eris (12c,68d,109c), Fria, frib (43d), frim (58d), frit (64c,67c), friz (39d), grid (17a,70d,119b,156d), grig (38c,70d,93a), grim (156a), grin, grip (159a), gris (61d), grit (137a,b), irid (38d,67c), Iris (53c,58a,111c), Iris (127c), kris (40b,95d), prig (112a,116c), prim (156b), trig (106a,148d,154b, 169d), trim (40a,106a,154b,160a,165c,169d), trin (169d), trio (104d,165a,169c), trip (85c), tris (122d), trit (34d,164c), Uria (14c,16d), urim (18d,23a,110a), writ (91a)

354

- - RI abri (61c,62c,144b), aeri (34a), agri (89b), Atri, auri (34a), bari (37c,79c), Bari (83d), Bori (110d,150c), buri (56b), Cori (138c), dari (38a,70b), Geri (183c), gyri (22d,131b), kari (14d), keri (75c,128b), kiri (86a,87c,115a,168c), kori (7d,77a), Kuri (191), lari (78a,101c), Lari (72c), lori (91b), Luri (191), mari (61d), Mari (16a), Neri, nori (8c,141c), Omri (18c,86d), pari (34a, 180a), peri (54b,116b,c,122b), puri (80d), qeri (75c), Rori (16b), sari (48b,65b,77b), seri (18b), Seri (192), Shri (17c,166c), siri (18b), sori (55c,64a), Tari (47d,69a), tori (101b), Turi (191), vari (34d,91b,134d,174d), veri (28b), weri (15c,27c)

R - - I rabi (38d,74a), Rabi (14b,117b), ragi (28b), rami (22d), rani (72c,77b,123c,127c), rati (189), ravi (61b), Ravi (16b), Reki (16a), Remi (10b), Reni (83d), rodi (98c), romi (72d), Rori (16b), roti (62c)

- - RK bark (115c), cark (26d,184d), cork (119d), dark (47a,67d,109b, 160b), dirk (40b), fork, hark (92d), jerk (153a), kirk (31a,139b), kurk (31a,139b), lark (19a,63d), lurk (92a,147d), mark (146b, 155a), Mark (52a,96a), mirk (41a,67d), murk (41a,67d), nark (81a,156d), park, perk (84d,93a), pork, Sark (28d), Turk (101d, 102d,106a,111d), work (64c,76b), yark (22c), york (38c), York (50b,c)

R - - K rack (32c,64b), raik (188,189), rank (31d,55d,70b,92c,94d,157c), reck (26d,75c), reek (49d,53c,64a,148d,149a), rick (74d,117d, 154d), rikk (49a), rink (147c,154a), risk (74d), rock (160b), rook (19b,29c,39a), ruck (39a,185a), rusk (23a)

- RL - orle (17b,56b,76a,144b,177a), orlo (56b,119c), Orly (8b)

- - RL birl (93c,131a,153c), burl (87c,169a), carl (115c,135d), Carl (96a), cirl (24c), curl (38d,73b,93b,131d), earl (107c), farl (138c, 140b), furl (132d), girl, harl (16b,56b,59a), herl (16b,59a), hurl (167c), jarl (40d,107d), Karl (96a), marl (32a,42c,55d), merl (20b), nurl (33b,87c), purl (87c,104c), yarl (40d,107d)

R - - L rail (16b,19b,c,37a,97b,138c,150c,177b), real (7a), reel (21b,40b, d,153c,154a,c,d,180d), rial (190), Riel (129a), rill (23c,102b, 132a,148d,157b), roil (44c,104b,156b,170d,176a), roll (134a, 160b), roti (103b,111c), rull (170b), ryal (110a,190), ryel (190)

- RM - arme (63a,179b), arms, army (78c), Erma (183c), Irma (96d)

- - RM barm (185b), berm (25d,90d,145c), corm (24b,38d,156a), derm (147c,158d), dorm, farm (165d), firm (154c,173d), form (54d, 143c), Garm (178c), germ (17d,99c,134d), harm (40b,81a), norm (15a,115a,128a,155a), perm (49b,97d), term (92b,105b,142b, 166b), turm (132d), warm (7c,75b,163b), worm, wurm (67c)

R - - M ream (18c,37d,50d,113d,171c), reem (18d), reim (112c), rhum (8c), riem (76c,112c,157c,164d), roam (178a), room (28d)

- RN - arna (24a,181b), Arnd (67a), Arne (35c,50c,134d), arni (24a, 181b), Arno (27a), arn't, erne (19c,d,47b,54b,141a), orna (169d, 182c), orne (169d,182c), Orne (25b), urna (133a)

- - RN barn (156d), Bern (160d), birn (31d), born, burn, carn (156c), cern (41c), corn (39d,95c,123a), darn (130b), dorn (164d), earn (42d,64b,99a), fern (142a), firn (67c,70c,106c,149b), garn (67d, 185b), horn (11a,105a,170b,182a), karn (156c), kern (59c,172a), Kern (132b), lorn (42d,60b), norn, Norn (69a,163d,174b), pern

355

(78a), **pirn** (21b,129a,179b), **sorn** (139a,d), **tarn** (87d,103d,120d), **tern** (19b,32d,72c,94a,138c,131b,160a), **torn** (130a), **turn** (28d, 131a,175a), **warn** (7b), **worn** (143b), **yarn** (154b,161b,184b)

R - - N **rain** (121d,162d), **rann** (175c), **rein** (29b,130c), **Rhin, rien** (62b), **roan** (78b,c,114c,128d,144a,181a), **roon** (41a,168b), **ruin** (42d)

RO - - **road** (37d,164d), **roam** (178a), **roan** (78b,c,114c,128d,144a, 181a), **roar** (145c), **robe** (65b), **Roch** (136c), **rock** (160b), **Roda** (107b), **rodd** (38d), **rode** (46c), **rodi** (98c), **roed, roer** (72d), **roey** (103d), **rohr** (72d), **roll** (44c,104b,156b,170d,176a), **rojo** (129a, 152c), **roka** (95a,168c,d), **roke** (174d,175b), **role** (114b), **roll** (134a,160b), **Roma** (83c), **Rome** (31c,51d), **romi** (72d), **romp** (63d), **rone** (127c,164b), **Rong** (88c), **rood** (38d,39a,88b), **roof** (78d), **rook** (19b,29c,39a), **room** (28d), **roon** (41a,168b), **Roos** (67a), **root** (53a), **ropa** (152a), **rope** (36d,88d,128b), **ropy** (157c, 176d), **Rori** (16b), **Rosa** (58d,134a,145d,183c), **rose** (33c), **Rose** (6a,50c,183c), **ross** (16c,161d), **Ross** (50c), **rosy** (21a,111a), **rota** (27c,30d,38a,79a,92d,133a,134a,b,180c), **rote** (130b,134b, 143a,b180c), **roti** (62c), **rotl** (103b,111c), **roto** (30a,122d,127b, 152c,171b), **roud** (57a,b), **roue** (41b,44c,127c,134b), **roup** (44a, 121d), **rout** (41d,44b,46b), **rove** (127d,132b,178a), **rowy** (157b), **Roxy** (183d)

· RO · **Aroa** (175b), **Arod** (86c), **aroo** (80c,82b), **arow** (92c,158b), **brob** (153c), **broo** (139a), **brow, croc** (13a,74a), **Crom, crop** (38b), **crow** (19a), **drop** (43d,54b,100b,114c,168b), **Eros** (11c,39c,68b, 97c,182d), **froe** (32a,167a,179d), **frog** (10a,17a,126d), **from, frot** (28c), **frow** (47a,167a), **grog** (92d,153d), **gros** (47a,53d), **Gros** (63a), **grot** (27d), **grow** (154b), **Irok** (55b), **iron** (55c,d,69d,81a, 97b,143b,149a,173d,179c), **Kroo** (191), **proa** (21b,26a,95c,d), **prod** (67d,80b,106b,120b), **prop** (159d), **prow** (21b,22c,144d, 156a), **trod, tron** (140d,180a), **trop** (62d,167a), **trot** (85b,93d, 112d), **trow** (18a,21a,159d,164c,170b), **troy** (161c,180a)

· · RO **aero** (8b,34a,b,58c,59a), **agro** (149d), **arro** (52c), **baro** (71a, 122c), **boro** (154b), **Boro** (193), **caro** (83a), **Caro** (183d), **cero** (57b,c,d,180b), **duro** (190), **Ebro** (132a), **faro** (65a), **Garo** (88c), **giro** (38c,167c), **gyro** (34d), **hero** (42b,124d,137b), **Hero** (90c), **hiro, inro** (84b,c,106c), **karo** (106d), **Lero** (82d), **loro** (19a,114b), **maro** (144d), **mero** (72a), **miro** (19a,106d,184a), **Miro** (113a, 151d), **moro** (19a,56c), **Moro** (100a,103a,117a,159a), **Nero** (8a, 126d,133a,150b,172c), **okro** (72c,175a), **otro** (151d), **pero** (152a), **Piro** (192), **Poro** (141d), **pyro, sero** (34d,88d,164b,178d), **taro** (13c,48c,49b,64b,112b,120a,133d,155c,170a,c), **tiro** (9b,17d, 108c), **toro** (38a,107a,152a,168c), **tyro** (9b,17d,108c), **zero** (31a, 84c,108c), **Zero** (118d)

R - - O **raio** (188), **redo** (165c), **Reno, rojo** (129a), **roto** (30a,122d,127b)

· RP · **arpa** (83b)

· · RP **carp** (27d,38d,40c,55a,56c,57a), **dorp** (73c,176b), **harp** (105a, 129a), **iarp** (51d), **ierp** (51d,141d), **tarp** (26b,178d), **terp** (12b, 123a), **torp** (54c), **turp, warp** (36c,165a,171c), **zarp** (120c)

R - - P **raip** (36d), **ramp** (65a,80b,127b,148b), **rasp** (56b,70d,140d), **reap** (7a,40a,74a), **repp** (53b,131a), **risp** (99a), **romp** (63d), **roup** (44a, 121d), **rump**

· RR ·   arra (47d,52c,82b), arro (52c), Irra (178a), orra (139c,d,140a)

· · RR   barr (49b), birr (180d), burr (123b), carr (120d,140a), curr (104c), darr (163c), dorr (32b), durr (70b), Herr (66c), Kerr, murr (72b,128b), nurr (67d), parr (136d,137a,147c), pirr (181a), purr (104c), turr (24d,105a), Tyrr (68c,109c,163d,178a), yarr (72a)

R · · R   rear (15b,23a,b,24a,51b,76d,127c), rier (180b), roar (145c), roer (72d), rohr (72d), ruer, Ruhr

· RS ·   Erse (28a,64b,82b), erst (60b), Ursa (17b,36b,43d)

· · RS   airs (123b), Bors (70b,134b), hers (124c), hors (62b), Lars (51d, 121b), Mars (68c,118d,119a,129a,178a), Mors (41b), ours (124c), pars (89d), sors (44d,89b)

R · · S   raas (91b), rais (26c,29d,75a,103b), Rais (106b), rats, reis (26c, 29d,75a,103b), Rems, revs (131a), Rhus (159a), Riis (9d), Riss (66a), Roos (67a), ross (16c,161d), Ross (50c), Russ (135b)

· RT ·   Arta (72b), arto (34a), arts (138c), arty, orts (60d), Urth (68d, 107d,163d)

· · RT   Bart (96b), Bert (96b), bort (43b), Bort (134b), cart (171d,175a, 177b), curt (145b,c), dart (13b,88a,100c,120b,153a,160c), dirt, fort (63d,157d), girt (50a), hart (41d,154d), hurt, mart (49d, 97a), Mart (96b,183d), mort (41b,47a,78b,136d), part (44d,60d, 121c,159c), pert (80a,93a,137c,154b), port (73d,136b,140c,170c, d,182b,c), Sart (82b,103b,170d), Sert (151d), sort (31d,39c,70b, 86b,153a), tart (114d), tert (31c,91a,185c), vert (71d,166a,171b), wart (124d), wert, wort (76a,95d,121d), yurt (101d)

R · · T   raft (27b,33c,58c,75b), rant (41c,127b,128a,161d), rapt (6c,27a, 50d), rect (117b), reft (32a,42c,44d,167b), rent (58a,77c,91b, 138b,153d,162c,167c), rest (15d,91b,104d,105a,115a,b,130a,b, 161b), rift (30c,32a,58a,110d), riot (44c,111d,170c,173d), root (53a), rout (41d,44b,46b), runt (47a,172d), rust (37b,112c,119a), ryot (115c)

RU · ·   ruay (189), rube (37d,135d,185d), Rube (96b), ruby (20a,65d, 179c), ruck (39a,185a), rudd (26d,57a,b), rude (134b,172b), ruer ruff (19b,33b,63d,137a), ruga (59b,185a), Ruhr, ruin (42d), rukh (53b,54a), rule (11b,26b,90b), rull (170b), rumb (120b), rump, rune (9b,67a,94a,95a,105c,107d,120a,141d,163d), rung (28c, 39a), runt (47a,172d), rupa (60b), ruru (19b,102c,106d), rusa, Rusa (41d,136d), ruse (13b,77c,157b,169c), rush, rusk (23a), Russ (135b), rust (37b,112c,119a), Ruta (76b,134d), rute (188), ruth (35b,118c), Ruth (105b,183c)

· RU ·   arui (11b,143d,144a,181c), arum (13a,39b,58d,92b,155c), Arum (66a), bruh (95a), brut (182c), Brut (23c), crus (91a,143c), crux (39a,151b), drub (17b,39c), drug (105d), drum (105a), drun (132b), erua (103c), eruc (37a,56a), grub (43c,88d), grum (102c), Grus (36b,c,38b), irus (109d), prutl, Prut (41a), true (7a,8d,37b, 54b,94c,149c), urus (14d,53a,112c)

· · RU   Aaru (6b,48d), baru (168c), ecru (17d,23d,172b), feru (37a,56a, 133d), guru (77b), maru (84c,144d), Meru (77a,103d), paru (57a), Peru, Puru (192), ruru (19b,102c,106d), Yaru (84d)

R · · U   Rahu (42b,48b), rimu (79d,106d,129a,168c), ruru (19b,102c, 106d)

- RV -   urva (38b)

RV - -   ryal (110a,190), ryel (190), ryme (178d), rynd (100a), ryot (115c), rype (19b,125a)

- RY -   Arya (80d), eryx (137a), oryx (11a), tryp (114a)

- - RY   adry (164c), aery (47b,51d,106c), airy (177a,176d), atry (141b), awry (13d,38d,171c), bury (81d), dory (21b,58b,144c), eery (172b,180a), ewry (133c), eyry (47b,106c), fury (157a), Gary, gory, jury (38a), lory (19a,114a), Mary (50c,126b,183c), miry, nary (108b), oary, sory (176d), spry (7a,107b), Tory (23c,36b, 94c,172a), vary (28d,43c), very (149c), wary (27d,176b), wiry (147a,167c)

R - - Y   racy (153b), rely (16b,170b), rily (176a), rimy (63d), roey (103d), ropy (157c,176d), rosy (21a,111a), rowy (157b), Roxy (183d), ruay (189), ruby (20a,65d,179c)

R - - Z   razz (131b)

SA - -   Saad (12b), saah (188), saal (66c,73b), Saan (24d), Saar (63b, 102d,132a), saba (56a,117a), Saba (143d), sabe, sack (43d,118a, 119d,182b), saco (189), sadd (33a,40b,58c,107b), sade (91d), sadh (77a), sado (26d,84d), sadr (94a), Sadr (155b), saer (163a), safe (141d,157d,174d), Safi (191), saga (79b,91a,138a,157a, 161b,c,168a), Saga, sage (13a,90d,100c,141c,145c,180b,183a), sago (54c,59b,113b,125b,155c), sagy, saha, sahh (188), Saho (6c), sahu (153d), saic (86b,91d,175d), said (174c), Said (42d, 101a,121b), sail (144c,185a), sain (20c,38d,48a), sair (140b, 150d), sais (48d,71d), Saka (10a), sake (84b,125d), saki (39c, 84b,102a), sala (152a,b,c), Sala (50c), sale (14c,61c,62b,c, 168b), salp (109c,148d), salt (35d,105b,123a,136c,141c,149d), sama (105c,169d), same (44d,79b), samh (56b), samp (70b,77d, 121b), sana (56a,166d), Sana (185d), sand (71d,146c), sane (128a), sang, sank, sano (152b), sans (63a,183b), sapa (70c), sapo (149c,166d), Sara (24d,183c), sard (26d,28d,65d,111a, 142b,156d), Sard, Sarg (96d,125c), sari (48b,65b,77b), Sark (28d), Sart (82b,103b,170d), sasa (55c), sash (18a,45c,67b, 182b), sass, sate (32d,52c,67d,70d,137c,159d), sati, Sati (49a, 126b,147b), Sauk (192), saul (48a,168c), Saul (18c,86d,115a), saum (189), save (52b,110c,123a,173c), sawk (188), sawn, saxe (20d,33c), saya (117a)

- SA -   asak (13d,168c169a), asar (67b), Esau (82c,84a,128c), Esay, Isar (41a,104c,132a), osar (51b,67b,131b), tsar (42d,49d,60b, 135c), usar (8d,16c), Usas (68d)

- - SA   ansa (73c,93d,137c), Ausa, Besa (68b,119c), bisa (11a), bosa (12a), casa (152b), Disa (111a), dosa (74b), Elsa (70a,93c,100d, 177b,183c), kasa (48a), kusa, Lisa (183d), masa (37a), mesa (49b,76d,119b,161a), Musa (16a), ossa (21d), Ossa (103d,110b, 164b), pasa (46a,127c,152c), pesa (190), Pisa (90c), rasa (51c), Rosa (58d,134a,145d,183c), rusa, Rusa (41d,136d), sasa (55c), Susa (49a), Tesa (80c), Ursa (17b,36b,43d), vasa (46d,114a, 160b,175d), Vasa, visa (114d), Xosa (86a)

S - - A   saba (56a,117a), Saba (143d), saga (79b,91a,138a,157a,161b,c, 168a), saha, Saka (10a), sala (152a,b,c), Sala (50c), sama (105c,169d), sana (56a,166d), Sana (185d), sapa (70c), Sara (24d,183c), sasa (55c), saya (117a), Seba (18c,39d), sera (11b,

358

20d,59a,83a,180d), **seta** (23b,27c,73a,b,123b,153c), **shea** (25a,
168c,d), **Shoa** (6c), **sida** (37a,126c,170a), **sika** (41d,84b), **sima**
(132b), **sina** (46c), **Sina** (102d,103d), **Sita** (127d), **siva** (67a,
120d), **Siva** (56d,77a), **skua** (19b,72c,84a,141a), **soda** (19a,
149d,181a), **sofa** (44d), **soga** (70d,152b), **Soga** (191), **Soia**, **soja**
(151b), **soka** (20c), **sola** (9a,48a,74b,118c,154a,167b), **soma**
(10c,21c,34a,48a,81d,136b), **sora** (19b,c,127b), **soya** (151b), **stoa**
(33c,121a,c), **Sula** (65a), **supa** (168c), **sura** (87c,113b,166d),
Susa (49a), **Syra**

- SB -   **isba** (135c)

S - - B   **scab** (80b,107d,157c), **scob** (42a), **Serb** (15d,148a,186c), **slab**
(148b), **Sleb** (12a), **slob** (173d), **slub** (171c), **snab** (23c,139a),
snib (54d,93c), **snob** (159c), **snub** (128c,148b), **sorb** (11d,103d,
134b,142d), **Sorb** (148a,180a), **stab** (14c,87a,117c), **stib** (19b,
47a,137a), **stub** (156c), **swab** (102b), **sweb** (160d), **swob** (102b)

SC - -   **scab** (80b,107d,157c), **scad** (31a,57a,78b,88d,137c), **scan** (52b,
93d,98a,116d,128b,c,140d), **scar** (31a,184d), **scat** (26b,67a,d,
126c,169c), **Scio**, **scob** (42a), **scon** (162c), **scop** (120a), **scot**
(14a,162b), **Scot** (64b,132c), **scow** (21a,58b), **scud** (32c,126c,
135b,160c), **scum** (129b), **scup** (57a,121b), **scur** (78b), **scut**
(145c,161b)

- SC -   **asci** (154a), **esca** (11c,44a,70c), **esce** (158d)

- - SC   **aesc** (12d,64d), **Bosc** (115c), **DDSC** (42a), **disc** (31b), **fisc** (52c,
134c)

S - - C   **saic** (86b,91d,175d), **spec**

S - - D   **Saad** (12b), **sadd** (33a,40b,58c,107b), **said** (174c), **Said** (42d,
101a,121b), **sand** (71d,146c), **sard** (26d,28d,65d,111a,142b,
156d), **Sard**, **scad** (31a,57a,78b,137c), **scud** (32c,126c,135b,
160c), **seed** (70b,111c,112c,119a,151b,154a), **seld** (103b), **Seid**
(42d,101a,171a), **send** (42c,44b,95c,121c,130a,144c,168b), **shad**
(27d,57a,b,c), **shed** (27a,90c,101b,144b), **shod**, **Sind**, **skid** (148b),
sled (40a), **slid**, **sned** (93d,125a), **snod** (169d), **sold**, **spad**
(105b), **Spad** (118d), **sped**, **spud** (121d,151c), **stad** (151b,167d,
176b), **stod** (40d,67d), **stud** (22b,25a,42d,54d,111c,143a,174a),
sudd (40b,58c,107b), **suid** (188), **surd** (82c,177a), **swad** (94d),
syed (103b), **syud** (103b)

SE - -   **seah** (188), **seal** (10c,d,54d,64c,96a,118b,128a), **seam** (85b,d,
160a,176d,185a), **Sean** (85b,96a), **sear** (23d,27d,72d,138c), **seat**
(98c,156b), **Seba** (18c,39d), **sebi** (34b), **sech** (97c), **seck** (173d),
sect (42b,54a,114c), **seed** (70b,111c,112c,119a,151b,154a), **seek**
(141c), **seel** (20c,32c,143b), **seem** (11c), **seen**, **seep** (110c,116a,
154b), **seer** (60a,124c,150c), **sego** (24b,25a,92b,174c), **sehr**
(66d), **seid** (103b), **Seld** (42d,101a,171a), **Selk** (77b), **Seim**
(120c), **sein** (146c), **seip** (110c), **Seir** (51b,94a,103d), **seis** (147b,
152c), **seit** (189), **Sejm** (120c), **self** (48d,80d), **sell** (97a,115c,
175b), **seme** (45c,138b,151b,154b,155c,157b), **semi** (34b,80b,
122c,d), **send** (42c,44b,95c,121c,130a,144c,168b), **senn** (76b),
Sens (63b), **sent**, **seps** (93b),142d), **sept** (31d,82b,143a,149c),
Sept (45b), **sera** (11b,20d,59a,83a,180d), **Serb** (15d,148a,186c),
sere (24d,46a,c,138c,183b), **Sere** (158b), **serf** (21d,148a), **seri**
(18b), **Seri** (192), **sero** (34d,88d,164d,178d), **Sert** (151d), **sesi**
(20b,57a,149b), **sess** (149c,162b), **seta** (23b,27c,73a,b,123b,

359

153c), **seth** (98d), **Seth** (7a,52b,68a,b,96a,98d), **seti** (34a), **Setl** (116d), **sett** (115a,156d), **seve** (63a,182c), **sewn, sext** (26b,111b, 147b)

· SE · **asea** (39b,177c), **asem** (9a,49a,69c), **Aser** (84a), **esek** (18d), **esel** (66b), **eser, lser** (49a), **oser** (61b), **used** (6d,73a), **usee, user** (49d), **uses** (18a), **yser**

· · SE **anse** (61d), **apse** (9b,20a,31a,128c,130a,142b,175a), **asse** (25a, 60d,74a), **base** (6a,43b,44b,51c,60c,79b,94b,122b), **bise** (182a), **bose** (163c), **case** (22c,36c,81c,91a,108c), **cise** (147b), **cose** (29b), **dose** (123a), **duse** (83c), **ease** (7c,8d,35a,100d,129d,130b, c,150c), **else** (18b,79b,111d), **ense** (139b,158c), **Erse** (28a,64b, 82b), **esse** (7a,18a,52d,89a,90a,159a,166c), **fuse** (98c), **hase** (74d), **hose** (156c), **huse** (180c), **ipse** (44d,89c), **Jose** (96a), **lose** (60a,100c), **lyse, mese** (71c), **mise** (8a,10a,70c), **Mose** (96b), **muse** (65b,93d,120d,164c), **Muse** (68d), **nase** (26b,75a,124b), **nose** (118d,125a,149b), **oese** (15d,119c), **Oise, Ouse** (132a, 185d), **owse, pise** (127d), **pose** (14c,15d), **rase** (42b,d,91d), **rese** (127b), **rise** (49d,80b,155a), **Rise** (110d,150c), **rose** (33c), **Rose** (6a,50c,183c), **ruse** (13b,77c,157b,169c), **sise** (62c,147b), **vase, vise** (31d,77d,114c), **wise** (136b)

S · · E **sabe, sade** (91d), **safe** (141d,157d,174d), **sage** (13a,90d,100c, 141c,145c,180b,183a), **sake** (84b,125d), **sale** (14c,61c,62b,c,168 b), **same** (44d,79b), **sane** (128a), **sate** (32d,52c,67d,70d,137c, 159d), **save** (52b,110c,123a,173c), **saxe** (20d,33c), **seme** (45c, 138b,151b,154b,155c,157b), **sere** (24d,46a,c,138c,183b), **Sere** (158b), **seve** (63a,182c), **shee** (82b), **shoe** (166a), **sice** (71d, 147b), **side** (13d,22a,b,54a,58a,89a,161b), **sime** (101d), **sine** (64c,66b,90a,97c,126a,163b,169d,183b), **sipe** (101a,110c,140b), **sire** (17d,55a,59d,124a,163b,166b), **sise** (62c,147b), **site** (93b), **sive** (146a), **size, skee** (149c), **Skye** (163c), **slee** (140b,148c), **sloe** (14a,20b,64a,119d,181c), **slue** (97b,148b,160a), **smee** (19b, 46c,d,118b,119d,141b,181b), **Smee** (116d), **snee** (40a,b,43d,87a), **soie** (62c), **soke** (44c,85d), **sole** (52c,57a,b,58b,d,110c,115d, 150a), **some** (114b,121c,126a), **sore** (23d,142c), **sote** (150c), **spae** (139c), **Spee** (66d,70b), **supe** (53a,154d), **sure** (173d), **syce** (71d), **syke** (194), **syne** (140b,147a), **sype** (110c)

S · · F **self** (48d,80d), **serf** (21d,148a), **souf** (146b), **stof** (135c), **surf** (23a)

SG · · **Sgau** (88c)

S · · G **sang, Sarg** (96d,125c), **shag** (73b,105b,161d,166d), **sing** (26d, 178a), **skag** (7d,46d), **skeg** (7d,86a,144d,157d,184a), **slag** (46c, 99a,138c,148d,177a), **slog** (157c,170b,177d), **slug** (46b,99b, 157c), **smug, snag** (11b,27b,35c,87c,124b,166a), **sneg** (139b), **snig** (45d), **snug** (35a,38b,165c), **Snug** (99d), **song** (12c,170c), **stag** (65a,98d), **stog** (155a), **sung, Sung** (30b), **swag** (22a,156c), **swig** (46a,72c)

SH · · **shad** (27d,57a,b,c), **shag** (73b,105b,161d,166d), **shah** (116c), **sham** (41c,55b,60d,80a,123a,b,146d), **Shan** (13c,80d,88c,101d), **shap, shat** (87d), **shaw** (164b), **Shaw** (50c,53b), **shay** (110c), **shea** (25a,168c,d), **shed** (27a,90c,101b,144b), **shee** (82b), **Shem** (107c), **Shen** (68a), **sher** (65d,165c), **shet, shew** (44c), **shih** (189), **Shik** (171a), **shim** (91d,144c,162a,179d), **shin** (91a,d,140b,

360

143c), ship, shir (36d,65d,165c), Shoa (6c), shod, shoe (166a), shoo (46b,67a,138b), shop, shoq (169a), shor (136d), Shor (162b), shot (9d,43d,90c,174d), shou (41d), show (42b,44c,96b), Shri (17c,166c), shul (161a), shun (15a,51b,52a), shut

- SH - Asha (191), ashy (113a,178a), Isha (174a), Tshi (69c), Usha (16a,150c)

- - SH bash, bish (120b), bosh, bush, cash (101c), cosh (35a,97c), cush (101c), Cush (51d,73c), dash (125c,162d), dish, fash (140c, 176a), fish, gash (40a), gish (102c), gosh, gush (35a,154c), hash, hish, hush (17b,146c), josh (85b), kish (16d,70c), Kish (137c), Kush, lash (58c,87b,165c,180d), losh (178b), lush (94d), mash (39b,156c), mesh (50d,106c), mush (97d), Nash (9c), Nish (19d), pish (36c,107d), posh (49b,148c), push (145c), rash (75a), resh (91d), rush, sash (18a,45c,67b,182b), sish (79b), sosh (81d), tash (154d), tosh (106a), tush (167b), wash, wish (53c)

S - - H saah (188), sadh (77a), sahh (188), samh (56b), sash (18a,45c, 67b,182b), seah (188), sech (97c), seth (98d), Seth (7a,52b,68a, b,96a,98d), shah (116c), shih (189), sigh, Sikh (77b), sinh (97c), sish (79b), soph, sosh (81d), such (146d)

SI - - siak (72d), sial (112a), Siam (163d,181a), sice (71d,147b), sick, sida (37a,126c,170a), side (13d,22a,b,54a,58a,89a,161b), sidi (103b,166b), sidy (123b), sier (57a,118b), sift (140d,142c,146b), sigh, sign (121c,146c), sika (41d,84b), Sikh (77b), silk (53b, 179c), sill (45c,76c,165a,182b), silo (59a,156d), silt (104b,142a), sima (132b), sime (101d), Simi (82d), simp (59c,146d), sina (46c), Sina (102d,103d), Sind, sine (64c,66b,90a,97a,126a,163b, 169d,183b), sing (26d,178a), sinh (97c), sink (41c,43c,46b, 158a), sino (34a), siol (82c), sion (125c,158c), Sion (75b,c,83a, 157d), sipe (101a,110c,140b), sire (17d,55a,59d,124a,163b, 166b), siri (18b), sise (62c,147b), sish (79b), sisi (121b), siss, sist (139b), Sita (127d), site (93b), sito (34b), siva (67a,120d), Siva (56d,77a), Sive (146a), size, sizy (176d), sizz

- SI - Asia (48a), Asin (102a), Hsia (30b,47c), Isis (68d,78c,111d), tsia (162c), Tsin (30b)

- - SI Absi (191), assi (77d), dasi (77a), desi (85d), kasi (116b), Lasi (191), nasi (34c,108a,115a), nisi (90a,173c), pasi (94b), sesi (20b,57a), sisi (121b), susi (53b,d)

S - - I Safi (191), saki (39c,84b,102a), sari (48b,65b,77b), sati, Sati (49a,126b,147b), sebi (34b), semi (34b,80b,122c,d), seri (18b), Seri (192), sesi (20b,57a,149b), seti (34a), Seti (116d), Shri (17c,166c), sidi (103b,166b), Simi (82d), siri (18b), sisi (121b), soli (12c,110c), sori (55c,64a), sufi (103a,116c), sugi (84b), suji (180c), susi (53b,d)

SK - - skag (7d,46d), skat (181b), Skat (155b), skee (149c), skeg (7d, 86a,144d,157d,184a), sken (164a), skeo (57d), skep (16d,17c, 77c), skew (148a,160c,171b,c), skey (185d), skid (148b), skil (57a), skim (67c), skin (53a,76c,115c,d), skio (57d), skip (110b, 114c,147c), skir, skit (145c), skiv (151b), skua (19b,72c,84a, 141a), Skye (163c), skyr (21d,151a), skyt (138c,140b)

- SK - Askr (107d)

- - SK bask (94d), bisk (120b,151a), bosk (164b), busk (17b,37b,55d,

361

161b), cask, cusk (57b), desk, disk (31b), dusk (171c), fisk (24d,52c,134c), husk (53a,78d,142a), mask (44a,45c), mosk (97b,103b), musk (116b), Omsk, pisk (9c,19b), risk (74d), rusk (23a), task (156b), Tosk (8c), tusk (167b)

S · · K   sack (43d,118a,119d,182b), sank, Sark (28d), Sauk (192)) sawk (188), seck (173d), seek (141c), Seik (77b), Shik (171a),siak (72d), sick, silk (53b,179c), sink (41c,43c,46b,158a), soak (46c, 137c), Sobk (38d), sock (157c,182a), sook (22a,25c,97a), souk (22a,97a), suck, sulk (159a), sunk

SL · ·   slab (148b), slag (46c,99a,138c,148d,177a), slam (180d,182d), slap (24a,128c,148c), slat (58b,89a,117c,184a), Slav (13c,40c, 48b,52a,120b,135b), slaw, slay, Sleb (12a), sled (40a), slee 140b,148c), slew (160a), sley (179b), slid, slim (148b,160a), slip (67c,119a), slit (40a), slob (173d), sloe (14a,20b,64a,119d, 181c), slog (157c,170b,177d), sloo (160a),. slop, slot (10d,11b, 41d,110d,167d,168a,181b), slow (43c), slub (171c), slue (97b, 148b,160a), slug (46b,99b,157c), slum, slur (44b,124c,148b, 168a)

· SL ·   isle (8b,53c,81d,86b,88a), Oslo (116d)

S · · L   saal (66c,73b), sail (144c,185a), saul (48a,168c), Saul (18c,86d, 115a), seal (10c,d,54d,64c,96a,118b,128a), seel (20c,32c,143b), sell (97a,115c,175b), shul (161a), sial (112a), sill (45c,76c, 165a,182b), siol (82c), skil (57a), soil (154d,159a,163c), soul (10d,125a,153c,176d)

SM · ·   smee (19b,46c,d,118b,119d,141b,181b), Smee (116d), smew (19b,46d,99a,137d), smug, smur (32c,46b,100c), smut (32d,44a, 119a,150c)

· SM ·   ismy (45a)

· · SM   kasm (189)

S · · M   saum (189), scum (129b), seam (85b,d,160a,176d,185a), seem (11c), Seim (120c), Sejm (120c), sham (41c,55b,60d,80a,123a,b, 146d), Shem (107c), shim (91d,144c,162a,179d), Siam (163d, 181a), skim (67c), slam (180d,182d), slim (148b,160a), slum, stem (29b,125a,154d,155a,156d), stom (34c), stum (70c,105c, 131a,173a), swam, swim (58c), swum

SN · ·   snab (23c,139a), snag (11b,27b,35c,87c,124b,166a), snap (23a, 36d,38b,48b,54d,56c,58c,149d), sned (93d,125a,140a), snee (40a,b,43d,87a), sneg (139b), snib (54d,93c), snig (45d), snip (32b,40a), snob (159c), snod (169d), snow, snub (128c,148b), snug (35a,38b,165c), Snug (99d), snup (149b)

· SN ·   asno (151d), esne (10c,45b,142c,148a,164d)

S · · N   Saan (24d), sain (20c,38d,48a), sawn, scan (52b,93d,98a,116d, 128b,c,140d), scon (162c), Sean (85b,96a), seen, sein (146c), senn (76b), sewn, Shan (13c,80d,88c,101d), Shen (68a), shin (91a,d,140b,143c), shun (15a,51b,52a), sign (121c,146c), sion (125c,158c), Sion (75b,c,83a,157d), sken (164a), skin (53a,76c, 115c,d), soon (123a,145c), sorn (139a,d), span (23b,107b,113a, 128b,162c), spin (131a,180d), spun, sten (72c,95a), stun (145a, 157d), sunn (56a), Svan (27d), swan (19b,33a)

SO · ·   soak (46c,137c), soap, soar (59a), Sobk (38d), sock (157c,182a), soco (22d), soda (19a,149d,181a), sofa (44d), soft (48b,95d,99d,

362

163a), soga (70d,152b), Soga (191), sohol, Soho (93c), Soia, soie (62c), soil (154d,159a,163c), soir (61c), soja (151b), soka (20c), soke (44c,85d), sola (9a,48a,74b,118c,154a,167b), sold, sole (52c,57a,b,58b,d,110c,115d,150a), soli (12c,110c), solo (12c,89a,110c), soma (10c,21c,34a,48a,81d,136b), some (114b, 121c,126a), song (12c,170c), sons (98d,109d), sook (22a,25c, 97a), soon (123a,145c), soot (20b,26c,88a), soph, Sopt (45b), sora (19b,c,127b), sorb (11d,103d,134b,142d), Sorb (148a,180a), sore (23d,142c), sori (55c,64a), sorn (139a,d), sors (44d,89b), sort (31d,39c,70b,86b,153a), sory (176d), sosh (81d), soso (99c, 114c,166d), sote (150c), souf (146b), souk (22a,97a), soul (10d, 125a,153c,176d), soup, sour, sous (62d,172c), soya (151b)

- SO - asok (13d), asom (18d), asop (180b), asor (75c,105a), Esop (53b,54a), esox (57b)

- - SO also (10b,18b,80a), Caso (82d), coso (152c), enso (34d,183b), huso (180c), ipso (89c), koso (6c,80d), Koso (192,193), Muso (192), peso (99c), piso (189), soso (99c,114c,166d), yeso (72d)

S - - O saco (189), sado (26d,84d), sago (54c,59b113b,125b,155c), Saho (6c), sano (152b), sapo (149c,166d), Scio, sego (24b,25a,92b, 174c), sero (34d,88d,164b,178d), shoo (46b,67a,138b),silo (59a, 156d), sino (34a), sito (34b), skeo (57d), skio (57d), sloo (160a), soco (22d), sohol, Soho (93c), solo (12c,89a,110c), soso (99c, 114c,166d), Sumo

SP - - spad (105b), Spad (118d), spae (139c), span (23b,107b,113a, 128b,162c), spar (22c,24c,64b,97b,100b,144d), spat (112c,126b, 134b), spec, sped, Spee (66d,70b), spes, Spes (69a,78a), spet (16c,57a,142c), spew (35a,49a), spex, spey, spin (131a,180d), spir (97c), spit (120a,132b,c), spot (93b,118c,154d,162a), spry (7a,107b), spud (121d,151c), spun (10d,67d,167d,168a), spur (10d,67d,167d,168a, 181b), sput (21c)

- SP - espy (44a,142a)

- - SP cusp (38c,78b,119a,120a,b), gasp (113c), hasp (31d,54d,153c), lisp (153b), rasp (56b,70d,140d), risp (99a), wasp, wisp (24b, 148c)

S - - P salp (109c,148d), samp (70b,77d,121b), scop (120a), scup (57a, 121b), seep (110c,116a,154b), seip (110c), shap, ship, shop, simp (59c,146d), skep (16d,17c,77c), skip (110b,114c,147c), slap (24a,128c,148c), slip (67c,119a), slop, snap (23a,36d,38b, 48b,54d,56c,58c,149d), snip (32b,40a), snup (149b), soap, soup, step (70b,112b,177b,d), stop (73b,111b), sump (28c,45d,100b), swap (168d), swop (168a)

S - - Q shoq (169a)

S - - R Saar (63b,102d,132a), sadr (94a), Sadr (155b), saer (163a), sair (140b,150d), scar (31a,184d), scur (78b), sear (23d,27d,72d, 138c), seer (60a,124c,150c), sehr (66d), Seir (51b,94a,103d), sher (65d,165c), shir (36d,65d,165c), shor (136d), Shor (162b), sier (57a,118b), skir, skyr (21d,151a), slur (44b,124c,148b,168a), smur (32c,46b,100c), soar (59a), soir (61c), sour, spar (22c,24c, 64b,97b,100b,144d), spir (97c), spur (10d,67d,167d,168a,181b), star (14a,21c,94c,100c), ster (158c,d), stir (8a,13a,35b,78d,100d, 104a), suer (124d)

363

- **SS** - asse (25a,60d,74a), **assi** (77d), **esse** (7a,18a,52d,89a,90a,159a, 166c), **ossa** (21d), **Ossa** (103d,110b,164b)

- - **SS** bass (57b,c,177a), **Bess** (76c,183d), **boss** (49d,157d), **buss** (87a, 148c), **cass** (140c,177a), **Cass** (147a), **cess** (91d,94c,162b), **coss** (98a), **cuss diss** (98b), **doss** (17c), **fass** (189), **fess** (23c,51b), **foss** (44d,100d), **fuss** (22b,35b), **hiss** (146a), **jass** (160d), **jess** (157a), **joss** (30b), **kiss** (148c), **koss** (188), **lass** (95b), **less** (100c, 108b,141d), **liss** (54b,58b,60c,129d,140a), **loss** (42c,123d,178b), **mass** (8a,24b,35b,142d), **mess** (22b,44b,77c,85d,104b,165c, 173d), **miss**, **moss** (91d,104c,114a,170c), **muss** (135b,173d), **ness** (26b,75a,124b), **pass** (110b,155c), **puss**, **Riss** (66a), **ross** (16c,161d), **Ross** (50c), **Russ** (135b), **sass**, **sess** (149c,162b), **siss**, **Tass** (107a,135d,151b), **Tess** (73d,164c,183d), **toss** (24a, 132d), **viss** (189)

- **S** - - **S** sais (48d,71d), **sans** (63a,183b), **sass**, **seis** (147b,152c), **sens** (63b), **seps** (93b,142d), **sess** (149c,162b), **siss**, **sons** (98d,109d), **sors** (44d,89b), **sous** (62d,172c), **spes**, **Spes** (69a,78a), **suds** (59a)

- **ST** - - stab (14c,87a,117c), **stad** (151b,167d,176b), **stag** (65a,98d), **star** (14a,21c,94c,100c), **stat** (72d), **stay** (72d,124c,130a,134a,162a), **stem** (29b,125a,154d,155a,156d), **sten** (72c,95a), **step** (70b, 112b,177b,d), **ster** (158c,d), **stet** (91b,123d),124c), **stev** (155b), **stew** (21c,44b,184d), **stib** (19b,47a,137a), **stir** (8a,13a,35b,78d, 100d,104a), **stoa** (33c,121a,c), **stod** (40d,67d), **stof** (135c), **stog** (155a), **stom** (34c), **stop** (73b,111b), **stot** (154d,155d,157d,179b, 186a), **stow** (112b), **stub** (156c), **stud** (22b,25a,42d,54d,111c, 143a,174a), **stum** (70c,105a,131a,173a), **stun** (145a,157d), **Styx** (29b,73a,105c)

- **ST** - asta (188), **Asta** (107a,164c), **Asti** (83d,182b), **esta** (152d,164c), **este** (152b,d,164c), **Este** (55c,83c,d,112d), **Esth** (16a,51d), **oste** (21d,83b)

- - **ST** bast (16c,56a,117b,184a), **Bast** (27b), **best** (41d,159c,160a), **bust**, **cast** (165b,167c), **cest** (18a,67b), **dost**, **dust**, **east**, **East** (111b), **erst** (60b), **fast** (56d,126c,141d,160c,173a,d), **fest**, **fist** (80c), **fust** (105c,143b), **gest** (7c,41d,52d,133c), **gist** (95c,118c), **gust**, **hast**, **hest** (35a), **hist** (25c,93d), **host** (13a,51d,104c), **jest** (169c), **just** (51b,54b), **kist** (29d,58a,139b), **last** (36c,50b,145a, 174c), **lest** (59d,163d), **list** (26d,27b,75b,83d,134a,138b,165d), **lost, lust** (41b), **mast** (17c,108d,120b,144d,152d), **mist** (46b,59b, 174d), **most, must** (70c,101a,106d,157d,182c), **myst** (71c,123b), **Nast** (9c,27a), **nest** (38b,74b,130d,149c,160b), **oast** (15d,86b, 112a), **oust** (44c,49a,52b,125d), **past** (25c,69d,165d), **pest** (108c, 116b,118d,170a), **pist** (25c), **post** (89a,95c,155d), **rest** (15d,91b, 104d,105a,115a,b,130a,b,161b), **rust** (37b,112c,119a), **sist** (139b), **test** (26a,51c,144a,169c,170c), **vast** (78d,79d), **vest** (32c, 177b), **wast, west, West** (9c,50b,109b), **wist** (87c), **zest** (55d, 72d)

- **S** - - **T** salt (35d,105b,123a,136c,141c,149d), **Sart** (82b,103b,170d), **scat** (26b,67a,d,126c,169c), **scot** (14a,162b), **Scot** (64b,132c), **scut** (145c,161b), **seat** (98c,156b), **sect** (42b,54a,114c), **seit** (189), **sent, sept** (31d,82b,143a,149c), **Sept** (45b), **Sert** (151d), **sett** (115a,156d), **sext** (26b,111b,147b), **shat** (87d), **shot** (9d,43d,90c, 174d), **shut, sift** (140d,142c,146b), **silt** (104b,142a), **skat** (181b),

364

Skat (155b), skit (145c), skyt (138c,140b), slat (58b,89a,117c, 184a), slit (40a), slot (10d,11b,41d,110d,167d,168a,181b), smut (32d,44a,119a,150c), soft (48b,95d,99d,163a), soot (20b,26c, 88a),Sopt (45b), sort (31d,39c,70b,86b,153a), spat (112c,126b, 134b), spet (16c,57a,142c), spit (120a,132b,c), spot (93b,118c, 154d,162a), sput (21c), stat (72d), stet (91b,123d,124c), stot (154d,155d,157d,179b,186a), suet (54d), suit (38a,58a,91a,112a, 119c,137c), swat (15d,20d,32d,157c), Swat (103a), swot

SU - - such (146d), suck, sudd (40b,58c,107b), suds (59a), suer (124d), suet (54d), sufi (103a,116c), sugi (84b), suit (38a,58a,91a,112a, 119c,137c), suji (180c), Suku (191), Sula (65a), suld (188), sulk (159a), Sulu (102c), Sumo, sump (28c,45d,100b), sung, Sung (30b), sunk, sunn (56a), supa (168c), supe (53a,154d), sura (87c,113b,166d), surd (82c,177a), sure (173d), surf (23a), Susa (49a), susi (53b,d), susu (20c), Susu (191), Susy (183d)

- SU - Asur (68c), Esus, tsun (30b), Usun (191)

- - SU ansu (11d), Apsu (29a), ausu (168c,180b), Jesu, masu (57a,84c), Nosu (27d), susu (20c), Susu (191), vasu (106c), Vasu (176d)

S - - U sahu (153d), Sgau (88c), shou (41d), Suku (191), Sulu (102c), susu (20c), Susu (191)

SV - - Svan (27d)

S - - V skiv (151b), Slav (13c,40c,48b,52a,120b,135b), stev (155b)

SW - - swab (102b), swad (94d), swag (22a,156c), swam, swan (19b, 33a), swap (168a), swat (15d,20d,32d,157c), Swat (103a), sway (104a), sweb (160d), swig (46a,72c), swim (58c), swiz (160c), swob (102b), swop (168a), swot, swow (100a), swum

S - - W scow (21a,58b), shaw (164b), Shaw (50c,53b), shew (44c), show (42b,44c,96b), skew (148a,160c,171b,c), slaw (160a), slew (160a), slow (43c), smew (19b,46d,99a,137d), snow (35a,49a), spew (35a,49a), stew (21c,44b,184d), stow (112b), swow (100a)

S - - X spex, Styx (29b,73a,105c)

SY - - syce (71d), syed (103b), syke (194), syne (140b,147a), sype (110c), Syra, syud (103b)

- - SY busy, cosy (149c), easy (54a,146d,149d,172b), Josy (183d), mosy (67d), nosy, rosy (21a,111a), Susy (183d)

S - - Y sagy, shay (110c), sidy (123b), sizy (176d), skey (185d), slay, sley (179b), sory (176d), Spey (7a,107b), stay (72d,124c, 130a,134a), Susy (183d), sway (104a)

S - - Z sizz, swiz (160c)

TA - - Taal (7d,88c,151a),taar (12b), tabi (84c,149d), tabu (59d,111d), tace (13a,155d), tack (28d,37d,54c), tact (43c,d,116a), tael (91d, 179d), Taft (29d), taha (179b), tahr (68a,76b), tail (11d,27d,59b, 143b), tain (166a), tair (68a,76d), tait (14d), tajo (152a,d), take, takt (105a,163a), Taku (80c), taky, tala (16d,113a,168c,d), talc (28d,63b,99c,100b,122a,149c), tale (91a,185b), tall (189), talk, tall (118d), Tama (192), tame (45a,b,66a), Tame, tamp (46b, 112b,121d,127d), tana (159a), Tana (87d), Tane (120d), tang (30b,58b,186b), tanh (97c), tank (175a,d), Tano (192), Taos (192), tapa (16c,32c,53b,56a,74b,104b,112b,113d,120d), tape (16a,19a,128d), tapu, tara (22a,55c,113a,168c), Tara (82b,c,

365

138b), **tare** (9a,18d,41a,176a,179d), **Tari** (47d,69a), **tarn** (87d, 103d,120d), **taro** (13c,48c,49b,64b,112b,120a,133d,155c,170a,c), **tarp** (26b,178d), **tart** (114d), **tash** (154d), **task** (156b), **Tass** (107a,135d,151b), **tate** (183a), **tatt** (87c), **tatu** (12d), **Tatu, taun** (188), **taut** (163b,165c), **Tave** (183d), **Tavy** (183d), **tawa** (106d, 168c), **taxi** (13a,125b), **taxo** (13a)

- **TA** - **atap** (113b), **atar** (58d,116b,134a), **Etah** (71d,51c), **etal** (89a), **etat** (62d), **Ptah** (48d,98c), **stab** (14c,87a,117c), **stad** (151b,167d, 176b), **stag** (65a,98d), **star** (14a,21c,94c,100c), **stat** (72d), **stay** (72d,124c,130a,134a,162a), **utac** (22d), **Utah** (180b), **utas** (49a, 109c)

- - **TA** **acta** (41d,123d,128d,164c), **Aeta** (94d,95d,100a,106b,117a), **alta** (89c,152d), **anta** (83d,117c,d,121a), **Anta** (164a), **Arta** (72b), **asta** (188), **Asta** (107a,164c), **atta** (58d,90c,97d,160c,173d), **Atta** (94d,95d,100a,106b,117a), **bata** (30a,142d), **beta** (71a,91c,141d), **bota** (189), **cata** (122c), **cota** (117a), **data** (54a), **dita** (117a), **esta** (152d,164c), **Etta** (183c), **gata** (143c), **geta** (84b,145a), **Gita, iota** (71a,85c,91c,114c,166c,176a,180d), **jota** (151c), **keta** (45a), **kota** (117a), **Kota** (45d), **lata** (85d,95d), **lota** (24c,121d, 178d), **Lota, meta** (132d,133a), **Meta, mota** (103a), **muta** (28d, 103a), **nata** (47c), **Nata** (15c), **nota** (15c,89c), **octa** (122c), **pata** (32c,160d), **pita** (9c,28b,56a,83a), **rata** (29d,56b,89d,96c,106d, 120c,168c), **rita, Rita** (37b,78d,183c), **rota** (27c,30d,38a,79a, 92d,133a,134a,b,180c), **Ruta** (76b,134d), **seta** (23b,27c,73a,b, 123b,153c), **Sita** (127d), **tota** (71d), **vata** (104a), **vita** (89c,92a), **vota** (133b), **weta** (93c), **yeta** 84c), **zeta** (71b,91c)

T - - A **taha** (179b), **taia** (16d,113a,168c,d), **Tama** (192), **tana** (159a), **Tana** (87d), **tapa** (16c,32c,53b,56a,74b,104b,112b,113d,120d), **tara** (22a,55c,113a,168c), **Tara** (82b,c,138b), **tawa** (106d,168c), **tcha** (162c), **teca, Teca** (192), **Teda** (191), **tela** (22d,98c,121b, 166a,179c), **tema** (12a,164a),**Tema, tera** (23d,84c), **tesa** (80c), **Tewa** (193), **Thea** (162c), **Tina** (183d), **tiza** (172a), **Toba** (80c), **Toda** (45d,76d), **toga** (132d,133a,b), **toia** (48a,80d,180a), **Toia** (85b), **Toma** (191), **tooa** (17c), **tora** (11a,44d,74a,75c,85c,90b, 102d,115d), **tota** (71d), **toxa** (153d), **tsia** (162c), **tuba** (105a, 137d), **tufa** (121b,177a), **tuia** (9a), **Tuia, tuna** (57a,b,123b), **tuza** (119d)

T - - B **theb** (188), **thob** (128a), **tomb**

TC - - **tcha** (162c), **tche** (13d,30b,105a), **tchi, Tchi, tchu**

- **TC -** **etch, itch**

T - - C **talc** (28d,63b,99c,100b,122a,149c)

T - - D **tend** (26d,80b,93d,100a), **thud, tied, tind** (86b), **toad** (10a,17a, 63d,126d), **toed, told** (129c), **trod, tund** (121d)

TE - - **teak** (41a,48a,168c), **teal** (19b,20d,46c,d), **team** (38c,72a,113a), **tean** (140c,167a), **tear** (67c,87b,130a), **teca, Teca** (192), **Tech, teck** (128b), **Teco** (192), **Teda** (191), **teel** (142d), **teem** (6b,121d), **teen** (139b,c,140b,158d), **teer** (25b,69d), **Tees** (108a), **teff** (6c), **tegg** (143d,171d), **tehr** (27c,68a), **Teig** (96a), **teil** (92b,c,168c), **teju** (151b), **tela** (22d,98c,121b,166a,179c), **tele** (34b,122c), **teli** (94b), **tell** (105d,129c,154b), **Tell** (160d), **tema** (12a,164a), **Tema, tend** (26d,80b,93d,100a), **tene** (34d,131b), **teng** (188), **tent** (26b, 115a), **Teos** (82a), **tera** (23d,84c), **term** (92b,105b,142b,166b),

366

tern (19b,32d,72c,94a,138c,141a,160a), **terp** (12b,123a), **tesa** (80c), **Tess** (73d,164c,183d), **test** (26a,51c,144a,169c,170c), **tete** (61d,73b,74d), **teth** (91d), **Tewa** (193), **text** (21c,140d), **teyi** (92b, c,168c)

· TE ·   **atef** (39a,48d), **aten** (150a,159b), **Ateo** (120d), **Ater** (18c), **ates** (160c), **Itea** (145d,160c,181d), **item** (6d,13b,42d,51a,90d,92d, 107a,113d,114c), **Iten** (192), **iter** (22d,76c,85c,89c,114c,132a,b, 133a,b), **Otea** (71a,82d), **stem** (29b,125a,154d,155a,156b), **sten** (72c,95a), **step** (70b,112b,177b,d), **ster** (158c,d), **stet** (91b,123d, 124c), **stev** (155b), **stew** (21c,44b,184d),

· · TE   **ante** (87a,89a,115b,120b,122b,125d,154d), **bate** (43c,91b,100d), **bete** (61a,107c), **bite** (29d,156b), **cate** (165c), **cete** (180b,c), **cite** (15a,98d,126d,159b), **cote** (19b,143d,144a,b), **cute** (39c), **date** (64a,153a), **dite** (150b), **dote** (17a,90b,94b,97a,112a,139d,165d), **ente** (70b,151d), **este** (152b,d,164c), **Este** (55c,83c,d,112d), **ette** (158a,c,d), **fate** (42d,52a,87a,94a), **fete** (55d,129b), **fute** (51c), **gate** (51a,121b), **gite** (62a,118d), **hate** (6a,43a), **Jete** (16a), **Jute** (37a,48a,56a,133d,136a), **Kate** (143c,183d), **kite** (19c,49a, 74c,d), **late** (128c), **lete**, **lite** (158c,d), **lote** (24c,94a), **lute** (11c, 28b,84d,105a,131d), **mate** (18c,35b,41d,113a,154a,162c), **mete** (9a,11d,22b,44c,45b,98a,121c), **mite** (12b,81b,82a,114a,c,148c,d, 181b), **mote** (114c,153a), **mute** (146c,153b), **Nate** (22b), **nete** (71c,108b,163d), **note** (98c,109b,124b,128d,130a,177c), **oste** (21d,83b), **pate** (39a,74d), **pete** (136b), **Pete**, **rate** (11d,14a,31d, 36b,51d,52a,70b,85c,112b,123b,127d,128a,138c,143a,174b), **rete** (106c,119c), **rite** (93a,131d), **rote** (130b,134b,143a,159d), **rute** (188), **sate** (32d,52c,67d,70d,137c,159d), **site** (93b), **sote** (150c), **tate** (183a), **tete** (61d,73b,74d), **tote** (27a,73c), **tute** (171b), **vite** (62b),**vote** (60b), **Vote** (56d), **Wate** (141a), **Wote** (191), **yate** (51d, 168c)

T · · E   **tace** (13a,155d), **take**, **tale** (91a,185b), **tame** (45a,b,66a), **Tame**, **Tane** (120d), **tape** (16a,19a,128d), **tare** (9a,18d,41a,176a,179d), **tate** (183a), **Tave** (183d), **tche** (13d,30b,105a), **tele** (34b,122c), **tene** (34d,131b), **tete** (61d,73b,74d), **thee** (124b), **tice** (9a,38c, 51a,185d), **tide** (39d,75d,109c,141c,159d), **tige** (118a), **tile** (31d,56d,72b,95b,133c,163c), **time** (47a,131a), **tine** (11b,124b,167b), **tipe** (168b), **tire** (15a,22a,52d,55a,179b,180d), **tobe** (7d,137b), **tode** (80a,148a), **tole** (9a,51a,99b,163a), **tome** (21d,177c), **tone** (6c,118c,150d), **tope** (24a,46b,57a,143c,151a), **tore**, **tote** (27a,73c), **tree** (11d,37a,66a,184b), **true** (7a,8d,37b, 54b,94c,149c), **tube** (118b,158a), **tuke** (26b,53b), **tule** (24b,27c), **tune** (8b,12c,98c), **tute** (171b), **twee**, **tyee** (29d), **tyke** (29d), **tyne**, **Tyne** (108a), **type** (31d,115a,155a), **tyre** (15a), **Tyre** (31b, 90d,117b)

T · · F   **teff** (6c), **tiff** (126b), **toff** (40d), **tref** (172b), **tuff** (121b,177a), **turf** (115c,149d,160b)

T · · G   **tang** (30b,58b,186b), **tegg** (143d,171d), **Teig** (96a), **teng** (188), **thug** (65a), **ting** (166a), **Ting** (30c), **tong** (30a,c,), **toug** (171a), **trig** (106a,148d,154b,169d), **tung** (110a,168c), **twig**

TH · ·   **Thai** (146a), **than** (35b), **thar** (68a,76d), **that** (42b,124b,129c), **thaw**, **Thea** (162c), **theb** (188), **thee** (124b), **them** (124b), **then**, **thew** (104c), **they** (124b), **thin** (43b,c,148b), **this** (42b,124b),

367

thob (128a), Thor (7c,68c,99c,100c,109c,165b), Thos (84a,181c), thou (124b), thud, thug (65a), thus (149c)

- TH - Otho (133a)

- - TH acth (13b), bath, Bath (50d,151c), beth, (91c), Beth (8c,183d), both, doth, Esth (16a,51d), Gath (117a), Goth (16c,163d), hath, Heth (77c), Hoth (20c), Jeth (102a), kath (14a), kith (63c), lath (157c), lith (34d,156c), loth (15a,173d), math (77a), moth, Moth (112d), muth (188), myth (8b,91a), Nath (155c), oath (119c, 150a), path (132a,134b), pith (37a,51c,67b,95c,97a,119b,126d), rath (76d,162d), ruth (35b,118c), Ruth (105b,183c), seth (98d), Seth (7a,52b,68a,b,96a,98d), teth (91d), Urth (68d,107d,163d), Voth (191), with (10b)

T - - H tanh (97c), tash (154d), Tech, teth (91d), toph (75c), tosh (106a), tush (167b)

TI - - Tiam, tiao, tiar (39a,75a,121a), Tibu (191), tice (9a,38c,51a, 185d), tick (12b,20d,97c), tide (39d,75d,109c,141c,159d), tidy (106a,111b), tied, tien (147d), tier (118a,134b), tiff (126b), tige (118a), tike (29d), Tiki (120c), tile (31d,56d,72b,95b,133c,163c), till (39c,101c,173d), tilt (26b,d,166a), time (47a,131a), Tina (183d), tind (86b), tine (11b,124b,167b), ting (166a), Ting (30c), Tino (136d), tint 33c,d,114d), tiny (100c,148c), tion (158b), Tiou (192), tipe (168b), tipi (181b), tire (15a,22a,52d,55a,179b,180d), tiro (9b,17d,108c), titi (20d,102a,145d,168d,181b), Tito (186c), tiza (172a)

- TI - Atik (155b), atip (14b,166a), atis (76d,102a), itis (158c), otic (14c,d,47b), Otis (9c,d,24d,82a,111a), stib (19b,47a,137a), stir (8a,13a,35b,78d,100d,104a)

- - TI anti (7d,111a,122c), Anti (193), Asti (83d,182b), biti (20b), Guti, Hati (48d), hoti, Inti (159b), jati (27b), jiti, joti, Leti (82d), liti (60d), Loti (63a,176a), neti (164a), rati (189), roti (62c), sati, Sati (49a,126b,147b), seti (34a), Seti (116d), titi (20d,102a, 145d,168d,181b), viti (176b), yati (76d), zati (21d)

T - - I tabi (84c,149d), tali (189), Tari (47d,69a), taxi (13a,125b), tchi, Tchi, teli (94b), Thai (146a), Tiki (120c), tipi (181b), titi (20d, 102a,145d,168d,181b), topi (37a,75a,118c), tori (101b), tshi, Tshi (69c), Tupi (192), Turi (191), tuwi (117a,168c), Tybi (102a)

- TK - Atka (11a)

T - - K tack (28d,37d,54c), talk, tank (175a,d), task (156b), teak (41a, 48a,168c), teck (128b), tick (12b,20d,97c), tock (7d,19b), tonk (173c), took, Tosk (8c), trek (85c,93c,99d,168b), tuck (156b), Turk (101d,102d,106a,111d), tusk (167b)

- TL - atle (136d,161d,169b), Atil (14c,72b,79a,107d)

- - TL roti (103b,111c)

T - - L Taal (7d,88c,151a), tael (91d,179d), tail (11d,27d,59b,143b), tall (118d), teal (19b,20d,46c,d), teel (142d), teil (92b,c,168c), tell (105d,129c,154b), Tell (160d), teyl (92b,c,168c), till (39c,101c, 173d), toil (46c,184c), toll (131c), tool (27c), tuel

TM - - T-men (168b)

- TM - atma (150d), atmo (34d,174d), Atmu (143a,159b), itmo (18b)

T - - M team (38c,72a,113a), teem (6b), term (92b,105b,142b,166b), them (124b), tiam, toom (139b), tram (170a), trim (40a,106a, 154b,160a,165c,169d), turm (132d)

- TN - etna (75b,153c,157a,175d,177a,c)

T - - N tain (166a), tarn (87d,103d,120d), taun (188), tean (140c,167a), teen (139b,c,140b,158d), tern (19b,32d,72c,94a,138c,141a,160a), than (35b), then, thin (43b,c,148b), tien (147d), tion (158b), T-men (168b), toon (80c,95b,168c), torn (130a), town (73c), tran (7a), trin (169d), tron (140d,180a), Tsin (30b), tsun (30b), tuan (95d,147b,166c), turn (28d,131a,175a), twin (45c,171d)

TO - - toad (10a,17a,63d,126d), Toba (80c), tobe (7d,137b), toby (8c, 85c,104b), Toby (96b,125c), tock (7d,19b), toco (19b,167c), Toda (45d,76d), tode (80a,148a), todo (22b,24d,35b,64c,156b), tody (19b,d,59a,166a), toed, toff (40d), toga (132d,133a,b), togs (32c), togt (77c), toho (79a), toil (46c,184c), toko (30c), tola (48a,80d,180a), Tola (85b), told (129c), tole (9a,51a,99b,163a), toll (131c), tolt, tolu (16a), Toma (191), tomb, tome (21d,177c), tone (6c,118c,150d), tong (30a,c), tonk (173c), tony, Tony (96b), tooa (17c), took, tool (27c), toom (139b), toon (80c,95b,168c), toot, tope (24a,46b,57a,143c,151a), toph (75c), topi (37a,75a, 118c), tops (159c), tora (11a,44d,74a,75c,85c,90b,102d,115d), tore, tori (101b), torn (130a), toro (38a,107a,152a,168c), torp (54c), tort (31c,91a,185c), Tory (23c,36b,94c,172a), tosh (106a), Tosk (8c), toss (24a,132d), tota (71d), tote (27a,73c), toto (8d, 15a,34d,89a,181a), toty (87b), toug (171a), toup (95d), tour (31b,85c), tout (61a,127a), town (73c), towy (58b), toxa (153d)

- TO - atom (101c,114c,180d), aton (150a,159b), atop (112a,174a), Eton (33b,50c,84a), itol (158b), Otoe (147b), stoa (33c,121a,c), stod (40d,67d), stof (135c), stog (155a), stom (34c), stop (73b, 111b), stot (154d,155d,157d,179b,186a), stow (112b), utor (90a, 166c)

- - TO acto (152b), alto (152b,176c), auto (34d), bito (7d,57d,168c), Boto (192), Buto (142d), Cato (132d,133a), ceto (34a), cito (89d, 126c), coto (16c,90b), dato (95c,102c,117a), Doto (141b), ecto (34c,122d), ento (34b,d), into (123a,183b), jato (173b), koto (84b), Leto (11c), ioto (65a,121d,178d), moto (104b), Nato (6a, 8d), nito (55c), octo (34a,89b,122c), onto (76a,174a), otto (58d, 116b,134a), Otto (14c,66d,67a,96a), pato (46d), peto (57a,177b), Peto (76a), pito (9c,28b,83a), roto (30a,122d,127b,152c,171b), sito (34b), Tito (186c), toto (8d,15a,34d),89a,181a), Tyto (16c), unto (166c), veto (94a,124a), Veto, Voto (192)

T - - O tajo (152a,d), Tano (192), taro (13c,48c,49b,64b,112b,120a,133d, 155c,170a,c), taxo (13a), Teco (192), tiao, Tino (136d), tiro (9b, 17d,108c), Tito (186c), toco (19b,167c), todo (22b,24d,35b,64c, 156b), toho (79a), toko (30c), toro (38a,107a,152a,168c), toto (8d,15a,34d,89a,181a), trio (104d,165a,169c), tuno (28b,168c), typo (35c,51b,123d), tyro (9b,17d,108c), Tyto (16c)

T - - P tamp (46b,112b,121d,127d), tarp (26b,178d), terp (12b,123a), torp (54c), toup (95d), trap (27b,67b,132b,149b), trip (85c), trop (62d,167a), tryp (114a), tump (60a,76d,103d), turp, tymp (20c), typp (185b)

TR - - tram (170a), tran (7a), trap (27b,67b,132b,149b), tray (128c, 136d,142d,143c), tree (11d,37a,66a,184b), tref (172b), trek (85c,

369

93c,99d,168b), **tres** (19a,52b,63a,152d,165a,175c), **tret** (9a,178b, 179d), **trey** (26c,165a), **trig** (106a,148d,154b,169d), **trim** (40a, 106a,154b,160a,165c,169d), **trin** (169d), **trio** (104d,165a,169c), **trip** (85c), **tris** (122d), **trit** (34d,164c), **trod, tron** (140d,180a), **trop** (62d,167a), **trot** (85b,93d,112d), **trow** (18a,21a,159d,164c, 170b), **troy** (161c,180a), **Troy, true** (7a,8d,37b,54b,94c,149c), **tryp** (114a)

· TR · **Atri, atry** (141b), **etre** (61a,c,62d,166c)

· · TR **natr** (189)

T · · R **taar** (12b), **tahr** (68a,76d), **tair** (68a,76d), **tear** (67c,87b,130a), **teer** (25b,69d), **tehr** (27c,68a), **thar** (68a,76d), **Thor** (7c,68c,99c, 100c,109c,165b), **tiar** (39a,75a,121a), **tier** (118a,134b), **tour** (31b, 85c), **tsar** (42d,49d,60b,135c), **turr** (24d,105a), **tyer, Tyrr** (68c, 109c,163d,178a), **tzar** (42d,49d,60b,135c)

TS · · **tsar** (42d,49d,60b,135c), **tshi, Tshi** (69c), **tsia** (162c), **Tsin** (30b), **tsun** (30b)

· · TS **Acts, arts** (138c), **cits, eats, lots, orts** (60d), **rats**

T · · S **Taos** (192), **Tass** (107a,135d,151b), **Tees** (108a), **Teos** (82a), **Tess** (73d,164c,183d), **this** (42b,124b), **Thos** (84a,181c), **thus** (149c), **togs** (32c), **toss** (24a,132d), **tres** (19a,52b, 63a,152d,165a,175c), **tris** (122d)

· TT · **atta** (58d,90c,97d,160c,173d), **Atta** (94d,95d,100a,106b,117a), **Attu, Etta** (183c), **ette** (158a,c,d), **otto** (58d,116b,134a), **Otto** (14c,66d,67a,96a)

· · TT **batt** (37c), **bitt** (54d,175c), **bott** (32a,88d), **butt** (27a,77b,127d, 162a,182b), **Catt** (9d), **gett** (44d), **Lett** (16a,90a,93a), **Matt, mitt** (56c), **mutt** (39c,101d), **Natt** (107b), **nett, Nott** (107b), **Pitt** (50d,155d), **pott** (113d), **putt** (69d), **sett** (115a,156d), **tatt** (87c), **watt** (173b,177c), **Watt** (82a)

T · · T **tact** (43c,d,116a), **Taft** (29d), **tait** (14d), **takt** (105a,163a), **tart** (114d), **tatt** (87c), **taut** (163b,165c), **tent** (26b,115a), **test** (26a, 51c,144a,169c,170c), **text** (21c,140d), **that** (42b,124b,129c), **tilt** (26b,d,166a), **tint** (33c,d,114d), **todt** (66b), **tolt, toot, tort** (31c, 91a,185c), **tout** (61a,127a), **tret** (9a,178b,179d), **trit** (34d,164c), **trot** (85b,93d,112d), **tuft** (24b,32d,38c), **twit** (162b,c)

TU · · **tuan** (95d,147b,166c), **tuba** (105a,137d), **tube** (118b,158a), **tuck** (156b), **tuel, tufa** (121b,177a), **tuff** (121b,177a), **tuft** (24b,32d, 38c), **tuke** (26b,53b), **tula** (9a), **Tula, tule** (24b,27c), **Tulu** (45d), **tump** (60a,76d,103d), **tuna** 57a,b,123b,170d), **tund** (121d), **tune** (8b,12c,98c), **tung** (110a,168c), **tuno** (28b,168c), **tunu** (28b), **tuny, Tupi** (192), **turf** (115c,149d,160b), **Turi** (191), **Turk** (101d, 102d,160a,111d), **turm** (132d), **turn** (28d,131a,175a), **turp, turr** (24d,105a), **tush** (167b), **tusk** (167b), **tute** (171b), **tutu** (16a, 106d,147d), **tuwi** (117a,168c), **tuza** (119d)

· TU · **atua** (120d), **Atum** (143a,159b), **etui** (27a,29b,62c,106b,148d, 166d,174b), **Otus** (67a), **stub** (156c), **stud** (22b,25a,42d,54d, 111c,143a,174a), **stum** (70c,105c,131a,173a), **stun** (145a,157d), **Utug** (159b), **utum** (19b,112c)

· · TU **actu** (7a,89a), **Attu, datu** (95c,102c,117a), **Ketu** (48b), **latu** (190), **mitu** (39d), **patu** (179b), **tatu** (12d), **Tatu, tutu** (16a,106d, 147d), **yutu** (19b,166a)

T - - U	tabu (59d,111d), Taku (80c), tapu, tatu (12d), Tatu, tchu, teju (151b), thou (124b), Tibu (191), Tiou (192), tolu (16a), Tulu (45d), tunu (28b), tutu (16a,106d,147d)
TW - -	twee, twig, twin (45c,171d), twit (162b,c)
T - - W	thaw, thew (104c), trow (18a,21a,159d,164c,170b)
TY - -	Tybi (102a), tyee (29d), tyer, tyke (29d), tymp (20c), tyne, Tyne (108a), type (31d,115a,155a), typo (35c,51b,123d), typp (185b), typy, tyre (15a), Tyre (31b,90d,117b), tyro (9b,17d,108c), Tyrr (68c,109c,163d,178a), Tyto (16c)
- TY -	etym (133d), itys (163b), Styx (29b,73a,105c)
- - TY	arty, city, Coty (63c), doty (43d), duty (109b,162b), Katy (183d), maty (80c), mity, pity (35b), toty (87b)
T - - Y	taky, Tavy (183d), they (124b), tidy (106a,111b), tiny (100c, 148c), toby (8c,85c,104b), Toby (96b,125c), tody (19b,d,59a, 166a), tony, Tony (96b), tory, Tory (23c,36b,94c,172a), toty (87b), towy (58b), tray (128c,136d,142d,143c), trey (26c,165a), troy (161c,180a), Troy, tuny, typy
TZ - -	tzar (42d,49d,60b,135c)
- TZ -	itza (192)
- - TZ	batz (190), litz (127b), untz (189)
UA - -	uang (131a)
- UA -	bual (182c), duab (157c), duad (171d), dual (45c,171d), duan (64b), duar, Duat (172d), Fuad (54d), Guam, guan (151b), guao (168c,169b), guar (46c,59d), juan (113a), Juan (96a), juar (100a), kuan (30b), Kuan (30c), Kuar (102a), Muav (66a), quad (33c,172a), quae (176b), quag (21c,102c), quai (88b,117c,180c), quan (190), quas (135c), quay (88b,117c,180c), ruay (189), tuan (95d,147b,166c), yuan (190), Yuan (30b,101d)
- - UA	aqua (152d,166c,178c), akua (120d), aqua (90a,178c), atua (120d), Erua (103c), skua (19b,72c,84a,141a), ulua (57a,74c), Ulua (141b)
U - - A	ueba (188), ulna (21d,39b), ulua (57a,74c), Ulua (141b), Ulva (141b), unca (49a), upia, Urfa (99a), Uria (14c,16d), urna (133a), Ursa (17b,36b,43d), urva (38b), Usha (16a,150c), uvea (53c,82b),
UB - -	uber (66b), Ubil (191)
- UB -	buba (170a), Bube (180b), Bubi (180b), Bubo (112c), cuba (189), Cuba (180b), cube (66b,150a), cubi (188), dubb (161c), hubb (118b), juba (106b), jube (28d), kuba (26d,189), Luba (191), lube (110a), Lubs (94c), Nuba (108c), nubk (30d,164d), rube (37d, 135d,185d), Rube (96b), ruby (20a,65d,179c), tuba (105a,137d), tube (118b,158a)
- - UB	blub, chub (40c,154c), club (39c), daub (148d), doub (189), drub (17b,39c), flub (22b), gaub (116c), glub (43c,88d), grub (43c,88d), knub (178b), slub (171c), snub (128c,148b), stub (156c)
- UC -	Auca (192), buck, cuca (33a,105d), duce (29d), duck (26b,53b, 179c), Duco, duct (170c), fuci (132c), huck (167d), juca (27a), juck (114c), luce (58c,117d), Luce (7b,35a), luck (28d), lucy, Lucy (183c), much, muck, ouch!, puca (68a), puce (33c,d,52a),

371

puck (44b,68a,77c,100c), Puck (99d,143b), ruck (39a,185a), such (146d), suck, tuck (156b), yuca (27a)

- - UC douc (101d), eruc (37a,56a)

U - - C Udic (108a), Utac (22d)

UD - - udad (143d,144a,181c), udal (76b,88b,131c), Udic (108a)

- UD - Aude, buda (83d), Buda, dude (40d), duds (32c,166d), Juda, Jude (11c,96a), judo (84b,85c,142b), Judy (125c,183d), kudu (11a), Ludd (23c), ludi (133b), ludo (65a,112b), mudd (188), nuda (39b), Nudd (23c), nude (16c,172d), pudu (41d), rudd (26d, 57a,b), rude (134b,172b), sudd (40b,58c,107b), suds (59a), wudu (102d)

- - UD baud (162d), Chud (191), feud (55d,126b,175b), foud (54d,144b), gaud (169d), laud (122a), loud (156a), maud (53d,71a,136d, 143c), Maud (181a,183c), Phud (110b), puud (189), roud (57a, b), scud (32c,126c,135b,160c), spud (121d,151c), stud (22b, 25a,42d,54d,111c,143a,174a), syud (103b), thud

U - - D udad (143d,144a,181c), used (6d,73a), uvid (101a)

UE - - ueba (188)

- UE - Auer (79a), duel, duet (104d,171d), euer (66d), fuel (65c), hued, juez (152b), kuel (44a), quei (189), ruer, suer (124d), suet (54d), tuel

- - UE ague (30a,55d,95c), blue (33c,98c,102c,150d,173a), clue, flue (8b,30a), gaue (67a), glue (7b,156a), moue (61d,62b), neue (66c), Niue (137d), roue (41b,44c,127c,134b), slue (97b,148b, 160a), true (7a,8d,37b,54b,94c,149c)

U - - E ulme (49c), unde (179a), unie (173a), unze (189), urde (86b), urge (42d,46b,79d,80a,b,81c,150a), usee

- UF - buff (134c,161d), Bufo (166c), cuff (148a), duff (125b), Dufy (63a), gufa (21b,99a), guff, huff (58a), kufa (21b,99a), luff (136b), muff, puff, (180d), ruff (19b,33b,63d,137a), sufi (103a, 116c), tufa (121b,177a), tuff (121b,177a), tuft (24b,32d,38c), yuft (135c)

- - UF pouf, souf (146b)

UG - - ugly

- UG - auge (123c,132b), Bugi (191), euge (180a), fuga, fugu (84b), gugu, huge, Hugh (96a), Hugo (63a,96a), juga (27a), kuge (84c), luge (148a), Lugh (28b), muga, ough, pugh, ruga (59b,185a), sugi (84b), vugg (28a,66a,132b), vugh (28a,66a,132b), Yuga (76d)

- - UG chug (53a), drug (105d), glug, joug (138d), plug (156d,184d), slug (46b,99b,157c), smug (35a,38b,165c), Snug (99d), thug (65a), toug (171a), Utug (159b)

U - - G uang (131a), Utug (159b)

- UH - buhl (81a), buhr (180d), Duhr (155b), Guha (191), guhr (47d), kuhl (53c), Ruhr

- - UH bruh (95a)

U - - H umph, Urth (68d,107d,163d), Utah (180b)

- UI - cuif (139a,d,140c), cuir (45c,62a), duim (188), duit (190), Duit (192), guib (11a), huia (19a,106d), luif, Muir (8b,142c), nuit

372

    (62b), **quid** (39b,166d), **quip** (183a,b), **quit** (90d,130c), **quiz**, **ruin** (42d), **suit** (38a,58a,91a,112a,119c,137c), **Yuit** (51c)

- - **UI**   **arui** (11b,143d,144a,181c), **equi** (122d), **etui** (27a,29b,62c,106b, 148d,166d,174b), **Maui** (120d)

U - - I   **Ubii** (191), **unci** (31d)

- **UJ** -   **fuji** (84b), **Fuji** (84d), **juju** (29b,55d), **puja** (77a), **suji** (180c)

- **UK** -   **bukh** (122a), **bukk** (122a), **cuke** (39b), **duke** (107c), **duku** (95d, 168c), **juke** (114c), **Kuki** (191), **kuku** (19a,106d), **luke**, **Luke** (52a,96a), **puka** (107a,168c), **puku** (11a), **rukh** (53b,54a), **Suku** (191), **tuke** (26b,53b), **wukf** (103a)

- - **UK**   **cauk** (139b), **dauk** (95c), **Sauk** (192), **souk** (22a,97a)

UL - -   **Ulam** (67b), **ulan** (27d,88a), **Ulex** (153c), **ullo** (6a,144a), **Ullr** (146b,164d), **ulme** (49c), **ulna** (21d,39b), **ulua** (57a,74c), **Ulua** (141b), **Ulva** (141b)

- **UL** -   **aula** (66c,73b), **aulu** (74c,168c), **bulb** (37a,172c), **bulk** (97b), **bull** (113c), **bult** (76d), **cull** (117c), **culm** (11a,32d,70d,145a, 156a), **cult** (141d,161c), **dull** (21a,32c,173a), **Dull** (94b), **fulk** (173a), **full** (7b,130b), **gula** (90a,101a,165b), **gulf** (6c), **gull** (32d, 41c,42a,72c,99b,141a), **Gulo** (183c), **gulp** (46a,79d,160a), **hula** (74b), **hule** (23a,134c), **hulk** (144d,173d), **hull** (141d,142a,144c, d), **hulu** (55b), **Jula**, **Jule** (183d), **July**, **kula** (189), **kuli** (27b), **lull** (25c,126d,150c), **lulu** (19a,57b,112c), **Lulu** (183d), **mule** (45b, 148b,153c,180b), **mulk** (60d), **mull** (53b,135a,164c), **null** (108c, 177a), **pule** (180d), **pulk** (37c,88d), **pull** (45a,78d), **pull** (45d, 167d), **pulp**, **pulu** (74c), **puly**, **rule** (11b,26b,90b), **rull** (170b), **Sula** (65a), **suld** (188), **sulk** (159a), **Sulu** (102c), **tula** (9a), **Tula**, **tule** (24b,27c), **Tulu** (45d), **vuln** (184d), **Yule** (30d), **zulu** (171d, 175d), **Zulu** (86a)

- - **UL**   **Aoul** (191), **azul** (151d), **baul** (18b), **caul** (16d,74d), **deul** (77b), **Elul** (102b), **foul** (173a), **Gaul** (10a,60d,63c), **goul** (102a), **haul** (27b,45d), **maul** (73c,96b), **paul**, **Paul** (96a), **poul** (190), **saul** (48a,168c), **Saul** (18c,86d,115a), **shul** (161a), **soul** (10d,125a, 153c,176d)

U - - L   **udal** (76b,88b,131c), **unal** (147a), **Ural** (135c), **uval** (70c)

UM - -   **umbo** (22b), **umph**

- **UM** -   **bump**, **Duma** (135c), **dumb** (153b), **dump**, **fume** (129a,149a, 157a), **fumy**, **Gump** (43b), **Hume** (50c), **hump** (124d), **jump**, **lump** (45a,160c), **mump** (29b,153d), **Numa** (133a), **numb**, **puma** (27b,37c,55b,103d), **Pume** (137b,175b,185b), **pump**, **rumb** (120 b), **rump**, **Sumo**, **sump** (28c,45d), **tump** (60a,76d,103d), **Yuma**

- - **UM**   **ahum**, **alum** (14a,45c), **arum** (13a,39b,58d,92b,155c), **Arum** (66a), **Atum** (143a,159b, **Baum** (9c,112c), **chum** (38d), **doum** (168c), **drum** (105a), **Geum** (76b), **glum** (102c,159a), **grum** (102c), **jhum**, **meum** (27a,89c), **Meum** (168c,180a), **odum** (168c,180a), **ogum** (82b), **ovum** (48d), **plum**, **rhum** (8c), **saum** (189), **scum** (129b), **slum**, **stum** (70c,105c,131a,173a), **swum**, **Ulam** (67b), **utum** (19b,112c)

U - - M   **urim** (18d,23a,110a), **utum** (19b,112c)

UN - -   **unal** (147a), **unau** (148c,171d), **unca** (49a), **unci** (31d), **unco** (140c), **unde** (179a), **undo** (11a,93d), **undy** (179a), **unie** (173a),

373

Unio (105c), unis (91b), unit (101c,110c,147a), unto (166c), untz (189), unze (189)

- UN - aune (188), aunt (129c), buna (161c), bund (49c,66c,90c), bung (119d,156d), bunk, bunn (25b), bunt (15d,180c), Cuna (193), dune (137a), dunk (43c,79d), Duns, dunt, fund (6d,101c,130c), Fung (191), Funj, funk (63d,113c), guna (106a,137b), gunj (70c), hung, hunh?, hunk, hunt (141c), June (183c), Jung (125a), junk (30a,134c), Juno (69c,85d,100c,126b), kung (125b), kunk (188), luna (103c), Luna (102b), lune (38c,73b,74d), lung, luny (38b), mund (124d), mung (70d), munj (70d), paun (18b), puna (10b, 33b,104a,119b,182a), pund (189), pung (22c,148b), punk (9b, 166a,167c), puno (182a), punt (21a,58b), puny (55b,179a), Qung (191), rune (9b,67a,94a,105c,107d,120a,141d,163d), rung (28c,39a), runt (47a,172d), sung, Sung (30b), sunk (56a), sunn (56a), tuna (57a,b,123b,170d), tund (121d), tune (8b,12c,98c), tung (110a,168c), tuno (28b,168c), tunu (28b), tuny, Yunx (184a), Zuni (125b)

· · UN Amun (86d,127d,159b,164a), Chun (30c), drun (132b), faun (56a,68b,137c,161a,184a), Idun (107d), jaun (113a), kaun (93d), laun (146b), loun (19a,b), maun (139d), noun (114b,158a), paun (18b), shun (15a,51b,52a), spun, stun (145a,157d), taun (188), tsun (30b), Usun (191), whun (64c,70a)

U · · N ulan (27d,88a), upon (6b), uran (101d), Usun (191), uzan (189)

- UO - buoy (28d,58c), quod (123d)

U · · O ullo (6a,144a), umbo (22b), unco (140c), undo (11a,93d), Unio (105c), unto (166c), upgo (13c)

UP · · upas (84d,120b,168c,d), upgo (13c), Upis (13b), upia, upon (6b)

- UP - dupe (27c,41c,72c,160c), Hupa (192), jupe (62b,84a), lupe (19a, 64a), Nupe (191), pupa (30d,81b,c), rupa (60b), supa (168c), supe (53a,154d), Tupi (192)

· · UP blup, caup, coup (20d,97c,157b,c,162d), gaup, loup (61d,62a, 90c,139d), Loup (193), noup (124b), plup, roup (44a,121d), scup (57a,121b), snup (149b), soup, toup (95d), yaup, youp (185d)

UR · · Ural (135c), uran (101d), urde (86b), Urdu (77b), urdy (86b), Urey (17b,36b,43d), Urth (68d,107d,163d), urus (14d,53a,112c), urva (150a), Uria (14c,16d), urim (18d,23a,110a), urna (133a), Ursa (17b,36b,43d), Urth (68d,107d,163d), urus (14d,53a,112c), urva (38b)

- UR - aura (44c,49c,66a,96b,158a,170d,177c), auri (34a), bura (182b), bure (61b), burg (22b,73c), buri (56b), burl (87c,169a), burn, burr (123c), bury (81d), cura (152c), curb (130c,146b), curd (99d), cure (123b), curl (38d,73b,131d), curr (104c), curt (145b, c), dura (153c), duro (190), durr (70b), furl (132d), fury (157a), guru (77b), hura (20a,137a), Hura, hurl (167c), hurt, jura, Jura, jure (90b), jury (38a), Kurd (48b,82a), Kure (84c), Kuri (191), kurk (31a,139b), lura (22d,82a), lure (41c,51a,54b,163a), lurg (96d,141b,184d), Lurl (191), lurk (92a,147d), mura (84d), Mura (192), mure (177d), murk (41a,67d), murr (72b,128b), nurl (33b, 87c), nurr (67d), ours (124c), pure (29b,172b,173c), puri (80d), purl (87c,104c), purr (104c), Puru (192), ruru (19b,102a,106d), sura (87c,113b,166d), surd (82c,177a), sure (173d), surf (23a),

374

turf (115c,149d,160b), Turl (191), Turk (101d,102d,106a,111d), turm (132d), turn (28d,131a,175a), turp, turr (24d,105a), Wurd, wurm (67c), yurt (101d)

· · UR Alur (191), Asur (68c), blur (35a), blur, caur (139a), Daur (139b), dour (67d,159a), ebur (89c), four (26c), gaur (112c, 181c), gour (112c,181c), hour, knur (67d,87c,107c), lour (13d, 63d), peur (61c), pour (162d), scur (78b), slur (44b,124c,148b, 168a), smur (32c,46b,100c), sour, spur (10d,67d,167d,168a, 181b), tour (31b,85c), your (124c)

U · · R uber (66b), Uilr (146b,164d), usar (8d,16c), user (49d), utor (90a,166c)

US · · usar (8d,16c), Usas (68d), used (6d,73a), usee, user (49d), uses (18a), Usha (16a,150c), Usun (191)

· US · Ausa, ausu (168c,180b), bush, busk (17b,37b,55d,161b), buss (87a,148c), bust, busy, cush (101c), Cush (51d,73c), cusk (57b), cusp (38c,78b,119a,120a,b), cuss, duse (83c), dusk (171c), dust, fuse (98c), fuss (22b,35b), fust (105c,143b), gush (35a,154c), gust, huse (180c), hush (17b,146c), husk (53a,78d,142a), huso (180c), just (51b,54b), kusa, Kush (73c), lush (94d), lust (41b), Musa (16a), muse (65b,93d,120d,164c), Muse (68d), mush (97d), musk (116b), Muso (192), muss (135b,173d), must (70c,101a, 106d,157d,182c), Ouse (132a,185d), oust (44c,49a,52b,125d), push, (145c), puss, rusa, Rusa (41d,136d), ruse (13b,77c,157b, 169c), rush, rusk (23a), Russ (135b), rust (37b,112c,119a), Susa (49a), susl (53b,d), susu (20c), Susu (191), Susy (183d), tush (167b), tusk (167b)

· · US acus (89d,118a), Apus (36b,c), avus (89b), cous (38a), crus (91a,143c), deus (68a,89b), Esus, gaus (67a), Grus (36b,c,38b), Ilus (88d,170b), Irus (109d), nous (81d,100a,128b), onus (24c, 93b,109b), opus (35c,105a,184c), Otus (67a), Pius (121a), plus (10b,102c), pous (188), Rhus (159a), sous (62d,172c), thus (149c), urus (14d,53a,112c), Zeus (135a)

U · · S unis (91b), upas (84d,120b,168c,d), Upis (13b), urus (14d,53a, 112c), uses (18a), Usas (68d), utas (49a,109c)

UT · · utac (22d), Utah (180b), utas (49a,109c), utor (90a,166c), Utug (159b), utum (19b,112c)

· UT · auto (34d), Buto (142d), butt (27a,77b,127d,162a,182b), cute (39c), duty (109b,162b), fute (51c), Guti, Jute (37a,48a,56a, 133d,136a), jute, lute (11c,28b,84d,105a,131d), muta (28d, 103a), mute (146c,153b), muth (188), mutt (39c,101d), putt (69d), Ruta (76b,134d), rute (188), ruth (35b,118c), Ruth (105b, 183c), tute (171b), tutu (16a,106d,147d), yutu (19b,166a)

· · UT abut (22a,167c), bhut (67a), blut (66b), bout (36c), brut (182c), Brut (23c), chutl, Cnut (40d,50c), gaut (88b,103d,132a), glut (52c,70a,137c,159d), gout, knut, Knut (40d,50c,96a), lout (15c, 22a,24b,45b,109a,157d), naut (141b), paut (140a), phut (24b), Phut (110b), pout (159a), prutl, Prut (41a), rout (41d,44b,46b), scut (145c,161b), shut, smut (32d,44a,119a,150c), sput (21c), taut (163b,165c), tout (61a,127a)

U · · T unit (101c,110c,147a)

· UU · puud (189)

375

U - - U   unau (148c,171d), Urdu (77b)

UV - -   uval (70c), uvea (53c,82b), uvic (70c), uvid (101a)

- UV -   cuvy (141a)

- UW -   tuwi (117a,168c)

- - UW   bouw (188), dauw (24c)

- UX -   buxy (115b), luxe (61c,62d,159c), puxy

- - UX   crux (39a,151b), eaux (178c), flux (28d,58d), jeux (61d), Vaux (63b)

U - - X   Ulex (153c)

- UY -   buyo (18b), cuya (39b), Puya (118b)

U - - Y   ugly, undy (179a), urdy (86b), Urey (14b,107c,138c)

UZ - -   uzan (189)

- UZ -   auzu (168c,180b), buzz, fuze (98c), fuzz (45d), guze (128d), huzz, Juza (155b), Muzo (192), tuza (119d), wuzu (102d), zuza (189)

- - UZ   Ghuz (171a)

U - - Z   untz (189)

VA - -   Vach (153b), vade (42c,67d,89b), vagi (38b), vail (94b,124a, 174b), vain (81a), vair (64c,154c), vale (54c,128a,174b), Vale (7c,109c), vali (171a,176a), Vali (7c,109c), vamp (80a,145a), vane (179b,182a), vang (72d,134a,140b), Vans (107d), vara (151d), vare (179b), vari (34d,91b,134d,174d), vary (28d,43c), vasa (46d,114a,160b,175d), Vasa, vase, vast (78d,79d), vasu (106c), Vasu (176d), Vaux (63b), Vayu (68c,182a), vaza (114a)

- VA -   aval (70c), Avar (27d,108a), Evan (96a), ivah (18d), ivan (40c, 85b,96a), kvas (135c), oval (48d,49c,127a), Svan (27d), uval (70c)

- - VA   Alva (151d), cava (116a,175b), Civa (56d), deva (23d,42a,42b, 56d,77a), diva (100d,123c), Hova (95a), Java (33a), jiva (77a), Jova (193), kava (18c,116a), kiva (28c,125b), lava (101c,151a, 177a), Neva (91b,132a), nova (20c,106d,155c,174d), peva (12d), siva (67a), Siva (56d,77a), Ulva (141b), urva (38b), viva (93d), Xova (193), yava

V - - A   vara (151d), vasa (46d,114a,160b,175d), Vasa, vaza (114a), Veda (77a,b), vega (110d,152c), Vega (155b), vela (98c,136b, 149d), Vela (36b,c), vena (90a,175a), vera (140c,151b,175c), Vera (183c), veta (104a), Vida (183c), vila (54b), vina (77a, 105a), Vira (191), visa (114d), vita (89c,92a), viva (93d), vola (89d,150a), vota (133b)

V - - B   verb (7a,114b,184b)

- - VD   NKVD (135d)

V - - D   veld (151a), vend (97a,115c,142b), Vend (10b,148a), verd (71d), void (11a,49d,108d,174b)

VE - -   veal, Veda (77a,b), veer (28d,144c,171b), vega (110d,152c), Vega (155b), veil (74d,76c), vein (20d,157b), vela (98c,136b, 149d), Vela (36b,c), veld (151a), velo (175b), vena (90a,175a), vend (97a,115c,142b), Vend (10b,148a), vent (8b,11b,110d, 112a), Veps (191), vera (140c,151b,175c), Vera (183c), verb

376

(7a,114b,184b), **verd** (71d), **veri** (28b), **vert** (71d,166a,171b), **very** (149c), **vest** (32c,177b), **veta** (104a), **veto** (94a,124a), **Veto**

- **VE** - **avec** (63a,183a), **aver** (7c,14a,15c,41c,95c,140d,155c,160b,184c), **Aves** (19d), **evea** (82a,95a), **even** (51a,58b,79d,91d,149a,173a), **ever** (9b,14b,80b), **evet** (48d,107a,136c,169d), **Ives** (9c,90b), **oven** (15d,78c,86b), **over** (6b,38c,80a,114d,130a), **uvea** (53c,82b)

- - **VE** **bave** (61d,146c), **cave** (27d), **cive** (110c), **cove** (17a,73d,107d), **Dave** (96b), **dive** (42b,74b,119d), **dove** (19a,117d), **eave** (133c), **five**, **gave**, **give** (79d,123a), **gyve** (55d,143b), **have** (92a), **hive** (17c), **hove** (92a), **Jave** (84d), **jive** (160c), **jove** (85d), **kive** (174d), **lave** (16d,178b), **leve** (62a), **live** (47c), **love** (163a), **move**, **nave** (30d,31a,78d,114b,180c), **neve** (56d,67c,70c,149b), **nove** (83b), **pave** (85a), **rave** (41c,157a,161d), **reve** (61c,104d), **rive** (32a,153d), **rove** (127d,132b,178a), **save** (52b,110c,123a,173c), **seve** (63a,182c), **sive** (146a), **Tave** (183d), **vive** (93d), **wave** (19a,59a,111c,131d,160c,172d), **wive** (97a), **wove**

V - - **E** **vade** (42c,67d,89b), **vale** (54c,128a,174b), **Vale** (7c,109c), **vane** (179b,182a), **vare** (179b), **vase** (31d,158a), **vice** (31d,158a), **vide** (89d,126a, 142a), **vile** (16c,56c), **vine** (32b), **vire** (11a,13b), **vise** (31d,77d, 114d), **vite** (62b), **vive** (93d), **voce** (83c,177a), **vole** (97d,104a, 148a,149b), **vote** (60b), **Vote** (56d)

- - **G** **vang** (72d,134a,140b), **voog** (28a,66a,132b), **vugg** (28a,66a, 132b)

- - **VH** **IHVH** (159d), **JHVH** (159d), **YHVH** (159d)

V - - **H** **Vach** (153b), **Voth** (191), **vugh** (28a,66a,132b)

VI - - **vial** (148c), **vice** (31d,158a), **Vida** (183c), **vide** (89d,126a,142a), **vier** (66c), **view** (93d,138b), **vila** (54b), **vile** (16c,56c), **vili** (54b), **Vili** (109c), **vill** (176b), **vily** (54b), **vina** (77a,105a), **vine** (32b), **vino** (92d,182b), **vint** (26c,182c), **viny**, **viol** (105a), **Vira** (191), **vire** (11a,13b), **visa** (114d), **vise** (31d,77d,114d), **viss** (189), **vita** (89c,92a), **vite** (62b), **viti** (176b), **viva** (93d), **vive** (93d), **vivo** (93a)

- **VI** - **avid** (47b,71a,186b), **avis** (89a), **Avis** (183c), **evil** (79c,95d,147a, 181a,185c), **Ovid** (132d,133b), **Ovis** (143d), **uvic** (70c), **uvid** (101a)

- - **VI** **Devi** (147b,153b), **divi**, **favi** (138a,165d), **hevi** (111d), **Kavi** (84d), **Levi** (84a,90c), **ravi** (61b), **Ravi** (16b)

V - - **I** **vagi** (38b), **vali** (171a,176a), **Vali** (7c,109c), **vari** (34d,91b,134d, 174d), **veri** (28b), **vili** (54b), **Vili** (109c), **viti** (176b), **vlei** (38c, 160a)

V - - **K** **volk** (66c,105d,116a,184c)

VL - - **vlei** (38c,160a), **vley** (160a)

V - - **L** **vail** (94b,124a,174b), **veal**, **vell**, (74d,76c), **vial** (148c), **vill** (176b), **viol** (105a)

V - - **N** **vain** (81a), **vein** (20d,157b), **vuln** (184d)

VO - - **voce** (83c,177a), **voet** (188), **Vogt**, **void** (11a,49d,108d,174b), **vola** (89d,150a), **vole** (97d,104a,148a,149b), **volk** (66c,105d,116a, 184c), **volt** (49b,78c,173b), **voog** (28a,66a,132b), **vota** (133b), **vote** (60b), **Vote** (56d), **Voth** (191), **Voto** (192)

- **VO** - **Avon** (143b), **Avow** (6d,36a,41c,112c), **evoe** (15b,130d,181c)

377

- - **VO**   levo (91a), pavo (115b), Pavo (36b,c), vivo (93a)

V - - O   velo (175b), veto (94,124a), Veto, vino (92d,182b), vivo (93a), Voto (192)

V - - P   vamp (80a,145a)

V - - R   vair (64c,154c), veer (28d,144c,171b), vier (66c)

- - **VS**   revs (131a)

V - - S   Vans (107d), Veps (191), viss (189)

V - - T   vast (78d,79d), vent (8b,11b,110d,112a), vert (71d,166a,171b), vest (32c,177b), vint (26c,182c), voet (188), Vogt, voit (49b,78c, 173b)

VU - -   vugg (28a,66a,132b), vugh (28a,66a,132b), vuln (184d)

- **VU -**   avus (89b), ovum (48d)

- - **VU**   kivu (170c)

V - - U   vasu (106c), Vasu (176d), Vayu (68c,182a)

V - - W   view (93d,138b)

V - - X   Vaux (63b)

- - **VY**   bevy (38a,58c), cavy (72b,120d,132c,157b), cuvy (141a), Davy (96b,136b), envy (41b), levy (14a,162b), Livy (132d,133a), navy (33c,58b), pavy (115b), pevy (91d,94c), Tavy (183d), wavy (147b,172d)

V - - Y   vary (28d,43c), very (149c), vily (54b), viny, vley (160a)

WA - -   Waac, waag (71d,101d), Wabi (192), Waco, wadd (109c), wade, wadi (46c,106a,109a,128a,132a), wady (109a,128a,132a), waeg (19b,72c,87a), waer (40b), Wafd (49a), waft (20d,58c), wage (27a,115b), walf (157b), wall (39b,88a), wain (177b), Wain, wait (26d,42b,92c,155d,162a), waka (26a), wake (134b,168a), wakf (103a), waky, wale (70b,131b,157c,163d,179a,180a,c,d), wali (171a), walk, wall, Walt (96b), wand (120b,132c,156a), wane (41c,43c), wang (189), want (41b,42d,87b,106b,122a), wany, wapp (54b,133d,145d), waqf (103a), ward (31c,55c,86b), ware (27d,35a), warf, warm (7c,75b,163b), warn (7b), warp (36c,165a, 171c), wart (124d), wary (27d,176b), wash, wasp, wast, Wate (141a), watt (173b,177c), Watt (82a), wave (19a,59a,111c,131d, 160c,172d), wavy (147b,172d), waxy (119c,149d), ways

- **WA -**   Awan (191), away (6b,69d,76a,109d,111d), Ewan, kwan (30b), swab (102b), swad (94d), swag (22a,156c), swam, swan (19b, 33a), swap (168a), swat (15d,20d,32d,157c), Swat (103a), sway (104a)

- - **WA**   biwa (93d,168c), dewa, Iowa (193), kawa (18c,116a), Iowa (19a), pawa (189), tawa (160d,168c), Tewa (193)

W - - A   waka (26a), Wega (155b), weka (58c,106d,107a,127b), weta (93c), whoa (156d)

W - - C   Waac

- - **WD**   dowd (143b), gawd (169c)

W - - D   wadd (109c), Wafd (49a), wand (120b,132c,156a), ward (31c, 55c,86b), week, weld (47c,85b,173c), wend (67d,123d), Wend (10b,148a), wild (38b,173d), wind (33b,39d,171c,185a), woad (20d,47c), wold (47c,60a,118d,174a,184d), wood, word (124b, 165c), Wurd, Wyrd (107d)

378

WE - -   weak (55b), weal (124d,157c,180c,d), wean (8d,42d), wear (50b),
          weed, week, weel (16d,57d,140d,180d), weep (39b,88a,104a),
          weet (19d), weft (39a,165a,184b), Wega (155b), Wegg (111d),
          weir (40b,57d), weka (58c,106d,107a,127b), weki (55c), weld
          (47c,85b,173c), Welf (67a), welk (65c,96d,141b), well, welt (36d,
          131b,145a,b,177b,d), wend (67d,123d), Wend (10b,148a), went
          (42c), wept, were (139b), werf (54d), weri (15c,27c), wert, west,
          West (9c,50b,109d), weta (93c)

- WE -   ewer (84d,85c,118c,181b), kwei (44a), Owen (96a,183c), sweb
          (160d), twee

- - WE   howe (77d), Howe (17a,82a), powe

W - - E   wade, wage (27a,115b), wake (134b,168a), wale (70b,131b,157c,
          163d,179a,180a,c,d), wane (41c,43c), ware (27d,35a), Wate
          (141a), wave (19a,59a,111c,131d,160c,172d), were (139b), whee,
          wide (133d), wife (154a), wile (13b,41c,157b,169c), wine, wipe,
          wire, wise (136b), wive (97a), woke, wore, Wote (191), wove

W - - F   waif (157b), wakf (103a), waqf (103a), warf, Welf (67a), werf
          (54d), wolf, woof (39a,163d,165a,179d), Wraf, wukf (103a)

W - - G   waag (71d,101d), waeg (19b,72c,87a), wang (189), Wegg (111d),
          Whig, wigg, wing (10d,58c,59a,118b,d), wong (56a)

WH - -   wham (157c), what (129c), whau (107a,168c), wheel, when
          (180d), whet (143c,156b), whew, whey (100a), Whig, whim (26c,
          54c,108c), whin (64c,70a,132b,181d), whip (58c,88d), whir (25c,
          181a), whit (166c), whiz (25c), whoa (156d), whom (42b), whool,
          whun (64c,70a), whyo (59d,65a)

- - WH   JHWH (159d), YHWH (159c)

W - - H   wash, wish (42d), with (10b)

WI - -   wick, wide (133d), widu (102d), wiel (140d,180d), wies (185a),
          wife (154a), wigg, wild (38b,173d), wile (13b,41c,157b,169c),
          wilk (65c,96d,141b), will (18b,43a,163c,177c), wilt (46b), wily
          (13b,38b,39c), wind (33b,39d,171c,185a), wine, wing (10d,58c,
          59a,118b,d), wink (107a), winy (176c), wipe, wire, wiry (147a,
          167c), wise (136b), wish (42d), wisp (24b,148c), wist (87c),
          with (10b), wive (97a)

- WI -   swig (46a,72c), swim (58c), swiz (160c), twig, twin (45c,171d),
          twit (162b,c)

- - WI   liwi (19a,74b), Kawi (84d), kiwi (11d,19a,58c), tuwi (117a,168c)

W - - I   Wabi (192), wadi (46c,106a,109a,128a,132a), wall (171a), weki
          (55c), weri (15c,27c)

- - WK   bowk (155d), cawk (133c), dawk (95c), gawk (146d), gowk
          (146d), hawk (19c,115a), sawk (188)

W - - K   walk (55b), weak (55b), week, welk (65c,96d,141b), wick, wilk (65c,
          96d,141b), wink (107a), work (64c,76b)

- - WL   bawl, bowl, cowl (101d), dowl, fowl, gowl (102a,140d,185b),
          howl (39b), jowl (29b), mewl (180d), pawl (43a,95a), yawl (136b,
          171d,175d), yowl

W - - L   wail (39b,88a), wall, weal (124d,157c,180c,d), weel (16d,57d,
          140d,180d), well, wiel (140d,180d), will (18b,43a,163c,177c),
          wool (58b,179c)

379

- - WM dawm (190)
W - - M warm (7c,75b,163b), wham (157c), whim (26c,54c,108c), whom (42b), worm, wurm (67c)
- - WN bawn (181a), dawn (14d,41b), down (149d), fawn (33c), gown, hewn, kawn (93d), lawn (20a,37c,53b,92c), lown (157d), mown, pawn (29c,119c), sawn, sewn, town (73c), yawn
W - - N wain (177b), Wain, warn (7b), wean (8d,42d), when (180d), whin (64c,70a,132b,181d), whun (64c,70a), woon (24c), worn (143b), wren (19b,c), Wren (50b), wynn (165d)
WO - - woad (20d,47c), woke, wold (47c,60a,118d,174a,184a), wolf, wong (56a), wont (6d,40a,73a,174c), wood, woof (39a,163d,165a, 179d), wool (58b,179c), woon (24c), word (124b,165c), wore, work (64c,76b), worm, worn (143b), wort (76a,95d,121d), Wote (191), wove
- WO - Lwow, swob (102b), swop (168a), swot, swow (100a)
W - - O Waco, whoo, whyo (59d,65a)
- - WP gawp, lowp (90c,139d), yawp
W - - P wapp (54b,133d,145d), warp (36c,165a,171c), wasp, weep (39b, 88a,104a), whip (58c,88d), wisp (24b,148c), wrap (32b,51a)
WR - - Wraf, wrap (32b,51a), wren (19b,c), Wren (50b), writ (91a)
- WR - awry (13d,38d,171c), ewry (133c)
W - - R waer (40b), wear (50b), weir (40b,57d), whir (25c,181a)
- WS - owse
- - WS mews (154c), news (165c)
W - - S ways, wies (185a)
- - WT newt (48d,136c,169d), nowt (106a,139a), yowt (139c)
W - - T waft (20d,58c), wait (26d,42b,92c,155d,162a), Walt (96b), want (41b,42d,87b,106b,122a), wart (124d), wast, watt (173b,177c), Watt (82a), weet (19d), weft (39a,165a,184b), welt (36d,131b, 145a,b,177b,d), went (42c), wept, wert, west, West (9c,50b, 109b), what (129c), whet (143c,156b), whit (166c), wilt (46b), wist (87c), wont (6d,40a,73a,174c), wort (76a,95d,121d), writ (91a)
WU - - wudu (102d), wukf (103a), Wurd, wurm (67c), wuzu (102d)
- WU - swum
W - - U whau (107a,168c), widu (102d), wudu (102d), wuzu (102d)
W - - W whew!
WY - - wynn (165d), Wyrd (107d)
- WY - Gwyn (40c,50b)
- - WY dewy (101a), jawy, nowy (194), rowy (157b), towy (58b)
W - - Y wady (109a,128a,132a), waky, wany, wary (27d,176b), wavy (147b,172d), waxy (119c,149d), whey (100a), wily (13b,38b,39c), winy (176c), wiry (147a,167c)
W - - Z whiz (25c)
- XA - axal (120b), exam, oxan (65c)
- - XA Bixa (145d), coxa (77b), doxa (48b), moxa (27d,30c), myxa (168c,169a), noxa, toxa (153d)

380

X - - A	xema (72c), Xema (12c), Xina (183d), Xosa (86a), Xova (193)
XE - -	xema (72c), Xema (12c), xeno (34d)
- XE -	oxea (153d), oxen (10c), oxer (55c)
- - XE	luxe (61c,62d,159c), Mixe (192), saxe (20d,33c)
X - - E	Xipe (15c)
XI - -	Xina (183d), Xipe (15c)
- XI -	axil (10c), axis (28b,41d,77c,153c), exit (114d), ixia (37a), Ixil (192), oxid (112c)
- - XI	dixi, taxi (13a,125b)
- XL -	axle (153c,180c), ixle (56a)
XM - -	Xmas
XO - -	Xosa (86a), Xova (193)
- XO -	axon (106c,153c)
- - XO	Moxo (192), myxo, taxo (13a)
X - - O	xeno (34d), xylo (35a,183d)
X - - S	Xmas
- - XT	next (106a), sext (26b,111b,147b), text (21c,140d)
XY - -	xylo (35a,183d)
- XY -	oxyl (112c)
- - XY	boxy, buxy (115b), doxy (129d), foxy (38b,39c,181d), mixy, pixy (154b), puxy, Roxy (183d), waxy (119c,149d)
YA - -	yage (23a), yaje (23a), Yaka (191), Yaki (193), Yale (173c), yali (171a), Yama (57a,68a), Yana (192,193), yang (30b,70a), yank, Yank, Yaou (30c), yapa (113b), Yapp (22a), yard (152d), yare (96b,124b,128b), yark (22c), yarl (40d,107d), yarn (154b,161b, 184b), yarr (72a), Yaru (48d), yate (51d,168c), yati (76d), yaup, yava, yawl (136b,171d,175d), yawn, yawp, yaya (113c,168c)
- YA -	ayah (108d), cyan, dyad (113a), Dyak (22b), Dyas (66a), eyah (95b,108d,111c), eyas (106c,173a), iyar (102b), kyah (19a), kyak (51c), kyar (33a), kyat (189), lyam (139a), Lyas (66a), pyal (175c), pyat (95b), ryal (110a,190)
- - YA	Alya (155b,c), Arya (80d), baya (179b), Baya (191), cuya (39b), Goya (151d), Hoya (14d), maya (77a,179b), Maya (23d,186c), Puya (118b), raya (19b,23c,76d,107d), saya (117a), soya (151b), yaya (113c,168c)
Y - - A	Yaka (191), Yama (57a,68a), Yana (192,193), yapa (113b), yava, yaya (113c,168c), yeta (84c), Yima (84a,116b,c), Ynca (193), yoga (10b,13c,77a), yuca (27a), Yuga (76d), Yuma
- YB -	gybe (144c), Tybi (102a)
- YC -	syce (71d)
- YD -	hyde (188), Hyde (45a)
- - YD	emyd (163a,167c)
Y - - D	yard (152d), yond (164d)
YE - -	yeah, yean (88a), year, yeas (177c), Yedo (166d), yegg (24c), yell (145c), yelp, yelt (151b), yeni (19b,161d), yeso (72d), yeta (84c)

- YE -   ayes (177c), byee (189), dyer, eyer, eyey (74b), oyer (38a,75b, 119c), oyes (38a,39b,75b), oyez (38a,39b,75b), pyet (95b), ryel (190), syed (103b), tyee (29d), tyer

- - YE   Daye (123d), Skye (163c)

Y - - E   yage (23a), yaje (23a), Yale (173c), yare (96b,124b,128b), yate (51d,168c), yoke (85b,92d,173c), yore (10b,69d,93c,110b,165d), Yule (30d)

- YG -   bygo (114c), zyga (134b)

Y - - G   yang (30b,70a), yegg (24c)

YH - -   YHVH (159d), YHWH (159d)

Y - - H   yeah, YHVH (159d), YHWH (159d), yodh (91d), yogh (10c,185a)

YI - -   Yima (84a,116b,c)

- YI -   ayin (91c)

- - YI   kiyi (185d)

Y - - I   Yaki (193), yali (171a), yati (76d), yeni (19b,161d), Yobi, yogi (76d)

- YK -   cyke (40c), dyke (49c,91d), fyke (15d), hykel, syke (194), tyke (29d)

Y - - K   yank, Yank, yark (22c), yolk, york (38c), York (50b,c)

- YL -   gyle (23b,174d), Hyla (10a,166d,169b), hyle (97c), kyle (57a, 139c), pyla (22d), pyle (34b), Pyle (9c,178a), Xylo (35a,183d)

- - YL   acyl (6d), amyl (155c), idyl (114d), noyl (87c), odyl (59d,79c), oxyl (112c), teyl (92b,c,168c)

Y - - L   yard (40d,107d), yawl (136b,171d,175d), yell (145c), yowl, ypil (117a,168c)

YM - -   Ymer (67a,131c), Ymir (67a,131c)

- YM -   cyma (101a,b), cyme (58d,69c), hymn (150c), ryme (178d), tymp (20c), zyme (55c)

- - YM   clym (12b), etym (133d), onym (162c)

YN - -   Ynca (193)

- YN -   dyna (34c), dyne (59d,173b), gyne (34b,55b,183c), jynx (78a), Jynx (184a), lynx (26c,181d), Lynx (36b), myna (19a,c,70b), rynd (100a), syne (140b,147a), tyne, Tyne (108a), wynn (165d)

- - YN   coyn (37a), Gwyn (40c,50b), llyn (120d,140a)

Y - - N   yarn (154b,161b,184b), yawn, yean (88a), yuan (190), Yuan (30b,101d)

YO - -   Yobi, yodh (91d), yoga (10b,13c,77a), yogh (10c,185a), yogi (76d), yoke (85b,92d,173c), yolk, yond (164d), yoop, yore (10b, 69d,93c,110b,165d), york (38c), York (50b,c), youp (185d), your (124c), yowl, yowt (139c)

- YO -   eyot (82d), ryot (115c)

- - YO   buyo (18b), cayo, coyo (15a,30c), Enyo (12c,69c,178a), Idyo (191), kayo (87c), Mayo (193), whyo (59d,65a)

Y - - O   Yedo (166d), yeso (72d)

YP - -   ypil (117a,168c)

- YP -   gyps, Gyps (71d), hype (185a), hypo (117b), hyps, rype (19b,

382

125a), **sype** (110c), **type** (31d,115a,155a), **typo** (35c,51b), **typp** (185b), **typy**

- - YP   **tryp** (114a)
Y - - P   **Yapp** (22a), **yaup, yawp, yelp, yoop, youp** (185d)
- YR -   **Byrd** (9c,120b), **byre** (38a), **eyra** (181d), **eyre** (23c,31b,85c), **Eyre, eyry** (47b,106c), **fyrd** (110a), **gyre** (31b,171b), **gyri** (22d, 131b), **gyro** (34d), **Lyra** (36b,74a), **lyre** (11c,81c,105a,111c), **Myra** (10a,31b,183c), **pyre** (64c), **pyro, Syra, tyre** (15a), **Tyre** (31b,90d,117b), **tyro** (9b,17d,108c), **Tyrr** (68c,109c,163d,178a), **Wyrd** (107d)
- - YR   **skyr** (21d,151a)
Y - - R   **yarr** (72a), **year, Ymer** (67a,131c), **Ymir** (67a,131c), **your** (124c), **Yser**
YS - -   **Yser**
- YS -   **cyst, lyse, myst** (71c,123b)
- - YS   **Alys** (183c), **Emys** (167c,171b), **days, Itys** (163b), **ways**
Y - - S   **yeas** (177c)
- YT -   **myth** (8b,91a), **Tyto** (16c)
- - YT   **skyt** (138c,140b)
Y - - T   **yelt** (151b), **yowt** (139c), **yuft** (135c), **Yuit** (51c), **yurt** (101d)
YU - -   **yuan** (190), **Yuan** (30b,101d), **yuca** (27a), **yuft** (135c), **Yuga** (76d), **Yuit** (51c), **Yule** (30d), **Yuma, Yunx** (184a), **yurt** (101d), **yutu** (19b,166a)
- YU -   **syud** (103b)
- - YU   **Vayu** (68c,182a)
Y - - U   **Yaou** (30c), **Yaru** (48d), **yutu** (19b,166a)
- YV -   **gyve** (55d,143b)
- YX -   **myxa** (168c,169a), **myxo**
- - YX   **Ceyx** (73b), **eryx** (137a), **onyx** (25d,28d,65d,142b), **oryx** (11a), **Pnyx** (71c), **Styx** (29b,73a,105c)
Y - - X   **Yunx** (184a)
- - YZ   **hayz**
ZA - -   **Zach** (96b), **zaim** (170d), **zain** (41a), **Zama** (73d,141d), **zany** (24a,32d,59c), **zarf** (39c,155a), **zarp** (120c), **zati** (21d)
- ZA -   **Azam** (166c), **azan** (102d), **czar** (42d,49d,60b,135c), **Izar** (65b, 103b), **Izar** (155b), **tzar** (42d,49d,60b,135c), **Uzan** (189)
- - ZA   **boza** (12a), **caza, Daza** (191), **Gaza** (117a), **itza** (192), **Juza** (155b), **onza** (189), **tiza** (172a), **tuza** (119d), **vaza** (114a), **zuza** (189)
Z - - A   **Zama** (73d,141d), **zeta** (71b,91c), **Zipa** (29d), **zira** (188), **Zola** (63a), **zona** (144c,186d), **zuza** (189), **zyga** (134b)
- ZB -   **ezba** (188)
Z - - B   **Zimb** (6c)
Z - - C   **zinc** (21a)
Z - - D   **Zend, zoid**
ZE - -   **zeal** (12c,55d), **zebu** (22d,80d,112c), **zein, Zeke** (96b), **zeme**

383

(55d,161b,180b), zemi (55d,161b,180b), Zend, Zeno (71b), zenu (143d), zero (31a,84c,108c), Zero (118d), zest (55d,72d), zeta (71b,91c), Zeus (135a)

- ZE - ezei (47a,85d)

- - ZE adze (40c,167a), bize (182a), coze (29b), daze (157d), doze (148a), faze (43d), fuze (98c), gaze, guze (128d), haze (100c, 174d), laze (79b), Laze (191), maze (87b,157d), naze (26b, 124b), noze (75a), ooze (53c,104b,116a), raze (42b,d,91d), size, unze (189)

Z - - E Zeke (96b), zeme (55d,161b,180b), zone (44c,50a,160a), zyme (55c)

Z - - F zarf (39c,155a)

Z - - G zing

- ZH - Azha (155b)

Z - - H Zach (96b)

ZI - - Zimb (6c), zinc (21a), zing, Zion (75b,c,83a,157d), Zipa (29d), zipp, Zips (40c), zira (188), zizz (181a)

- - ZI cazi (103a), gazi, kazi (103a), Lazi (191), Nazi

Z - - I zati (21d), zemi (55d,161b,180b), Zuni (125b)

Z - - L zeal (12c,55d)

Z - - M zaim (170d), zoom

Z - - N zain (41a), zein, Zion (75b,c,83a,157d), zoon (43a)

ZO - - Zoar, Zoas (20b), zobo (186b), zodi, zogo (136a), zoid, Zola (63a), zona (144c,186d), zone (44c,50a,160a), zoom, zoon (43a)

- ZO - Azof (20b,135d), azon (127b), Azov (20b,135d), mozo (152b), Muzo (192)

- - ZO bozo (55b), Idzo (191), kozo (113d,168c), lazo (88d,128b,133d),

Z - - O Zeno (71b), zero (31a,84c,108c), Zero (118d), zobo (186b), zogo (136a)

Z - - P zarp (120c), zipp

- ZR - Ezra (96a)

Z - - R Zoar

Z - - S Zeus (135a), Zips (40c), Zoas (20b)

Z - - T zest (55d,72d)

ZU - - zulu (171d,175d), Zulu (86a), Zuni (125b), zuza (189)

- ZU - azul (151d)

- - ZU anzu (11d), auzu (168c,180b), Enzu (102b), wuzu (102d)

Z - - U zebu (22d,80d,112c), zenu (143d), zulu (171d,175d), Zulu (86a)

ZY - - zyga (134b), zyme (55c)

- - ZY cazy (103a), cozy (149c), dazy, dozy, gazy, hazy (174b), Jozy, kazy (103a), lazy, oozy (148b), sizy (176d)

Z - - Y zany (24a,32d,59c)

- - ZZ bizz, buzz, fuzz (45d), huzz, jazz, razz (131b), sizz, zizz (181a)

Z - - Z zizz (181a)

384